SQL Server™ 2000 Stored Procedure & XML Programming

Second Edition

Dejan Šunderić

McGraw-Hill/Osborne

New York   Chicago   San Francisco
Lisbon   London   Madrid   Mexico City   Milan
New Delhi   San Juan   Seoul   Singapore   Sydney   Toronto

The McGraw·Hill Companies

McGraw-Hill/Osborne
2100 Powell Street, 10th Floor
Emeryville, California 94608
U.S.A.

To arrange bulk purchase discounts for sales promotions, premiums, or fund-raisers, please contact **McGraw-Hill**/Osborne at the above address. For information on translations or book distributors outside the U.S.A., please see the International Contact Information page immediately following the index of this book.

SQL Server™ 2000 Stored Procedure & XML Programming, Second Edition

   4567890 CUS CUS 01987654

ISBN 0-07-222896-2

Publisher	Brandon A. Nordin
Vice President & Associate Publisher	Scott Rogers
Acquisitions Editor	Lisa McClain
Project Editor	Janet Walden
Acquisitions Coordinator	Athena Honore
Technical Editor	Deborah Bechtold
Development Editor	Tom Woodhead
Copy Editor	William McManus
Proofreader	Laurie Stewart
Indexer	Valerie Robbins
Computer Designers	Carie Abrew, Tara A. Davis, Lucie Ericksen
Illustrators	Lyssa Wald, Melinda Moore Lytle, Kathleen Fay Edwards
Series Designer	Peter F. Hancik
Cover Series Designer	Pattie Lee

This book was composed with Corel VENTURA™ Publisher.

Writing a book isn't easy, but living with someone
who is writing a book can be, at times, even harder.
I would like to thank my family for their patience,
understanding, and inspiration.

Acknowledgments

I wish to thank all the people who helped to make this book a reality,
in particular:

- ► **Tom Woodhead**, for straightening the winding course of my writings.
- ► **Olga Baranova**, who created several examples for Chapters 10, 11, and 15.
- ► **Wendy Rinaldi** and **Lisa McClain**, for the opportunity to do this project.
- ► **Athena Honore** and **Janet Walden**, for their patience, expertise, and hard work.
- ► **Deborah Bechtold**, for her expertise and hard work beyond the call of duty.

About the Author

Dejan Šunderić is the principal consultant at Trigon Blue, Inc. (www.trigonblue.com). He specializes in database and application development for Internet and Windows platforms.

Projects that he has been involved with cover B2C and B2B e-commerce, financial, document-management, mortgage, asset management, insurance, real-estate, IT supply chain, process control, communication, data warehouse, and OLAP systems. Dejan has worked as a database architect, database and application developer, database administrator, team leader, project manager, writer, and technical trainer.

He is the author of *SQL Server 2000 Stored Procedure Programming* (www .trigonblue.com/stored_procedure.htm), coauthor of *Windows 2000 Performance Tuning and Optimization*, and three other books, as well as numerous technical articles for several computer and professional publications.

His career started in Belgrade, Yugoslavia where he graduated on Faculty of Electrical Engineering. In 1995 he moved to Toronto, Canada and he is currently in Pittsburgh, U.S.A. He holds certifications for Microsoft Certified Solution Developer (MCSD), Microsoft Certified Database Administrator (MCDBA), and Certified SQL Server Programmer Master Level. Dejan is a member of Toronto SQL Server User Group (www.tssug.com), Visual Basic Developer's Online Group (www.visualbyte.com/vbdogs), Pittsburgh SQL Server User Group (www.pssug.com), and Professional Association for SQL Server (www.sqlpass.org).

Dejan can be contacted by email (dejan's username on hotmail.com server; to avoid spam filter, put *sp_book* in the subject) or the book's web site (www .trigonblue.com/sqlxml).

Contents at a Glance

Contents

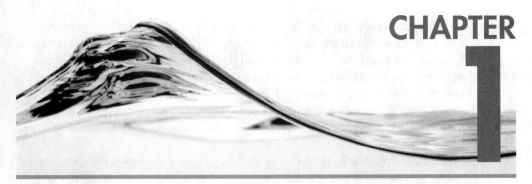

CHAPTER 1

Introduction

Welcome to *SQL Server 2000 Stored Procedure & XML Programming.* This book identifies and describes the key concepts, tips and techniques, and best practices the professional developer needs to master in order to take full advantage of stored procedures in the SQL Server development environment.

Microsoft SQL Server is the relational database management system (RDBMS) of choice for a growing number of business organizations and professional database and application developers. The reasons for this growing popularity are quite simple:

▶ **Integration**   No other RDBMS integrates as fully and cleanly with applications and integrated development environments (IDEs) designed to run on the ubiquitous Microsoft Windows platform.

▶ **Ease of use**   SQL Server provides Enterprise Manager and Query Analyzer to allow DBAs to design, develop, deploy, and manage database solutions. These interfaces automate repetitive tasks and provide simple ways to perform complex operations. SQL Server integrates seamlessly with development tools such as Visual Basic and Visual Interdev to allow developers to design and develop client/server or Internet solutions rapidly.

▶ **Flexibility**   You can use different features within SQL Server to achieve similar results. (Of course, with flexibility comes choice, and choice means that the developer is responsible for choosing the most appropriate means of achieving an end. This book will help you make those choices.)

▶ **Power**   SQL Server makes large amounts of data available to large numbers of concurrent users while maintaining the security and integrity of the data. At the time of this writing, SQL Server holds the record in TPC-C benchmark tests for performance and price/performance (see www.tpc.org).

When I began working with SQL Server, reference materials relating to the development and deployment of stored procedures were rare and not particularly helpful. These materials described basic concepts, but the examples presented were often trivial and not complex enough to be applied to real-world situations in which aspects such as error handling, debugging, naming conventions, and interfaces to other applications are critical. As the legions of application developers and development DBAs migrate from Microsoft Access to SQL Server, and as SQL Server becomes the leading database for mission-critical application development, the need for more advanced work on SQL Server stored procedures becomes even more critical.

Who Should Read This Book

This book has been written to fill this gap, and thus it has been written with a wide audience in mind. Ideally, it will be neither the first nor the last book you read on SQL Server, but it may be the one you refer to and recommend the most. Above all, this book has been written to help professional developers get the most out of SQL Server stored procedures and SQLXML extensions and to produce quality work for their clients.

If you are an experienced SQL Server developer, you will find this book to be an essential reference text full of tips and techniques to help you address the development issues you encounter in the course of your day-to-day development activities.

If you have some experience with SQL Server development, but substantially more in other programming environments such as Visual Basic, you will find this book useful as a tool to orient yourself with the SQL Server environment and become proficient more quickly with SQL Server stored procedure and SQLXML concepts and methods. You will be able to incorporate effective, swift stored procedures into Visual Basic code and SQLXML methods and queries into your client Windows or web applications.

If you are a novice SQL Server developer, the concepts, tips, and techniques you will learn in reading this book and working through the exercises will help you attain the knowledge, skills, and good habits that will help you become an accomplished professional.

I hope that this book remains close to your workstation for a long time. Indeed, in the course of this book's useful life, you may in turn be all three of the users just described.

What You Will Find in This Book

Each chapter in this book (aside from the one you are reading, which is introductory in nature) will provide conceptual grounding in a specific area of the SQL Server development landscape. The first 12 chapters are dedicated to stored procedure programming, and Chapters 13, 14, and 15 are focused on XML programming on SQL Server 2000.

As you may have gathered, this chapter describes the content of this book, as well as its intended audience, and describes a sample database that we will use throughout the book to demonstrate stored procedure development.

Chapter 2, "The SQL Server Environment," provides a 30,000-foot overview of the Transact-SQL language, SQL Server tools, and stored procedure design.

Chapter 3, "Stored Procedure Design Concepts," explores SQL Server stored procedure design in greater detail, with particular attention paid to the different types of stored procedures, their uses, and their functionality.

Chapter 4, "Basic Transact-SQL Programming Constructs," describes Transact- SQL, the ANSI SQL-92–compliant programming language used to write scripts in SQL Server. This chapter summarizes data types, variables, flow control statements, and cursors in the context of SQL Server 2000.

Chapter 5, "Functions," describes the extensive set of built-in functions available in SQL Server 2000 and how to use them in various common situations.

Chapter 6, "Composite Transact-SQL Constructs: Batches, Scripts, and Transactions," describes the various ways in which you can group Transact-SQL statements for execution.

Chapter 7, "Debugging and Error Handling," provides a coherent approach to the identification and resolution of defects in code and a coherent strategy for handling errors as they occur.

Chapter 8, "Special Types of Procedures," describes user-defined, system, extended, temporary, global temporary, and remote stored procedures as well as other types of procedures in Transact-SQL, such as user-defined functions, table-valued user-defined functions, After triggers, Instead-of triggers, standard SQL views, indexed views, INFORMATION_SCHEMA views, and local and distributed partitioned views.

Chapter 9, "Advanced Stored Procedure Programming," introduces some advanced techniques for coding stored procedures, such as dynamically constructed queries, optimistic locking using timestamps, and nested stored procedures.

Chapter 10, "Interaction with the SQL Server Environment," focuses on the ways in which you can use system and extended stored procedures to interact with the SQL Server environment, and discusses the ways in which user-defined stored procedures can help you leverage the existing functionality of various elements within the SQL Server environment.

Chapter 11, "Source Code Management and Database Deployment," demonstrates how you can manage and deploy Transact-SQL source code from development to the test and production environment. It explains and demonstrates two alternative approaches—one using Visual Studio .NET and the other, more traditional, using scripts developed in Transact-SQL and VBScript.

Chapter 12, "Stored Procedures for Web Search Engines," presents an example of how to use stored procedures in a web application that queries the database system. Several optimization techniques are used to avoid typical design problems and improve the performance.

Chapter 13, "Introduction to XML for Database Developers," introduces XML as the markup language for information exchange and publishing, and then focuses on complementary features and technologies like DTDs, XML Schemas, and XPath as they are used in SQL Server 2000.

Chapter 14, "Publishing Information Using SQLXML," describes methods for returning an XML stream instead of a recordset from SQL Server 2000.

Chapter 15, "Modifying Databases Using SQLXML," describes several methods for parsing XML and updating database tables.

The appendix, "T-SQL and XML Data Types in SQL Server 2000," provides you with tables that list data types in use in SQL Server 2000 and the way they map.

Requirements

To make full use of this book, you will need access to a server running one of the following versions of SQL Server 2000 or SQL Server 2000 (64-bit):

▶ **Enterprise Edition**   Supports all features and scales to enterprise level; supports up to 32 CPUs and 64GB RAM

▶ **Standard Edition**   Scales to the level of departmental or workgroup servers; supports up to four CPUs and 2GB RAM

▶ **Evaluation Edition**   Supports all features of Enterprise Edition; use is limited to 120 days; available for download over the Web

Stored Procedure Programming Requirements

You can also perform most of the stored procedure programming–oriented activities described in this book using a stand-alone PC with Windows 98, Windows 2000, or Windows NT Workstation to run one of the following versions of Microsoft SQL Server 2000:

▶ **Personal Edition**   Designed for mobile or stand-alone users and applications; does not support some advanced features, such as fail-over clustering, publishing of transactional replications, OLAP Server, or Full Text Search; supports up to two CPUs

▶ **Developer Edition**   Licensed to be used only as a development and test server, although it supports all features of Enterprise Edition

▶ **Desktop Engine**   Distributable but stripped-down version that software vendors can package and deploy with their systems; part of Microsoft Access and Visual Studio; also known as MSDE; does not contain administrative tools such as Enterprise Manager, Query Analyzer, and Books Online; does not support advanced features such as Analysis Services and replication; database size is limited to 2GB

Although MSDE is compatible with all other versions of SQL Server 2000 and thus makes an excellent development tool in a stand-alone environment, the absence of administrative tools such as Enterprise Manager and Query Analyzer means that some of the information you find in this book will not be usable right away. I recommend that you obtain some other version (such as Developer Edition or Evaluation Edition), or at least buy a Server/Per-Seat Client Access License (CAL) that will allow you to use administrative tools against MSDE.

XML Programming Requirements

To explore and use XML programming features, you need to install and use:

► **XML for SQL Server Web release (SQLXML)**   I recommend that you download and install at least SQLXML 3.0, Service Pack 1.

► **Microsoft SOAP Toolkit**   Download version 2, Service Pack 2 or newer.

► **Microsoft XML Core Services (MSXML)**   Use version 4, Service Pack 1 or newer. Earlier versions were called Microsoft XML Parser.

► **Internet Information Services (IIS)**   Use version 5 or newer.

► **Internet Explorer**   Use version 5 or newer.

Sample Database and Other Resources

You may have noticed that this book does not include a CD. SQL Server development is a dynamic field, as you will see if you compare the first and second editions of this book. Rather than increase the cost of the book by adding a CD, which would be out of date almost before it hits the bookstore, the publisher and I have chosen to make additional resources available for download via the Web. In addition to the sample database (more information on that in just a bit) that I have created and will use through most of this book, other resources available include:

► **Several tools for source code management and database deployment**   Set of T-SQL, VBScript and .NET tools for generating, managing, and deploying code of database objects.

► **Sample SQLXML code**   Visual Studio .NET sample projects for demonstrating use of SQLXML managed classes.

▶ **Periodic updates**   As noted earlier, SQL Server development is a dynamic field, and thus a book on SQL Server needs to be dynamic to meet the evolving needs of its audience. Reader feedback is important to me. Check my web site (www.trigonblue.com) for periodic updates on issues raised by readers.

▶ **Author's web site**   Aside from being the source of the sample database and periodic update downloads, the Trigon Blue web site provides a wealth of excellent reference materials and links. Visit the site often for SQL Server and e-business news. While you're there, have a look at the many articles and white papers, and check out Trigon Blue's many product and service offerings.

The subject of the Asset sample database created for this book is an asset management system within a fictional organization. Although the database is based on real-world experience within financial institutions, it is also applicable in many other environments.

The main purpose of the database is to track assets. Assets are defined as equipment, and all variations in their content, attributes, and shape are recorded as values of properties. The Inventory table tracks location, status, leasing information, and who is currently using each asset. To transfer an asset from one location to another, to assign assets to a different owner or department, to request maintenance, or to request upgrades or new assets, users of the database use orders and order items. Activities performed to complete the order are recorded in the charge log and interdepartment invoices are generated. There are lookup tables used to track provinces, lease frequencies, statuses, and other details.

Sample Database Installation

You should download this database and install it on your server before you begin to read the rest of this book. To download and install the sample Asset database:

1. Visit **www.trigonblue.com/sqlxml**

2. Click the Download Sample DB link.

3. Click the Asset sample database link to start the download. When prompted, opt to save the file to disk. Remember the location to which you saved the file.

4. Unzip the contents of the Zip file into the Data folder of the machine on which SQL Server is installed (usually \Program Files\Microsoft SQL Server\MSSQL\Data).

5. Make sure that SQL Server is running. If necessary, run SQL Server Service Manager from Programs | MS SQL Server or use the system tray icon. If necessary, start the SQL Server service.

6. Run Query Analyzer (select Programs | MS SQL Server | Query Analyzer).

7. You will be prompted to connect to SQL Server. Type the server name and log in as system administrator (sa). If the password has not been set, leave the password blank (an empty string).

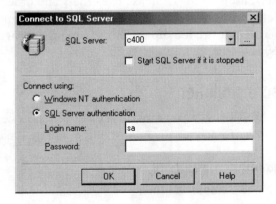

Query Analyzer opens a query window pointing to the *master* database.

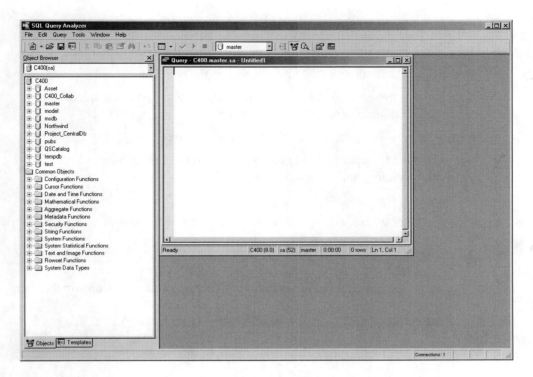

8. Type the following text in the query window:

```
EXEC sp_attach_db 'Asset',
     'E:\Program Files\Microsoft SQL Server\MSSQL\Data\Asset_data.mdf',
     'E:\Program Files\Microsoft SQL Server\MSSQL\Data\Asset_log.ldf'
```

If the location of the folder containing the Asset database file is different from the one shown in the command, change the command.

9. To attach the database, select Query | Execute from the menu bar. SQL Server attaches the database. The database is now ready for use.

Purpose and Design of the Sample Database

The Asset database is designed to track and manage assets within an organization. This database allows users to

▶   Track features of assets

▶   Search for assets with specific features

- ▶ Record the current location and status of an asset
- ▶ Track the person and organizational unit to which the asset is assigned
- ▶ Note how an asset is acquired and the cost of the acquisition
- ▶ Keep parameters concerning leases (for example, lease payments, lease schedules, and lease vendors used to obtain assets)
- ▶ Identify assets for which lease schedules have expired
- ▶ Record orders to departments in charge of services such as acquisition, disposal, servicing, and technical support
- ▶ Monitor the processing of orders
- ▶ Manage the costs associated with actions taken on order items

Database Diagram

Figure 1-1 shows the physical implementation of the Asset entity relationship diagram.

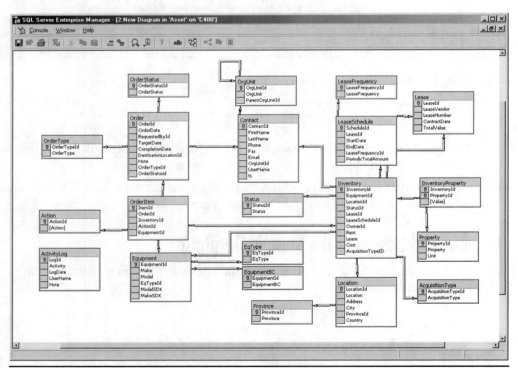

Figure 1-1   *A database diagram of the Asset database*

Description of Assets

The following illustration shows the tables involved in the description of each asset. Detailed information about deployed equipment and their features is essential for the proper management of current inventory as well as future upgrades and acquisitions.

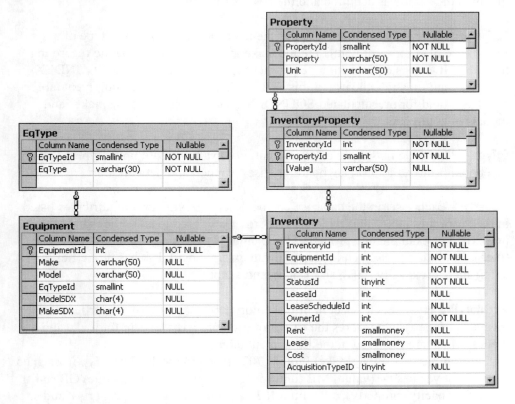

Information in these asset description tables allows users to

▶ Manage a list of standard equipment deployed within the organization

▶ Manage a list of attributes (properties) that can be used to describe assets

▶ Manage a list of attributes for each asset

▶ Obtain a summary of equipment deployed within the organization

▶ Make decisions about the deployment of a software package based on the capabilities of existing equipment in the field

▶ Find obsolete pieces of equipment that need to be disposed of and replaced with new equipment

Inventory   The central table in the Asset database is the Inventory table. It is designed to track the assets currently deployed within an organization. The most important information about an asset indicates what kind of equipment it is. This table also stores information about the asset's current location and its status, as well as the way in which the asset was acquired and the cost of acquisition.

Equipment   The Equipment table stores the make and model of each type of asset. Each piece of equipment with a unique make and model has a separate record in this table. It groups equipment by equipment type. To accommodate SOUNDEX searches (and illustrate the use of this SOUNDEX function), the Equipment table also has a field for precalculated SOUNDEX codes representing the makes and models of equipment.

EqType   This table lists types of equipment. For example, equipment types include notebook, printer, monitor, keyboard, mouse, scanner, and network hub.

Property   Each asset in the database can be described with a set of attributes listed in the Properties table. This table also records a unit used to store the value of the property. For example, the properties (and units of measure) of a monitor are size (inch), resolution (pixel), and type, while an external hard disk has properties (and units) such as capacity (GB), size (inch), and adapter.

InventoryProperty   Each Asset in the Inventory table has a set of properties. The InventoryProperty table stores the values of each property (except for make and model, which are recorded in the Equipment table).

For example, a Toshiba (Make) Protégé 7020 (Model) notebook (EqType) assigned to an employee has 64 (value) MB (unit) of RAM (property), 4.3 (value) GB (unit) of HDD capacity (property), a Pentium II 333 (value) processor (property), and so on. Another employee is using an upgraded version of the same equipment with 128 (value) MB (unit) of RAM (property), 6.4 (value) GB (unit) of HDD capacity (property), a Pentium II 366 (value) processor (property), and so on.

Deployment of Assets

This following set of tables keeps track of the location in which an asset is deployed and the person and organizational unit to which the asset is assigned.

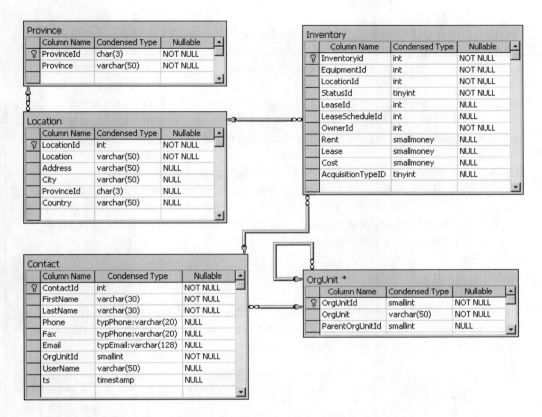

The information in these asset deployment tables allows users to

► Manage a list of locations within an organization

► Manage a list of persons working within an organization

► Retrieve contact information about persons to whom assets are assigned

► Generate reports about assets deployed by province and organizational unit

► Retrieve a list of assets assigned to a particular person

► Manage relationships between organizational units

► Assign person(s) to organizational units

Location   The Location table stores information about the physical location of the deployed asset. Each location has a name and an address as attributes.

Province   This table contains a list of provinces and states. The primary key is the abbreviation of the province/state. The presence of this table is essential for reports, which will aggregate asset deployment by location, province/state, and country.

Contact   This table contains a list of persons involved in the asset management process. It includes persons with assets assigned to them, persons completing and approving orders, and persons performing maintenance and support.

OrgUnit   Each contact is assigned to some organizational unit within the organization. The OrgUnit table records relationships between companies, cost centers, departments, and the like. This table is designed as a recursive table: an organizational unit can be part of some other organizational unit. This quality also reflects the need for rapid changes in today's work environment due to change of ownership, restructuring, and so on.

Leasing Tables

An important aspect of asset management is the tracking of lease information. It helps management avoid payment of penalties associated with late returns or the failure to return leased assets to the leasing vendor:

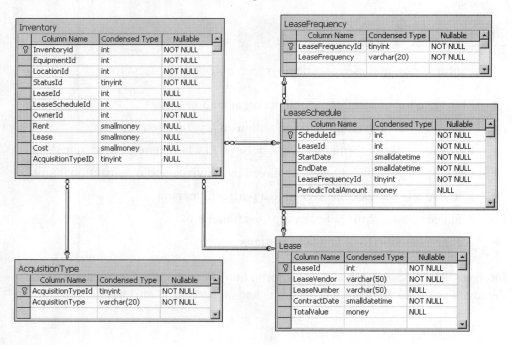

The information in the lease tables allows users to

▶ Keep track of the assets associated with each lease

▶ Manage lease schedules to keep track of the start, end, and duration of lease periods

▶ Identify assets that need to be returned to a lease vendor

▶ Generate reports on assets deployed by lease schedule and lease contract

▶ Retrieve a list of assets obtained from a particular lease vendor

▶ Retrieve the total value of lease payments, lease schedules, and lease contracts

Lease   The Lease table contains information about lease contracts. It records the name of the lease vendor, the number of the lease that the vendor is using to track the contract, the date the contract was signed, and the total value of assets assigned to the lease.

LeaseSchedule   Assets obtained through one lease contract might not be received on the same date. An asset might also be under a different payment regime and lease duration. Therefore, each lease contains a set of lease schedules. Each schedule is recorded in the LeaseSchedule table and is described with a start date, an end date, and the frequency of payments. This table also tracks the total value of payments per lease term.

LeaseFrequency   LeaseFrequency is a lookup table that contains all possible values for lease frequency including monthly, semimonthly, biweekly, and weekly.

AcquisitionType   AcquisitionType is a lookup table that lists possible acquisition types including lease, purchase, and rent.

Order Tables

Orders are the primary means of managing assets within the organization. Users can request new assets and the disposal of obsolete assets. They can request maintenance and technical support. Authorized personnel can monitor orders and react to them, associate a cost with their execution, and generate invoices. The following tables are used to store information about orders:

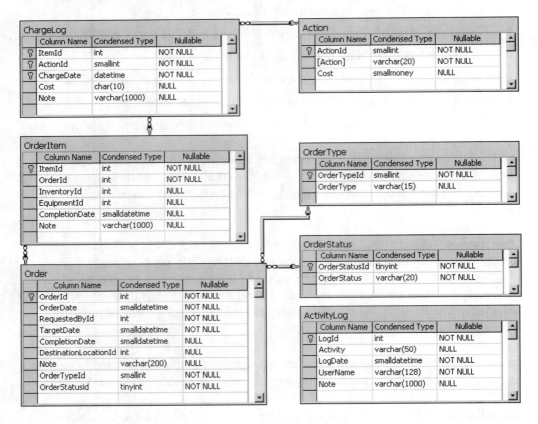

The information in these order tables allows users to

▶ Request new equipment

▶ Request technical support

▶ Request maintenance

▶ Execute scheduled maintenance

▶ Track the status of orders

▶ Assign a staff member to execute the order

▶ Approve the execution of orders

- ▶ Manage a list of actions and the default costs associated with them
- ▶ Track costs associated with each activity
- ▶ Generate interdepartmental invoices
- ▶ Request the transfer of assets
- ▶ Request the disposal of obsolete assets
- ▶ Generate summaries and reports on performed activities

Order   Users can record requests in the Order table. At that time, the order date and target date are recorded. General request requirements are recorded as an order type, and special requirements are recorded as a note. The person making the request is recorded, as well as the person approving the request and assigning the order for execution. If the order is a transfer request, the table also records a destination for the asset. Users can track the status of the order, and once it is completed, its completion date is set. At that point, one organizational unit is billed for performed actions, and once the order is paid, the payment is noted on the order and funds are assigned to the organizational unit completing the order.

OrderItem   The OrderItem table records assets that need the intervention of authorized personnel or new equipment that needs to be purchased. Special requests are recorded in the Note field.

Action   The Action table manages the list of activities needed to complete a request as well as the default cost associated with each.

ChargeLog   Actions performed on an order item to complete an order will be recorded in the ChargeLog table. This table will be used to generate an invoice after completion of the order.

OrderStatus   The OrderStatus table is used as a lookup table to manage the status of orders. It contains statuses such as

- ▶ Ordered
- ▶ In-process
- ▶ Canceled
- ▶ Deferred
- ▶ Completed

OrderType   The OrderType table is used as a lookup table to store the general requirements of the order. It contains values such as

- ▶ Requisition
- ▶ Transfer
- ▶ Support
- ▶ Scrap
- ▶ Repair

ActivityLog   This table is not related specifically to the recording of orders. Rather, it is a repository for audit trail information. Most of the time it is populated by a trigger associated with some specific database change.

CHAPTER 2

The SQL Server Environment

Y ou already know that SQL Server is a full-featured and powerful database management system. You may also be experienced in some or many aspects of this system. But before you proceed to become an expert in application development using SQL Server stored procedures, we should probably take a step back and look at the "big picture" to ensure that we share the same conceptual grounding.

To attain this conceptual grounding, I will start with a 30,000-ft. overview that will cover the following topics:

▶   A brief introduction to SQL Server tools

▶   A quick overview of stored procedure design

I have written this overview to enable people who are in a hurry to learn the basics and then get down to developing complex stored procedures to retrieve, manipulate, update, and delete data, and address a variety of business problems. I am going to assume that you have already had an opportunity to work with SQL on SQL Server, or some other database system, and that you understand common database concepts. The purpose of this overview is to define the terminology that you will use as the foundation on which to build your knowledge of programming in the SQL Server environment. I will direct you to other books that will help to develop your knowledge of related SQL Server conceptual and development topics:

▶   *SQL Server 2000: A Beginner's Guide* by Dušan Petkovic (McGraw-Hill/Osborne, 2000)

▶   *SQL Server 2000 Design & T-SQL Programming* by Michelle Poolet and Michael D. Reilly (McGraw-Hill/Osborne, 2000)

SQL Server 2000 Tools

All versions of SQL Server 2000 except Microsoft Desktop Engine (MSDE) are delivered with the following management tools:

▶   Service Manager

▶   Query Analyzer

▶   Enterprise Manager

▶   DTS and Import/Export Data

- ► osql
- ► isql
- ► SQL Server Profiler
- ► Client Network Utility
- ► Server Network Utility

The following sections discuss the preceding tools as well as online resources.

Service Manager

The SQL Server database server is implemented as the following services:

- ► SQL Server (MSSQL)
- ► SQL Server Agent (SQLAgent)
- ► Distributed Transaction Coordinator (MSDTC)
- ► SQL Mail

The database server is actually implemented as the SQL Server (MSSQL) service. It receives queries from users, executes them, sends responses to calling applications, and manages data in database files.

SQL Server Agent (SQLAgent) is an automation service that manages the scheduled execution of tasks and notifies administrators of problems that occur on the server.

Distributed Transaction Coordinator (MSDTC) is a service that manages *two-phase commit* transactions spanned over multiple servers. This service ensures that changes that need to be made to data stored on different servers complete successfully.

SQL Mail is used to send and receive e-mail. It is possible to configure SQL Server to perform such tasks as receiving requests and returning result sets through e-mail to notify administrators of the success status of scheduled tasks and of encountered errors.

On Windows NT Server and Windows 2000 Server, MSSQL, SQLAgent, and Distributed Transaction Coordinator services can be started or stopped, as can any other service, using the Services icon in Control Panel. In Windows 9*x* environments, the only way to start and stop these services is to use Service Manager. On Windows 2000, you can also use the `net start` command from the command prompt. SQL Mail service can be controlled from the Support Services node in Enterprise Manager. You will see in the "Enterprise Manager" section later in this chapter how to control SQL Mail.

When the Service Manager applet is running, you can choose the current service and server using combo boxes and then use the appropriate button to start, pause, or stop the current service.

During SQL Server installation, Service Manager is set to run minimized in the system tray. You can investigate the execution status of the current service by hovering the mouse pointer over the icon in the system tray, or by right-clicking the icon and selecting Properties from the pop-up menu. The icon will be displayed with a green arrow if running, and a red block if not running.

Query Analyzer

Query Analyzer is a Windows application for designing, debugging, and executing Transact-SQL (T-SQL) statements (such as queries) against a SQL Server database. This application is a descendant of isql (a text-based tool) and ISQL/W (a Windows-based tool). Before Enterprise Manager was introduced in SQL Server 6.0, administrators relied on isql to manage servers and databases and to execute queries.

Query Analyzer is an MDI application that can contain one or more Query windows. You can use Query windows to enter and execute a batch of Transact-SQL statements. The Query window contains two major components: the Query pane and the Results pane (see Figure 2-1).

The *Query pane* is a Transact-SQL syntax-sensitive editor. Because it is syntax-sensitive, users can type Transact-SQL statements in the pane and Query Analyzer uses different colors to distinguish keywords, variables, comments, and constants.

Object Browser   Query pane   Query Analyzer toolbar

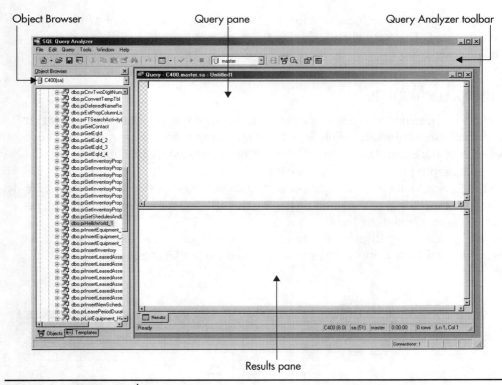

Figure 2-1   *Query Analyzer*

Results pane

The *Results pane* displays the result of the code executed in the Query pane. Earlier versions of SQL Server displayed results only in the form of text. Since SQL Server 7.0, Query Analyzer has been able to display result sets in the form of a grid, display messages separately, and diagram the way that SQL Server will execute the query (that is, the execution plan).

The *Query Analyzer toolbar* contains icons for managing the contents of the window. A noteworthy option is the DB combo box, which selects and displays the current database.

The *Object Browser* is a window that allows users to explore database objects or access predefined Transact-SQL code templates. Users can check for the existence of a database object; explore its contents (that is, view records in a table); execute and debug objects such as stored procedures; view the structure and dependencies of an object; view and edit extended properties of the object; drag the name of a database object to the Query window or a script object to the Query window, file, or Clipboard. This very useful addition to Query Analyzer is available only in SQL Server 2000.

Enterprise Manager

Enterprise Manager was introduced in SQL Server 6.0 as a tool to simplify server and database administration on SQL Server. It was an innovation and a huge success when introduced, and over time, Microsoft has improved its functionality. Now, all competing products include equivalent tools.

Enterprise Manager visually represents database objects stored on the server and provides tools for accessing and managing them. There are two main components—the Console tree and the Details pane (see Figure 2-2).

The *Console tree* displays database and server objects in a hierarchy designed for easy navigation. It works in the same way as any other GUI tree object. You can

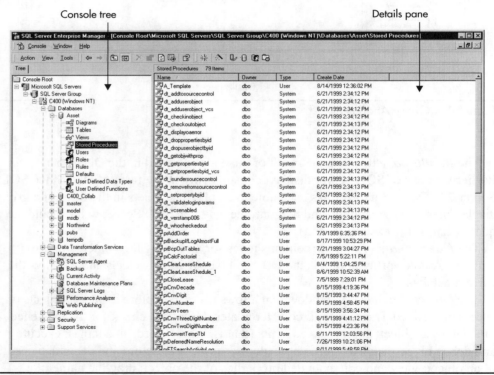

Figure 2-2   *Enterprise Manager*

click the + symbol next to any node on the tree or press the RIGHT ARROW key on the keyboard to expand the node. When you right-click a node, a context-sensitive menu is displayed.

The *Details pane* shows details of the node (object) selected in the Console tree. If the user selects a folder with tables or stored procedures, the Details pane lists the tables or stored procedures in the current database. The behavior of the Details pane is quite similar to that of Windows Explorer.

If you select certain objects in the Console tree, such as a database or a server, the Details pane can display the *taskpad*—a complex report showing the state of the database or server that can also be used to manage the database or server (see Figure 2-3). Taskpads are implemented as HTML pages. Activities can be initiated by clicking links within the taskpad.

Enterprise Manager has been developed as a Microsoft Management Console (MMC) snap-in. A *snap-in* is simply a program designed to run inside MMC. Other BackOffice server management tools can also run inside MMC. This design is the reason there are two major toolbars within the Enterprise Manager interface. The top one contains options (under Console and Window) to let the user control the MMC and its snap-ins. The lower one is the Enterprise Manager toolbar, in which you will find menus and icons for administering servers and databases.

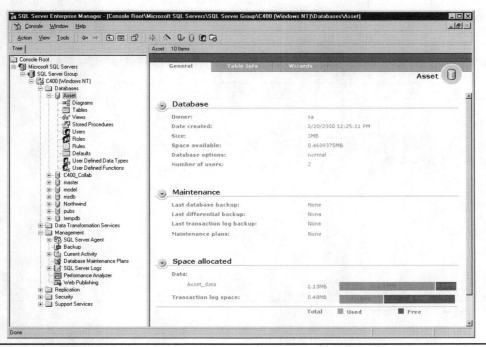

Figure 2-3   *The taskpad*

As I mentioned earlier, SQL Mail service can be controlled from the Support Services node in Enterprise Manager.

DTS and Import/Export Data

Data Transformation Services (DTS) is a component of SQL Server that enables administrators to transfer data and objects between servers and databases. It is not limited to export from and import to SQL Server. It can also be used between any ODBC- or OLE DB–compliant databases, including Oracle, Sybase SQL Server, Access, and FoxPro, and between other storage types such as text files, Excel spreadsheets, and Outlook files.

The tangible part of DTS is the DTS Wizard, which can be started from Enterprise Manager (the Data Transformation Services node) or the Windows menu (Import and Export Data). In the screens that follow, you can specify the source and target data locations as well as the transformation to be performed on the data. The result of the DTS Wizard is also a package that could be further managed using tools within the Data Transformation Services node in Enterprise Manager. Figure 2-4 shows such a package in DTS Designer. A package can transform data, run SQL scripts, load files from the Internet, send e-mails, run ActiveX (VBScript and JavaScript) tasks, copy SQL Server objects, run command shell processes, and so on. Unfortunately, this exciting topic is beyond the scope of this book.

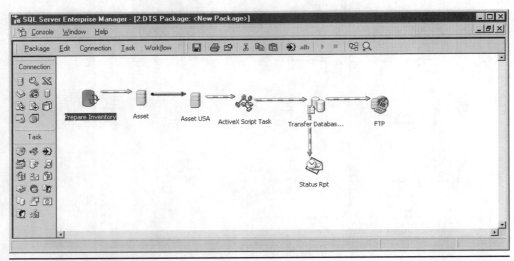

Figure 2-4   *DTS Designer*

osql and isql

Before Query Analyzer (and ISQL/W—ISQL for Windows), DBAs used a command line utility called *isql* to run Transact-SQL statements against the server (see Figure 2-5).

Tools such as isql are reminiscent of UNIX environments, and they are seldom used now that GUI applications like Query Analyzer are available.

Another tool that works from the command prompt is *osql*. It was introduced in SQL Server 7.0. The major difference between these two command line utilities lies in the API each uses to connect to SQL Server databases: osql uses ODBC to connect, and isql uses DB-Library. isql does not support all SQL Server 2000 features because DB-Library is an API developed for SQL Server 6.5.

SQL Server Profiler

SQL Server Profiler is a component of SQL Server designed to monitor activities on servers and in databases (see Figure 2-6).

You can use this utility to capture queries against a database, the activities of a particular user application, login attempts, failures, errors, and transactions. It is often used to improve the performance of a system, and you can also use it to troubleshoot and debug stored procedures and T-SQL scripts.

```
Command Prompt - isql -SC400 -Usa                                    _ □ ×
C:\Documents and Settings\Dsunderic>isql/?
isql: unknown option ?
usage: isql                [-U login id]         [-P password]
  [-S server]              [-H hostname]         [-E trusted connection]
  [-d use database name]   [-l login timeout]    [-t query timeout]
  [-h headers]             [-s colseparator]     [-w columnwidth]
  [-a packetsize]          [-e echo input]       [-x max text size]
  [-L list servers]        [-c cmdend]
  [-q "cmdline query"]     [-Q "cmdline query" and exit]
  [-n remove numbering]    [-m errorlevel]
  [-r msgs to stderr]
  [-i inputfile]           [-o outputfile]
  [-p print statistics]    [-b On error batch abort]
  [-O use Old ISQL behavior disables the following]
      <EOF> batch processing
      Auto console width scaling
      Wide messages
      default errorlevel is -1 vs 1
  [-? show syntax summary (this screen)]

C:\Documents and Settings\Dsunderic>isql -SC400 -Usa
Password:
1> use asset
2> select * from Equipment
3> go_
```

Figure 2-5 *The isql command line utility*

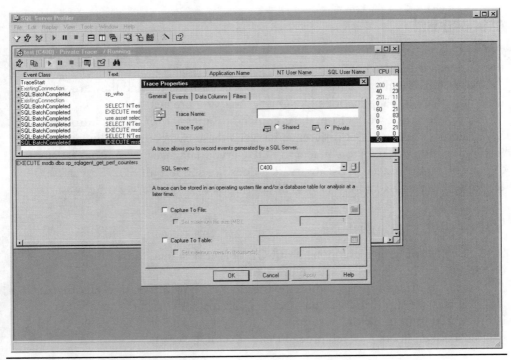

Figure 2-6 *SQL Server Profiler*

Client Network Utility

SQL Server client tools can use different protocols to communicate with SQL Server:

► Named pipes

► TCP/IP

► Multiprotocol

► NWLink IPX/SPX

► AppleTalk

► Banyan VINES

► Shared memory

For each protocol, Microsoft has designed a DLL communication library, referred to as a *Network Library* or *NetLib*.

The *Client Network Utility* is designed to select the protocol and NetLib to be used by other client tools. It is possible to specify a *default network library* and exceptions on a per-server basis.

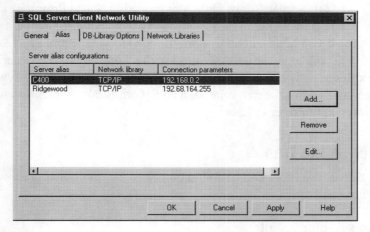

Server Network Utility

The *Server Network Utility* is designed to control network protocols and network ports that SQL Server 2000 instance uses to listen for requests:

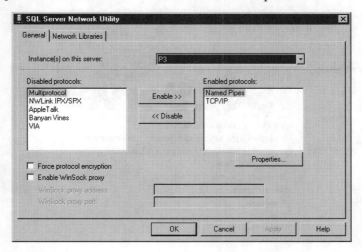

The Help Subsystem and SQL Server Books Online

Traditionally, due to the nature of the environment, SQL Server client tools (including Enterprise Manager and Query Analyzer) have been light on context-sensitive help, but SQL Server has a subsystem that is a great tool for browsing through its documentation—*SQL Server Books Online.* This subsystem contains the complete set of documentation—which used to be delivered on paper—in the form of an online, searchable, indexed hierarchy of documents.

You can start SQL Server Books Online by selecting Start | Programs | Microsoft SQL Server 2000 | Books Online (see Figure 2-7). You can also launch it from Query Analyzer if you highlight a keyword in the Query pane and press SHIFT-F1.

In the Contents tab, you can browse through the hierarchy of the material as in Windows Explorer, or you can switch to the Index tab to see a list of keywords or to the Search tab to define search criteria. The Favorites tab enables you to record pages that you want to refer to later.

SQL Server on the Web

Many SQL Server resources can be found on the Web. Traditional places are Microsoft sites such as:

- ► www.microsoft.com/sql
- ► msdn.microsoft.com

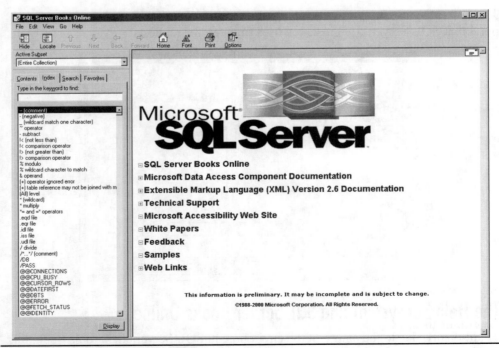

Figure 2-7   *SQL Server Books Online*

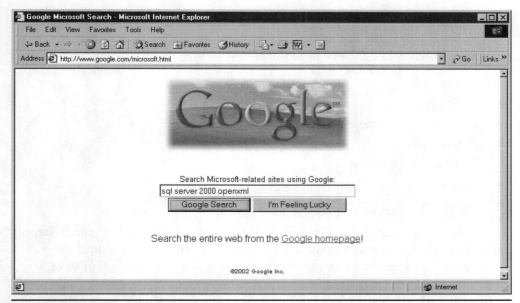

Figure 2-8   *Microsoft-related Google search*

I was always able to find information quicker on Google.com. Later, I discovered that it has a specialized tool that searches only Microsoft-related sites (see Figure 2-8).

Basic Operations with Stored Procedures

This section will serve as a primer to introduce you to the concepts of executing, creating, and editing stored procedures. We will walk through the usage of the most important SQL Server client tools. Since Transact-SQL is just another programming language, we will follow a tradition first established by an unknown programmer and start with a trivial Hello World example.

What Are Stored Procedures?

Stored procedures are database objects that encapsulate collections of Transact-SQL statements on the server for later repetitive use. Although stored procedures use nonprocedural Transact-SQL statements, they are in essence procedural. They define algorithms that determine how operations should be performed.

Stored procedures are the T-SQL equivalents of subroutines in other programming languages. Developers of custom database applications can use all major programming constructs while building stored procedures:

- ► Variables
- ► Data types
- ► Input/output parameters
- ► Return values
- ► Conditional execution
- ► Loops
- ► Comments

SQL Server includes a set of *system stored procedures* designed for administering the system. Their role is to provide information, set configuration, control the environment, manage user-defined objects, and schedule and run custom tasks.

Execution of Stored Procedures from Query Analyzer

The execution of stored procedures from Enterprise Manager or Query Analyzer is very simple. Let's try it using the system stored procedure sp_who, which lists all users and processes connected to the system.

1. Run Query Analyzer (Start | Programs | Microsoft SQL Server 2000 | Query Analyzer). The Query Analyzer application prompts you for a server, login name, and password, as shown in the following illustration. If the application is unable to connect to the server, you should check whether the Microsoft SQL Server service is running and whether you correctly typed the name of the server and/or your login name and password.

TIP

*If you have not changed the server since installation, you can use **sa** as the login name and an empty string (blank) as the password. The name of your machine is the name of the SQL Server. If you are working on the machine that has SQL Server installed, you can always use "**(local)**" or a simple dot "." to refer to the current machine as the server to which you want to connect.*

2. Once you have logged in successfully, the application opens the Query window that you use to write code. In the Query pane, type the following code:

```
exec sp_who
```

NOTE

Query Analyzer uses different colors to distinguish keywords, variables, comments, and constants.

3. To run the stored procedure, you can select Query | Execute, click the green arrow on the toolbar, or press CTRL-E. The application will split the screen to display both query and results (see Figure 2-9).

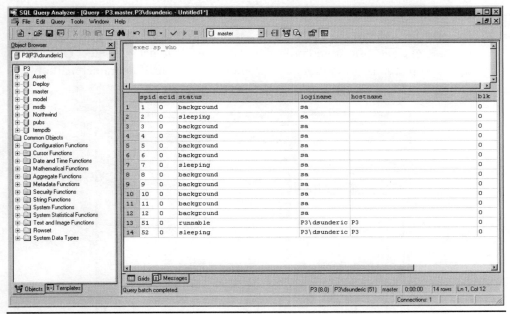

Figure 2-9   *Execution of stored procedures from Query Analyzer*

4. You can click the Messages tab to see whether SQL Server has returned any messages along with the result (such as the number of records, a warning, or an error). This stored procedure lists active processes on the current server and the login names of the users who started them.

5. Select Query | Results in Text and then execute the query again (Query | Execute). Query Analyzer displays the result set in the form of text. Messages are mixed with result sets in this case, which is the way in which Query Analyzer has always worked in past versions (see Figure 2-10).

NOTE

Before we continue, please ensure that you have installed the sample Asset database. If you have not already installed it, review the download and installation instructions in Chapter 1.

You can also use the Object Browser in Query Analyzer to list, execute, and edit stored procedures:

1. If the Object Browser is not already present on the screen, select Tools | Object Browser to display it (see Figure 2-11).

2. Expand the node for the *master* database and expand the Stored Procedures node. Right-click the stored procedure sp_who in the list and select Open from the pop-up menu. Query Analyzer prompts you to specify parameters (not required in this case) and execute the stored procedure.

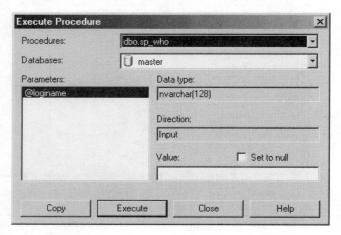

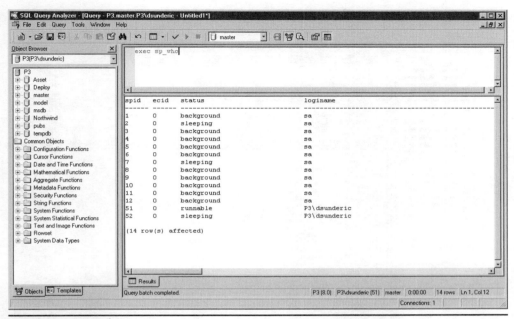

Figure 2-10   *Results in text*

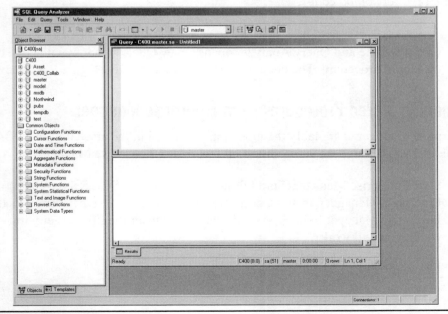

Figure 2-11   *The Object Browser*

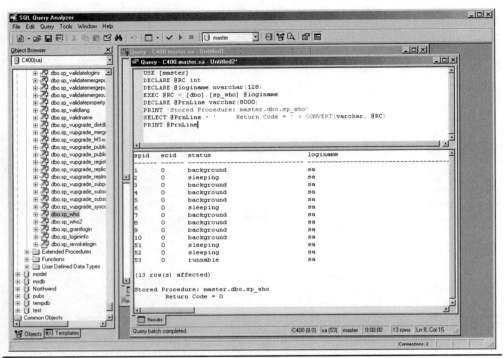

Figure 2-12 *Supporting code*

3. Click Execute and Query Analyzer opens a new Query window with code of the stored procedure. The code is executed automatically (Figure 2-12 above).

Managing Stored Procedures from Enterprise Manager

Enterprise Manager is arguably the most important tool in the arsenal of the DBA. I will lead you through the most important features of Enterprise Manager:

1. Start Enterprise Manager (Start | Programs | Microsoft SQL Server 2000 | Enterprise Manager). In some cases (for example, if you have never opened Enterprise Manager before), you will have to register the first server with which you will work.

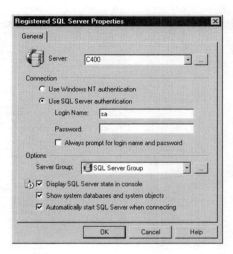

NOTE

Before you can work with a server in Enterprise Manager, you need to register it.

2. Again, you need to provide the name of the server, your login name, and your password. You can accept default values for the Server Group option and all other choices under Options. If the connection parameters are correct, Enterprise Manager displays a window for managing SQL Server.

3. Click the + symbol to expand the SQL Server Group node.

4. Expand your server node (again, click the + symbol).

5. Expand the Databases node.

6. Expand the Asset sample database.

7. Click Stored Procedures and watch as a list of stored procedures is displayed in the Details pane (see Figure 2-13).

8. In this list, find a stored procedure named prGetEqId, and right-click. When you right-click an object in the Details pane, a context-sensitive menu appears with options to let you perform operations such as deleting and renaming the stored procedure or creating a new stored procedure.

9. Select Properties on the pop-up menu. The application opens a window to allow you to view and edit the stored procedure (see Figure 2-14). See the sidebar "The Structure of Stored Procedures" for more information.

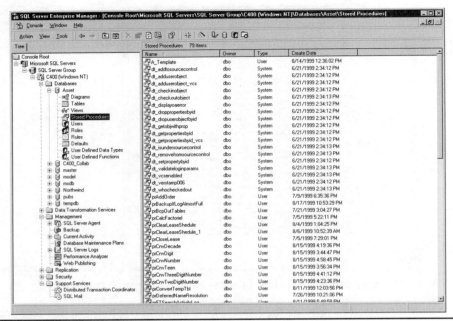

Figure 2-13 *List of stored procedures in Enterprise Manager*

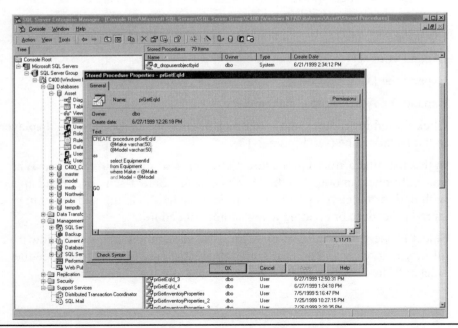

Figure 2-14 *Properties of a stored procedure*

NOTE

Don't worry. In the following chapters, I will give you detailed descriptions of all these objects and their components.

10. Close the Properties window.

11. Right-click anywhere in the Details pane and select New Stored Procedure from the pop-up menu. Enterprise Manager displays a Properties window with a template for the stored procedure (see Figure 2-15).

12. Replace the template with the following code:

```
Create procedure prHelloWorld_1 As
    Select 'Hello world'
    Select * from Inventory
```

13. Click the Check Syntax button to verify the syntax of the procedure.

14. Click OK. The procedure is compiled and stored in the database. You will be able to see it in the list of stored procedures.

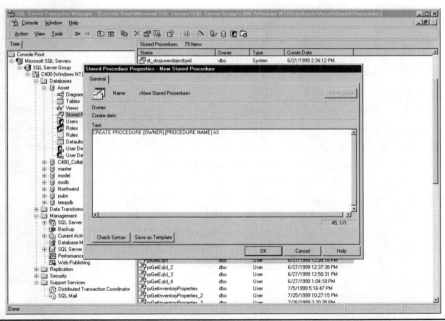

Figure 2-15   *A template of a new stored procedure*

NOTE

Earlier versions of Enterprise Manager did not display the stored procedure in the list automatically. The user had to refresh the screen by right-clicking the database name and selecting Refresh from the menu.

This scenario still arises on occasion. For example, if you create a stored procedure (or change something in the database) using some other tool, you will need to refresh the list in Enterprise Manager.

You can switch to Query Analyzer to run the newly created stored procedure:

1. On the Tools menu, select SQL Server Query Analyzer, switch to the Asset database, and type the following code:

    ```
    Exec prHelloWorld_1
    ```

NOTE

Query Analyzer will always open and connect to the current server when opened from within Enterprise Manager, but will not necessarily default to the current database.

2. Execute it (choose Query | Execute).

The Structure of Stored Procedures

We will pause a minute to explain the structure of a stored procedure. The prGetEqId stored procedure encapsulates a relatively simple Select statement for later use. It returns a recordset containing values from the EquipmentId column. The recordset will contain only records with the specified Make and Model.

The code of a stored procedure consists of a *header* and a *body*. The header of the stored procedure defines external attributes of the stored procedure—its *name* and a list of one or more *parameters*. The prGetEqId stored procedure has two parameters. Parameter names must start with the @ character. The developer must also define a data type for each parameter. The header must begin with the Create Procedure keyword and finish with the As keyword.

The body of the stored procedure contains the Transact-SQL statements to be executed when the stored procedure runs. In this case, there is just one Select statement using the procedure parameters.

Editing Stored Procedures in Enterprise Manager

The easiest way to edit stored procedures is to use Enterprise Manager. You simply need to display the Properties window for the stored procedure:

1. Verify that the Stored Procedures node in the Asset database is still open in Enterprise Manager.

2. Right-click the prHelloWorld_1 stored procedure and select Properties. The Properties window displays the stored procedure code.

Editing Stored Procedures in Query Analyzer

Before Enterprise Manager was released in Microsoft SQL Server 6.0, administrators used isql (the ancestor of Query Analyzer) to do most of the work. It is still possible to edit stored procedures in the traditional way using Query Analyzer.

Traditionally, DBAs included the code for deleting (dropping) the original stored procedure and then re-creating the stored procedure (with the changed code):

1. Launch Query Analyzer.

2. Make sure that you are in the Asset database.

3. Type the following code in the Query pane:

```
DROP PROCEDURE prHelloWorld_1
GO

CREATE PROCEDURE prHelloWorld_1
AS
    SELECT 'Hello Dejan'
    SELECT * from Inventory
RETURN 0
GO
```

4. Execute the code by selecting Query | Execute.

SQL Server will first delete the existing stored procedure and then re-create it (with the new code).

The trouble with this method (dropping and then re-creating) is that you also drop some attributes associated with the stored procedure (such as permissions), which also affects other dependent objects. Since Microsoft SQL Server 7.0, it is possible to use the Alter Procedure statement to modify an existing stored procedure without affecting permissions and other dependent objects:

```
ALTER PROCEDURE prHelloWorld_1
AS
    SELECT 'Hello World again!'
    SELECT * from Inventory
RETURN 0

GO
```

You may have noticed the Go command in the previous two examples. This command is not a SQL statement. It is not even part of the T-SQL language. It is a signal to Query Analyzer (and some other tools, such as isql and osql) to treat the SQL statements as one set—a *batch*. All statements in a batch are compiled and executed together.

In SQL Server 2000, it is possible to use the Object Browser to edit stored procedures:

1. If the Object Browser is not already present on the screen, select Tools | Object Browser to display it.

2. Open the Asset database and then its list of stored procedures.

3. Find and right-click prHelloWorld_1 in the list and select Edit. Query Analyzer displays a Query window with the code of the stored procedure in it (see Figure 2-16).

Figure 2-16   *The Query window displays the stored procedure's code.*

NOTE

Do not be confused by the additional Set Quoted_Identifier and Set Ansi_Nulls statements. They are present just to set an optimal environment for the execution of the Alter Procedure statement. When they are present, the client session settings are ignored during the stored procedure execution.

4. Once you are satisfied with changes in the code, you can simply execute it (Query | Execute).

Syntax Errors

Sooner or later you will make a typo, and the server will react with an error. Let's deliberately cause a problem to see how the server reacts.

1. Verify that you are in Query Analyzer and that Asset is your current database. We will attempt to alter the code of prHelloWorld_1.

NOTE

There are two ways to type comments in the Transact-SQL language. If you type two dashes (- -), the rest of that line will be ignored by the server. Code stretched over multiple lines can be commented out by using /* and */ as delimiters at either end of the comment.

2. We will comment out the second line (the keyword As):

```
Alter Procedure prHelloWorld_1
--As
Select 'Hello World again!'
    Select * from Inventory
Return 0
Go
```

3. As soon as you execute this code, the server reports an error (see Figure 2-17). Keep in mind that SQL Server is not a perfect compiler. Some error messages that it reports may not contain sufficient details or may even be misleading. The rule of thumb is simple: check your basic syntax first.

TIP

If you double-click the error message in the Results pane, Query Analyzer will try to return the cursor to the line containing the error in the Query pane (actually, to the first line that appears after the last statement that executed correctly). This is very useful when you are executing a long batch.

Figure 2-17   *An error in Query Analyzer*

Another advantage the Alter statement has over the Drop/Create approach is that the stored procedure remains intact after an unsuccessful attempt such as we produced in this example.

You have made your first steps in the development of stored procedures in Transact-SQL. The next chapter explores SQL Server stored procedure design in greater detail.

Naming Conventions

One of the most important things you can do to improve the quality and readability of your code is to use standards to name variables, procedures, and objects in your database. We will now go though the importance of using naming conventions and describe one used in this book.

Why Bother?

Unfortunately, many developers dislike, and avoid using, standards. Their usual explanation is that standards stifle their creativity, or that the constant need to comply with standards distracts them from what they are really being paid to do. While there may be some truth in these claims, compliance with reasonable standards is another one of those habits that differentiates the professional from the amateur (not to mention the prima donna). Often, however, the problem lies not in the presence or content of a standard but in the spirit of its enforcement. Frequently, organizations (or the people in them) get carried away. They forget the reasons for enforcing standards, and the standards become an end in themselves.

There are several valid reasons for introducing naming conventions:

► The main reason for the existence of naming conventions is to make code readable, understandable, and easy to remember.

► A standard allows developers to speak a common "language" that will help the team to communicate more efficiently.

► Team members will be able to understand and learn parts of the code with which they are not familiar.

► New team members will have to learn only one standard way of coding instead of having to learn the distinct coding habits of individual team members.

► Time will be saved and confusion avoided, since it will be easier to define and identify unique names for objects and variables.

If you are developing a project on your own, you might go through it without implementing a standard (or without being aware that you actually have a standard). However, in most cases, the introduction of a standard becomes critical, such as when the following conditions exist:

► More than one developer is working on the project.

► The code or project will be maintained or reviewed by other developers who are not currently members of the team.

► The application under development is too complex for one person to analyze all aspects at once and requires different components to be designed and implemented separately.

Conventions do not have to be complicated. To demonstrate this point, consider this simple example. If you name a variable @OrderNum, you will become confused about its contents because the name does not convey its purpose clearly. Does it contain the total number of orders or the index of a particular order? To resolve this confusion, you could establish a convention that indexes are named with "Id" and totals with "Count" at the end of the name. In this case, the variable becomes @OrderId or @OrderCount.

Naming Objects and Variables

The naming of objects should take into account the following details:

► Entity description
► Name length
► Abbreviations
► Name formatting

Entity Description

It is common knowledge that variables, procedures, and objects should be named after the entities or processes that they represent. Therefore, just to type a full description is a good start. The advantages of this approach are

► Nobody will be confused about the purpose or contents.
► It makes for easy-to-read code, since no cryptic abbreviations are used.
► It makes the entity name easy to understand and memorize, since the description closely matches the entity.

Just compare the names in the following table:

Good	Bad
@CurrentDate	@D
@ActivityCount	@ActNum
@EquipmentType	@ET
CalculateOrderTotal	RunCalc

NOTE

Such descriptions are usually just the basis for a name. Standards generally prescribe the use of different prefixes or suffixes to further describe other attributes such as the type of object, the data type of a variable, and the scope.

A very common mistake is to use computer-oriented terminology instead of business-oriented terminology. For example, ProcessRecord is a confusing name for a procedure. It should be replaced with a business description of the process, such as CompleteOrder.

Name Length

Unfortunately, if you are too literal in naming procedures according to their business descriptions, you end up with names like

▶   PickupReconciliationInventoryIdentifier

▶   TotalAmountOfMonthlyPayments

▶   GetParentOrganizationalUnitName

Although SQL Server supports the use of identifiers up to 128 characters long, research has shown that code in which most variable names are between 8 and 15 characters in length is easiest to develop, read, debug, and maintain. This fact does not imply that all of your variables must have lengths in that range, but you can use it as a rule of thumb.

Another rule of thumb is to try to limit names to three words. Otherwise, names become too long, and thus more difficult to use and maintain.

You could go to an extreme in the other direction, as well. If you are using a variable as a temporary counter in a loop, you could name it @I. But even in that case, it might be easier to understand your code if you name it @OrderItem.

Abbreviations

A simple way to reduce the length of a name is to abbreviate it. If you can find an abbreviation in a thesaurus or dictionary, you should use it. You will avoid potential confusion. If not, you can simply remove vowels (except at the beginning of the word) and duplicate letters from each word, as in these examples:

▶   Current = Crnt

▶   Address = Adr

- ► Error = Err
- ► Average = Avg

You could also use the first letters of words or the first few letters of a word, but make sure that the names you create will not be confused with other, more common abbreviations. For example, you could abbreviate Complete Order Management to COM, but Visual Basic programmers might assume it stands for "component."

If you do not want to confuse readers of your code (such as the fellow programmers trying to maintain it months after you have taken early retirement and moved to a remote tropical island), you should *avoid* using phonetic abbreviations like

- ► 4tran (Fortran)
- ► xqt (execute)
- ► b4 (before)

Abbreviations are great, but you should be careful not to confuse your colleagues. Try to be consistent. If you start abbreviating one word, you should do the same in all occurrences (variables, procedures, objects). It is potentially confusing to abbreviate the word Equipment as Eq in one case and leave the full word in another case. You will cause confusion as to which to use and whether they are equivalent.

To avoid confusion, you can write a description (using full words) in comments beside the declaration of a variable, in the definition of an object, or in the header of a procedure; for example:

```
declare @ErrCd int  -- Error Code
```

Ideally, the use of abbreviations should be defined, documented, and enforced as a naming convention and therefore applied consistently by everyone on the team.

Name Formatting

I have seen people have endless debates about formatting identifiers. To underscore or not to underscore—that is the question:

- ► LeaseScheduleId
- ► lease_schedule_id

The truth is: it does not matter. You should avoid mixing these two conventions because developers will never know what they have used for which variable.

Unfortunately, you can catch even Microsoft developers mixing them. They are just human beings, after all.

In some rare cases, I believe it is justifiable to mix these two conventions in one identifier. For example, I like to note modification statements at the end of the name of a trigger (insert and update trigger on OrderItem table):

```
trOrderItem_IU
```

I also use an underscore to divide table names joined with a foreign key (such as a foreign key between Order and OrderItem tables):

```
fk_Order_OrderItem
```

Suggested Convention

In computer science theory, you can find several well-documented formal conventions. The most famous one is the Hungarian convention (http://msdn.microsoft.com/isapi/msdnlib.idc?theURL=/library/techart/hunganotat.htm). I will present a convention that is rather informal and tailored for use in Transact-SQL. You do not have to follow it literally, but you should have a good reason to break any rule.

TIP

Rules are made to be broken, but only if the solution is thereby improved.

Variables

Variable identifiers should consist of two parts:

▶ The *base part,* which describes the content of the variable
▶ The *prefix,* which describes the data type of the variable

Table 2-1 shows data type abbreviations that should be used as prefixes.

Data Type	Prefix	Example
char	chr	@chrFirstName
varchar	chv	@chvActivity
nchar	chrn	@chrnLastName
nvarchar	chvn	@chvnLastName

Table 2-1   *Data Type Prefixes*

Data Type	Prefix	Example
text	txt	@txtNote
ntext	txtn	@txtnComment
datetime	dtm	@dtmTargetDate
smalldatetime	dts	@dtsCompletionDate
tinyint	iny	@inyActivityId
smallint	ins	@insEquipmentTypeId
integer	int	@intAsset
bigint	inb	@inbGTIN
numeric or decimal	dec	@decProfit
real	rea	@reaVelocity
float	flt	@fltLength
smallmoney	mns	@mnsCost
money	mny	@mnyPrice
binary	bin	@binPath
varbinary	biv	@bivContract
image	img	@imgLogo
bit	bit	@bitOperational
timestamp	tsp	@tspCurrent
uniqueidentifier	guid	@guidOrderId
sql_variant	var	@varPrice
cursor	cur	@curInventory
table	tbl	@tblLease

Table 2-1   *Data Type Prefixes* (continued)

Database Objects

Names of database objects should consist of two parts:

▶ The *base part,* which describes the content of the object

▶ The *prefix,* which describes the type of database object

Table 2-2 shows database object abbreviations that should be used as prefixes.

Database Object	Prefix	Example
Table	(no prefix)	Activities
Column	(no prefix)	ActivityId
View	v	vActivities
Stored procedure	pr	prCompleteOrder
Trigger	tr	trOrder_IU
Default	df	dfToday
Rule	rul	rulCheckZIP
Index	ix	ix_LastName
Primary key	pk	pk_ContactId
Foreign key	fk	fk_Order_OrderType
User-defined data type	udt	udtPhone
User-defined functions	fn	fnDueDates

Table 2-2   *Database Object Prefixes*

NOTE

Tables and columns should not have prefixes describing the object type.

Triggers

Names of triggers should consist of three parts:

► The *prefix* (tr), which implies the database object type

► The *base part,* which describes the table to which the trigger is attached

► The *suffix,* which shows modification statements (Insert, Update, and Delete)

The following is an example of a trigger name:

```
trOrder_IU
```

If more than one trigger per modification statement is attached to the table, the base part should contain the name of the table and a reference to a business rule implemented by a trigger:

► **trOrderCascadingDelete_D**   Delete trigger on Order table that implements cascading deletes of order items.

▶ **trOrderItemTotal_D**   Delete trigger on Order table that maintains a total of order item prices.

SQL Server 2000 has an additional type of trigger—*Instead-of* triggers (reviewed in detail in Chapter 8). To differentiate them from standard triggers (called *After* triggers in SQL Server 2000 documentation), you should use a different naming convention for them. For example, to represent the Instead-of delete trigger on the Order table, you could use "itr" as a prefix:

```
itr_Order_D
```

Stored Procedures

The base name of a stored procedure should usually be created from a verb followed by a noun to describe the process the stored procedure performs on an object, as in these examples:

▶ prGetEquipment
▶ prCloseLease

You can also adopt the opposite role—noun followed by verb:

▶ prEquipmentGet
▶ prLeaseClose

If the procedure performs several tasks, all of those tasks should become part of the procedure name. It is okay to make procedure names longer than variable names. You should be able to pack a name into between 20 and 40 characters.

Some developers use the sp_ prefix in front of the base name of a stored procedure. This prefix should be reserved for system stored procedures that reside in the *master* database and that are accessible from all databases.

You should also avoid computer-oriented or fuzzy names like these:

▶ prProcessData
▶ prDoAction

Names such as these are often a symptom of a poorly designed stored procedure.

CHAPTER 3

Stored Procedure Design Concepts

A *stored procedure* is a set of T-SQL statements that is compiled and stored as a single database object for later repetitive use. They are the equivalent of subroutines and functions in other programming languages. Upon completion of this chapter, you will be able to do the following:

▶ Create a stored procedure

▶ Explain the elements of a stored procedure

▶ List ways to return information from a stored procedure

▶ Pass input parameters to a stored procedure

▶ Receive output parameters from a stored procedure

▶ Receive a return value from a stored procedure

▶ Explain where stored procedures are stored on SQL Server

▶ Explain the compilation and reuse of stored procedures

Anatomy of a Stored Procedure

We can describe a stored procedure in terms of

▶ Composition

▶ Functionality

▶ Syntax

Composition

Logically, a stored procedure consists of

▶ A *header* that defines the name of the stored procedure, the input and output parameters, and some miscellaneous processing options. You can think of it as an API (application programming interface) or declaration of the stored procedure.

▶ A *body* that contains one or more Transact-SQL statements to be executed at runtime.

Creating Stored Procedures

Let's look at the simplified syntax for implementing the core functionality of stored procedures:

```
CREATE PROC[EDURE] procedure_name
    [ {@parameter data_type} [= default] [OUTPUT] ] [,...n]
AS
    sql_statement [...n]
```

The following is an example of a stored procedure:

```
Create Procedure prGetEquipment
    @chvMake varchar(50)
as
    Select *
    from Equipment
    where Make = @chvMake
```

This Transact-SQL statement creates a stored procedure named prGetEquipment
with one input parameter. During execution, prGetEquipment returns a result set
containing all records from the Equipment table having a Make column equal to the
input parameter.

Please, be patient and do not create the procedure in the Asset database yet. If you
try to create a stored procedure that already exists in the database, SQL Server will
report an error. You can reproduce such an error if you run the same statement for
creating a stored procedure twice. For example:

```
Server: Msg 2729, Level 16, State 5, Procedure prGetEquipment, Line 3
Procedure 'prGetEquipment' group number 1 already exists in the database.
Choose another procedure name.
```

As I have shown in Chapter 2, one way to change a stored procedure is to drop
and re-create it. There are two ways to prevent the error just described. One way is to
use an Alter Procedure statement to change the stored procedure. I will explain this
technique in the next section. The traditional way to prevent this error is to delete a
stored procedure (using the Drop Procedure statement) and then create it again:

```
Drop Procedure prGetEquipment
go

Create Procedure prGetEquipment
    @intEqTypeId int
as
    Select *
    from Equipment
    where EqTypeId = @intEqTypeId
go
```

If you are not sure whether a stored procedure exists, you can write a piece of code to check for its existence. If you do not, SQL Server will report an error when you try to drop a stored procedure that does not exist. This code takes advantage of the fact that SQL Server records each database object in the sysobjects table (see "Storing Stored Procedures," later in this chapter). It also uses programming constructs I have not yet introduced in this book. For now, do not worry about the details. All will become clear later.

```
if exists (select * from sysobjects
          where id = object_id('prGetEquipment ')
    and OBJECTPROPERTY(id, 'IsProcedure') = 1)
drop procedure prGetEquipment
GO

Create Procedure prGetEquipment
    @intEqTypeId int
as
    Select *
    from Equipment
    where EqTypeId = @intEqTypeId
go
```

NOTE

Most of the stored procedures in this book already exist in the database. If you just try to create them, SQL Server will complain. If you are sure that the code that you have typed is correct, you can drop the original stored procedure and put yours in its place. Or you can alter the original stored procedure and use your code instead.

It is much better to rename your stored procedure. All stored procedures in the Asset database start with the pr prefix. You could start yours, for example, with up (for user procedure). I follow a similar practice when I create several versions of the same stored procedure to illustrate a point or a technique. I merely change the stored procedure's suffix by adding a version number (for instance, _1, _2, and so on).

Altering Stored Procedures

The other way to change a stored procedure is to use the Alter Procedure statement:

```
Alter Procedure prGetEquipment
    @intEqTypeId int
as
    Select *
    from Equipment
    where EqTypeId = @intEqTypeId
go
```

The syntax of this statement is identical to the syntax of the Create Procedure statement (except for the keyword). The main reason for using this statement is to avoid undesirable effects on permissions and dependent database objects. For more details about permissions, see Chapter 10.

The Alter Procedure statement preserves all aspects of the original stored procedure. The object identification number (id column) of the procedure from the sysobjects table remains the same, and all references to the stored procedure are intact. Therefore, it is much better to use the Alter Procedure statement than to drop and re-create the procedure. For more details about the sysobjects table and the object identification number (id column), see "Storing Stored Procedures," later in this chapter.

Limits

When you are creating or changing a stored procedure, you should keep in mind the following limits:

- ▶ The name of the procedure is a standard Transact-SQL identifier. The maximum length of any identifier is 128 characters.

- ▶ Stored procedures may contain up to 2100 input and output parameters.

- ▶ The body of the stored procedure consists of one or more Transact-SQL statements. The maximum size of the body of the stored procedure is 128MB.

Functionality

Stored procedures can be used to

- ▶ Return information to the caller
- ▶ Modify data in databases
- ▶ Implement business logic in data tier
- ▶ Control access to data
- ▶ Improve performance of the system
- ▶ Reduce network traffic
- ▶ Perform other actions and operations (such as process e-mail, execute operating system commands and processes, and manage other SQL server objects)

There are four ways to receive information from a stored procedure:

- ▶ Result set
- ▶ Output parameters

► Return value

► Global cursor

Returning Result Sets

To obtain a result set from a stored procedure, insert a Transact-SQL statement that returns a result set into the body of the stored procedure. The simplest way is by using a Select statement, but you could also call another stored procedure.

It is also possible to return several result sets from one stored procedure. Such a stored procedure will simply contain several Select statements. You should note that some client data-access methods (such as ADO) can access all result sets, but others will receive just the first one or possibly even report an error.

Input and Output Parameters

Let's add a new procedure to the Asset database:

```
Create procedure prGetEqId
     @chvMake varchar(50),
     @chvModel varchar(50)
as
     select EquipmentId
     from Equipment
     where Make = @chvMake
     and Model = @chvModel
```

This is a very simple stored procedure. It uses two input parameters to receive the make and model, and returns identifiers of equipment that matches the specified make and model.

Physically, the stored procedure encapsulates just one Select statement. The header and body of the procedure are divided by the keyword As. The header of the stored procedure contains a list of parameters delimited with a comma (,) character. Each parameter is defined with an identifier and a data type. Parameter identifiers must begin with the at sign (@).

You can use the following statement to execute the stored procedure:

```
Execute prGetEqId 'Toshiba', 'Portege 7020CT'
```

The keyword Execute is followed by the name of the stored procedure. Since the stored procedure requires two parameters, they are provided in the form of a comma-delimited list. In this case, they are strings, so they must be delimited with single quotation marks.

The keyword Execute is not needed if the stored procedure is executed in the first statement of a batch:

```
prGetEqId 'Toshiba', 'Portege 7020CT'
```

However, I recommend you use it. It is a good habit that leads to clean code. You can use its shorter version (Exec) to save keystrokes:

```
Exec prGetEqId 'Toshiba', 'Portege 7020CT'
```

The execution will return a result set containing just one value in one record:

```
EquipmentId
-----------
1

(1 row(s) affected)
```

Stored procedures can return output parameters to the caller. To illustrate, we will create a stored procedure similar to the previous one, but having one critical difference: this new stored procedure contains an additional parameter. The direction of the parameter is controlled by including the keyword Output after the data type:

```
Create procedure prGetEqId_2
    @chvMake varchar(50),
    @chvModel varchar(50),
    @intEqId int output
as

    select @intEqId = EquipmentId
    from Equipment
    where Make = @chvMake
    and Model = @chvModel
```

The Select statement does not return a result set, as the previous one did. Instead, it assigns an output parameter, @EqId, with the selected value.

NOTE

This stored procedure is not perfect. It may seem correct at first glance, but there is a potential problem with it. More than one piece of equipment (that is, more than one record) could correspond to the criteria. I will address this issue in detail in the chapters to follow.

In this case, we require a more complicated batch of Transact-SQL statements to execute the stored procedure. We must define the variable that will receive the output value. The parameter must be followed by the Output keyword to indicate that a value for the parameter will be returned by the procedure. At the end of the batch, the result of the stored procedure is displayed using the Select statement:

```
Declare @intEqId int
Execute prGetEqId_2 'Toshiba', 'Portege 7020CT', @intEqId OUTPUT
Select @intEqId 'Equipment Identifier'
```

The batch returns the value of the variable as an output parameter:

```
Equipment Identifier
--------------------
1

(1 row(s) affected)
```

NOTE

A typical error is to forget to mark parameters in Execute statements with Output. The stored procedure will be executed, but the value of the variable will not be returned.

Return Value

An alternative way to send values from a stored procedure to the caller is to use a *return value*. Each stored procedure can end with a Return statement. The statement can be followed by an *integer* value that can be read by the caller. If the return value is not explicitly set, the server will return the default value—zero (0).

Because return values are limited to integer data types, they are most often used to signal an status or error code to the caller. We will examine this use later. First, let's explore its functionality in some unorthodox examples.

In the following example, the value returned by the procedure will be assigned to the local variable and finally returned to the caller:

```
Create Procdure prGetEqId_3
     @chvMake varchar(50),
     @chvModel varchar(50)
as

Declare @intEqId int

Select @intEqId  = EquipmentId
from Equipment
where Make = @chvMake
and Model = @chvModel

Return @intEqId
```

The same functionality could be achieved even without a local variable, since a Return statement can accept an integer expression instead of an integer value:

```
Create Procedure prGetEqId_3
     @chvMake varchar(50),
     @chvModel varchar(50)
as
   Return (select EquipmentId
           from Equipment
           where Make = @chvMake
           and Model = @chvModel)
```

To execute the stored procedure and access the returned value, we require the following lines of code:

```
Declare @intEqId int
Execute @intEqId = prGetEqId_3 'Toshiba', 'Portege 7020CT'
Select @intEqId 'Equipment Identifier'
```

Notice the difference in assigning a value. The local variable must be inserted before the name of the stored procedure. The result of the batch is the returned value:

```
Equipment Identifier
--------------------
1

(1 row(s) affected)
```

This solution, however, is not a perfect way to transfer information from a stored procedure to a caller. In the first place, it is limited by data type. Only integers can be returned this way (including int, smallint, and tinyint). This method is used primarily to return status information to the caller:

```
Create Procedure prGetEqId_2
     @chvMake varchar(50),
     @chvModel varchar(50),
     @intEqId int output
As
     select @intEqId = EquipmentId
     from Equipment
     where Make = @chvMake
     and Model = @chvModel
Return @@error
```

In this example, the stored procedure will potentially return an error code. @@error is a global variable/scalar function that contains an error number in the case of failure or a zero in the case of success. To execute the stored procedure, use the following code:

```
Declare     @intEqId int,
            @intErrorCode int
Execute @intErrorCode = prGetEqId_2 'Toshiba',
                                    'Portege 7020CT',
                                    @intEqId output
Select @intEqId result, @intErrorCode ErrorCode
```

The result will look like this:

```
result      ErrorCode
----------- -----------
1           0

(1 row(s) affected)
```

An ErrorCode of 0 indicates the stored procedure was executed successfully without errors.

Default Values

If the stored procedure statement has parameters, you must supply values for the parameters in your Exec statement. If a user fails to supply them, the server reports an error. It is possible, however, to assign default values to the parameters so that the user is not required to supply them. Default values are defined at the end of a parameter definition, behind the data types. All that is needed is an assignment (=) and a value.

Add this new procedure to the Asset database:

```
Create Procedure prGetEqId_4
    @chvMake varchar(50) = '%',
    @chvModel varchar(50) = '%'
as
    Select *
    from Equipment
    where Make Like @chvMake
    and Model Like @chvModel
```

The procedure is designed as a small search engine that accepts T-SQL wild cards. You can execute this stored procedure with normal values:

```
Execute prGetEqId_4 'T%', 'Portege%'
```

The result set will consist of records that match the criteria:

```
EquipmentId Make                    Model                   EqTypeId
----------- --------------------- ----------------------- --------
1           Toshiba               Portege 7020CT          1

(1 row(s) affected)
```

If one parameter is omitted, as follows, the procedure will behave, since the value that was defined as a default has been supplied:

```
Execute prGetEqId_4 'T%'
```

The server will return the following result set:

```
EquipmentId Make                    Model                   EqTypeId
----------- --------------------- ----------------------- --------
1           Toshiba               Portege 7020CT          1

(1 row(s) affected)
```

Even both parameters may be skipped:

```
Execute prGetEqId_4
```

The server will return all records that match the default criteria:

```
EquipmentId Make                    Model                   EqTypeId
----------- --------------------- ----------------------- --------
1           Toshiba               Portege 7020CT          1
2           Sony                  Trinitron 17XE          3

(2 row(s) affected)
```

Passing Parameters by Name

You do not have to follow parameter order if you pass parameters by name. You must type the name of the parameter and then assign a value to it. The parameter name must match its definition, including the @ sign.

This method is sometimes called *passing parameters by name*. The original method can be referred to as *passing parameters by position*. In the following example, the server will use T% for the second parameter and a default value, %, for the first one:

```
Execute prGetEqId_4 @Model = 'T%'
```

The result of the search will be the following:

```
EquipmentId Make                    Model                    EqTypeId
----------- ----------------------- ------------------------ --------
2           Sony                    Trinitron 17XE           3

(1 row(s) affected)
```

The opportunity to skip parameters is just one reason for passing parameters by name. Even more important is the opportunity to create a method that makes code more readable and maintainable. And, if a developer makes a mistake and assigns a value to a nonexistent parameter, the error will be picked up by SQL Server.

TIP

Although passing parameters by position can be a little faster, passing parameters by name is preferable.

Syntax

The following is the complete syntax for the creation of a stored procedure:

```
CREATE PROC[EDURE] procedure_name [;number]
    [
        {@parameter data_type} [VARYING] [= default] [OUTPUT]
    ]
    [,...n]
[WITH {    RECOMPILE
        | ENCRYPTION
        | RECOMPILE, ENCRYPTION }
]
[FOR REPLICATION]
AS
    sql_statement [...n]
```

When you create a stored procedure using With Encryption, the code of the stored procedure is encrypted and then saved in the database. SQL Server will be able to use the encrypted version of the source code to recompile the stored procedure when needed, but none of the users (not even the system administrator) will be able to obtain it.

NOTE

That was the theory. In reality, you should not count on SQL Server encryption to protect your code. It is possible to find on the Internet the means to defeat SQL Server encryption. Copyright and good support are much better protection for the company's interests when you deploy stored procedures on the server of your client.

Keep in mind that you will not be able to change a stored procedure if you create the procedure using With Encryption. You must preserve its code somewhere else (ideally in a source code management system like Visual SourceSafe, described in Chapter 11). For more details about storage and encryption of stored procedures, see "Storing Stored Procedures," later in this chapter.

As a developer, you might decide to recompile a stored procedure each time it is used. To force compilation, you should create the stored procedure using With Recompile. Recompiling for each use may improve or degrade the performance of the stored procedure: although the compilation process is extra overhead when you are executing the stored procedure, SQL Server will sometimes recompile the stored procedure differently (and more economically) based on the data it is targeting. You will find more details about compilation and reasons for recompiling a stored procedure later in this chapter.

[*;number*] is an optional integer value that can be added to the name of a stored procedure. In this way, a user can create a group of stored procedures that can be deleted with a single Drop Procedure statement. Procedures will have names such as

- ▶ prListEquipment;1
- ▶ prListEquipment;2
- ▶ prListEquipment;3

Numbering of stored procedures is sometimes used during development and testing, so that all nonproduction versions of a procedure can be dropped simultaneously and quickly.

Stored procedures that include the For Replication option are usually created by SQL Server to serve as a filter during the replication of databases.

An output parameter for a stored procedure can also be of the `cursor` data type. In such a case, the structure of the result set contained by the cursor might vary. The [Varying] option will notify SQL Server to handle such cases. But it is too early to talk about cursors. We will return to cursors in the next chapter.

All of these options involve rarely used features. Some of them will be covered in more detail later in this book, but some are simply too esoteric.

Types of Stored Procedures

There are many types of stored procedures:

- ▶ User-defined
- ▶ System
- ▶ Extended

▶ Temporary

▶ Global temporary

▶ Remote

There are also database objects, which are very similar in nature:

▶ Triggers

▶ Views

▶ User-defined functions

As you can infer from the name, *user-defined stored procedures* are simply plain stored procedures assembled by administrators or developers for later use. All the examples we have discussed so far in this chapter have been such stored procedures.

Microsoft delivers a vast set of stored procedures as part of SQL Server. They are designed to cover all aspects of system administration. Internally, *system stored procedures* are just regular stored procedures. Their special features result from the fact that they are stored in system databases (*master* and *msdb*) and they have the prefix sp_. This prefix is more than just a convention. It signals to the server that the stored procedure should be accessible from all databases without putting the database name as a prefix to fully qualify the name of the procedure. For example, you can use sp_spaceused to examine usage of the current database; such as disk space for data and indexes (see Figure 3-1).

We will examine all types of stored procedures in more detail in Chapter 8.

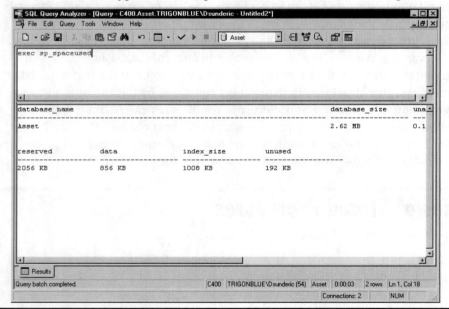

Figure 3-1   *Using sp_spaceused*

Compilation

Transact-SQL is not a standard programming language, nor is Microsoft SQL Server a standard environment for program execution, but the process of compiling the source code for a stored procedure and its execution bear some resemblance to the compilation and execution of programs in standard programming languages.

The Compilation and Execution Process

When a developer executes any batch of T-SQL statements, SQL Server performs the following three steps:

1. Parse the batch.
2. Compile the batch.
3. Execute the batch.

Parsing

Parsing is a process during which the Microsoft SQL Server *command parser module* first verifies the syntax of a batch. If no errors are found, the command parser breaks the source code into logical units such as keywords, identifiers, and operators. The parser then builds an internal structure that describes the series of steps needed to perform the requested operation or to extract the requested result set from the source data. If the batch contains a query, this internal structure is called a *query tree,* and if the batch contains a procedure, it is called a *sequence tree.*

Compilation

In this step, a sequence tree is used to generate an execution plan. The *optimizer module* analyzes the ways that information can be retrieved from the source tables. It attempts to find the fastest way that uses the smallest amount of resources (that is, processing time). It also complements the list of tasks that need to be performed (for instance, it checks security, it verifies that constraints are enforced, and it includes triggers if they need to be incorporated in processing). The result is an internal structure called an *execution plan.*

Execution

The execution plan is then stored in the procedure cache, from which it is executed. Different steps in the execution plan will be posted to different modules of the relational engine to be executed: DML manager, DDL manager, stored procedure manager, transaction manager, or utility manager. Results are collected in the form of a result set and sent to the caller.

Reuse of Execution Plans

Execution plans remain in the procedure cache for a while. If the same or some other user issues a similar batch, the relational engine first attempts to find a matching execution plan in the procedure cache. If it exists, it will be reused. If it does not exist, Microsoft SQL Server parses and compiles a batch.

If SQL Server requires more memory than is available, it might remove some execution plans from memory. There is a sophisticated "aging" algorithm that takes into account how long ago and how many times an execution plan is used. If there is an abundance of memory, it is possible that execution plans will remain in the cache indefinitely.

Reuse of Query Execution Plans

A simple query can be reused only in two scenarios. First, the query text of the second query must be identical to the text of the query described by the execution plan in the cache. Everything has to match—spaces, line breaks, indentation—even case on case-sensitive servers.

The second scenario may occur when the query contains fully qualified database objects to reuse execution plans:

```
Select *
from Asset.dbo.Inventory
```

Parameterized Queries

The designers of SQL Server have created two methods to improve the reuse of queries that are not designed as stored procedures:

▶ Autoparameterization

▶ The sp_executesql stored procedure

We will cover the first of these methods in the following section and the second one in Chapter 9.

Autoparameterization

When a Transact-SQL statement is sent to SQL Server, it attempts to determine whether any of its constants can be replaced with parameters. Subsequent queries that use the same template will reuse the same execution plan.

For example, let's say that SQL Server receives the following ad hoc query:

```
SELECT FirstName, LastName, Phone, Fax, Email, OrgUnitId, UserName
FROM Asset.dbo.Contact
where ContactId = 3
```

It will try to parameterize it in the following manner and create an execution plan:

```
SELECT FirstName, LastName, Phone, Fax, Email, OrgUnitId, UserName
FROM Asset.dbo.Contact
where ContactId = @P1
```

After this, all similar queries will reuse the execution plan:

```
SELECT FirstName, LastName, Phone, Fax, Email, OrgUnitId, UserName
FROM Asset.dbo.Contact
where ContactId = 11
```

SQL Server applies autoparameterization only when a query's template is "safe"— that is, when the execution plan will not be changed and the performance of SQL Server will not be degraded if parameters are changed.

NOTE

SQL Server might decide to create and use a different execution plan even if the query is based on the same field. For example, imagine that you are querying a table with contact information using the Country field. If your company is operating predominantly in North America, SQL Server might carry out a query for Denmark contacts based on the index on the Country field and a query for USA contacts as a table scan.

SQL Server attempts autoparameterization on Insert, Update, and Delete statements too. In fact, the query must match a set of four templates in order for SQL Server to attempt autoparameterization:

```
Select {* | column-list}
From table
Where column-expression
[Order by column-list]

Insert table
Values ({constant | NULL | Default} [, ...n])

Update table
set column-name = constant
where column-expression

Delete table
Where column-expression
```

Note that a *column-expression* is an expression that involves only column names, constants, the And operator, and comparison operators: <, >, =, >=, <=, and <>.

SQL Server is more forgiving about formatting the query when autoparameterization is used, but it still does not allow changes in capitalization or changes in the way an object is qualified.

Reuse of Stored Procedure Execution Plans

Stored procedures do not have the limitations associated with ad hoc queries, and that is the main reason stored procedures are reused more often then queries.

The reuse of execution plans is one of the main reasons why the use of stored procedures is a better solution than the use of ad hoc queries. For example, if you execute a query three times, SQL Server will have to parse, recompile, and execute it three times. A stored procedure will most likely be parsed and recompiled only once—just before the first execution.

NOTE

Someone might argue that the time needed to compile is insignificant compared with the time needed to execute a query. That is sometimes true. But the SQL Server query engine in this version compares dozens of new processing techniques in order to select the best one to process the query or stored procedure. Therefore, the time needed to recompile a stored procedure is greater in this version than it used to be in earlier versions.

The execution plan consists of two parts. One is reentrant and can be used concurrently by any number of processes. The other part contains the data context; that is, the parameters to be used during execution. Although this part can be reused, it cannot be used by another process concurrently, so more instances of this part will be created.

The execution plan will be removed from the procedure cache when a process called *lazywriter* concludes that the execution plan has not been used for a while and SQL Server needs more memory, or when the execution plan's dependent database objects are changed in any of the following ways:

▶   The amount of data is significantly changed

▶   Indexes are created or dropped

▶   Constraints are added or changed

▶   Distribution statistics of indexes are changed

▶   sp_recompile was explicitly called to recompile the stored procedure or trigger

I was impressed with the way that lazywriter determines which execution plans are obsolete. Microsoft SQL Server 2000 contains a sophisticated emulation of the aging process. When SQL Server creates an execution plan, it assigns it a "compilation cost factor." The value of this factor depends on the expense required to create the execution plan in terms of system resources. For example, a large execution plan might be assigned a compilation cost factor of 8, while a smaller one might be assigned a factor of 2. Each time the execution plan is referenced by a connection, its age is incremented by the value of the compilation cost factor. Thus, if the compilation cost factor of the execution plan is 8, each reference to the execution plan adds 8 to its "age."

SQL Server uses the lazywriter process to decrement the age of the execution plan. The lazywriter process periodically loops through the execution plans in the procedure cache and decrements the age of each execution plan by 1. When the age of an execution plan reaches 0, SQL Server deallocates it, provided that the system is in need of the resources and no connection is currently referencing the execution plan.

If a dependent database object is deleted, the stored procedure will fail during execution. If it is replaced with a new object (new object identification number) with the same name, the execution plan does not have to be recompiled and will run flawlessly. Naturally, if the structure of the dependent object is changed so that objects that the stored procedure is referencing are not present or not compatible any more, the stored procedure will fail, resulting in a run-time error.

Recompiling Stored Procedures

SQL Server is intelligent enough to recompile a stored procedure when a table referenced by that stored procedure changes. Unfortunately, SQL Server does not recompile when you add an index that might help execution of the stored procedure. The stored procedure will be recompiled only when the procedure cache is flushed (which usually happens only when SQL Server is restarted).

To force compilation of a stored procedure, a DBA can use sp_recompile:

```
Exec sp_recompile prListOrders
```

This task can be very tedious if many stored procedures and/or triggers depend on a table for which an index was added. Fortunately, it is possible to name the table for which dependent objects should be recompiled:

```
Exec sp_recompile Orders
```

This statement will recompile all triggers and stored procedures that depend on the Orders table. When a stored procedure or a trigger is specified as a parameter, only that stored procedure or trigger will be recompiled. If you use a table or a view as a parameter, all dependent objects will be recompiled.

 TIP

Do not forget to recompile dependent objects after you add an index to a table. Otherwise, SQL Server will not be able to use them.

A developer might also decide to recompile a stored procedure each time it is used. A typical example is when a stored procedure is based on a query, the execution and performance of which depend on the value used as a criterion. We discussed such an example earlier, in the section "Autoparameterization."

In that example, when a user requests orders from the USA, the selectivity of the index might be such that it is better for the query to do a table scan. If a user requests orders from a country that rarely appears in the particular database, the query engine might decide to use the index. To force SQL Server to evaluate these options every time, the developer should use the With Recompile option while designing the stored procedure:

```
Create Procedure prListOrders
     @Country char(3)
With Recompile
as
     Select *
     from Orders
     where Country =  @Country
```

The execution plan of a stored procedure created in this manner will not be cached on SQL Server.

It is also possible to force recompilation of a stored procedure during execution using the With Recompile option:

```
Exec prListOrders 'USA' With Recompile
```

Storing Stored Procedures

Stored procedures are persistent database objects, and Microsoft SQL Server stores them in system tables to preserve them when their execution plan is removed from the procedure cache or when SQL Server is shut down.

When the Create Procedure statement is executed, Microsoft SQL Server creates a new record in the sysobjects table of the current database (see Figure 3-2).

This system table contains all types of database objects; it is sometimes useful to filter it by object type using the xtype field.

NOTE

Microsoft does not recommend direct use of system tables in production system code because it reserves the right to change them. Microsoft recommends usage of INFORMATION_SCHEMA views or system stored procedures instead. We will cover these objects in Chapter 8.

	name	id	xtype	uid	info	status	base_schema_ver	replinfo	pare
124	prGetInventoryProper...	1218103380	P	1	0	1610612736	0	0	0
125	prDeferredNameResolution	1250103494	P	1	0	1610612736	48	0	0
126	prListInventoryEquipment	1282103608	P	1	0	536870912	0	0	0
127	prInsertLeasedAsset_1	1298103665	P	1	0	1610612736	16	0	0
128	prInsertLeasedAsset_2	1314103722	P	1	0	1610612736	32	0	0
129	prInsertLeasedAsset_3	1330103779	P	1	0	1610612736	0	0	0
130	prInsertLeasedAsset_4	1346103836	P	1	0	1610612736	16	0	0
131	prInsertLeasedAsset_5	1362103893	P	1	0	1610612736	112	0	0
132	prInsertLeasedAsset_6	1378103950	P	1	0	1610612736	32	0	0
133	OrgUnit	1381579960	U	1	3	1610616098	64	0	0
134	prInsertLeasedAsset_7	1394104007	P	1	0	1610612736	0	0	0
135	PK_OrgUnit	1397580017	PK	1	0	32	0	0	1381
136	prClearLeaseShedule	1410104064	P	1	0	1610612736	48	0	0

Figure 3-2 *Content of sysobjects table*

The source code of the stored procedure is recorded in the syscomments system table (unless the stored procedure is encrypted). To see the source code, execute sp_helptext or query the syscomments system table directly (see Figure 3-3).

The source code is stored in a field named text. The data type of this field is varchar(4000). Fortunately, this does not mean that stored procedures are limited to 4000 characters. If the stored procedure is larger than 4000 characters, SQL Server allocates additional records with an incremented colid field. Since this field is declared as smallint, a stored procedure can be 32K * 4000 bytes ≈ 125MB long. In versions before SQL Server 2000 and SQL Server 7.0, colid was byte and text was varchar(255), so stored procedures were limited to 255 * 255 ≈ 64KB.

You can hide the source code for a stored procedure if you encrypt it during creation. After you create the stored procedure using With Encryption, none of the users (not even the system administrator) will be able to see it on the server. Keep in mind that you can (and should) keep source code in a separate external script file.

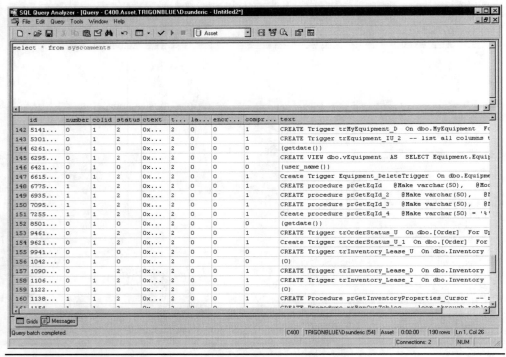

Figure 3-3 Content of syscomments table

NOTE

Before this feature was introduced in SQL Server, developers achieved the same effect by setting the syscomments.text associated with the stored procedure to null. SQL Server was able to run the stored procedure without any problem. Unfortunately, this solution caused problems during SQL Server upgrades, since setup programs expected to use the text of stored procedures in order to recompile the stored procedures in the new environment. The inclusion of the With Encryption clause eliminated this issue.

Managing Stored Procedures

SQL Server Enterprise Manager and Query Analyzer are primary tools that you will use to control the environment and manage stored procedures.

We will review the ways that you can use Enterprise Manager and Query Analyzer to

▶ List stored procedures

▶ View code of stored procedures

- ▶ Rename stored procedures
- ▶ Delete stored procedures
- ▶ List dependent and depending objects

Listing Stored Procedures

The easiest way to list stored procedures in a database is to view them from
Enterprise Manager. All you need to do is follow these steps:

1. Open Enterprise Manager.

2. Expand the server group (click +).

3. Expand the server.

4. Expand the database.

5. Click the Stored Procedures node in a tree; Enterprise Manager lists the stored
   procedures in the Details pane (see Figure 3-4).

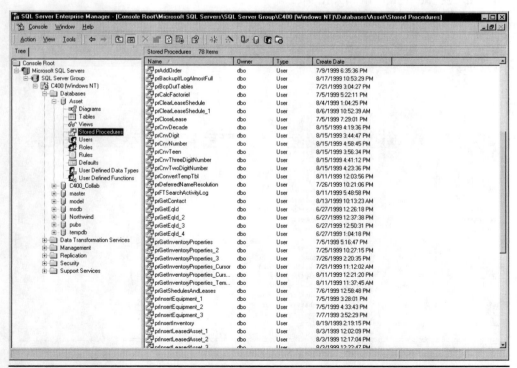

Figure 3-4   *Listing stored procedures in Enterprise Manager*

There are two ways to list stored procedures from Query Analyzer. I have shown how to use the Object Browser in the previous chapter. The traditional way is based on Transact-SQL. SQL Server is delivered with the system stored procedure sp_stored_procedures. It lists stored procedures in the current database:

1. Open Query Analyzer.

2. Switch the current database to Asset.

3. Set Query Analyzer to display results in a grid (Query | Results In Grid).

4. Type and execute **sp_stored_procedures** (Query | Execute). The program will show the list of stored procedures in the current database (see Figure 3-5).

The stored procedure sp_stored_procedures retrieves a list of stored procedures from the sysobjects system table in the database. If you want to see the sysobjects table's contents, execute the following statement:

```
Select *
from sysobjects
```

You can see the results in Figure 3-6.

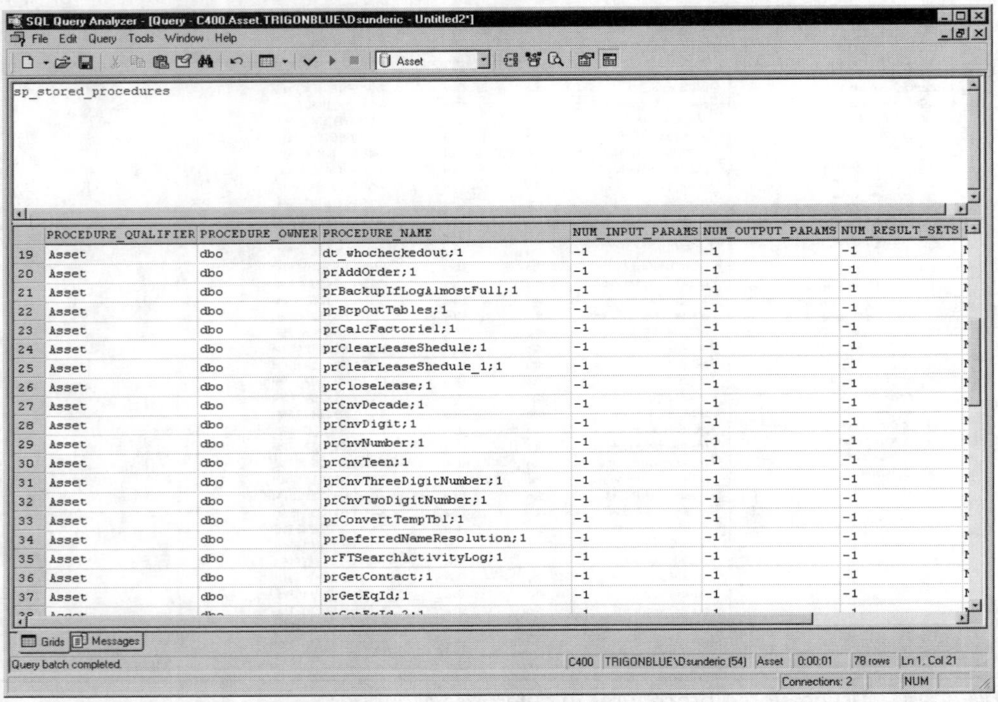

Figure 3-5 *Listing stored procedures in Query Analyzer*

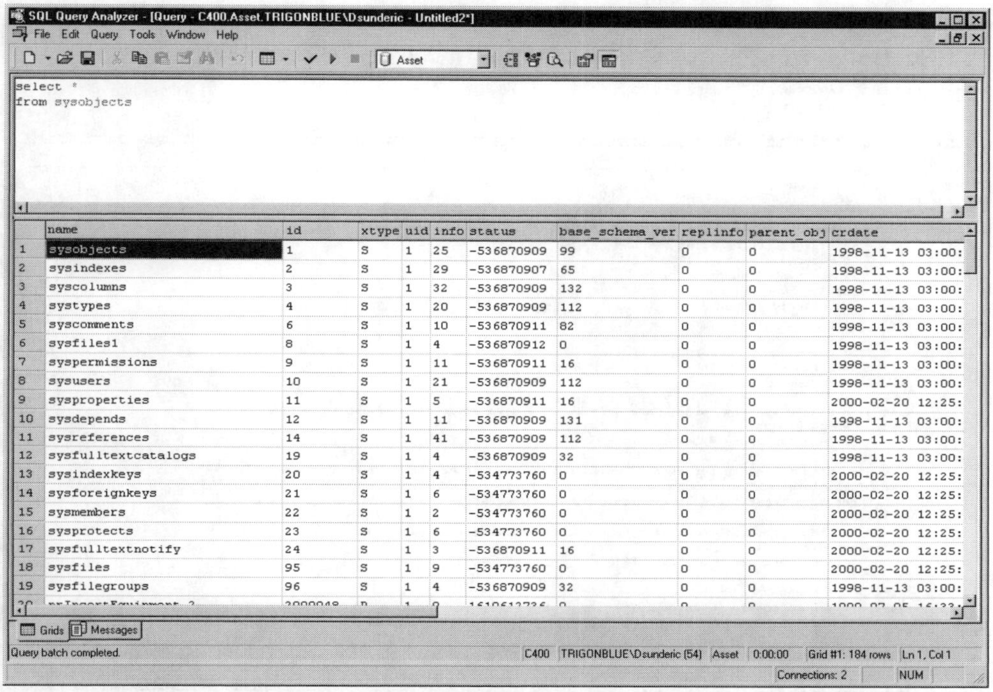

Figure 3-6   *A list of database objects in sysobjects*

To see just user-defined stored procedures, you need to filter the database objects with xtype set to 'P':

```
Select *
from sysobjects
where xtype = 'P'
```

Viewing Code of Stored Procedures

I have already shown you in Chapter 2 how to display a stored procedure from Enterprise Manager. You just double-click its name and the program displays it in an editor. I have also shown that you can use the Object Browser in Query Analyzer to achieve the same task. You just need to find the stored procedure in the Object Browser, right-click, and then select Edit from the menu; Query Analyzer displays it in a new Query window.

It is a little bit more difficult to display a stored procedure in the traditional way using Transact-SQL. You need to use the sp_helptext system stored procedure. The database that contains the stored procedure must be the current database, and you must supply the name of the stored procedure as a parameter (see Figure 3-7).

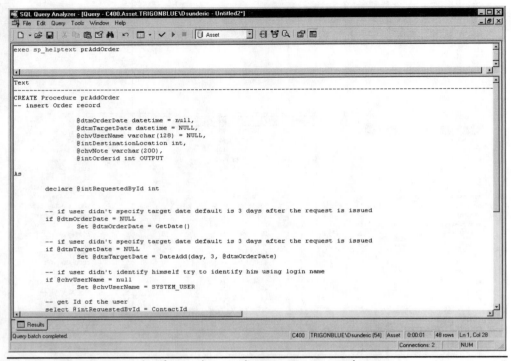

Figure 3-7 *Viewing code of stored procedures in Query Analyzer*

NOTE

You can also use sp_helptext to view the code of other database objects such as triggers, views, defaults, and rules.

If you now want to save the code of the stored procedure, you can copy it through the Clipboard to your Query pane, or you can save Results from Query Analyzer in a text file:

1. Click the Results pane of Query Analyzer.
2. Select File | Save and specify a name for the file. Verify that the File Format is set to ANSI.

The result will be saved to an ANSI file, which you can edit in any text editor, such as Notepad. You can also open it in the Query pane:

1. Click the Query pane in Query Analyzer.
2. Select File | Open and specify the name of the file.

Renaming Stored Procedures

There are several ways to change the name of a stored procedure. If you use sp_rename or a command of Enterprise Manger, SQL Server will change the name of the object in the sysobjects table, but it will not affect code of the stored procedure. You might receive unexpected results if you try to execute the Create Procedure statement or the Alter Procedure statement after that.

sp_rename was designed to change the names of all database objects (including tables, views, columns, defaults, rules, and triggers). In fact, the versatility of this stored procedure is the reason the code is not changed in the previous example. The stored procedure is designed only to change the names of objects in the sysobjects table.

Database objects with code such as stored procedures, views, and user-defined functions require a different strategy. It is better to drop them and create them again. Again, do not forget to change all associated objects, such as permissions, at the same time. The Alter Procedure statement cannot help us in this case, since we need to change the name of the stored procedure.

NOTE

This operation is not something that you should perform very often. It could be problematic if you were to do it on a production server. SQL Server contains a procedure cache—a part of the memory where it keeps compiled versions of stored procedures. You should flush the procedure cache to force all dependent stored procedures (which refer to the stored procedure by its old name) to recompile. You can use DBCC FREEPROCCACHE, or you can simply restart SQL Server and the procedure cache will be emptied.

Deleting Stored Procedures

To delete a stored procedure from Enterprise Manager, right-click the name of the stored procedure in the list and select Delete. It is also simple to delete a stored procedure using the Object Browser in Query Analyzer: right-click the name of the stored procedure in the list and select Delete.

Drop Procedure is a Transact-SQL statement for deleting a stored procedure. To use it, you must supply the name of the stored procedure as a parameter:

```
DROP PROCEDURE prTest2
```

Objects that are referencing the stored procedure that has been dropped will not be able to run properly after this.

Listing Dependent and Depending Objects

If you plan to perform some dramatic action, such as deleting or renaming a database object, you should first investigate which objects will be affected by it. Microsoft SQL Server keeps a list of dependencies between objects in the sysdepends system table in each database. To view this list in Enterprise Manager:

1. Right-click the name of the database object.
2. Select All Tasks.
3. Click Display Dependencies, and SQL Server will display a list of dependencies.

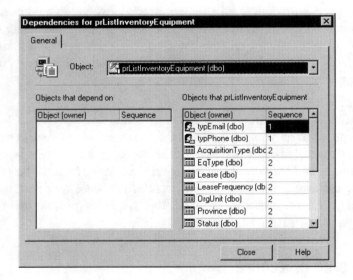

The program displays two lists. The list to the left shows objects that reference the selected object (dependent). The list to the right shows objects that are referenced by the object (depending). In the case of prListInventoryEquipment, since no object in the database is using it, the list to the left is empty.

4. Use the drop-down list box at the top to change the selected object. You can also double-click any dependent or depending object and SQL Server will display a form showing its dependencies.
5. Select vEquipment and the program will display the following form. From this form, we can conclude that this view is based on two tables and that it is referenced in one stored procedure.

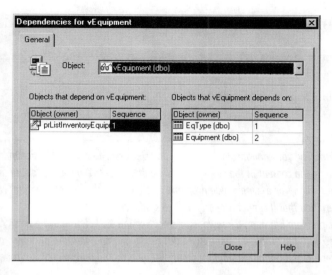

The system stored procedure sp_depends has a similar function. It can also return one or two result sets—one for dependent objects and one for depending objects. If you execute the following statement in Query Analyzer,

```
exec sp_depends prListLeasedAssets
```

you will see a result like that shown in Figure 3-8.

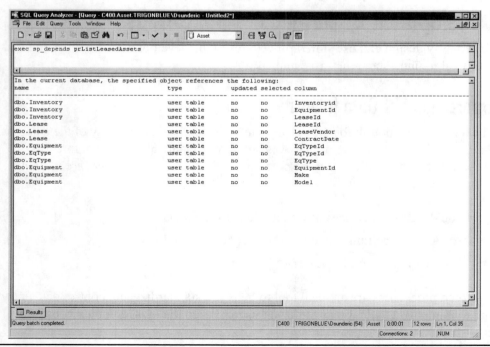

Figure 3-8   *Dependent and depending objects*

The Object Browser can also be used to display a list of dependencies:

1. Expand the node of a database object (for example, the prListLeasedAssets stored procedure).

2. Expand the Dependencies node.

NOTE

Unfortunately, you cannot completely rely on SQL Server to get a list of dependencies. It does not update the content of the sysdepends table in all cases. You can reproduce and observe this behavior when, for example, you drop and re-create a table. However, in that case, SQL Server will warn you that it cannot properly update sysdependencies.

This problem has been a known issue since version 4.21, but in SQL Server 7.0 and SQL Server 2000, the problem is even more difficult to manage, because of deferred name resolution. Therefore, if SQL Server displays an empty list, you should open the source code and check it!

Neither of these methods will show you dependencies between objects outside of the current database.

The Role of Stored Procedures in the Development of Database Applications

To properly design and use stored procedures in the development of applications, it is critical to understand their role and advantages.

Enforcement of Data Integrity

The most important task for each DBA is to maintain the data integrity of the database that he or she is managing. If a DBA is not almost fanatical about data integrity, the results for the database will be potentially disastrous. During my career, I have encountered databases with

▶ 106 different provinces of Canada (one of them was France)

▶ An Address column filled with "Guest had frozen Fish."

▶ Nine ways to write HP LaserJet III…

Stored procedures are an ideal tool to help you standardize and control data entry, and to implement validation of information and even the most complex constraints.

Consistent Implementation of Complex Business Rules and Constraints

Transact-SQL stored procedures are powerful enough to implement even the most complex business rules because they can combine both procedural and set-oriented statements. Everything that is too complicated to be implemented using other constraints and that is procedural and not just set-oriented can be implemented in the form of a stored procedure. These are complex and important considerations and will be expanded upon throughout the remainder of this book.

NOTE

Naturally, stored procedures are not the only way to implement business logic on the server. Three-tier architecture envisions implementation of business services on a middleware server.

Modular Design

Stored procedures allow developers to encapsulate business functionality and provide callers with a simple interface. Stored procedures behave like a black box. The caller does not have to know how they are implemented, just what they do, what input is required, and what output will be generated. From a development standpoint, this also reduces the complexity of the design process. You do not need to know how a stored procedure is implemented. You just need to reference it in your application or your own procedures.

Maintainability

System design is a cyclic process. Every system needs to be reviewed, changed, and improved. By hiding database structure details behind stored procedures, database administrators can reduce or hopefully eliminate the need to change all other components (that is, client applications and middleware components) of the system whenever they change the database structure.

Microsoft has achieved the same goal with system stored procedures and system tables. Although you can use the contents of system tables directly in your applications, you should base your code on system stored procedures, because Microsoft reserves the right to change tables from version to version but has promised to keep the interface and functionality of stored procedures intact.

Another advantage is that stored procedures are implemented on the server and can be maintained centrally. If the business logic is implemented in the client application, a huge effort will be needed to deploy changes.

Reduced Network Traffic

One of the major disadvantages of file-server architecture is high network traffic due to the fact that entire files are being transferred across the network. If a client/server system is well designed, the client will receive just the information it needs, which is usually just a slight portion of the database, thus significantly reducing the network traffic.

If a client/server system is implemented with even more of the processing/business logic on the server (that is, using stored procedures), even less data will be transferred back and forth through the network.

Faster Execution

Stored procedures have several performance advantages over ad hoc queries. Stored procedures are cached in a compiled form on the database server, so when they need to be used, the server does not have to parse and recompile them again.

A developer can optimize a stored procedure's code so that every user will use the best possible method to perform an action.

Enforcement of Security

One sign of a well-designed database system is that it prevents users from directly accessing the tables and forces them to use stored procedures to perform specific functions. It is also easier to manage a set of stored procedures by functionality than to manage table- and column-level permissions.

CHAPTER 4

Basic Transact-SQL Programming Constructs

All modern relational database management systems are based on an implementation of SQL (Structured Query Language). Most vendors have extended SQL into a more sophisticated programming language. The ANSI committee has standardized the language several times, of which ANSI SQL-92 is the latest specification. Unfortunately (or fortunately—depending on your point of view), each vendor has created its own version of this specification to extend ANSI SQL.

The language in use in Microsoft SQL Server is called Transact-SQL (T-SQL). It complies with the Entry Level ANSI SQL-92 standard, and you can use this ANSI SQL–compliant language to select, update, insert, and delete records from tables.

T-SQL Identifiers

All databases, servers, and database objects in SQL Server (such as tables, constraints, stored procedures, views, columns, and data types) must have unique names, or *identifiers*. They are assigned when an object is created, and used thereafter to identify the object. The identifier for the object may, if needed, be changed.

The following are the rules for creating identifiers:

▶ Identifiers in SQL Server 2000 may have between 1 and 128 characters. There are exceptions to this rule: certain objects are limited (for instance, temporary tables can have identifiers up to only 116 characters long). Before Microsoft SQL Server 7.0, identifiers were limited to 30 characters.

▶ The first character of the identifier must be a letter, underscore (_), at sign (@), or number sign (#). The first letter must be defined in the Unicode 2.0 standard. Among other letters, Latin letters a–z and A–Z can be used as a first character. Some characters (@ and #) have special meanings in T-SQL. They act as signals to SQL Server to treat their carriers differently.

▶ Subsequent characters must be letters from the Unicode 2.0 standard, or decimal digits, or one of the special characters @, #, _, or $.

▶ SQL Server reserved words should not be used as object identifiers.

▶ Identifiers cannot contain spaces or other special characters except for @, #, _, or $.

TIP

You can check which identifiers are valid by using the system stored procedure sp_validname.

If the identifier does not comply with one of the previous rules, it is referred to as a *delimited identifier,* and it must be delimited by double quotes (" ") or square brackets ([ ]) when referenced in T-SQL statements. You can change the default behavior if you use the Set Quoted_Identifier Off statement. The role of single and double quotes will be reversed. Single quotes will delimit identifiers, and double quotes will delimit strings.

As an interim migration aid, you can specify the compatibility mode in which SQL Server will run using the system stored procedure sp_dbcmptlevel. Changing the compatibility mode will affect the way in which SQL Server interprets identifiers. You should check Books Online for more information if you are running in any compatibility mode other than 80.

NOTE

The designers of Microsoft SQL Server have created a special system data type called `sysname` *to control the length of identifiers. You should use it—instead of* `nvarchar(128)`—*for variables that will store database object identifiers. If Microsoft again changes the way identifiers are named, procedures using sysname will automatically be upgraded.*

The following are valid identifiers:

- ▶ Cost
- ▶ Premium36
- ▶ prCalcCost
- ▶ idx_User
- ▶ @@Make
- ▶ #Equipment
- ▶ [First Name]
- ▶ "Equipment ID"
- ▶ [User]
- ▶ [User.Group]

NOTE

Although delimiters can be used to assign identifiers that are also keywords (such as User) to objects, this practice is not recommended. You will save a substantial amount of time if you use regular identifiers.

Database Object Qualifiers

The complete name of a database object consists of four identifiers, concatenated in the following manner:

```
[[[server.][database].][owner].]database_object
```

Each of these identifiers must comply with the rules described in the previous section. *Server, database,* and *owner* are often referred to as *database object qualifiers.* The complete name of the object is often referred to as the *fully qualified name, or four-part name.* You do not have to use all the qualifiers all the time. *Server* and *database* are (naturally) the names of the server and the database in which the object is stored. You can omit the server name and/or the database name if the database object is located in the current database and/or on the current server.

Owner is the name of the user that created the object. If the object was created by the user that created the database (or any member of the db_owner fixed database role or sysadmin server role), SQL Server will record the owner as dbo. In other cases, the username of whoever created the object will be assigned as the object owner.

When you are referencing the object, if you do not specify the name of the owner, SQL Server will automatically try to find the named object owned by the current user. If such an object does not exist, SQL Server will try to locate the named object with the owner listed as dbo. (Actually, this is the reason you should always explicitly specify dbo.)

For example, when you are connected to the Asset database on the SQLBox server, instead of typing

```
SQLBox.Asset.dbo.prInventoryList
```

you can use any of the following:

```
prInventoryList
dbo.prInventoryList
Asset.dbo.prInventoryList
Asset..prInventoryList
SQLBox.Asset..prInventoryList
SQLBox...prInventoryList
SQLBox..dbo.prInventoryList
```

NOTE

You can also use consecutive periods to skip qualifiers.

Data Types

Data types specify the type of information (such as number, string, picture, date) that can be stored in a column or a variable.

SQL Server recognizes 27 *system-defined data types*. Apart from these data types, you can create *user-defined data types* to fulfill specific needs.

The following are the categories of system-defined data types:

- ▶ Character strings
- ▶ Unicode character strings
- ▶ Date and time
- ▶ Interoximate numeric
- ▶ Exact numeric
- ▶ Moger numbers
- ▶ Appnetary
- ▶ Binary
- ▶ Special

NOTE

In some cases, you can use different identifiers to refer to a data type in T-SQL code. For example, the `char` *data type can be referenced as* `character`, *and* `varchar` *can be referenced as* `character varying`. *Some of these synonyms are based on ANSI SQL-92 standard requirements.*

Character Strings

Character data types store character strings. The three different character types vary in length and storage characteristics:

- ▶ `char`
- ▶ `varchar`
- ▶ `text`

The `char` data type is used to store strings of fixed size. As noted earlier, the maximum size of this data type is 8000 characters, which is a significant increase over the 255-character limit in early versions. When a variable or a table column is assigned with a string that is shorter than its nominal size, it is padded with trailing spaces to fill the specified field length.

The `varchar` data type stores strings of variable size up to 8000 characters long. When a character value whose length is less than the nominal size is assigned to the column or variable, SQL Server does not add trailing spaces to it, but records it as is. `varchar` data types occupy two additional bytes in order to record the length of the string.

NOTE

Maintenance of this information requires some additional computation during I/O operation, but that time is usually countered by savings in the space required. A record using such columns occupies less space, and more records fit into a single page. Therefore, SQL Server reads more records when accessing data, and it is more likely that a single page contains the information that the user is looking for.

The `text` data type is used to store huge amounts of data. One field can store up to 2GB ($2^{31} - 1$ bytes) of information. Only a 16-byte pointer to this data is stored in the table. Therefore, additional processing overhead is involved with the use of text columns. There are special functions for processing text values.

The following command creates a table with three fields using different character string data types:

```
Create table Contacts(ContactId char(8),
                      Name varchar(50),
                      Note text)
```

Character constants are delimited from the rest of the Transact-SQL code with quotes. For example, the following statement inserts contact information:

```
insert into Contacts (ContactId, Name, Note)
values ('CO-92-81', 'Tom Jones', 'Tom@trigon.com')
```

Unicode Character Strings

Microsoft SQL Server 2000 has three character data types for storing Unicode data—using non-ASCII character sets. They are equivalent to the `char`, `varchar`, and `text` data types and are called

▶ `nchar`

▶ `nvarchar`

▶ `ntext`

The main difference between these new data types and the older character data types is that the new data types can hold Unicode characters, which occupy 2 bytes per character. Therefore, the maximum string length that they can store is half that of the corresponding older data types (4000 for `nchar` and `nvarchar`).

The following statement creates the same table, but using Unicode data types:

```
Create table Contacts_2(ContactId nchar(8),
                        Name nvarchar(50),
                        Note ntext)
go
```

Unicode character constants are also delimited with quotes but are prefixed with N':

```
insert into Contacts_2 (ContactId, Name, Note)
values (N'CO-92-81', N'Tom Jones', N'Tom@trigonblue.com')
```

This N' prefix might look a little odd, but you will get used to it. Microsoft documentation is full of samples with Unicode constants. It was some time before I discovered the reason Microsoft uses N' as a prefix. It stands for "National." In fact, acceptable alternative identifiers for these data types are

- ► `National char`
- ► `National char varying`
- ► `National text`

TIP

Typically, it is not a problem if you omit the N' prefix on constants. SQL Server automatically converts the string to its Unicode equivalent. Naturally, it is better to insert it whenever you are dealing with Unicode columns or variables, but it is not a big problem. The CPU will just have to perform a couple of extra cycles to make the conversion.

However, there are cases in which it becomes a problem. When your string constant is part of a query criterion, then the presence of the N' prefix might significantly affect execution of the query. If the column is defined as a non-Unicode string and the criterion is specified with the N' prefix, SQL Server converts every row of the table to compare it with the Unicode constant. As a result, the query performs a table scan instead of using an index.

Date and Time Data Types

SQL Server supports two data types for storing date and time:

- ► `datetime`
- ► `smalldatetime`

The main difference between these two data types is in the amount of space they occupy. `datetime` occupies 8 bytes and `smalldatetime` only 4 bytes. The difference between the two types is the precision of the date stored, and the range of dates that can be used. The precision of `smalldatetime` is one minute, and it covers dates from January 1, 1900, through June 6, 2079, which is usually more than enough. The precision of `datetime` is 3.33 ms, and it covers dates from January 1, 1753, to December 31, 9999.

Date and time constants are written in Transact-SQL with quote delimiters (as are character strings):

```
update Contacts_2
Set DateOfBirth = '2/21/1965 10:03 AM'
where ContactId = 'CO-92-81'
```

TIP

SQL Server supports many different date and time formats. The Convert() function accepts a parameter that controls the format of date and time functions (explained in detail in Chapter 5).

If time is not specified in a constant, SQL Server automatically assigns a default value—12:00 A.M. (midnight). You should keep in mind that SQL Server always records time as a part of these data types. Thus, if you want to select all contacts born on a particular day, you should *not* use something like this:

```
select *
from Contacts_2
where DateOfBirth = '2/21/1965'
```

This statement would extract records with DateOfBirth set to midnight of that day. Such a solution might be acceptable if all other applications recording values in the field also make the same mistake. A proper solution would be

```
select *
from Contacts_2
where DateOfBirth >= '2/21/1965' and DateOfBirth < '2/22/1965'
```

Integer Numbers

Integers are whole numbers. Traditionally, SQL Server supported 1-, 2-, and 4-byte integers. SQL Server 2000 introduces an 8-byte integer. The `bit` data type is used to store 1 or 0, to represent logical true and false values. The following table lists integer data types, their storage size, and range of values.

Data Type	Storage Size	Minimum	Maximum
int	4 bytes	−2,147,483,648 (−2G)	2,147,483,647 (2G − 1)
smallint	2 bytes	−32768 (−32K)	32767 (32K − 1)
tinyint	1 byte	0	255 (2^8 − 1)
bigint	8 bytes	−9,223,372,036,854,775,808 (-2^{63})	9,223,372,036,854,775,807 (2^{63}−1)
bit	1 bit	0	1

The great thing about the `int` data types is that they can store huge numbers in a small space. For this reason, they are often used for key values. If the data type of the primary key is `int`, the table can store up to four billion records.

TIP

We are starting to see computers with billions of records — both OLTP and data warehousing systems are getting bigger and bigger, and there are also some implementations of distributed databases that can use integers higher than two billion. In those cases you could use `bigint` *for primary keys.*

Integer constants do not need delimiters:

```
update Inventory_2
Set StatusId = 3,
    Operational = 0
Where InventoryId = 3432
```

Approximate Numbers

Decimal numbers are often stored in `real` and `float` data types, also known as *single* and *double precision*. Their advantage is that they do not occupy much space but they can hold large ranges of numbers. The only trouble is that they are not exact. They store a binary representation of the number that is often approximately, but not exactly, equal to the original decimal number.

Precision is the number of significant digits in the number, and *scale* is the number of digits to the right of the decimal point. For example, the number 123456.789 has a precision of 9 and a scale of 3. The precision of `real` numbers is up to 7 digits, and the precision of `float` numbers is up to 15 digits. For this reason, they are ideal for science and engineering (where, for example, you may not care about a couple of meters when you are measuring the distance between the Earth and the Moon), but they are not adequate for the financial industry (where a company budget has to be exact to the last cent).

To record the number 234,000,000,000 in mathematics, you can use 234×10^9, and in Transact-SQL, you can use 234E9. This is known as *scientific notation*. The number after E is called the *exponent*, and the number before E is called the *mantissa*. This notation can be used to store small constants, too. In mathematics, 0.000000000234 can be written as 0.234×10^{-9}, and in Transact-SQL, it can be written as 0.234E-9.

SQL Server uses the IEEE 754 standard to store these numbers. When a `float` or `real` variable or column is assigned a number, SQL Server first converts the decimal number to its binary representation. This conversion is the reason these values are approximately, but not exactly, equal to the decimal version. This is why they are referred to as *approximate numbers*. Therefore, you should not rely on the equivalence of two such numbers. You should limit their use in Where clauses to < and > operators and avoid the use of the = operator.

Exact Numbers

The `decimal` or `numeric` data type does not use approximations when storing numbers. Unfortunately, it requires much more space than the `real` and `float` data types. When a `decimal` column or a variable is defined, you have to specify its scale and precision.

SQL Server can store `decimal` numbers with a maximum precision of 38. Scale can be less than or equal to the precision.

In the next example, Weight and Height columns have precision 5 and scale 2—the columns can have up to two digits after the decimal point and up to three digits before.

```
Create table Patient (PatientId int,
                      FullName varchar(30),
                      Weight decimal(5,2),
                      Height decimal(5,2),
                      ADP smallint,
                      BDZ tinyint)
go
```

`decimal` constants do not need delimiters either:

```
insert into Patient (PatientId, FullName, Weight, Height, ADP, BDZ)
values (834021, 'Tom Jones', 89.5, 188.5, 450, 11)
```

Monetary Data Types

The `money` and `smallmoney` data types are a compromise between the precision of `decimal` numbers and the small size of `real` numbers. `smallmoney` occupies 4 bytes and uses the same internal structure as `int` numbers. The data can have up to four digits after the decimal point. For this reason, you can store numbers ranging from –214,768.3648 to 214,768.3647 in the `smallmoney` data type. The `money` data type uses the same structure for storing information as the `bigint` data type. It occupies 8 bytes for storage, so its values must range from –922,337,203,685,477.5808 to +922,337,203,685,477.5807.

Monetary constants can be preceded by $ or one of 17 other currency symbols (listed in SQL Server Books Online):

```
update Inventory_2
Set Rent = $0,
LeaseCost = $119.95
Where InventoryId = 3432
```

Binary Data Types

Binary data types are used to store strings of bits. SQL Server supports three basic binary data types, the attributes of which are similar to character data types:

- ► `binary`
- ► `varbinary`
- ► `image`

The `binary` and `varbinary` data types can store up to 8000 bytes of information, and `image` can store up to 2GB of data. The following example creates a table that has two binary columns:

```
CREATE TABLE MyTable (
    Id int,
    BinData varbinary(8000),
    Diagram image)
go
```

Binary constants are written as hexadecimal representations of bit strings and prefixed with 0x (zero and x):

```
Update MyTable
Set BinData = 0x82A7210B
where Id = 121131
```

Special Data Types

The following sections cover the special data types.

timestamp

The `timestamp` data type is not designed to store date or time information, but rather is a binary value that serves as a version number of the record. The value is updated every time the record is updated, and the value is unique in the database. It is used to implement optimistic locking. You can find more details about this subject in "Optimistic Locking Using Timestamp Values" Chapter 9. Only one field in a table can be defined as the `timestamp` value. It occupies 8 bytes.

uniqueidentifier

The `uniqueidentifier` data type stores 16-byte binary values. These values are often called *globally unique identifiers (GUIDs)*. When a system generates a new GUID value, it is guaranteed that the same value cannot be produced again, neither on the same computer nor on any other computer in the world. GUIDs are generated using the identification number of the network card and a unique number obtained from the computer's clock. Manufacturers of network cards guarantee that the identification number of a network card will not be repeated in the next 100 years.

A `uniqueidentifier` constant is usually presented as

- ► **Character string**   '{BB7DF450-F119-11CD-8465-00AA00425D90}'
- ► **Binary constant**   0xaf16a66f7f8b31d3b41d30c04fc96f46

However, you will rarely type such values. In Transact-SQL, GUIDs should be generated using the NEWID function. There is also a Win32 API function that can produce a GUID value.

`uniqueidentifier` values are used relatively often for implementations of web applications and distributed database systems. In web applications, designers might use the `uniqueidentifier` data type to generate a unique identifier before the record is sent to the database. In distributed systems, this data type serves globally unique identifiers.

sql_variant

The `sql_variant` data type is based on the same idea as the `variant` data type in Visual Basic. It is designed to allow a single variable, column, or parameter to store values in different data types. Internally, variant objects record two values:

- ► The actual value
- ► The metadata describing the variant: base data type, maximum size, scale, precision, and collation

The following statement creates a lookup table that can store values of different types:

```
Create table Lookup(
   LookupGroupId tinyint,
   LookupId smallint,
   LookupValue sql_variant)
Go
```

Before SQL Server 2000, more than one field was needed to store lookup values of different data types.

The following statements illustrate how you can insert different types of values in one column:

```
Insert Lookup (LookupGroupId, LookupId, LookupValue)
Values (2, 34, 'VAR')
Insert Lookup (LookupGroupId, LookupId, LookupValue)
Values (3, 22, 2000)
Insert Lookup (LookupGroupId, LookupId, LookupValue)
Values (4, 16, '1/12/2000')
Insert Lookup (LookupGroupId, LookupId, LookupValue)
Values (4, 11, $50000)
```

A `sql_variant` object can store values of any data type *except:*

▶ text

▶ ntext

▶ image

▶ timestamp

▶ sql_variant

But there are more serious restrictions on their use:

▶ `sql_variant` columns *can* be used in *indexes* and *unique keys* if the total length of the data in the key is shorter than 900 bytes.

▶ `sql_variant` columns *cannot* have an `identity` property.

▶ `sql_variant` columns *cannot* be part of a computed column.

▶ You *must use functions for converting data types* when assigning values from `sql_variant` objects to objects of other data types.

▶ The comparison of `sql_variant` values has complex rules and is prone to errors.

▶ `sql_variant` values are automatically converted to `nvarchar(4000)` when accessed from client applications using OLE DB Provider for SQL

Server 7.0 or the SQL Server ODBC Driver from SQL Server version 7.0. If stored values are longer then 4000 characters, SQL Server will return just the first 4000 characters.

▶ `sql_variant` values are automatically converted to `varchar(255)` when accessed from client applications using the SQL Server ODBC Driver from SQL Server version 6.5 or earlier, or using DB-Library. If stored values are longer than 255 characters, SQL Server will return just the first 255 characters.

▶ `sql_variant` columns are not supported in the Like predicate.

▶ `sql_variant` columns do not support full-text indexes.

▶ `sql_variant` objects cannot be concatenated using the + operator, even if the stored values are strings or numeric. The proper solution is to convert values before concatenation.

▶ Some functions—Avg(), Identity(), IsNumeric(), Power(), Radians(), Round(), Sign(), StDev() StDevP(), Sum(),Var(), VarP()—do not support `sql_variant` parameters.

TIP

You should be very conservative in using the `sql_variant` *data type. Its use has serious performance and design implications.*

table

The `table` data type is used to store a recordset for later processing. In some ways, this data type is similar to a temporary table. You cannot use this type to define a column. It can only be used as a *local variable* to *return the value of a function.*

NOTE

You will find more information about `table` *variables in the "Table Variables" section later in this chapter, and information about functions in Chapters 5 and 8.*

The Cursor Data Type

This is a special kind of data type that contains references to cursors. You will see in the "Cursors" section later in this chapter that cursors are programming constructs that are designed to allow operations on records one at a time. It is not possible to define a column of this type. It can be used only for variables and stored procedure output values.

User-Defined Data Types

You can define custom data types in the database. These new types are based on system-defined data types and are accessible only in the database in which they are defined. You can define them from Enterprise Manager, or using the system stored procedure sp_addtype:

```
Exec sp_addtype Phone, varchar(20), 'NOT NULL'
Exec sp_addtype typPostalCode, varchar(7), 'NULL'
```

The first parameter is the name of the new data type, the second parameter is the system-defined data type on which it is based, and the third parameter defines the nullability of the new data type. When the command is executed, the server adds the type to the systype table of the current database. New types can be based on any system-defined type except `timestamp`.

TIP

A fascinating aspect of user-defined data types is that you can change them in one step across the database. For example, if you decide that decimal(19,6) *is not big enough for you monetary values, you can replace it with* decimal(28,13). *You can simply run the script that first changed the data type and then re-create all database objects that are referencing it. This feature is very useful during the development stage of a database. Unfortunately, when a database is already in the production phase, tables contain data, and this feature becomes a lot more complicated.*

The designers of Microsoft SQL Server have included one special data type with the server—`sysname`. It is used to control the length of Transact-SQL identifiers. When the server is working in default mode, the length of this type is set to 128 characters. When the compatibility level is set to 65 or 60, the length is shortened to 30 characters. You should use it to define columns and variables that will contain Transact-SQL identifiers.

Variables

Variables in Transact-SQL are the equivalent of variables in other programming languages, but due to the nature of the Transact-SQL language, their use and behavior are somewhat different.

There are two types of variables in Transact-SQL:

► Local variables
► Global variables

Local Variables

The major difference between the two types of variables is their scope. The scope of local variables is a batch (a set of T-SQL statements that is sent to SQL Server and executed simultaneously). This restriction implicitly includes a single stored procedure (because stored procedures are defined in a batch). This is a significant limitation. However, several workarounds can be used as solutions to this problem.

A stored procedure cannot access variables defined in other stored procedures. One way to pass values to and from stored procedures is to use parameters. Keep in mind that you are passing only the values associated with the variables, not references, as you can in some other programming languages.

Another way to transfer value between stored procedures or between batches is the use of more permanent database objects such as tables or temporary tables.

Let's review basic operations with local variables.

Declaring Variables

Before you can do anything with a local variable, you need to declare it. Declaration consists of the reserved word Declare and a list of variables and their respective data types.

The names of variables must comply with the rules for identifiers:

▶ They must begin with @:

```
Declare @LastName varchar(50)
```

▶ It is possible to define several variables in a single Declare statement. You just need to separate them with commas:

```
Declare   @LastName varchar(50),
          @FirstName varchar(30),
          @BirthDate smalldatetime
```

▶ You can also define variables based on user-defined data types:

```
Declare @OfficePhone phone
```

NOTE

You cannot define the nullability of the variable, as you can with table columns. This does not mean that variables cannot contain null values. In fact, before assignment, the value of each variable is null. It is also possible to explicitly set the value of each variable to null.

Assigning Values with the Select Statement

There are several ways to assign a value to a local variable. In early versions of SQL Server, the only way to do this was to use a modification of the Select statement:

```
Select @LastName = 'Smith'
```

It is also possible to assign several variables in the same statement:

```
Select      @LastName = 'Smith',
            @FirstName = 'David',
            @BirthDate = '2/21/1965'
```

NOTE

It is necessary to assign a value of an appropriate data type to the variable; however, there are some workarounds. In some cases, the server will perform an implicit conversion from one data type to another. SQL Server also includes a set of functions for explicit conversion. Convert() and Cast() can be used to change the data type of the value (see Chapter 5). Some data types are not compatible, so explicit conversion is the only solution.

Quite often, variables are assigned values from the result set of the Select statement:

```
Select      @Make = Equipment.Make,
            @Model = Equipment.Model,
            @EqType = Equipment.EqType
From EqType INNER JOIN Equipment
    ON EqType.EqTypeId = Equipment.EqTypeId
Where EquipmentId = 2
```

There are some potential problems associated with this approach. How will the server assign values if the result set contains multiple records, or no records?

If more than one record is returned in the result set, a variable will be assigned the values from the *last* record. The only trouble is that we cannot predict which record will be the last, because this position depends on the index that the server uses to create the result set.

It is possible to create workarounds to exploit these facts (that is, to use hints to specify an index or use minimum and/or maximum functions to assign extreme values). The recommended solution, however, is to narrow the search criteria so that only one record is returned.

The other behavior that might cause unexpected results is the case in which a result set does not return any records. It is a common belief and expectation of many developers that the variable will be set to null. This is absolutely incorrect. The content of the variable *will not be changed* in this case.

Observe the following example, or try to run it against the Asset database:

```
Declare     @make varchar(50),
            @model varchar(50),
            @EqType varchar(50)

Select      @Make = 'ACME',
            @Model = 'Turbo',
```

```
        @EqType = 'cabadaster'

Select    @Make = make,
          @Model = Model,
          @EqType = EqType.EqType
From EqType INNER JOIN Equipment
    ON EqType.EqTypeId = Equipment.EqTypeId
Where EquipmentId = -1

Select @make make, @model model, @EqType EqType
```

Since the Equipment table does not have a record with the identifier set to −1, the variables will keep their original values. Only if the values of the variables were not previously set will they continue to contain a null value.

The variable can be assigned with any Transact-SQL expression such as a constant, or a calculation, or even a complete Select statement that returns a single value:

```
Select    @Make = Make,
          @Model = Model,
          @EquipmentName = Make + ' ' + Model,
          @EqType = (select EqType
                      from EqType
                      where EqTypeId = Equipment.EqTypeId)
From Equipment
Where EquipmentId = 2
```

There is one combination of statements and expressions that will result in a syntax error. It is not possible to return a result set from the Select statement and to assign a variable in the same Select statement:

```
Select    Make,
          @Model = Model    -- wrong
From Equipment
Where EquipmentId = 2
```

Assigning Values with the Set Statement

In SQL Server 2000 and SQL Server 7.0, the syntax of the Set statement has been expanded to support the assignment of local variables. In earlier versions, it was possible to use the Set statement only to declare cursor variables. Today, Microsoft is proclaiming this as a preferred method for assigning variables:

```
Set @LastName = 'Johnson'
```

Use of the Set statement is preferable, since it makes code more readable and reduces the opportunity to make a mistake (assign a variable and return a result set at the same time).

There is just one problem with the Set statement—it is not possible to assign several values with one statement. You will be forced to write code like this:

```
Set      @Make = 'ACME'
Set      @Model = 'Turbo'
Set      @EqType = 'cabadaster'
```

Assigning Values in the Update Statement

The ability to set the values of local variables in an Update statement is a feature that is buried deep in the oceans of SQL Server Books Online. It is an element that was designed to solve concurrency issues when code needs to read and update a column concurrently:

```
Update Inventory
Set @mnsCost = Cost = Cost * @fltTaxRate
Where InventoryId = @intInventoryId
```

Displaying the Values of Variables

The value of a variable can be displayed to the user by using a Select or a Print statement:

```
Select @LastName
Print @FirstName
```

It is possible to include a local variable in a result set that will be returned to the user:

```
Select    make "Selected make",
          Model "Selected Model",
          @Model "Original model"
From Equipment
Where EquipmentId = 2
```

Global Variables

Global variables constitute a special type of variable. The server maintains the values in these variables. They carry information specific to the server or a current user session. They can be examined from anywhere, whether from a stored procedure or a batch. In the SQL Server 7.0 and SQL Server 2000 documentation, Microsoft refers to them as *scalar functions,* meaning that they return just one value. Since you can still find references to global variables in some documentation, and since I would like to use some of them in this chapter, I will review them both here and in the next chapter, which is dedicated to functions.

Global variable names begin with an @@ prefix. You do not need to declare them, since the server constantly maintains them. They are system-defined functions and you cannot declare them.

Let's review the principal global variables/scalar functions.

@@identity

This is a function/global variable that you will use frequently. It is also a feature that generates many of the questions on Usenet newsgroups.

One column in each table can be defined as the Identity column, and the server will automatically generate a unique value in it. This is a standard technique in Microsoft SQL Server for generating *surrogate keys* (keys whose values are just numbers and do not carry any information). Usually, such columns will be set to assign sequential numbers:

```
Create table Eq (EqId int identity(1,1),
                Make varchar(50),
                Model varchar(50),
                EqTypeId int)
```

The @@identity global variable allows you to get the last identity value generated in the current session. It is important to read the value as soon as possible (that is, in the next Transact-SQL statement). Otherwise, it might happen that you initiate, for example, another stored procedure or a trigger that inserts a record to a different table with an Identity column. In such a case, SQL Server overwrites the number stored in @@identity with the new value. In the following example, a record will be inserted and a new identifier will immediately be read:

```
Declare @intEqId int
Insert into Eq(Make, Model, EqTypeId)
Values ('ACME', 'Turbo', 2)
Select @intEqId = @@identity
```

If one Transact-SQL statement inserts several records into a table with an Identity column, @@identity will be set to the value from the last record:

```
Declare @intEqId int
Insert into Equipment(Make, Model, EqTypeId)
   Select Make, Model, EqTypeID
   From NewEquipment
Select @intEqId = @@identity
```

You will use this function very often. One of the most common types of stored procedures that you will write will just insert a record and return its new key to the caller.

@@error

After each Transact-SQL statement, the server sets the value of this variable to an integer value:

- ▶ **0**   If the statement was successful
- ▶ **Error number**   If the statement has failed

This global variable is the foundation of all methods for error handling in the Microsoft SQL Server environment. It is essential to examine the value of this variable before any other Transact-SQL statement is completed, because the value of @@error will be reset. Even if the next statement is only a simple Select statement, the value of the @@error variable will be changed after it. In the following example, let's assume that an error will occur during the Update statement. @@error will contain the error code only until the next statement is executed; even the command for reading the @@error value will reset it. If it was completed successfully, SQL Server will set @@error to 0. The only way to preserve the @@error value is to immediately read it and store it in a local variable. Then it can be used for error handling.

```
Update Equipment
Set EqTypeId = 3
Where EqTypeId = 2
Select @intErrorCode = @@error
```

If it is necessary to read more than one global variable immediately after a statement, all such variables should be included in a single Select statement:

```
Declare    @intEqId int,
           @intErrorCode int
Insert into Equipment(Make, Model, EqTypeId)
Values ('ACME', 'Turbo', 2)
Select    @intEqId = @@identity,
          @intErrorCode = @@Error
```

The @@error variable will be set to an error number only in the case of errors, not in the case of warnings. Supplementary information that the server posts regarding errors or warnings (that is, severity, state, and error messages) are not available inside a stored procedure or a batch. Only the error number is accessible from a stored procedure or a batch. Further components of error messages can be read only from the client application.

You will find more details about use of the @@error function in the "Error Handling" section in Chapter 7.

@@rowcount

After each Transact-SQL statement, the server sets the value of this variable to the total number of records affected by it. It can be used to verify the success of selected operations:

```
select Make, Model, EqTypeid
into OldEquipment
from Equipment
where EqTypeid = 2

if @@rowcount = 0
    Print "No rows were copied!"
```

NOTE

Certain statements (like the If statement) will set @@rowcount to 0, and certain statements (like Declare) will not affect it.

Rowcount_big() is a function introduced in SQL Server 2000. It returns the number of affected records in the form of a `bigint` number.

TIP

When you try to update an individual record, SQL Server will not report an error if your Where clause specifies a criterion that does not qualify any records. SQL Server will not update anything, and you might, for example, think that the operation was successful. You can use @@rowcount to identify such cases.

Table Variables

SQL Server 2000 introduces the `table` data type. A statement declaring a variable for `table` initializes the variable as an empty table with a specified structure. As a table definition, such a statement includes definitions of columns with their data type, size, precision, optional primary key, unique and check constraints, and indexes. All elements have to be defined during the declaration. It is not possible to alter or add them later.

The following batch declares a variable for `table`, inserts rows, and returns them to the user:

```
Declare @MyTableVar table
    (Id int primary key,
     Lookup varchar(15))

Insert @MyTableVar values (1, '1Q2000')
```

```
Insert @MyTableVar values (2, '2Q2000')
Insert @MyTableVar values (3, '3Q2000')

Select * from @MyTableVar
Go
```

Because of their nature, `table` variables have certain limitations:

▶ `table` variables can only be part of the Select, Update, Delete, Insert, and Declare Cursor statements.

▶ `table` variables can be used as a part of the Select statement everywhere tables are acceptable, except as the destination in a Select...Into statement:

```
Select LookupId, Lookup
Into @TableVariable      -- wrong
From Lookup
```

▶ `table` variables can be used in Insert statements except when the Insert statement collects values from a stored procedure:

```
Insert into @TableVariable    -- wrong
    Exec prMyProcedure
```

▶ Unlike temporary tables, `table` variables always have a *local scope.* They can be used only in the batch, stored procedure, or function in which they are declared.

▶ The scope of cursors based on `table` variables is limited to the scope of the variable (the batch, stored procedure, or function in which they are defined).

▶ `table` variables are considered to be nonpersistent objects, and therefore they will not be rolled back after a Rollback Transaction statement.

TIP

If possible, use `table` *variables instead of temporary tables.* `table` *variables have less locking overhead and therefore are faster.*

Flow-Control Statements

Flow-control statements from T-SQL are rather rudimentary compared to similar commands in other modern programming languages such as Visual Basic and C++. Their use requires knowledge and some skill to overcome their lack of user friendliness. However, on a positive note, they allow the creation of very complex procedures.

This section covers the use of the following Transact-SQL statements and programming constructs:

▶ Comments
▶ Statement block
▶ If…Else
▶ While…Break
▶ Break
▶ Continue
▶ GoTo
▶ WaitFor
▶ Begin…End

Comments

You can include comments inside the source code of a batch or a stored procedure; these comments are ignored during compilation and execution by SQL Server. It is a common practice to accompany source code with remarks that will help other developers to understand the your intentions.

Comments can also be a piece of Transact-SQL source code that you do not want to execute for a particular reason (usually while developing or debugging). Such a process is usually referred to as *commenting out* the code.

Single-Line Comments

There are two methods to indicate a comment. A complete line or part of the line can be marked as a comment if the user places two hyphens (--) at the beginning. The remainder of the line becomes a comment. The comment ends at the end of the line:

```
-- This is a comment. Whole line will be ignored.
```

You can place the comment in the middle of a Transact-SQL statement. The following example comments out the last column:

```
Select LeaseId, LeaseVendor --, LeaseNumber
From Lease
Where ContractDate > '1/1/1999'
```

This type of comment can be nested in another comment defined with the same or a different method:

```
-- select * from Equipment -- Just for debugging
```

This commenting method is compatible with the SQL-92 standard.

Multiline Comments: /* ... */

The second commenting method is native to SQL Server. It is suitable for commenting out blocks of code that can span multiple lines. Such a comment must be divided from the rest of the code with a pair of delimiters—(/*) and (*/):

```
/*
This is a comment.
All these lines will be ignored.
*/

/* List all equipment. */
select * from Equipment
```

Comments do not have a length limit. It is best to write as much as is necessary to adequately document the code.

SQL Server documentation forbids the nesting of multiline comments. In different versions and in different tools, the following may or may not generate a syntax error:

```
/* This is a comment.
/* Query Analyzer will understand the following delimiter
as the end of the first comment. */
   This will generate a syntax error in some cases. */
Select * from Equipment
```

If you type this code in Query Analyzer, the program will not color the last line of explanation as a comment. (I am not sure you will be able to see a difference on the paper.) However, during the execution in Query Analyzer, the third line of the comment is ignored and will return a result set without reporting a syntax error (see Figure 4-1).

Single-line comments can be nested inside multiline comments:

```
/*
-- List all equipment.
Select * from Equipment
*/
```

In Chapter 6, when I discuss batches, I will illustrate the restriction that multiline comments cannot span more than one batch.

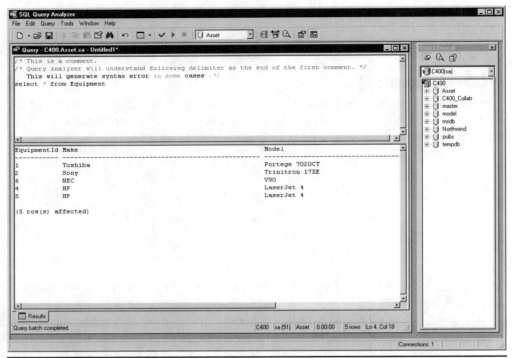

Figure 4-1 *Problems with comments*

Documenting Code

Again, your comments will be of benefit to other developers who read your code; your comments will be better still if you make their presence in the code as obvious as possible. It is a favorable, although not required, practice to accompany comment delimiters with a full line of stars, or to begin each commented line with two stars:

```
/***************************************************************
** File: prInsertEquipment.sql
** Name: prInsertEquipment
** Desc: Insert equipment and equipment type
**       (if not present).
**
** Return values: ErrorCode
**
** Called by:   middleware
**
** Parameters:
```

```
** Input                          Output
** ----------                     -----------
** Make                           EqId
** Model
** EqType
**
** Auth: Dejan Sunderic
** Date: 1/1/2000
**********************************************************************
** Change History
**********************************************************************
** Date:          Author:       Description:
** --------       --------      ------------------------------------
** 11/1/2003      DS            Fixed:49. Better error handling.
** 11/2/2003      DS            Fixed:36. Optimized for performance.
**********************************************************************/
```

Inserting two stars at the beginning of each line serves two purposes:

▶ They are a visual guide for your eye. If you comment out code this way, you will not be in doubt whether a piece of code is functional or commented out.

▶ They force SQL Server to report a syntax error if somebody makes an error (for example, by nesting comments or by spanning comments over multiple batches).

The preceding example is based on part of a SQL script for creating a stored procedure generated by Visual InterDev. It is very useful to keep track of all these items explicitly, especially Description and Change History. It is a personal choice to be more elaborate in describing stored procedures, but if you are, your comments can be used as instant design documentation.

Occasionally, developers believe that this type of header is sufficient code documentation, but you should consider commenting your code throughout. It is important to comment not *how* things are being done, but *what* is being done. I recommend that you write your comments to describe what a piece of code is attempting to accomplish, then write the code itself. In this way, you create design documentation that eventually becomes code documentation.

Statement Blocks: Begin…End

The developer can group several Transact-SQL statements by using Begin…End statements in a logical unit. Such units are then typically used in flow-control statements to execute a group of Transact-SQL statements together. Flow-control statements, such as If and While, can incorporate a single statement or a statement block to be executed when certain conditions are met.

```
Begin
     Transact-SQL statements
End
```

There must be one or more Transact-SQL statements inside a block. If there is only one statement inside, you could remove the Begin and End keywords. Begin and End must be used as a pair. If a compiler does not find a matching pair, it will report a syntax error.

Begin and End can also be nested, but this practice is prone to errors. However, if you are cautious and orderly, there should not be a problem. An excellent way to avoid such problems is to indent the code:

```
Begin

    Insert Order(OrderDate, RequestedById,
                TargetDate, DestinationLocation)
    Values(@OrderDate, @ContactId,
           @TargetDate, @LocId)

    Select    @ErrorCode = @@Error,
              @OrderId = @@Identity

    if @ErrorCode <> 0
    begin
        RaiseError('Error occurred while inserting Order!', 16,1)
        Return @@ErrorCode
    end
End
```

Conditional Execution: The If Statement

The If statement is the most common flow-control statement. It is used to examine the value of a condition and to change the flow of code based on the condition. First, let us review its syntax:

```
If boolean_expression
     {Transact-SQL_statement | statement_block}
[else
     {Transact-SQL_statement | statement_block}]
```

When the server encounters such a construct, it examines the value of the Boolean expression. If this value is True (1), it executes the statements or the statement block that follows it. The Else component of the statement is optional. It includes a single statement or a statement block that will be executed if the Boolean expression returns a value of False (0).

The following code sample tests the value of the @ErrorCode variable. If the variable contains a 0, the server inserts a record in the Order table and then records the value of the identity key and any error that may have occurred in the process.

```
If @ErrorCode = 0
Begin
     Insert Order(OrderDate,  RequestedById,
           TargetDate, DestinationLocation)
     Values(@dtOrderDate,  @intContactId,
           @dtTargetDate, @intLocId)

     Select    @intErrorCode = @@Error,
               @intOrderId = @@Identity
End
```

Let us take a look at a more complex case. The following stored procedure inserts a record in the Equipment table and returns the ID of the record to the caller. The stored procedure accepts the equipment type, make, and model as input parameters. The stored procedure must then find out if such an equipment type exists in the database and insert it if it does not.

```
Create Procedure prInsertEquipment_1
-- store values in equipment table.
-- return identifier of the record to the caller.
    (
          @chvMake varchar(50),
          @chvModel varchar(50),
          @chvEqType varchar(30)
    )
As
declare    @intEqTypeId int,
           @intEquipmentId int

-- read Id of EqType
Select @intEqTypeId = EqTypeId
From EqType
Where EqType = @chvEqType
-- does such eqType already exists in the database
If  @intEqTypeId IS NOT NULL
     --insert equipment
     Insert Equipment (Make, Model, EqTypeId)
     Values (@chvMake, @chvModel, @intEqTypeId)
Else
```

```
          --if it does not exist
      Begin
            -- insert new EqType in the database
            Insert EqType (EqType)
            Values (@chvEqType)

            -- get id of record that you've just inserted
            Select @intEqTypeId = @@identity

            --insert equipment
            Insert Equipment (Make, Model, EqTypeId)
            Values (@chvMake, @chvModel, @intEqTypeId)
      End
Select @intEquipmentId = @@identity

-- return id to the caller
return @intEquipmentId
```

There are a few items that could be changed in this stored procedure, but the
importance of this example is to illustrate a use of the Else statement.

One item that could be improved upon is the process of investigating the EqType
table with the Exists keyword. Its use here is similar to its use in the Where clause.
It tests for the presence of the records in the subquery:

```
If [NOT] Exists(subquery)
    {Transact-SQL_statement | statement_block}
[else
    {Transact-SQL_statement | statement_block}]
```

The stored procedure prInsertEquipment can be modified to use the Exists
keyword:

```
    . . .
If  Exists (Select EqTypeId From EqType Where EqType = @chvEqType)
    . . .
```

Naturally, if you use the Not operator, the encapsulated statement will be executed
if the subquery does not return records:

```
Alter Procedure prInsertEquipment_2
-- store values in equipment table.
-- return identifier of the record to the caller.
    (
        @chvMake varchar(50),
        @chvModel varchar(50),
        @chvEqType varchar(30)
```

```
        )
As
declare    @intEqTypeId int,
           @intEquipmentId int


-- does such eqType already exists in the database
If  Not Exists (Select EqTypeId From EqType Where EqType = @chvEqType)
    --if it does not exist
    Begin
            -- insert new EqType in the database
            Insert EqType (EqType)
            Values (@chvEqType)

            -- get id of record that you've just inserted
            Select @intEqTypeId = @@identity
    End
else
    -- read Id of EqType
    Select @intEqTypeId = EqTypeId
    From EqType
    Where EqType = @chvEqType

--insert equipment
Insert Equipment (Make, Model, EqTypeId)
Values (@chvMake, @chvModel, @intEqTypeId)

Select @intEquipmentId = @@identity

-- return id to the caller
Return @intEquipmentId
```

Both If and Else statements can be nested:

```
Create Procedure prInsertEquipment_3
-- store values in equipment table.
-- return identifier of the record to the caller.
    (
            @chvMake varchar(50),
            @chvModel varchar(50),
            @chvEqType varchar(30),
            @intEquipmentId int
    )
As
declare @intEqTypeId int,
        @ErrorCode int
```

```
-- does such eqType already exists in the database
If  Not Exists (Select EqTypeId From EqType Where EqType = @chvEqType)
      --if it does not exist
      Begin
            -- insert new EqType in the database
            Insert EqType (EqType)
            Values (@chvEqType)

            -- get id of record that you've just inserted
            Select @intEqTypeId = @@identity,
                  @ErrorCode = @@Error
            If @ErrorCode <> 0
                begin
                      Select 'Unable to insert Equipment Type. Error: ',
                            @ErrorCode
                      Return 1
                  End
      End
Else
      Begin
            -- read Id of EqType
            Select @intEqTypeId = EqTypeId

            From EqType
            Where EqType = @chvEqType
            Select @ErrorCode = @@Error

            If @ErrorCode <> 0
                begin

                    Select 'Unable to get Id of Equipment Type. Error: ',
                            @ErrorCode
                      Return 2
                  End
      End

--insert equipment
Insert Equipment (Make, Model, EqTypeId)
Values (@chvMake, @chvModel, @intEqTypeId)

-- return id to the caller
Select @intEquipmentId = @@identity,
      @ErrorCode = @@Error

If @ErrorCode <> 0
      Begin
```

```
        Select 'Unable to insert Equipment. Error: ', @ErrorCode
        Return 3
    End

-- return id to the caller
Select @intEquipmentId = @@identity

Return @intEquipmentId
```

There is no limit to the number of levels. However, this capability should not be abused. The presence of too many levels is a sure sign that a more in-depth study should be made concerning code design.

Looping: The While Statement

Transact-SQL contains only one statement that allows looping:

```
While Boolean_expression
    {sql_statement | statement_block}
    [Break]
    {sql_statement | statement_block}
    [Continue]
```

If the value of the Boolean expression is True (1), the server will execute one or more encapsulated Transact-SQL statement(s). From inside the block of statements, this execution can be controlled with the Break and Continue statements. The server will interrupt the looping when it encounters a Break statement. When the server encounters a Continue statement, it will ignore the rest of the statements and restart the loop.

NOTE

Keep in mind that loops are primarily tools for third-generation languages. In such languages, code was written to operate with records one at a time. Transact-SQL is a fourth-generation language and is written to operate with sets of information. It is possible to write code in Transact-SQL that will loop through records and perform operations on a single record, but you pay for this feature with severe performance penalties. However, there are cases when such an approach is necessary.

It is not easy to find bona fide examples to justify the use of loops in Transact-SQL. Let us investigate a stored procedure that calculates the factorial of an integer number:

```
Create Procedure prCalcFactorial
-- calculate factorial
-- 1! = 1
```

```
-- 3! = 3 * 2 * 1
-- n! = n * (n-1)* . . . 5 * 4 * 3 * 2 * 1
     @inyN tinyint,
     @intFactorial int OUTPUT
As

Set @intFactorial = 1

while @inyN > 1
begin
     set @intFactorial = @intFactorial * @inyN
     Set @inyN = @inyN - 1
end

return 0
```

Another example could be a stored procedure that returns a list of properties assigned to an asset in the form of a string:

```
Create Procedure prGetInventoryProperties
/*
Return comma-delimited list of properties that are describing asset.
i.e.: Property = Value Unit;Property = Value Unit;Property = Value
 Unit;Property = Value Unit;Property = Value Unit;...
*/
     (
          @intInventoryId int,
          @chvProperties varchar(8000) OUTPUT
     )

As

declare @intCountProperties int,
        @intCounter int,
        @chvProperty varchar(50),
        @chvValue varchar(50),
        @chvUnit varchar(50)

Create table #Properties(
        Id int identity(1,1),
        Property varchar(50),
        Value varchar(50),
        Unit varchar(50))

-- identify Properties associated with asset
insert into #Properties (Property, Value, Unit)
```

```
    select Property, Value, Unit
    from InventoryProperty inner join Property
    on InventoryProperty.PropertyId = Property.PropertyId
    where InventoryProperty.InventoryId = @intInventoryId

-- set loop
select @intCountProperties = Count(*),
       @intCounter = 1,
       @chvProperties = ''
from #Properties

-- loop through list of properties
while @intCounter <= @intCountProperties
begin
    -- get one property
    select @chvProperty = Property,
        @chvValue = Value,
        @chvUnit = Unit
    from #Properties
    where Id = @intCounter

    -- assemble list

    set @chvProperties = @chvProperties + '; '
                        + @chvProperty + '='
                        + @chvValue + ' ' +  @chvUnit

    -- let's go another round and get another property
    set @intCounter = @intCounter + 1
end

drop table #Properties
return 0
```

Unconditional Execution: The GoTo Statement

The GoTo statement forces the server to continue the execution from a *label*:

```
GoTo label
...
label:
```

The *label* has to be within the same stored procedure or batch. It is not important whether the *label* or the GoTo statement is defined first in the code. The *label* can even exist without the GoTo statement. On the contrary, the server will report an error if it encounters a GoTo statement that points to a nonexistent label.

The following stored procedure uses the GoTo statement to interrupt further processing and display a message to the user when an error occurs:

```
Create Procedure prCloseLease
-- Clear Rent, ScheduleId, and LeaseId on all assets associated
-- with specified lease.

    @intLeaseId int
As
    -- delete schedules
    Update Inventory
    Set Rent = 0,
        LeaseId = null,
        LeaseScheduleId = null
    Where LeaseId = @intLeaseId
    If @@Error <> 0 Goto PROBLEM_1

    -- delete schedules
    Delete from LeaseSchedule
    Where LeaseId = @intLeaseId
    If @@Error <> 0 Goto PROBLEM_2

    -- delete lease
    Delete from Lease
    Where LeaseId = @intLeaseId
    If @@Error <> 0        Goto PROBLEM_3
    Return 0

PROBLEM_1:
    Select 'Unable to update Inventory!'
    Return 50001
PROBLEM_2:
    Select 'Unable to remove schedules from the database!'
    Return 50002
PROBLEM_3:
    Select 'Unable to remove lease from the database!'
Return 50002
```

NOTE

The stored procedure is only an academic example. It would be better to use transactions and rollback changes in case of errors. I will describe transactions in Chapter 6.

Scheduled Execution: The WaitFor Statement

There are two ways to schedule the execution of a batch or stored procedure in SQL Server. One way is based on the use of SQL Server Agent. The other way is to use the WaitFor statement. The WaitFor statement allows the developer to specify the time when, or a time interval after which, the remaining Transact-SQL statements will be executed:

```
WaitFor {Delay 'time' | Time 'time'}
```

There are two variants to this statement. One specifies the delay (time interval) that must pass before the execution can continue. The time interval specified as a parameter of the statement must be less than 24 hours. In the following example, the server will pause for one minute before displaying the list of equipment:

```
WaitFor Delay '00:01:00'
     Select * from Equipment
```

The other variant is more significant. It allows the developer to schedule a time when the execution is to continue. The following example runs a full database backup at 11:00 P.M.:

```
WaitFor Time '23:00'
     Backup Database Asset To Asset_bkp
```

There is one problem with this Transact-SQL statement. The connection remains blocked while the server waits to execute the statement. Therefore, it is much better to use SQL Server Agent than the WaitFor statement to schedule jobs.

Cursors

Relational databases are designed to work with sets of data. In fact, the purpose of the Select statement, as the most important statement in SQL, is to define a set of records. In contrast, end-user applications display information to the user record by record (or maybe in small batches). To close the gap between these conflicting requirements, RDBMS architects have invented a new class of programming constructs—*cursors*.

Many types of cursors are implemented in various environments using different syntax, but all cursors work in a similar fashion:

1. A cursor first has to be defined and its features have to be set.
2. The cursor must be populated.

3. The cursor has to be positioned (*scrolled*) to a record or block of records that needs to be retrieved (*fetched*).

4. Information from one or more current records is fetched, and then some modification can be performed or some action can be initiated based on the fetched information.

5. Optionally, Steps 3 and 4 are repeated.

6. Finally, the cursor must be closed and resources released.

Cursors can be used on both server and client sides. SQL Server and the APIs for accessing database information (OLE DB, ODBC, DB-Library) all include sets of functions for processing cursors.

SQL Server supports three classes of cursors:

▶ Client cursors

▶ API server cursors

▶ Transact-SQL cursors

The major difference between Transact-SQL cursors and other types of cursors is their purpose. Transact-SQL cursors are used from stored procedures, batches, functions, or triggers to repeat custom processing for each row of the cursor. Other kinds of cursors are designed to access database information from the client application. We will review only Transact-SQL cursors.

Transact-SQL Cursors

Processing in Transact-SQL cursors has to be performed in the following steps:

1. Use the Declare Cursor statement to create the cursor based on the Select statement.

2. Use the Open statement to populate the cursor.

3. Use the Fetch statement to change the current record in the cursor and to store values into local variables.

4. Do something with the retrieved information.

5. If needed, repeat Steps 3 and 4.

6. Use the Close statement to close the cursor. Most of the resources (memory, locks, and so on) will be released.

7. Use the Deallocate statement to deallocate the cursor.

NOTE

Transact-SQL cursors do not support processing blocks of records. Only one record can be fetched at a time.

It is best to show this process through an example. We will rewrite the stored procedure that we used to illustrate the use of the While statement. The purpose of this stored procedure is to collect the properties of a specified asset and return them in delimited format (Property = Value Unit;). The final result should look like this:

```
CPU=Pentium II;RAM=64 MB;HDD=6.4 GB;Resolution=1024x768;Weight=2 kg;
```

Here is the code for the new instance of the stored procedure:

```
Alter Procedure prGetInventoryProperties_Cursor
/*
Return comma-delimited list of properties that are describing asset.
Property = Value unit;Property = Value unit;Property = Value unit;
Property = Value unit;Property = Value unit;Property = Value unit;...
*/
        (
                @intInventoryId int,
                @chvProperties varchar(8000) OUTPUT,
                @debug int = 0
        )

As

declare    @intCountProperties int,
           @intCounter int,
           @chvProperty varchar(50),
           @chvValue varchar(50),
           @chvUnit varchar(50),
           @insLenProperty smallint,
           @insLenValue smallint,
           @insLenUnit smallint,
           @insLenProperties smallint

Set @chvProperties = ''

Declare @CrsrVar Cursor

Set @CrsrVar = Cursor For
     select Property, Value, Unit
     from InventoryProperty inner join Property
     on InventoryProperty.PropertyId = Property.PropertyId
```

```
        where InventoryProperty.InventoryId = @intInventoryId

Open @CrsrVar

Fetch Next From @CrsrVar
Into @chvProperty, @chvValue, @chvUnit

While (@@FETCH_STATUS = 0)
Begin

    Set @chvUnit = Coalesce(@chvUnit, '')

    If @debug <> 0
        Select @chvProperty Property,
                @chvValue [Value],
                @chvUnit [Unit]

    -- check will new string fit
    Select @insLenProperty = DATALENGTH(@chvProperty),
            @insLenValue = DATALENGTH(@chvValue),
            @insLenUnit = DATALENGTH(@chvUnit),
            @insLenProperties = DATALENGTH(@chvProperties)


    If @insLenProperties + 2 + @insLenProperty + 1 +
        @insLenValue + 1 + @insLenUnit > 8000
    Begin
        Select 'List of properties is too long (> 8000 char)!'
        Return 1
    End

    -- assemble list
    Set @chvProperties = @chvProperties + @chvProperty + '='
                        + @chvValue + ' ' + @chvUnit + '; '
    If @debug <> 0
        Select @chvProperties chvProperties

    Fetch Next From @CrsrVar
    Into @chvProperty, @chvValue, @chvUnit

End

Close @CrsrVar
Deallocate @CrsrVar

Return 0
```

The stored procedure will first declare a cursor:

```
Declare @CrsrVar Cursor
```

The cursor will then be associated with the collection of properties related to the specified asset:

```
Set @CrsrVar = Cursor For
    Select Property, Value, Unit
    From InventoryProperty inner join Property
    On InventoryProperty.PropertyId = Property.PropertyId
    Where InventoryProperty.InventoryId = @intInventoryId
```

Before it can be used, the cursor needs to be opened:

```
Open @CrsrVar
```

The content of the first record can then be fetched into local variables:

```
Fetch Next From @CrsrVar
Into @chvProperty, @chvValue, @chvUnit
```

If the fetch was successful, we can start a loop to process the complete recordset:

```
While (@@FETCH_STATUS = 0)
```

After the values from the first record are processed, we read the next record:

```
    Fetch Next From @CrsrVar
    Into @chvProperty, @chvValue, @chvUnit
```

Once all records have been read, the value of @@fetch_status is set to −1 and we exit the loop. We need to close and deallocate the cursor and finish the stored procedure:

```
Close @CrsrVar
Deallocate @CrsrVar
```

Now, let's save and execute this stored procedure:

```
Declare @chvRes varchar(8000)
Exec prGetInventoryProperties_Cursor 5, @chvRes OUTPUT
Select @chvRes Properties
```

SQL Server will return the following:

```
Properties
---------------------------------------------------------------------
----------------------------
CPU=Pentium II ; RAM=64 MB; HDD=6.4 GB; Resolution=1024x768 ; Weight
=2 kg; Clock=366 MHz;
```

Cursor-Related Statements and Functions

Let's review statements and functions that you need to utilize to control cursors.

The Declare Cursor Statement

The Declare Cursor statement declares the Transact-SQL cursor and specifies its behavior and the query on which it is built. It is possible to use syntax based on the SQL-92 standard or native Transact-SQL syntax. I will display only the simplified syntax. If you need more details, refer to SQL Server Books Online.

```
Declare cursor_name Cursor
For select_statement
```

The name of the cursor is an identifier that complies with the rules set for local variables.

The Open Statement

The Open statement executes the Select statement specified in the Declare Cursor statement and populates the cursor:

```
Open { { [Global] cursor_name } | cursor_variable_name}
```

The Fetch Statement

The Fetch statement reads the row specified in the Transact-SQL cursor:

```
Fetch    [    [ Next | Prior | First | Last
                | Absolute {n | @nvar}
                | Relative {n | @nvar}
            ]
            From
        ]
{ { [Global] cursor_name } | @cursor_variable_name}
[Into @variable_name[,...n] ]
```

This statement can force the cursor to position the current record at the Next, Prior, First, or Last record. It is also possible to specify the Absolute position of the record or a position Relative to the current record.

If the developer specifies a list of global variables in the Into clause, those variables will be filled with values from the specified record.

If the cursor has just been opened, you can use Fetch Next to read the first record.

@@fetch_status

@@fetch_status is a function (or global variable) that returns the success code of the last Fetch statement executed during the current connection. It is often used as an exit criterion in loops that fetch records from a cursor.

Success Code	Description
0	Fetch was completely successful.
−1	The Fetch statement tried to read a record outside the recordset (last record was already read) or the Fetch statement failed.
−2	Record is missing (for example, somebody else has deleted the record in the meantime).

@@cursor_rows

As soon as the cursor is opened, the @@cursor_rows function (or global variable) is set to the number of records in the cursor (you can use this variable to loop through the cursor also).

When the cursor is of a dynamic or keyset type, the @@cursor_rows function will be set to a negative number to indicate it is being asynchronously populated.

The Close Statement

The Close statement closes an open cursor, releases the current recordset, and releases locks on rows held by the cursor:

```
Close { { [Global] cursor_name } | cursor_variable_name }
```

This statement must be executed on an opened cursor. If the cursor has just been declared, SQL Server will report an error.

The Deallocate Statement

After the Close statement, the structure of the cursor is still in place. It is possible to open it again. If you do not plan to use it any more, you should remove the structure as well, by using the Deallocate statement:

```
Deallocate { { [Global] cursor_name } | @cursor_variable_name}
```

Problems with Cursors

Cursors are a valuable but dangerous tool. Their curse is precisely the problem they are designed to solve—the differences between the relational nature of database systems and the record-based nature of client applications.

First of all, cursors are procedural and thus contradict the basic idea behind the SQL language—that is, to define what is needed in a result, not how to get it.

Performance penalties are an even larger problem. Regular SQL statements are set-oriented and much faster. Some types of cursors lock records in the database and prevent other users from changing them. Other types of cursors create an additional copy of all records and then work with them. Both approaches have performance implications.

Client-side cursors and API server cursors are also not the most efficient way to transfer information between server and client. It is much faster to use a "fire hose" cursor, which is actually not a cursor at all. You can find more details about "fire hose" cursors in *Hitchhiker's Guide to Visual Basic and SQL Server,* 6th edition, by William Vaughn (Microsoft Press, 1998).

The Justified Uses of Cursors

The rule of thumb is to avoid the use of cursors whenever possible. However, in some cases, such avoidance is not possible.

Cursors can be used to perform operations that cannot be performed using set-oriented statements. It is acceptable to use cursors to perform processing based on statements, stored procedures, and extended stored procedures, which are designed to work with one item at a time. For example, the sp_addrolemember system stored procedure is designed to set an existing user account as a member of the SQL Server role. If you can list users that need to be assigned to a role, you can loop through them (using a cursor) and execute the system stored procedure for each of them.

Excessive processing based on a single row (for example, business logic implemented in the form of an extended stored procedure) can also be implemented using a cursor. If you implement such a loop in a stored procedure instead of in a client application, you can reduce network traffic considerably.

Another example could be the export of a group of tables from a database to text files using bcp. The bcp utility is a command-prompt program that can work with one table at a time. To use it within a stored procedure, you need to execute it using the xp_cmdshell extended stored procedure, which can run just one command at a time:

```
Create Procedure prBcpOutTables
--loop through tables and export them to text fields
     @debug int = 0
As

Declare    @chvTable varchar(128),
           @chvCommand varchar(255)

Declare @curTables Cursor
```

```
-- get all USER-DEFINED tables from current database
Set @curTables = Cursor FOR
    select name
     from sysobjects
     where xType = 'U'

Open @curTables

-- get first table
Fetch Next From @curTables
Into @chvTable

-- if we successfully read the current record
While (@@fetch_status = 0)
Begin

    -- assemble DOS command for exporting table
    Set @chvCommand = 'bcp "Asset..[' + @chvTable
                    + ']" out C:\sql7\backup\' + @chvTable
                    + '.txt -c -q -Sdejan -Usa -Pdejan'
    -- during test just display command
    If @debug <> 0
        Select @chvCommand chvCommand

    -- in production execute DOS command and export table
    If @debug = 0
        Execute xp_cmdshell @chvCommand, NO_OUTPUT

    Fetch Next From @curTables
    Into @chvTable

End

Close @curTables
Deallocate @curTables

Return 0
```

If you execute this stored procedure (without specifying the @debug parameter), SQL Server will execute the following sequence of command-prompt commands to export tables:

```
bcp "Asset..[AcquisitionType]" out C:\sql7\backup\AcquisitionType.txt -c -q
-Sdejan -Usa -Pdejan
bcp "Asset..[MyEquipment]" out C:\sql7\backup\MyEquipment.txt -c -q
```

```
-Sdejan -Usa -Pdejan
bcp "Asset..[Equipment]" out C:\sql7\backup\Equipment.txt -c -q
-Sdejan -Usa -Pdejan
bcp "Asset..[EqType]" out C:\sql7\backup\EqType.txt -c -q
-Sdejan -Usa -Pdejan
bcp "Asset..[ActivityLog]" out C:\sql7\backup\ActivityLog.txt -c -q
-Sdejan -Usa -Pdejan
bcp "Asset..[OrderType]" out C:\sql7\backup\OrderType.txt -c -q
-Sdejan -Usa -Pdejan
bcp "Asset..[OldEquipment]" out C:\sql7\backup\OldEquipment.txt -c -q
-Sdejan -Usa -Pdejan
bcp "Asset..[Property]" out C:\sql7\backup\Property.txt -c -q
-Sdejan -Usa -Pdejan
bcp "Asset..[OrderStatus]" out C:\sql7\backup\OrderStatus.txt -c -q
-Sdejan -Usa -Pdejan
...
```

TIP

In Chapter 9, in the "A While Loop with Min() or Max() Functions" section, I will demonstrate another method for looping through a set of records using the While statement. Personally, I seldom use cursors; I prefer to use the method demonstrated in Chapter 9.

Functions

Microsoft has done a fantastic job providing database administrators and developers with an extensive set of built-in functions for SQL Server. In SQL Server 2000, you are now also able to create your own functions. We will cover the design of user-defined functions in detail in Chapter 8 and focus here on the uses and attributes of built-in functions.

Using Functions

Functions are Transact-SQL elements that are used to evaluate zero or more input parameters and return data to the caller. The syntax for calling a function is

```
Function_name ([parameter] [,...n])
```

For example, the Sin() function has the following syntax:

```
Sin(float_expression)
```

So, to display the sine of 45 degrees, you would use:

```
SELECT Sin(45)
```

Some functions accept more than one parameter, and some do not require parameters at all. For example, the GetDate() function, which returns the current date and time on the system clock to the caller, accepts no parameters. We will use the GetDate() function to illustrate the most common ways to use functions in Transact-SQL.

In Selection and Assignment

Functions can be used to represent a value or a part of a value to be assigned or selected in a Set or Select statement. In the following example, two variables are populated using values stored in the selected record and a third variable is populated using a function:

```
Select  @chvMake = Make,
        @Model = Model,
        @dtsCurrentDate = GetDate()
from Equipment
where EquipmentID = @intEqId
```

As previously noted, this use is not limited to the Select statement. Values can be assigned in the Set statement, displayed in the Print statement, stored in a table using Update and Insert, or even used as parameters for other functions:

```
Create Procedure prInsertNewSchedule
     @intLeaseId int,
     @intLeaseFrequencyId int
As

     Insert LeaseSchedule(LeaseId, StartDate,
                          EndDate, LeaseFrequencyId)
     Values (@intLeaseId,                GetDate(),
          DateAdd(Year, 3, GetDate()), @intLeaseFrequencyId)

return @@Error
```

This procedure inserts the current date using the GetDate() function in the StartDate column. The EndDate column is calculated using the DateAdd() function, which accepts the GetDate() function as one parameter. It is used to set the end date three years from the current date. This was just an example of the usage of functions. You will be able to see more details about GetDate() and DateAdd() in the "Date and Time Functions" section of this chapter.

As Part of the Selection Criteria

Functions are often used in the Where clause of Transact-SQL statements:

```
SELECT Inventory.InventoryId
FROM LeaseSchedule INNER JOIN Inventory
     ON LeaseSchedule.ScheduleId = Inventory.LeaseScheduleId
WHERE (LeaseSchedule.EndDate < GetDate())
AND (Inventory.Rent <> 0)
```

This Select statement selects the lease schedules that have reached the end of the term by comparing the EndDate to the current date.

In Expressions

You can also use functions anywhere you can use an expression, such as in an If statement, which requires a Boolean expression to determine further execution steps:

```
If @dtmLeaseEndDate < GetDate()
     Begin
          ...
     end
```

As Check and Default Constraints

Functions can also be used to define Check and Default constraints:

```
ALTER TABLE [dbo].[Order] (
     [OrderId] [int] IDENTITY (1, 1) NOT null ,
     [OrderDate] [smalldatetime] NOT null ,
     [RequestedById] [int] NOT null ,
     [TargetDate] [smalldatetime] NOT null ,
     [CompletionDate] [smalldatetime] null ,
     [DestinationLocationId] [int] null
) ON [PRIMARY]

GO

ALTER TABLE [dbo].[Order] WITH NOCHECK ADD
   CONSTRAINT [DF_Order_OrderDate] DEFAULT (GetDate()) FOR [OrderDate],
   CONSTRAINT [PK_Order] PRIMARY KEY  CLUSTERED
 (
   [OrderId]
 )  ON [PRIMARY]
GO
```

In this case, the Order table will automatically set the OrderDate field to the current date if a value is not supplied.

Instead of Tables

Because SQL Server 2000 has a new `table` data type, it is also possible for a function to return a recordset. Such functions are referred to as *table-valued functions*. These functions can be used in T-SQL statements anywhere tables are expected. In the following example, the result of the function is joined with a table (EqType) to produce a new result set:

```
declare @dtmLastMonth datetime
set @dtmLastMonth = DateAdd(month, -1, GetDate())
Select *
from dbo.fnNewEquipment (@dtmLastMonth) NewEq
inner join EqType
on NewEq.EqTypeId = EqType.EqTypeId
```

To reference any user-defined function including a table-valued function, you must specify the object owner along with the function name (*owner.function*). The

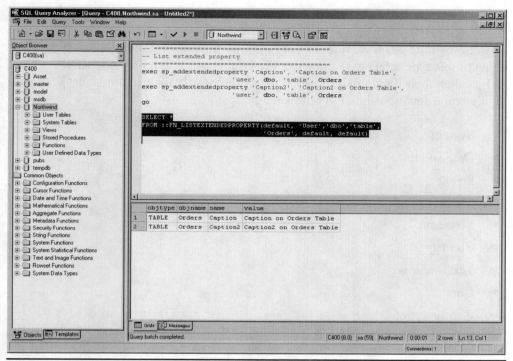

Figure 5-1   *Using table-valued user-defined functions*

only exception to this rule is in the use of built-in table-valued functions. In this case, you must place two colons (::) in front of the function name. For example, the fn_ListExtendedProperty() function lists properties of the database object (see Figure 5-1). For more details about extended properties, see Chapter 9.

Types of Functions

There are three primary groups of built-in functions, distinguishable by the type of result that is returned:

▶   Scalar

▶   Aggregate

▶   Rowset

Scalar Functions

Most of the time when we refer to functions, we are thinking of the scalar type. The name of this type refers to the fact that these functions return only one value.

Based on their functionality (although not necessarily their return values), we can divide scalar functions into the following groups:

► System
► Date and time
► String
► Mathematical
► Metadata
► Security
► Text and image
► Cursor
► Configuration
► System statistical

We will not be able to cover in detail all the built-in functions available in SQL Server 2000, but we will discuss the key functions that you will use most frequently. You can find complete documentation of all built-in functions in SQL Server Books Online.

System Functions

System functions return information related to the Microsoft SQL Server environment. They are used to return object names and identifiers, the current user, the current database, session, application, and login; to investigate the data type of an expression; and to perform conversions between data types.

Let's examine some of the system functions that are likely to be more frequently used and look at some examples.

Conditional Expression: Case   In other programming languages, Case is considered to be a flow-control programming construct. In earlier versions of SQL Server documentation, Case was classified as an expression. Since SQL Server 7.0, it is classified as a function, which is mathematically more correct. However, all of these classifications are more or less true.

The Case function/expression enables the user to evaluate an expression and to return the value associated with the result of the expression. For example, the Case function/expression in the following stored procedure returns the approximate number of days associated with a leasing schedule:

```
Create Procedure prLeasePeriodDuration
-- return approximate number of days associated with lease frequency
    @inyScheduleFrequencyId tinyint,
    @insDays smallint OUTPUT
As
Declare @chvScheduleFrequency varchar(50)

Select @chvScheduleFrequency = ScheduleFrequency
From ScheduleFrequency
where ScheduleFrequencyId = @inyScheduleFrequencyId
select @insDays =
    Case @chvScheduleFrequency
         When 'monthly' then 30
         When 'semi-monthly' then 15
         When 'bi-weekly' then 14
         When 'weekly' then 7
         When 'quarterly' then 92
         When 'yearly' then 365
    END
return
```

The Case function/expression works much like a Select statement with nested If statements. In fact, most of the time, you can write equivalent code using nested If statements.

There are two types of Case function/expressions:

▶ Simple Case function/expressions

▶ Searched Case function/expressions

A simple Case function/expression has the following syntax:

```
Case input_expression
    WHEN when_expression THEN result_expression
        [...n]
    [
        ELSE else_result_expression
    ]
END
```

The previous example used this kind of Case function/expression. SQL Server attempts to match the *input_expression* with one of the *when_expression*s. If it is successful, it returns the *result_expression* associated with the first matching *when_expression*. An Else clause is also part of the Case function/expression. If the value of the *input_expression* is not equal to either of the *when_expression*s, the function returns the value of the *else_result_expression*.

A searched Case function/expression is very similar. The only difference is that it does not have an *input_expression*. The complete criteria are inside the When clause in the form of a Boolean expression:

```
Case
    WHEN Boolean_expression THEN result_expression
        [...n]
    [
        ELSE else_result_expression
    ]
END
```

SQL Server returns the *result_expression* associated with the first *Boolean_expression*, which is True. If all *Boolean_expressions* are false, SQL Server returns the *else_result_expression*.

In the following example, a searched Case function/expression has to be used because the *Boolean_expression*s have different operators (= and Like):

```
Create Procedure prListLeaseInfo
-- list all lease contract information
As

Select LeaseVendor [Lease Vendor],
        LeaseNumber [Lease Number],
        Case -- some vendors have id of sales reps
            -- incorporated in lease numbers
            When LeaseVendor = 'Trigon FS'
                THEN SUBSTRING( LeaseNumber, 5, 12)
            When LeaseVendor Like 'EB%'
                THEN SUBSTRING( LeaseNumber, 9, 8)
            When LeaseVendor Like 'MMEX%'
                THEN SUBSTRING( LeaseNumber, 7, 6)
            When LeaseVendor = 'DAFS'
                THEN SUBSTRING( LeaseNumber, 8, 11)
            Else 'Unknown'
        end [Lease Agent],
        ContractDate [Contract Date]
        from Lease
```

TIP

Although both examples use Case functions/expressions as a part of the Select statement, keep in mind that you can use it anywhere that you can place an expression. This flexibility might come in very handy in some situations.

Getting Information about Data   You can use numerous functions to return information about expressions, the most important of which are the following:

► IsDate()
► IsNumeric()
► DataLength()
► Binary_CheckSum()

IsDate() is a function that is used to determine whether an expression is a valid date. It is particularly useful when you need to read data from text files. If the result of this function is 1 (true), SQL Server guarantees that you will be able to convert the data to the datetime data type. IsDate() uses the following syntax:

```
IsDate(expression)
```

In the following stored procedure, SQL Server verifies that Lease Data (received as a string) can be converted to a datetime value. It then stores this result with the rest of the parameters in the Lease table.

```
Create Procedure prLoadLeaseContract
-- insert lease contract information and return id of lease

        @chvLeaseVendor varchar(50),
        @chvLeaseNumber varchar(50),
        @chvLeaseDate varchar(50),
        @intLeaseId int OUTPUT
As
Declare @intError int

-- test validity of date
if IsDate(@chvLeaseDate) = 0
begin
     Raiserror ('Unable to Convert to date.', 16, 1)
     return 1
end

insert into Lease(LeaseVendor, LeaseNumber, ContractDate)
```

```
values (@chvLeaseVendor, @chvLeaseNumber,
        Convert(smalldatetime, @chvLeaseDate))

select    @intError = @@Error,
          @intLeaseId = @@identity

return @intError
```

You can use the IsNumeric() function to determine whether it is possible to convert a character value or expression into one of the numeric data types (int, smallint, tinyint, real, float, money, smallmoney, decimal, or numeric). IsNumeric() uses the following syntax:

```
IsNumeric(expression)
```

The DataLength() function returns the number of bytes used to store or display an expression. This information is particularly useful when processing variable-length character data types.

NOTE

DataLength() returns the number of bytes used to store the expression, not the number of characters, as Len() function. For example, each character in the nvarchar *data type (or any of the Unicode data types) uses 2 bytes.*

The DataLength() function uses the following syntax:

```
DataLength(expression)
```

If you assign a string value to a variable, and that value is too long, SQL Server will not report an error. It will simply truncate the value and assign it. The following stored procedure was originally designed without verifying that the list of properties will fit into the output variable. Since SQL Server 2000 and SQL Server 7.0 support data lengths up to 8000 characters using the varchar data type, it is unlikely that you will exhaust the available storage very often. However, experienced developers do not rely on such expectations (just think of the Y2K problem).

This stored procedure uses the DataLength() function to evaluate whether the resulting string is longer then 8000 characters before the strings are concatenated:

```
Alter Procedure prGetInventoryProperties
-- return comma-delimited list of properties describing asset.
-- i.e.: Property = Value unit;Property = Value unit;Property
-- = Value unit;
```

```
        (
                @intInventoryId int,
                @chvProperties varchar(8000) OUTPUT
        )

As

declare @intCountProperties int,
        @intCounter int,
        @chvProperty varchar(50),
        @chvValue varchar(50),
        @chvUnit varchar(50),
        @insLenProperty smallint,
        @insLenValue smallint,
        @insLenUnit smallint,
        @insLenProperties smallint

Create table #Properties(
        Id int identity(1,1),
        Property varchar(50),
        Value varchar(50),
        Unit varchar(50))

-- identify Properties associated with asset
insert into #Properties (Property, Value, Unit)
        select Property, Value, Unit
        from InventoryProperty inner join Property
        on InventoryProperty.PropertyId = Property.PropertyId
        where InventoryProperty.InventoryId = @intInventoryId

-- set loop
select    @intCountProperties = Count(*),
          @intCounter = 1,
          @chvProperties = ''
from #Properties

-- loop through list of properties
while @intCounter <= @intCountProperties
begin
        -- get one property
        select @chvProperty = Property,
               @chvValue = Value,
               @chvUnit = Unit
        from #Properties
        where Id = @intCounter
```

```
        -- check will new string fit
        select @insLenProperty = DataLength(@chvProperty),
               @insLenValue = DataLength(@chvValue),
               @insLenUnit = DataLength(@chvUnit),
               @insLenProperties = DataLength(@chvProperties)

        if @insLenProperties + 2 + @insLenProperty
            + 1 + @insLenValue + 1 + @insLenUnit > 8000
        begin
            select 'List of properties is too long '
                    + '(over 8000 characters)!'
            return 1
        end

        -- assemble list
        set @chvProperties = @chvProperties + '; '
                            + @chvProperty + '='
                            + @chvValue + ' '
                            + @chvUnit

        -- let's go another round and get another property
        set @intCounter = @intCounter + 1
end

drop table #Properties
return 0
```

SQL Server 2000 introduces the Binary_CheckSum() function, which calculates the binary checksum of a specified expression or set of table columns. It is designed to detect changes in a record. This function uses the following syntax:

```
Binary_CheckSum(*|expression[,...n])
```

TIP

Binary_CheckSum() is a much-needed tool for data warehousing projects. It allows DBAs to detect and handle the problem of "slowly changing dimensions" type 2 and 3.

The following stored procedure compares the binary checksum of columns containing new information with the checksum of columns already stored in the table; if the values do not match, the new data will be inserted into the table:

```
CREATE Procedure prUpdateEquipment
-- Check if values were changed in the meanwhile
-- Update values in equipment table.
```

```
        @intEquipmentId int,
        @chvMake varchar(50),
        @chvModel varchar(50),
        @intEqTypeId int,
        @debug int = 0
As
declare @intNewEquipmentBC int

set @intNewEquipmentBC = Binary_CheckSum(@chvMake,
                                        @chvModel,
                                        @intEqTypeId)

if @debug <> 0
    Select @intNewEquipmentBC NewBC
if @debug <> 0
    select EquipmentBC OldBC
    from EquipmentBC
    where EquipmentId = @intEquipmentId

if not exists (Select EquipmentBC
            from EquipmentBC
            where EquipmentId = @intEquipmentId)
    insert EquipmentBC (EquipmentId, EquipmentBC)
        select @intEquipmentId,
            Binary_CheckSum(Make, Model, EqTypeId)
        from Equipment
         where EquipmentId = @intEquipmentId

-- Check if values were changed in the meanwhile
if @intNewEquipmentBC <> (Select EquipmentBC
                        from EquipmentBC
                        where EquipmentId = @intEquipmentId)
begin
    if @debug <> 0
        select 'Information will be updated.'

    -- update information
    update Equipment
    Set  Make = @chvMake,
        Model = @chvModel,
        EqTypeId = @intEqTypeId
    where EquipmentId = @intEquipmentId

    if exists(select EquipmentId
            from    EquipmentBC
            where   EquipmentId = @intEquipmentId)
```

```
            update EquipmentBC
            Set EquipmentBC = @intNewEquipmentBC
            where EquipmentId = @intEquipmentId
    else
            insert EquipmentBC (EquipmentId, EquipmentBC)
            values (@intEquipmentId, @intNewEquipmentBC)
end
return
```

NOTE

Binary_CheckSum() is case-sensitive. It evaluates columns/expressions differently depending on the case (uppercase/lowercase) used in the column or expression. This might seem unusual since most SQL Server behavior depends on the code page that you select during installation.

If the default is selected, SQL Server ignores the case of characters when matching them. The nature of the algorithm used to implement the Binary_CheckSum() function is such that it cannot work that way.

Functions for Handling null Values   SQL Server is equipped with a set of three functions to help ease the pain of using null in your database system:

```
NullIf(expression, expression)
IsNull(check_expression, replacement_value)
Coalesce(expression [,...n])
```

NullIf() returns null if two expressions in the function are the same value. If the expressions are not equivalent, the function returns the value of the first expression.

This function can be useful when calculating the average of columns that accept null values. For example, let's assume that the author of the Asset database has created constraints or stored procedures such that a user can leave the value of the Inventory.Rent column as either null or zero when equipment is not leased. In this case, the Avg() function for calculating the average of the column will eliminate records containing null from the average but keep records with zero. It is not that the Avg() function is implemented improperly, but rather that our design can be improved. It is possible to implement a workaround using the NullIf() function:

```
select    AVG(Rent) [average without nulls],
          AVG(NullIf(Rent, 0)) [average without nulls and zeros]
from Inventory
```

An average calculated in this way will be different from an average calculated in the standard way:

```
average without nulls average without nulls and zeros
--------------------- -------------------------------
```

```
100.0000                   150.0000
(1 row(s) affected)
```

```
Warning: Null value eliminated from aggregate.
```

The IsNull() function examines the *check_expression*. If its value is null, the function returns the *replacement_value*. If the value of the *check_expression* is not null, the function returns the *check_expression*.

Let's suppose you want to calculate an average based on the total number of computers in the Inventory table. You can use the IsNull() value to replace null values during the calculation:

```
select AVG(Rent) [Eliminating nulls],
       AVG(ISNULL(rent, 0)) [with nulls as zeros]
from Inventory
```

The average price of computers that counts nulls as zeroes is less than the average that ignores computers with the price set to null:

```
Eliminating nulls  with nulls as zeros
-----------------  -------------------
100.0000               75.0000

(1 row(s) affected)
```

```
Warning: Null value eliminated from aggregate.
```

The last line is a warning that refers to the fact that null values are excluded when Avg() is calculated.

NOTE

The name of this function is confusing, especially if you are a Visual Basic programmer as well. It cannot be used to test whether the value of an expression is null. You should use these operators instead:

```
If expression IS null
If expression IS NOT null
```

The Coalesce() function is often used to coalesce (unite) values that are split into several columns. The result of the function is the first non-null expression. This function uses the following syntax:

```
COALESCE(expression [,...n])
```

In the following example, we coalesce values from three columns (Rent, Lease, and Cost) into one value (Acquisition Cost). Coalesce() evaluates the input expressions and returns the first non-null value.

```
SELECT Inventory.Inventoryid,
       Equipment.Make + ' ' + Equipment.Model Equipment,
       AcquisitionType.AcquisitionType,
       COALESCE(Inventory.Rent, Inventory.Lease, Inventory.Cost) [Cost]
FROM Inventory INNER JOIN AcquisitionType ON
     Inventory.AcquisitionTypeID = AcquisitionType.AcquisitionTypeId
            INNER JOIN Equipment
       ON Inventory.EquipmentId = Equipment.EquipmentId
```

The result contains just one column, showing the cost of acquisition:

```
Inventoryid Equipment                          AcquisitionType Cost
----------- ---------------------------------- --------------- ---------
5           Toshiba Portege 7020CT             Purchase        1295.0000
6           Toshiba Portege 7020CT             Rent             200.0000
8           Toshiba Portege 7020CT             Lease             87.7500
10          Toshiba Portege 7020CT             Lease             99.9500
```

Conversion Functions   The Cast() and Convert() functions are used to explicitly convert the information in one data type to another specified data type. There is just one small difference between these two functions: Convert() allows you to specify the format of the result, whereas Cast() does not.

Their syntax is

```
Cast(expression AS data_type)
Convert(data_type[(length)], expression [, style])
```

In this case, *expression* is any value or expression that you want to convert, and *data_type* is the new data type. The following statement concatenates two strings and an error number and returns them as a string:

```
Select "Error ["+Cast(@@Error as varchar)+"] has occurred."
```

The result is an error number integrated with a sentence, which might be useful in an error handling situation:

```
--------------------------------------------------
Error [373] has occurred.
```

In the Convert() function, *style* refers to the formatting style used in the conversion of date and time (datetime, smalldatetime) or numeric (money, smallmoney, `float`, `real`) expressions to strings (`varchar`, `char`, `nvarchar`, `nchar`). The following command displays the current date in default and German style:

```
select GetDate() standard, Convert(varchar, GetDate(), 104) German
```

The result is

```
standard                     German
-------------------------    ------------------------------
2003-07-11 11:45:57.730      11.07.2003
```

Table 5-1 lists formatting styles that you can use when converting `datetime` to character or character to `datetime` information.

Style with 2-Digit Year	Style with 4-Digit Year	Standard	Format
–	0 or 100	Default	mon dd yyyy hh:miAM (or PM)
1	101	USA	mm/dd/yy
2	102	ANSI	yy.mm.dd
3	103	British/French	dd/mm/yy
4	104	German	dd.mm.yy
5	105	Italian	dd-mm-yy
6	106	–	dd mon yy
7	107	–	mon dd, yy
8	108	–	hh:mm:ss
–	9 or 109	Default + milliseconds	mon dd yyyy hh:mi:ss:mmmAM (or PM)
10	110	USA	mm-dd-yy
11	111	Japan	yy/mm/dd
12	112	ISO	yymmdd
-	13 or 113	Europe default + milliseconds	dd mon yyyy hh:mm:ss:mmm(24h)
14	114	–	hh:mi:ss:mmm(24h)
–	20 or 120	ODBC canonical	yyyy-mm-dd hh:mi:ss(24h)
–	21 or 121	ODBC canonical (with milliseconds)	yyyy-mm-dd hh:mi:ss.mmm(24h)
–	130	Kuwaiti	dd/mm/yyyy hh:mi:ss.mmmAM
–	131	Kuwaiti	dd mm yyyy hh:mi:ss.mmmAM

Table 5-1 *Formatting Styles for `datetime` Information*

The following table lists formatting styles that you can use when converting monetary values to character information:

Value	Output
0 (default)	Two digits behind decimal point No commas every three digits Example: 1234.56
1	Two digits behind decimal point Commas every three digits Example: 1,234.56
2	Four digits behind decimal point No commas every three digits Example: 1234.5678

In the following example, we format a monetary value:

```
Select    $12345678.90,
          Convert(varchar(30), $12345678.90, 0),
          Convert(varchar(30), $12345678.90, 1),
          Convert(varchar(30), $12345678.90, 2)
```

The result is

```
------------- ------------- --------------- -------------
12345678.9000 12345678.90   12,345,678.90   12345678.9000
```

The following table lists formatting styles that you can use when converting float or real values to character information:

Value	Output
0 (default)	In scientific notation, when needed; 6 digits maximum
1	8 digits always in scientific notation
2	16 digits always in scientific notation

TIP

Microsoft recommends using the Cast() function whenever the formatting power of Convert() is not required, because Cast() is compatible with the ANSI SQL-92 standard.

When you specify the target data type of variable length as a part of the Cast() or Convert() functions, you should include its length, too. If you do not specify length, SQL Server assigns a default length of 30. Therefore, the previous example could be written as

```
Select    $12345678.90,
          Convert(varchar, $12345678.90, 0),
          Convert(varchar, $12345678.90, 1),
          Convert(varchar, $12345678.90, 2)
```

You need to use conversion functions when you do any of the following:

▶ Supply a Transact-SQL statement or function with a value in a specific data type

▶ Set the format of a date or number

▶ Obtain a value that uses an exotic data type

In some cases, SQL Server automatically (that is, behind the scenes) converts the value if the required data type and the supplied data type are compatible. For example, if some function requires a `char` parameter, you could supply a `datetime` parameter and SQL Server will perform an *implicit conversion* of the value. In the opposite direction, you must use an *explicit conversion*—that is, you must use conversion functions. If it is not possible to convert the expression to the specified data type, SQL Server raises an error.

TIP

SQL Server Books Online includes a table that lists which data types can be converted to other data types and which kind of conversion (explicit or implicit) is required.

Information about the Current Session   The following functions return information associated with the current session (for instance, how you logged on to the server, your username in the database, the name of the server, the permissions you have in the current database, and so on):

Function	Description
App_Name()	Name of the application that opened the session.
Host_Id()	ID of the computer hosting the client application.
Host_Name()	Name of the computer hosting the client application.

Function	Description
Permissions()	Bitmap that specifies permissions on a selected column, a database object, or the current database.
Current_User	Name of the database user; same as User_Name().
Session_User	Name of the database user who owns the current session.
System_User	Name of the server login that owns the current session. If the user has logged on to the server using Microsoft Windows NT Authentication, this function returns the Windows NT login.
User_Name()	Name of the database user; same as Current_User.

The following stored procedure uses the System_User function to identify the user adding an order to the system:

```
Create Procedure prAddOrder
-- insert Order record

    @dtmOrderDate datetime = null,
    @dtmTargetDate datetime = null,
    @chvUserName varchar(128) = null,
    @intDestinationLocation int,
    @chvNote varchar(200),
    @intOrderid int OUTPUT

As

    declare     @intRequestedById int

    -- If user didn't specify order date
    -- default is today.
    if @dtmOrderDate = null
        Set @dtmOrderDate = GetDate()

    -- If user didn't specify target date
    -- default is 3 days after request date.
    if @dtmTargetDate = null
        Set @dtmTargetDate = DateAdd(day, 3, @dtmOrderDate)

    -- if user didn't identify himself
    -- try to identify him using login name
    if @chvUserName = null
        Set @chvUserName = System_User

    -- get Id of the user
    select @intRequestedById = ContactId
    from Contact
```

```
where UserName = @chvUserName

-- if you cannot identify user report an error
If @intRequestedById = null
begin
    Raiserror('Unable to identify user in Contact table!', 1, 2)
    return 1
end

-- and finally create Order
Insert into [Order](OrderDate, RequestedById, TargetDate,
                    DestinationLocationId,  Note)
Values (@dtmOrderDate, @intRequestedById, @dtmTargetDate,
        @intDestinationLocation,    @chvNote)

set @intOrderid = @@identity
```

```
return 0
```

Functions for Handling Identity Values   *Identity* columns are used in SQL Server tables to automatically generate unique identifiers for each record. Numbers that are generated in this manner are based on two values—*identity seed* and *identity increment.* SQL Server starts assigning identity values from an identity seed, and every row is given a value that is greater than the previous one by the value specified in the identity increment (or less than that value if you use a negative increment value).

In Chapter 4, we covered the use of the @@identity function/global variable. It returns the last value generated by SQL Server while inserting record(s) into the table with an identity value:

```
Declare @intEqId int
Insert into Equipment(Make, Model, EqTypeId)
Values ('ACME', 'Turbo', 2)
Select @intEqId = @@identity
Select @intEqId [EqId]
```

The Ident_Seed() and Ident_Incr() functions return to the user the values of the seed and the increment for the selected table or view:

```
Select IDENT_SEED('Inventory'), IDENT_INCR('Inventory')
```

The Identity() function allows a user to generate identity values while using the Select…Into command. Let me remind you that this command selects records and immediately inserts them into a new table. Without it, you would be forced to create a new table with an identity column and then insert the selected records into the table. With it, everything can be achieved in one step:

```
SELECT    Identity(int, 1,1) AS ID,
          Property.Property,
          InventoryProperty.Value,
          Property.Unit
INTO #InventoryProperty
FROM InventoryProperty INNER JOIN Property ON
     InventoryProperty.PropertyId = Property.PropertyId
WHERE (InventoryProperty.InventoryId = 12)
```

Ident_Current() returns the last identity value set for a specified table (in any scope of any process). To use it, just supply the table name as a parameter:

```
Select Ident_Current('Equipment')
```

The Scope_Identity() function, new with SQL Server 2000, returns the last identity value generated in the scope of the current process. We will discuss in detail usage of the Scope_Identity() function and the problems it solves in the "Using Identity Values" section of Chapter 9.

Date and Time Functions

The following set of functions is designed to process data and time values and expressions.

Get (Current) Date   GetDate() is the function that you will probably use more often than any other date and time function. It will return the system time in `datetime` format.

We have already demonstrated the use of this function in the first section of this chapter, "Using Functions."

GetUtcDate() is the function that returns the date and time for the Greenwich time zone, also known as Universal Time Coordinate (UTC).

Extracting Parts of Date and Time   From time to time, you will need to extract just one component of the date and time value. The basic functionality necessary to achieve this end is implemented in the following three functions:

```
DAY(date)
MONTH(date)
YEAR(date)
```

These functions require expressions of the `datetime` or `smalldatetime` data type, and they all return the corresponding integer value.

The DatePart() and DateName() functions provide similar functionality, but they are more flexible:

```
DatePart(datepart, date)
DateName(datepart, date)
```

The user can specify which component of the date to obtain by supplying a *datepart* constant from Table 5-2 (you can use either the full name or the abbreviation).

DatePart() then returns the value of the *datepart*, and DateName() returns the string that contains the appropriate name. Naturally, DateName() is not meaningful in some cases (for example, year, second) and SQL Server will return the same value as it would for DatePart(). The following Select statement shows how can you use data functions:

```
SELECT    GetDate()'Date',
          DateName(month, GetDate()) AS 'Month Name',
          DatePart(yyyy, GetDate()) AS 'Year'
```

Datepart — Full	Datepart — Abbreviation
Millisecond	ms
Second	ss, s
Minute	mi, n
Hour	hh
weekday	dw
Week	wk, ww
dayofyear	dy, y
Day	dd, d
Month	mm, m
Quarter	qq, q
Year	yy, yyyy

Table 5-2 *Dateparts and Abbreviations Recognized by SQL Server*

Notice that the first parameter is not a character parameter. You cannot fill it using an expression or variable. SQL Server will return:

```
Date                         Month Name        Year
-------------------------    ---------------   -----------
2003-02-20 00:45:40.867      February          2003
```

Date and Time Calculations   Transact-SQL contains two functions for performing calculations on date and time expressions:

```
DateAdd(datepart, number, date)
DateDiff(datepart, startdate, enddate)
```

DateAdd() is used to add a *number* of *datepart* intervals to the specified *date* value. DateDiff() returns the number of *datepart* intervals between a *startdate* and an *enddate*. Both of these functions use a value from Table 5-2, shown in the previous section, to specify *datepart*. The following stored procedure uses these functions to list the due dates for leases:

```
Alter Procedure prListTerms
-- return list of due days for the leasing
    @dtsStartDate smalldatetime,
    @dtsEndDate smalldatetime,
    @chvLeaseFrequency varchar(20)
As
set nocount on

declare @insDueDates smallint -- number of intervals

-- calculate number of DueDates
select @insDueDates =
    Case @chvLeaseFrequency
        When 'monthly'
            then DateDiff(month, @dtsStartDate, @dtsEndDate)
        When 'semi-monthly'
            then 2 * DateDiff(month, @dtsStartDate, @dtsEndDate)
        When 'bi-weekly'
            then DateDiff(week, @dtsStartDate, @dtsEndDate)/2
        When 'weekly'
            then DateDiff(week, @dtsStartDate, @dtsEndDate)
        When 'quarterly'
            then DateDiff(qq, @dtsStartDate, @dtsEndDate)
        When 'yearly'
            then DateDiff(y, @dtsStartDate, @dtsEndDate)
```

```
    END

-- generate list of due dates using temporary table
Create table #DueDates (ID int)

while @insDueDates >= 0
begin
    insert #DueDates (ID)
    values (@insDueDates)

    select @insDueDates = @insDueDates - 1
end

-- display list of Due dates
select ID+1, Convert(varchar,
    Case
        When @chvLeaseFrequency = 'monthly'
            then DateAdd(month,ID, @dtsStartDate)
        When @chvLeaseFrequency = 'semi-monthly'
        and ID/2 =  CAST(ID as float)/2
            then DateAdd(month, ID/2, @dtsStartDate)
        When @chvLeaseFrequency = 'semi-monthly'
        and ID/2 <> CAST(ID as float)/2
            then DateAdd(dd, 15,
                        DateAdd(month, ID/2, @dtsStartDate))
        When @chvLeaseFrequency = 'bi-weekly'
            then DateAdd(week, ID*2, @dtsStartDate)
        When @chvLeaseFrequency = 'weekly'
            then DateAdd(week, ID, @dtsStartDate)
        When @chvLeaseFrequency = 'quarterly'
            then DateAdd(qq, ID, @dtsStartDate)
        When @chvLeaseFrequency = 'yearly'
            then DateAdd(y, ID, @dtsStartDate)
    END , 105) [Due date]
from #DueDates
order by ID

-- wash the dishes
drop table #DueDates

return 0
```

You can see the result of the stored procedure in Figure 5-2.

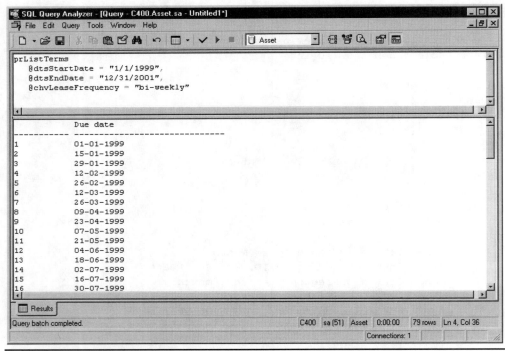

Figure 5-2 *Execution prListTerms*

String Functions

Microsoft SQL Server supports an elaborate set of string functions. (Who would expect such a thing from a tool developed in C?)

Basic String Manipulation   The Len() function uses the following syntax:

```
Len(string_expression)
```

This function returns the length of a string in characters. The input parameter can be any kind of string expression. DataLength(), a similar system function, returns the number of bytes occupied by the value.

```
declare @chvEquipment varchar(30)
set @chvEquipment = 'Toshiba Portege 7020CT'
select Len(@chvEquipment)
```

The result is

```
-----------
    22
```

The following two functions return the number of characters from the left or right side of the string:

Left(*character_expression*, *integer_expression*)

Right(*character_expression*, *integer_expression*)

Early versions of Microsoft SQL Server contained only the Right() function:

```
declare @chvEquipment varchar(30)
set @chvEquipment = 'Toshiba Portege 7020CT'
select Left(@chvEquipment, 7) Make, Right(@chvEquipment, 14) Model
```

The result of this batch is

```
Make      Model
-------   --------------
Toshiba   Portege 7020CT
```

Before the introduction of the Left() function, developers had to implement its functionality using the SubString() function:

```
SubString(expression, start, length)
```

The SubString() function returns a set (*length*) of characters from the string (*expression*) starting from a specified (*start*) character. The *expression* can be any character, `text`, `image`, or `binary` data type. Because of this data type flexibility, the *length* and *start* parameters are based on the number of *bytes* when the *expression* is of the `text`, `image`, `binary`, or `varbinary` data types, rather than on the number of characters. In the case of Unicode data types, one character occupies 2 bytes. If you specify an odd number, you may get unexpected results in the form of split characters.

The following batch extracts part of a string:

```
declare @chvEquipment varchar(30)
set @chvEquipment = 'Toshiba Portege 7020CT'
select SubString(@chvEquipment, 9, 7)
```

The result set is

```
-------
Portege
```

The CharIndex() function returns the index of the first occurrence of a string (*expression1*) within a second string (*expression2*):

```
CharIndex(expression1, expression2 [, start_location])
```

There is an optional parameter that allows you to specify the start location for the search:

```
Create Procedure prSplitFullName
-- split full name received in format 'Sunderic, Dejan'
-- into last and first name
-- default delimiter is comma and space ', ',
-- but caller can specify other
    @chvFullName varchar(50),
    @chvDelimiter varchar(3) = ', ',
    @chvFirstName varchar(50) OUTPUT,
    @chvLastName varchar(50) OUTPUT
As
set nocount on

declare @intPosition int

Set @intPosition = CharIndex(@chvDelimiter, @chvFullName)

If @intPosition > 0
begin
    Set @chvLastName = Left(@chvFullName, @intPosition - 1)
    Set @chvFirstName = Right(@chvFullName,
        Len(@chvFullName) - @intPosition - Len(@chvDelimiter) )
end
else
    return 1

return 0
```

All of these string functions might look to you like a perfect tool for searching table columns, but there is just one problem with this application. If you apply a conversion function inside the Where clause of a Select statement, SQL Server does not use the index to query the table. Instead, it performs a table scan—even if the index exists. For example, you should not use the CharIndex() function to identify records with a particular string pattern:

```
select *
from Equipment
where CharIndex('Portege', Model) > 0
```

The Like operator with wild card characters is a much better choice if the string that you are looking for is at the beginning of the field:

```
select *
from Equipment
where Model like 'Portege%'
```

The PatIndex() function is similar to the CharIndex() function:

```
PatIndex('%pattern%', expression)
```

The major difference is that it allows the use of wild card characters in the search pattern:

```
Set @intPosition = PATINDEX('%,%', @chvFullName)
```

Again, if you use this function to search against a table column, SQL Server ignores the index and performs a table scan.

TIP

In earlier versions of SQL Server, PatIndex() was the only reasonable (although not very fast) way to query the contents of text columns and variables. Since version 7.0, SQL Server has had a new feature — Full-Text Search — that allows linguistic searches against all character data and works with words and phrases instead of with character patterns. Basically, Microsoft has included Index Server in the Standard and Enterprise editions of SQL Server 7.0 and 2000.

String Conversion   The following two functions remove leading and trailing blanks from a string:

```
LTrim(character_expression)
RTrim(character_expression)
```

In the following query, we use both of them at the same time:

```
select LTrim(RTrim('   Dejan Sunderic   '))
```

The following functions convert a string to its uppercase or lowercase equivalent:

```
Upper(character_expression)
Lower(character_expression)
```

Use the Str() function to convert numeric values to strings:

```
Str(float_expression[, length[, decimal]])
```

The *length* parameter is an integer that specifies the number of characters needed for the result. This parameter includes everything: sign, digit, and decimal point. If necessary to fit the output into the specified length, SQL Server will round the value before converting it. If you do not specify a length, the default length is ten characters, and the default decimal length is 0.

SQL Server provides a number of functions for representing the conversion from character types to ASCII codes and vice versa:

```
Char(integer_expression)
ASCII(character_expression)
NChar(integer_expression)
Unicode(character_expression)
```

The Char() and NChar() functions return characters with the specified integer code according to the ASCII and Unicode standards:

```
select NChar(352) + 'underi' + NChar(263)
```

Depending on fonts, operating systems, language settings, and other criteria, you may get proper or improper results from this expression (see Figure 5-3).

There is another interesting use of the Char() function. You can use it to insert control characters into output. For example, you can add tabulators Char(9) or carriage returns Char(13). In the past, this was a very important way to format output.

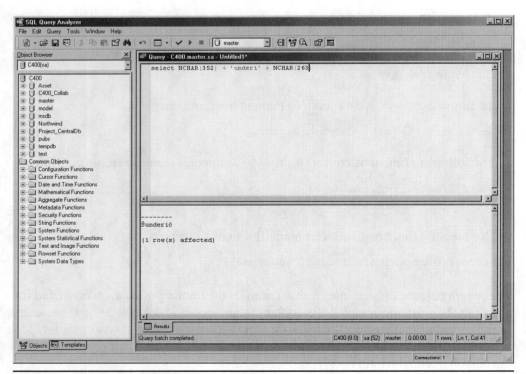

Figure 5-3   *Using Unicode characters*

The ASCII() and Unicode() functions perform the opposite operation. They return the integer that corresponds to the first character of an expression (see Figure 5-4).

The following two functions generate a string of a specified length (*integer_expression*) and fill it with spaces or a specified character:

```
Space(integer_expression)
Replicate(character_expression, integer_expression)
```

For example:

```
select Space(4) + Replicate('*', 8)
```

This statement returns a useless result, but these functions were used at one time primarily to format output:

```
-----------
        ********
```

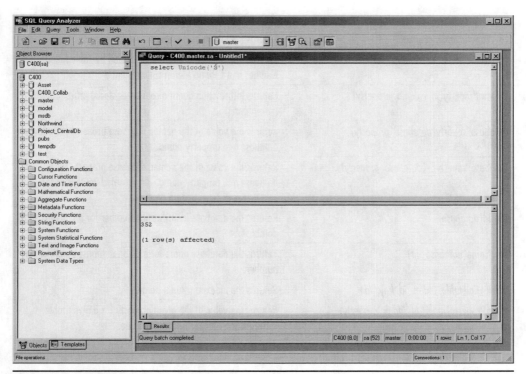

Figure 5-4   *Identifying Unicode character*

Use the Stuff() function to stuff a string:

```
Stuff(character_expression1, start, length, character_expression2)
```

SQL Server removes a *length* of *character_expression1*, beginning at the specified *start* point, and replaces it with *character_expression2*. The specified length does not have to match that of *character_expression2*:

```
select Stuff('Sunderic, Dejan', 9, 2, Char(9))
```

This query replaces the comma and space in the target string with a tabulator:

```
------------------
Sunderic    Dejan
```

Metadata Functions

These functions are like a drill that you can use to obtain information about a database and database objects. The following table contains a partial list of metadata functions:

Function	Description
Col_Length(*table*, *column*)	Returns the length of the column.
Col_Name(*table_id*, *column_id*)	Returns the name of the column specified by Table Identification Number and Column Identification Number.
ColumnProperty(*id*, *column*, *property*)	Returns information about a column or stored procedure parameter.
DatabaseProperty(*database*, *property*)	Returns the value of the named database property for a given database and property name.
DatabasePropertyEx(*database*, *property*)	Returns the value of the named database property for a given database and property name. The returned value is of the `sql_variant` data type.
Db_Id(*database*)	Returns the database identification number for the given database.
Db_Name(*database_id*)	Returns the database name for a given database identification number.
Index_Col(*table*, *index_id*, *key_id*)	Returns the indexed column name.
IndexProperty(*table_id*, *index*, *property*)	Returns the value of the given property for a given table identification number and index name.

Function	Description
Object_Id(*object*)	Returns the identification number of the given object.
Object_Name(*object_id*)	Returns the database object name for the given object identification number.
ObjectProperty(*id, property*)	Returns information about the specified property for a given object's identification number.
@@ProcID	Returns the identification number of the current stored procedure.
Sql_Variant_Property(*expression, property*)	Returns the value of the given property for a given expression.
TypeProperty(*type, property*)	Returns information about the data type.

The Sql_Variant_Property() function retrieves information about the sql_variant data type, introduced in SQL Server 2000. It returns specified *property* information about data stored in or obtained from the *expression* parameter. You can specify one of the following properties to be returned:

Property	Output
BaseType	The SQL Server data type
Precision	Number of digits of the base type
Scale	Number of digits behind decimal point
TotalBytes	Number of bytes required to store data and metadata
Collation	Collation of the data
MaxLength	Maximum length in bytes

The Sql_Variant_Property() function uses the following syntax:

```
SQL_Variant_Property(expression, property)
```

The *property* parameter must be specified in the form of a string:

```
SELECT    SQL_Variant_Property(Lookup,'BaseType'),
          SQL_Variant_Property(Lookup,'Precision'),
          SQL_Variant_Property(Lookup,'Scale')
FROM      Lookup
WHERE     LookupGroupId = 16
AND       LookupId = 4
```

Aggregate Functions

Aggregate functions perform an operation on a set of records and return a single value. They can be used in the following situations:

- The selection list of the Select statement
- A Having clause
- A Compute clause

Function	Description
Avg([All | Distinct] *expression*)	Returns the average value in the group.
Count([All | Distinct] *expression* |*)	Counts the number of items in the group.
Count_Big([All | Distinct] *expression* |*)	Counts the number of items in the group. The result is returned in the form of a `bigint` number.
Grouping(*Column_Name*)	Creates an additional column with a value of 1 when a row is added by the CUBE or ROLLUP operator or 0 if it is not the result of a CUBE or ROLLUP operator.
Max(*expression*)	Returns the maximum value in the expression.
Min(*expression*)	Returns the minimum value in the expression.
Sum(*expression*)	Returns the sum of the expression's values.
StDev(*expression*)	Returns the statistical standard deviation for the values in the expression.
StDevP(*expression*)	Returns the statistical standard deviation for the population for the values in the expression.
Var(*expression*)	Returns the statistical variance of the values in the expression.
VarP(*expression*)	Returns the statistical variance for the population for the values in the expression.

Except for the Count() function, all aggregate functions ignore records that have null in the specified field from the set:

```
select Avg(Rent) [Average Rent] from Inventory
```

As you can see, SQL Server will even print a warning about nulls:

```
Average Rent
------------
200.0000
```

```
(1 row(s) affected)

Warning: Null value eliminated from aggregate.
```

You apply Count() on a specific field:

```
select Count(Rent) [Rentals] from Inventory
```

SQL Server will count only records that do not have null in the Rent field:

```
Rentals
------------
241

(1 row(s) affected)

Warning: Null value eliminated from aggregate.
```

You can apply Count() on all fields:

```
select Count(*) [Assets] from Inventory
```

SQL Server counts all records in the table:

```
Assets
------------
7298

(1 row(s) affected)
```

Rowset Functions

Functions of this type are distinguished from other functions in that they return a complete recordset to the caller. They cannot be used (as is the case for scalar functions) in any place where an expression is acceptable. They can be used in Transact-SQL statements only in situations where the server expects a table reference. An example of such a situation is the From clause of the Select statement.

The OpenQuery() function is designed to return a recordset from a linked server. It can be used as a part of Select, Update, Insert, and Delete Transact-SQL statements. The Query parameter must contain a valid SQL query in the dialect of the linked server, since the query will be executed (as-is—as a pass-through query) on the linked server. This function uses the following syntax:

```
OpenQuery(linked_server, 'query')
```

NOTE

Linked servers are OLE DB data sources that are registered on the local SQL server. After registration, the local server knows how to access data on the remote server. All that is needed in your code is a reference to the name of the linked server.

You can register a linked server to be associated with the Northwind.mdb sample database either from Enterprise Manager or using the following code:

```
EXEC sp_addlinkedserver
    @server = 'Northwind_Access',
    @provider = 'Microsoft.Jest.OLEDB.4.0',
    @srvproduct = 'OLE DB Provider for Jet',
    @datasrc = 'c:\program files\Microsoft '
            + 'Office2000\Office\Samples\northwind.mdb'
Go
```

Then, you can use the OpenQuery() function to return records from the linked server:

```
SELECT *
FROM OpenQuery(Northwind_Access, 'SELECT * FROM Orders')
```

OpenRowSet() is very similar to the OpenQuery() function:

```
OpenRowset(
'provider_name',
{'datasource';'user_id';'password' | 'provider_string' },
{ [catalog.][schema.]object | 'query'}
)
```

It is designed for connecting to a server that is not registered as a linked server. Therefore, you must supply both the connection parameters and the query in order to use it. There are several options for defining the connection, such as OLE DB, ODBC, and OLE DB for ODBC, along with two options for specifying a result set: a pass-through query or a valid name for a database object.

The following query joins one table from the remote SQL server with two tables on the local SQL server:

```
SELECT a.au_lname, a.au_fname, titles.title
FROM OpenRowset('MSDASQL',
     'DRIVER={SQLServer};SERVER=Toronto;UID=sa;PWD=pwd',
     pubs.dbo.authors) AS a
        INNER JOIN titleauthor
```

```
       ON a.au_id = titleauthor.au_id
            INNER JOIN titles
            ON titleauthor.title_id = titles.title_id
```

The OpenDataSource() function is more similar to OpenRowset() than to OpenQuery(). It allows the caller to specify connection parameters inside the four-part database object name. It can be used in T-SQL in every position where a linked server can be used. The following example joins tables on the local server with tables on the remote server:

```
SELECT a.au_lname, a.au_fname, titles.title
FROM OpenDataSource('SQLOLDB',
    'DataSource=Toronto;User ID=sa; Password=pwd).pubs.dbo.authors as a
        INNER JOIN titleauthor
        ON a.au_id = titleauthor.au_id
            INNER JOIN titles
            ON titleauthor.title_id = titles.title_id
```

TIP

Although OpenRowset() and OpenDataSource() will work fine, if you plan repetitive use of some data source, you should consider registering a linked server and using OpenQuery(). The execution of OpenQuery() will be considerably faster.

Depending on the features of the OLE DB provider, you can also use these functions to delete, update, or insert information on other servers.

Composite Transact-SQL Constructs: Batches, Scripts, and Transactions

169

Transact-SQL statements can be grouped and executed together in a variety of ways. They can be

▶ Compiled as a part of a stored procedure, user-defined function, or trigger

▶ Written and executed individually or in groups from client utilities in the form of batches

▶ Grouped and stored in external script files that can be opened and executed from various client utilities

▶ Grouped in transactions that succeed completely or fail completely

This chapter discusses batches, scripts, and transactions.

It is not necessary to run examples from the text against the Asset database, but if you do, you must first make sure that the database contains the following table by executing the following script against the Asset database:

```
Create Table Part(PartId int identity,
            Make varchar(50),
            Model varchar(50),
            Type varchar(50))
```

This table is used to illustrate the concepts discussed in this chapter. Some of the changes are destructive, so existing tables such as Equipment will not be used, which may be needed for other purposes later.

Batches

A *batch* is a set of Transact-SQL statements that are sent to and executed by SQL Server as a single unit. The most important characteristic of a batch is that it is parsed and executed on the server as an undivided entity. In some cases, batches are created implicitly. For example, if you execute a set of Transact-SQL statements from Query Analyzer, the program will treat that set as one batch and do so invisibly:

```
Insert Into Part (Make, Model, Type)
Values ('Toshiba', 'Portege 7010CT', 'notebook')

Insert Into Part (Make, Model, Type)
Values ('Toshiba', 'Portege 7020CT', 'notebook')

Insert Into Part (Make, Model, Type)
Values ('Toshiba', 'Portege 7030CT', 'notebook')
```

Some tools, such as Query Analyzer, osql, and isql, use the Go command to divide Transact-SQL code into explicitly set batches. In the following example, the code for dropping a stored procedure is in one batch and the code for creating a new stored procedure is in another. The batch is explicitly created using the Go command.

```
If Exists (Select * From sysobjects
          Where id = object_id(N'[dbo].[prPartList]')
          And OBJECTPROPERTY(id, N'IsProcedure') = 1)
     Drop Procedure [dbo].[prPartList]
Go

Create Procedure prPartList
As
     Select * from Part
Return 0
Go
```

In Query Analyzer, you can highlight part of the code and execute it. Query Analyzer treats the selected piece of code as a batch and sends it to the server and ignores the rest of the code (see Figure 6-1).

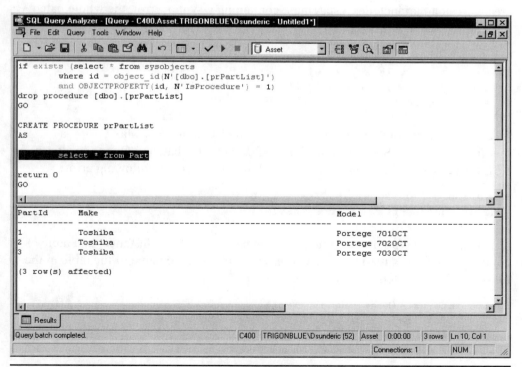

Figure 6-1   *Executing selected code in Query Analyzer*

In other utilities and development environments, batches may be divided in some other manner. In ADO, OLEDB, ODBC, and DB-Library, each command string prepared for execution (in the respective object or function) is treated as one batch.

Using Batches

Batches reduce the time and processing associated with transferring statements from client to server, as well as that associated with parsing, compiling, and executing Transact-SQL statements. If you need to execute a set of 100 insert commands against a database, it is preferable to group them in one batch rather than send them to the server as 100 separate statements. The overhead involved in sending 100 separate statements and receiving 100 separate results is very high. Network traffic will be increased unnecessarily, and the whole operation will be slower for the user.

Batches and Errors

The fact that the batch is compiled as an undivided entity has interesting implications for statements that contain syntax errors. Results will vary according to whether the syntax error occurs in a statement or in the name of a database object. If you create a batch that includes a statement containing a syntax error, the whole batch will fail to execute.

Consider the following batch:

```
Insert into Part (Make, Model, Type)
Values ('Toshiba', 'Portege 7020CT', 'Notebook')
Selec * from Part
```

It consists of two commands, the second of which contains a syntax error—a missing letter in the Select keyword. If you execute this batch in Query Analyzer, SQL Server will not compile or execute it but will return the following error:

```
Server: Msg 170, Level 15, State 1, Line 3
Line 3: Incorrect syntax near 'Selec'
```

If you make a typo in the name of the database object (for instance, in a table or column name), the situation is very different. Note that the name of the table in the following Insert statement is incorrect:

```
Insert into art (Make, Model, Type)
Values ('Toshiba', 'Portege 7020CT', 'Notebook')
Select * from Part
```

In this example, the application will notice an error and stop execution as soon as it encounters it:

```
Server: Msg 208, Level 16, State 1, Line 1
Invalid object name 'art'.
```

SQL Server executes the batch in three steps: it parses, compiles, and then executes. In the first phase, SQL Server verifies batch syntax. It focuses on the sequence of keywords, operators, and identifiers. The first batch used a statement with an error in a keyword. SQL Server picked up the error during the parsing phase.

The error in the second batch (an invalid object name) was picked up during execution. To further demonstrate this fact, let's investigate the following example, where the error is in the second statement:

```
Insert into Part (Make, Model, Type)
Values ('Toshiba', 'Portege 7020CT', 'Notebook')
Select * from art
```

In this case, the application behaves differently:

```
 (1 row(s) affected)
```

```
Server: Msg 208, Level 16, State 1, Line 1
Invalid object name 'art'.
```

Both commands are parsed and compiled, then the first command is executed, and finally the second command is canceled. Users with experience of earlier versions of Microsoft SQL Server remember that such a scenario would produce very different results in those earlier versions.

Microsoft SQL Server 2000 supports deferred name resolution (actually introduced in SQL Server 7.0). *Deferred name resolution* allows the server to compile Transact-SQL statements even when dependent objects do not yet exist in the database. This feature can prove to be very useful when you are creating or transferring objects from one database or server to another. You do not have to worry about dependencies and the order in which objects are created. Unfortunately, the introduction of this feature also has some strange secondary effects. In the case of the last example:

▶ The server has successfully compiled a batch, since the name resolution is not part of the compilation.

▶ The first command was executed without a problem.

▶ When a problem was encountered in the second command, the server canceled all further processing and returned a runtime error.

Keep this problem in mind when writing batches. Developers in modern programming languages like Visual Basic or Visual C++ usually employ sophisticated error-handling strategies to avoid situations like this. Transact-SQL also contains programming constructs for error handling. We will explore them in the next chapter.

The situation could be worse. Particular runtime errors (for example, constraint violations) do not stop execution of the batch. The following case attempts to use an Insert statement to insert a value in the identity column:

```
Select PartId, Make + ' ' + Model Part from Part
Insert into Part (PartId, Make, Model, Type)
Values (1, 'IBM', 'Thinkpad 390D', 'Notebook')
Select PartId, Make + ' ' + Model Part from Part
Go
```

The result is a "partial failure":

```
PartId      Part
----------- -------------------------------------------------
1           Toshiba Portege 7020CT

(1 row(s) affected)

Server: Msg 544, Level 16, State 1, Line 1
Cannot insert explicit value for identity column in table
'Part' when IDENTITY_INSERT is set to OFF.
PartId      Part
----------- ----------------------------------
1           Toshiba Portege 7020CT

(1 row(s) affected)
```

In some cases, "partial success" may be tolerable, but in the real world it is generally not acceptable.

Let's investigate a case in which several batches are written, divided by a Go statement, and executed together. Although the user has issued a single command to execute them, the client application will divide the code into batches and send them to the server separately. If an error occurs in any batch, the server will cancel its execution. However, this does not mean that execution of the other batches is canceled. The server will try to execute the next batch automatically.

In some cases, this may be useful, but in most cases, it may not be what the user expects to happen. In the following example, one column needs to be deleted from the Part table. One way to perform this action (very popular until we were spoiled with fancy tools like Enterprise Manager or the Alter Table...Drop Column statement) would be to do the following:

1. Create a provisional table to preserve the information that is currently in the Part table.

2. Copy information from the Part table to the provisional table.

3. Drop the existing Part table.

4. Create a Part table without the column you want to delete.

5. Copy the preserved information back to the Part table.

6. Drop the table.

The code necessary to implement this functionality could be created in a set of five batches:

```
Create Table TmpPart (PartId int,
                      Make varchar(50),
                      Model varchar(50))
GO


Insert into TmpPart (PartId, Make, Model)
Select PartId, Make, Model from Part
GO


Drop Table Part
GO


Create Table Part (PartId int,
                   Make varchar(50),
                   Model varchar(50))
GO


Insert into Part (PartId, Make, Model)
Select PartId, Make, Model from TmpPart
Go


Drop Table TmpPart
GO
```

In theory, this set of batches would work perfectly. However, there is just one problem—it doesn't take errors into account. For example, if a syntax error occurs in the first batch, the temporary table will not be created. Part information will not be preserved in it, and when the code drops the table, the information will be lost. To observe a method that you can use to handle errors, read the next chapter.

DDL Batches

Data Definition Language (DDL) is that part of Transact-SQL dedicated to the creation and modification of database objects. Some DDL statements must stand alone in the batch, including the following statements:

- ► Create Procedure
- ► Create Trigger
- ► Create Default
- ► Create Rule
- ► Create View
- ► Set Showplan_Text
- ► Set Showplan_All

If any of these statements is combined with other statements in a batch, the batch will fail. Create statements must stand alone because every other statement that follows them will be interpreted as a part of the Create statement. Set Showplan_Text and Set Showplan_All must stand alone in the batch because they are setting how SQL Server 2000 processes the batch and execution plan.

Self-Sufficient Content

During compilation, the batch is converted into a single execution plan. For this reason, the batch must be self-sufficient. In the real world, this concept has vast implications for the scope of database objects, variables, and comments.

Scope of Objects

Some DDL statements can be inside batches together with other commands, but keep in mind that the resulting object will not be accessible until the batch is completed. For example, it is not possible to add new columns to the table and to access those new columns in the same batch. Therefore, the following batch will fail:

```
Alter Table Part ADD Cost money NULL
select PartId, Cost from Part
Go
```

The Select statement is not able to access the Cost column, and the whole batch will fail:

```
Server: Msg 207, Level 16, State 3, Line 1
Invalid column name 'Cost'.
```

Therefore, the batch has to be divided in two:

```
Alter Table Part ADD Cost money NULL
Go
Select PartId, Cost from Part
Go
```

NOTE

Some DDL statements can be combined with DML statements that reference them. For example, it is possible to create a table and insert records into it in the same batch.

Scope of Variables

All (local) variables referenced in a batch must also be declared in that batch. The following code will result in the failure of the second batch:

```
Declare @Name as varchar (50)
Go
Select @Name = 'Dejan'
Go
```

Scope of Comments

Comments must be started and finished within the same batch. Ignoring this requirement will result in some very interesting outcomes, because Go commands are preprocessed on the client side, before the code is sent to the server. Take a look at the comment in the following sample:

```
Select * From Part
Go
Update Part
Set Type = 'desktop'
Where Type = 'PC'
/*
Go

Update Part
Set Type = 'Notebook'
```

```
Where Type = 'Laptop'
Go
Select * from Part
Go
Update Part
Set Type = 'desktop'
Where Type = 'computer'
Go
*/
Select * from Part
Go
```

To developers of other programming languages, this might look perfectly legal. Query Analyzer will even change the color of the code that is commented out. Unfortunately, this code is a complete disaster. Due to errors, the server will cancel execution of parts that the user expects to run and execute other parts that are commented out:

```
PartId        Make          Model             Type
-----------   ------------- ----------------- ------------------
1             Toshiba       Portege 7020CT    Laptop
(1 row(s) affected)

Server: Msg 113, Level 15, State 1, Line 2
Missing end comment mark '*/'.


(1 row(s) affected)

PartId        Make          Model             Type
-----------   ------------- ----------------- ------------------
1             Toshiba       Portege 7020CT    Notebook
(1 row(s) affected)

Server: Msg 170, Level 15, State 1, Line 4
Line 4: Incorrect syntax near '/'.
```

The first batch is the only batch that will behave in accordance with our intention. The second batch fails because the comments are not complete:

```
Update Part
Set Type = 'desktop'
Where Type = 'PC'
/*
```

The third batch is executed because the server is not aware of our intention to comment it out:

```
Update Part
Set Type = 'Notebook'
Where Type = 'Laptop'
```

The fourth batch is also executed, again because the server is not aware of our intention to comment it out:

```
Select * from Part
```

The fifth batch is also executed:

```
Update Part
Set Type = 'desktop'
Where Type = 'computer'
```

The last batch fails:

```
*/
Select * from Part
```

If you want to comment out the Go command, you must use two dashes as a comment marker at the beginning of the row:

```
--Go
```

Scripts

A *script* is usually defined as a collection of Transact-SQL statements (in one or more batches) in the form of an external file. Client tools, such as Query Analyzer, isql, osql, and Enterprise Manager, usually have support for managing script files.

Scripts are usually stored in plain text files with a .sql extension. This makes them manageable from any text editor as well as from many sophisticated tools, such as the Microsoft application for code control, Visual SourceSafe.

Query Analyzer has the usual features (File | Open, Save) of any text editor. isql and osql are command-line utilities that allow the user to specify script files with code to be executed against the server.

Database Scripting

One of the most exciting features in Enterprise Manager is the ability to perform reverse engineering on the database without the need for external tools. The result of this process is a script that contains DDL statements, which can be used to re-create the database objects included in the script. This script can be used to

▶ Explore user and system database objects

▶ Back up source code

▶ Establish a source control process

▶ Transfer the complete database (or just some objects) to another server (and/or another database)

The process of database scripting is very simple. Select a database in Enterprise Manager and runs Tools | Generate SQL Script. SQL Server prompts you to specify the objects to be scripted. You can select all database objects or all objects of a specific type by selecting the appropriate check box. You can also select individual objects by transferring them from the Object On Database list to the Objects To Be Scripted list.

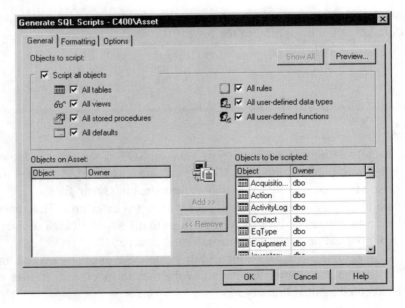

On the Formatting tab, you can specify the format in which each database object is to be scripted. A small preview template helps you to make the right choice among several options.

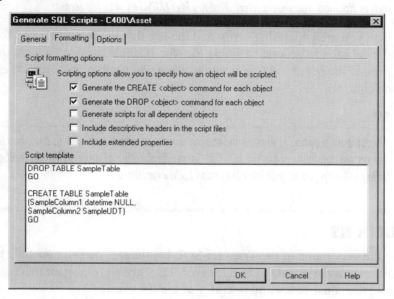

The Options tab allows you to specify options for supporting objects such as indexes, triggers, constraints, logins, users, roles, and permissions. The ability to specify a file format is very important for multilanguage environments.

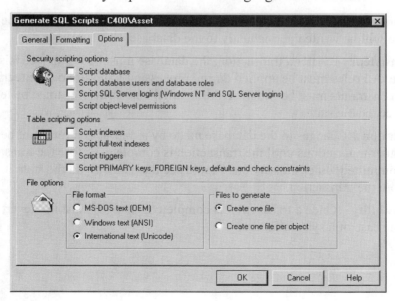

TIP

If you want to be able to open a script file from regular editors (that do not support Unicode) such as Notepad, you should select Windows Text (ANSI) as your file format.

The reason you are generating script and the use that you have planned for it will influence the decision to generate a single file (for example, when you want to transfer the object) or one file per object (for example, when you want to use scripts to establish source code control).

TIP

Use database scripting to explore the sample databases associated with this book and the sample and system databases published with SQL Server. Exploration of other styles and methods in coding will help you to gain knowledge and build experience.

Transactions

Even from the very name of the Transact-SQL language, you can conclude that *transactions* play a major role in SQL Server. They are an important mechanism for enforcing the consistency and integrity of the database.

A transaction is the smallest unit of work in SQL Server. To qualify a unit of work as a transaction, it must satisfy the following four criteria, often referred to as the ACID test:

▶ **Atomicity**   All data changes must be completed successfully, or none of them will be written permanently to the database.

▶ **Consistency**   After a transaction, the database must be left in a consistent state. All rules must be applied during processing to ensure data integrity. All constraints must be satisfied. All internal data structures must be left in an acceptable state.

▶ **Isolation**   Changes to the database made by a transaction must not be visible to other transactions until the transaction is complete. Before the transaction is committed, other transactions should see the data only in the state it was in before the transaction.

▶ **Durability**   Once a transaction is completed, changes must not revert even in the case of a system failure.

Autocommit Transactions

In fact, every Transact-SQL statement is a transaction. When it is executed, it either finishes successfully or is completely abandoned. To illustrate this, let's try to delete all records from the EqType table. Take a look at the following diagram:

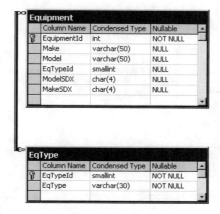

A foreign key relationship exists between the EqType and Equipment tables. The foreign key prevents the deletion of records in the EqType table that are referenced by records in the Equipment table.

Let's try to delete them anyway. You can see the result of such an attempt in Figure 6-2.

Two Select statements that will count the number of records in EqType are placed around the Delete statement. As expected, the Delete statement is aborted because of the foreign key. The count of records before and after the Delete statement is the same, which confirms that all changes made by the Delete statement were canceled. So the database remains in the state that it was in before the change was initiated.

If there were no errors, SQL Server would automatically commit the transaction (that is, it would record all changes) to the database. This kind of behavior is called *autocommit*.

In this case, SQL Server deleted records one after the other from the EqType table until it encountered a record that could not be deleted because of the foreign key relationship, at which point the operation was canceled.

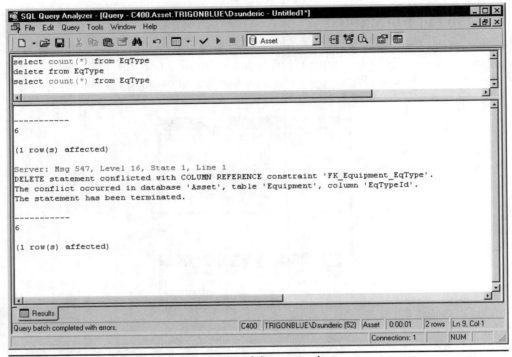

Figure 6-2 *Complete failure of attempt to delete records*

Explicit Transactions

The most popular and obvious way to use transactions is to give explicit commands to start or finish the transaction. Transactions started in this way are called *explicit transactions*. You can group Transact-SQL statements into a single transaction using the following statements:

▶ Begin Transaction

▶ Rollback Transaction

▶ Commit Transaction

If anything goes wrong with any of the grouped statements, all changes need to be aborted. The process of reversing changes is called *rollback* in SQL Server terminology. If everything is in order with all statements within a single transaction, all changes are recorded together in the database. In SQL Server terminology, these changes are *committed* to the database.

I will demonstrate the use of these processes on the prClearLeaseSchedule stored procedure. Its main purpose is to set monthly lease amounts to zero for each asset associated with an expired lease schedule. It also sets the total of the lease amounts to zero. These two operations must be performed simultaneously to preserve the integrity of the database.

```
Create Procedure prClearLeaseShedule
-- Set value of Lease of all equipment
-- associated with expired Lease Schedule to 0.
-- Set total amount of Lease Schedule to 0.

    @intLeaseScheduleId int
As

Begin Transaction

-- Set value of Lease of all equipment
-- associated with expired Lease Schedule to 0
Update Inventory
Set Lease = 0
Where LeaseScheduleId = @intLeaseScheduleId

If @@Error <> 0 goto PROBLEM

-- Set total amount of Lease Schedule to 0
Update LeaseSchedule
Set PeriodicTotalAmount = 0
Where ScheduleId = @intLeaseScheduleId
If @@Error <> 0 goto PROBLEM

Commit Transaction
Return 0

PROBLEM:
Print ' Unable to eliminate lease amounts from the database!'
Rollback Transaction
Return 1
```

Before the real processing starts, the Begin Transaction statement notifies SQL Server to treat all of the following actions as a single transaction. It is followed by two Update statements. If no errors occur during the updates, all changes are committed to the database when SQL Server processes the Commit Transaction statement, and finally the stored procedure finishes. If an error occurs during the updates, it is detected by If statements and execution is continued from the PROBLEM label. After displaying a message to the user, SQL Server rolls back any changes that occurred during processing.

We will review more complex transactions (including nested transactions) and ways to process errors in the next chapter.

Implicit Transactions

The third transaction mode is called the *implicit transaction*. To use this mode, you must set the Set Implicit_Transactions On statement for the connection. Any of the following statements will serve as an implicit start to a transaction:

- ▶ Alter Table
- ▶ Create
- ▶ Delete
- ▶ Drop
- ▶ Fetch
- ▶ Grant
- ▶ Insert
- ▶ Open
- ▶ Revoke
- ▶ Select
- ▶ Truncate Table
- ▶ Update

To finish the transaction, you must use the Commit Transaction or Rollback Transaction statement. After that, any of the preceding commands will start a new implicit transaction.

Transaction Processing Architecture

An explanation of how transactions are implemented in Microsoft SQL Server will give you some insight into many processes.

Every change to the database is recorded in a transaction log before it is written to the appropriate tables. In SQL Server 2000, transaction logs are implemented in separate files (or sets of files) with the extension .ldf. All modifications are written to this file chronologically. The records in this transaction log can later be used to roll back the transaction (thus providing atomicity) or to commit the changes to the database (thus providing durability). Two types of records can be stored in transaction logs:

▶ Logical operations performed (for instance, insert, delete, and start of transaction)
▶ Before and after images of the changed data (that is, copies of data before and after the change is made)

NOTE

The transaction log does not record queries that are executed against the database (since they do not modify its content).

The transaction log mechanism helps to resolve many issues:

▶ If a client application loses its connection before a transaction is finished, SQL Server will detect a problem and roll back changes, to ensure consistency.
▶ If the machine loses power during processing, SQL Server will recover the database when services are restored. All transactions that were recorded in the transaction log in an undivided manner (that is, as part of a complete transaction set) are rolled forward (written to data tables) as if nothing unusual has happened. All transactions that were not completed before the problem occurred are rolled back (deleted) from the database.

NOTE

The transaction log also plays an important role in the implementation of backups in SQL Server. When a user starts a full backup, SQL Server records a complete snapshot of the data tables in backup files. At that point, SQL Server marks the current position in the transaction log and continues to record all changes to the database in the transaction log. Transactions logged during the process are also recorded as part of the full backup. When the backup is complete, SQL Server makes another mark in the transaction log. At the time of the next backup, a transaction log backup will suffice. To restore the database, an administrator first uses the full backup and then one or more transaction log backups that have been run since the full backup. SQL Server runs through the transaction log and applies changes to the data tables.

Nested Transactions

SQL Server allows you to nest transactions. Basically, this feature means that a new transaction can start even though the previous one is not complete:

```
Begin transaction
...
     Begin transaction
     ...
     Commit transaction
...
Commit transaction
```

Usually this situation occurs when one stored procedure containing a transaction calls another stored procedure that also contains a transaction. In the following example, prCompleteOrder completes an order by setting its completion date and changing the status of the order, and then looping through associated order items and calling prCompleteOrderItem to complete each of them; prCompleteOrderItem sets the completion date of an order item to the last ChargeLog date associated with that OrderItem. Both of these procedures contain a transaction.

```
Alter Procedure prCompleteOrder_1
-- complete all orderItems and then complete order
@intOrderId int,
@dtsCompletionDate smalldatetime

As
set nocount on

Declare @intErrorCode int,
        @i int,
        @intCountOrderItems int,
        @intOrderItemId int

Select @intErrorCode = @@Error

If @intErrorCode = 0
    Begin Transaction

-- complete order
If @intErrorCode = 0
Begin
     Update [Order]
     Set CompletionDate = @dtsCompletionDate,
```

```
            OrderStatusId = 4 -- completed
        Where OrderId = @intOrderId

        Select @intErrorCode = @@Error
End


-- loop through OrderItems and complete them
If @intErrorCode = 0
Begin
        Create Table #OrderItems(
            id int identity(1,1),
            OrderItemId int)

        Select @intErrorCode = @@Error
End


-- collect orderItemIds
If @intErrorCode = 0
Begin
        Insert Into #OrderItems(OrderItemId)
            Select ItemId
            From OrderItem
            Where OrderId = @intOrderId
            Select @intErrorCode = @@Error
End


If @intErrorCode = 0
Begin
        Select @intCountOrderItems = Max(Id),
            @i = 1
        From #OrderItems

        Select @intErrorCode = @@Error
End


while @intErrorCode = 0 and @i <= @intCountOrderItems
Begin
        If @intErrorCode = 0
        Begin
            Select @intOrderItemId = OrderItemId
            From #OrderItems
            Where id = @I
            Select @intErrorCode = @@Error
        End
```

```
     If @intErrorCode = 0
          Exec @intErrorCode = prCompleteOrderItem_1 @intOrderItemId


     If @intErrorCode = 0
          Set @i = @i + 1
End


If @intErrorCode = 0 and @@trancount > 0
     Commit Transaction
Else
     Rollback Transaction
return @intErrorCode
Go



Alter Procedure prCompleteOrderItem_1
-- Set CompletionDate of OrderItem to date
-- of last ChargeLog record associated with OrderItem.
     @intOrderItemId int
As
set nocount on
Declare @intErrorCode int
Select @intErrorCode = @@Error


If @intErrorCode = 0
     Begin Transaction


-- Set CompletionDate of OrderItem to date
-- of last ChargeLog record associated with OrderItem.
If @intErrorCode = 0
Begin
     update OrderItem
     Set CompletionDate = (Select Max(ChargeDate)
                           from ChargeLog
                           where ItemId = @intOrderItemId)
     Where ItemId = @intOrderItemId

     Select @intErrorCode = @@Error
End


If @intErrorCode = 0
Begin
     exec @intErrorCode = prNotifyAccounting intOrderItemId
End
```

```
If @intErrorCode = 0 and @@trancount > 0
    Commit Transaction
Else
    Rollback Transaction
Return @intErrorCode
```

In the case of nested transactions, no Commit statements except the outer one will save changes to the database. Only after the last transaction is committed will all changes to the database become permanent. Up to that point, it is still possible to roll back all changes.

The interesting question is how SQL Server knows which transaction is the last one. It keeps the number of opened transactions in the @@trancount global variable for each user connection. When SQL Server encounters a Begin Transaction statement, it increments the value of the @@trancount, and when SQL Server encounters a Commit Transaction statement, it decrements the value of the @@trancount. Therefore, the only effect of a nested (internal) Commit Transaction statement is a change to the @@trancount value. Only the outer Commit Transaction statement (when @@trancount = 1) stores changes in data tables rather than in the transaction log.

The following is a purely academic example that does not perform any real processing, but it demonstrates the effect of nested transactions on the @@trancount global variable:

```
print 'Trancount = ' + Convert(varchar(4), @@trancount)
BEGIN TRANSACTION
    print 'Trancount = ' + Convert(varchar(4), @@trancount)
    BEGIN TRANSACTION
    print 'Trancount = ' + Convert(varchar(4), @@trancount)
    COMMIT TRANSACTION
    print 'Trancount = ' + Convert(varchar(4), @@trancount)
COMMIT TRANSACTION
print 'Trancount = ' + Convert(varchar(4), @@trancount)
```

Each transactional statement will increment and decrement the @@trancount:

```
Trancount = 0
Trancount = 1
Trancount = 2
Trancount = 1
Trancount = 0
```

An interesting inconsistency to observe is in the behavior of the Rollback Transaction statement. No matter how many transaction levels deep execution extends, the Rollback Transaction statement will cancel all changes caused by all transactions (and bring the @@trancount value down to zero). In fact, if you execute an additional Rollback Transaction statement after the first one, SQL Server will report an error.

```
print 'Trancount = ' + Convert(varchar(4), @@trancount)
BEGIN TRANSACTION
    print 'Trancount = ' + Convert(varchar(4), @@trancount)
    BEGIN TRANSACTION
    print 'Trancount = ' + Convert(varchar(4), @@trancount)
    ROLLBACK TRANSACTION
    print 'Trancount = ' + Convert(varchar(4), @@trancount)
ROLLBACK TRANSACTION
print 'Trancount = ' + Convert(varchar(4), @@trancount)
```

The following is the result of this example:

```
Trancount = 0
Trancount = 1
Trancount = 2
Trancount = 0
Server: Msg 3903, Level 16, State 1, Line 8
The ROLLBACK TRANSACTION request has no corresponding BEGIN TRANSACTION.
Trancount = 0
```

TIP

I have to admit that I had many problems with this issue at one time. Be careful.

To prevent this error, you need to test for the value of the @@trancount variable before you execute the Rollback Transaction statement. A simple way to test for this value works something like this:

```
if @@trancount > 0
Rollback Transaction
```

You will find a much better solution in Chapter 7.

Named Transactions

Transaction statements can be named. The name must be a valid SQL Server identifier (that is, no more than 128 characters), but SQL Server will read only the first 32 characters:

```
Begin Tran[saction][transaction_name|@transaction_name_variable]
Commit Tran[saction][transaction_name|@transaction_name_variable]
Rollback [Tran[saction][transaction_name|@transaction_name_variable]]
```

I know that this sounds like a perfect tool for resolving some issues with nested transactions. Unfortunately, in nested transactions, only the names of outer transactions are recorded by SQL Server. If you try to roll back any of the inner transactions, errors occur. The following listing is an academic demonstration of such an attempt:

```
BEGIN TRANSACTION t1
    BEGIN TRANSACTION t2
    ROLLBACK TRANSACTION t2
ROLLBACK TRANSACTION t1
```

SQL Server will return an error:

```
Server: Msg 6401, Level 16, State 1, Line 3
Cannot roll back t2. No transaction or savepoint of that name was found.
```

TIP

You can see that you need to know the name of the outer transaction that has called all other stored procedures/transactions. This is not a practical requirement, especially when your stored procedure will be called from more than one stored procedure. Therefore, I recommend that you do not use transaction names.

Savepoints

SQL Server contains a mechanism for rolling back only part of a transaction. This statement may seem to contradict the basic idea of a SQL Server transaction as I have explained it, but it can be justified in some cases. Microsoft recommends *savepoints* to be used if it is more expensive to check will change be valid in advance (for example, because of a slow connection) and operation has high probability of success. For example, assume that you are trying to reserve a set of plane tickets (or to get a set of some other resources) using different companies (distributed database system). Each leg of a journey has to be booked separately. If the reservation fails, you will roll back just that leg of the journey, not all reservations that you already successfully made. Only in the case that it is impossible to find any alternative for the remaining part of the journey will you roll back the complete transaction.

To mark a savepoint in a transaction, use the following statement:

```
Save Tran[saction]{savepoint_name|@savepoint_variable}
```

The savepoint's name is also a SQL Server identifier, but SQL Server reads only the first 32 characters.

To roll back part of the transaction, you must use the savepoint name or variable:

```
Rollback Tran[saction]{savepoint_name|@savepoint_variable}
```

NOTE

Rollback Transaction statements without a savepoint will roll back the complete transaction.

Savepoints do not save anything to the database. They just mark the point to which you can roll back a transaction. Resources (like locks) also stay in place after a Save Transaction statement. They are released only when a transaction has been completed or canceled.

The following procedures are designed to store an order and set of order items in a database. The prScrapOrderSaveItem stored procedure uses savepoints to roll back the insertion of a particular item.

```
Create Procedure prScrapOrder
-- save order information.

    @dtsOrderDate smalldatetime,
    @intRequestedById int,
    @dtsTargetDate smalldatetime,
    @chvNote varchar(200),
    @insOrderTypeId smallint,
    @inyOrderStatusId tinyint
As
    Set nocount on

    Insert [Order](OrderDate,    RequestedById,
                   TargetDate,   Note,
                   OrderTypeId,  OrderStatusId)
    Values (@dtsOrderDate,       @intRequestedById,
            @dtsTargetDate,      @chvNote,
            @insOrderTypeId,     @inyOrderStatusId)

Return @@identity
Go
```

```
Create Procedure prScrapOrderSaveItem
-- Saves order item.
-- If error occurs, this item will be rolled back,
-- but other items will be saved.

-- demonstration of use of Save Transaction
-- must be called from sp or batch that initiates transaction
    @intOrderId int,
    @intInventoryId int,
    @intOrderItemId int OUTPUT
As
    Set nocount on
    Declare    @intErrorCode int,
               @chvInventoryId varchar(10)

    -- name the transaction savepoint
    Set @chvInventoryId = Convert(varchar, @intInventoryId)

    Save Transaction @chvInventoryId

    -- Set value of Lease of all equipment associated
    -- with expired Lease Schedule to 0
    Insert OrderItem (OrderId, InventoryId)
    Values (@intOrderId, @intInventoryId)

    Select @intOrderItemId = @@identity,
           @intErrorCode = @@Error

    If @intErrorCode <> 0
    Begin
        Rollback Transaction @chvInventoryId
        Return @intErrorCode
    End

Return 0
Go
```

Let's assume that the caller is some external application that is trying to fulfill an order by adding a line item by line item. If one line item fails, the application will detect an error, roll back to the last savepoint, and try to add some other line item.

The stored procedures are designed in such a manner that a transaction must be initiated by the caller. You can test the stored procedures by using the following batch:

```
Declare    @intOrderId int,
           @intOrderItemId int

Begin Tran

Exec @intOrderId = prScrapOrder @dtsOrderDate = '1/10/2003',
                         @intRequestedById = 1,
                         @dtsTargetDate = '1/1/2004',
                         @chvNote = NULL,
                         @insOrderTypeId = 3, -- scrap
                         @inyOrderStatusId = 1 -- ordered
Exec prScrapOrderSaveItem @intOrderId,
                          5,
                          @intOrderItemId OUTPUT
Exec prScrapOrderSaveItem @intOrderId,
                          6,
                          @intOrderItemId OUTPUT
Exec prScrapOrderSaveItem @intOrderId,
                          8,
                          @intOrderItemId OUTPUT

Commit Tran
```

In nested transaction statements, transaction names are ignored, or can cause errors. If you are using transactions in stored procedures, which could be called from within other transactions, do not use transaction names. In the previous example, although stored procedures with transaction names are called from a batch (it could have been implemented as a stored procedure), the transaction itself was not nested.

Locking

Let me remind you of the requirements represented by the so-called ACID test. The isolation requirement means that changes to the database made by a transaction are not visible to other transactions that are themselves in an intermediate state at the time of that transaction's completion, and that before the transaction is committed, other transactions can see data only in the state it was in before the transaction.

To satisfy the isolation requirement, SQL Server uses *locks*. A lock is a restriction placed on the use of a resource in a multiuser environment. It prevents other users (that is, processes) from accessing or modifying data in the resource. SQL Server automatically acquires and releases locks on resources in accordance with the actions a user performs. For example, while the user is updating a table, nobody else can modify (and in some cases, even see) records that are already updated. As soon as all updates connected to the user action are completed, the locks are released and the records become accessible.

There is just one problem with this process. Other users have to wait for the resource to become available again—they are *blocked.* Such blocking can lead to performance problems or even cause a process to fail. The use of locking is a trade-off between data integrity and performance. SQL Server is intelligent enough to handle most problems, and it does a great job in preventing problems. It is also possible to control locking using *transaction isolation levels* and *optimizer hints,* both of which are described in the next section.

Locks can have different levels of *granularity.* They can be acquired on

► Rows

► Pages

► Keys

► Ranges of keys

► Indexes

► Tables

► Databases

SQL Server automatically acquires a lock of the appropriate granularity on a resource. If SQL Server determines during execution that a lock is no longer adequate, it dynamically changes the lock's granularity.

Locks are acquired by connection. Even if two connections are initiated from the same application, one can block the other.

The type of lock acquired by SQL Server depends on the effect that the change statement will have on the resource. For example, different locks are applied for the Select statement and the Update statement. There are five lock types:

► **Shared (read) locks**   Usually acquired for operations that do not modify data (that is, read operations). Another transaction can also acquire a nonexclusive lock on the same record, and thus the lock is shared. The shared lock is released when the transaction moves on to read another record.

► **Exclusive (write) locks**   Acquired for statements that modify data (such as Insert, Update, and Delete). Only one exclusive lock on a resource can be held at a time. An exclusive lock can be acquired only after other locks on the resource (including shared locks) are released.

▶ **Update locks**   Resemble shared locks more than they do exclusive locks. They are used to notify SQL Server that a transaction will later modify a resource. They prevent other transactions from acquiring exclusive locks. Update locks can coexist with shared locks. Just before the resource is modified, SQL Server promotes the update lock to an exclusive lock.

▶ **Intent locks**   Set on an object of higher granularity to notify SQL Server that a process has placed a lock of lower granularity inside the object. For example, if a transaction places a lock on a page in a table, it will also place an intent lock on the table. The intent lock means that SQL Server does not have to scan the whole table to find out if a process has placed a lock on some page or record inside, in order to place a table lock for another transaction. In fact, there are three different types of intent locks: IS (intent share), IX (intent exclusive), and SIX (shared with intent exclusive).

▶ **Schema locks**   Prevent the dropping or modifying of a table or index while it is in use. There are two types of schema locks. Sch-S (schema stability) locks prevent table or index drops. Sch-M (schema modification) locks ensure that other transactions cannot access the resource while it is being modified.

Transaction Isolation Levels and Hints

You can change the default behavior of SQL Server using *transaction isolation levels* or *lock hints*. Transaction isolation levels set locking at the connection level, and lock hints set locking at the statement level. SQL Server can work on four different transaction isolation levels:

▶ **Serializable**   The highest level in which transactions are completely isolated. The system behaves as though the transactions are occurring one after another. SQL Server will hold locks on both data and key records until the end of the transaction. This may lead to some performance issues.

▶ **Repeatable Read**   Forces SQL Server to place shared locks on data records and hold them until the transaction is completed. Unfortunately, it allows *phantoms*, which occur when a transaction reads a range of records. There is no guarantee that some other concurrent transaction will not add records that fall in the range or modify keys of records so that they fall out of the range. If the uncommitted transaction repeats the read, the result will be inconsistent.

▶ **Read Committed**   The default level in SQL Server. SQL Server places shared locks while reading. It allows phantoms and *nonrepeatable reads*. There is no guarantee that the value of the record that a transaction reads multiple times during execution will stay consistent. Some other transaction could change it.

▶ **Read Uncommitted**   The lowest level of isolation in SQL Server. It ensures that physically corrupt data is not read. SQL Server will not place shared locks, and it will ignore exclusive locks. You will have the fewest performance issues when using this level, but you will also likely have many data integrity problems. It allows phantoms, nonrepeatable reads, and *dirty reads* (everybody can see the content of the changed record, even if a transaction is not yet committed and could potentially be rolled back).

The isolation level is specified in the Set statement. For example:

```
Set Transaction Isolation Level Repeatable Read
```

Locking hints change the behavior of the locking manager as it processes a single Transact-SQL statement. They overwrite behavior set by the transaction isolation level. The following table describes hints that can be used to control locking:

Hints	Description
Holdlock or Serializable	Holds a shared lock until a transaction is completed. The lock will not be released when the resource is no longer needed, but rather when the transaction is completed.
Nolock	This hint applies only to Select statements. SQL Server will not place shared locks, and it will ignore exclusive locks.
Updlock	Uses update instead of shared locks while reading a table.
Rowlock	Specifies the granularity of locks at the row level.
Paglock	Specifies the granularity of locks at the page level.
Tablock	Specifies the granularity of locks at the table level.
Tablockx	Specifies the granularity of locks at the table level and the type of lock to be exclusive.
Readcommitted	Equivalent to the default isolation level (Read Committed).
Readpast	This hint is applicable only in Select statements working under the Read Committed isolation level. Result sets created with this hint will not contain records locked by other transactions.
Readuncommitted	Equivalent to the Read Uncommitted isolation level.
Repeatableread	Equivalent to the Repeatable Read isolation level.

Locking hints can be used in Select, Insert, Update, or Delete statements. They are set after the table reference in SQL statements (for example, in the From clause of a Select statement or in the Insert clause of an Insert statement). Their scope is just the table that they are used for. For example, the following command will hold a lock until the transaction is completed:

```
Select *
From Inventory With (HOLDLOCK)
Where InventoryId = @intInventoryId
```

Nobody will be able to change data records that were read and keys that match the criteria of this table until the transaction is completed. Therefore, this table cannot have phantoms, nonrepeatable reads, or dirty reads.

The next example demonstrates the use of hints in an Update statement and the use of more than one hint in a statement:

```
Update Inventory With (TABLOCKX, HOLDLOCK)
Set StatusId = 4
Where StatusId = @intStatusId
```

The complete table will be locked for the duration of the transaction.

Distributed Transactions

Microsoft Distributed Transaction Coordinator (MS DTC) is a component that allows you to span transactions over two or more servers while maintaining transactional integrity.

Servers in this scenario are called *resource managers,* and MS DTC performs the function of transaction manager. In fact, all those resource managers do not even have to be Microsoft servers; they just have to be compatible with MS DTC. For example, it is possible to execute a single transaction against databases on Microsoft SQL Server and Oracle.

When transactions are distributed over different resource managers, different mechanisms have to be applied by the transaction coordinator to compensate for problems that might occur in such an environment. A typical problem is network failure. For example, everything might be executed properly by each individual resource manager, but if the transaction coordinator is not informed due to a network failure, the result is the same as if one of the resource managers had failed, and the transaction will be rolled back.

The mechanism for dealing with such problems is called the *two-phase commit (2PC).* As the name implies, it consists of two phases:

▶ **Prepare phase**   Starts when a transaction manager receives a request to execute a transaction. It notifies the resource managers and informs them of the work that needs to be done. The resource managers perform all changes and even write everything from the transaction log in memory to the disk. When everything is completed, each resource manager sends a status message indicating success or failure to the transaction manager.

▶ **Commit phase**   Starts when the transaction manager receives messages from resource managers. If the resource managers successfully complete the preparation phase, the transaction manager sends a Commit command to the resource managers. Each of them makes the changes permanently to the database and reports the success of the operation to the transaction manager. If any of the resource managers reports failure during the preparation phase, the transaction manager will send a Rollback command to all resource managers.

From a developer's point of view, distributed transactions are very similar to regular transactions. The major difference is that you need to use the following statement to start the transaction:

```
Begin Distributed Tran[saction]  [transaction_name]
```

Distributed transactions can also be started implicitly, by executing a query or stored procedure that will be run against distributed servers.

Transactions are completed with regular Commit or Rollback statements. The following stored procedure updates two tables in a local database and then updates information in a remote database using a remote stored procedure:

```
Alter Procedure prClearLeaseShedule_distributed
-- Set value of Lease of all equipment associated to 0
-- Set total amount of Lease Schedule to 0.
-- notify lease company that lease schedule is completed
    @intLeaseScheduleId int
As
    Declare @chvLeaseNumber varchar(50),
            @intErrorCode int

    -- Verify that lease has expired
    If GetDate() <  (Select EndDate
                    From LeaseSchedule
                    Where ScheduleId = @intLeaseScheduleId)
```

```
        Raiserror ('Specified lease schedule has not expired yet!', 16,1)
If @@Error <> 0
Begin
        Print 'Unable to eliminate lease amounts from the database!'
        Return 50000
End

-- get lease number
Select @chvLeaseNumber = Lease.LeaseNumber
From Lease
Inner Join    LeaseSchedule
On Lease.LeaseId = LeaseSchedule.LeaseId
Where (LeaseSchedule.ScheduleId = @intLeaseScheduleId)

Begin Distributed Transaction

-- Set value of Lease of all equipment associated to 0
Update Inventory
Set Lease = 0
Where LeaseScheduleId = @intLeaseScheduleId
If @@Error <> 0 Goto PROBLEM

-- Set total amount of Lease Schedule to 0
Update LeaseSchedule
Set PeriodicTotalAmount = 0
Where ScheduleId = @intLeaseScheduleId
If @@Error <> 0 Goto PROBLEM

-- notify lease vendor
Exec @intErrorCode = lease_srvr.LeaseShedules..prLeaseScheduleComplete
                    @chvLeaseNumber, @intLeaseScheduleId

If @intErrorCode <> 0 GoTo PROBLEM

Commit Transaction
Return 0

PROBLEM:
    print 'Unable to complete lease schedule!'
    Rollback Transaction
Return 50000
```

Apart from a reference to the remote stored procedure, the only thing that needed to be done was to use the Distributed keyword to start the transaction. Everything else was managed by MS DTC.

Typical Locking Problems

Transactions are a powerful weapon in the hands of a programmer, but improper use can cause substantial damage. I will try to forewarn you of some typical problems.

A Never-Ending Story

The worst thing that you can do is to explicitly open a transaction and then forget to close it. All changes sent to the database through that connection will become part of that transaction; resources normally released at the end of a transaction are held indefinitely; other users cannot access resources; and eventually, your server chokes.

Spanning a Transaction over Batches

A transaction can span batches. SQL Server counts transactions over the connection, so it is "legal" to issue two batches like this over one connection:

```
Begin Transaction
update Inventory
set Lease = 0
where LeaseScheduleId = 141
Go

update LeaseSchedule
Set PeriodicTotalAmount = 0
where ScheduleId = 141
Commit Transaction
Go
```

However, I cannot think of any justification for doing so, and you significantly increase the probability of error. For example, you could easily forget to finish the transaction.

There are some cases in which it is justified for a transaction to span batches. For example, when a DDL statement must be in a separate batch.

Rollback Before Begin

Sometimes you might set your error handling so that all errors that occur in a stored procedure are treated in the same way. Naturally, you will include a statement to roll back the transaction. If an error occurs before the transaction starts, the stored procedure will jump to the error handling code and another error will occur:

```
Create Procedure prClearLeaseShedule_1
-- Set value of Lease of all equipment associated
-- with expired Lease Schedule to 0
```

```
-- Set total amount of Lease Schedule to 0.

    @intLeaseScheduleId int
As

    -- Verify that lease has expired
    If GetDate() < (select EndDate
                    from LeaseSchedule
                    where ScheduleId = @intLeaseScheduleId)
        raiserror ('Specified lease schedule has not expired yet!',
16,1)

    -- If error occurs here,
    -- server will execute Rollback before transaction is started!
    if @@Error <> 0 goto PROBLEM

    Begin Transaction

    -- Set value of Lease of all equipment associated
    -- with expired Lease Schedule to 0
    update Inventory
    set Lease = 0
    where LeaseScheduleId = @intLeaseScheduleId
    if @@Error <> 0 goto PROBLEM

    -- Set total amount of Lease Schedule to 0
    update LeaseSchedule
    Set PeriodicTotalAmount = 0
    where ScheduleId = @intLeaseScheduleId
    if @@Error <> 0 goto PROBLEM

    commit transaction
    return 0

PROBLEM:

print 'Unable to eliminate lease amounts from the database!'
    rollback transaction
return 1
```

Multiple Rollbacks

Unlike Commit statements, only one Rollback statement is required to close a set
of nested transactions. In fact, if more than one Rollback statement is executed, SQL
Server will raise another error.

Long Transactions

SQL Server places locks on data that has been modified by a transaction, to prevent other users from further changing the data until the transaction is committed. This feature can lead to problems if a transaction takes "too long" to complete.

NOTE

There is no exact definition of "too long." The longer a transaction works, the greater the likelihood that problems will occur.

Some of the problems that might occur if a long transaction is present in the database include the following:

► Other users are blocked. They will not be able to access and modify data.

► The transaction log fills up. (SQL Server 2000 and SQL Server 7.0 can be configured to automatically increase the size of the transaction log, but you could fill your disk as well.)

► Most of the time, transaction log work is performed in memory. If all available memory is used before the transaction is complete, SQL Server will start saving changes to disk, thus reducing the overall performance of the server.

TIP

You should be particularly aware of concurrency problems because they are the problems most likely to happen. While you are developing applications, you will probably work alone (or in a small group) on the server, but the situation will change drastically when you place 50, 250, or 5000 concurrent users on the production server.

CHAPTER
7

Debugging and
Error Handling

Debugging and error handling seem like such negative topics. By admitting debugging as a necessary phase of development and error handling as a required practice, we seem to admit to weakness in our abilities as developers. But we are not the computers themselves: we cannot account for all contingencies when we write code. So, to find the error of our ways after the fact, we need a coherent approach to the identification and resolution of defects in our code and a coherent strategy for handling errors in our code as they occur.

Debugging

The process of debugging is an integral part of both the development and stabilization phases of software production.

What Is a "Bug"?

You have probably heard errors and defects found in software referred to as "bugs." This word has found its way into our everyday language and reality so that we now seem to regard the bug as normal and inevitable—like death and taxes. However, not many people know how this term actually entered the language.

It happened in the dim, distant technological past when computers occupied whole rooms (if not buildings). On one occasion, technicians were investigating a malfunction on such a computer. Much to their surprise, they found the cause of the circuit malfunction to be a large moth that had been attracted by the heat and glow of the machine's vacuum tubes. Over time, all computer-related errors (particularly the ones that were difficult to explain) came to be known as bugs.

Sometimes we anthropomorphize bugs—give them human attributes. They can seem in turn capricious and malicious, but the bugs we experience in application and database development are not related to mythological folk such as gremlins. Bugs are very real, but their causes are inevitably human. Computers bear no malice toward users or developers, compilers do not play practical jokes, and operating systems are not being stubborn when they refuse to operate as expected. No, when you encounter an error, you can be sure that it was you or another programmer who caused it. What you need to do is find the offending code and fix it, but to find bugs efficiently and painlessly, you need to establish a debugging process—a formal routine with well-defined steps and rules.

The Debugging Process

The objectives of the debugging process are to identify and resolve the defects present in a software product. This process consists of two phases:

1. Identification
2. Resolution

Identification

The identification phase consists of two primary activities:

1. Stabilize the error.
2. Find the source of the error.

Stabilize the Error   In most cases, identifying the error consumes 95 percent of your debugging time, whereas fixing it often requires just a few minutes. The first step in identifying an error is to stabilize (or isolate) the error. You must make the error repeatable. What this means is that you must find a test case that causes the error to recur predictably. If you are not able to reproduce the error, you will not be able to identify its cause nor will you be able to fix it.

But we need to qualify the test case in another way. It is not enough to create a test case that will cause the error to occur predictably. You must also strive to simplify the test case in order to identify the minimum circumstances under which the error will occur. Refining the test case is certainly the most difficult aspect of debugging, and cultivating this skill will greatly enhance your debugging efficiency, while removing a large part of the frustration. Stabilizing the error answers the question, "What is the error?" With this knowledge in hand, you can go on to answer the question, "Why does the error occur?"

Find the Source of the Error   After you identify the minimum circumstances under which the error will occur, you can proceed to find the source of the error. If your code is properly structured and well written, this search should not be a difficult task. You can apply a variety of tools at this point:

► **Your brain**   The most important debugging tool at your disposal is your brain. If you can follow the program's execution and understand its logic, you will be able to understand the problem as well. When you have learned everything your test cases can teach you, you can create a hypothesis, and then prove it through further testing.

▶ **SQL Server**   Some errors will be clearly reported by SQL Server. Be sure that your client application picks up and displays all error messages reported by the server. Also, try using Query Analyzer to execute your stored procedures without the client application. Naturally, you should take care to use the same parameters that were passed from the client application when you produced the error.

▶ **SQL Profiler**   Some errors will occur only when the application is executing stored procedures and queries in SQL Server. Too often, the application does not properly collect all error information, and then application and database developers play ping-pong blaming each other for the reported defect. SQL Profiler can resolve such disputes. It can be configured to collect information about events such as stored procedures, transactions, and server, database, and session events. When you analyze the collected data, you will be able to determine which of the stored procedure's calls and parameters are responsible for the individual errors.

▶ **T-SQL Debugger**   An integral part of Visual Studio is the T-SQL Debugger. It enables you to set breakpoints in your code and pause execution to investigate and change the contents of local variables, functions, and input and output parameters. The T-SQL Debugger lets you step through the code of your stored procedures and triggers. It is fully integrated with many development environments and lets you move from Visual Basic, JavaScript, C++, or any other client code into a Transact-SQL statement. Query Analyzer in SQL Server 2000 also contains a T-SQL Debugger. It has features similar to the tool provided in Visual Studio.

Resolution

Resolving defects in code is usually much easier than finding those defects, but do not take this phase too lightly. At this point in the development cycle, when the product shipping date is looming large, you may be tempted by the "quick fix." Resist this temptation: it often causes developers to introduce new errors while fixing the old ones. It is seldom an issue of carelessness or incompetence, but rather of increased pressure to fix and ship a product.

The resolution phase consists of two primary activities:

1. Develop the solution in a test environment.
2. Implement the solution in the production environment.

Develop the Solution in a Test Environment   To consistently resolve defects in your code, you need to assemble two critical ingredients—a test environment and source code control.

▶ **Test environment**   SQL Server is especially susceptible to errors generated in haste to solve a problem because a stored procedure is compiled and saved as a single action. If you are trying to resolve defects on the production system, you are performing brain surgery *in vivo*.

Although it is possible to perform fixes in a production environment, it is always much better to step back, spend adequate time understanding the problem, and then attempt to solve the problem outside of the production environment.

If a test environment does not exist or if the existing test environment is outdated, you may be tempted to save time with a "quick and dirty" fix. Before you go down this path, however, you should consider the resources that would be required to reverse the changes made if you happen to make a mistake. Anything you do, you should be able to undo quickly and easily.

Let it be understood, loud and clear: you need a test environment!

▶ **Source code control**   Keep source code of your procedures and database objects. Source code control gives you a snapshot of your application at critical points in the development cycle and allows you to "turn back the clock." It gives you the ability to reverse changes if you find they have introduced new problems or failed to solve the existing one. Visual SourceSafe, which is examined in Chapter 11, is a perfect tool for this function.

Source code control works best if you take a patient approach to debugging. You should save versions often to help you identify the source of errors when they occur. It is a poor practice to make multiple changes per version. Old and new errors tend to overlap and lead you to incorrect conclusions.

Implement the Solution in the Production Environment   Once you are satisfied with the change, you should implement it in the production environment. Then test. Then test again. You should not assume that it will work in the production environment because it worked in the test environment. If, after stringent testing, everything is still functioning properly, you should then look for other places in the code and database structure where similar errors may exist.

Debugging Tools and Techniques

Modern development environments contain sophisticated tools to help you debug your applications. The T-SQL Debugger in Visual Studio and the T-SQL Debugger in Query Analyzer are examples of these tools, and will help you to identify and fix problems in your code. I will first examine the T-SQL Debugger in Visual Studio, and then in Query Analyzer. However, even if your development environment does not support the T-SQL Debugger, there are techniques you can employ to achieve the same results. I will discuss these techniques in "Poor Man's Debugger" later in this chapter.

T-SQL Debugger in Visual Studio

The T-SQL Debugger is a dream tool for developers working in Visual Studio to find errors in a Microsoft SQL Server environment, but there is a downside: the T-SQL Debugger from Visual Studio is difficult to install and configure. This difficulty arises from the nature of the environment and the complexity of the components required for debugging.

The T-SQL Debugger was initially released as a part of Visual C++ 4.2. Now it is a component of the Enterprise Edition of all Visual Studio tools (such as Visual Basic and Visual InterDev).

Requirements   Before you continue, make sure that your development environment fulfills the following requirements:

▶ Microsoft SQL Server 7.0 or 2000 (or Microsoft SQL Server 6.5 with Service Pack 2 or later) must be installed. At the time of publication, the T-SQL Debugger was not compatible with Desktop Engine (MSDE).

▶ Microsoft SQL Server must be running on Windows NT 4 Server or Windows 2000 Server or higher.

▶ Client-side tools must be installed on workstations with Windows 9x, Windows NT 4, or Windows 2000.

▶ You must have the Enterprise Edition of one Visual Studio development tool such as Visual Basic or Visual InterDev.

Configuration   The T-SQL Debugger is a complex tool that relies on the synchronous behavior of many components. Because all of these components are delivered with different versions of various programs, the biggest challenge that you face is to force all of these components to work together. You can achieve this end by following these configuration steps:

1. Install debugging components on your SQL Server machine.

2. Set up a valid user account (not a system account).

3. Verify that DCOM is properly configured.

Install debugging components: The installation of debugging components is different for each development tool. First, check the documentation for details. When you are installing the T-SQL Debugger, use the Custom Setup option to make sure that the SQL Server Debugging components are installed.

In Visual Studio 6.0, the setup program is in the Sqldbg_ss folder on Disc 2. You may need to reinstall SQL Server Debugging if the Application Event Log contains error messages referring to missing DLLs containing "SDI" in their names. For example:

```
17750: Cannot load the DLL SDI, or one of the DLLs it references.
Reason: 126 (The specified module could not be found.).
```

You should check the Application Event Log for messages like this one if your debugger is not working.

With some development tools, you need to perform an additional step to enable the T-SQL Debugger. For example, in Visual Basic you need to access the Add In Manager and select T-SQL Debugger To Be Loaded.

Set up a valid user account (not a system account): SQL Server can run as a service under the virtual LocalSystem account or under a real user account with adequate privileges. For debugging purposes, it must run under a real user account. To set up a user account under Windows 2000:

1. Open the Control Panel and then Administrative Tools.

2. Open the Services applet.

3. Select the MSSQLServer service and then right-click.

4. When the context menu appears on the screen, select Properties.

5. The program will display the Properties dialog box. Switch to the Log On tab (see Figure 7-1).

6. Select This Account and type the username in the text box.

7. Type the password for the account in the Password text box.

8. Type the password again in the Confirm Password text box, and then click OK to close the dialog box.

9. Right-click the MSSQLServer service again, and choose Restart from the menu.

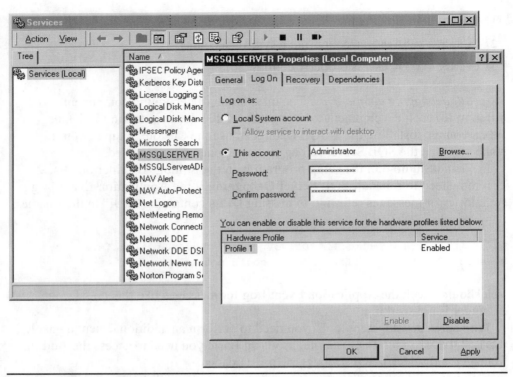

Figure 7-1 *Setting services*

TIP

I use an Administrator account that was created by the system during Windows NT setup, but it is not classified as a local system account.

Verify that DCOM is properly configured: SQL Server uses DCOM to communicate between the client workstation and the database server during debugging.

TIP

If both the T-SQL Debugger and SQL Server are running on the same machine during debugging, you will not need to configure DCOM.

When Microsoft SQL Server is installed on a server machine, all DCOM settings are configured to support DCOM for cross-machine debugging. However, due to security issues, administrators occasionally have unrestricted access to the server through DCOM. If you have followed all the instructions in your development tool's documentation and your debugger is still not working, check DCOM configuration:

1. Run dcomcnfg.exe from the command prompt. The Distributed COM Configuration Properties window appears.
2. Open the Default Security tab.
3. In Default Access Permissions, click Edit Default.
4. If the Everyone group already has Allow Access permission, your DCOM configuration is okay. If it does not, add the user that you plan to use (apply *domain\user* format).
5. Assign Allow Access permission to the new user.
6. If the System group does not have Allow Access permission, add it.

SQL Server Debugging Interface   Microsoft developers have defined a DLL with a set of functions to be called before each Transact-SQL statement. This tool is called the SQL Server Debugging Interface (SDI). The core of SDI is a pseudo-extended stored procedure called sp_sdidebug. It is defined in the sysobjects table as an extended stored procedure, although it is based on an external DLL file. Its name includes the prefix "sp" so that it can be accessed from all databases as a system stored procedure. When the debugger executes this stored procedure, it loads the DLL, which provides access to SQL Server internal state information.

NOTE

SDI adds substantial overhead and makes the machine run more slowly. For this reason, you should never use the T-SQL Debugger on a production machine.

Using the T-SQL Debugger in Visual Studio   This section demonstrates the use of the T-SQL Debugger from Visual InterDev. The major difference between debugging stored procedures and debugging within other programming languages is that you do not need to run the application to debug a single procedure.

1. Open Data View in Visual InterDev.
2. Open Stored Procedures and right-click the prGetInventoryProperties_3 stored procedure.
3. When you click Debug, the T-SQL Debugger starts the procedure and prompts you for input parameters (see Figure 7-2). Use the Value combo box to select <DEFAULT> or Null, or enter an appropriate value.

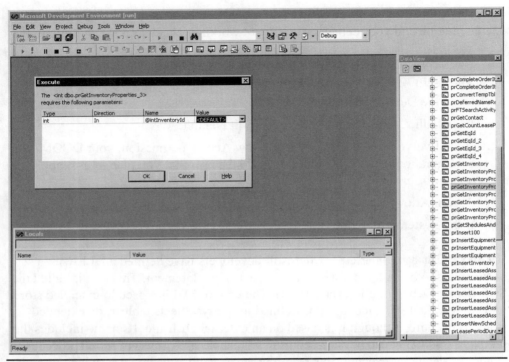

Figure 7-2 *Setting input parameters in the T-SQL Debugger*

4. Click OK. The T-SQL Debugger opens the source code of the procedure and pauses on the first executable statement. A small yellow arrow on the left border marks the position of the statement to be executed next. The commands in the Debug menu become enabled, as do two more windows, described next, that enable you to examine the state of the environment, as shown in Figure 7-3.

▶ **Locals window** Allows you to scroll through the local variables and parameters of the stored procedure and to see its current contents and data type:

Name	Value	Type
@chvProperties	'CPU=Pentium II ; RAM=64 MB; '	varchar(28)
@insLenProperties	17	smallint
@insLenUnit	2	smallint
@insLenValue	2	smallint
@insLenProperty	3	smallint
@chvUnit	'MB'	varchar(2)
@chvValue	'64'	varchar(2)
@chvProperty	'RAM'	varchar(3)
@intCounter	3	int
@intCountProperties	6	int
@intInventoryId	5	int

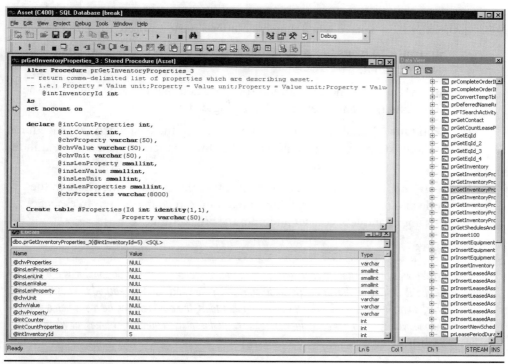

Figure 7-3   *The T-SQL Debugger*

As the stored procedure's code is executed, the values of variables change. To help you follow the execution, the T-SQL Debugger colors the values of variables that were changed in the previous statement. The Locals window allows you to change values of variables interactively during execution of the code. This window has more than one tab, but only this one has meaning in the T-SQL Debugger. The other tabs are used to debug client applications.

▶   **Watch window**   Has a similar function to the Locals window. You can type, or drag from the code, a Transact-SQL expression to be evaluated in this window. This feature is useful when you want to investigate the values of expressions in If, While, Case, and other similar statements. The Watch window also contains an Output tab, which displays result sets returned by the Select statement and messages sent from the Print statement.

5.   Click the Debug menu. The majority of commands available on the Debug menu target execution control. Most of the time, you will use the Step Into or Step Over commands to step through a stored procedure. These commands

execute one Transact-SQL statement at a time. The difference between them is in the way they behave when they encounter a nested stored procedure:

► **Step Into**   Opens the code of the nested stored procedure and lets you step through it.

► **Step Over**   The nested stored procedure is treated as any other Transact-SQL statement and is executed in a single step.

► **Step Out**   Enables you to execute the rest of the nested stored procedures without pause and halts only when the stored procedure is completed in the calling stored procedure.

► **Run To Cursor**   Enables you to position the cursor somewhere in the code and to execute everything to that point in a single step. In essence, this command lets you set a temporary breakpoint.

NOTE

Breakpoints *are markers in code that serve to stop execution when certain conditions are met. In the T-SQL Debugger, the only such condition is when the execution has reached the position of the breakpoint. In Visual Basic, Visual C++, and other tools, the condition can be met when a variable changes value, when a breakpoint has been reached a selected number of times, or when a Boolean expression is true.*

6. Right-click a line of code containing an executable Transact-SQL statement, then choose Insert Breakpoint on the Debug menu. SQL Server marks that position with a red dot on the left border. The breakpoint makes it unnecessary to step through the code. Just run it and it will stop when execution reaches the breakpoint. From this point, you can either explore variables or continue to step through the code, as shown in Figure 7-4.

If you want to continue until another breakpoint is reached, use the Debug | Start menu item.

One of my favorite features in the Visual Basic debugger is the ability to continue execution from the position of the cursor. Unfortunately, due to the architecture of the T-SQL Debugger, the Set Next Step command is not available.

T-SQL Debugger in Query Analyzer

Query Analyzer in SQL Server 2000 also contains a T-SQL Debugger. It seems that Microsoft has decided to resolve its support nightmare that was introduced with the setup and configuration of the T-SQL Debugger in Visual Studio by providing a tool in Query Analyzer that is much more robust, as well as easier to configure.

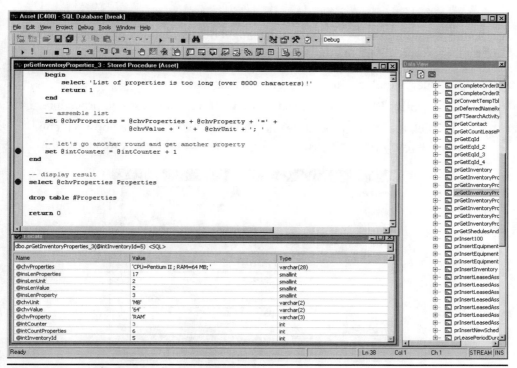

Figure 7-4   *Breakpoints in the T-SQL Debugger*

Requirements   The requirements for using the T-SQL Debugger in Query Analyzer are quite simple:

▶ You must have Microsoft SQL Server 2000 installed (any version other than the Desktop Engine or Desktop Edition).

▶ Microsoft SQL Server 2000 must be running on Windows NT 4 Server or Windows 2000 Server (or higher).

▶ Client-side tools must be installed on workstations with Windows 98, Windows ME, Windows NT 4, or Windows 2000.

Configuration   T-SQL Debugger setup is quite simple. Just make sure that you select the Debugger Interface from among the Development Tools during SQL Server setup. If you did not select it during the initial setup, you can simply run Setup again and add this component.

Using the T-SQL Debugger in Query Analyzer   The T-SQL Debugger in Query Analyzer has features similar to the Visual Studio Debugger. Although the interface is a little different, it is quite intuitive. To use it, follow these steps:

1. Open Query Analyzer and connect to the database.

2. Use the Object Browser or Object Search to find a target stored procedure.

3. Right-click the stored procedure and choose Debug from the pop-up menu. Query Analyzer prompts you to supply parameters for the stored procedure:

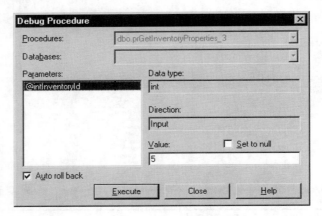

4. Click each parameter in the Parameters list and type the value. When you are done, click Execute; SQL Server launches the T-SQL Debugger window (see Figure 7-5).

The T-SQL Debugger opens the source code for the procedure and pauses on the first executable statement. A small yellow arrow on the left border marks the position of the statement to be executed next. You will not be able to edit the stored procedure's code, but you can use buttons on the window's toolbar to step through the stored procedure, and you can use the panels in the lower part of the window to investigate local and global variables, view the callstack, and view the result of the procedures.

The left section of the middle portion of the window allows you to monitor, and even set, values for local variables and parameters of the stored procedure.

The middle section allows you to monitor values of global variables. Naturally, all values are not initially present, but you can type them yourself. The right section lists (nested) procedures in the order in which they are called. The lower part of the window displays the result as it would be in the Results pane of the Query window.

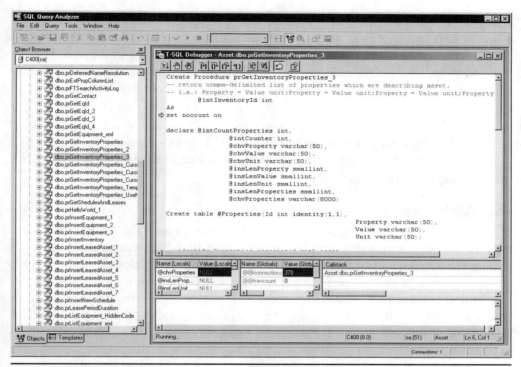

Figure 7-5   *The T-SQL Debugger window in Query Analyzer*

The buttons on the toolbar of the T-SQL Debugger window control the execution of the code. Most of the time you will use the Step Into and Step Over buttons. These commands have the same effect as those in Visual Studio—they allow you to execute one Transact-SQL statement at a time. Again, the difference between them is in the way they behave when they encounter a nested stored procedure (a procedure that is executed from the procedure that you are debugging). If you choose Step Into (F11), the T-SQL Debugger opens the code of the nested stored procedure and lets you step through it. If you choose Step Over (F10), the nested stored procedure is treated as any other Transact-SQL statement and is executed in a single step. The Step Out (SHIFT-F11) command enables you to execute the rest of the nested stored procedures without pause and halts only when the stored procedure is completed in the calling stored procedure. Run To Cursor (CTRL-F10) enables you to position the cursor somewhere in the code and to execute everything to that point in a single step.

It is also possible to use breakpoints in Query Analyzer. As explained earlier, *breakpoints* are markers in code that serve to stop execution when certain conditions are met. In the T-SQL Debugger, the only such condition is when the execution has reached the position of the breakpoint. To set (or remove) a breakpoint, you can click a line of code and then click the Toggle Breakpoints button (or press F9). Again, the program marks the breakpoint with a big red dot at the beginning of the line. Then, you can simply run the procedure using the Go button (F5). It is not necessary to step through the code. The program stops execution when it encounters a breakpoint.

NOTE

The T-SQL Debugger in Query Analyzer has one small limitation—it is not possible to open more than one T-SQL Debugger, and only one stored procedure can be debugged at a time (along with any nested stored procedures).

Poor Man's Debugger

You can debug your stored procedures even if you do not have the T-SQL Debugger (that is, if your environment does not comply with all the requirements). Before debuggers became part of the programming environment, developers used simple techniques to print the contents of variables and follow the execution of code. Some programming languages include commands (for instance, Assert in Visual Basic 6.0) that are active only during debugging. In others, you simply add print commands during the development stage and comment them out before releasing the code into production.

In Transact-SQL, I use a very simple technique that allows me to view the contents of the variables and recordsets when I am testing a stored procedure from Query Analyzer. I add one additional parameter with the default set to 0 to the stored procedure:

```
@debug int = 0
```

In the stored procedure, at all important points, I add code that tests the value of the @debug variable and displays the values of selected variables or result sets:

```
if @debug <> 0
    select    @chvProperty Property,
              @chvValue [Value],
              @chvUnit [Unit]
. . .

if @debug <> 0
    select * from #Properties
```

I do not use the Print statement for this purpose because

▶ It does not support the display of result sets.

▶ In older versions, it was impossible to concatenate a string inside a Print statement.

▶ Some utilities handle messages from the Print statement differently than they do the result set from the Select statement.

▶ If the procedure was moved into production without removing the debug code, the debug code would not be executed due to the value of the variable. If Print statements were inadvertently left in procedures when they were moved into production, this would present a problem for the application.

In the following example, you can see a stored procedure that is designed to support this kind of testing:

```
Alter Procedure prGetInventoryProperties_2
-- Return comma-delimited list of properties
-- which are describing asset.
-- i.e.: Property=Value unit;Property=Value unit;...        (
        @intInventoryId int,
        @chvProperties varchar(8000) OUTPUT,
        @debug int = 0

As
set nocount on

declare    @intCountProperties int,
           @intCounter int,
           @chvProperty varchar(50),
           @chvValue varchar(50),
           @chvUnit varchar(50),
           @insLenProperty smallint,
           @insLenValue smallint,
           @insLenUnit smallint,
           @insLenProperties smallint

declare @chvProcedure sysname
set @chvProcedure = 'prGetInventoryProperties_2'

if @debug <> 0
    select '**** '+ @chvProcedure + 'START ****'

Create table #Properties(Id int identity(1,1),
                         Property varchar(50),
                         Value varchar(50),
                         Unit varchar(50))
```

```
-- identify Properties associated with asset
insert into #Properties (Property, Value, Unit)
    select Property, Value, Unit
    from InventoryProperty inner join Property
    on InventoryProperty.PropertyId = Property.PropertyId
    where InventoryProperty.InventoryId = @intInventoryId

if @debug <> 0
    select * from #Properties

-- set loop
select @intCountProperties = Count(*),
    @intCounter = 1,
    @chvProperties = ''
from #Properties

-- loop through list of properties
while @intCounter <= @intCountProperties
begin
    -- get one property
    select    @chvProperty = Property,
              @chvValue = Value,
              @chvUnit = Coalesce(Unit, '')
    from #Properties
    where Id = @intCounter

    if @debug <> 0
        select    @chvProperty Property,
                  @chvValue [Value],
                  @chvUnit [Unit]

    -- check will new string fit
    select @insLenProperty = DATALENGTH(@chvProperty),
           @insLenValue = DATALENGTH(@chvValue),
           @insLenUnit = DATALENGTH(@chvUnit),
           @insLenProperties = DATALENGTH(@chvProperties)

    if @insLenProperties + 2
      + @insLenProperty + 1
      + @insLenValue + 1
      + @insLenUnit > 8000
```

```
        begin
            select 'List of properties is too long '
            + '(over 8000 characters)!'
            return 1
        end

        -- assemble list
        set @chvProperties = @chvProperties + @chvProperty
                + '=' + @chvValue + ' ' +  @chvUnit + '; '
        if @debug <> 0
            select @chvProperties chvProperties

        -- let's go another round and get another property
        set @intCounter = @intCounter + 1
end

drop table #Properties

if @debug <> 0
    select '**** '+ @chvProcedure + 'END ****'

return 0
```

To debug or test a stored procedure, I execute the stored procedure from Query Analyzer with the @debug parameter set to 1:

```
declare @chvResult varchar(8000)
exec prGetInventoryProperties_2
    @intInventoryId = 5,
    @chvProperties = @chvResult OUTPUT,
    @debug = 1

select @chvResult Result
```

Remember that you can pass parameters either by name or by position. The result of the execution will be an elaborate printout like the one shown in Figure 7-6.

Execution in the Production Environment   In production, the stored procedure is called without a reference to the @debug parameter. Here, SQL Server assigns a default

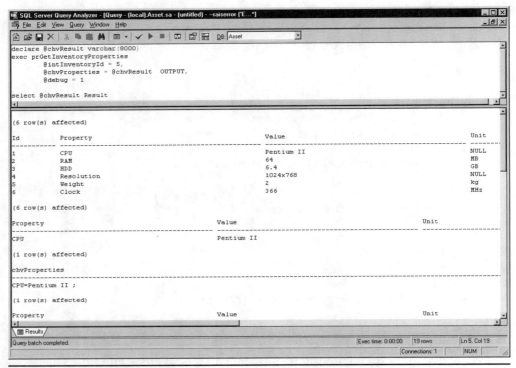

Figure 7-6 *Poor man's debugger*

value to the parameter (0), and the stored procedure is executed without debug statements:

```
exec prGetInventoryProperties_2
        @intInventoryId = 5,
        @chvProperties = @chvResult OUTPUT
```

Nested Stored Procedures   Two tricks can help you debug a set of nested stored procedures (that is, when a stored procedure calls another stored procedure). It is a useful practice to display the name of the stored procedure at the beginning and end of the stored procedure:

```
declare @chvProcedure sysname
set @chvProcedure = 'prGetInventoryProperties_2'

if @debug <> 0
```

```
      select '**** '+ @chvProcedure + 'START ****'
...
if @debug <> 0
      select '**** '+ @chvProcedure + 'END ****'

return 0
```

When you call a nested stored procedure, you need to pass the value of the @debug parameter to it as well. In this way, you will be able to see its debugging information.

```
exec prGetInventoryProperties @intInventoryId,
                              @chvProperties OUTPUT,
                              @debug
```

SQL Profiler

SQL Profiler allows you to monitor and capture events on an instance of SQL Server. You can configure it to capture all events, or just a subset that you need to monitor. It lets you do the following:

► Capture T-SQL statements that are causing errors

► Debug individual stored procedures or T-SQL statements

► Monitor system performance

► Collect the complete T-SQL load of a production system and replay it in your test environment

SQL Profiler can collect external events initiated by end users (such as batch starts or login attempts), as well as internal events initiated by the system (such as individual T-SQL statements from within a stored procedure, table or index scans, objects locks, and transactions).

Using SQL Profiler

SQL Profiler is an MDI application that contains one or more trace windows. A *trace window* allows you to first configure events, filters, and data columns, and then to collect data from the server that is being audited.

After you start SQL Profiler, the first thing you should do is open a new trace window (File | New | Trace) and select the server to be audited. You will be prompted to configure trace properties either manually or by choosing a predefined template (in the Template Name list box):

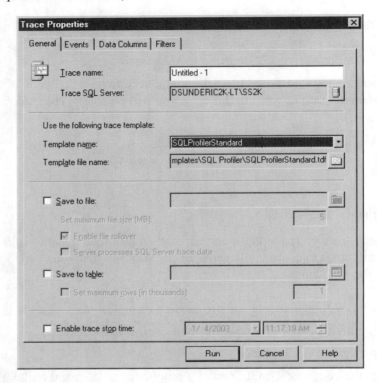

There are numerous templates available, some of the most useful of which are the following:

- ► **SQLProfilerStandard.tdf**   Collects information about connections, stored procedures, and batches that are executed against the server

- ► **SQLProfilerT-SQL_SPs.tdf**   Collects information about individual stored procedures and all T-SQL statements initiated within the stored procedure

- ► **SQLProfilerSP_Counts.tdf**   Displays stored procedures and the number of times they have been executed

- ► **SQLProfilerT-SQL_Replay.tdf**   Collects all T-SQL statements that have been executed against the server to allow you to replay them later (against the same or some other server)

By default, data is collected on the screen, but it can also be stored in a file or in a database table. The latter two options allow you to preserve the data for future use and further analysis.

On the corresponding tabs of the Trace Properties window, you can specify events and data columns to be recorded. Some data columns are not applicable for some events, and SQL Server will leave them empty. It takes a little time and experimentation to learn which are the most useful. I recommend you analyze some of the templates and see how they are built.

Filters provide you with a way to avoid information overload. For example, you can decide to monitor only those activities performed just by a particular user, or all activities except those initiated by SQL Profiler in a specific database.

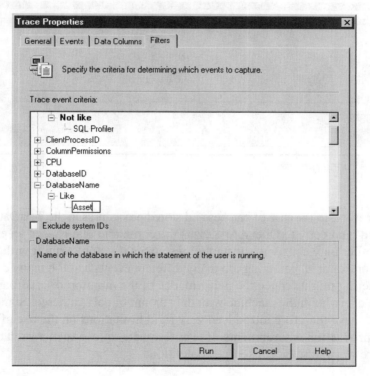

When you have finished modifying the trace properties, you run the trace. Profiler starts to collect data and display it on the screen (see Figure 7-7).

When you have gathered enough data, you can pause or stop data collection without closing the window. The top pane displays all specified data columns. In the bottom pane, SQL Profiler displays the complete content of the TextData column for

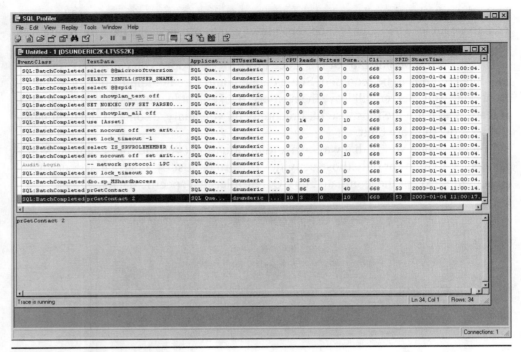

Figure 7-7   *A running trace*

the selected event. In the case of batches and stored procedures in the TextData column, you can find (and copy to Query Analyzer) the command that caused an error.

SQL Profiler may consume substantial resources if you just run it without careful planning. For example, gathering too many different events and too many data columns without filtering might reduce the performance of the monitored server; and the trace itself might overwhelm the machine with the amount of data gathered. Some database departments have therefore introduced very rigid limitations on the use of SQL Profiler in production environments. It is unfortunate to lose such a valuable tool, but there are ways to reduce resource contention:

▶ Do not run SQL Profiler on the server that you are monitoring.

▶ If the volume of the gathered data is an issue, save it to a file (not to the screen or a database table). Storing trace data in a database table allows you to analyze it with the full power of SQL Server tools, but it might also introduce a performance problem. Ideally, gather data in a file and then periodically load it to a database table.

▶ To reduce network contention on a busy production server, add a new network connection dedicated to SQL Profiler (in other words, an additional NIC and additional network).

▶ Use PerfMon to track the impact of SQL Profiler on the production system.

Typical Errors

You should keep the following issues in mind when you are writing your code and testing Transact-SQL programs:

▶ Handling null

▶ Assignment of variable from the result set

▶ No records affected

▶ Wrong size or data type

▶ Default length

▶ Rollback of triggers

▶ Warnings and lower-priority errors

▶ Nested comments

▶ Deferred name resolution

▶ Cursors

▶ Overconfidence

Handling Null

Many errors are a result of the inadequate treatment of null values in Transact-SQL code. Developers often forget that local variables or table columns might contain null. If such a value becomes part of any expression, the result will also be null.

The proper way to test the value of an expression for null is to use the Is Null or Is Not Null clause. Microsoft SQL Server treats the use of = Null as another way to type Is Null (when Set Ansi_Nulls is set to Off), but <> Null is not the equivalent of Is Not Null. The result of such an expression is always simply null. It will never be true, and stored procedures will always skip statements after the If statement when you use the <> Null clause.

```
If @intInventoryId IS NULL
...
If @intInventoryId = NULL
```

```
...
If @intInventoryId IS NOT NULL
...
If @intInventoryId <> NULL   -- WRONG!!!
...
```

Assignment of Variable from the Result Set

Earlier, I discussed assigning the value for a variable using the result set of the Select statement. This technique is fine when the result set returns only one record. However, if the result set returns more than one record, the variable is assigned using the value from the last record in the recordset—not perfect, but in some cases, you can live with it. It is sometimes difficult to predict which record will be returned last in the recordset. It depends on both the query and the index that SQL Server has used.

A more serious problem occurs when the recordset is empty. The values of the variables are changed in this case, and the code is vulnerable to several mistakes. If you do not expect the result set to be empty, your stored procedure will fail. If you expect the values of the variables to be null, your stored procedure will function correctly only immediately after it is started (that is, in the first iteration of the process). In such a case, the local variables are not yet initialized and will contain null. Later, when variables are initialized, their values will remain unchanged. If you are testing the contents of the variables for null to find out if the record was selected, you will just process the previous record again.

No Records Affected

Developers sometimes assume that SQL Server will return errors if a Transact-SQL statement affects no records. Unfortunately, this error is semantic rather than syntactic and SQL Server will not detect it.

To identify this type of error, use the @@rowcount function rather than the @@error function:

```
declare @intRowCount int
declare @intErrorCode int

update Inventory
Set StatusId = 3
where InventoryID = -11

select @intRowCount = @@rowCount,
       @intErrorCode = @@error

if @intRowCount = 0
```

```
begin
     select 'Record was not updated!'
     --return 50001
end
```

Wrong Size or Data Type

I can recall one occasion when a colleague of mine spent two days going through a complicated data conversion process to find out why his process was consistently failing. In one of the nested stored procedures, I had declared the variable as `tinyint` instead of `int`. During the testing phase of the project, everything worked perfectly because the variable was never set to a value higher than 255. However, a couple of months later in production, the process started to fail as values climbed higher.

Similar problems can occur if you do not fully understand the differences between similar formats (for example, `char` and `varchar` or `money` and `smallmoney`), or if you fail to synchronize the sizes of data types (for instance, `char`, `varchar`, `numeric`, and other data types of variable size).

Default Length

A similar problem can occur when a developer does not supply the length of the variable data type and SQL Server assigns a default length.

For example, the default length of the `varchar` data type is 30. Most of the time SQL Server reports an error if the length is omitted, but not in all cases. In the Convert() function, for example, the user need only specify the data type:

```
Convert(varchar, @intPropertyId)
```

If the resulting string is short enough, you will not have any problems. I recall a colleague who employed this method for years without any problems, and then….

Unfortunately, other statements and functions behave as expected. If you declare a variable and assign it like so:

```
Declare @test varchar
Set @test = '12345678901234567890123345677890'
Select datalength(@test), @test
```

SQL Server will allocate just one byte to the string and return the following:

```
----------- ----
1           1

(1 row(s) affected)
```

Rollback of Triggers

In different versions of SQL Server, triggers react differently in rollback transaction statements. When a trigger is rolled back in SQL Server 7.0 or SQL Server 2000, the complete batch that initiated the trigger fails and the execution continues from the first statement of the next batch. Version 4.2 behaves in a similar manner. In version 6.0, processing continues in the trigger, but the batch is canceled. In version 6.5, the processing continues in both the trigger and the batch. It was the responsibility of the developer to detect errors and cascade out of the process (in other words, go out of all nested procedures and triggers).

Warnings and Lower-Priority Errors

Warnings do not stop the execution of a stored procedure. In fact, you cannot even detect them from within the SQL Server environment.

Low-level errors, which are detectable using the @@error function, do not abort the execution either. Unfortunately, there are also errors that abort processing completely, so that the error handlers in stored procedures do not process the error.

Nested Comments

Only single-line comments (--) can be nested. Nested multiline comments (/* */) may be treated differently by different client tools.

I recommend that you put one or two stars (**) at the beginning of each line that is commented out. In this manner, the problem will be obvious if the comments are nested and SQL Server starts to compile part of the code that you consider to be commented out:

```
/*************************************************************
**      select *
**      from #Properties
*************************************************************/
```

Deferred Name Resolution

It is possible (in Microsoft SQL Server 7.0 and Microsoft SQL Server 2000) to create database objects (such as stored procedures and triggers) that refer to other database objects that do not yet exist within the database. In previous versions, this would have been treated as a syntax error. This feature helps tremendously when you need to generate a database structure and objects using script. Unfortunately, this introduces a number of risks. If, as in the following example, you make a typo in the name of the table from which you want to retrieve records, SQL Server will not report a syntax error during compilation but will report a runtime error during execution.

```
Create Procedure prDeferredNameResolution
As
     set nocount on
     select 'Start'
     select * from NonExistingTable
     select 'Will execution be stopped?'
return
```

If you attempt to run this stored procedure, SQL Server will return the following:

```
-----
Start

Server: Msg 208, Level 16, State 1,
Procedure prDeferredNameResolution, Line 7
Invalid object name 'NonExistingTable'.
```

The execution will be stopped. Even an error handler written in Transact-SQL will not be able to proceed at this point.

Cursors

Be very cautious when you use cursors: test the status after each fetch; place error handling after each command; do not forget to close and deallocate the cursor when you do not need it any more. There are many rules and regulations for using cursors, and some of them might seem trivial, but even the smallest mistake can halt the execution of your code.

Overconfidence

The overconfidence that comes with routine may be your worst enemy. If you perform the same or similar tasks over and over again, you can lose focus and skip basic steps. Do not put code into production before it is thoroughly tested; do not place bug fixes directly into production; use error handling even if the code seems straightforward and the chance for error slight.

Error Handling

A developer's effective use of error handling procedures is often an excellent indicator of his or her experience in that particular programming language. Those of us who deal with a C or Visual Basic environment are accustomed to a whole set of feature-rich error handling objects, procedures, and functions. Compared with those, T-SQL seems rather inadequate. You can employ only one function and a few procedures for setting or raising errors. However, the apparent limitations of the tool set still do not justify sloppy solutions.

This section starts by investigating how errors can be returned to a caller. Then, it discusses the concept of error handling and offers a comprehensive methodology for implementation. It also discusses some alternative techniques involving the Set Xact_Abort On statement.

Raiserror

An important tool for implementing error handling is the Raiserror statement. Its main purpose is to return a user-defined or system-defined message to the caller. Open Query Analyzer and execute the following statement:

```
Raiserror ('Error occurred!', 0, 1)
```

The server will display an error message in the Result pane (see Figure 7-8).

The second and third parameters indicate the severity and state of the error.

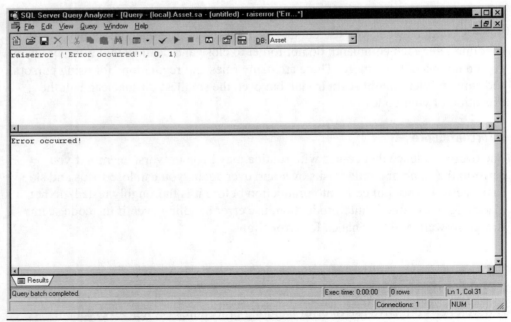

Figure 7-8   *Using Raiserror*

Naturally, this statement does more than return this meager result. It also sets the value of the @@error function to the number of the error that you have raised. If you do not specify an error number (as was the case in the previous example), SQL Server will assign the default of 50000.

You can also display errors that are predefined in SQL Server if you reference them by their numbers, and you can define your own errors using the sp_addmessage system stored procedure:

```
Exec sp_addmessage 50001,
                   16,
                   'Unable to update Total of LeaseSchedule'
```

Then you can display this message using the following statement:

```
Raiserror (50001, 16, 1)
```

The server will return the following:

```
Server: Msg 50001, Level 16, State 1, Line 1
Unable to update Total of LeaseSchedule
```

You can set the state and severity of the error, record the error in the SQL Server Error Log, and even record the error in the Windows NT Error Log:

```
Raiserror (50001, 16, 1) WITH LOG
```

Enterprise Manager contains a tool for displaying and editing error messages. To start it, click a server node and then choose Tools | Manage SQL Server Messages.

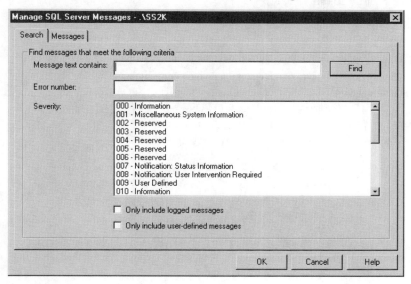

Using Error Handling

Since T-SQL is so laconic (critics may say feature poor), development DBAs commonly express themselves in a very concise manner. DBAs frequently write ad hoc scripts for one-time use or manual execution, and they thus neglect the need for consistent error handling.

Logic that is fine in standard languages like Visual Basic or C frequently does not work in T-SQL. For example, an error may occur in T-SQL, but if T-SQL does not consider it fatal, processing will continue. Also, if the error is fatal, all processing will stop. The process does not react: it is just killed.

Why Bother?

For many, the question is why be concerned with implementing error handling at all? Let us review this question through the following example:

```
Create Procedure prInsertLeasedAsset_1
-- Insert leased asset and update total in LeaseSchedule.
-- (demonstration of imperfect solution)
            (
            @intEquipmentId int,
            @intLocationId int,
            @intStatusId int,
            @intLeaseId int,
            @intLeaseScheduleId int,
            @intOwnerId int,
            @mnyLease money,
            @intAcquisitionTypeID int
            )
As
set nocount on

begin transaction

-- insert asset
insert Inventory(EquipmentId,          LocationId,
                 StatusId,             LeaseId,
                 LeaseScheduleId,      OwnerId,
                 Lease,                AcquisitionTypeID)
values (         @intEquipmentId,      @intLocationId,
                 @intStatusId,         @intLeaseId,
                 @intLeaseScheduleId,  @intOwnerId,
                 @mnyLease,            @intAcquisitionTypeID)
```

```
-- update total
update LeaseSchedule
Set PeriodicTotalAmount = PeriodicTotalAmount + @mnyLease
where LeaseId = @intLeaseId

commit transaction

return
```

This may seem like a trivial example, and it is true that in all probability nothing would go wrong, but imagine that an error occurs on the Update statement. The error could be for any reason—overflow, violation of a constraint, or inadequate security privileges, for example. As explained earlier, transactions do not automatically roll back when an error occurs. Instead, SQL Server simply commits everything that was changed when it encounters the Commit Transaction statement as if nothing unusual had happened. Unfortunately, from that moment on, the total of the lease schedule will have the wrong value.

Tactics of Error Handling

Most developers recognize the importance of this issue and place error handling in critical positions in their code. The result would be something like the following:

```
Create Procedure prInsertLeasedAsset_2
-- Insert leased asset and update total in LeaseSchedule.
-- (demonstration of not exactly perfect solution)
    (
        @intEquipmentId int,
        @intLocationId int,
        @intStatusId int,
        @intLeaseId int,
        @intLeaseScheduleId int,
        @intOwnerId int,
        @mnyLease money,
        @intAcquisitionTypeID int
    )
As
set nocount on

begin transaction

-- insert asset
insert Inventory(EquipmentId,          LocationId,
```

```
                    StatusId,             LeaseId,
                    LeaseScheduleId,      OwnerId,
                    Lease,                AcquisitionTypeID)
values (            @intEquipmentId,      @intLocationId,
                    @intStatusId,         @intLeaseId,
                    @intLeaseScheduleId,  @intOwnerId,
                    @mnyLease,            @intAcquisitionTypeID)
If @@error <> 0
Begin
    Print 'Unexpected error occurred!'
    Rollback transaction
    Return 1
End


-- update total
update LeaseSchedule
Set PeriodicTotalAmount = PeriodicTotalAmount + @mnyLease
where LeaseId = @intLeaseId

If @@error <> 0
Begin
    Print 'Unexpected error occurred!'
    Rollback transaction
    Return 1
End

commit transaction

return 0
```

This kind of solution contains substantial repetition—especially if your business logic requires more than two Transact-SQL statements to be implemented. A more elegant solution is to group codes into a generic error handling procedure:

```
Create Procedure prInsertLeasedAsset_3
-- Insert leased asset and update total in LeaseSchedule.
-- (demonstration of not exactly perfect solution)
    (
        @intEquipmentId int,
        @intLocationId int,
        @intStatusId int,
        @intLeaseId int,
        @intLeaseScheduleId int,
        @intOwnerId int,
        @mnyLease money,
```

```
            @intAcquisitionTypeID int
    )
As
set nocount on

begin transaction

-- insert asset
insert Inventory(EquipmentId,         LocationId,
                 StatusId,            LeaseId,
                 LeaseScheduleId,     OwnerId,
                 Lease,               AcquisitionTypeID)
values (         @intEquipmentId,     @intLocationId,
                 @intStatusId,        @intLeaseId,
                 @intLeaseScheduleId, @intOwnerId,
                 @mnyLease,           @intAcquisitionTypeID)
If @@error <> 0 GOTO ERR_HANDLER

-- update total
update LeaseSchedule
Set PeriodicTotalAmount = PeriodicTotalAmount + @mnyLease
where LeaseId = @intLeaseId
If @@error <> 0 GOTO ERR_HANDLER

commit transaction

return 0

ERR_HANDLER:
    Print 'Unexpected error occurred!'
    Rollback transaction
    Return 1
```

This is better, but it does not deal with all the issues that need to be handled.

A typical error that beginners in T-SQL make is to check the value of a global variable and then try to return or process it. Such an attempt is usually the result of a good intention, such as wanting to notify the user of an error that has occurred.

```
Create Procedure prInsertLeasedAsset_4
-- Insert leased asset and update total in LeaseSchedule.
-- (demonstration of not exactly perfect solution)
    (
            @intEquipmentId int,
            @intLocationId int,
            @intStatusId int,
```

```
        @intLeaseId int,
        @intLeaseScheduleId int,
        @intOwnerId int,
        @mnyLease money,
        @intAcquisitionTypeID int
    )
As
set nocount on

begin transaction

-- insert asset
insert Inventory(EquipmentId,           LocationId,
                StatusId,               LeaseId,
                LeaseScheduleId,        OwnerId,
                Lease,                  AcquisitionTypeID)
values (        @intEquipmentId,        @intLocationId,
                @intStatusId,           @intLeaseId,
                @intLeaseScheduleId,    @intOwnerId,
                @mnyLease,              @intAcquisitionTypeID)
If @@error <> 0 GOTO ERR_HANDLER

-- update total
update LeaseSchedule
Set PeriodicTotalAmount = PeriodicTotalAmount + @mnyLease
where LeaseId = @intLeaseId
If @@error <> 0 GOTO ERR_HANDLER

commit transaction

return 0

ERR_HANDLER:
    Print 'Unexpected error occurred: '
        + Convert(varchar, @@error) -- this will
                                    -- not work,
                                    -- as expected

    Rollback transaction
    Return @@error
```

Although something like this could work in Visual Basic, for example, in this case the stored procedure will return 0 as an error number. SQL Server sets the value of the @@error variable after each statement. It treats each statement separately, so the value of @@error is set to 0 subsequently when the If statement is (successfully) executed. Thus the Print statement displays 0 as an error number, and eventually the stored procedure will also return 0.

A Coherent Error Handling Methodology

This section presents a single comprehensive error handling methodology. The fundamental idea is that *all* SQL statements within a stored procedure should be covered by this error handling solution. Any time an unexpected error occurs, a stored procedure should stop further processing. When a nested stored procedure stops processing, so should the stored procedures that called it.

The basic feature of this solution is to follow all SQL statements with a statement that reads the contents of the @@error function, and to use an If statement to check whether the previous command completed successfully:

```
Create Procedure prInsertLeasedAsset_5
-- Insert leased asset and update total in LeaseSchedule.
     (
          @intEquipmentId int,
          @intLocationId int,
          @intStatusId int,
          @intLeaseId int,
          @intLeaseScheduleId int,
          @intOwnerId int,
          @mnyLease money,
          @intAcquisitionTypeID int
     )
As
set nocount on

Declare @intErrorCode int
Select @intErrorCode = @@error

begin transaction

If @intErrorCode = 0
begin
     — insert asset
     insert Inventory(EquipmentId,           LocationId,
                      StatusId,               LeaseId,
                      LeaseScheduleId,        OwnerId,
                      Lease,                  AcquisitionTypeID)
```

```
    values (           @intEquipmentId,      @intLocationId,
                       @intStatusId,         @intLeaseId,
                       @intLeaseScheduleId,  @intOwnerId,
                       @mnyLease,            @intAcquisitionTypeID)
    Select @intErrorCode = @@error
end

If @intErrorCode = 0
begin
    — update total
    update LeaseSchedule
    Set PeriodicTotalAmount = PeriodicTotalAmount + @mnyLease
    where LeaseId = @intLeaseId
    Select @intErrorCode = @@error
end

If @intErrorCode = 0
    COMMIT TRANSACTION
Else
    ROLLBACK TRANSACTION

return @intErrorCode
```

If an error occurs, the If statements prevent further execution and pass control to the end of the procedure. Changes will be rolled back, and the stored procedure returns the value of the @intErrorCode variable to the calling stored procedure or script. This variable can then be used to notify the calling procedure that there was a problem.

Nested Stored Procedures

The calling stored procedure might have the same error handling system in place. In such a case, calls to the stored procedures should treat the returned values as error codes:

```
...
If @ErrorCode = 0
Begin
    execute @intErrorCode = MyStoredProcedure @parm1, @param2...
End
```

The method works like a cascade that stops all further processing in a whole set of nested stored procedures.

Interfacing to Other Environments

This error handling structure is very useful even in cases when a stored procedure is called from another programming environment, such as Visual Basic or Visual C++. The return value of a stored procedure can be retrieved, and the error can be handled by the calling application.

```
conn.Open "provider=sqloledb;data source=sqlserver;" + _
"user id=sa;password=;initial catalog=Asset"

With cmd
    Set .ActiveConnection = conn
    .CommandText = "prInsertLeasedAsset_5"
    .CommandType = adCmdStoredProc
    .Parameters.Refresh
    .parameters(1).Value =  4
    .parameters(2).Value =  1
    .parameters(3).Value =  1
    .parameters(4).Value =  1
    .parameters(5).Value =  1
    .parameters(6).Value =  1
    .parameters(7).Value = 99.95
    .parameters(8).Value =  1
    Set rs = .Execute()
    lngReturnValue = .Parameters(0).Value
end with
If lngReturnValue <> 0 Then
    MsgBox "Procedure has failed!"
    Exit Sub
Else
    MsgBox "Procedure was successful"
end if
```

Other Functions

Cases should be handled with the same Select statement that reads @@error when you wish to read the value of other functions immediately after the statement. You often require such a technique when you are using identity columns.

```
    insert Inventory(EquipmentId,        LocationId,
                     StatusId,           LeaseId,
                     LeaseScheduleId,    OwnerId,
                     Lease,              AcquisitionTypeID)
    values (         @intEquipmentId,    @intLocationId,
```

```
                         @intStatusId,          @intLeaseId,
                         @intLeaseScheduleId,  @intOwnerId,
                         @mnyLease,             @intAcquisitionTypeID)
      Select @intErrorCode = @@error,
             @intInventoryId = @@identity
```

Transaction Processing

You can integrate transaction processing perfectly with this solution. Review Chapter 6 to remind yourself why Rollback and Commit statements must be treated differently.

At the beginning of a stored procedure or transaction, you should add the following code:

```
Declare @intTransactionCountOnEntry int
If @intErrorCode = 0
Begin
    Select @intTransactionCountOnEntry = @@TranCount
    BEGIN TRANSACTION
End
```

At the end of the procedure (and/or transaction), you should complete the transaction:

```
If @@TranCount > @intTransactionCountOnEntry
Begin
    If @intErrorCode = 0
        COMMIT TRANSACTION
    Else
        ROLLBACK TRANSACTION
End
```

The solution will also perform well in the case of nested stored procedures. All procedures are rolled back using the same cascading mechanism.

The local variable @TransactionCountOnEntry is used to track the number of opened transactions upon entry into a stored procedure. If the number is unaffected within the stored procedure, there is no reason to commit or roll back (using either the Commit or Rollback statement) within the procedure. The finished stored procedure looks like this:

```
Alter Procedure prInsertLeasedAsset_6
-- Insert leased asset and update total in LeaseSchedule.
        (
         @intEquipmentId int,
```

```
            @intLocationId int,
            @intStatusId int,
            @intLeaseId int,
            @intLeaseScheduleId int,
            @intOwnerId int,
            @mnyLease money,
            @intAcquisitionTypeID int,
            @intInventoryId int OUTPUT
            )
As
set nocount on

Declare @intErrorCode int,
        @intTransactionCountOnEntry int

Select @intErrorCode = @@error

If @intErrorCode = 0
Begin
    Select @intTransactionCountOnEntry = @@TranCount
    BEGIN TRANSACTION
End


If @intErrorCode = 0
begin
    -- insert asset
    insert Inventory(EquipmentId,          LocationId,
                     StatusId,             LeaseId,
                     LeaseScheduleId,      OwnerId,
                     Lease,                AcquisitionTypeID)
    values (         @intEquipmentId,      @intLocationId,
                     @intStatusId,         @intLeaseId,
                     @intLeaseScheduleId,  @intOwnerId,
                     @mnyLease,            @intAcquisitionTypeID)
    Select @intErrorCode = @@error,
           @intInventoryId = @@identity
end

If @intErrorCode = 0
begin
    -- update total
    update LeaseSchedule
    Set PeriodicTotalAmount = PeriodicTotalAmount + @mnyLease
    where LeaseId = @intLeaseId
```

```
        Select @intErrorCode = @@error
end

If @@TranCount > @intTransactionCountOnEntry
Begin
    If @@error = 0
        COMMIT TRANSACTION
    Else
        ROLLBACK TRANSACTION
End

return @intErrorCode
```

Xact_Abort

SQL Server does, in fact, have an equivalent to the On Error Go To command used by Visual Basic. The Set Xact_Abort statement forces SQL Server to roll back the complete transaction and stop further processing on the occurrence of any error:

```
create Procedure prInsertLeasedAsset_7
-- Insert leased asset and update total in LeaseSchedule.
-- (demonstration of imperfect solution)
        (
        @intEquipmentId int,
        @intLocationId int,
        @intStatusId int,
        @intLeaseId int,
        @intLeaseScheduleId int,
        @intOwnerId int,
        @mnyLease money,
        @intAcquisitionTypeID int
        )
As
set nocount on
SET XACT_ABORT ON
begin transaction

-- insert asset
insert Inventory(EquipmentId,        LocationId,
                 StatusId,           LeaseId,
                 LeaseScheduleId,    OwnerId,
                 Lease,              AcquisitionTypeID)
values (         @intEquipmentId,    @intLocationId,
```

```
               @intStatusId,        @intLeaseId,
               @intLeaseScheduleId, @intOwnerId,
               @mnyLease,           @intAcquisitionTypeID)

-- update total
update LeaseSchedule
Set PeriodicTotalAmount = PeriodicTotalAmount + @mnyLease
where LeaseId = @intLeaseId

commit transaction

return (0)
```

Unfortunately, this solution presents a problem. This statement will also completely stop execution of the current batch. The error can still be detected and handled from the client application, but inside the Transact-SQL code, SQL Server will treat it as a fatal error.

Another problem is that the Set Xact_Abort statement does not detect "compilation" errors. According to SQL Server Books Online: "Compile errors, such as syntax errors, are not affected by Set Xact_Abort." Unfortunately, because of deferred name resolution, compilation errors can occur at runtime as well. By editing the stored procedure from the previous example, the Update statement references a nonexistent table:

```
-- update total
update LeaseSchedule_NON_EXISTING_TABLE
Set PeriodicTotalAmount = PeriodicTotalAmount + @mnyLease
where LeaseId = @intLeaseId
```

Next, run the stored procedure:

```
Exec prInsertLeasedAsset_8
           @intEquipmentId = 100,
           @intLocationId = 1,
           @intStatusId = 1,
           @intLeaseId = 1,
           @intLeaseScheduleId = 1,
           @intOwnerId = 1,
           @mnyLease = 5000,
           @intAcquisitionTypeID = 1
-- test transaction
select *
from Inventory
```

```
where EquipmentId = 100
and LocationId = 1
```

SQL Server simply stops the execution of the stored procedure without a rollback:

```
Server: Msg 208, Level 16, State 1, Procedure prInsertLeasedAsset_8, Line 30
Invalid object name 'LeaseSchedule_NON_EXISTING_TABLE'.
Server: Msg 266, Level 16, State 1, Procedure prInsertLeasedAsset_8, Line 36
Transaction count after EXECUTE indicates that a COMMIT or ROLLBACK
TRANSACTION statement is missing. Previous count = 0, current count = 1.
EquipmentId LocationId  StatusId Lease
----------- ----------- -------- ------------
100         1           1        5000.0000
```

This is a potentially significant problem. The official response concerning my support question on this matter was that SQL Server is behaving as specified in SQL Server Books Online. Developers have different expectations—in the case of an error, the transaction should be rolled back. This explanation makes it sound like the Set Xact_Abort statement is useless. Fortunately, the stored procedure will be promoted to production only after detailed unit testing, and therefore it should not reference nonexistent tables.

However, there is an additional problem: only the stored procedure with the syntax error is aborted. Assume that the stored procedure is executed as a nested stored procedure and that the compilation error occurs in the inner stored procedure. The earlier procedure is split into two procedures to demonstrate this scenario:

```
Create Procedure prUpdateLeaseSchedule
    @intLeaseId int,
    @mnyLease int
as
update LeaseSchedule_NON_EXISTING_TABLE
set PeriodicTotalAmount = PeriodicTotalAmount + @mnyLease
where LeaseId = @intLeaseId

return (0)
GO

create Procedure prInsertLeasedAsset_9
-- Insert leased asset and update total in LeaseSchedule.
-- (demonstration of compilation error in nested stored procedure)
        (
        @intEquipmentId int,
        @intLocationId int,
```

```
            @intStatusId int,
            @intLeaseId int,
            @intLeaseScheduleId int,
            @intOwnerId int,
            @mnyLease money,
            @intAcquisitionTypeID int
            )
As
set nocount on
SET XACT_ABORT ON
begin transaction

-- insert asset
insert Inventory(EquipmentId,        LocationId,
                 StatusId,           LeaseId,
                 LeaseScheduleId,    OwnerId,
                 Lease,              AcquisitionTypeID)
values (         @intEquipmentId,    @intLocationId,
                 @intStatusId,       @intLeaseId,
                 @intLeaseScheduleId, @intOwnerId,
                 @mnyLease,          @intAcquisitionTypeID)

-- update total
exec prUpdateLeaseSchedule @intLeaseId, @mnyLease

commit transaction

return (0)
GO
```

Now run them:

```
Exec prInsertLeasedAsset_9
        @intEquipmentId = 200,
        @intLocationId = 1,
        @intStatusId = 1,
        @intLeaseId = 1,
        @intLeaseScheduleId = 1,
        @intOwnerId = 1,
        @mnyLease = 5000,
        @intAcquisitionTypeID = 1
-- test transaction
select EquipmentId, LocationId, StatusId, Lease
from Inventory
```

```
where EquipmentId = 200
and LocationId = 1
```

SQL Server simply stops the execution of the inner stored procedure, but the outer stored procedure continues as though nothing has happened (and even commits the transaction):

```
Server: Msg 208, Level 16, State 1, Procedure prUpdateLeaseSchedule, Line 5
Invalid object name 'LeaseSchedule_NON_EXISTING_TABLE'.
EquipmentId LocationId  StatusId Lease
----------- ----------- -------- ------------
200         1           1        5000.0000
```

At the time, my expectation was that the Set Xact_Abort statement would abort further execution of everything, as it does in case or runtime errors. Unfortunately, it does not behave in that way. This is potentially very dangerous, but as I said before, problems such as this should be caught during QA phase.

Another Coherent Error Handling Methodology

On a recent .NET project I was involved with, there were many errors when we mixed different types of transactions—COM+, DTC, ADO, and T-SQL. Therefore, we decided not to mix them. We went even further and decided not to nest any transactions. If the caller initiates a transaction, the nested procedure skips its own initiation of the transaction. Furthermore, the transaction should be closed only from within the procedure that initiated it.

The following procedure records the number of opened transactions on the entry. The Begin Tran statement is preceded by the If statement that initiates the transaction only if the procedure is not already in one transaction:

```
create procedure dbo.prEquipment_Insert
-- insert equipment (and if necessary equipment type)
-- (demonstration of alternative method for error handling and
transaction
processing)
        @chvMake varchar(50),
        @chvModel varchar(50),
        @chvEqType varchar(50),
        @intEqupmentId int OUTPUT
AS
```

```
set xact_abort on
set nocount on

declare @intTrancountOnEntry int,
        @intEqTypeId int

set @intTrancountOnEntry = @@tranCount

-- does such EqType already exist in the database
If  not exists (Select EqTypeId From EqType Where EqType = @chvEqType)
--if it does not exist
Begin
    if @@tranCount = 0
        BEGIN TRAN

    -- insert new EqType in the database
    Insert EqType (EqType)
    Values (@chvEqType)

    -- get id of record that you've just inserted
    Select @intEqTypeId = @@identity
End
else
begin
    -- read Id of EqType
    Select @intEqTypeId
    From EqType
    Where EqType = @chvEqType
end

--insert equipment
Insert Equipment (Make, Model, EqTypeId)
Values (@chvMake, @chvModel, @intEqTypeId)

Select @intEqupmentId = @@identity

if @@tranCount > @intTrancountOnEntry
    COMMIT TRAN

return 0
```

The Commit Tran statement will similarly be executed only if the transaction is initiated in the current procedure.

The following procedure demonstrates the way to return logic errors to the caller. Notice that I am using both Raiserror and Return statements. It is very important to use the Return statement to communicate an error to the caller because the caller might not be able to detect the effect of the Raiserror statement.

```
ALTER Procedure dbo.prInsertInventory_XA
-- insert inventory record , update inventory count and return Id
-- (demonstration of alternative method for error handling and
transaction
processing)

    @intEquipmentId int,
    @intLocationId int,
    @inyStatusId tinyint,
    @intLeaseId int,
    @intLeaseScheduleId int,
    @intOwnerId int,
    @mnsRent smallmoney,
    @mnsLease smallmoney,
    @mnsCost smallmoney,
    @inyAcquisitionTypeID int,
    @intInventoryId int output

As
declare @intTrancountOnEntry int
set nocount on
set xact_abort on
set @intTrancountOnEntry = @@tranCount

if @@tranCount = 0
   begin tran

Insert into dbo.Inventory (EquipmentId, LocationId, StatusId,
        LeaseId, LeaseScheduleId, OwnerId,
        Rent, Lease, Cost,
        AcquisitionTypeID)
values (@intEquipmentId, @intLocationId, @inyStatusId,
        @intLeaseId, @intLeaseScheduleId, @intOwnerId,
        @mnsRent, @mnsLease, @mnsCost,
        @inyAcquisitionTypeID)

select @intInventoryId = Scope_Identity()
```

```
update dbo.InventoryCount
Set InvCount = InvCount + 1
where LocationId = @intLocationId

if @@rowcount <> 1
begin
-- business error
   Raiserror(50133, 16, 1)
   if @@tranCount > @intTrancountOnEntry
      rollback tran
   return 50133
end

if @@tranCount > @intTrancountOnEntry
   commit tran

return 0
```

The following procedure demonstrates detection of logic errors from the nested
stored procedure:

```
Create procedure prInventory_Insert_XA
-- insert new inventory and new equipment
-- (demonstration of alternative method for error handling and transaction
processing)
    @chvMake varchar(50),
    @chvModel varchar(50),
    @chvEqType varchar(30),
    @intLocationId int,
    @inyStatusId tinyint,
    @intLeaseId int,
    @intLeaseScheduleId int,
    @intOwnerId int,
    @mnsRent smallmoney,
    @mnsLease smallmoney,
    @mnsCost smallmoney,
    @inyAcquisitionTypeID int,
    @intInventoryId int output,
    @intEquipmentId int output
as

Set nocount on
set xact_abort on
```

```
declare @intError int,
        @intTrancountOnEntry int

set @intError = 0
set @intTrancountOnEntry = @@tranCount

if @@tranCount = 0
    begin tran

-- is equipment already in the database
if not exists(select EquipmentId
              from Equipment
              where Make = @chvMake
              and Model = @chvModel)
EXEC @intError = dbo.prEquipment_Insert @chvMake, @chvModel,    @chvEqType,
                                        @intEquipmentId OUTPUT


if @intError > 0
begin
    if @@tranCount > @intTrancountOnEntry
        rollback tran
    return @intError
end

exec @intError = dbo.prInsertInventory_XA
        @intEquipmentId,      @intLocationId,     @inyStatusId,
        @intLeaseId,          @intLeaseScheduleId, @intOwnerId,
        @mnsRent,             @mnsLease,          @mnsCost,
        @inyAcquisitionTypeID, @intInventoryId output

if @intError > 0
begin
    if @@tranCount > @intTrancountOnEntry
        ROLLBACK TRAN
    return @intError
end

if @@tranCount > @intTrancountOnEntry
    COMMIT TRAN

return 0
```

If an error has been returned, the current stored procedure will roll back the transaction (using Rollback Transaction) if a transaction has been initiated in it. The caller stored procedure can also be designed so that it knows about all (or some) error codes that can be returned from a nested stored procedure. Then it is possible to write code that will handle the errors.

To test it, run the following:

```
declare @intError int,
        @intInvId int,
        @intEqId int
begin tran

exec @intError = prInventory_Insert_XA
    @chvMake = 'Compaq',
    @chvModel = 'IPaq 3835',
    @chvEqType = 'PDA',
    @intLocationId = 12,
    @inyStatusId = 1,
    @intLeaseId = null,
    @intLeaseScheduleId = 1,
    @intOwnerId = 411,
    @mnsRent = null,
    @mnsLease = null,
    @mnsCost = $650,
    @inyAcquisitionTypeID = 1,
    @intInventoryId = @intInvId output,
    @intEquipmentId = @intEqId output
if @intError = 0
   commit tran
else
   rollback tran
select @intError Err
select * from Inventory where InventoryId = @intInvId
select * from Equipment where EquipmentId = @intEqId
```

In the case of an error, SQL Server returns the error message and rolls back the transaction:

```
Server: Msg 50133, Level 16, State 1, Procedure prInsertInventory_XA, Line 48
Unable to update inventory count.
Err
-----------
50133
(1 row(s) affected)
```

```
Inventoryid EquipmentId LocationId  StatusId LeaseId LeaseScheduleId
----------- ----------- ----------- -------- ------- ---------------

(0 row(s) affected)

EquipmentId Make                                               Model
----------- -------------------------------------------------- -------

(0 row(s) affected)
```

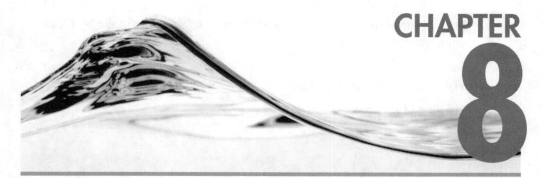

CHAPTER 8

Special Types of Procedures

This chapter examines other types of procedures available in the SQL Server environment:

- ▶ Special types of stored procedures
- ▶ User-defined functions
- ▶ Triggers
- ▶ Views

Some of these procedures are just special types of stored procedures, whereas others are completely different types of database objects. However, they all share a common attribute: they are used to describe or implement an algorithm for the purpose of achieving some result.

Types of Stored Procedures

There are six types of stored procedures:

- ▶ User-defined
- ▶ System
- ▶ Extended
- ▶ Temporary
- ▶ Global temporary
- ▶ Remote

User-Defined Stored Procedures

As you may infer from the name, user-defined stored procedures are simply groups of Transact-SQL statements assembled by administrators or developers and compiled into a single execution plan. The design of this type of stored procedure is the primary focus of this book.

System Stored Procedures

Microsoft delivers a vast set of stored procedures as a part of SQL Server. They are designed to cover all aspects of system administration. Before Microsoft SQL Server 6.0, you had to use scripts from isql to control the server and their databases. Although administrators today customarily use Enterprise Manager, system stored procedures are still very important, since Enterprise Manager uses the same system stored procedures, through SQL-DMO, behind the scenes.

NOTE

SQL-DMO stands for SQL Distributed Management Objects. It is a collection of objects designed to manage the SQL Server environment. You can use it to create your own Enterprise Manager or automate repetitive tasks. It is interesting that it does not support the return of a recordset to the caller. You should use other objects (such as ADO) to achieve this result.

System stored procedures are stored in the system databases (*master* and *msdb*), and they have the prefix sp_. This prefix is more than just a convention. It signals to the server that the stored procedure is located in the *master* database and that it should be accessible from all databases without the user needing to insert the database name as a prefix to fully qualify the name of the procedure:

```
Exec sp_who      -- instead of exec master..sp_who
```

It also signals to the server that the stored procedure should be executed in the context of the current database. For example, the script shown in Figure 8-1 will return information about the current database, and not the *master*.

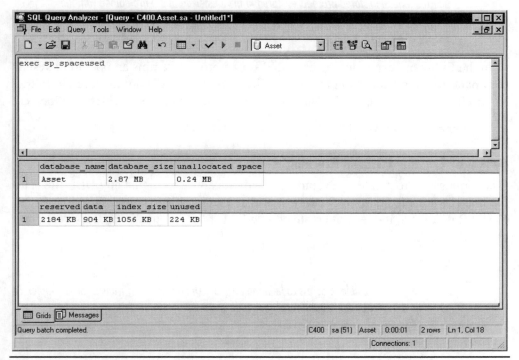

Figure 8-1   *The system procedure works in the context of the current database.*

NOTE

There is a small behavioral inconsistency between stored procedures in the master database and the msdb database. Stored procedures in the msdb database are delivered with SQL Server, but they must be referenced with the database name (for example: msdb..sp_update_job), and they do not work in the context of the current database. In this respect, you can understand them as "system-supplied stored procedures" rather than as "system stored procedures" as we have defined them.

Extended Stored Procedures

Certain SQL Server features cannot be implemented through Transact-SQL statements. The designers of SQL Server have developed a way to use the functionality encapsulated in special DLL libraries written in languages such as C or C++. Extended stored procedures are actually these C functions encapsulated in DLL files. They have a wrapper stored in the *master* database that uses the prefix xp_. Using this wrapper, you can access them just as you would any other stored procedure.

NOTE

Selected extended stored procedures stored in the master database are named with the prefix sp_ to allow users to access them from any database (such as sp_execute, sp_executesql, and sp_sdidebug).

In the following example, the extended stored procedure runs an operating system command to list all scripts in the BINN directory. Since it is not declared with the sp_ prefix, you must qualify its name with that of the database in which it is located:

```
Exec master..xp_cmdshell 'dir c:\mssql7\binn\*.sql'
```

Design of Extended Stored Procedures

It is not possible to create an extended stored procedure from just any DLL file. The file must be prepared in a special way. It is also not possible to create these files from Visual Basic, since it does not create classic DLL files, but just in-process versions of COM objects.

NOTE

Fortunately, it is possible to access code in the form of COM objects from Transact-SQL. Chapter 11 describes the creation and execution of such code in detail.

The development of extended stored procedures is based on the use of the Open Data Services API (ODS API). In the past, it was a tedious job and the developer had to perform all tasks manually. Nowadays, the process is automated in the Enterprise Edition of Visual C++ through the Extended Stored Proc Wizard. I will quickly demonstrate its use.

With the proper initialization code, the Extended Stored Proc Wizard generates Win32 DLL projects that contain an exported function. You should change the content of the exported function to perform the job of the future extended stored procedure. The wizard includes the header file (srv.h) and a library (opends60.lib) needed for using ODS in the code.

To create an extended stored procedure:

1. In Visual C++ Enterprise Edition, select File | New. The New dialog box should appear with the Projects tab opened. You need to set the name of the project. You could and should also use the name of the extended stored procedure as the name of the project. Extended stored procedure names commonly begin with the xp_ prefix.

2. Select Extended Stored Proc Wizard from the list of project types:

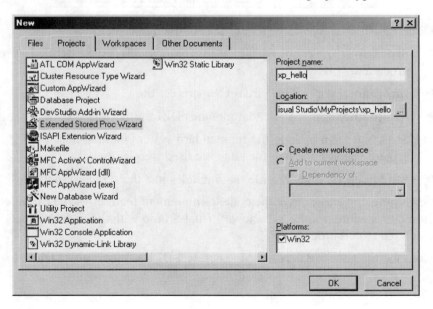

3. When you click OK, the program will launch the Extended Stored Proc Wizard. It prompts you to name your extended stored procedure:

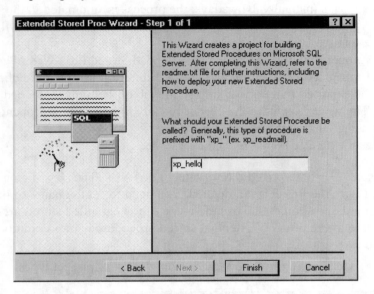

4. Click Finish. The wizard generates the following project files:

   ▶ **proc.cpp**   The exported Win32 function, which is the extended stored procedure

   ▶ **[projname].dsp**   The Visual C++ project file

   ▶ **[projname].cpp**   A file that includes DLL initialization code

   ▶ **StdAfx.h**   An include file for standard system include files, or project-specific include files that are used frequently

   ▶ **StdAfx.cpp**   A source file that includes just the standard includes

5. Open proc.cpp and change the code to implement features of the extended stored procedure. Figure 8-2 shows Visual Studio with the code of the extended stored procedure.

6. Compile the generated project to generate a DLL—**[projname].DLL**.

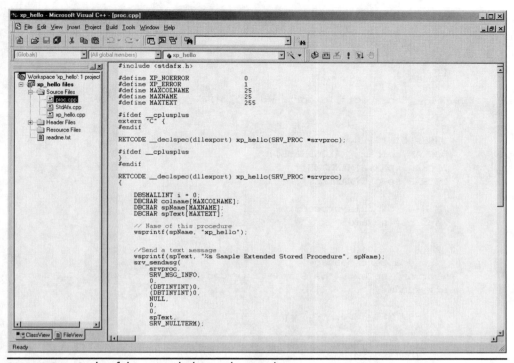

Figure 8-2   *Code of the extended stored procedure*

The following code listing shows the contents of proc.cpp. It contains the
exported Win32 function xp_hello. The function was generated by the wizard,
and it returns a simple message and a recordset that contains three records.

```
#include <stdafx.h>
#define XP_NOERROR              0
#define XP_ERROR               1
#define MAXCOLNAME            25
#define MAXNAME               25
#define MAXTEXT              255

#ifdef __cplusplus
extern "C" {
#endif
```

```
RETCODE __declspec(dllexport) xp_hello(SRV_PROC *srvproc);

#ifdef __cplusplus
}
#endif

RETCODE __declspec(dllexport) xp_hello(SRV_PROC *srvproc)
{

    DBSMALLINT i = 0;
    DBCHAR colname[MAXCOLNAME];
    DBCHAR spName[MAXNAME];
    DBCHAR spText[MAXTEXT];

    // Name of this procedure
    wsprintf(spName, "xp_hello");


    //Send a text message
    wsprintf(spText, "%s Sample Extended Stored Procedure", spName);
    srv_sendmsg(
        srvproc,
        SRV_MSG_INFO,
        0,
        (DBTINYINT)0,
        (DBTINYINT)0,
        NULL,
        0,
        0,
        spText,
        SRV_NULLTERM);


    //Set up the column names
    wsprintf(colname, "ID");
    srv_describe(srvproc, 1, colname, SRV_NULLTERM, SRVINT2,
                sizeof(DBSMALLINT), SRVINT2, sizeof(DBSMALLINT), 0);

    wsprintf(colname, "spName");
    srv_describe(srvproc, 2, colname, SRV_NULLTERM, SRVCHAR, MAXNAME,
                SRVCHAR, 0, NULL);

    wsprintf(colname, "Text");
    srv_describe(srvproc, 3, colname, SRV_NULLTERM, SRVCHAR, MAXTEXT,
                SRVCHAR, 0, NULL);


    // Update field 2 "spName", same value for all rows
    srv_setcoldata(srvproc, 2, spName);
```

```
    srv_setcollen(srvproc, 2, strlen(spName));


    // Send multiple rows of data
    for (i = 0; i < 3; i++) {

        // Update field 1 "ID"
        srv_setcoldata(srvproc, 1, &i);

        // Update field 3 "Text"
        wsprintf(spText,
"%d) Sample rowset generated by the %s extended stored procedure", i,
spName);

        srv_setcoldata(srvproc, 3, spText);
        srv_setcollen(srvproc, 3, strlen(spText));

        // Send the entire row
        srv_sendrow(srvproc);
    }


    // Now return the number of rows processed
    srv_senddone(srvproc, SRV_DONE_MORE | SRV_DONE_COUNT,
                 (DBUSMALLINT)0, (DBINT)i);

    return XP_NOERROR ;
}
```

TIP

If you are fluent enough in the techniques required to create extended stored procedures, you should not be spending your time creating business applications. You should be working on more fundamental stuff like operating systems or RDBMSs and devoting your time to hacking. Let the rest of us collect the easy money.

Registering the Extended Stored Procedure

Once the DLL is compiled, the extended stored procedure has to be registered on the server before it can be used:

1. Copy the xp_hello.dll file to the SQL Server \...\Binn folder.

2. Register the new extended stored procedure using the SQL Server Enterprise Manager, or by executing the following SQL command:

```
sp_addextendedproc 'xp_hello', 'XP_HELLO.DLL'
```

Once the extended stored procedure is registered, you can test it using Query Analyzer (see Figure 8-3).

You should carefully test the new extended stored procedure. If you find out that it is not working as expected or that you need to make some modification, you need to unregister (drop) the extended stored procedure by using the following SQL command:

```
sp_dropextendedproc 'xp_hello'
```

When the extended stored procedure is executed in SQL Server, it is loaded into memory. It stays there until SQL Server is shut down or until you issue a command to remove it from memory:

```
DBCC xp_hello(FREE)
```

To register an extended stored procedure from Enterprise Manager, right-click the Extended Stored Procedures node in the *master* database and select New Extended

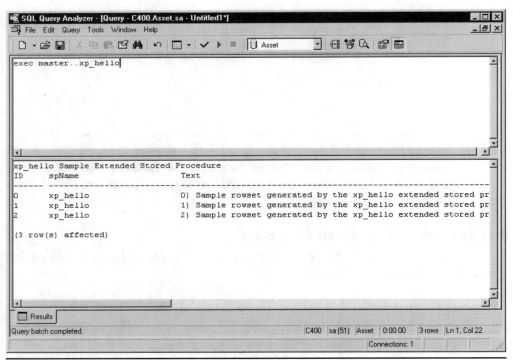

Figure 8-3   *Using the extended stored procedure*

Stored Procedure. Enterprise Manager prompts you for the name of the extended stored procedure and the location of the DLL file:

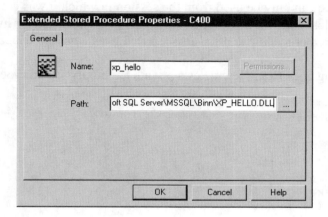

It is also simple to remove an extended stored procedure using Enterprise Manager. You merely right-click it and select Delete from the pop-up menu.

NOTE

The trouble with extended stored procedures is that they work in the address space of SQL Server. Therefore, an extended stored procedure that doesn't behave properly could crash SQL Server. Such a problem is not likely to occur because SQL Server monitors the behavior of extended stored procedures. If an extended stored procedure attempts to reference memory outside of its address space, SQL Server will terminate it. Commonsense programming practices (using error checking, doing exception handling, and thoroughly testing final code) will further reduce the possibility of errors.

Temporary Stored Procedures

Temporary stored procedures are related to stored procedures as temporary tables are related to tables. You use them when you expect to reuse the execution plan of a stored procedure within a limited time frame. Although you can achieve the same functionality with a standard user-defined stored procedure, temporary stored procedures are a better solution because you do not have to worry about maintenance issues (such as dropping the stored procedure).

Temporary stored procedures reside in the *tempdb* database and must be named with the prefix #. You create them in the same way you create user-defined stored procedures. The only change is the use of a # as a name prefix. This prefix signals the server to create the procedure as a temporary stored procedure. This kind of stored procedure can only be used from the session in which it was created. When the session is closed, it will be dropped automatically. This behavior indicates why this type of stored procedure is often also referred to as a *private temporary stored procedure*.

The following code example creates a private temporary stored procedure:

```
Create Procedure #prGetId
    @Make varchar(50),
    @Model varchar(50)
as
    Select EquipmentId
    from Equipment
    where Make = @Make
    and Model = @Model
```

Sometimes, all user-defined stored procedures in *tempdb* are referred to as temporary stored procedures. This is incorrect because there are major differences between the two. For example, user-defined stored procedures stored in the *tempdb* database are accessible to all authorized users and are not limited to the session in which they were created. These stored procedures stay in *tempdb* until the server is shut down, at which time the complete content of *tempdb* is flushed.

Global Temporary Stored Procedures

Global temporary stored procedures are related to temporary stored procedures as global temporary tables are related to private temporary tables. They also reside in the *tempdb* database, but they use the prefix ##. You create them in the same way you create temporary stored procedures. The only difference is that they are visible and usable from all sessions. In fact, permissions are not required and the owner cannot even deny other users access to them.

When the session that has created the procedure is closed, no new sessions will be able to execute the stored procedure. After all instances of the stored procedure already running are finished, the procedure is dropped automatically.

The following code example creates a global temporary stored procedure:

```
Create Procedure ##prInsertEquipment
    @Make varchar(50),
    @Model varchar(50),
```

```
        @EqType varchar(50)
as
        declare @EqTypeId smallint
        select @EqTypeId = EqTypeId   -- This is OK in a perfect world,
        from EqType                   -- but it is based on the
        Where EqType = @EqType        -- unreasonable assumption that
                                      -- you can identify the key using
                                      -- the description.
        Insert Equipment (Make, Model, EqTypeId)
        Values (@Make, @Model, @EqTypeId)
```

Remote Stored Procedures

This type is actually a user-defined stored procedure that resides on a remote server. The only challenge implicit in this type of stored procedure is that the local server has to be set to allow the remote use of stored procedures.

For more information, search SQL Server Books Online using the following string: How to set up a remote server to allow the use of remote stored procedures.

TIP

Microsoft, in fact, considers this mechanism as a legacy of older versions of SQL Server. Heterogeneous queries are the recommended way to execute stored procedures or access tables on other servers.

User-Defined Functions

The ability to design user-defined Transact-SQL functions is a new feature in SQL Server 2000. In earlier versions, you were only able to use built-in functions.

Design of User-Defined Functions

User-defined functions can be created using the Create Function statement, changed using Alter Function, and deleted using Drop Function. You can use sp_help and sp_stored_procedures to get information about a function, and sp_helptext to obtain its source code. From Enterprise Manager, you can use the same technique to manage user-defined functions as you used to create and manage stored procedures.

Functions can accept zero, one, or more input parameters, and must return a single return value. The returned value can be scalar, or it can be a table. Input parameters can be values of any data type except `timestamp`, `cursor`, and `table`. Return values can be of any data type except `timestamp`, `cursor`, `text`, `ntext`, and `image`.

The Create Function statement has the following syntax:

```
Create Function [owner_name.]function_name
(
    [ {@parameter_name scalar_data_type [= default]} [,...n] ]
)
returns scalar_data_type
        |Table
        |return_variable Table({column_def|table_constraint}[,…n])
[With {Encryption|Schemabinding}[,…n] ]
[As]
{Begin function_body End}
| Return [(] {value|select-stmt} [)]
```

The following example produces a function that will return the quarter for a specified date:

```
Create Function fnQuarterString
-- returns quarter in form of '3Q2000'.
    (
    @dtmDate datetime
    )
Returns char(6) -- quarter like 3Q2000
As
Begin
    Return (DateName(q, @dtmDate) + 'Q' + DateName(yyyy, @dtmDate))
End
```

As I mentioned in Chapter 5, and as you can see in Figure 8-4, to reference a function, you must specify both the object owner and the object identifier.

The function in the previous example had just one Return statement in the body of the function. In fact, a function can be designed with flow control and other Transact-SQL statements. A function can even contain more than one Return statement. Under different conditions, they can serve as exit points from the function. The only requirement is that the last statement in the function body be an unconditional

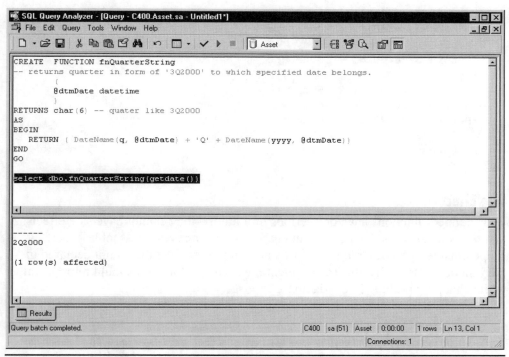

```
CREATE   FUNCTION fnQuarterString
-- returns quarter in form of '3Q2000' to which specified date belongs.
         (
         @dtmDate datetime
         )
RETURNS char(6) -- quater like 3Q2000
AS
BEGIN
    RETURN ( DateName(q, @dtmDate) + 'Q' + DateName(yyyy, @dtmDate))
END
GO

select dbo.fnQuarterString(getdate())
```

```
------
2Q2000

(1 row(s) affected)
```

Figure 8-4 *Using a function by specifying an object owner and an object identifier*

Return statement. The following function illustrates this principle in returning a date three business days after the specified date:

```
Create Function fnThreeBusDays
-- returns date 3 business day after the specified date
     (@dtmDate datetime)
Returns datetime
As
Begin
Declare @inyDayOfWeek tinyint
Set @inyDayOfWeek = DatePart(dw, @dtmDate)
Set @dtmDate = Convert(datetime, Convert(varchar, @dtmDate, 101))

If @inyDayOfWeek = 1 -- Sunday
     Return DateAdd(d, 3, @dtmDate )
```

```
If @inyDayOfWeek = 7 -- Saturday
    Return DateAdd(d, 4, @dtmDate )
If @inyDayOfWeek = 6 -- Friday
    Return DateAdd(d, 5, @dtmDate )
If @inyDayOfWeek = 5 -- Thursday
    Return DateAdd(d, 5, @dtmDate )
If @inyDayOfWeek = 4 -- Wednesday
    Return DateAdd(d, 5, @dtmDate )

Return DateAdd(d, 3, @dtmDate )
End
```

Side Effects

User-defined functions have one serious limitation—they cannot have side effects. A *function side effect* is any permanent change to resources (such as tables) that have a scope outside of the function (such as a nontemporary table that is not declared in the function). Basically, this requirement means that a function should return a value while changing nothing in the database.

TIP

In some development environments like C or Visual Basic, a developer can write a function that can perform some additional activities or changes, but it is a matter of good design and discipline not to abuse that opportunity.

SQL Server prevents you from creating side effects by limiting which Transact-SQL statements can be used inside a function:

▶ Assignment statements (Set or Select) referencing objects local to the function (such as local variables and a return value)

▶ Flow control statements

▶ Update, Insert, and Delete statements that update local table variables

▶ Declare statements that define local variables or cursors

▶ Statements that declare, open, close, fetch, and deallocate local cursors (the only Fetch statements allowed are ones that retrieve information from a cursor into local variables)

Use of Built-in Functions

User-defined functions cannot call built-in functions that return different data on each call, such as these:

@@CONNECTIONS	@@TIMETICKS
@@CPU_BUSY	@@TOTAL_ERRORS
@@IDLE	@@TOTAL_READ
@@IO_BUSY	@@TOTAL_WRITE
@@MAX_CONNECTIONS	GetDate()
@@PACK_RECEIVED	NewId()
@@PACK_SENT	Rand()
@@PACKET_ERRORS	TextPtr()

Notice that GetDate() is among the forbidden functions. If you try to use it inside a user-defined function, SQL Server will report an error, as shown in Figure 8-5.

Encryption

As is the case with stored procedures, functions can be encrypted so that nobody can see their source code. You just need to create or alter the function using the With Encryption option.

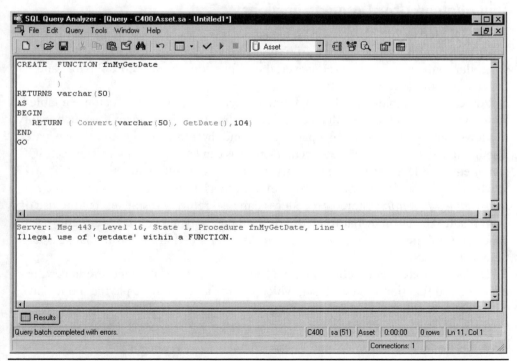

Figure 8-5   *Limitation on use of built-in functions in user-defined functions*

Schema-Binding

A new option, With Schemabinding, allows developers to *schema-bind* a user-defined function to database objects (such as tables, views, and other user-defined functions) that it references. Once the function is schema-bound, it is not possible to make schema changes on underlying objects. All attempts to drop the objects and all attempts to alter underlying objects (which would change the object schema) will fail.

A function can be schema-bound only if all of the following criteria are satisfied:

▶ All existing user-defined functions and views referencing the objects referenced by the function must already be schema-bound.

▶ All database objects that the function references must reside in the same database as the function. References to database objects cannot have server or database qualifiers. Only object owner qualifiers and object identifiers are allowed.

▶ The user who executes the Create (or Alter) Function statement must have References permissions on all referenced database objects.

Table-Valued User-Defined Functions

Since SQL Server 2000 has a `table` data type, it is possible to design a user-defined function that returns a table. The primary use of table-valued user-defined functions is similar to the use of views. However, these functions are far more flexible and provide additional functionality.

You can use a table-valued user-defined function anywhere you can use a table (or view). In this respect, table-valued user-defined functions implement the functionality of views, but functions can have parameters, and therefore are dynamic. Views are also limited to a single Select statement. Functions can have one or more Transact-SQL statements inside, enabling them to implement more complex functionality. That is why functions of this type are often referred to as *multistatement table-valued user-defined functions*. Stored procedures can also return a result set, but the use of such result sets is somewhat limited. For example, only a result set returned by a function (and not a stored procedure) can be referenced in the From clause of a Select statement.

To demonstrate this functionality, the following Select statement references the user-defined function fnDueDays(), which returns a list of lease payment due dates. The statement returns a list of remaining payments and due dates.

```
select DD.TermId, DD.DueDate, Inventory.Lease
from dbo.fnDueDays('1/1/2000','1/1/2004','monthly') DD, Inventory
where InventoryId = 8
and DD.DueDate > GetDate()
```

The result looks like this:

```
TermId      DueDate                     Lease
----------- --------------------------- ------------
3           2000-04-01 00:00:00         87.7500
4           2000-05-01 00:00:00         87.7500
5           2000-06-01 00:00:00         87.7500
6           2000-07-01 00:00:00         87.7500
7           2000-08-01 00:00:00         87.7500
...
```

The stored procedure prListTerms has functionality similar to the functionality of the fnDueDates() function. But to perform additional filtering of the result set returned by the stored procedure, you would first need to load the result set into a temporary table:

```
Create Table #tbl(TermId int, DueDate smalldatetime)

Insert Into #Tbl(TermId, DueDate)
    Exec prListTerms '1/1/2000','1/1/2004','monthly'

Select #tbl.TermId, #tbl.DueDate, Inventory.Lease
From #tbl, Inventory
Where InventoryId = 8
And #tbl.DueDate > GetDate()

Drop Table #tbl
```

This is much more complicated than using the comparable function.
Let's investigate the internals of the fnDueDate() function:

```
Create Function fnDueDays
-- return list of due days for the leasing
(
    @dtsStartDate smalldatetime,
    @dtsEndDate smalldatetime,
    @chvLeaseFrequency varchar(20)
)
Returns @tblTerms table
    (
    TermID int,
    DueDate smalldatetime
    )

As
```

```
Begin

Declare @insTermsCount smallint -- number of intervals
Declare @insTerms smallint -- number of intervals

-- calculate number of terms
Select @insTermsCount =
  Case @chvLeaseFrequency
    When 'monthly'
            then DateDIFF(month, @dtsStartDate, @dtsEndDate)
    When 'semi-monthly'
            then 2 * DateDIFF(month, @dtsStartDate, @dtsEndDate)
    When 'bi-weekly'
            then DateDIFF(week, @dtsStartDate, @dtsEndDate)/2
    When 'weekly'
            then DateDIFF(week, @dtsStartDate, @dtsEndDate)
    When 'quarterly'
            then DateDIFF(qq, @dtsStartDate, @dtsEndDate)
    When 'yearly'
            then DateDIFF(y, @dtsStartDate, @dtsEndDate)
  End

-- generate list of due dates
Set @insTerms = 1
While @insTerms <= @insTermsCount
Begin
  Insert @tblTerms (TermID, DueDate)
  Values (@insTerms, Convert(smalldatetime, CASE
        When @chvLeaseFrequency = 'monthly'
            then DateADD(month,@insTerms, @dtsStartDate)
        When @chvLeaseFrequency = 'semi-monthly'
        and @insTerms/2 =  Cast(@insTerms as float)/2
            then DateADD(month, @insTerms/2, @dtsStartDate)
        When @chvLeaseFrequency = 'semi-monthly'
        and @insTerms/2 <> Cast(@insTerms as float)/2
            then DateADD(dd, 15,
                        DateADD(month, @insTerms/2, @dtsStartDate))
        When @chvLeaseFrequency = 'bi-weekly'
            then DateADD(week, @insTerms*2, @dtsStartDate)
        When @chvLeaseFrequency = 'weekly'
            then DateADD(week, @insTerms, @dtsStartDate)
        When @chvLeaseFrequency = 'quarterly'
            then DateADD(qq, @insTerms, @dtsStartDate)
        When @chvLeaseFrequency = 'yearly'
            then DateADD(y, @insTerms, @dtsStartDate)
        End , 105))
```

```
        Select @insTerms = @insTerms + 1
End

Return
End
```

Let me point out to you a few differences between these functions and scalar functions. User-defined functions that return a table have a table variable definition in the Returns clause:

```
...
Returns @tblTerms table
    (
    TermID int,
    DueDate smalldatetime
    )
...
```

In the body of the function, there are statements that fill the contents of the table variable:

```
...
    Insert @tblTerms (TermID, DueDate)
    Values (@insTerms, Convert(smalldatetime, CASE
                        When @chvLeaseFrequency = 'monthly'
...
```

The Return statement at the end of the function does not specify a value. As soon as it is reached, SQL Server returns the contents of the table variable to the caller:

```
Return
End
```

Inline Table-Valued User-Defined Functions

An *inline table-valued user-defined function* is a special type of table-valued user-defined function. Its purpose is to implement parameterized views.

The syntax of an inline table-valued user-defined function is a bit different from the syntax of other functions:

```
Create Function [owner_name.]function_name
(
    [ {@parameter_name scalar_data_type [= default]} [,...n] ]
```

```
)
Returns Table
        [With {Encryption|Schemabinding}[,...n] ]
[As]
| Return (select-stmt)
```

You do not have to define the format of the return value. It is enough to specify just the Table keyword. An inline table-valued function does not have the body of a function. A result set is created by a single Select statement in the Returns clause. It is best to demonstrate this feature with an example. The following function returns only a segment of a table based on a role the user belongs to. The idea is that a manager or any other employee can see only equipment from his own department:

```
Create Function fn_DepartmentEquipment
    ( @chvUserName sysname )
Returns table
As
Return (
      Select InventoryId, Make + ' ' + model Model, Location
      From Inventory inner join Contact C
      On Inventory.OwnerId = C.ContactId
            Inner Join Contact Manager
            On C.OrgUnitId = Manager.OrgUnitId
                  Inner Join Equipment
                  On Inventory.EquipmentId = Equipment.EquipmentId
                        Inner Join Location
                        On Inventory.LocationId = Location.LocationId
      Where Manager.UserName = @chvUserName
      )
Go
```

You can use this function in any place where a view or table is allowed, such as in a Select statement:

```
Select *
From fn_DepartmentEquipment ('dejans')
Go
```

Figure 8-6 shows the result of such a statement.

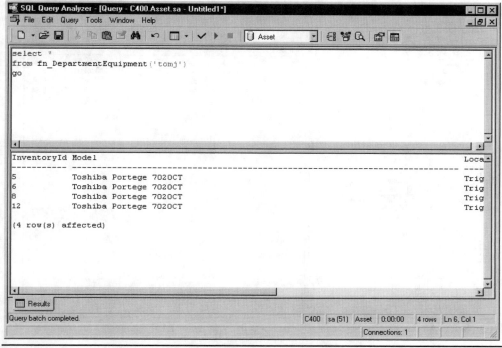

Figure 8-6   *Using an inline table-valued user-defined function*

Managing User-Defined Functions in Enterprise Manager

You can access user-defined functions from Enterprise Manager, as shown in Figure 8-7.

If you double-click a function, SQL Server displays a modal form for editing its properties (that is, code and permissions). This editor is identical to the editor you use to edit stored procedures (see Figure 8-8).

If you right-click a function and select New User Defined Function, SQL Server opens a form with a template for creating a new function (see Figure 8-9).

Once you have written or changed the function, you can click the Check Syntax button to verify it, then click OK or Apply to compile and save it.

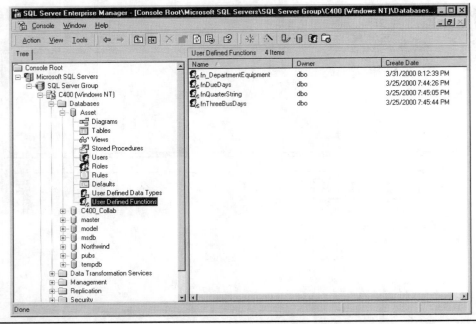

Figure 8-7 Managing user-defined functions in Enterprise Manager

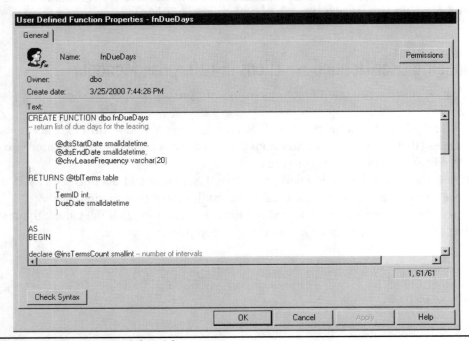

Figure 8-8 Editing user-defined functions

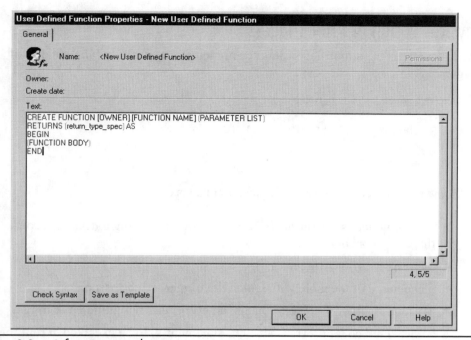

Figure 8-9   *A function template*

Triggers

Triggers are a unique type of procedure. Triggers are very similar to events—a type of procedure in certain programming languages such as Visual Basic. Events in Visual Basic are initiated by the system when certain actions occur (for instance, a form is loaded, a text box receives focus, or a key is pressed).

Triggers are associated with a table in a database and executed by SQL Server when a specific change occurs in the table. The change could be the result of the following modification statements:

▶ Insert

▶ Update

▶ Delete

SQL Server 7.0 and earlier versions recognized only one type of trigger. In SQL Server 2000, this type is called an *After trigger.* SQL Server 2000 introduces a new type—an *Instead-of trigger.* In the following sections, we first examine the standard (After) triggers and then introduce the new Instead-of trigger.

Physical Design of After Triggers

The following is the simplified syntax for implementing the core functionality of triggers:

```
Create Trigger trigger_name
On table
{After { [Delete] [,] [Insert] [,] [Update] }
   As
      sql_statement [...n]
```

As a stored procedure, a trigger logically consists of

▶ A *header*, which is a Transact-SQL statement for creating a trigger. It consists of three components:

  ▶ The name of the trigger

  ▶ The name of the table with which the trigger will be associated

  ▶ A modification statement (that is, an event) that will initiate the trigger

▶ A *body*, which contains Transact-SQL statement(s) to be executed at runtime.

The following example first creates a new table called MyEquipment, and then populates it with Make and Model information from the Equipment table, and finally creates a trigger. The trigger is named trMyEquipment_D and is associated with the MyEquipment table. It is fired after a Delete statement is executed against the table. Its function is very simple—it notifies the user regarding actions and the number of records that have been deleted.

```
Create Table MyEquipment
     (Id int identity,
      Description varchar(500))
GO

-- populate table
Insert MyEquipment(Description)
     Select Make + ' ' + Model from Equipment
GO

Create Trigger trMyEquipment_D
On dbo.MyEquipment
After Delete  -- For Delete
```

```
As
     Print 'You have just deleted '
          + Cast(@@rowcount as varchar)
          + ' record(s)!'
Go
```

To execute the trigger, you need to execute the Delete statement:

```
Delete MyEquipment
Where Id = 2
```

SQL Server returns the following:

```
You have just deleted 1 record(s)!

(1 row(s) affected)
```

You can also execute the Delete statement to delete multiple records:

```
Delete MyEquipment
```

Even in this case, the trigger will *not* be fired once for each record. You will receive just one message:

```
You have just deleted 4 record(s)!

(4 row(s) affected)
```

For this reason, it is important to design your trigger to handle actions against multiple records. You will see more reasons in following paragraphs.

Inserted and Deleted Virtual Tables

SQL Server maintains two temporary virtual tables during the execution of a trigger: *Deleted* and *Inserted*. These tables contain all the records inserted or deleted during the operation that fired the trigger. You can use this feature to perform additional verification or additional activities on affected records.

You are probably wondering if there is an Updated table. No. Because an Update can be performed as a combination of the Delete and Insert statements, records that were updated will appear in both the Deleted and Inserted tables.

SQL Server does not create both tables in all cases. For example, in a trigger fired during a Delete statement, only a Deleted virtual table is accessible. A reference to an Inserted virtual table will cause an error.

The following table summarizes the presence of virtual tables in the relevant Transact-SQL statements:

Modification Statement	Deleted	Inserted
Insert	N/A	New records
Update	Old version of updated records	New version of updated records
Delete	Deleted records	N/A

The following modifies the trigger from the previous section to display which records are deleted:

```
Alter Trigger trMyEquipment_D
On dbo.MyEquipment
After Delete      -- For Delete
As
    Select 'You have just deleted following '
        + Cast(@@rowcount as varchar)
        + ' record(s)!'

    Select * from deleted
go
```

When you delete all records from the MyEquipment table, SQL Server returns the following:

```
----------------------------------------------------------------
You have just deleted following 5 record(s)!

(1 row(s) affected)

Id          Description
----------- ----------------------------------------------------
1           Toshiba Portege 7020CT
2           Sony Trinitron 17XE
3           NEC V90
4           HP LaserJet 4
5           HP LaserJet 4

(5 row(s) affected)
```

You can use values from these tables, but you cannot modify them directly. If you need to perform some operation on records that were inserted, for example, you should not try to change them in the Inserted table. The proper method would be to issue a regular Transact-SQL statement against the original table. In the Where or From clause, you can reference the virtual table (Inserted) and in that way limit the subset of the original table that you are targeting.

In the following example, the trigger calculates a SOUNDEX code for the Make and Model of the Equipment records affected by the Insert or Update statement that has fired the trigger:

```
Alter Trigger trEquipment_IU
On dbo.Equipment
After Insert, Update     -- For Insert, Update
As
    -- precalculate ModelSDX and MakeSDX field
    -- to speed up use of SOUNDEX function
    update Equipment
    Set ModelSDX = SOUNDEX(Model),
        MakeSDX = SOUNDEX(Make)
    where EquipmentId IN (Select EquipmentId from Inserted)
```

What Triggers a Trigger?

A trigger is executed *once for each modification statement* (Insert, Update, or Delete). An After trigger is fired *after* the modification statement finishes *successfully*. If a statement fails for another reason (for example, foreign key or check constraints), the trigger is not invoked. For example, the Equipment table has the following Delete trigger:

```
Alter Trigger Equipment_DeleteTrigger
On dbo.Equipment
After Delete      -- For Delete
As
Print 'One or more rows are deleted in Equipment table!'
```

If you attempt to delete all records from the table:

```
delete Equipment
```

SQL Server aborts the execution because there is a foreign key relationship with the Inventory table. The execution is aborted before the trigger is invoked:

```
Server: Msg 547, Level 16, State 1, Line 1
DELETE statement conflicted with COLUMN REFERENCE constraint
'FK_Inventory_Equipment'. The conflict occurred in database
'Asset', table 'Inventory', column 'EquipmentId'.
The statement has been terminated.
```

A trigger and developer might have different definitions of what is a successfully finished modification to a table. The trigger will fire even when a modification statement affected zero records. The following example is based on the assumption that the record with EquipmentId set to 77777 does not exist in the database:

```
Delete Equipment
Where EquipmentId = 77777
```

SQL Server nonchalantly prints from the trigger:

```
One or more rows are deleted in Equipment table!
```

Full Syntax of After Triggers

After triggers were the only type of triggers before SQL Server 2000. After triggers in SQL Server 2000 have the same syntax as before except that the keyword For is replaced with After:

```
Create Trigger trigger_name
On table
[With Encryption]
{
    {After { [Delete] [,] [Insert] [,] [Update] }
        [With Append]
         [Not For Replication]
        As
            sql_statement [...n]
    }
    |
    {After { [Insert] [,] [Update] }
        [With Append]
        [Not For Replication]
        As
        {    If Update (Column)
            [{And | Or} Update (Column)]
                [...n]
            | If (Columns_Updated()
                            {bitwise_operator}
                            updated_bitmask)
                { comparison_operator} column_bitmask [...n]
        }
            sql_statement [ ...n]
    }
}
```

If a trigger is defined with the With Encryption clause, SQL Server encrypts it so that its code remains concealed. Keep in mind that you need to preserve the source code in a script outside SQL Server if you plan to modify it later.

The Not For Replication clause indicates that SQL Server should not fire a trigger during replication of the table.

The With Append clause is used only when the compatibility mode of SQL Server is set to a value less than 70. For more details, refer to SQL Server Books Online.

It is possible to determine which columns were updated during the Update operation. Transact-SQL includes two functions that you can use within the trigger—Update() and Columns_Updated():

```
If Update (column)
sql_statement [ ...n]


If (Columns_Updated() {bitwise_operator} updated_bitmask)
                    {comparison_operator} column_bitmask [...n]
    sql_statement [ ...n]
```

You can now modify your previously used trigger to update only the fields that were changed:

```
Alter Trigger trEquipment_IU
On dbo.Equipment
After Insert, Update    -- For Insert, Update
As
    -- precalculate ModelSDX and MakeSDX field
    -- to speed up use of SOUNDEX function
    if Update(Model)
        update Equipment
        Set ModelSDX = SOUNDEX(Model)
        where EquipmentId IN (Select EquipmentId from Inserted)

    if Update(Make)
        update Equipment
        Set MakeSDX = SOUNDEX(Make)
        where EquipmentId IN (Select EquipmentId from Inserted)
    go
```

The Update() function might not perform exactly as you expect. In fact, it returns True for columns that were *referenced* during the Transact-SQL statement rather than for columns that were actually *changed*. For example, if you issue the following

Update statement, SQL Server references the `Make` column of all records, and the trigger recalculates the SOUNDEX code in all records:

```
Update Equipment
Set Make = Make
```

TIP

This behavior might cause some problems for you if you forget about it. However, in some cases, you can use it to your advantage. For example, to speed up the upload of information to the table, you can temporarily disable triggers (see the "Disabling Triggers" section, later in this chapter). Later, when you want to execute the triggers (for example, to verify their validity and/or perform additional activities), you can use this feature to initiate triggers for records that are present in the table.

Too often, developers forget that the presence of a Default constraint in a column causes the Update() function to return True for that column during the execution of the Insert statement. This will occur even if the Insert statement did not reference the column itself.

The Columns_Updated() function operates with a bitmap that is related to the positions of columns. You can investigate its contents if you use an integer bitmask. To test whether the third column in a table was updated, you can use the following:

```
if Columns_Updated() & 3 = 3
        print 'Column 3 was updated!'
```

The ampersand (&) is a *binary and* operator, with which you can test the value of the flag.

Naturally, hard-coding the order of columns does not make much sense. The real value of this function is as a means of looping through all the columns that were updated and performing specified actions.

The following trigger loops through columns and displays which ones were updated:

```
Create Trigger trEquipmentN_IU_2
-- list all columns that were changed
On dbo.EquipmentN
after Insert, Update
As

    Set Nocount Off
    declare @intCountColumn int,
            @intColumn int
```

```
-- count columns in the table
Select @intCountColumn = Count(Ordinal_position)
From Information_Schema.Columns
Where Table_Name = 'EquipmentN'

Select Columns_Updated() "COLUMNS UPDATED"
Select @intColumn = 1

-- loop through columns
while @intColumn <= @intCountColumn
begin
    if Columns_Updated() & @intColumn = @intColumn
        Print 'Column ('
            +   Cast(@intColumn as varchar)
            + ') '
            + Col_Name(Object_ID('EquipmentN'), @intColumn)
            + ' has been changed!'
    set @intColumn = @intColumn + 1
End
```

Use the following statement to test this trigger:

```
Insert EquipmentN(Make, Model, EqTypeID)
Values('Acme', '9000', 1)
```

Handling Changes on Multiple Records

The following example is a trigger designed to record the name of the user that changed the status of an order in the ActivityLog table, along with some additional information:

```
Create Trigger trOrderStatus_U_1
On dbo.[Order]
After Update     -- For Update
As
    declare @intOldOrderStatusId int,
            @intNewOrderStatusId int

    If Update (OrderStatusId)
    Begin

        select @intOldOrderStatusId = OrderStatusId from deleted
        select @intNewOrderStatusId = OrderStatusId from inserted
```

```
Insert into ActivityLog( Activity,
                         LogDate,
                         UserName,
                         Note)
  values ( 'Order.OrderStatusId',
           GetDate(),
           User_Name(),
           'Value changed from '
           + Cast( @intOldOrderStatusId as varchar)
           + ' to '
           + Cast((@intNewOrderStatusId) as varchar)
         )
End
```

This method is far from perfect. Can you detect the problem?

It records the user who has changed the status of an order only when the user changes no more than a single order:

```
select @intOldOrderStatusId = OrderStatusId from deleted
```

Let me remind you that if the Select statement returns more than one record, the variable(s) will be filled with values from the last record. This is sometimes all that is required. If you have restricted access to the table and the only way to change the status is through a stored procedure (which allows only one record to be modified at a time), then this is sufficient.

Unfortunately, there is always a way to work around any restriction and possibly issue an Update statement that will change the status of all tables. The following is the proper solution:

```
Alter Trigger trOrderStatus_U
On dbo.[Order]
After Update -- For Update
As
    If Update (OrderStatusId)
    begin

        Insert into ActivityLog( Activity,
                                 LogDate,
                                 UserName,
                                 Note)
        Select   'Order.OrderStatusId',
                 GetDate(),
                 User_Name(),
```

```
                    'Value changed from '
                    + Cast( d.OrderStatusId as varchar)
                    + ' to '
                    + Cast( i.OrderStatusId as varchar)

            from deleted d inner join inserted i
            on d.OrderId = i.OrderId
    end
```

In this case, a set operation is used and one or more records from the Deleted and Inserted virtual tables will be recorded in the ActivityLog.

Nested and Recursive Triggers

A trigger can fire other triggers on the same or other tables when it inserts, updates, or deletes records in them. This technique is called *nesting triggers*.

If a trigger changes records in its own table, it can fire another instance of itself. Such an invocation is called *direct invocation of recursive triggers*.

There is another scenario in which recursive invocation of triggers might occur. The trigger on one table might fire a trigger on a second table. The trigger on the second table might change the first table again, and the first trigger will fire again. This scenario is called *indirect invocation of recursive triggers*.

All these scenarios might be ideal for implementing referential integrity and business rules, but they might also be too complicated to design, understand, and manage. If you are not careful, the first trigger might call the second, then the second might call the first, then the first the second, and so on.

Very often, the SQL Server environment is configured to prevent this kind of behavior. To disable nested triggers and recursive triggers, you need to use the stored procedure sp_configure to set the Nested Triggers server option and use the Alter Table statement to set the Recursive_Triggers option to Off mode. Keep in mind that recursive triggers will be disabled automatically if you disable nested triggers.

Trigger Restrictions

The following are the trigger restrictions, none of which usually cause any difficulties:

▶ The trigger must be created with the first statement in a batch.

▶ The name of the trigger is its Transact-SQL identifier, and therefore must be no more than 128 characters long.

▶ The trigger's name must be unique in the database.

▶ A trigger can only be associated with one table, but one table can have many triggers. In the past, only one trigger could be associated with one modification statement on one table. Now, each required function can be implemented in a separate trigger. By implementing these features in separate triggers, you assure that the triggers will be easier to understand and manage.

▶ Triggers cannot be nested to more than 32 levels, nor can they be invoked recursively more than 32 times. Attempting to do so causes SQL Server to return an error.

▶ A trigger must not contain any of following Transact-SQL statements:

Alter Database	Drop Database
Alter Procedure	Drop Default
Alter Table	Drop Index
Alter Trigger	Drop Procedure
Alter View	Drop Rule
Create Database	Drop Table
Create Default	Drop Trigger
Create Index	Drop View
Create Procedure	Grant
Create Rule	Load Database
Create Schema	Load Log
Create Table	Reconfigure
Create Trigger	Restore Database
Create View	Restore Log
Deny	Revoke
Disk Init	Truncate Table
Disk Resize	Update Statistics

Instead-of Triggers

Instead-of triggers are executed instead of the modification statement that has initiated them. The following trigger is executed when an attempt is made to delete records from the MyEquipment table. It will report an error instead of allowing the deletion:

```
Create Trigger itrMyEquipment_D
On dbo.MyEquipment
instead of Delete
As
    -- deletion in this table is not allowed
    raiserror('Deletion of records in MyEquipment '
            + 'table is not allowed', 16, 1)
GO
```

Instead-of triggers are executed after changes to base tables occur in Inserted and Deleted virtual tables, but before any change to the base tables is executed. Therefore, the trigger can use information in the Inserted and Deleted tables. In the following example, a trigger tests whether some of the records that would have been deleted are in use in the Equipment table:

```
Create Trigger itrEqType_D
On dbo.EqType
instead of Delete
As
If exists(select *
    from Equipment
    where EqTypeId in (select EqTypeId
                        from deleted)
    )
    raiserror('Some recs in EqType are in use in Equipment table!',
            16, 1)
else
    delete EqType
    where EqTypeId in (select EqTypeId from deleted)
GO
```

Instead-of triggers are initiated before any constraints. This behavior is very different from that of After triggers. Therefore, the code for an Instead-of trigger must perform all checking and processing that would normally be performed by constraints.

Usually, an Instead-of trigger executes the modification statement (Insert, Update, or Delete) that initiates it. The modification statement does not initiate the trigger again. If some After triggers and/or constraints are defined on the table or view, they will be executed as though the Instead-of trigger does not exist.

A table or a view can have only one Instead-of trigger (and more than one After trigger) per modification type.

Triggers on Views

Instead-of triggers can be defined on views also. In the following example, a trigger is created on a view that displays fields from two tables:

```
Create View dbo.vEquipment
AS
Select Equipment.EquipmentId,
       Equipment.Make,
       Equipment.Model,
       EqType.EqType
From Equipment Inner Join EqType
On Equipment.EqTypeId = EqType.EqTypeId
Go

Create Trigger itr_vEquipment_I
On dbo.vEquipment
instead of Insert
As

-- If the EqType is new, insert it
If exists(select EqType
          from inserted
          where EqType not in (select EqType
                               from EqType))
    -- we need to insert the new ones
    insert into EqType(EqType)
        select EqType
        from inserted
        where EqType not in (select EqType
                             from EqType)

-- now you can insert new equipment
Insert into Equipment(Make, Model, EqTypeId)
Select inserted.Make, inserted.Model, EqType.EqTypeId
From inserted Inner Join EqType
On inserted.EqType = EqType.EqType

GO

Insert Into vEquipment(EquipmentId, Make, Model, EqType)
Values (-777, 'Microsoft', 'Natural Keyboard', 'keyboard')
```

The trigger first examines whether the Inserted table contains EqType values that do not exist in EqTable. If they exist, they will be inserted in the EqType table. At the end, values from the Inserted table are added to the Equipment table.

The previous example illustrates one unusual feature in the use of Instead-of triggers on views. Since EquipmentId is referenced by the view, it can (and must) be specified by the modification statement (Insert statement). The trigger can (and will) ignore the specified value since it is inserted automatically (`EquipmentId` is an identity field in the base table). The reason for this behavior is that the Inserted and Deleted tables have different structures from the base tables on which the view is based. They have the same structure as the Select statement inside the view.

Columns in the view can be nullable or not nullable. The column is nullable if its expression in the Select list of the view satisfies one of the following criteria:

▶ The view column references a base table column that is nullable.

▶ The view column expression uses arithmetic operators or functions.

If the column does not allow nulls, an Insert statement must provide a value for it. This is the reason a value for EquipmentId column was needed in the previous example. An Update statement must provide values for all nonnullable columns referenced by the Set clause in a view with an Instead-of update trigger.

NOTE

You must specify values even for view columns that are mapped to `timestamp`, *Identity, or computed base table columns.*

You can use the `AllowNull` property of the ColumnProperty() function (table function) to examine which fields are nullable from code.

NOTE

The previous code example is much more important than you might think. It allows you to insert a whole set of records at one time into the view (actually to the set of base tables behind the view). Before Instead-of triggers, you had to do this record by record with a stored procedure. This capability is very useful for loading information into a SQL Server database. For example, you can load information from a denormalized source (such as a flat file) and store it in a set of normalized, linked tables.

Another unusual feature of Instead-of triggers is the fact that they support `text`, `ntext`, and `image` columns in Inserted and Deleted tables. After triggers cannot handle these data types. In base tables, `text`, `ntext`, and `image` columns actually contain pointers to the pages holding data. In Inserted and Deleted tables, `text`, `ntext`, and `image` columns are stored as continuous strings within each row. No pointers are stored in these tables, and therefore the use of the Textptr() and Textvalid() functions and the Readtext, Updatetext, and Writetext statements is not permitted. All other uses are valid, such as references in the Select list or Where clause, or use of Charindex(), Patindex(), or Substring() functions.

Trigger Order of Execution

SQL Server 7.0 introduced the idea that more than one trigger could be created per modification statement. However, the execution order of such triggers could not be controlled. In SQL Server 2000, it is possible to define which After trigger to execute first and which to execute last against a table. For example, the following statement will set trInventory_I to be the first trigger to be executed in the case of an Insert modification statement:

```
Exec sp_settriggerorder @triggername = 'trInventory_I',
                        @order = 'first',
                        @stmttype = 'INSERT'
```

The @order parameter must have one of these values: 'first', 'last', or 'none'. The value 'none' is used to reset the order of the execution of the trigger after it has been specified. The @smttype parameter must have one of these values: 'INSERT', 'UPDATE', or 'DELETE'.

Since only one Instead-of trigger can be associated with a table, and since it is executed before any other trigger (or constraint), it is not possible to set its order.

Alter Trigger statements reset the order of the trigger. After altering the trigger, you must execute the sp_SetTriggerOrder statement to set it again.

Managing Triggers

You can manage triggers using GUI tools such as Enterprise Manager, Query Analyzer Object Browser, or Visual Database Tools. Other methods include using Transact-SQL statements within tools like Query Analyzer.

Managing Triggers in Enterprise Manager

You can access triggers from Enterprise Manager by right-clicking the table with which the trigger is associated and selecting All Tasks | Manage Triggers from the pop-up menus.

SQL Server displays a modal form for editing trigger properties (see Figure 8-10). This editor is very similar to the editor you use to edit stored procedures.

SQL Server initially fills the form with a template for creating a new trigger. If you want to access a trigger that is already defined for the table, use the Name list box to select it.

Once you have created or modified the trigger, you can click the Check Syntax button to verify it, then click OK or Apply to attach it to the table. You can delete triggers by selecting the trigger from the drop-down list and clicking the Delete button.

Managing Triggers in the Query Analyzer Object Browser

You can access triggers from the Object Browser when you open the tree node under the table with which the trigger is associated. When you open the Triggers node, Query Analyzer displays a list of triggers. You can right-click any trigger and the program will offer you the usual options (for instance, Edit and Delete).

Managing Triggers Using Transact-SQL Statements

SQL Server has a rich pallet of system stored procedures for managing triggers from Transact-SQL.

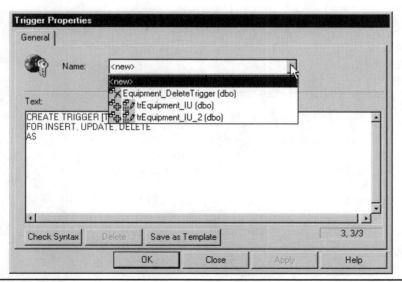

Figure 8-10   *Editing triggers*

Listing Triggers   To list triggers associated with a table, use the system stored procedure sp_helptrigger:

```
sp_helptrigger 'Order'
```

The server returns the list of triggers associated with the specified table and displays the type of trigger found in the isupdate, isdelete, isinsert, isafter, and isinteadof columns:

trigger_name	owner	isupdate	isdelete	isinsert	isafter	isinteadof
trOrderStatus_U	dbo	1	0	0	1	0
trOrderStatus_U_1	dbo	1	0	0	1	0

```
(2 row(s) affected)
```

Viewing Triggers   You can obtain the code for a trigger using the system stored procedure sp_helptext:

```
sp_helptext 'trOrderStatus_U'
```

The server returns the code for the specified trigger:

```
Text
------------------------------------------------------------------------
CREATE Trigger trOrderStatus_U
On dbo.[Order]
After Update      -- For Update
As
     If Update (OrderStatusId)
     Begin

          Insert into ActivityLog( Activity,
                                   LogDate,
                                   UserName,
                                   Note)
          Select        'Order.OrderStatusId',
                        GetDate(),
                        USER_NAME(),
                        'Value changed from '
                        + Cast( d.OrderStatusId as varchar)
                        + ' to '
                        + Cast( i.OrderStatusId as varchar)
```

```
        From deleted d inner join inserted i
        On d.OrderId = i.OrderId
    End
```

Deleting Triggers   A trigger can be deleted, as can all other database objects, using the appropriate Drop statement:

```
Drop Trigger 'Orders_Trigger1'
```

Modifying Triggers   Earlier in this chapter, you saw details of the syntax of a Transact-SQL statement for creating triggers. Triggers can be modified using the Alter Trigger statement. Since the features of the Alter Trigger and Create Trigger statements are identical, we will not explore the syntax a second time.

It is much better to use the Alter Trigger statement to modify a trigger than to drop and then re-create the trigger. During the period between dropping and creating a trigger, a user might make a change to the table, the consequence of which is that the rules that are usually enforced by the trigger will not be enforced.

NOTE

Keep in mind that the order of execution is lost when the trigger is altered—you must reset it again using sp_SetTriggerOrder.

Renaming Triggers   Triggers are often renamed using Transact-SQL statements designed for the creation and modification of triggers, such as Alter Trigger. As with all other database objects, a trigger can be forced to change its name using the following system stored procedure:

```
Exec sp_rename 'Orders_Trigger1', 'trOrders_IU'
```

The first parameter is the current name of the database object, and the second parameter is the new name of the object.

Disabling Triggers   It is possible to temporarily disable and enable triggers without dropping them:

```
Alter Table [Order] Disable Trigger trOrders_IU
```

After the execution of this statement, the specified trigger will not fire, but it will still be associated with the table. This technique is often used to load large amounts of data into a table without initiating the business logic encapsulated in a trigger.

Trigger Design Recommendations

Since triggers are relatively complex database objects, it is easy to create design, performance, or maintainability problems inside your database. Therefore, I will spend some time pointing out a proper way to use them.

Go out ASAP

Triggers take time to execute. If your server is very busy and/or other users are locking resources in the database, execution might take much more time than expected. On the other hand, locks that you (or rather SQL Server) have placed in the database while the trigger is executing will not be released until the trigger is finished. Thus, your trigger may increase competition for resources and affect other users and their sessions.

For these reasons, you should always try to exit a trigger as soon as possible. For example, you could start (almost) every trigger with the following test:

```
If @@rowcount = 0
    Return
```

It will abort further execution of the trigger if no records were changed.

Keep in mind that this If clause must occur at the very beginning of the trigger. If you put it after any other statement, @@rowcount will return the number of records affected by that statement. For example, if you put a simple Print statement at the beginning of the trigger and then this test, the remainder of the trigger will not be executed:

```
Alter Trigger trOrderStatus_U
On dbo.[Order]
After Update   -- For Update
As

Print 'Start of trOrderStatus_U'
If @@Rowcount = 0  -- This is always true
                   -- and the rest will NEVER be executed.
    Return

    If Update (OrderStatusId)
    Begin

        Insert into ActivityLog( Activity,
                                 LogDate,
                                 UserName,
```

```
                                Note)
        Select    'Order.OrderStatusId',
                  GetDate(),
                  USER_NAME(),
                  'Value changed from '
                  + Cast( d.OrderStatusId as varchar)
                  + ' to '
                  + Cast( i.OrderStatusId as varchar)

        From deleted d inner join inserted i
        On d.OrderId = i.OrderId
    End
```

Make It Simple

It is true that triggers are suitable for implementing complex business rules, particularly if those business rules are too complex to be handled by simpler database objects such as constraints. However, just because you are using them to handle complex business rules, you do not have to make your code so complex that it is difficult to understand and follow. It is challenging enough to work with triggers: keep them as simple as possible.

Divide and Conquer

In earlier versions of Microsoft SQL Server, only one trigger per modification statement could be associated with a table. This physical restriction led developers to produce poor code. Features that were not related had to be piled up in a single trigger. However, this restriction no longer applies. There is no reason to couple the code for multiple triggers. Each distinct piece of functionality can be implemented in a separate trigger (except in the case of Instead-of triggers).

Do Not Use Select and Print Inside a Trigger

The Print and Select commands are very useful in triggers during the debugging process. However, they can be very dangerous if left in a trigger after it has been introduced into production. These statements generate additional result sets, which might cause the client application to fail if it is not able to handle them or does not expect them.

Do Not Use Triggers at All

If you can implement the required functionality using constraints, do not use triggers!

If you can implement the required functionality using stored procedures, and if you can prevent users from accessing your tables directly, do not use triggers! Triggers are more difficult to implement, debug, and manage. You will save both time and money for your company or your client if you can find simpler ways to implement the required functionality.

Transaction Management in Triggers

A trigger is always part of the transaction that initiates it. That transaction can be explicit (when SQL Server has executed Begin Transaction). It can also be implicit—basically, SQL Server treats each Transact-SQL statement as a separate transaction that will either succeed completely or fail completely.

It is possible to abort the entire transaction from inside the trigger by using Rollback Transaction. This command, shown in action next, is valid for both implicit and explicit transactions:

```
Alter Trigger trOrderStatus_U
On dbo.[Order]
After Update     --For Update
As

    If @@Rowcount = 0
        Return

    If Update (OrderStatusId)
    Begin

        Insert into ActivityLog( Activity,
                                 LogDate,
                                 UserName,
                                 Note)
        Select    'Order.OrderStatusId',
                  GetDate(),
                  USER_NAME(),
                  'Value changed from '
                  + Cast( d.OrderStatusId as varchar)
                  + ' to '
                  + Cast( i.OrderStatusId as varchar)

        From deleted d inner join inserted i
        On d.OrderId = i.OrderId

        If @@Error <> 0
        Begin
```

```
            RAISERROR ("Error in trOrderStatus_U", 16, 1)
            Rollback Transaction
        End
    End
```

In this trigger, SQL Server investigates the presence of the error and rolls back the complete operation if it is unable to log changes to the ActivityLog table.

The processing of Rollback Transaction inside a trigger differs from its processing inside a stored procedure. It also differs in different versions of Microsoft SQL Server.

When a Rollback statement is encountered in a stored procedure, changes made since the last Begin Transaction are rolled back, but the processing continues.

In Microsoft SQL Server 2000, when a Rollback statement is executed within a trigger, a complete batch is aborted and all changes are rolled back. SQL Server continues to process from the beginning of the next batch (or stops if the next batch does not exist).

Microsoft SQL Server 7.0 and 4.2 and all versions of Sybase SQL Server behaved in this manner. In Microsoft SQL Server 6.0, execution was continued through the trigger, but the batch was canceled. Version 6.5 went to an opposite extreme. Execution of both the trigger and the batch was continued. It was the responsibility of the developer to detect an error and stop further processing.

Using Triggers

In SQL Server, triggers may have the following roles:

▶ To enforce data integrity, including referential integrity and cascading deletes

▶ To enforce complex business rules too complex for Default and Check constraints

▶ To log changes and send notification to administrators via e-mail

▶ To maintain derived information (computed columns, running totals, aggregates, and so on)

Triggers can be implemented to replace all other constraints on a table. A typical example is the use of a trigger to replace the functionality enforced by a foreign key constraint.

It is possible to implement *cascading deletes* using triggers. For example, if you do not have a foreign key between the Inventory and InventoryProperty tables, you might implement a trigger to monitor the deletion of Inventory records and to delete all associated InventoryProperty records.

Check and Default constraints are limited in that they can base their decision only on the context of current records in the current tables. You can implement a trigger that functions in a manner similar to Check constraints and that verifies on the contents of multiple records or even on the contents of other tables.

Triggers can be set to create an audit trail of activities performed on a table. For example, you might be interested in obtaining information on who changed the contents of, or specific columns in, the Lease table, and when that user made the changes.

It is possible to create a trigger to notify you when a specific event occurs in the database. For example, in a technical support system, you might send e-mail to the person responsible for dispatching technical staff, to inform that person that a request for technical support has been received. In an inventory system, you might automatically generate a purchase order if the quantity of an inventory item falls below the specified level.

Triggers are suitable for computing and storing calculated columns, running totals, and other aggregates in the database. For example, to speed up reporting, you might decide to keep a total of ordered items in an order table.

Cascading Deletes

Usually, referential integrity between two tables is implemented with a foreign key, such as in the following illustration:

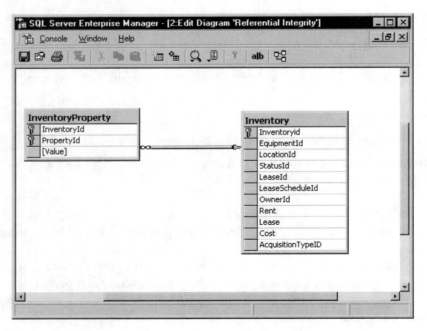

In such cases, a foreign key prevents the user from deleting records from a parent table (Inventory) if a record is referenced in a linked table (InventoryProperty). The only way to delete the record would be to use the following code:

```
Delete InventoryProperty
Where InventoryId = 222

Delete Inventory
Where InventoryId = 222
```

In some cases, the system design requirements might call for *cascading deletes,* which automatically delete records from the linked table when the record in the parent table is deleted. In this case, only one command is required to delete any instance of an asset with an InventoryId value of 222:

```
Delete Inventory
Where InventoryId = 222
```

SQL Server 2000 introduces cascading referential integrity constraints that can implement this behavior. In SQL Server 7.0 and earlier versions, you had to use triggers to implement cascading operations. The following example creates two new tables (without a foreign key), populates them with a few records, and creates a trigger that will implement a cascading delete:

```
Create Table MyInventory
    (
    Inventoryid int Not Null Identity (1, 1),
    EquipmentId int Null,
    LocationId int Null,
    StatusId tinyint Null,
    LeaseId int Null,
    LeaseScheduleId int Null,
    OwnerId int Null,
    Rent smallmoney Null,
    Lease smallmoney Null,
    Cost smallmoney Null,
    AcquisitionTypeID tinyint Null
    )
Go

Alter Table MyInventory Add Constraint
    PK_Inventory Primary Key Nonclustered
    (
```

```
        Inventoryid
        )
Go

Create Table MyInventoryProperty
        (
        InventoryId int Not Null,
        PropertyId smallint Not Null,
        Value varchar(50) Null
        )
Go
Alter Table MyInventoryProperty Add Constraint
        PK_InventoryProperty Primary Key Nonclustered
        (
        InventoryId,
        PropertyId
        )
Go

Create Trigger trMyInventory_CascadingDelete_D
On MyInventory
After Delete     --For delete
As

If @@Rowcount = 0
        Return
Delete MyInventoryProperty
where InventoryId In (Select InventoryID from deleted)
Go

Insert into myInventory(EquipmentId) Values (1)
Insert into myInventory(EquipmentId) Values (2)
Insert into myInventory(EquipmentId) Values (3)
Insert into myInventory(EquipmentId) Values (4)
Insert into myInventory(EquipmentId) Values (5)

Insert into myInventoryProperty(InventoryId, PropertyId, Value)
Values (1, 1, 'ACME')
Insert into myInventoryProperty(InventoryId, PropertyId, Value)
Values (1, 2, 'Turbo')
Insert into myInventoryProperty(InventoryId, PropertyId, Value)
Values (1, 3, '311')
Insert into myInventoryProperty(InventoryId, PropertyId, Value)
Values (2, 1, 'ACME')
```

```
Insert into myInventoryProperty(InventoryId, PropertyId, Value)
Values (2, 2, 'TurboPro')
Insert into myInventoryProperty(InventoryId, PropertyId, Value)
Values (2, 3, '312')
Go

Delete MyInventory
Where InventoryId = 1

Select * from myInventory
Select * from myInventoryProperty
```

Aggregates

Imagine that users of an Asset database are often clogging the Inventory table. One operation that they perform often is the execution of reports that prepare the sum of all monthly lease payments per lease schedule. If the sum were prepared in advance, the report would be available in an instant, the table would be less clogged, and the user would experience fewer locking and deadlocking problems.

To provide this functionality, you could create one or more triggers to maintain the `PeriodicTotalAmount` field in the LeaseSchedule table. The field will contain the sum of lease payments for assets in the Inventory table that are associated with a lease schedule.

It is possible to implement diverse solutions for this task. This solution is based on separate triggers for different modification statements.

The Insert trigger is based on a relatively complex Update statement with a subquery based on the contents of the Inserted table. Each new record increments the total in the related lease schedule.

The Coalesce statement is used to replace nulls with zeros in the calculation. The trigger evaluates the number of records affected by the modification statement at the beginning and, if no records are affected, aborts further execution.

This solution executes properly even when multiple records are inserted with one statement:

```
Create Trigger trInventory_Lease_I
On dbo.Inventory
after Insert      -- For Insert
As

If @@Rowcount = 0
    return
```

```
-- add inserted leases to total amount
Update LeaseSchedule
Set LeaseSchedule.PeriodicTotalAmount =
    LeaseSchedule.PeriodicTotalAmount
    + Coalesce(i.Lease, 0)
from LeaseSchedule inner join inserted i
    on LeaseSchedule.ScheduleId = i.LeaseScheduleId

Go
```

The Delete trigger is very similar to the previous trigger. The main difference is that the values from the Deleted table are subtracted from the total, as shown here:

```
Create Trigger trInventory_Lease_D
On dbo.Inventory
After Delete      -- For delete
As

If @@Rowcount = 0
    Return

-- subtract deleted leases from total amount
Update LeaseSchedule
Set LeaseSchedule.PeriodicTotalAmount =
    LeaseSchedule.PeriodicTotalAmount
    - Coalesce(d.Lease, 0)
from LeaseSchedule inner join deleted d
    on LeaseSchedule.ScheduleId = d.LeaseScheduleId
Go
```

The Update trigger is the most complicated. The calculation of a total is performed only if the Lease and LeaseScheduleId fields are referenced by the Update statement. The trigger then subtracts the Lease amounts from the deleted records and adds the Lease amounts from the inserted records to the related totals.

```
Create Trigger trInventory_Lease_U
On dbo.Inventory
After Update  -- For Update
As

if @@Rowcount = 0
    return
```

```
If Update (Lease) or Update(LeaseScheduleId)
begin
    -- subtract deleted leases from total amount
    Update LeaseSchedule
    Set LeaseSchedule.PeriodicTotalAmount =
            LeaseSchedule.PeriodicTotalAmount
            - Coalesce(d.Lease, 0)
    From LeaseSchedule inner join deleted d
        On LeaseSchedule.ScheduleId = d.LeaseScheduleId

    -- add inserted leases to total amount
    Update LeaseSchedule
    Set LeaseSchedule.PeriodicTotalAmount =
            LeaseSchedule.PeriodicTotalAmount
            + Coalesce(i.Lease, 0)
    From LeaseSchedule inner join inserted i
        On LeaseSchedule.ScheduleId = i.LeaseScheduleId

End
Go
```

Views

Views are database objects that behave like stored queries or virtual tables. There are
several types of views, and they differ in internal design and purpose:

- Standard SQL views
- Dynamic views
- INFORMATION_SCHEMA views
- Indexed views
- Partitioned views

Design of Standard SQL Views

In their basic form, views are designed simply as queries enclosed inside a Create
View statement:

```
CREATE VIEW dbo.vInventory
AS
SELECT dbo.Inventory.Inventoryid, dbo.Equipment.Make, dbo.Equipment.Model,
```

```
dbo.Location.Location, dbo.Status.Status, dbo.Contact.FirstName,
dbo.Contact.LastName, dbo.Inventory.Cost, dbo.AcquisitionType.AcquisitionType,
dbo.Location.Address, dbo.Location.City, dbo.Location.ProvinceId,
dbo.Location.Country, dbo.EqType.EqType, dbo.Contact.Phone,
dbo.Contact.Fax, dbo.Contact.Email, dbo.Contact.UserName,
dbo.Inventory.Rent, dbo.Inventory.EquipmentId, dbo.Inventory.LocationId,
dbo.Inventory.StatusId, dbo.Inventory.OwnerId, dbo.Inventory.AcquisitionTypeID,
dbo.Contact.OrgUnitId
FROM dbo.EqType
RIGHT OUTER JOIN dbo.Equipment
ON dbo.EqType.EqTypeId = dbo.Equipment.EqTypeId
   RIGHT OUTER JOIN dbo.Inventory
      INNER JOIN dbo.Status
      ON dbo.Inventory.StatusId = dbo.Status.StatusId
         LEFT OUTER JOIN dbo.AcquisitionType
         ON dbo.Inventory.AcquisitionTypeID =
            dbo.AcquisitionType.AcquisitionTypeId
   ON dbo.Equipment.EquipmentId = dbo.Inventory.EquipmentId
            LEFT OUTER JOIN dbo.Location
            ON dbo.Inventory.LocationId = dbo.Location.LocationId
               LEFT OUTER JOIN dbo.Contact
               ON dbo.Inventory.OwnerId = dbo.Contact.ContactId
```

After a view is created, it can be used in the same way as any other table:

```
SELECT dbo.vInventory.EquipmentId, dbo.vInventory.Make,
dbo.vInventory.Model, dbo.vInventory.Status
FROM dbo.vInventory
WHERE LocationId = 2
```

Although data is accessible through a view, it is not stored in the database inside a view. When the view is referenced in a query, SQL Server simply processes the Select statement behind the view and combines the data with the rest of the query:

```
EquipmentId Make                 Model            Status
------------------------------------------------------------
1           Toshiba              Portege 7020CT   Active
6           NEC                  V90              Ordered
5           Bang & Olafson       V4000            Active
1           Toshiba              Portege 7020CT   Active
34          Toshiba              Portege 7030CT   Active
(5 row(s) affected)
```

A view is often created on a query that joins many tables and contains aggregate functions:

```
Create View vInventoryCost
WITH SCHEMABINDING
as
select ET.EqType, e.Make, e.Model, Sum(Cost) TotalCost, Count(*) [Count]
from dbo.Inventory I
inner join dbo.Equipment e
on i.EquipmentId = e.EquipmentId
    inner join dbo.EqType ET
    on e.EqTypeId = ET.EqTypeId
where Cost is not null
group by ET.EqType, e.Make, e.Model
```

Syntax

Views can be created and edited by simply executing Create View and Alter View statements:

```
{CREATE}|{ALTER} VIEW view_name [ ( column [ ,...n ] ) ]
[ WITH < view_option > [ ,...n ] ]
AS
select_statement
[ WITH CHECK OPTION ]
```

It is not necessary to specify column names in the header of the view. The view just transfers column names from the Select statement if they are uniquely identified. You just need to make sure that column names are not repeated and that all computed columns also have names assigned (for example, you can add aliases to computed columns).

As with stored procedures and functions, views can be encrypted so that nobody can see their source code. You just need to create or alter it using the With Encryption view option.

The With Schemabinding option allows you to *schema-bind* a view to database objects (such as tables, views, and user-defined functions) that it references. Once the function is schema-bound, it is not possible to make schema changes on the underlying objects. All attempts to drop the objects and all attempts to alter underlying objects (which would change the object schema) will fail. When this option is used, all objects inside the view must be referenced using two-part names (owner.dbobject).

The View_Metadata option specifies that SQL Server will return information about the view's columns (not base table columns) to client-side APIs. This feature might be useful for making views with triggers that are updateable.

Design View in Enterprise Manager

When a query is complicated, it is sometimes easier to create it in the Design View window of Enterprise Manager (see Figure 8-11). You can launch it from the context-sensitive menu of the View node in Enterprise Manger. It consists of four components: the Diagram pane (for managing tables visually), the Grid pane (for managing columns), the SQL pane (for editing SQL statements), and the Results pane (for displaying and editing data). This window is used in a manner similar to the Query Design window in Microsoft Access or Visual Studio, so I will not spend more time describing it here.

Security

Typically, a user does not need permissions on underlying base tables and views when the user has permission to access a view. There are two exceptions—SQL Server checks permissions if all underlying tables and views do not belong to the same database, or when base objects belong to different owners.

Standard SQL Views in Execution Plans

It is a common misconception that SQL Server creates, stores, and reuses an execution plan of a view. The idea behind this wishful thinking is that SQL Server would optimize the execution plan of the view, so when it is referenced from a stored procedure or a query,

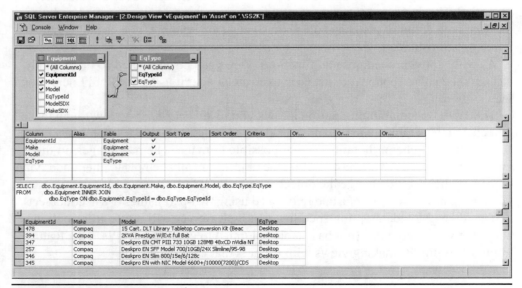

Figure 8-11 *Design View window*

SQL Server would just include it in the execution plan of the caller. Although this might sound like a good idea (time would be saved since recompilation would not be necessary and since the "optimal" plan will be used), SQL Server has a better solution.

There is another common misconception about view execution. Although I used the phrase "virtual table" to describe views, SQL Server does not execute the view, create a result set in memory, and then process the rest of the query.

When a SQL view is referenced with other tables in a query, SQL Server compiles everything again and creates a new optimal execution plan. Other elements of the query (joins with other tables, additional criteria, and the list of required columns) typically change the nature of the query significantly so that a new execution plan works better than simply reusing the execution plan of a view.

 NOTE

Execution plans of other types of views are constructed differently, and I will discuss them "Indexed Views in Execution Plans" and "Execution Plans of Distributed Partitioned Views," later in this chapter.

Limitations of Views

Keep in mind that views have the following limitations:

▶ A view can contain up to 1024 columns.

▶ A view can be based on tables and other views, but not on temporary tables or table variables.

▶ It is possible to have only 32 levels of nested views.

▶ The Select statement in a view cannot have an Into clause (it cannot create a new table as a side effect).

▶ A view cannot have Compute and Compute By clauses.

▶ Only Instead-of triggers can be created on a view (not After triggers).

▶ An Order By clause can be used in the view only together with a Top clause.

The last statement points to a very cool workaround if you need to order the results in a view—the attempt to create a view using just the Order By clause will result in a syntax error:

```
Server: Msg 1033, Level 15, State 1, Procedure vInventory_Ordered, Line 25
The ORDER BY clause is invalid in views, inline functions, derived tables,
and subqueries, unless TOP is also specified.
```

To solve this problem, add Top 100 Percent to it:

```
Create VIEW dbo.vInventory_Ordered
AS
SELECT TOP 100 PERCENT
dbo.Inventory.Inventoryid, dbo.Equipment.Make, dbo.Equipment.Model
FROM dbo.Equipment
    RIGHT OUTER JOIN dbo.Inventory
    ON dbo.Equipment.EquipmentId = dbo.Inventory.EquipmentId
order by dbo.Equipment.Make, dbo.Equipment.Model
```

Editing Data Using Views

It is possible to modify data in base tables through a view:

```
Update dbo.vInventory
Set Cost = 2000
Where InventoryId = 1234
```

SQL Server has to be able to identify rows and fields that clearly need to be modified. The view cannot contain derived columns (columns based on calculated values such as aggregate functions or expressions).

If a view is created using With Check Option, SQL Server does not accept changes on records that will fall out of scope of the view after modification. For example, a manager who can see Inventory for his own location cannot assign it to some other location:

```
CREATE VIEW vInventoryTrigonTower
AS
SELECT *
FROM dbo.vInventory
WHERE LocationId = 2
WITH CHECK OPTION
GO

update dbo.vInventoryTrigonTower
set LocationId = 10
where InventoryId = 6
```

SQL Server will generate an error:

```
Server: Msg 550, Level 16, State 1, Line 1
The attempted insert or update failed because the target view
either specifies WITH CHECK OPTION or spans a view that specifies
```

```
WITH CHECK OPTION and one or more rows resulting from the operation
did not qualify under the CHECK OPTION constraint.
The statement has been terminated.
```

   With standard SQL views, it is not possible to modify data in more then a single base table. However, when an Instead-of trigger is placed on a view, the trigger can issue separate statements that modify individual base tables. See "Triggers on Views," earlier in this chapter, for a detailed example and discussion of this method. It is very interesting and useful.

Dynamic Views

Compared with stored procedures, views have one serious limitation—they do not support parameters. Fortunately, you can use a table-valued user-defined function as a *dynamic view,* which do support parameters (you can also call them *parameterized views*):

```
Create Function fnInventoryByLocationId(
        @LocationId int)
Returns Table
AS
Return (SELECT *
        FROM dbo.vInventory
        WHERE LocationId = @LocationId)
```

They can be referenced in the From clause of a Select statement, which makes them work like a view:

```
select *
from dbo.fnInventoryByLocationId (2)
```

INFORMATION_SCHEMA Views

SQL Server 2000 contains a group of system views that are used to obtain metadata. Their names consist of three parts. The first part is the database name (optional); the second part is always INFORMATION_SCHEMA (as opposed to being the database owner, which is why these views are so named); and the third part references the type of metadata that the view contains.

   In Figure 8-12, you can see the usage of an INFORMATION_SCHEMA.TABLES view. It returns the names of all tables (and views—virtual tables) that the current user has permission to see in the current database. INFORMATION_SCHEMA

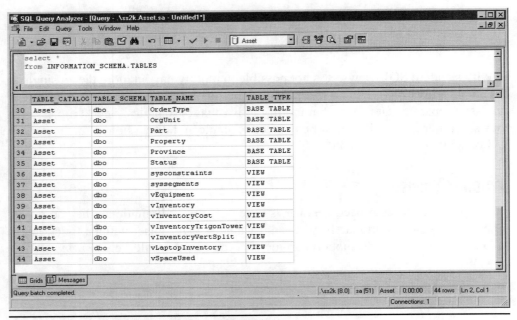

Figure 8-12 *Using INFORMATION_SCHEMA views*

views work like system stored procedures—they are defined in the *master* database, but they return information in the context of the current database (or the database that is referenced in the first part of the name).

The INFORMATION_SCHEMA views are designed to be compatible with SQL-92 naming standards. Therefore, instead of database, owner, object, and user-defined data types INFORMATION_SCHEMA views are named with catalog, schema, object, and domain as a third parts of the name, respectively.

Microsoft recommends that you reference these views (as well as system stored procedures) instead of directly referencing system tables in your procedures.

Indexed Views

It is possible to *materialize* a view—to create a table in the database that will contain all the data that is referenced by a view. This technique can significantly improve the performance of a Select statement when SQL Server has to join many tables, and return or aggregate a large number of records.

When you create a *unique clustered index* on a view, SQL Server materializes the view. Records are saved in the database in the same manner that clustered indexes on regular tables are stored:

```
Create View vLaptopInventory
WITH SCHEMABINDING
as
select i.Inventoryid, i.EquipmentId, i.StatusId, e.Make, e.Model
from dbo.Inventory I
inner join dbo.Equipment e
on i.EquipmentId = e.EquipmentId
where EqTypeId = 1
GO

CREATE UNIQUE CLUSTERED INDEX idxvLaptopInventory
ON vLaptopInventory (InventoryID)
```

Although the index references only a subset of columns, the index (indexed view) contains all columns in the leaf-level nodes (as does every clustered index).

Indexed View Limitations

There are many limitations with which a view must comply to be converted to an indexed view:

▶ The view must be created using the With Schemabinding option.

▶ The view must reference only tables—not other views, derived tables, rowset functions, or subqueries.

▶ All base tables must have the same owner as the view.

▶ The view cannot join tables from more than one database.

▶ The view cannot contain an outer or self-join.

▶ The view cannot have a Union clause, Top clause, Order By clause, or Distinct keyword.

▶ Some aggregate functions are not allowed: Count(*) [use Count_Big(*) instead], Avg(), Max(), Min(), Stdev(), Stdevp(), Var(), or Varp(). But all of these aggregate functions can be reengineered using valid functions [such as Sum() and Count_Big(*)].

▶ If a query contains a Group By clause, it must contain Count_Big(*) in the Select list.

▶ The view and all base tables must be created with Set Ansi_Nulls On.

▶ All tables and user-defined functions in the view must be referenced using two-part names (owner.dbobject).

- ► All columns must be explicitly specified—Select * is not allowed.

- ► The view cannot contain `text`, `ntext`, or `image` columns.

- ► Having, Rollup, Cube, Compute, and Compute By clauses are not allowed.

- ► The same table column must not be converted to more than a single view column.

- ► You can only create indexed views in SQL Server 2000 Enterprise Edition or SQL Server 2000 Developer Edition.

- ► The Create Index statement and all subsequent Insert, Update, and Delete statements must be executed with the following option settings (explicitly or implicitly):

```
Set ANSI_NULLS ON
Set ANSI_PADDING ON
Set ANSI_WARNINGS ON
Set ARITHABORT ON
Set CONCAT_NULL_YIELDS_NULL ON
Set QUOTED_IDENTIFIERS ON
Set NUMERIC_ROUNDABORT OFF
```

Indexed Views in Execution Plans

Optimizer treats indexed views as tables. SQL Server simply joins them with other tables. There is one exception—Optimizer can use an indexed view even when the view is not explicitly referenced in the query (when the query is referencing only some of the base tables). SQL Server compares the cost of the execution plan with base tables and the execution plan with the indexed view and chooses the cheapest one.

You can force SQL Server to ignore the indexed view using the Expand View hint. Conversely, you can also force SQL Server to use the indexed view using the Noexpand hint.

Nonclustered Indexes on Views

Once a clustered index is added to a view, you can add more nonclustered indexes:

```
CREATE INDEX idxvLaptopInventory_MakeModel
ON vLaptopInventory (Make, Model)
```

Performance Implications

Indexed views typically improve the performance of data warehouse systems and other systems that predominantly have queries that read data. On the other hand, indexed views can reduce the performance of OLTP systems. Updates to an indexed view become part of transactions that modify the base tables. This fact may increase the cost of OLTP transactions and offset the savings achieved on read operations.

Partitioned Views

Views can be a very useful tool for managing very large databases (VLDBs). Typically, data warehouse systems contain huge volumes of uniform data. A textbook example is a retailer that collects information about sales over years. Some analyses would process many years of data, but others would focus on only a few months or the current year. If everything were in a single table, queries and management of data would become increasingly difficult. In such a scenario, the retailer's sales information would be split into several horizontally partitioned tables such as OrderItem2000, OrderItem2001, and OrderItem2002. For analyses (queries) that span all tables, you can create a view that puts them all together:

```
Create View vOrderItem
as
select * from OrderItem2000
UNION ALL
select * from OrderItem2001
UNION ALL
select * from OrderItem2002
```

Horizontal and Vertical Partitioning

Views based on multiple instances of the same table are called *partitioned views*. A *horizontal partitioning* occurs when different subsets of records are stored in different table instances (as in the preceding example).

It is also possible to do *vertical partitioning*—to put columns in separate tables based on the frequency with which they are needed. On "wide" tables, each record occupies a substantial amount of space. Since each data page is limited to 8KB, a smaller number of records can fit onto a single data page. As a result, the number of IO operations needed to access a large number of records is much higher. To reduce it, we can put frequently used fields in one table and other fields in a second table. The tables will have a one-to-one relationship. In the following example, the InventorySum table has been split into InventoryPrim and InventorySec tables:

```
CREATE TABLE [dbo].[InventoryPrim] (
    [Inventoryid] [int]        NOT NULL ,
    [Make]        [varchar] (50) NULL ,
    [Model]       [varchar] (50) NULL ,
```

```
    [Location]      [varchar]  (50) NULL ,
    [FirstName]     [varchar]  (30) NULL ,
    [LastName]      [varchar]  (30) NULL ,
    [UserName]      [varchar]  (50) NULL ,
    [EqType]        [varchar]  (50) NULL ,
    CONSTRAINT [PK_InventoryPrim] PRIMARY KEY  CLUSTERED
    (
        [Inventoryid]
    )  ON [PRIMARY]
) ON [PRIMARY]
GO


CREATE TABLE [dbo].[InventorySec] (
    [Inventoryid]       [int]       NOT NULL ,
    [AcquisitionType]  [varchar] (12) NULL ,
    [Address]           [varchar] (50) NULL ,
    [City]              [varchar] (50) NULL ,
    [ProvinceId]        [char]    (3)  NULL ,
    [Country]           [varchar] (50) NULL ,
    [EqType]            [varchar] (50) NULL ,
    [Phone]             [typPhone]    NULL ,
    [Fax]               [typPhone]    NULL ,
    [Email]             [typEmail]    NULL ,
    CONSTRAINT [PK_InventorySec] PRIMARY KEY  CLUSTERED
    (
        [Inventoryid]
    )  ON [PRIMARY]
) ON [PRIMARY]
GO
```

The following creates a view that joins them:

```
create view vInventoryVertSplit
as
select IP.Inventoryid, IP.Make,       IP.Model,
       IP.Location,    IP.FirstName, IP.LastName,
       IP.UserName,    IP.EqType,     ISec.AcquisitionType,
       ISec.Address,   ISec.City,     ISec.ProvinceId,
       ISec.Country,   ISec.Phone,    ISec.Fax,
       ISec.Email
from dbo.InventoryPrim IP
full join dbo.InventorySec ISec
on IP.Inventoryid = ISec.Inventoryid
```

The following creates a query that references only fields from one table:

```
SET STATISTICS PROFILE ON
SELECT Make, Model, Location, UserName
FROM dbo.vInventoryVertSplit
where Inventoryid = 1041
```

In this case, SQL Server realizes that there is no need to access both tables:

```
Make      Model                         Location     UserName
--------- ----------------------------- ------------ ----------
Compaq    18.2GB 10K RPM Ultra2 Disk Dr Royal Hotel  PMisiaszek

(1 row(s) affected)


Rows Executes StmtText
---- -------- ---------------------------------------------------------
1    1        SELECT [Make]=[Make],[Model]=[Model],[Location]=[Locatio
1    1          |--Clustered Index Seek(OBJ:(Asset.dbo.InventoryPrim.P
(2 row(s) affected)
```

Unfortunately, this is not always the case. If we remove criteria from the previous Select statement, SQL Server accesses both tables (although the columns selected are in only one table):

```
Rows Executes StmtText
---- -------- ---------------------------------------------------------
980  1        SELECT [Make]=[Make],[Model]=[Model],[Location]=[Locatio
980  1          |--Merge Join(Full Outer Join, MERGE:(InventorySec.Inv
980  1             |--Clustered Index Scan(OBJ:(Asset.dbo.InventorySec.
980  1             |--Clustered Index Scan(OBJ:(Asset.dbo.InventoryPrim
```

NOTE

You can always force SQL Server to use just one table if you reference the table and not the view.

Distributed Partitioned Views

If all base tables of a view are stored on a single server, it is called a *local partitioned view*. If the underlying tables of a view are stored on separate servers, it is called a *distributed partitioned view*. Distributed partitioned views are always created on tables that are horizontally partitioned. In the following example, the vSales view on server Alpha references tables on servers Beta and Gamma:

```
Create view vSales
as
select * from Sales.dbo.OrderItem2000
UNION ALL
select * from Beta.Sales.dbo.OrderItem2001
UNION ALL
select * from Gamma.Sales.dbo.OrderItem2002
```

That's the basic idea, but it is not that simple. I will discuss all the details and then show a complete example.

Servers that host horizontally partitioned tables and that work together are called *federated servers.* This technology is one of the major new features of SQL Server 2000 and it has allowed Microsoft to beat the competition consistently on TPC-C benchmarks since it became available in the Beta version of SQL Server 2000.

The strategy of splitting the transaction and query load among a set of distributed servers is often called *scaling-out* (as opposed to *scaling-up,* which refers to the brute force method of simply applying bigger and faster hardware instead).

Partitioned tables are split based on a *partitioning key*—a column that determines which of the partitioned tables/federated servers the record will fall into. In the previous example, the partitioning key is a year. A partitioning key should be selected to ensure that the majority of queries are served from a single table/server. The success of a federated server project depends largely on the selection of an appropriate partitioning key.

NOTE

You do not have to have multiple physical servers to test federated servers. You can install several instances of SQL Server on the same machine to develop and test the solution. Naturally, it would be pointless to implement federated servers that way in a production environment.

By way of example, assume that your Asset database is serving a Canadian company and that it is functionally divided into three divisions—one serves the Canadian market, the second the U.S. market, while the third serves the international market (see Figure 8-13). This schema is very good when reporting is typically done per division.

You will partition the table using the Country column as a partitioning key. To assist the resolution of the distributed partitioned view, make Country the first field of the primary key and create Check constraints to prevent entry of records from an

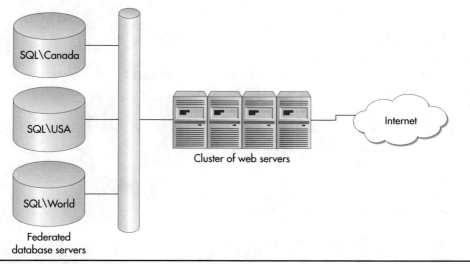

Figure 8-13   *Federated servers*

incorrect geographic location. It is very important that data ranges do not overlap and that a single record can end up only on a single server. The following Create Table statements should be executed on the respective servers:

```
-- on Canada server
CREATE TABLE [dbo].[InventoryCanada] (
    [Inventoryid] [int] NOT NULL ,
    [Make] [varchar] (50) NULL ,
    [Model] [varchar] (50) NULL ,
    [Location] [varchar] (50) NULL ,
    [FirstName] [varchar] (30) NULL ,
    [LastName] [varchar] (30) NULL ,
    [AcquisitionType] [varchar] (12) NULL ,
    [Address] [varchar] (50) NULL ,
    [City] [varchar] (50) NULL ,
    [ProvinceId] [char] (3) NULL ,
    [Country] [varchar] (50) NOT NULL ,
    [EqType] [varchar] (50) NULL ,
    [Phone] [typPhone] NULL ,
    [Fax] [typPhone] NULL ,
    [Email] [typEmail] NULL ,
    [UserName] [varchar] (50) NULL ,
    CONSTRAINT [PK_InventoryCanada] PRIMARY KEY  CLUSTERED
```

```
   (
      [Country],
      [Inventoryid]
   )  ON [PRIMARY] ,
   CONSTRAINT [chkInventoryCanada] CHECK ([Country] = 'Canada')
) ON [PRIMARY]
GO
------------------------------------------------------------------
-- on US server
CREATE TABLE [dbo].[InventoryUSA] (
   [Inventoryid] [int] NOT NULL ,
   [Make] [varchar] (50) NULL ,
   [Model] [varchar] (50) NULL ,
   [Location] [varchar] (50) NULL ,
   [FirstName] [varchar] (30) NULL ,
   [LastName] [varchar] (30) NULL ,
   [AcquisitionType] [varchar] (12) NULL ,
   [Address] [varchar] (50) NULL ,
   [City] [varchar] (50) NULL ,
   [ProvinceId] [char] (3) NULL ,
   [Country] [varchar] (50) NOT NULL ,
   [EqType] [varchar] (50) NULL ,
   [Phone] [typPhone] NULL ,
   [Fax] [typPhone] NULL ,
   [Email] [typEmail] NULL ,
   [UserName] [varchar] (50) NULL ,
   CONSTRAINT [PK_InventoryUS] PRIMARY KEY  CLUSTERED
   (
      [Country],
      [Inventoryid]
   )  ON [PRIMARY] ,
   CONSTRAINT [chkInventoryUSA] CHECK ([Country] = 'USA')
) ON [PRIMARY]
GO
------------------------------------------------------------------
-- on World server
CREATE TABLE [dbo].[InventoryWorld] (
   [Inventoryid] [int] NOT NULL ,
   [Make] [varchar] (50) NULL ,
   [Model] [varchar] (50) NULL ,
   [Location] [varchar] (50) NULL ,
   [FirstName] [varchar] (30) NULL ,
   [LastName] [varchar] (30) NULL ,
   [AcquisitionType] [varchar] (12) NULL ,
```

```
[Address] [varchar] (50) NULL ,
[City] [varchar] (50) NULL ,
[ProvinceId] [char] (3) NULL ,
[Country] [varchar] (50) NOT NULL ,
[EqType] [varchar] (50) NULL ,
[Phone] [typPhone] NULL ,
[Fax] [typPhone] NULL ,
[Email] [typEmail] NULL ,
[UserName] [varchar] (50) NULL ,
CONSTRAINT [PK_InventoryWorld] PRIMARY KEY  CLUSTERED
(
    [Country],
    [Inventoryid]
)  ON [PRIMARY] ,
CONSTRAINT [chkInventoryWorld] CHECK ([Country] in ('UK',
        'Ireland', 'Australia'))
) ON [PRIMARY]
GO
```

Create linked servers that reference all other servers that will participate in the distributed partitioned view on each server. In the current example, on server Canada, you need to create linked servers that reference the USA and World servers; on server USA, create linked servers that reference the Canada and World servers; and on the World server, create linked servers that reference the Canada and USA servers.

```
exec sp_addlinkedserver N'(local)\USA', N'SQL Server'
GO
exec sp_addlinkedserver N'(local)\WORLD', N'SQL Server'
GO
```

 NOTE

As you can see, I am running these statements against three instances of SQL Server 2000 running on the same physical machine.

To achieve better performance, it is necessary to set each linked server with the Lazy Schema Validation option. In the current example, on Canada server, you should execute

```
USE master
EXEC sp_serveroption '(local)\USA', 'lazy schema validation', 'true'
EXEC sp_serveroption '(local)\World', 'lazy schema validation', 'true'
```

Other servers should be set with the option for their linked servers. After that, the partitioned view will request metadata that describes the underlying table only if it is really needed.

Create distributed partitioned views that reference the local table and two tables on remote servers. On Canada Server, you should execute

```
Create view vInventoryDist
as
select * from Asset.dbo.InventoryCanada
UNION ALL
select * from [(local)\USA].Asset.dbo.InventoryUSA
UNION ALL
select * from [(local)\World].Asset.dbo.InventoryWorld
```

Now, you can test the distributed partitioned view. Figure 8-14 shows the query that calls all three servers. The highlighted part of the result shows that the view is redirecting parts of the query to other servers. Figure 8-15 shows execution of the same query against database objects.

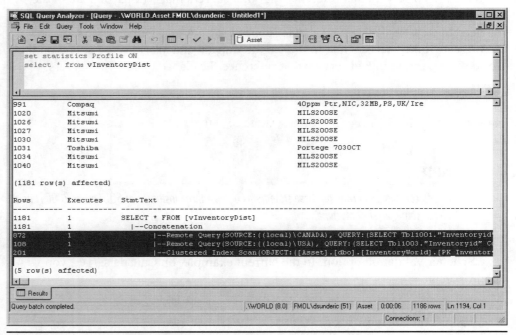

Figure 8-14   *Usage of distributed partitioned view*

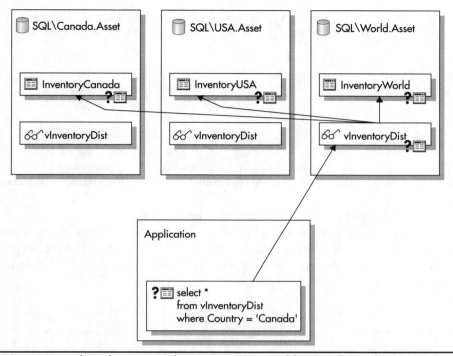

Figure 8-15   *Distributed partitioned view connects to tables on all member servers*

Execution Plans of Distributed Partitioned Views

If the query contains a criterion based on the partitioning key, SQL Server evaluates
which servers contain matching data and executes the query against them only:

```
set statistics Profile ON
select * from vInventoryDist
where Country = 'UK'

Rows Executes StmtText
---- -------- ------------------------------------------------------------
154        1 SELECT * FROM [vInventoryDist] WHERE [Country]=@1
154        1 |--Compute Scalar(DEFINE:([InventoryWorld].[Inventoryid
154        1    |--Clustered Idx Seek(OBJ:([Asset].[dbo].[InventoryWo
```

The profile shows that the query was executed on the local server. In a case in which the data resides on another server, the profile would look like this:

```
set statistics Profile ON
select * from vInventoryDist
where Country = 'CANADA'

Rows Executes StmtText
---- -------- ---------------------------------------------------------------
872        1 SELECT * FROM [vInventoryDist] WHERE [Country]=@1
872        1  |--Compute Scalar(DEFINE:([(local)\CANADA].[Asset].[d
872        1     |--Remote Query(SOURCE:((local)\CANADA), QUERY:(SE
```

Figure 8-16 shows how the view will route the query to the remote server.

It is necessary to create partitioned views on two other servers with identical names. In that way, an application can get the data through the view on any of the servers. The views will reroute the query to the server that contains the data that is needed (see Figure 8-17).

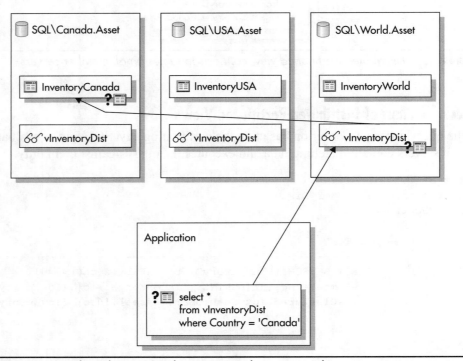

Figure 8-16   *Distributed partitioned view routes the query to the remote server*

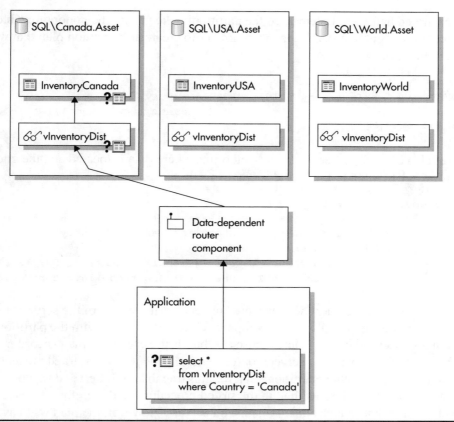

Figure 8-17   *Data-dependent routing*

The system will achieve better performance if the partitioned view does not have to perform query routing—that is, if the application knows which server contains the data needed and therefore sends the query to the appropriate server. This technique is often called *data-dependent routing.*

NOTE

If the application is that intelligent, you might wonder why you need distributed partitioned views. Well, not all queries can be served from a single server. Some queries require data that is located on more than one server, and a distributed partitioned view would give you access to it.

The selection of a partitioning key and implementation of a Check constraint have a critical impact on the performance of the system. You would have seen this fact demonstrated had you implemented the partitioning key using the nonoptimizable argument (an argument that leads the optimizer to create an execution plan that will ignore indexes):

```
...
 CONSTRAINT [chkInventoryWorld] CHECK ([Country] <>'USA'
                                   and [Country] <>'Canada'))
) ON [PRIMARY]
```

In such a case, SQL Server cannot determine where data is located and the query will always be routed to the World server as well:

```
Rows  Executes StmtText
----  -------- ----------------------------------------------------------
872        1 SELECT * FROM [vInventoryDist] WHERE [Country]=@1
872        1 |--Concatenation
872        1 |--Remote Query(SOURCE:((local)\CANADA), QUERY:(SELECT
0          1   |--Clustered Idx Seek(OBJ:(Asset.dbo.InventoryWorld.P
```

As you can see, the query was executed unnecessarily on one of the servers—no records were returned. SQL Server compares Check constraints with the partition key ranges specified in the Where clause and builds the execution plan accordingly.

You might think that SQL Server won't do such a good job when stored procedures are used against distributed partitioned views. It is true that SQL Server does not know which parameter will be specified in the stored procedure, and therefore it creates an execution plan that runs the query against all servers. However, the plan will have dynamic filters that serve as conditional logic and execute only the queries that are needed. To demonstrate, I will create a stored procedure that references the view:

```
CREATE PROCEDURE prInventoryList
    @chvCountry varchar(50)
AS

SELECT *
FROM vInventoryDist
WHERE Country = @chvCountry
```

I will now execute it so that you can review the profile:

```
set statistics Profile ON
exec prInventoryList 'CANADA'
```

The execution plan will contain queries against all tables:

```
Rows Executes StmtText
---- -------- -------------------------------------------------------
872        1 select * from vInventoryDist where Country = @chvCoun
872        1 |--Concatenation
872        1 |   |--Clustered Index Seek(OBJECT:([Asset].[dbo].[
0          1 |--Filter(WHERE:(STARTUP EXPR([@chvCountry]='USA')))
0          0 |   |--Remote Query(SOURCE:(.\USA), QUERY:(SELECT C
0          1 |--Filter(WHERE:(STARTUP EXPR([@chvCountry]='Ireland
0          0 |       |--Remote Query(SOURCE:(.\World), QUERY:(SELECT
```

But two of these queries are not executed (as you can see in the Executes column). Figure 8-18 shows a graphical representation of the execution plan with dynamic filters.

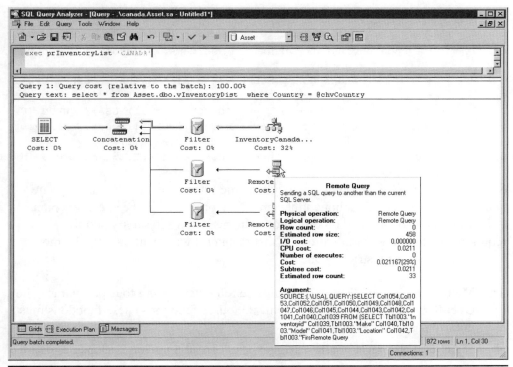

Figure 8-18   *Execution plan with dynamic filers*

Updateable Distributed Partitioned Views

Distributed partitioned views in SQL Server 7.0 were not updateable. On SQL Server 2000 Enterprise Edition and Developer Edition servers, data can be modified through a distributed partitioned view:

```
set xact_abort on
update vInventoryDist
set UserName = 'unknown'
where UserName is null
and Country = 'Canada'
```

I needed to set the Xact_Abort option because each such statement is treated as a distributed transaction. Therefore, Distributed Transaction Coordinator must be running on each server. The result will look like this:

```
(2 row(s) affected)

Rows Executes StmtText
---- -------- --------------------------------------------------------------
0           1 update vInventoryDist set UserName = 'unknown' where Use
0           1 |--Sequence
0           1    |--Remote Query(SOURCE:((local)\CANADA), QUERY:(UPDAT
0           1       |--Filter(WHERE:(STARTUP EXPR(0)))
0           0       |  |--Remote Query(SOURCE:((local)\USA), QUERY:(UP
0           1       |--Clustered Index Update(OBJECT:(Asset.dbo.Invent
0           1          |--Filter(WHERE:(STARTUP EXPR(0)))
0           0             |--Clustered Index Seek(OBJECT:(Asset.dbo.Inv
```

Note that SQL Server has again created dynamic filters, and only the appropriate queries will be executed, although they are all incorporated in the execution plan.

Unfortunately, views and modification statements have to satisfy additional requirements to allow modifications in that manner. I will mention only the most interesting and most restrictive ones:

▶ Member tables on other servers must be referenced using four-part names, the OpenRowset function, or the OpenDataSource function. These functions must not use pass-through queries.

▶ Member tables must not have triggers and cascading deletes or updates defined.

▶ All columns of a member table must be included in the distributed partitioned view. The order of the columns must be identical.

▶ The column definitions in all base tables must match (data type, scale, precision, collation).

▶ Ranges of partition key values in member tables must not overlap.

▶ There can be only one Check constraint on the partitioning column and it may use only these operators: BETWEEN, AND, OR, <, <=, >, >=, =.

▶ Tables cannot have identity values (otherwise, Insert statements will fail).

▶ Partitioning keys cannot have defaults, allow nulls, be computed columns, or be timestamp values.

▶ `smallmoney` and `smalldatetime` columns on remote tables are automatically converted to `money` and `datetime`. Since all data types must match, the local table must use `money` and `datetime`. To avoid confusion it is best not to use `smallmoney` and `smalldatetime`.

It is sometimes possible to work around some of these rules—you can create an Instead-of trigger to modify the member tables directly. Unfortunately, in that case, query optimizer might not be able to create an execution plan as good as the one that would be created for a view that follows all the rules.

Scalability and Performance of Distributed Systems

Federated servers and distributed partitioned views are not a magic bullet that will solve all your problems. Note that distributed partitioned views are primarily designed to improve scalability of the system, not its performance. Although these two parameters might seem similar to you, there is a significant difference. Performance refers to the speed of execution of the system (or of individual transactions), while scalability refers to the ability to increase transactional load or the number of concurrent users without significant performance degradation. For example, if a metric describing system performance is 100 percent on a single server, adding another server might cause performance to fall to, for example, 50 percent. In this case, end users would notice improvements only after a third server is added (3×50 percent). But the advantage is that we now have a system with nearly *linear scalability*—every additional server would increase performance by another 50 percent.

Federated servers (like other distributed database systems) are also more difficult to manage. Even "simple" operations, such as backups and restores, become very complicated. Promotion of hot fixes or new code in a production environment requires significant manual intervention or development of specialized tools.

It is very important to evaluate the pros and cons of this design before you start. A rule of thumb is that all other options should be explored and exhausted first, and only then should scaling out be attempted. The game plan should be something like this:

1. Optimize the database and the application.
2. Scale up the server.
3. Scale out the system.

A Poor Man's Federated Server

It is possible to create a distributed system without the use of distributed partitioned views. For example, if you are in a business that has only a few, large customers (with a heavy transactional load), you could create a single database per customer instead of storing all transactions in the same database. Then, you could divide databases between several servers or install each one on a separate dedicated server. An application can be designed to direct each query or transaction to the appropriate server—to perform data-dependent routing.

A similar design would be applicable for an organization that can easily be partitioned into its suborganizations, based, for example, on geographic locations.

The key requirement is that there be no (or very little) need to aggregate data on the complete system—that is, to run queries (or transactions) that span multiple servers.

Using SQL Views

SQL views can have different roles in your database system. Their basic role is to customize table data, but there are more complex roles. You can use standard SQL views to implement security and to ease export and import of data, or you can use the other types of views to achieve performance improvement.

Export and Import

Because they can transform and join data from one or more tables, standard SQL views are useful for exporting data out of your database system. Standard SQL views alone are not convenient for importing data, since you can insert data only in one base table at the time. Fortunately, you can add an Instead-of trigger to the view and then you will be able to modify multiple base tables (see "Triggers on Views" earlier in this chapter).

Security Implementation

Standard SQL views are the preferred means of setting security when users are accessing the database through generic tools for accessing and editing database information (such as Access or Excel). Different users could have permissions to use different views with different filters on tables:

```
CREATE VIEW vInventoryTrigonTower
AS
SELECT *
FROM dbo.vInventory
WHERE LocationId = 2
```

Using this technique, developer can also "filter" which columns are accessible by certain users. For example, you could allow only users from the accounting or human resources departments to view and edit salary data in a table containing employee information.

Reduce Complexity

Views are a very nice way to simplify queries. As shown in Figure 8-19, I've created a vSpaceUsed view, which lists all database tables and their sizes. Its results are very similar to the results of sp_spaceused. In the past, I used this procedure to get the size of tables. As you may remember, Microsoft recommends that developers use

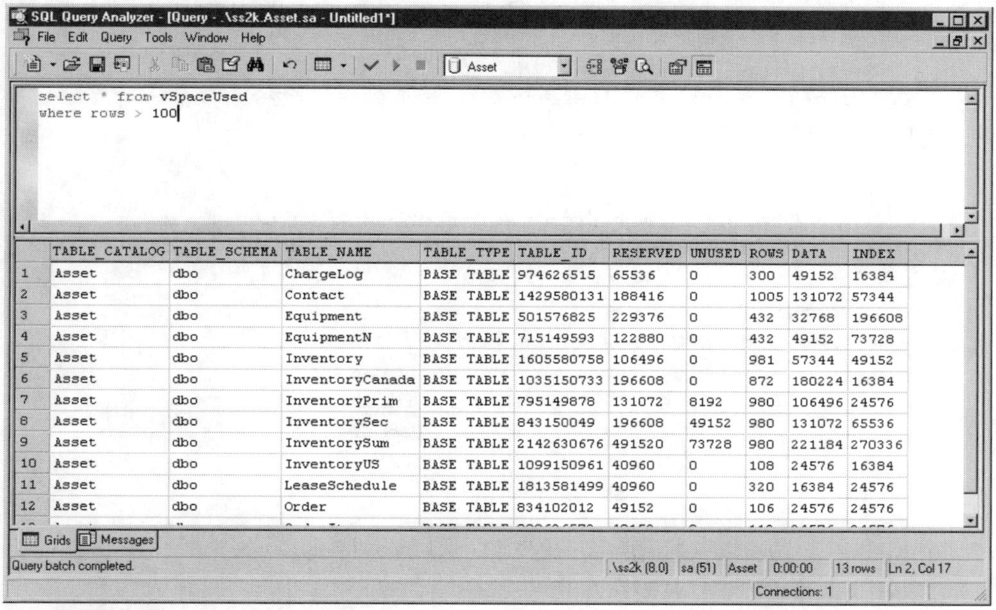

Figure 8-19   *Using vSpaceUsed*

system procedures, instead of querying system tables directly, since the structure of tables might change between SQL Server versions. Unfortunately, sp_spaceused returns data about a single object only, and I often need a recordset that contains all tables. So, instead of calling sp_spaceused in a loop to collect data in the temporary table, I created a view that returns all data that I might be interested in:

```sql
create view vSpaceUsed
as
select  distinct TOP 100 PERCENT
        db_name()               as TABLE_CATALOG
    , user_name(obj.uid)     as TABLE_SCHEMA
    , obj.name               as TABLE_NAME
    , case obj.xtype
        when 'U' then 'BASE TABLE'
        when 'V' then 'VIEW'
      end                    as TABLE_TYPE
    , obj.ID                 as TABLE_ID
    , Coalesce((select sum(reserved)
                from sysindexes i1
                where i1.id = obj.id
                and i1.indid in (0, 1, 255))
            *   (select d.low from master.dbo.spt_values d
                where d.number = 1 and d.type = 'E')
        , 0)               as RESERVED
    , Coalesce((select Sum (reserved) - sum(used)
                from sysindexes i2
                where i2.indid in (0, 1, 255)
                and id = obj.id)
            * (select d.low from master.dbo.spt_values d
                where d.number = 1    and d.type = 'E')
        , 0)               as UNUSED
    , case obj.xtype
        when 'U' then Coalesce((select i3.rows
                                from sysindexes i3
                                where i3.indid < 2
                                and i3.id = obj.id), 0)
        when 'V' then NULL
      end                  as [ROWS]
    ,   Coalesce
        (   (    (select sum(dpages)    from sysindexes
                where indid < 2 and id = obj.id
            ) + (select isnull(sum(used), 0) from sysindexes
                where indid = 255 and id = obj.id
                )
```

```
     ) * (select d.low from master.dbo.spt_values d
            where d.number = 1 and d.type = 'E'
        ), 0)          as [DATA]
   , Coalesce(
       ((select sum(reserved)
       from sysindexes i1
       where i1.id = obj.id
       and i1.indid in (0, 1, 255)
       ) - ( (select sum(dpages) from sysindexes
            where indid < 2 and id = obj.id
          ) + (select isnull(sum(used), 0) from sysindexes
               where indid = 255 and id = obj.id)
        ) )
   * (select d.low from master.dbo.spt_values d
      where d.number = 1 and d.type = 'E')
      , 0)          as [INDEX]
from sysobjects obj
where obj.xtype in ('U', 'V')
and    permissions(obj.id) != 0
order by db_name(), user_name(obj.uid), obj.name
```

The view has a very complex structure, but its use is very simple. You just need to reference a table in a SQL statement (see Figure 8-19).

Performance Improvement

Views are often used as a mechanism for improving system performance. When an index is added to the view, SQL server typically does not have to query and join underlying tables—the request will be satisfied using data from the indexed view. Unfortunately, this feature can also degrade overall performance if the system is mostly modifying underlying tables.

Distributed partitioned views can divide the execution of workload between servers and provide an exciting new way to linearly scale out the performance of the system. Unfortunately, this is not a magic bullet either—if typical queries need data from multiple servers, performance may be degraded.

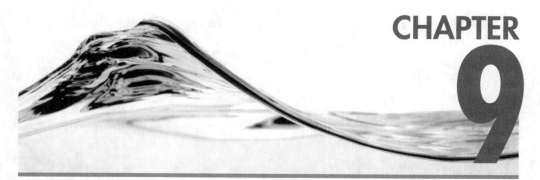

Advanced Stored Procedure Programming

T his chapter introduces some advanced techniques for coding stored procedures, including

► Dynamically constructed queries

► Optimistic locking using `timestamp` values

► Full-text searches and indexes

► Nested stored procedures

► Temporary tables

► Parameterized queries

► Inserting the results of a stored procedure into a table

► Techniques for generating unique identifiers and potential problems associated with their use

► The `uniqueidentifier` (GUID) data type

► Additional looping methods

► Property management—using extended properties

Dynamically Constructed Queries

This section examines some ways in which you can construct queries dynamically, including

► Executing a string statement

► Querying by form

► Using parameterized queries

Executing a String

Transact-SQL contains a variation of the Execute statement that you can use to run a batch recorded in the form of a character string:

```
EXEC[UTE] ({@string_variable | [N]'tsql_string'} [+...n])
```

You can supply a Transact-SQL batch in the form of a character string, a variable, or an expression:

```
Exec ('select * from Contact')
```

The Execute statement allows you to assemble a batch or a query dynamically. This might look like magic to you:

```
declare @chvTable sysname
set @chvTable = 'Contact'
Exec ('select * from ' + @chvTable)
```

The Execute statement is necessary because the following batch, which you might expect to work, will actually result in a syntax error:

```
declare @chvTable sysname
set @chvTable = 'Contact'
select * from @chvTable  -- this will cause an error
```

The error occurs because SQL Server expects a table name, and will not accept a string or a variable, in a From clause.

It is important to realize that you are dealing with two separate batches in the example with the Execute statement. You can use the variable to assemble the second batch, but you cannot reference variables from the batch that initiated the Execute statement in the string batch. For example, the following code will result in a syntax error:

```
declare @chvTable sysname
set @chvTable = 'Contact'
Exec ('select * from @chvTable')
```

The server will return:

```
Server: Msg 137, Level 15, State 2, Line 1
Must declare the variable '@chvTable'.
```

NOTE

Even if you were to declare the variable in the second batch, the Select statement would fail because you cannot use a string expression or variable in the From clause.

You cannot use a database context from the other batch, either:

```
Use Asset
exec ('Use Northwind select * from Employees')
select * from Employees    -- Error
```

Query By Form

One of the simplest ways to create a search form in a client application is to list all the fields in a table as text boxes on a form. The user will fill some of them in, and they can be interpreted as search criteria.

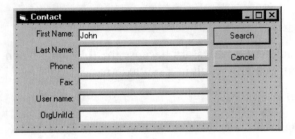

The trouble with this kind of solution is that, most of the time, the user will leave blank most of the text boxes. This does not mean that the user wants to find only those records in which the values of the blank fields are set to empty strings, but rather that those fields should not be included in the criteria. Stored procedures have a static structure, but something dynamic would be more appropriate to launch this kind of query.

The following stored procedure assembles a character-string query. The contents of the Where clause are based on the criteria that were specified (that is, fields that were not set to null). When all components are merged, the query returns a list of matching contacts:

```
Create Procedure prQbfContact_1
-- Dynamically assemble a query based on specified parameters.
    (
            @chvFirstName      varchar(30)    = NULL,
            @chvLastName       varchar(30)    = NULL,
            @chvPhone          typPhone       = NULL,
            @chvFax            typPhone       = NULL,
            @chvEmail          typEmail       = NULL,
            @insOrgUnitId      smallint       = NULL,
            @chvUserName       varchar(50)    = NULL,
            @debug             int            = 0
    )
As
set nocount on

Declare @intErrorCode int,
```

```
            @intTransactionCountOnEntry int,
            @chvQuery varchar(8000),
            @chvWhere varchar(8000)
Select @intErrorCode = @@Error,
       @chvQuery = 'SET QUOTED_IDENTIFIER OFF SELECT * FROM Contact',
       @chvWhere = ''

If @intErrorCode = 0 and @chvFirstName is not null
Begin
    Set @chvWhere = @chvWhere + ' FirstName = "'
                 + @chvFirstName + '" AND'
    Select @intErrorCode = @@Error
End


If @intErrorCode = 0 and @chvLastName is not null
Begin
    Set @chvWhere = @chvWhere + ' LastName = "'
                 + @chvLastName + '" AND'
    Select @intErrorCode = @@Error
End


If @intErrorCode = 0 and @chvPhone is not null
Begin
    set @chvWhere = @chvWhere + ' Phone = "' + @chvPhone + '" AND'
    Select @intErrorCode = @@Error
End


If @intErrorCode = 0 and @chvFax is not null
Begin
    set @chvWhere = @chvWhere + ' Fax = "' + @chvFax + '" AND'
    Select @intErrorCode = @@Error
End


If @intErrorCode = 0 and @chvEmail is not null
Begin
    set @chvWhere = @chvWhere + ' Email = "' + @chvEmail + '" AND'
    Select @intErrorCode = @@Error
End


If @intErrorCode = 0 and @insOrgUnitId is not null
Begin
    set @chvWhere = @chvWhere + ' OrgUnitId = '
                 + @insOrgUnitId + ' AND'
    Select @intErrorCode = @@Error
End
```

```
If @intErrorCode = 0 and @chvUserName is not null
Begin
    set @chvWhere = @chvWhere + ' UserName = "' + @chvUserName + '"'
    Select @intErrorCode = @@Error
End

if @debug <> 0 select @chvWhere chvWhere

-- remove ' AND' from the end of string
If @intErrorCode = 0 And
    Substring(@chvWhere, Len(@chvWhere) - 3, 4) = ' AND'
Begin
    set @chvWhere = Substring(@chvWhere, 1, Len(@chvWhere) - 3)
    Select @intErrorCode = @@Error
     if @debug <> 0 select @chvWhere chvWhere
End

If @intErrorCode = 0 and Len(@chvWhere) > 0
Begin
    set   @chvQuery = @chvQuery + ' WHERE ' + @chvWhere
    Select @intErrorCode = @@Error
End

if @debug <> 0
    select @chvQuery Query

-- get contacts
If @intErrorCode = 0
Begin
    exec (@chvQuery)
    Select @intErrorCode = @@Error
End

return @intErrorCode
```

The procedure is composed of sections that test the presence of the criteria in each parameter and add them to the Where clause string. At the end, the string with the Select statement is assembled and executed. Figure 9-1 shows the result of the stored procedure (along with some debugging information).

TIP

You are right if you think that this solution can probably be implemented more easily using client application code (for example, in Visual Basic).

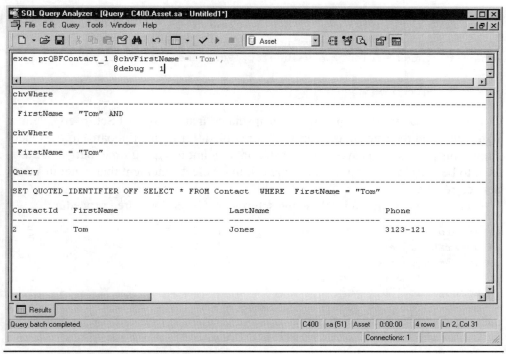

Figure 9-1   *The results of Query By Form*

Data Script Generator

Database developers often need an efficient way to generate a set of Insert statements to populate a table. In some cases, data is already in the tables, but it may need to be re-created in the form of a script to be used to deploy it on another database server, such as a test server.

One solution is to assemble an Insert statement dynamically for every row in the table using a simple Select statement:

```
select 'Insert dbo.AcquisitionType values('
        + Convert(varchar, AcquisitionTypeId)
        + ', ''' + AcquisitionType
        + ''')' from dbo.AcquisitionType
```

When you set Query Analyzer to Result In Text and execute such a statement, you get a set of Insert statements for each row:

```
----------------------------------------------------------------
Insert dbo.AcquisitionType values(1, 'Purchase')
```

```
Insert dbo.AcquisitionType values(2, 'Lease')
Insert dbo.AcquisitionType values(3, 'Rent')
Insert dbo.AcquisitionType values(4, 'Progress Payment')
Insert dbo.AcquisitionType values(5, 'Purchase Order')

(5 row(s) affected)
```

The Insert statements can now be encapsulated inside a pair of Set Insert_Identity statements and then saved as a script file or copied (through Clipboard) to the Query Pane. This process can save you a substantial amount of typing time, but you still have to be very involved in creating the original Select statement that generates the desired results.

An alternative solution is to use the setup_DataGenerator stored procedure:

```
alter proc setup_DataGenerator
-- generate a set of Insert statements
-- that can reproduce content of the table.
    @table sysname = 'Equipment',
    @debug int = 0
-- debug:  setup_DataGenerator @debug = 1
as

declare @chvVal varchar(8000)
declare @chvSQL varchar(8000)
declare @chvColList varchar(8000)

set @chvColList = ''
set @chvVal = ''

SELECT @chvVal = @chvVal
    + '+'',''+case when ' + [COLUMN_NAME]
    + ' is null then ''null'' else '
    + case when DATA_TYPE in ('varchar', 'nvarchar', 'datetime',
                                'smalldatetime', 'char', 'nchar')
                then '''''''''+convert(varchar(8000),'
            else '+ convert(varchar(8000),'
        end
    + convert(varchar(8000),[COLUMN_NAME])
    + case when DATA_TYPE in ('varchar', 'nvarchar', 'datetime',
                                'smalldatetime','char', 'nchar')
                then ')+'''''''''
            else ')'
        end
    + ' end '
FROM       [INFORMATION_SCHEMA].[COLUMNS]
```

```
where      [TABLE_NAME] = @table
order by [ORDINAL_POSITION]

set @chvVal = substring(@chvVal, 6, len(@chvVal))

if @debug <> 0 select @chvVal [@chvVal]

-- get column list
SELECT    @chvColList = @chvColList
                     + ',' + convert(varchar(8000),[COLUMN_NAME])
FROM      [INFORMATION_SCHEMA].[COLUMNS]
where      [TABLE_NAME] = @table
order by [ORDINAL_POSITION]

if @debug <> 0 select @chvColList [@chvColList]

-- remove first comma
set @chvColList = substring(@chvColList, 2, len(@chvColList))

-- assemble a command to query the table to assemble everything
set @chvSQL = 'select ''Insert dbo.' + @table
     + '(' + @chvColList +') values (''+'
     + @chvVal + ' + '')''from ' +@table

-- get result
if @debug <> 0 select @chvSQL chvSQL
exec(@chvSQL)
```

The procedure is based on the way SQL Server behaves when a recordset is assigned to a variable. This behavior was discussed in Chapter 4, but let me remind you: SQL Server loops through the records and assigns them each, one by one, to the variable. Each change overwrites the previous change and, finally, the value of the last row is assigned to the variable. This value stays in the variable after the statement has completed. You can use this behavior to produce a comma-delimited list of column names:

```
declare @chvColList varchar(8000)
declare @table sysname
set @chvColList = ''
set @ table = 'Equipment'

SELECT    @chvColList = @chvColList + ',' + [COLUMN_NAME]
FROM      [INFORMATION_SCHEMA].[COLUMNS]
where      [TABLE_NAME] = @table
```

```
order by [ORDINAL_POSITION]

select @ chvColList
```

If you execute this batch, you get the following:

```
------------------------------------------------------------
,EquipmentId,Make,Model,EqTypeId,ModelSDX,MakeSDX
```

> **NOTE**
>
> *You should not use this method for application code, but it is okay to use it for noncritical tasks, such as in a utility to manage code. If you use it, keep in mind that you should use Coalesce() or IsNull() in cases in which the column is nullable.*

The procedure assembles another string using this method—part of the final string that will be used to gather data. It is designed in a similar manner, but the code is more complex, to handle nullability of columns and to insert different delimiters for different data types. In the final step before execution, these strings are put together in a Select statement that will retrieve data from the table:

```
select 'Insert dbo.Equipment(EquipmentId,Make,Model,
                             EqTypeId,ModelSDX,MakeSDX)
        values ('
          + case
                when EquipmentId is null then 'null'
                else + convert(varchar(8000),EquipmentId)
            end
     + ',' + case
                when Make is null then 'null'
                else '''' + convert(varchar(8000),Make) + ''''
            end
     + ',' + case
                when Model is null then 'null'
                else '''' + convert(varchar(8000),Model) + ''''
            end
     + ',' + case
                when EqTypeId is null then 'null'
                else + convert(varchar(8000),EqTypeId)
            end
     + ',' + case
                when ModelSDX is null then 'null'
                else '''' + convert(varchar(8000),ModelSDX) + ''''
            end
```

```
    + ',' + case
            when MakeSDX is null then 'null'
            else '''' + convert(varchar(8000),MakeSDX) + ''''
        end
    + ')'
from Equipment
```

The result is set of Insert statements:

```
-----------------------------------------------------------------
Insert dbo.Equipment(EquipmentId,Make,Model,EqTypeId,ModelSDX,MakeSDX)
values (478,'Trigon',
'15 Cart. DLT Library Tabletop Conversion Kit (Beac',1,null,null)
Insert dbo.Equipment(EquipmentId,Make,Model,EqTypeId,ModelSDX,MakeSDX)
values (394,'Trigon','2KVA Prestige W/Ext full Bat',1,null,null)
Insert dbo.Equipment(EquipmentId,Make,Model,EqTypeId,ModelSDX,MakeSDX)
values (347,'Trigon',
'DeskSys EN CMT PIII 733 10GB 128MB 48xCD NT',1,null,null)
...
```

Using the sp_executesql Stored Procedure

In Chapter 3, you saw that an important advantage stored procedures have over ad
hoc queries is their capability to reuse an execution plan. SQL Server, and developers
working in it, can use two methods to improve the reuse of queries that are not designed
as stored procedures. The first of these is autoparameterization, covered in Chapter 3.
This section focuses on the second of these methods: using a stored procedure to
enforce parameterization of a query.

If you know that a query will be re-executed with different parameters and that
reuse of its execution plan will improve performance, you can use the sp_executesql
system stored procedure to execute it. This stored procedure has the following syntax:

```
sp_executesql [@stmt =] stmt
[

    {, [@params =] N'@parameter_name data_type [,...n]' }
    {, [@param1 =] 'value1' [,...n] }

]
```

The first parameter, @stmt, is a string containing a batch of Transact-SQL statements.
If the batch requires parameters, you must also supply their definitions as the second
parameter of the sp_executesql procedure. The parameter definition is followed by

a list of the parameters and their values. The following script executes one batch twice, each execution using different parameters:

```
EXECUTE sp_executesql
   @Stmt = N'SELECT * FROM Asset.dbo.Contact WHERE ContactId = @Id',
   @Parms = N'@Id int',
   @Id = 11
EXECUTE sp_executesql
   @Stmt = N'SELECT * FROM Asset.dbo.Contact WHERE ContactId = @Id',
   @Parms = N'@Id int',
   @Id = 313
```

There is one unpleasant requirement to this exercise. If all database objects are not *fully qualified* (that is, hard-coded with the database name and object owner), the SQL Server engine will not reuse the execution plan.

In some cases, you may be able to ensure that all database objects are fully qualified. However, this requirement becomes a problem if you are building a database that will be deployed under a different name or even if you use more than one instance of the database in your development environment (for example, one instance for development and one for testing).

The solution is to obtain the name of a current database using the Db_Name() function. You can then incorporate it in a query:

```
Declare @chvQuery nvarchar(200)
Set @chvQuery = N'Select * From ' + DB_NAME()
                + N'.dbo.Contact Where ContactId = @Id'
EXECUTE sp_executesql @stmt = @chvQuery,
                      @Parms = N'@Id int',
                      @Id = 1
EXECUTE sp_executesql @stmt = @chvQuery,
                      @Parms = N'@Id int',
                      @Id = 313
```

Solutions based on this stored procedure are better than solutions based on the execution of a character string. The execution plan for the latter is seldom reused. It might happen that it will be reused only when parameter values supplied match those in the execution plan. Even in a situation in which you are changing the structure of a query, the number of possible combinations of query parameters is finite (and some of them are more probable than others). Therefore, reuse will be much more frequent if you force parameterization using sp_executesql.

When you use Execute, the complete batch has to be assembled in the form of a string each time. This requirement also takes time. If you are using sp_executesql, the batch will be assembled only the first time. All subsequent executions can use the same string and supply an additional set of parameters.

Parameters that are passed to sp_executesql do not have to be converted to characters. That time is wasted when you are using Execute, in which case parameter values of numeric type must be converted. By using all parameter values in their native data type with sp_executesql, you may also be able to detect errors more easily.

Security Implications

As a reminder, the following are two security concerns that are important in the case of dynamically assembled queries:

▶ Permissions on underlying tables

▶ SQL injection

Permissions on Underlying Tables

The fact that a caller has permission to execute the stored procedure that assembles the dynamic query does not mean that the caller has permission to access the underlying tables. You have to assign these permissions to the caller separately. Unfortunately, this requirement exposes your database—someone might try to exploit the fact that you are allowing more than the execution of predefined stored procedures.

SQL Injection

Dynamically assembled queries present an additional security risk. A malicious user could use a text box to type something like:

```
Acme' DELETE INVENTORY --
```

A stored procedure (or application) can assemble this into a query, such as

```
Select *
from vInventory
Where Make = 'Acme' DELETE INVENTORY --'
```

The quote completes the parameter value and, therefore, the Select statement, and then the rest of the query is commented out with two dashes. Data from an entire table could be lost this way.

Naturally, a meticulous developer, such as you, would have permissions set to prevent this kind of abuse. Unfortunately, damage can be done even using a simple Select statement:

```
Acme' SELECT * FROM CUSTOMERS --
```

In this way, your competitor might get a list of your customers:

```
Select *
from vInventory
Where Make = 'Acme' SELECT * FROM CUSTOMERS --'
```

A hack like this is possible not just on string parameters; it might be even easier to perform on numeric parameters. A user can enter the following:

```
122121 SELECT * FROM CUSTOMERS
```

The result might be a query such as this:

```
Select *
from vInventory
Where InventoryId = 122121 SELECT * FROM CUSTOMERS
```

Fortunately, it's not too difficult to prevent this. No, you do not have to parse strings for SQL keywords. It's much simpler. The application must validate the content of text boxes. If a number or date is expected, the application must make sure that values really are of numeric or date data types. If text (such as a T-SQL keyword) is added, the application should prompt the user to supply a value of the appropriate data type.

Unfortunately, if a text box is used to specify a string, there is little that you can validate. The key is to prevent the user from adding a single quote (') to the query. There are several ways to do this. The quote is not a legal character in some types of fields (such as keys, e-mails, postal codes, and so forth) and the application should not accept it in such fields. In other types of fields (such as company names, personal names, descriptions, and so on), use of quotes may be valid. In that case, in the procedure that assembles the string, you should replace a single quote—char(39)—with two single quotes—char(39) + char(39)—and SQL Server will find a match for the string:

```
set @chvMake = Replace(@chvMake, char(39), char(39) + char(39))
```

The dynamic query will become a query that works as expected:

```
Select *
from vInventory
Where Make = 'Dejan''s Computers Inc.'
```

In the case in which someone tries to inject a SQL statement, SQL Server will just treat it as a part of the parameter string:

```
Select *
from vInventory
Where Make = 'Dejan'' SELECT * FROM CUSTOMERS --'
```

Another possibility is to replace a single quote—char(39)—with a character that looks similar onscreen but that is stored under a different code, such as (`)—char(96). Naturally, you have to make this substitution for all text boxes (on both data entry and search pages). In some organizations, this substitution might be inappropriate, since existing databases may already contain quotes.

NOTE

You are at risk not only when you are passing strings directly from a GUI into the stored procedure that is assembling a query, but also when an application is reading the field with injected SQL into a variable that will be used in a dynamic query. A user might attempt to weaken security with some administrative procedure—there is no need for direct interaction with the code by the attacker. Therefore, you should convert all string input parameters and local variables that are participating in the dynamic assembly of the query.

You also might want to prevent users from injecting special characters (such as wild cards) into strings that will be used in Like searches. The following function will make a string parameter safe for use in dynamic queries:

```
CREATE FUNCTION dbo.fnSafeDynamicString
-- make string parameters safe for use in dynamic strings
   (@chvInput varchar(8000),
    @bitLikeSafe bit = 0) -- set to 1 if string will be used in LIKE
RETURNS varchar(8000)
AS
BEGIN
   declare @chvOutput varchar(8000)
   set @chvOutput = Replace(@chvInput, char(39), char(39) + char(39))
   if @bitLikeSafe = 1
   begin
      -- convert square bracket
      set @chvOutput = Replace(@chvOutput, '[', '[[]')
      -- convert wild cards
      set @chvOutput = Replace(@chvOutput, '%', '[%]')
      set @chvOutput = Replace(@chvOutput, '_', '[_]')
   end
   RETURN (@chvOutput)
END
```

You can test the function with the following:

```
SELECT 'select * from vInventory where Make = '''
    + dbo.fnSafeDynamicString ('Dejan' + char(39) + 's Computers Inc.', 0)
    + ''''
```

This test simulates a case in which a user enters the following text on the screen:

```
Dejan' s Computers Inc.
```

The result becomes:

```
-----------------------------------------------------------------
select * from vInventory where Make = 'Dejan''s Computers Inc.'
(1 row(s) affected)
```

In the case of a Like query, you must prevent the user from using wild cards. The following query simulates a case in which a user enters % in the text box. It also assumes that the application or stored procedure is adding another % at the end of the query.

```
SELECT 'select * from vInventory where Make like '''
    + dbo.fnSafeDynamicString ('%a', 1)
    + '%'''
```

When you set the second parameter of the function to 1, the function replaces the first % character with [%], in which case it will not serve as a wild card:

```
---------------------------------------------
select * from vInventory where Make = '[%]a%'
(1 row(s) affected)
```

Optimistic Locking Using timestamp Values

When more than one user is working in a database, you might expect some concurrency problems to appear. The most common problem is the following: User A reads a record. User B also reads the record and then changes it. Any changes that user A now decides to commit to the database will overwrite the changes that user B made to it, without knowing that user B already changed it. Two standard solutions for this kind of problem are the following:

▶ Pessimistic locking

▶ Optimistic locking

In the *pessimistic locking* scenario, user A acquires a lock on the record so that nobody can change it until user A is finished with it. User A is a pessimist and expects that someone will attempt to change the record while user A is editing it.

NOTE

I will not go into the details of how locks are implemented. Locks are covered in detail in other SQL Server books. At this time, it is important to know that it is possible to mark a record so that nobody else can change it.

When user A changes the record, the lock is released and user B can now access the updated record and change it.

The trouble with this solution is that user A might go out for lunch—or on vacation—and, if user A didn't close the application that retrieved the record, the lock will not be released. This scenario is one of the reasons why this kind of solution is not recommended in a client/server environment.

In the *optimistic locking* scenario, user A locks the record only while he or she is actually performing the change. User A is an optimist who believes that nobody while change the record while user A is editing it. A mechanism in SQL Server will notify other users if somebody has changed the record in the meantime. The user can then decide either to abandon their changes or to overwrite the updated record.

A simple way to find out whether somebody has changed a record since the time user A read it would be to compare all fields. To run this comparison, user A must keep both an "original" and a "changed" record and needs to send them both to the server. Then, a process on the server must compare the original record with the current record in the table to make sure that it wasn't changed. Only then can the record be updated with the changed record. This process is obviously slow and increases network traffic, but there are solutions in the industry that use precisely this method.

timestamp

SQL Server has a `timestamp` data type. It is used for versioning records in a table. When you insert or update a record in a table with a `timestamp` field, SQL Server "timestamps" the change. Figure 9-2 demonstrates such behavior.

The table is created with a `timestamp` field. When a record is inserted, SQL Server automatically sets its value. When the record is updated, SQL Server increases the value of the `timestamp`.

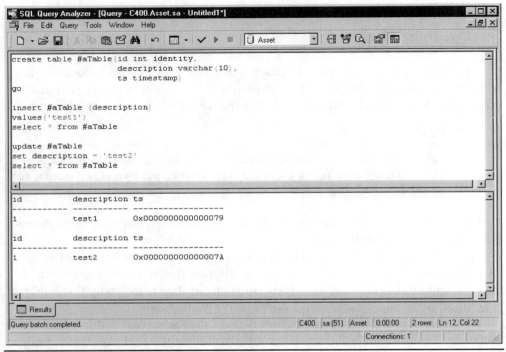

Figure 9-2   *Use of the* `timestamp` *data type*

It is important to realize that `timestamp` values are not actually a kind of timekeeping. They are just binary values that are increased with every change in the database and, therefore, are unique within the database. You should not make any assumptions about their values and growth. Somebody (or some process) might change something in the database concurrently, and even two changes that you executed consecutively might not have consecutive `timestamp` values.

To make sure that nobody has changed a record in the meantime, you might decide to update it like this:

```
update #aTable
set description = 'test3'
where id = 1
and ts = 0x000000000000007A  -- not a perfect solution
```

The record will be updated only if the `timestamp` is unchanged. The trouble with this solution is that you will not know what happens after the statement is executed. Maybe everything is okay and the record has been successfully changed. It is possible that the record was not updated because the `timestamp` was changed, but it is also possible that the record is not in the table any more.

TSEqual() Function

The SQL Server TSEqual() function (no longer described in SQL Server Books Online) compares `timestamp` values in the table and the Transact-SQL statement (see Figure 9-3). If they do not match, this function raises an error 532 and aborts the statement. This function allows you to write code that handles errors properly (for example, the user can be prompted for further action). If you executed the previous Update statement, the following one should cause SQL Server to force an error:

```
update #aTable
set description = 'test4'
where id = 1
and TSEQUAL(ts, 0x000000000000007A)
```

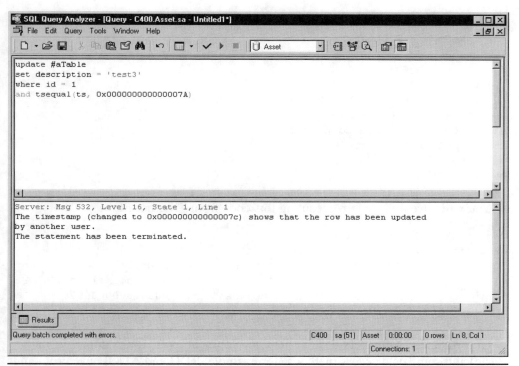

Figure 9-3   *The use of the TSEqual() function*

You can use this function in stored procedures to implement optimistic locking:

```
Create Procedure prUpdateContact_1
-- update record from contact table
-- prevent user from overwriting changed record
    (
            @intContactId int,
            @chvFirstName varchar(30),
            @chvLastName varchar(30),
            @chvPhone typPhone,
            @chvFax typPhone,
            @chvEmail typEmail,
            @insOrgUnitId smallint,
            @chvUserName varchar(50),
            @tsOriginal timestamp
    )
As
Set nocount on

Update Contact
Set FirstName = @chvFirstName,
    LastName = @chvLastName,
    Phone = @chvPhone,
    Fax = @chvFax,
    Email = @chvEmail,
    OrgUnitId = @insOrgUnitId,
    UserName = @chvUserName
Where ContactId = @intContactId
and TSEQUAL(ts, @tsOriginal)

Return @@Error
```

You will have no problem executing this code from Transact-SQL:

```
Declare @intErrorCode int
Exec @intErrorCode = prUpdateContact_1
                    1,         'Dejan',    'Sunderic',
                    '121-1111', '111-1112', 'dejans@hotmail.com',
                    1,         'dejans',   0x00000000000009C3
Select @intErrorCode ErrorCode
```

Unfortunately, some versions of client development tools (for example, Visual Basic) and some data access methods (for example, RDO and ADO) have problems retrieving and using timestamp values.

Before you implement 50 stored procedures in this manner, you should test whether your client development tools support timestamp values. If they do not, you must implement a workaround.

timestamp Conversion

The first workaround that comes to mind is to pass the timestamp as some other data type. Binary(8) and varchar are the first options most people try. Unfortunately, client tools usually do not support binary data types either. The trouble with varchar is that SQL Server converts the timestamp to an empty string.

One solution that works is based on the conversion of the timestamp to a datetime or money data type (sounds strange, doesn't it?). Conversion in the opposite direction results in the same timestamp as well. You can test this workaround using the following code:

```
declare @dtmOriginal datetime,
        @tsOriginal timestamp

Set @tsOriginal = 0x00000000000009C3

select @dtmOriginal = Convert(datetime, @tsOriginal)
select @dtmOriginal, Convert (timestamp, @dtmOriginal)
```

NOTE

Both of these data types are 8 bytes long, as is the timestamp *data type. Converted* datetime *or* money *values do not have any meaning. Although "timestamp" sounds as if it contains date information, it is, as previously stated, just a sequential number that is increased with every database change.*

The stored procedure has to be modified as follows:

```
Create Procedure prUpdateContact
-- update conrecord from contact table
-- prevent user from overwriting changed record
    (
        @intContactId int,
        @chvFirstName varchar(30),
        @chvLastName varchar(30),
        @chvPhone typPhone,
        @chvFax typPhone,
        @chvEmail typEmail,
```

```
                @insOrgUnitId smallint,
                @chvUserName varchar(50),
                @dtmOriginalTS datetime
        )
As
set nocount on
declare    @tsOriginalTS timestamp,
           @intErrorCode int


set @intErrorCode = @@Error


if @intErrorCode = 0
begin
     Set @tsOriginalTS = Convert(timestamp, @dtmOriginalTS)
     set @intErrorCode = @@Error
end



if @intErrorCode = 0
begin
     Update Contact
     Set FirstName = @chvFirstName,
         LastName = @chvLastName,
         Phone = @chvPhone,
         Fax = @chvFax,
         Email = @chvEmail,
         OrgUnitId = @insOrgUnitId,
         UserName = @chvUserName
     where ContactId = @intContactId
     and TSEqual(ts, @tsOriginalTS)

     set @intErrorCode = @@Error
end

return @intErrorCode
```

Naturally, you have to read records using a stored procedure that will convert the timestamp to a datetime or money data type, too:

```
Create Procedure prGetContact
-- get Contact record with timestamp converted to datetime
    (
        @intContactId int
    )
As
```

```
set nocount on

SELECT ContactId,
       FirstName,
       LastName,
       Phone,
       Fax,
       Email,
       OrgUnitId,
       UserName,
       Convert(datetime, ts) dtmTimestamp
FROM Contact
where ContactId = @intContactId

return @@Error
```

Full-Text Search and Indexes

The Standard and Enterprise editions of SQL Server 2000 include *Microsoft Search Service,* a search engine that allows *full-text indexing and querying* like the search engines used to query the Web. You can search for combinations of words and phrases. It allows linguistic searches whereby the engine also matches variations of the original word (singular, plural, tenses, and so on). The result may be a simple list or a table that ranks how well the results match the search criteria. Part of the criteria may also be the proximity of words and phrases—that is, how close one word is to another.

These capabilities are different from those of standard database search engines, in which you can do the following:

▶ Search for an exact match of a word or phrase

▶ Use wild card characters and the Like operator to search for character patterns

▶ Use indexes only if a pattern matches the beginning of the field

Microsoft Search Service was first introduced as a component of Internet Information Server. At that time, it was called Index Server.

I will not go into the details of Microsoft Search Service's architecture and administration, except to note that

▶ Full-text indexes are not stored in databases but in files (usually in C:\ Program Files\Microsoft SQL Server\MSSQL\FTDATA).

► You have to set the full-text index search capability and create full-text catalogs on tables and columns explicitly.

► A table must have a unique index based on a single field to be indexed in this manner.

I will focus on full-text search capabilities. The two most important predicates are Contains and Freetext. They are designed to be used in the Where clause of a Select statement.

The Contains predicate returns true or false for records that contain specified keywords. Variations of this predicate accommodate linguistic searches for variations of words and for words that are in proximity to other words. For more details, see SQL Server Books Online.

Freetext orders the search engine to evaluate specified text and extract "important" words and phrases. It then constructs queries in the background to be executed against the table.

The following stored procedure implements different forms of full-text search on the `ActivityLog.Note` field:

```
Alter Procedure prFTSearchActivityLog
-- full-text search of ActivityLog.Note
-- this will only work if you enable full-text search
    (
          @chvKeywords varchar(255),
          @inySearchType tinyint
    )
As
set nocount on
--------- Constants -----------
declare    @c_Contains int,
           @c_FreeText int,
           @c_FormsOf int

Set        @c_Contains = 0
Set        @c_FreeText = 1
Set        @c_FormsOf = 2
--------- Constants -----------

if @inySearchType = @c_Contains
    exec ('select * from Activity Where Contains(Note, '
          + @chvKeywords + ')')
else if @inySearchType = @c_FreeText
    exec ('select * from Activity Where FreeText(Note, '
```

```
            + @chvKeywords + ')')
else if @inySearchType = @c_FormsOf
    exec ('select * from Activity '
          + 'Where FreeText(Note, FORMSOF(INFLECTIONAL,'
          + @chvKeywords + ')')

Return
```

NOTE

Full-text search has additional features related to the use of ContainsTable and FreeText table and the use of the Formsof, Near, and Weight keywords, but the description of these features is beyond the scope of this chapter and this book.

Nested Stored Procedures

Nested stored procedures are simply stored procedures that were called by other stored procedures. Using SQL Server 2000, it is possible to do 32 levels of nesting. You can investigate current nesting level using the @@nestlevel function.

This section explores methods for passing recordsets between a nested stored procedure and its caller.

Using Temporary Tables to Pass a Recordset to a Nested Stored Procedure

Some programming languages (such as Visual Basic and Pascal) use the concept of global and module variables. These types of variables are very useful for passing complex parameters (like arrays or recordsets) to a procedure when its parameter list supports only basic data types.

The same problem exists with stored procedures. You cannot pass a recordset through a parameter list to a stored procedure from the current batch or stored procedure, and neither recordsets nor local variables from the outer stored procedure (or batch) are visible to the inner stored procedure unless they are passed as a parameter to that procedure.

Unfortunately, SQL Server does not support user-defined global variables. Modules, and therefore module variables, do not even exist in Transact-SQL.

One way to pass a recordset is to create and fill a temporary table and then reference that temporary table from the inner stored procedure, which will be able to see and access its contents. The following example consists of two stored procedures. The first is business-oriented and collects a list of properties associated with an inventory asset. The list is implemented as a temporary table:

```
Alter Procedure prGetInventoryProperties_TempTbl_Outer
/*
Return comma-delimited list of properties
that are describing asset.
i.e.: Property = Value unit;Property = Value unit;Property =
Value unit; Property = Value unit; Property = Value unit; Property =
Value unit;
*/
    @intInventoryId int
As
set nocount on

declare     @chvProperties varchar(8000)

Create table #List(Id int identity(1,1),
                  Item varchar(255))

-- identify Properties associated with asset
insert into #List (Item)
    select Property + '=' + Value + ' ' +  Coalesce(Unit, '') + '; '
    from InventoryProperty inner join Property
    on InventoryProperty.PropertyId = Property.PropertyId
    where InventoryProperty.InventoryId = @intInventoryId

-- call sp that converts records to a single varchar
exec prConvertTempTbl @chvProperties OUTPUT

-- display result
select @chvProperties Properties

drop table #List

return 0
go
```

The second stored procedure, the nested stored procedure, is not business-oriented—unlike the caller stored procedure, the nested stored procedure does not implement the business rule. It simply loops through the records in the temporary table (which was created in the calling stored procedure) and assembles them into a single `varchar` variable:

```
Alter Procedure prConvertTempTbl
-- Convert information from Temporary table to a single varchar
```

```
        @chvResult varchar(8000) output
As
set nocount on

declare @intCountItems int,
        @intCounter int,
        @chvItem varchar(255),
        @insLenItem smallint,
        @insLenResult smallint

-- set loop
select @intCountItems = Count(*),
       @intCounter = 1,
       @chvResult = ''
from #List

-- loop through list of items
while @intCounter <= @intCountItems
begin
    -- get one property
    select @chvItem = Item
    from #List
    where Id = @intCounter

    -- check will new string fit
    select @insLenItem = DATALENGTH(@chvItem),
           @insLenResult = DATALENGTH(@chvResult)

    if @insLenResult + @insLenItem > 8000
    begin
        print 'List is too long (over 8000 characters)!'
        return 1
    end

    -- assemble list
    set @chvResult = @chvResult + @chvItem

    -- let's go another round and get another item
    set @intCounter = @intCounter + 1
end

return 0
go
```

You can execute this example from Query Analyzer, as shown in Figure 9-4.

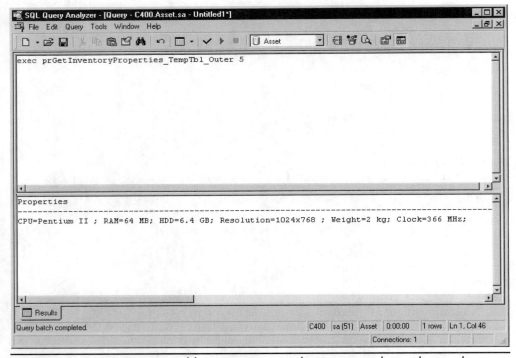

Figure 9-4   *Using temporary tables to pass a recordset to a nested stored procedure*

You may question when this kind of solution is justified and whether these stored procedures are coupled. It is true that neither of these stored procedures can function without the other. If you have other stored procedures that also use prConvertTempTbl, I would consider this solution justified.

Using a Cursor to Pass a Recordset to a Nested Stored Procedure

Similar solutions can be implemented using cursors. Cursors are also visible to, and accessible from, nested stored procedures.

The following example also consists of two stored procedures. The first is business-oriented and creates a cursor with properties associated with specified inventory:

```
create Procedure prGetInventoryProperties_Cursor_Nested
/*
Return comma-delimited list of properties
that are describing asset.
```

```
i.e.: Property = Value unit;Property = Value unit;Property =
Value unit; Property = Value unit; Property = Value unit; Property =
Value unit;
*/
     (
          @intInventoryId int,
          @chvProperties varchar(8000) OUTPUT,
          @debug int = 0
     )
As

Select @chvProperties = ''

Declare curItems Cursor For
     Select Property + '=' + [Value] + ' '
             + Coalesce([Unit], '') + '; ' Item
     From InventoryProperty Inner Join Property
     On InventoryProperty.PropertyId = Property.PropertyId
     Where InventoryProperty.InventoryId = @intInventoryId

Open curItems

Exec prProcess_Cursor_Nested @chvProperties OUTPUT, @debug

Close curItems
Deallocate curItems

Return 0
Go
```

The second stored procedure is generic and converts information from a cursor into a single variable:

```
Create Procedure prProcess_Cursor_Nested
-- Process information from cursor initiated in calling sp.
-- Convert records into a single varchar.
     (
          @chvResult varchar(8000) OUTPUT,
          @debug int = 0
     )

As

Declare    @intCountProperties int,
           @intCounter int,
```

```
            @chvItem varchar(255),
            @insLenItem smallint,
            @insLenResult smallint

Fetch Next From curItems
Into @chvItem

While (@@FETCH_STATUS = 0)
Begin

    If @debug <> 0
        Select @chvItem Item

    -- check whether new string will fit
    Select @insLenItem   = DATALENGTH(@chvItem),
           @insLenResult = DATALENGTH(@chvResult)

    If @insLenResult + @insLenItem > 8000
    Begin
        Select 'List is too long (over 8000 characters)!'
        Return 1
    End

    -- assemble list
    If @insLenItem > 0
        Set @chvResult = @chvResult + @chvItem

    If @debug <> 0
        Select @chvResult chvResult

    Fetch Next From curItems
    Into @chvItem

End

Return 0
Go
```

You can execute this code from Query Analyzer, as shown in Figure 9-5.

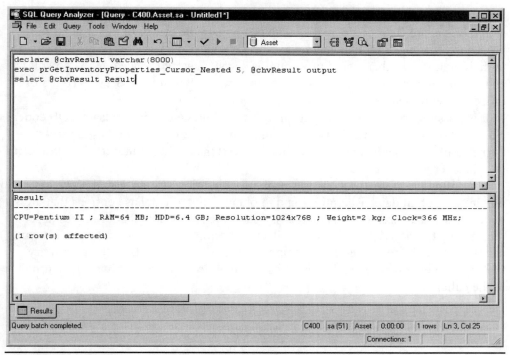

```
declare @chvResult varchar(8000)
exec prGetInventoryProperties_Cursor_Nested 5, @chvResult output
select @chvResult Result
```

```
Result
--------------------------------------------------------------------------------
CPU=Pentium II ; RAM=64 MB; HDD=6.4 GB; Resolution=1024x768 ; Weight=2 kg; Clock=366 MHz;

(1 row(s) affected)
```

Figure 9-5   *Using a cursor to pass a recordset to a nested stored procedure*

How to Process the Result Set of a Stored Procedure

From time to time, you will encounter stored procedures that return result sets that
you need to process. This is not as simple as it sounds.

One option is to receive the result set in a client application or middleware component
and process it from there. Sometimes this option is not acceptable, for a variety of
reasons. For example, the result set might be too big, in which case network traffic
could be considerably increased. Since the result set needs to be transferred to the
middleware server before it is processed, the performance of the system could be
degraded. There might be security implications—for example, you may determine
that a user should have access only to a segment of a result set and not to the complete
result set.

An alternative option is to copy the source code of the stored procedure into your stored procedure. This could be illegal, depending on the source of the original stored procedure. It also reduces the maintainability of your code, since you have two copies to maintain; if the other stored procedure is a system stored procedure, Microsoft can change its internals with the release of each new version of SQL Server. Your stored procedure will then need to be changed.

It is possible to collect the result set of a stored procedure in Transact-SQL code. You need to create a (temporary) table, the structure of which matches the structure of the result set exactly, and then redirect (insert) the result set into it. Then you can do whatever you want with it.

The following stored procedure uses the sp_dboption system stored procedure to obtain a list of all database options and to obtain a list of database options that are set on the Asset database. Records that have a structure identical to that of the result set as returned by the stored procedure are collected in temporary tables. The Insert statement can then store the result set in the temporary table. The contents of the temporary tables are later compared and a list of database options not currently set is returned to the caller.

```
Create Procedure prNonSelectedDBOption
-- return list of non-selected database options

    @chvDBName sysname

As

Set Nocount On

Create Table #setable
    (
        name nvarchar(35)
    )
Create Table #current
    (
        name nvarchar(35)
    )

-- collect all options
Insert Into #setable
    Exec sp_dboption

-- collect current options
Insert Into #current
    Exec sp_dboption @dbname = @chvDBName
```

```
-- return non-selected
Select name non_selected
From #setable
Where name not in ( Select name
                        From #current
                  )

Drop Table #setable
Drop Table #current

Return 0
```

The only trouble with this method is that you need to know the structure of the result set of the stored procedure in advance in order to create a table with the same structure, although this is not a problem for user-defined stored procedures. It used to be a problem for system stored procedures, but SQL Server Books Online now provides information regarding the result sets generated by these stored procedures.

NOTE

Unfortunately, it is not possible to capture the contents of a result set if a stored procedure returns more than one result set, as is the case with sp_spaceused when no table name is specified.

This technique also works with the Exec statement. For example, if you try to collect a result set from the DBCC command in this way, SQL Server will return an error. But you can encapsulate the DBCC statement in a string and execute it from Exec.

The following stored procedure returns the percentage of log space used in a specified database:

```
Create Procedure prLogSpacePercentUsed
-- return percent of space used in transaction log for
-- specified database
    (
        @chvDbName sysname,
        @fltPercentUsed float OUTPUT
    )

As
Set Nocount On

Declare @intErrorCode int

Set @intErrorCode = @@Error
```

```
If @intErrorCode = 0
Begin
     Create Table #DBLogSpace
               (    dbname sysname,
                    LogSizeInMB float,
                    LogPercentUsed float,
                    Status int
               )
     Set @intErrorCode = @@Error
End

-- get log space info. for all databases
If @intErrorCode = 0
Begin
     Insert Into #DBLogSpace
          Exec ('DBCC SQLPERF (LogSpace)')
     set @intErrorCode = @@Error
end

-- get percent for specified database
if @intErrorCode = 0
begin
     select @fltPercentUsed = LogPercentUsed
     from #DBLogSpace
     where dbname = @chvDbName

     set @intErrorCode = @@Error
end

drop table #DBLogSpace

return @intErrorCode
```

You can test this stored procedure from Query Analyzer, as shown on Figure 9-6.

These techniques were extremely important before SQL Server 2000. It is now possible to use the `table` data type as a return value for user-defined functions. You learned how to use table-valued user-defined functions in Chapter 8. Unfortunately, it is still not possible to use a `table` variable as the output parameter of a stored procedure.

You have another option available when you want to pass a result set (or multiple result sets) to a calling stored procedure—you can use the `cursor` data type as the output parameter of a stored procedure. In the following example,

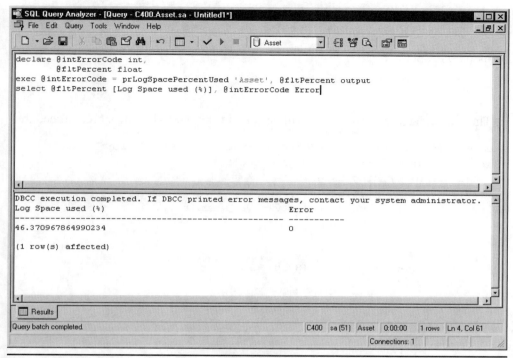

Figure 9-6   *Percentage of log space used in specified database*

prGetInventoryProperties_CursorGet creates and opens a cursor. The content of the cursor is then returned to the calling procedure.

```
Create Procedure prGetInventoryProperties_CursorGet
-- Return Cursor that contains properties
-- that are describing selected asset.

    (
        @intInventoryId int,
        @curProperties Cursor Varying Output
    )

As

Set @curProperties = Cursor Forward_Only Static For
    Select Property, Value, Unit
    From InventoryProperty inner join Property
```

```
        On InventoryProperty.PropertyId = Property.PropertyId
        Where InventoryProperty.InventoryId = @intInventoryId

Open @curProperties

Return 0
```

The preceding stored procedure will be called from the following stored procedure:

```
Create Procedure prGetInventoryProperties_UseNestedCursor
-- return comma-delimited list of properties
-- that are describing asset.
-- i.e.: Property = Value unit;Property = Value unit;
-- Property = Value unit;Property = Value unit;...

    (
        @intInventoryId int,
        @chvProperties varchar(8000) OUTPUT,
        @debug int = 0
    )

As

Declare @intCountProperties int,
        @intCounter int,
        @chvProperty varchar(50),
        @chvValue varchar(50),
        @chvUnit varchar(50),
        @insLenProperty smallint,
        @insLenValue smallint,
        @insLenUnit smallint,
        @insLenProperties smallint

Set @chvProperties = ''

Declare @CrsrVar Cursor

Exec prGetInventoryProperties_CursorGet @intInventoryId,
                                        @CrsrVar Output

Fetch Next From @CrsrVar
Into @chvProperty, @chvValue, @chvUnit

While (@@FETCH_STATUS = 0)
```

```
Begin

    Set @chvUnit = Coalesce(@chvUnit, '')

    If @debug <> 0
        Select @chvProperty Property,
               @chvValue [Value],
               @chvUnit [Unit]

    -- check whether new string will fit
    Select @insLenProperty = DATALENGTH(@chvProperty),
           @insLenValue = DATALENGTH(@chvValue),
           @insLenUnit = DATALENGTH(@chvUnit),
           @insLenProperties = DATALENGTH(@chvProperties)

    If @insLenProperties + 2
       + @insLenProperty + 1
       + @insLenValue + 1 + @insLenUnit > 8000
    Begin
        Select 'List of properties is too long (over 8000 chrs)!'
        Return 1
    End

    -- assemble list
    Set @chvProperties = @chvProperties
                       + @chvProperty + '='
                       + @chvValue + ' '
                       + @chvUnit + '; '
    If @debug <> 0
        Select @chvProperties chvProperties

    Fetch Next From @CrsrVar
    Into @chvProperty, @chvValue, @chvUnit

End

Close @CrsrVar
Deallocate @CrsrVar

Return 0
```

It is the responsibility of the caller to properly close and deallocate the cursor at the end.

> **TIP**
>
> *You should not use a cursor as an output parameter of a stored procedure unless you have to. Such a solution is inferior because procedures are coupled and prone to errors. If you are working with SQL Server 2000, you should use table-valued user-defined functions as part of your Select statements instead.*

Using Identity Values

In previous chapters, I introduced the function of identity values in a table. They are used to generate surrogate keys—unique identifiers based on sequential numbers.

A Standard Problem and Solution

Identity values are similar to the `autonumber` data type in Access tables. But there is one difference that generates many questions in Usenet newsgroups among developers who are used to Access/DAO behavior. When you insert a record into a table, the value of the `autonumber` fied is immediately available in Access. Unfortunately, due to the nature of the client/server environment, this is not the case in SQL Server.

The best way to insert a record into a SQL Server table and obtain an identity key is to use a stored procedure. The following stored procedure, prInsertInventory, presents such a solution. A new record is inserted into a table and the key is read using the @@identity function.

```
Create Procedure prInsertInventory
-- insert inventory record and return Id
    @intEquipmentId int,
    @intLocationId int,
    @inyStatusId tinyint,
    @intLeaseId int,
    @intLeaseScheduleId int,
    @intOwnerId int,
    @mnsRent smallmoney,
    @mnsLease smallmoney,
    @mnsCost smallmoney,
    @inyAcquisitionTypeID int,
    @intInventoryId int output

As
Set Nocount On

Declare @intErrorCode int
Select @intErrorCode = @@Error
```

```
If @intErrorCode = 0
Begin
    Insert into Inventory (EquipmentId, LocationId, StatusId,
                    LeaseId, LeaseScheduleId, OwnerId,
                    Rent, Lease, Cost,
                    AcquisitionTypeID)
        Values (        @intEquipmentId, @intLocationId, @inyStatusId,
                    @intLeaseId, @intLeaseScheduleId, @intOwnerId,
                    @mnsRent, @mnsLease, @mnsCost,
                    @inyAcquisitionTypeID)

    Select @intErrorCode = @@Error,
            @intInventoryId = @@identity
End

Return @intErrorCode
```

Identity Values and Triggers

Unfortunately, the previous solution does not always work as you might expect.
SQL Server has a bug/feature that can change a value stored in the @@identity
global variable. If the table in which the record was inserted (in this case, Inventory)
has a trigger that inserts a record into some other table with an identity key, the value
of that key will be recorded in @@identity.

You can reproduce this behavior using the following script. It must be executed
against the *tempdb* database.

```
Create Table a (a_id int identity(1,1),
                a_desc varchar(20),
                b_desc varchar(20))
Go

Create Table b (b_id int identity(1,1),
                b_desc varchar(20))
Go

Create Trigger tr_a_I
On dbo.a
After Insert      -- For Insert
As

If @@Rowcount = 0
    Return

Insert Into b (b_desc)
```

```
     Select b_desc from inserted
Go
```

Now execute this batch:

```
Insert into b (b_desc)
Values ('1')

Insert into a (a_desc, b_desc)
Values ('aaa', 'bbb')

Select @@identity [IdentityValue]
```

Query Analyzer returns the following result:

```
(1 row(s) affected)


(1 row(s) affected)


IdentityValue
----------------------------------------
2

(1 row(s) affected)
```

The first Insert statement adds the first record to table b. The second Insert statement adds the first record in a table. Because there is a trigger on the table, another record (the second one) will be inserted into table b, and the value of @@identity will be set to 2. If there was no trigger, the Select statement would return a value of 1.

Last Identity Value in the Scope

The problem with identity values and triggers has been resolved in the proper manner with SQL Server 2000. The new Scope_Identity() function returns the last identity value generated in the current scope of the current process. The following example adds this function to the code executed earlier against the *tempdb* database:

```
Insert into b (b_desc)
Values ('1')

Insert into a (a_desc, b_desc)
```

```
Values ('aaa', 'bbb')


Select @@identity [@@Identity], SCOPE_IDENTITY() [SCOPE_IDENTITY()]
```

When you execute it, notice that the Scope_Identity() function returns the proper result:

```
(1 row(s) affected)

(1 row(s) affected)

@@Identity                               SCOPE_IDENTITY()
---------------------------------------  ----------------------------
4                                        2

(1 row(s) affected)
```

NOTE

You now should use Scope_Identity() instead of the @@identity function.

GUIDs

Distributed environments have different requirements for the generation of unique keys. A typical example is a database of sales representatives who are carrying notebook computers with local databases installed on them. These users do not have to be connected to a central database. They do the majority of their work locally and then replicate the information in their local database to the central database once in a while. The use of identity fields as a unique key will lead to unique key violations, unless the key is composite and consists of an identity field and another field that is unique to the user. Another solution could be to divide key ranges between users (for example, by setting an identity seed differently in each database). Each of these solutions has different limitations.

One way to generate unique keys is to use GUIDs (globally unique identifiers). The `uniqueidentifier` data type was discussed in Chapter 4. When a column in a table is assigned this data type, it does not mean that its (unique) value will be generated automatically. The unique value must be generated using the NewID() function.

Typically, a GUID value is generated as a default value of a table, as shown in the following code:

```
Create Table Location(
 LocationId uniqueidentifier NOT NULL DEFAULT newid(),
 Location varchar(50) not null,
 CompanyId int NOT NULL,
 PrimaryContactName varchar(60) NOT NULL,
 Address varchar(30) NOT NULL,
 City varchar(30) NOT NULL,
 ProvinceId varchar(3) NULL,
 PostalCode varchar(10) NOT NULL,
 Country varchar(20) NOT NULL,
 Phone varchar(15) NOT NULL,
 Fax varchar(15) NULL
)
Go
```

You can also generate a GUID in a stored procedure:

```
Create Procedure prInsertLocation
 @Location varchar(50),
 @CompanyId int,
 @PrimaryContactName varchar(60),
 @Address varchar(30) ,
 @City varchar(30) ,
 @ProvinceId varchar(3) ,
 @PostalCode varchar(10),
 @Country varchar(20) ,
 @Phone varchar(15),
 @Fax varchar(15),
 @LocationGUID uniqueidentifier OUTPUT

AS
Set @LocationGUID  = NewId()

Insert Into Location (Location_id, Location, CompanyId,
                      PrimaryContactName, Address, City,
                      ProvinceId, PostalCode, Country,
                      Phone, Fax)
values (@LocationGUID, @Location, @CompanyId,
        @PrimaryContactName, @Address, @City,
        @ProvinceId, @PostalCode, @Country,
        @Phone, @Fax)
Return @@error
```

The stored procedure will return the GUID value to the caller.

A While Loop with Min() or Max() Functions

It is possible to iterate through a table or recordset using a While statement with the aggregate() function, which returns extreme values: Min() and Max(). Take a look at the following batch:

```
declare Value int
-- get first value
Select @Value = MIN(Value)
From aTable

-- loop
While @Value is not null
Begin
    -- do something instead of just displaying a value
    Select @Value value

    -- get next value
    Select @Value = MIN(Value)
    From aTable
    Where Value > @Value
End
```

The first Select statement with the Min() function obtains a first value from the set (table):

```
Select @Value = MIN(Value)
From aTable
```

The next value is obtained in a loop as a minimal value bigger than the previous one:

```
Select @Value = MIN(Value)
From aTable
Where Value > @Value
```

If no records qualify as members of the set, an aggregate() function will return null. You can then use null as a criterion to exit the loop:

```
While @Value is not null
```

To demonstrate this method, the following rewrites prSpaceUsedByTables, which displays the space used by each user-defined table in the current database:

```
Create Procedure prSpaceUsedByTables_4
-- loop through table names in current database
    -- display info about amount of space used by each table

-- demonstration of while loop

As
Set nocount on
Declare @TableName sysname

-- get first table name
Select @TableName = Min(name)
From sysobjects
Where xtype = 'U'

While @TableName is not null
Begin

    -- display space used
    Exec sp_spaceused  @TableName

    -- get next table
    Select @TableName = Min(name)
    From sysobjects
    Where xtype = 'U'
    And name > @TableName
End

Return 0
```

This was just an academic example. Naturally, the proper solution includes a temporary table to collect all results and display them at the end in one recordset. Note that I am not talking about a temporary table such as the one used in Chapter 4 for looping using a While statement.

You can step backward through the recordset if you use the Max() function and if you compare the old record and the remainder of the set using the < operator.

TIP

This method may be a quick solution for problems that require iteration. However, solutions based on set operations usually provide superior performance.

Looping with sp_MSForEachTable and sp_MSForEachDb

You can find and review the sp_MSForEachTable and sp_MSForEachDb system stored procedures in the *master* database, but they are not documented in SQL Server Books Online. Microsoft has designed them to support writing a single statement that can perform the same activity on all databases on the current server or on all tables in the current database.

To demonstrate this, set Query Analyzer to Result In Text and execute the following:

```
exec sp_MSforEachDb
@Command1 = "Print '?'",
@Command2 = "select count(name) from ?.dbo.sysobjects where xtype = 'U'"
```

SQL Server returns a count of user-defined tables from each database on the current server:

```
Asset
----------
36

DEPLOY
----------
0

master
----------
10
...
```

The @Command1 and @Command2 parameters are used to specify the actions that the stored procedure will execute against each database. The database name was replaced with a question mark. It is possible to specify up to three commands (using @Command3). Behind the scenes, the stored procedure will open a cursor for the records in the sysdatabases table (which contains a list of existing databases) and dynamically assemble a batch that will be executed against each record in a loop.

The following command creates a report about space usage of each database:

```
exec sp_MSforEachDb @Command1 = "use ? exec sp_Spaceused"
```

It is even more interesting to run sp_spaceused against all tables in the current database:

```
exec sp_MSforEachTable @Command1 = "sp_spaceused '?'"
```

Unfortunately, the result is not nicely aligned in either text or grid mode.

You can also get a number of records in each table:

```
exec sp_MSforEachTable
    @Command1 = "Print '?'",
    @Command2 = "select Count(*) from ?"
```

In the last two queries, the result is not ordered as you might expect. It simply follows the order of records in systables (in other words, the order of creation). If you want to order it by table name, you must use the @whereand parameter:

```
exec sp_MSforEachTable
    @command1 = "exec sp_spaceused '?'",
    @whereand = "order by name"
```

This parameter was originally designed to allow you to add a Where clause, but since the query is dynamically assembled, you can sneak an Order By clause into it as well.

You can use the @replacechar parameter to specify a different placeholder for database and table names. This parameter is useful when your commands require the use of a question mark—for example, as a wild card in the Like clause.

If a command should be executed only once before or after the loop, you should use the @precommand and @postcommand parameters.

Property Management

One of the features that I have always wanted to see in SQL Server is the capability to add descriptions to database objects. Microsoft Access already has this feature. Naturally, you could be even more ambitious. It would be helpful on some projects to be able to store additional attributes such as field formats, input masks, captions, and the location and size of screen fields in the database. The more things you manage centrally, the fewer maintenance and deployment issues you will have later in production.

SQL Server 2000 introduces *extended properties.* You can define extended properties, store them in the database, and associate them with database objects. Each database object can have any number of extended properties, and an extended property can store a sql_variant value up to 7500 bytes long.

SQL Server 2000 introduces three stored procedures and one function for managing extended properties. The sp_addextendedproperty, sp_updateextendedproperty, and sp_dropextendedproperty stored procedures are used to create, change, or delete extended properties, respectively. They all have very unusual syntax. The following example examines this syntax in sp_addextendedproperty:

```
sp_addextendedproperty
    [@name =]{'property_name'}
    [, [@value =]{'extended_property_value'}
        [, [@level0type =]{'level0_object_type'}
        , [@level0name =]{'level0_object_name'}
            [, [@level1type =]{'level1_object_type'}
            , [@level1name =]{'level1_object_name'}
                    [, [@level2type =]{'level2_object_type'}
                    , [@level2name =]{'level2_object_name'}
                    ]
            ]
        ]
    ]
```

Here, @name and @value are the name and value of the extended property. Other parameters define the name and type of the object with which the extended property will be associated. For this reason, database objects are divided into three levels:

1. User, user-defined type
2. Table, view, stored procedure, function, rule, default
3. Column, index, constraint, trigger, parameter

If you want to assign an extended property to an object of the second level, you must also specify an object of the first level. If you want to assign an extended property to an object of the third level, you must also specify an object of the second level. For example, to specify an extended property Format to be associated with the column Phone in the table Contact, you must specify the owner of the table:

```
Exec sp_addextendedproperty 'Format', '(999)999-9999',
                'user', dbo,
                    'table', Contact,
                        'column', Phone
```

The fn_ListExtendedProperty() function is designed to list the extended properties of an object. It requires that you specify objects in the same manner as the stored procedures do. You can see the result set returned by the function in Figure 9-7.

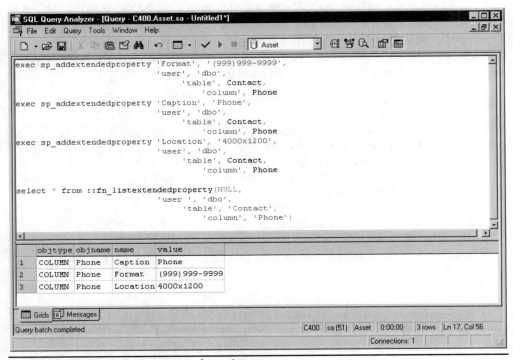

Figure 9-7   *Extended properties of an object*

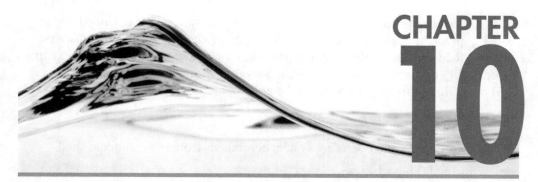

CHAPTER
10

Interaction with the SQL Server Environment

T his chapter focuses on the ways you can use system and extended stored procedures to interact with the SQL Server environment. It also discusses the ways user-defined stored procedures can help you leverage the existing functionality of elements within the SQL Server environment.

By the end of this chapter, you will be able to do the following:

▶ Use OLE Automation in Transact-SQL

▶ Run programs and operating system commands from the command shell

▶ Execute DTS packages

▶ Implement looping in DTS packages

▶ Manage jobs in Job Scheduler

▶ Read and write Registry entries

▶ Use the e-mail capabilities of SQL Server to notify users of events on the server

▶ Use the e-mail capabilities of SQL Server to send queries, process them, and receive result sets

▶ Publish the contents of the database on the Web

▶ Perform administration tasks with stored procedures

▶ Manage application security

Execution of OLE Automation/COM Objects

Microsoft has developed several technologies that enable developers to encapsulate code and custom objects into executable components. These components can then be invoked by other applications developed in the same (or any other) programming language that supports these kinds of components. Through the years, this technology has been known by different names: OLE, OLE Automation, COM, DCOM, Automation, ActiveX, COM+ ... and the saga continues.

SQL Server can initiate code components and access the properties and methods exposed by them. A set of system stored procedures (with the prefix sp_OA) has been designed and implemented in SQL Server to help you accomplish such tasks.

NOTE

When Microsoft first unveiled this feature in SQL Server, code components were known as "OLE Automation objects." For this reason, Microsoft attached the OA prefix to these stored procedure names, and I used OLE Automation Objects in the title of the section.

To demonstrate the use of OLE Automation on a simple Visual Basic function:

1. Create the DjnToolkit ActiveX DLL project in Visual Basic and then create a DjnTools class.

2. Create a method called SpellNumber, which ignores the input value (currency amount) and returns a constant string (see Figure 10-1).

NOTE

Even if you run the object from the Visual Basic IDE (instead of compiling and installing it), you will still be able to access it from Transact-SQL code. This is an important feature for debugging the object.

The stored procedure shown in the code on the following page first initiates the COM object using the sp_OACreate system stored procedure. It obtains a token @intObject, which is used from that point to access the class.

Figure 10-1   *A COM object created in Visual Basic*

The sp_OAMethod stored procedure is used to execute class methods. The return value and input parameter of the method are placed at the end of the stored procedure's parameter list.

Before the stored procedure is complete, the COM object must be destroyed using sp_OADestroy.

If an automation error occurs at any point, sp_OAGetErrorInfo can be used to obtain the source and description of the most recent error:

```
Alter Procedure prSpellNumber
-- demo of use of Automation objects
    @mnsAmount money,
    @chvAmount varchar(500) output,
    @debug int = 0

As
set nocount on

Declare @intErrorCode int,
        @intObject int,  -- hold object token
        @bitObjectCreated bit,
        @chvSource varchar(255),
        @chvDesc varchar(255)

Select @intErrorCode = @@Error

If @intErrorCode = 0
    exec @intErrorCode = sp_OACreate 'DjnToolkit.DjnTools',
                                        @intObject OUTPUT

If @intErrorCode = 0
    Set @bitObjectCreated = 1
else
    Set @bitObjectCreated = 0

If @intErrorCode = 0
    exec @intErrorCode = sp_OAMethod @intObject,
                                      'SpellNumber',
                                      @chvAmount OUTPUT,
                                      @mnsAmount

If @intErrorCode <> 0
begin
```

```
        Raiserror ('Unable to obtain spelling of number', 16, 1)
        exec sp_OAGetErrorInfo @intObject,
                               @chvSource OUTPUT,
                               @chvDesc OUTPUT
        Set @chvDesc = 'Error ('
                     + Convert(varchar, @intErrorCode)
                     + ', ' + @chvSource  + ') : ' + @chvDesc
        Raiserror (@chvDesc, 16, 1)
end

if @bitObjectCreated = 1
    exec  sp_OADestroy @intObject

return @intErrorCode
```

Once you are sure that communication between Transact-SQL and Visual Basic code is working, you can write code in Visual Basic that converts numbers to text. Since this is not a book about Visual Basic, I will not go into detail on that subject.

There is an even better example on how to use these stored procedures in Chapter 11.

Data Type Conversion

Keep in mind that code components and Transact-SQL code use different data types. You have to set compatible data types on both sides to allow the OLE Automation system stored procedures to automatically convert data between them. You can identify most of the compatible data types using common sense (for example, `varchar`, `char`, and `text` types in SQL Server translate to the `String` data type in Visual Basic, and the `int` SQL Server data type translates to the `Long` data type). However, some data types deserve special attention.

When values are passed from SQL Server to Visual Basic, `binary`, `varbinary`, and `image` are converted to a one-dimensional `Byte` array. Any Transact-SQL value set to null is converted to a `Variant` set to null. `Decimal` and `numeric` are converted to `String` (not `currency`).

When values are passed from Visual Basic to SQL Server, `Long`, `Integer`, `Byte`, `Boolean`, and `Object` are converted to the `int` data type. Both `Double` and `Single` data types are converted to `float`. Strings shorter than 255 characters are converted to `varchar`, and strings longer then 255 characters are converted to the `text` data type. One-dimensional `Byte()` arrays shorter than 255 characters become `varbinary` values, and those longer than 255 become `image` values.

Running Programs

Before Microsoft included support for OLE Automation and COM in SQL Server, administrators ran command prompt programs and commands using the xp_cmdshell extended stored procedure:

```
xp_cmdshell {'command'} [, no_output]
```

When xp_cmdshell is executed, a *command* string is passed to the command shell of the operating system to be executed. Any rows of text that are normally displayed by the command shell are returned by the extended stored procedure as a result set. There is also an option to ignore the output.

The status of the execution is returned as an output parameter of the extended stored procedure. Its value is set to 0 if execution was successful and 1 if execution failed. In Windows 95 and Windows 98, the value will always be set to 0.

Figure 10-2 shows the use of the command prompt instruction to list files in the Backup folder. This output can be received in a temporary table and further processed in Transact-SQL code.

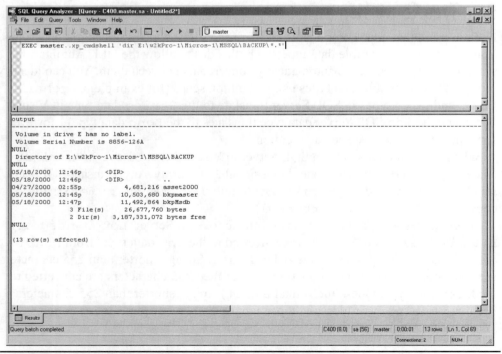

Figure 10-2   *Using xp_cmdshell to run commands and programs*

The following batch copies files from the Backup folder to another drive:

```
exec master..xp_cmdshell 'copy e:\w2kPro~1\Mocros~1\'
                    + 'MSSQL\BACKUP\*.* m:', no_output
```

Running Windows Script Files

The Windows Script Host enables users to write and execute scripts in VBScript, JavaScript, and other languages compatible with the Windows environment. It was initially developed as an additional component, but it is now integrated into the Windows 98, Me, 2000, and XP platforms.

Script files usually have .vbs and .js extensions. They are executed from the Windows environment using wscript.exe or from the command prompt using csript.exe.

Execution of script files can also be initiated from Transact-SQL code. The following statement runs a demo script that starts Excel and populates a worksheet with information:

```
exec xp_cmdshell 'c:\windows\command\cscript.exe '
    + 'c:\windows\samples\wsh\Excel.vbs', NO_OUTPUT
```

Running/Looping Through DTS Packages

Data Transformation Services (DTS) is a SQL Server tool used for the visual design and execution of data transformation routines. These routines are stored on a server as DTS packages. Naturally, their design and management are beyond the scope of this book, but I will show you how to run a DTS package from a stored procedure.

SQL Server 2000 includes the dtsrun.exe utility, which allows you to execute DTS packages from the command prompt. We can simply call it using xp_cmdshell:

```
exec xp_cmdshell 'dtsrun /SA1000 /Udbo /E /NExportData '
                + '/ADatabase:8=Asset7 /AServer:8=A1000', NO_OUTPUT
```

One of the features that you might wish to use, but that is missing from DTS, is looping. The tool simply does not allow you to create tasks to be executed in a loop. The solution is to use a scripting language (such as T-SQL or VBScript) to launch a group of tasks (organized into a single DTS package) in a loop. The following procedure loops though a list of databases and executes a DTS package with a database name as an input parameter (a global variable in DTS terminology):

```
ALTER PROCEDURE   dbo.prDbLoop_DTS
--  loop through Asset databases
--  run the DTS package for each of them
    @debug int = 0
As
set nocount on
declare @intCount int,
        @intCounter int,
        @chvDOS varchar(2000),
        @chvDB sysname,
        @chvServer sysname

Declare @intErrorCode int,
        @chvProcedure sysname

set @chvProcedure = 'prDbLoop_DTS'
if @debug <> 0
    select '**** '+ @chvProcedure + ' START ****'
Select @intErrorCode = @@Error


If @intErrorCode = 0
Begin
    Create table #db(Id int identity(1,1),
                     Name sysname)
    Select @intErrorCode = @@Error
End

If @intErrorCode = 0
Begin
    insert into #db (Name)
        select Name from master.dbo.sysdatabases
        where name like 'Asset%'

    Select @intErrorCode = @@Error
End


If @intErrorCode = 0
Begin
    -- set loop
```

```
    select @intCount = Count(*),
           @intCounter = 1,
           @chvServer = @@SERVERNAME
    from #db
    Select @intErrorCode = @@Error
End


-- loop through list of databases
while @intErrorCode = 0 and @intCounter <= @intCount
begin
    -- get db
    If @intErrorCode = 0
    Begin
        select @chvDB = Name
        from #db
        where Id = @intCounter

         Select @intErrorCode = @@Error
    End


    If @intErrorCode = 0
    Begin
        SELECT   @chvDOS = 'dtsrun /S' + @chvServer
                   + ' /Udbo /E /NExportData'
                   + ' /ADatabase:8=' + @chvDB
                   + ' /AServer:8=' + @chvServer
        Select @intErrorCode = @@Error
    End


    If @intErrorCode = 0
    Begin
        if @debug = 0
            EXEC master.dbo.xp_cmdshell @chvDOS, no_output
        else
            select @chvDOS
        Select @intErrorCode = @@Error
    End

    -- let's go another round and get another property
    If @intErrorCode = 0
    Begin
        set @intCounter = @intCounter + 1
        Select @intErrorCode = @@Error
```

```
      End
end

drop table #db

if @debug <> 0
   select '**** '+ @chvProcedure + ' END ****'
return @intErrorCode
```

If you run the procedure, it will generate and execute the following set of commands:

```
dtsrun /SA1000 /Udbo /E /NExportData /ADatabase:8=Asset7 /AServer:8=A1000
dtsrun /SA1000 /Udbo /E /NExportData /ADatabase:8=Asset2000 /AServer:8=A1000
dtsrun /SA1000 /Udbo /E /NExportData /ADatabase:8=Asset2000_2 /AServer:8=A1000
```

Interacting with the NT Registry

Developers of client applications in a 32-bit environment often use the Registry as a repository for application configuration data and defaults. The Registry is a database (but not an RDBMS) that stores configuration information centrally.

SQL Server exposes the following extended stored procedures for manipulating the Registry:

Extended Stored Procedure	Purpose
xp_regread	Reads a Registry value
xp_regwrite	Writes to the Registry
xp_regdeletekey	Deletes a key
xp_regdeletevalue	Deletes a key's value
xp_regenumvalues	Lists names of value entries
xp_regaddmultistring	Adds a multi string (zero-delimited string)
xp_regremovemultistring	Removes a multi string (zero-delimited string)

xp_regread

This stored procedure enables you to read the value of the Registry key located on the specified path of the specified subtree:

```
xp_regread subtree,
           path,
           key,
           @value   OUTPUT
```

In the following example, this extended stored procedure reads the root directory of the SQL Server installation:

```
declare @chvSQLPath varchar(255)
exec master..xp_regread
       'HKEY_LOCAL_MACHINE'
     ,'SOFTWARE\Microsoft\MSSQLServer\Setup'
     ,'SQLPath',@chvSQLPath    OUTPUT
select   @chvSQLPath SQLPath
go
```

xp_regwrite

This stored procedure enables you to write a new value to the Registry key located on the specified path of the specified subtree:

```
xp_regwrite subtree,
            path,
            key,
            datatype,
            newvalue
```

In the following example, this extended stored procedure adds one value to the Setup key:

```
exec master..xp_regwrite
       'HKEY_LOCAL_MACHINE'
     ,'SOFTWARE\Microsoft\MSSQLServer\Setup'
     ,'Test'
     ,'REG_SZ'
     ,'Test'
go
```

TIP

You should be very careful when writing and deleting Registry keys using Transact-SQL. It is often a better idea (performance-wise) to store most of your configuration parameters in a special table in the application database.

Jobs

One valuable administrative feature of Microsoft SQL Server is the capability to launch the execution of custom jobs at specified times. Each job has properties such as name, description, schedule, and a list of operators to be notified in case of success, completion, or failure, as well as a list of steps that will be performed as part of the job and actions to be taken after completion of a job. These steps can be defined as Transact-SQL code, Active Script code, or operating system commands.

Administration of Jobs

This section looks at the basics of job creation from Enterprise Manager to show the potential of this feature, but it will not go into too much detail. The following exercise creates a job that performs a backup of the transaction log if it is more then 95 percent full. It is based on the prBackupIfLogAlmostFull stored procedure.

   You can create a job using a wizard or directly from the Enterprise Manager tree:

1. Open Enterprise Manager and expand the local server in the tree pane.

2. Expand Management, then SQL Server Agent. Make sure that it is running.

3. Click Jobs; SQL Server displays a list of existing jobs.

4. Right-click Jobs and choose New Job. Enterprise Manager displays a New Job Properties dialog box.

5. Fill in the General tab with the information shown in the following illustration:

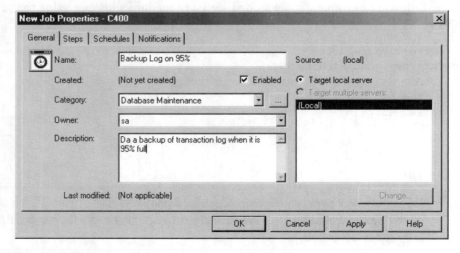

6. Click the Steps tab.

7. Click New to start creating the first step. The application displays the New Job Step dialog box.

8. In the Step Name field, type **do backup**.

9. Select Transact-SQL Script in the Type list.

10. Specify Asset as the working database.

11. You can either populate the Command text box with script from the file (using the Open button) or, as in this case, enter code manually for the execution of a stored procedure:

```
exec prBackupIfLogAlmostFull 'Asset', 95
```

The dialog box should look like this:

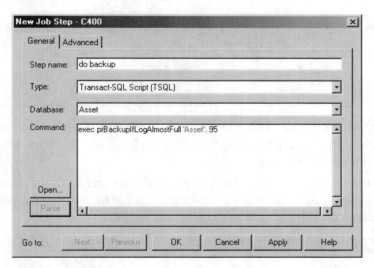

12. Click the Advanced tab to see other options. You can specify behavior in the case of successful or unsuccessful completion, the log file to record the output of the script, and retry options. For this exercise, accept the default values and close the dialog box. SQL Server returns you to the Steps tab of the New Job Properties dialog box.

13. You will create only one step for this job, so now you can click the Schedules tab to set a schedule.

14. Click the New Schedule button to display the New Schedule dialog box.

15. Name the schedule **Every 5 min**.
The Schedule Type is set to Recurring, but the default frequency is not what you want. Click the Change button. The Edit Recurring Job Schedule dialog box appears.

16. Select Daily in the Occurs group.

17. Set Daily Frequency to Occurs Every 5 Minute(s), as shown here:

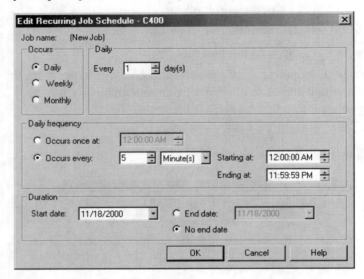

18. Click OK to close the dialog box; the application displays a message describing the schedule. Close the message box; the application returns you to the New Job Properties dialog box.

19. Click the Notifications tab to set activities that will occur when the job completes. It is possible to page or send e-mail to operators, write the status to the Windows NT application event log, or automatically delete the job:

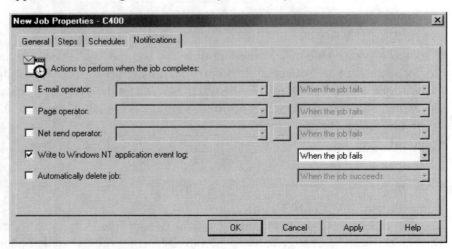

20. Accept the default values and click OK to close the dialog box.

Keep in mind that SQL Server will execute this job every five minutes from now on. If you want to disable it, you can edit the job or just right-click the job in Enterprise Manager and select Disable Job from the pop-up menu.

All of the functionality in this job is actually provided by the prBackupIfLogAlmostFull stored procedure. The only requirement that such a stored procedure must comply with is that it must return a success status (0 in the case of success; any other number represents an error code). SQL Server Agent uses this value to determine the completion status of the job and potentially execute subsequent steps. Returning a success status is a highly recommended practice when the stored procedure works inside the job.

The prBackupIfLogAlmostFull stored procedure calls the prLogSpacePercentUsed stored procedure to obtain the amount of log space available in the database. If the limit is reached, it creates a backup device using the sp_addumpdevice system stored procedure and performs a backup of the transaction log.

```
CREATE Procedure prBackupIfLogAlmostFull
-- Do backup of transaction log
-- if percent of space used is bigger than @fltPercentLimit
    (
        @chvDbName sysname,
        @fltPercentLimit float,
        @debug int = 0
    )
As
set nocount on

declare    @intErrorCode int,
           @fltPercentUsed float,
           @chvDeviceName sysname,
           @chvFileName sysname

set @intErrorCode = @@Error

-- how much of log space is used at the moment
if @intErrorCode = 0
    exec @intErrorCode = prLogSpacePercentUsed @chvDbName,
                                    @fltPercentUsed OUTPUT

-- if limit is not reached, just go out
if @intErrorCode = 0 and @fltPercentUsed < @fltPercentLimit
```

```
          return 0

if @intErrorCode = 0
begin
      Select @chvDeviceName = @chvDbName
                            + Convert(Varchar, GetDate(), 112),
             @chvFileName   = 'C:\PROGRAM FILES\MICROSOFT.SQL SERVER'
                            + '\MSSQL\BACKUP\bkp'
                            + @chvDeviceName
                            + '.dat'
      set @intErrorCode = @@Error
end

if @debug <> 0
      select @chvDeviceName chvDeviceName,
             @chvFileName chvFileName

if @intErrorCode = 0
begin
      EXEC sp_addumpdevice 'disk', @chvDeviceName, @chvFileName
      set @intErrorCode = @@Error
end

-- 15061 it is OK if dump device already exists
if @intErrorCode = 0 or @intErrorCode = 15061
begin
      BACKUP LOG @chvDbName TO @chvDeviceName
      set @intErrorCode = @@Error
end

return @intErrorCode
```

TIP

Some might argue that such a stored procedure and job are not needed in Microsoft SQL Server 2000 because it can increase the size of a transaction log automatically if it approaches its specified limit. This is true, but it's valid only if you can afford unlimited storage. If your disk resources are limited, it is a much better solution to clear the log.

An Alternative to Job Scheduler

Microsoft has developed Job Scheduler into a relatively sophisticated tool, with these features:

▶ Steps are included as components of jobs to allow better control.

▶ You can continue or even stop execution from different points, depending on the success or failure of each step.

▶ Operators can be notified according to predefined criteria.

▶ Each step can be coded in a different language (including Transact-SQL, ActiveX Scripts, operating system commands, or commands that call replication and maintenance services and utilities).

In the past, the only way to create a complex job was to code everything in Transact-SQL. Now, simpler jobs can be implemented using steps. If you really need a sophisticated solution, you still need the power of Transact-SQL or ActiveX Script.

SQL Server includes a set of stored procedures and extended stored procedures inside Enterprise Manager that can achieve everything that you can do within Job Scheduler. They reside in the *msdb* database. (This database is used by SQL Server Agent to hold information about jobs, schedules, and operators.)

The following paragraphs will quickly review some of these stored procedures.

Stored Procedures for Maintaining Jobs

The sp_help_job stored procedure returns information about jobs. If no parameters are specified, the stored procedure returns a result set with a list of jobs and their attributes. If the job name (or ID) is specified, the stored procedure returns an additional result set that describes the job's steps, schedules, and target servers.

The sp_add_job, sp_delete_job, and sp_update_job stored procedures are used to create, delete, and change existing jobs, respectively.

The sp_add_jobstep and sp_add_jobschedule stored procedures are designed to associate a schedule and steps with an existing job. Naturally, there are corresponding stored procedures that allow you to delete or update schedules and steps and obtain information about them.

The following example creates a single-step job to perform a backup of the transaction log and assigns a nightly schedule to it:

```
USE msdb
EXEC sp_add_job @job_name = 'Asset Backup Log',
    @enabled = 1,
    @description = 'Backup transaction Log of Asset database',
    @owner_login_name = 'sa'

EXEC sp_add_jobserver @job_name = 'Asset Backup Log',
```

```
        @server_name = 'DSUNDERIC\ss2k'

EXEC sp_add_jobstep @job_name = 'Asset Backup Log',
    @step_name = 'Backup Log',
    @subsystem = 'TSQL',
    @server =   'DSUNDERIC\ss2k',
    @command = ' BACKUP LOG Asset TO bkpAssetLog',
    @retry_attempts = 5,
    @retry_interval = 5

EXEC sp_add_jobschedule @job_name = 'Asset Backup Log ',
    @name = 'Nightly Backup',
    @freq_type = 4,        -- daily
    @freq_interval = 1, -- every 1 day
    @active_start_time = '000000' -- midnight
```

It is much easier to create jobs, schedules, and steps from Enterprise Manager, but the previous script might be useful for deploying a job from a development or test environment into a production environment. You can also use sp_start_job to instruct SQL Server Agent to run the job immediately, as in the following example:

```
USE msdb
EXEC sp_start_job @job_name = 'Asset Backup Log'
```

There is also an orthogonal stored procedure, sp_stop_job, that is designed to stop execution of a job that is in progress.

Once a job is completed, SQL Server Agent will record its completion status in the job history. You can view the history of a job using sp_help_jobhistory, and you can delete old records from the history using sp_purge_jobhistory.

Operators and Alerts

SQL Server Agent also maintains a list of operators and a list of alerts.

Operators are administrators who should be notified of predefined events configured in SQL Server. The system keeps track of the operator's network, e-mail, and pager addresses, as well as a timetable indicating when the operator is available during the week (and weekends).

Alerts are events that can occur in SQL Server, such as specific errors, errors of a certain severity, and conditions that can occur in a database, as well as the actions that need to be taken to handle the event (such as sending a message to the operator or executing a job).

There is also a third type of object that serves as a link between alerts and operators. *Notifications* are used to assign and send a message to operator(s) to handle alerts.

Naturally, there are stored procedures to manage these lists of operators and alerts:

▶ sp_help_operator, sp_add_operator, sp_delete_operator, sp_update_operator

▶ sp_help_alert, sp_add_alert, sp_delete_alert, sp_update_alert

▶ sp_help_notification, sp_add_notification, sp_delete_notification, sp_update_notification

SQL Server and the Web

SQL Server is not designed as a tool for publishing content to the Web, but support for the basic tasks is built into it. You can do the following with SQL Server:

▶ Publish the contents of the database on the Web

▶ Create a web page based on the result of a query

▶ Use HTML templates to format result sets

▶ Update a web page periodically or on demand to incorporate changes to the database

▶ Set a database to update a web page whenever underlying tables are changed

Many tools and technologies are available that are suitable for creating web applications, but Visual InterDev is one that you should investigate before others because of the seamless integration between it and SQL Server.

NOTE

Web publishing from SQL Server is available only from the Standard and Enterprise Editions of SQL Server 2000

Web Assistant

The easiest way to generate web pages is to use the Web Assistant Wizard:

1. From Enterprise Manager, select Tools | Wizards. The Select Wizard tree appears.

2. Expand the Management subtree, select the Web Assistant Wizard, then click OK.

3. Click Next to open the second page; the wizard prompts you for the database to be used as a source of information.

4. The next page prompts you for the name of the web page you want to generate. You will also have to specify the type of query you want to use to get a result set from the database. The query can be a stored procedure, an ad hoc query, or a selection of table columns to be assembled into a query by the wizard.

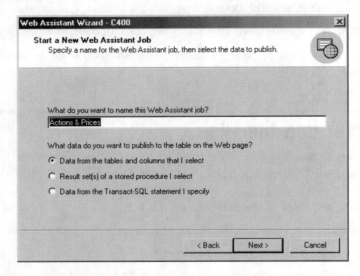

5. Select the first option (Data From The Tables And Columns That I Select) and click Next, and the wizard will prompt you to select a table and the columns that should appear in the result set.

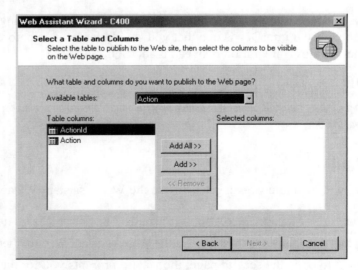

6. Select the table and columns you want to include, and click Next.

7. The wizard gives you the option to filter the recordset you have defined. You can type a Where clause, use list boxes to specify columns, operators, and the values of criteria, or accept the default to return all rows. When you have finished specifying criteria, click Next.

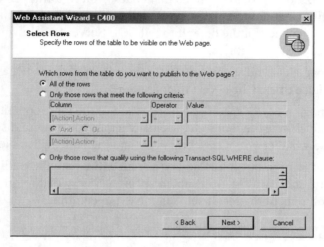

8. The next page prompts you to schedule the job to create a web page. You can also specify that the web page needs to be generated at scheduled intervals or when data changes. SQL Server will schedule a recurring job or create triggers that will fire when the table changes. The trouble with using a recurring job is that changes will not be published immediately to the Web; the trouble with the trigger approach is that the generation of the web page will become part of (that is, overhead for) the transaction. Accept the default and click Next to continue.

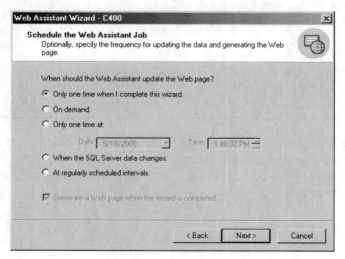

9. Specify the location of the web page to be generated. Click Next to continue.

10. The Web Assistant Wizard then asks you to format the web page. It prompts you to specify a predefined template that you want to use, or to specify that you want the wizard to provide options that enable you to format all elements of the page. I will talk about templates in "Web Page Templates" later in this chapter. In this case, just accept the default to tell SQL Server to help you format the page. Click Next to continue.

11. The next page lets you specify titles for the page and the table, and specify font sizes for those titles. Click Next to continue.

12. The next page lets you specify the formatting of the table containing the result set. You can change the font style, decide whether you want to display columns, and choose whether you want borders around the table. Click Next to continue.

13. The next page prompts you to add one or an entire list of hyperlinks to the page. If you specify a list, you should specify a query that returns labels and links as columns of the result set. Click Next to continue.

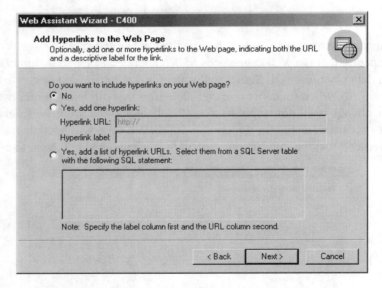

14. The next page provides options that are helpful if the table is very long. You can limit the number of rows that you want to display on the page or decide to create a set of linked pages with a specified number of rows on each page. Click Next to continue.

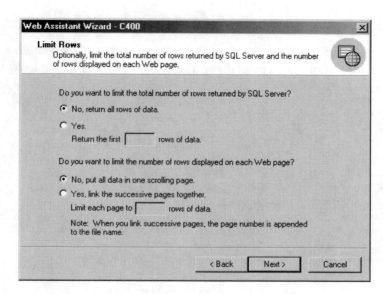

15. The final page allows you to save and execute the command for creating the web task that you have defined. Click the Write Transact SQL To File button to save the script created by the wizard, and then click Finish to execute the script.

Web Task Stored Procedures

Everything that the Web Assistant does can be accomplished using a set of three stored procedures:

▶ sp_makewebtask

▶ sp_runwebtask

▶ sp_dropwebtask

These stored procedures are designed to manage *web tasks,* which are just regular jobs. You can see them in the SQL Server Agent's list of jobs.

NOTE

The reason these stored procedures use "webtask" in their names is that they were introduced in SQL Server 6.5. At that time, jobs were called tasks.

sp_makewebtask

This stored procedure creates a job that produces an HTML document containing the result set of a query (or a stored procedure). The syntax of the command looks terrifying:

```
sp_makewebtask [@outputfile =] 'outputfile', [@query =] 'query'
    [, [@fixedfont =] fixedfont]
    [, [@bold =] bold]
    [, [@italic =] italic]
    [, [@colheaders =] colheaders]
    [, [@lastupdated =] lastupdated]
    [, [@HTMLHeader =] HTMLHeader]
    [, [@username =] username]
    [, [@dbname =] dbname]
    [, [@templatefile =] 'templatefile']
    [, [@webpagetitle =] 'webpagetitle']
    [, [@resultstitle =] 'resultstitle']
    [
        [, [@URL =] 'URL', [@reftext =] 'reftext']
        | [, [@table_urls =] table_urls, [@url_query =] 'url_query']
    ]
    [, [@whentype =] whentype]
    [, [@targetdate =] targetdate]
    [, [@targettime =] targettime]
    [, [@dayflags =] dayflags]
    [, [@numunits =] numunits]
    [, [@unittype =] unittype]
    [, [@procname =] procname ]
    [, [@maketask =] maketask]
    [, [@rowcnt =] rowcnt]
    [, [@tabborder =] tabborder]
    [, [@singlerow =] singlerow]
    [, [@blobfmt =] blobfmt]
    [, [@nrowsperpage =] n]
    [, [@datachg =] table_column_list]
    [, [@charset =] characterset]
    [, [@codepage =] codepage]
```

Fortunately, there is usually no need for you to start populating all of these parameters by hand. Use Web Assistant to create the script, and save the command during the final step of the wizard. You can later modify it using Query Analyzer.

The @whentype parameter specifies when the web task should be executed. The default value is 1, meaning that a web task should be created and executed immediately.

A job set with the default value of 1 will actually be created, executed, and then deleted. However, most of the other settings will leave the job for SQL Server Agent to launch.

When sp_makewebtask is executed, several database objects are created. A new record is added to the list of jobs in the *msdb* database. A new stored procedure is created in the database specified by the @dbname parameter. The new stored procedure has the same name as the job. It encapsulates the query that returns the recordset to be published (@query). If the web task is designed to update a web page whenever underlying data changes, the wizard also creates a trigger to run the job.

For discussion of other parameters, consult SQL Server Books Online.

sp_runwebtask

This is a stored procedure for managing web tasks that you use more often than others. It is designed to run an existing web task:

```
sp_runwebtask [[@procname =] 'procedurename']
    [,[@outputfile =] 'outputfile'
```

The result of the web task is an HTML file (`outputfile`) that can be specified by either the sp_runwebtask or the sp_makewebtask stored procedure.

sp_dropwebtask

This stored procedure is designed to delete web tasks. It deletes all objects that belong to the web task (for example: job, stored procedure with query, triggers):

```
sp_dropwebtask [[@procname =] 'procedurename']
              [,[@outputfile =] 'outputfile'
```

Web Page Templates

The best way to format your web page is to use a *template file,* which is an ordinary HTML file with placeholders for incorporating a result set.

There are two types of placeholders:

▶   <%insert_data_here%>
▶   <%begindetail%>, <%enddetail%>

<%insert_data_here%>

This placeholder is used to mark the spot where SQL Server is to place a complete result set. The placeholder is formatted as a regular HTML table.

The following code has been extracted from such a template file:

```
<html>

<head>
<title>Price List</title>
</head>

<body>
<H1>Price List<H1>

<%insert_data_here%>
</body>

</html>
```

Naturally, you can enrich your template with logos, links, additional text, and other elements. A simple trick is to design your page first in an HTML editor such as FrontPage and add the table placeholder later.

<%begindetail%>, <%enddetail%>

If you want more control over the look of your table, you can use these placeholders. They mark the beginning and end of the HTML code that will be replicated for each row in the result set. Between them, you should use the <%insert_data_here%> placeholder to mark the position where each field should be inserted.

The following code was generated in FrontPage. It is a simple page that uses a table with two rows and three columns. I have inserted the column heading in the first row and then marked a block around the next record with the <%begindetail%> and <%enddetail%> tags. Inside each table cell in the row, I have inserted a placeholder for the fields.

```
<html>

<head>
<title>Price List</title>
</head>

<body>

<table border="1" width="336">
  <tr>
    <td>Action ID</td>
```

```
      <td>Action</td>
      <td>List Price</td>
   </tr>
<%begindetail%>
   <tr>
      <td><%insert_data_here%></td>
      <td><%insert_data_here%></td>
      <td><%insert_data_here%></td>
   </tr>
<%enddetail%>
</table>

</body>

</html>
```

Of course, the point of this whole exercise is to create a more complex layout. You can also include code for hyperlinks and more complex formatting options.

E-Mail

SQL Server has the capability to interact with administrators and users via e-mail. Usually, operators are notified by SQL Server when specific events occur. You can use the Alert and Operator mechanisms to implement and define this behavior.

This feature is an alternative to standard methods of processing errors, such as recording critical errors in the Error Log. If SQL Server is in critical need of attention, and your operators do not possess pagers, SQL Server can send e-mail to them. This approach is also practical for notifying administrators of successfully completed jobs.

Another common use for SQL Mail is to process e-mail that contains database queries. Remote users can send queries to SQL Server and have it return result sets to them.

SQL Server can also send messages that include result sets in the form of a report to one or more users. Although these result sets are rather crude (just ASCII text), it is possible to envision and create an application that uses this capability to notify management when some change occurs in the database.

SQL Server 2000 contains two services that handle e-mail. The MSSQLServer service contains a component called *SQL Mail* that processes all extended stored procedures that use e-mail. SQL Server Agent contains a separate e-mail capability in a component often called *SQLAgentMail*.

I will not go into detail on the implementation and configuration of these services. Refer to SQL Server Books Online and the Microsoft Support web site for more details.

Extended Stored Procedures for Working with E-Mail

To implement custom behavior and features, you need to use extended stored procedures and build your own code in the form of stored procedures. These stored procedures can be executed from a client application or by the Job Scheduler. See Table 10-1 for a list of extended stored procedures available for processing e-mail.

xp_sendmail

This stored procedure can send a text message and/or query result to the list of recipients. The following statement will notify an administrator that the transaction log is almost full:

```
EXEC xp_sendmail
    @recipients = 'SQLAdmin',
    @Message = 'The transaction log of Asset database is over 95% full.'
```

NOTE

You cannot use e-mail addresses in the @recipients parameter. The stored procedure expects the name of a contact that is defined in the address book of an e-mail client application.

The next example sends the result set of the query to the receiver. It could be a job that periodically lists all databases and their log usage and sends this information to the database administrator:

```
Exec xp_sendmail
    @recipients = 'SQLAdmin',
    @query = 'DBCC SQLPERF (LogSpace)'
```

A query can be returned in the form of an attached file:

```
Exec xp_sendmail
    @recipients = 'SQLAdmin; NetAdmin',
    @query = 'DBCC SQLPERF (LogSpace)',
    @subject = 'Transaction Log usage',
    @attach_results = 'TRUE'
```

Attachment files are also used to overcome the message size limit of 8000 characters:

```
create table #Message(msg text)

Insert into #Message
```

```
values ('You can put more then 8000 chrs in a text field.')

Exec xp_sendmail
    @recipients = 'SQLAdmin; NetAdmin',
    @query = 'select * from #Message',
    @attach_results = 'TRUE'

drop #Message
```

xp_readmail

This extended stored procedure can be used to

▶ Read a single message

▶ Return a list of e-mail messages and their contents

When the stored procedure is executed without a specified @messageid parameter, SQL Server will return a recordset that contains a list of all messages in the SQL Server mailbox. The result set will contain fields to identify the following:

▶ Message ID

▶ Subject

▶ Body of message

▶ Sender

▶ Recipient list

Extended Stored Procedure	Use
xp_sendmail	Sends e-mail
xp_readmail	Returns a message in the form specified by output parameters
xp_findnextmsg	Finds a pointer to the next e-mail message
sp_processmail*	Reads incoming e-mail messages with queries in them; returns the result sets to the message senders
xp_deletemail	Deletes a message from the inbox
xp_startmail	Runs an administrative procedure that starts SQL Mail
xp_stopamail	Runs an administrative procedure that stops SQL Mail

*Actually, sp_processmail is a Transact-SQL system stored procedure, not an extended stored procedure.

Table 10-1 *Extended Stored Procedures for Working with E-Mail*

- ► CC list
- ► BCC list
- ► Attachments
- ► Date received
- ► Read status
- ► Message type

To read a single message, you must specify the @messageid parameter. You can retrieve this ID either from the previous list or by using the xp_findnextmsg extended stored procedure.

```
EXEC @intStatus = xp_findnextmsg
                  @msg_id = @intMessageId OUTPUT
EXEC @intStatus = xp_readmail
                  @msg_id = @intMessageId,
                  @originator = @chvOriginator OUTPUT,
                  @cc_list = @chvCC OUTPUT,
                  @bcc_list = @chvBCC OUTPUT,
                  @subject = @chvSubject OUTPUT,
                  @message = @query OUTPUT
```

Unfortunately, this extended stored procedure can only read messages in segments that are no longer than 255 characters. Two parameters control where to start reading and the length of the message. Using these parameters, you can implement a loop that will read the whole message. See SQL Server Books Online for an example of such a procedure.

sp_processmail

This system stored procedure reads e-mail messages from the inbox, executes the queries specified in them, and returns a result set to the sender and all recipients specified on the CC list. It is usually used internally within a job that is periodically executed on the SQL Server.

The following statement can be placed in the Job Scheduler and executed periodically to process e-mail that contains the string 'Asset' in the subject against the Asset database. A result set is returned in the form of a comma-separated value (CSV) attachment file:

```
exec sp_processmail @Subject = 'Asset',
                    @filetype = 'CSV',
                    @separator = ',',
                    @dbuse =  'Asset'
```

The sp_processmail stored procedure uses xp_readmail, xp_deletemail, xp_findnextmsgl, and xp_sendmail to process messages.

TIP

Open this stored procedure and study its code. It is a good example of Transact-SQL code.

Security

Implementing security on SQL Server is not difficult, but you need to have a good understanding of its security architecture before you can define and implement an effective and manageable security solution.

Security Architecture

A user (a person or application) has to go through four levels of security before performing an action on a database object:

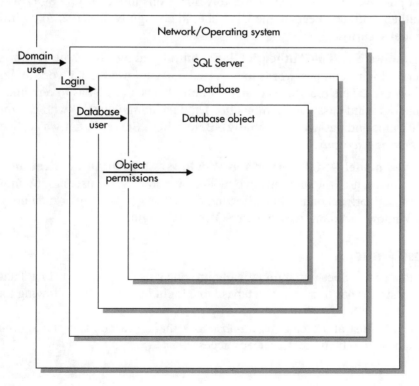

Network/OS Access

A user needs access to the client computer, operating system, and network on which the server is located. Usually, this access is the responsibility of technical support specialists or network administrators. However, in smaller environments, this responsibility may fall to a DBA or developer instead.

Server Access

The first level of security that pertains strictly to SQL Server allows a client to access a server. This security level is always the responsibility of database administrators.

SQL Server supports three security models:

▶ **SQL Server Authentication**   Requires a login and password from each user. These may be different from his or her network login and password and may be different from one instance of SQL Server to another. This model was the first to be developed; it was implemented by Sybase. Before SQL Server 7.0, it was called *standard security.* In fact, in SQL Server 7.0 and SQL Server 2000, it is not possible to configure a server to work in this mode only. If SQL Server Authentication is needed, the DBA should configure the server to use mixed model security.

▶ **Windows NT/2000 Authentication**   Introduced by Microsoft, it allows SQL Server logins and passwords to be based on Windows NT network logins and passwords. This practice is easier for both the user (who has to remember only one login and password combination) and the administrator (who can manage all logins and passwords centrally). Before SQL Server 7.0, it was called *integrated security.*

▶ **Mixed model—SQL Server and Windows NT/2000 Authentication**   A combination of the previous two models, it allows some users to log in with their network account while allowing other users (who may or may not have a Windows account) to use their SQL Server login.

Database Access

Access to a server does not automatically provide a user with access to a database. An administrator has to assign a database to a login in one of the following manners:

▶ The administrator creates a *database user* that corresponds to the login in each database to which the user needs access.

▶ The administrator configures a database to treat a login/database user as a member of a *database role*. Such a user inherits all permissions from the role.

▶ The administrator sets a login to use one of the *default user accounts*: guest or database owner (dbo).

Once access to a database has been granted, the user can see all database objects because the object definitions are stored in system tables to which every user has read access.

Permissions

Permissions are the final level of SQL Server security. To have access to user-defined database objects, a user has to have *permissions* to perform actions on them. There are three types of permissions in SQL Server:

▶ **Object permissions**   Allow a user to read and change data and execute stored procedures

▶ **Statement permissions**   Allow a user to create and manage database objects

▶ **Implied permissions**   Allow members of fixed roles and owners of database objects to perform activities that are not part of the object or statement permissions

Roles   Users can be granted permissions individually or as members of a *database role*. Roles are the SQL Server equivalent to groups in Windows NT or roles in Microsoft Transaction Server.

In earlier versions of SQL Server, a user could belong to only one role. This restriction led to some pretty unrefined security solutions. A user can now be a member of many database roles. Therefore, roles can be used to provide a sophisticated security model, managing access to the required functionality and database objects.

Object Permissions   The following table indicates which object permissions are applicable to which database objects:

	Table	View	Stored Procedure	User-Defined Function	Column
Select	X	X		X	X
Update	X	X			X
Insert	X	X			

	Table	View	Stored Procedure	User-Defined Function	Column
Delete	X	X			
Reference	X				X
Execute			X	X	

Database users can be given Select, Update, Insert, and Delete permissions to tables and views. This access level means that the user can read, write, delete, or change data in the respective tables or views. Reference permission allows a user to use a foreign key constraint to validate an entry to a column or table. Permissions to select, update, and reference can also be handled at the column level.

To access a stored procedure or a user-defined function, a user has to have Execute permission on it.

Statement Permissions   Database users can be granted the following permissions to create and manage other databases or database objects:

► Create Database

► Create Table

► Create View

► Create Default

► Create Rule

► Backup Database

► Backup Log

Implementing Security

You can implement a security solution using Enterprise Manager or system and extended stored procedures. Security stored procedures can also be used to manage security or implement some additional security features from a client application.

Selection of Security Model

You select a security model in the SQL Server Properties dialog box.

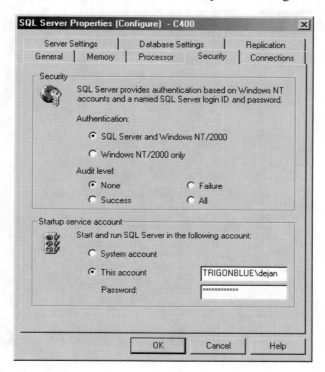

To open this dialog, select Tools | SQL Server Configuration Properties.

Managing Logins

To create a login, expand the Security branch of the SQL server in Enterprise Manager, right-click Logins, and select New Login from the pop-up menu. To manage an existing login, right-click the login in the list pane and select Properties. The application opens the SQL Server Login Properties dialog box to enable you to manage login properties. You can select a name and type of login, password, default database and language, and membership in Server Roles.

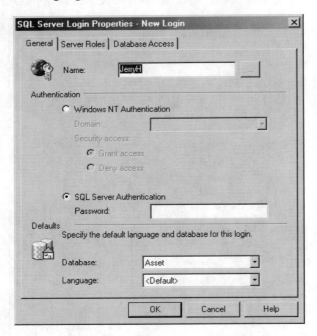

Alternatively, you can use sp_addlogin and sp_droplogin to manage SQL Server logins:

```
EXEC sp_droplogin 'tomjones'
EXEC sp_addlogin @loginame='tomj',@passwd='T.Pwd',@defdb='Asset'
```

A password of a SQL Server login can be changed using sp_password:

```
exec sp_password @old='T.Pwd',@new='jso83-au82',@loginname='tomj'
```

The Database Access tab controls the databases the user can access and the user's membership in roles.

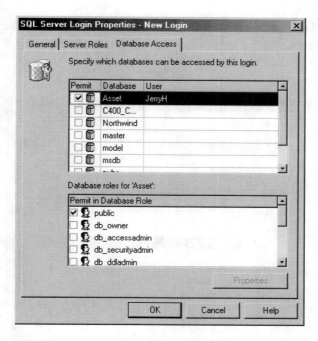

You can also grant logins using stored procedures. You can use sp_grantlogin to create a login on SQL Server. To give a Windows user access to a SQL server, only the name of the user is required as a parameter:

```
exec sp_grantlogin @login = 'Accounting\TomB'
```

However, when you create a login for SQL Server, you usually specify an authentication password and a default database as well:

```
exec sp_addlogin @login='TomB',@passwd='password',@defdb='Asset'
```

Granting Database Access

As you have seen, database access can be granted to a login during the login's creation. There is also a way to grant access to additional databases after the login has been created. Database users can be managed from the Users node of a database in Enterprise Manager. You can both manage existing users and create new users.

Login names have to be selected from the list box. The User Name list box is set by default to the name of the login. This default is not required, but it simplifies user management. In the Database Role Membership section, you check all databases to which you want to grant the user membership.

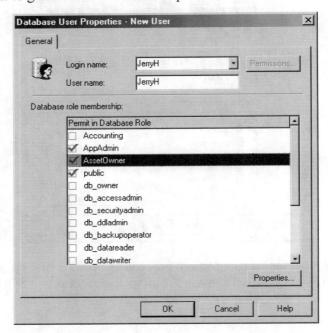

You can perform the same operation from Transact-SQL.

To grant access to the database, use sp_grantdbaccess:

```
exec sp_grantdbaccess @loginname='TomB', @name_in_db='TomB'
```

In this case, login TomB will become associated with the new TomB user in the current database.

You can review access using sp_helpusers and revoke access using sp_revokedbaccess.

To assign a user to a user-defined database role, you issue a command such as

```
exec sp_addrolemember @rolename='Management', @membername='TomB'
```

You can review membership using sp_helprolemember and revoke it using sp_droprolemember. You can create roles using sp_addrole:

```
exec sp_addrole @rolename='Management'
```

You can remove roles using sp_droprole. To view a list of roles, use sp_helpfixeddbroles and sp_helproles.

Assigning Permissions

The system of permissions controls user and role access to database objects and statements. Permissions can exist in one of following three states:

▶ **Granted** Means that a user has permission to use an object or statement.

▶ **Denied** Means that a user is not allowed to use a statement or object, even if the user has previously inherited permission (that is, the user is a member of a role that has permission granted).

▶ **Revoked** Means that records that were stored for that security account (that is, the records granting or revoking permissions) are removed from the sysprotects table.

Physically, a record is stored in the sysprotects table for each user (or role) and object (or statement) for which permission has been granted or denied.

Because of their physical implementation, permissions are cumulative. For example, a user can receive permissions from one role and other permissions from some other role. Or, the user can be denied permissions that have been granted to all other members of a role.

You can control statement permissions from the Permissions tab of a database's Properties dialog box. You can set object permissions using the Permissions button in a database object's Properties dialog box. In both cases, you see a list of users and roles:

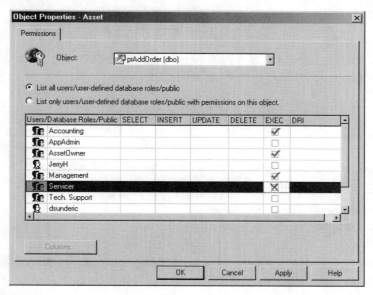

An administrator can grant (☑), deny (☐), or revoke (☒) permissions.

Grant Statement   To grant statement permission, an administrator can issue a Grant statement with the following syntax:

```
Grant {ALL | statement_name_1
      [, statement_name_2, … statement_name_n]
      }
To account_1[, account_2, … account_n]
```

To grant object permission, an administrator can issue a Grant statement with the following syntax:

```
Grant {All [Privileges]| permission_1[,permission_2, … permission_n]}
{
    [column_1, column_2, … column_n] ON {table | view }
    | On {table | view } [column_1, column_2, … column_n]
    | On {stored_procedure }
}
To account_1[, account_2, … account_n]
[With Grant Option]
As {group | role}
```

The following statement allows JohnS (SQL Server login) and TomB from the Accounting domain (Windows domain user) to create a table in the current database:

```
Grant Create Table
To JohnS, [Accounting\TomB]
```

The following statement allows members of the AssetOwners role to view, store, delete, and change records in the Inventory table:

```
Grant Select, Insert, Update, Delete
On Inventory
To AssetOwner
```

When you grant a user object permission using WITH GRANT OPTION, the user will also be able to grant that permission to other users:

```
GRANT SELECT ON Contact TO roleHR
WITH GRANT OPTION
```

Deny Statement   The Deny statement is used to explicitly negate permissions. Its syntax is basically the same as the syntax of the Grant statement (except that the keyword Deny is used).

The following statement prevents TomB from the Accounting domain from creating a database:

```
Deny Create Database
To [Accounting\TomB]
```

The following statement prevents JohnS from deleting and changing records from the Inventory table, even though he has inherited rights to view, store, delete, and change records as a member of the AssetOwners role:

```
Deny Update, Delete
On Inventory
To JohnS
```

A Deny statement, even at the user level, will supercede all Grant permissions, whether at the user or role level.

Revoke Statement   The Revoke statement is used to deactivate statements that have granted or denied permissions. It has the same syntax as the Grant and Deny statements (except that the keyword Revoke is used).

It is easy to understand that permission can be removed using the Revoke statement. It is a little more challenging to understand how a permission can be granted by revoking it. To help you understand this concept, consider the following example in which a user, JohnS, is a member of the AssetOwners role, which has permission to insert, update, select, and delete records from the Inventory table:

```
exec sp_addrolemember 'AssetOwner', 'JohnS',
```

The administrator then decides to deny JohnS permission to delete and update records from Inventory:

```
Deny Update, Delete
On Inventory
To JohnS
```

After a while the administrator issues the following statement:

```
Revoke Update, Delete
On Inventory
To JohnS
```

In effect, this command has granted Update and Delete permission on the Inventory table to JohnS.

Since the Revoke statement removes records from the sysprotects table in the current database, the effect of the Revoke statement is to return permissions to their original state. Naturally, this means that the user will not have access to the object (or statement). In that respect, its effect is similar to the Deny statement. However, there are two major differences between revoked and denied permissions: the Revoke statement does not prevent permissions from being granted in the *future*; and the Revoke statement doesn't supercede any other granted permissions provided by membership in other roles, whereas Deny does supercede those permissions.

Synchronization of Login and Usernames

Chapter 11 discusses in detail deploying/moving databases from one server to another. The problem you will encounter in this situation is a mismatch between users and logins. This problem is a result of the fact that records in the sysusers table of the copied database point to the records in the syslogins table with matching sid fields. Unfortunately, same sid value might be used by different logins on two different servers. It is also possible that login with specific sid value does not yet exist on a new server. One solution is to create and manage a script that re-creates logins and users on the new server after a database is copied.

Another solution is to dynamically assemble a script to create logins on the target server:

```
SET NOCOUNT ON
SELECT 'EXEC sp_addlogin @loginame = ''' + loginname + ''''
,', @defdb = ''' +  'tempdb'+ ''''
,', @deflanguage = ''' + language + ''''
,', @encryptopt = ''skip_encryption'''
,', @passwd ='
, cast(password AS varbinary(256))
,', @sid ='
, sid
FROM syslogins
WHERE name NOT IN ('sa')
AND isntname = 0

SELECT 'EXEC sp_grantlogin @loginame = ''' + loginname + ''''
FROM syslogins
WHERE loginname NOT IN ('BUILTIN\Administrators')
AND isntname = 1
```

```
select 'EXEC sp_addsrvrolemember '''+loginname+''', ''sysadmin'''
from syslogins
where sysadmin = 1
union
select 'EXEC sp_addsrvrolemember '''+loginname+''', ''securityadmin'''
from syslogins
where securityadmin = 1
union
select 'EXEC sp_addsrvrolemember '''+loginname+''', ''serveradmin'''
from syslogins
where serveradmin = 1
union
select 'EXEC sp_addsrvrolemember '''+loginname+''', ''setupadmin'''
from syslogins
where setupadmin = 1
union
select 'EXEC sp_addsrvrolemember '''+loginname+''', ''processadmin'''
from syslogins
where processadmin = 1
union
select 'EXEC sp_addsrvrolemember '''+loginname+''', ''diskadmin'''
from syslogins
where diskadmin = 1
union
select 'EXEC sp_addsrvrolemember '''+loginname+''', ''dbcreator'''
from syslogins
where dbcreator = 1
union
select 'EXEC sp_addsrvrolemember '''+loginname+''', ''bulkadmin'''
from syslogins
where bulkadmin = 1


-----------------------------------------
select 'Run these after dbs are created:'

select ' EXEC sp_defaultdb @loginame = ''' + loginname + ''''
,', @defdb = ''' + Coalesce(dbname, 'tempdb') + ''''
FROM syslogins
where name NOT IN ('sa')
AND isntname = 0
---------------------------------------


select ' EXEC sp_defaultdb @loginame = ''' + loginname + ''''
```

```
,', @defdb = '''' + Coalesce(dbname, 'tempdb') + ''''
FROM syslogins
WHERE loginname NOT IN ('BUILTIN\Administrators')
AND isntname = 1
```

When executed on the source server, the script generates one group of commands to be executed before deployment, and one group to be executed after the databases are deployed on the target server. The first group re-creates logins, preserves their IDs and passwords, and then renews their membership in server roles. The second group sets their default databases.

SQL Server also offers the sp_change_users_login procedure. You can use it to display the mapping between the user and login:

```
exec sp_change_users_login @Action = 'Report'
```

Note that using sp_change_users_login with @Action='Report' does not accept parameters for user or login names.

You can set a login manually for a single user:

```
exec sp_change_users_login @Action = 'Update_one',
                           @UserNamePattern = 'TomB',
                           @LoginName = 'TomB'
```

SQL Server can also match database users to logins with the same name:

```
exec sp_change_users_login @Action = 'Auto_Fix',
                           @UserNamePattern = '%'
```

For each user, SQL Server tries to find a login with the same name and to set the login ID.

TIP

sp_change_users_login with 'Auto_Fix' does a decent job, but the cautious DBA should inspect the results of this operation.

Managing Application Security Using Stored Procedures, User-Defined Functions, and Views

When permissions are granted on complex objects like stored procedures, user-defined functions, or views, the user does not need to have permissions on the underlying objects within or referenced by it. This characteristic is illustrated in the following example:

```
Create Database Test
Go

sp_addlogin @loginame = 'AnnS',
            @passwd = 'password',
            @defdb = 'test'
GO
Use Test

Exec sp_grantdbaccess @loginame = 'AnnS',
                      @name_in_db = 'AnnS'
Go

Create Table aTable(
     Id int identity(1,1),
     Description Varchar(20)
     )
Go

Create Procedure ListATable
as
     Select * from aTable
go

Create Procedure InsertATable
     @Desc varchar(20)
as
     Insert Into aTable (Description)
     Values (@Desc)
Go

Deny Select, Insert, Update, Delete
On Atable
To Public

Grant Execute
On InsertATable
To Public

Grant Execute
On ListATable
```

```
To Public
Go
```

A table is created along with two stored procedures for viewing and inserting records into it. All database users are prevented from using the table directly but are granted permission to use the stored procedures.

 NOTE

All database users are automatically members of the Public role. Whatever permissions are granted or denied to the Public role are automatically granted or denied to all database users.

After this script is executed, you can log in as AnnS in Query Analyzer and try to access the table both directly and through stored procedures. Figure 10-3 illustrates such attempts.

There are two exceptions to the rule I have just described:

▶ If the owner of the stored procedure is not the owner of the database objects by the stored procedure, SQL Server will check the object's permissions on each underlying database object. Usually, this is not an issue because all objects should be owned by the dbo user.

▶ If you are executing a character string batch in a stored procedure, you still need to set permissions on all underlying objects.

Stored procedures, user-defined functions, and views are important tools for implementing sophisticated security solutions in a database. Each user should have permissions to perform activities tied to the business functions for which he or she is responsible and to view only related information. It is also easier to manage security in a database on a functional level than on the data level. Therefore, client applications should not be able to issue ad hoc queries against tables in a database. Instead, they should execute stored procedures.

Users should be grouped in roles by the functionality they require, and roles should be granted execute permissions to related stored procedures. Since roles are stored only in the current database, using them helps you avoid problems that occur during the transfer of the database from the development to the production environment.

Managing Application Security Using a Proxy User

Security does not have to be implemented on SQL Server. If the application is developed using three-tier architecture, objects can use roles, users, and other

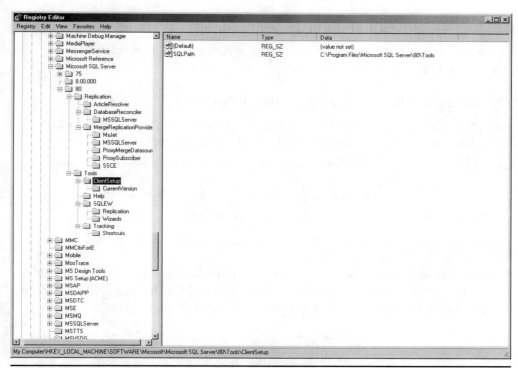

Figure 10-3   *Stored procedures are accessible even when underlying objects are not.*

security features of Microsoft Transaction Server (on Windows NT) or Component Services (in Windows 2000) to implement security. Security is sometimes also implemented inside the client application.

In both cases, database access is often accomplished through a single database login and user. Such a user is often called a *proxy user*.

NOTE

The worst such solution occurs when the client application developer completely ignores SQL Server security and achieves database access using the sa login. I have seen two variants on this solution.

One occurs when the developer hard-codes the sa password inside an application. The administrator is then prevented from changing the password (or the application will stop functioning) and the security of the entire SQL Server is exposed.

The other occurs when a developer stores login information in a file or Registry so that it can be changed later. Unfortunately, it can also be read by unauthorized people, and again, SQL Server security is compromised.

Managing Application Security Using Application Roles

Application roles are designed to implement security for particular applications. They are different from standard database roles in that

▶ Application roles require passwords to be activated.

▶ They do not have members. Users access a database via an application. The application contains the name of the role and its password.

▶ SQL Server ignores all other user permissions when the application role is activated.

To create an application role, administrators should use sp_addapprole:

```
Exec sp_addapprole @rolename = 'Accounting', @password = 'password'
```

Permissions are managed using Grant, Deny, and Revoke statements in the usual manner.

A client application (or a middle-tier object) should first log in to SQL Server in the usual manner and then activate the application role using sp_setapprole:

```
Exec sp_setapprole @rolename = 'Accounting', @password = 'password'
```

Source Code Management and Database Deployment

IN THIS CHAPTER:

The Concept of Source Code Management

Database Deployment

S *ource code control* (or *version control*) is typically introduced in development environments in which more than one developer needs to work with the same piece of code. It allows development organizations and their members to

▶ Manage code centrally

▶ Manage multiple versions of the same code

▶ Track change history

▶ Compare versions

▶ Prevent or allow developers from modifying the same piece of code at the same time

▶ Synchronize deployment of all modifications needed to implement a single feature or bug fix

The problem that you will face relatively often is that, while you develop your database (and application) in a development environment, you must deploy the database first in a test environment and then in a production environment. Initially, you need to deploy the complete database, but later you will have to update the database with design changes and hotfixes.

In this chapter, I will introduce methods and tools for source code management and database deployment. I will present solutions using two different approaches. One approach is for developers who have Visual Studio .NET (and who are probably doing both database and application development). The other, more traditional, approach is geared toward SQL Server specialists who are working with traditional database development tools. I will use the tools that are delivered with SQL Server, as well as tools that I have developed, to automate some processes.

The Concept of Source Code Management

Microsoft provides source code control software as an integral part of its development environment under the name Visual SourceSafe. This application allows developers to control their most valuable asset—source code. You can also use the Visual SourceSafe database to manage other file types such as web content, documentation, and test data, but our focus in this chapter is on how to use Visual SourceSafe to manage database objects.

Introduction to Microsoft Visual SourceSafe

Microsoft's primary purpose in delivering Visual SourceSafe as a part of its Visual Studio .NET suite of development tools is to provide a project-oriented means of storing and organizing code that allows developers to spend more time developing their projects and less time managing them. The emphasis is on ease of use and integration with a wide range of development tools. SQL Server developers can benefit greatly from this ease of use and integration, not only with regard to source code, but also as a means of organizing related files such as project documentation and test data.

As with SQL Server, there are different ways to use Visual SourceSafe. It is essentially a client/server application, but if you are an independent developer, your development workstation will likely also be your application server, database server, and source code server. Of course, if you are an independent developer, you may be wondering why you have a need for source code control at all. I will discuss this issue later in the chapter. For now, you can take my word that source code control is just as important for the solo developer working on a simple project as it is for a large development team working on a complex, component-based project.

If you are a member of a development team, the Visual SourceSafe client will allow you to work with local copies of code while preventing other members of your team from overwriting your changes while you have the code checked out from the Visual SourceSafe database. The benefit of this simple concept is obvious, but you have to work with and become comfortable with Visual SourceSafe before its many other benefits will become just as obvious. After you have posted your source code, you can

▶ Get the current version of all files.

▶ Check out a copy of a file that needs to be changed. Visual SourceSafe is, by default, configured to prevent all other developers from changing the file until it is returned (checked in) to the Visual SourceSafe database.

▶ View differences between a local version of a source code file and the latest version stored in the Visual SourceSafe database.

▶ Label versions of files to identify them with a particular release of a software product.

▶ Retrieve older versions of a particular file or a complete set of project files.

▶ View changes between any two versions of a source code file.

▶ Share common files between separate projects.

▶ Make a single backup copy of the complete source code and all supporting files.

▶ Create branches of source code files to separately manage multiple versions of a software project.

▶ Merge code in different branches of the source code file.

Administering the Visual SourceSafe Database

Before you can use Visual SourceSafe, you need to create users and assign privileges to them.

When you install Visual SourceSafe, you create just two users: *Admin* and *Guest*. The Admin user has all privileges in the database and can also create other users. The Guest user is initially limited to read-only access to source code files. Both users are created with their password set to an empty string (that is, blank). Since this state constitutes a threat to your source code, your first step should be to set the Admin password using Visual SourceSafe Administrator (User | Change Password). When you are done, create a user for yourself (Users | Add User) with the appropriate permissions.

TIP

If your Visual SourceSafe username and password match your operating system username and password, you will not have to type them each time you open Visual SourceSafe on the local system. Visual SourceSafe can be configured to use them automatically.

With Visual SourceSafe, you can assign more refined permission levels, such as Add, Rename, Delete, Check In, Check Out, Destroy, and Read. To activate this wide-ranging control, click Tools | Options | Project Security and check the Enable Project Security option.

Adding Database Objects to Visual SourceSafe in Visual Studio .NET

To demonstrate the implementation of source code control in a database project, you add code from your sample Asset database in Visual Studio .NET:

1. Create the Asset database project in Visual Studio .NET.

2. Open Solution Explorer.

3. Make sure that the Asset database is one of the Database References. If the reference does not already exist, right-click Database References and select New Database Reference to create one that points to the Asset database.

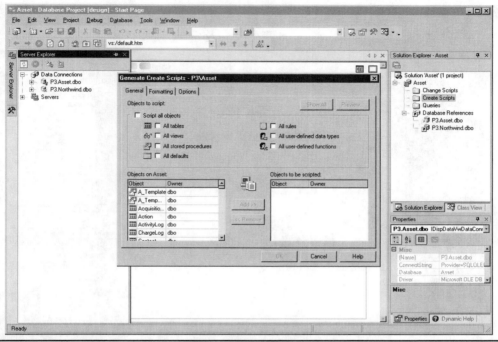

Figure 11-1   *The Generate Create Scripts dialog box*

4. In the Server Explorer, expand the Data Connections node.

5. Right-click the Asset data connection and choose Generate Create Script. The program prompts you for objects to be scripted (see Figure 11-1 above).

6. Select Script All Objects, and then switch to the Options tab and select the Script Database, Script Object-level Permissions, Windows Text (ANSI), and Create One File per Object options.

7. When the program prompts for the folder, accept ...\Asset\Change Scripts. The program will then create a set of script files for the database objects (see Figure 11-2).

8. Select File | Source Control | Add Solution to Source Control. Visual Studio .NET will prompt you to log in to the Visual SourceSafe Common database:

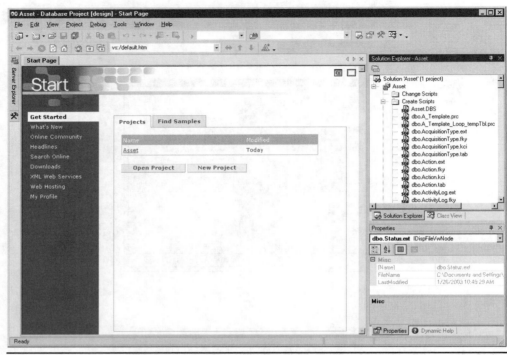

Figure 11-2   *Create scripts*

9. If your Visual SourceSafe database is stored locally, you can keep the Common database. If your Visual SourceSafe database is not stored locally, use the Browse button to locate the shared srcsafe.ini file.

> **NOTE**
>
> *On my machine, the Visual SourceSafe database is located in the C:\Program Files\Microsoft Visual Studio\Common\VSS folder. My computer, in this case, is a development workstation, as well as the database server and Visual SourceSafe server.*
>
> *If the Visual SourceSafe client is installed on the same machine as SQL Server, the location of the Visual SourceSafe database that you need to specify in this text box should be relative to the server machine. If you are developing from a workstation that is separate from the "development" server, you have to be careful how you enter the location of the Visual SourceSafe database. You should use the server's absolute path (for example: C:\Program Files\Microsoft Visual Studio\Common\VSS) regardless of whether you have that drive mapped on your workstation using another drive letter (such as S:).*

10. Visual SourceSafe prompts you to add a project to Visual SourceSafe. Name the project (you can also type a comment to describe the project).

Visual SourceSafe creates a project and locks all *Create scripts* (scripts that can be used to drop and create objects from scratch). You can see a small lock icon beside each Create script in Solution Explorer:

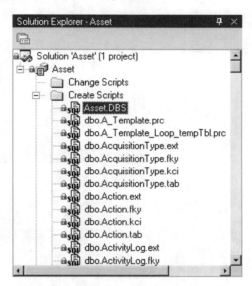

NOTE

From this moment, you must check out a Create script before you can change it.

Managing Create Scripts in Visual Studio .NET

When Create scripts are locked, you can open them for viewing in the editor, but Visual Studio .NET will prevent you from changing them until you check them out.

To view a Create script, right-click the script you want to review and select Open. Visual Studio .NET opens a copy of the Create script but marks it "read-only."

The following list demonstrates how to change a stored procedure:

1. Close the window with the read-only version of the Create script.

2. Right-click the script for a stored procedure and select Check Out from the pop-up menu. The program prompts you for confirmation and comment:

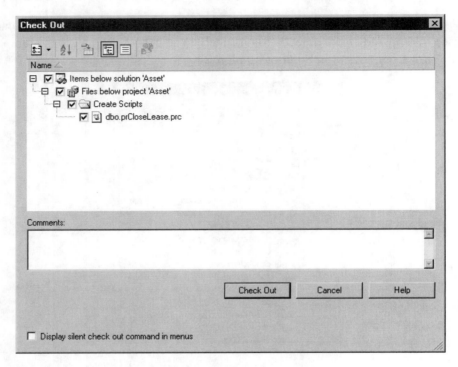

3. Make some trivial change to the stored procedure.

4. Save the changes (File | Save) in the change file.

5. Right-click the file and choose Check In from the menu. The program prompts you for confirmation and comment again.

TIP

Take the time to describe what changes you made in your comment. This will be incredibly helpful if some detective work is required later.

6. Click Check In. Visual Studio .NET saves the changes in Visual SourceSafe and locks the Create script.

7. At this point, the stored procedure does not yet exist in SQL Server. You must right-click the file and select Run to add it to the default database. Visual Studio .NET opens the Database Output pane to show the results (and possibly errors) of the execution (see Figure 11-3).

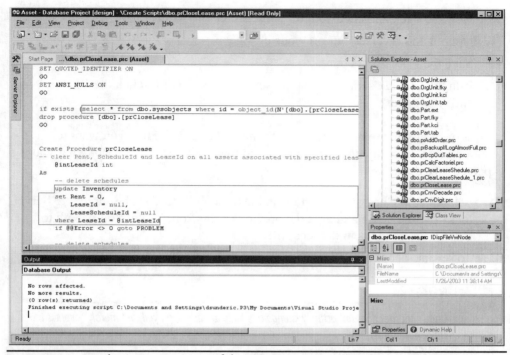

Figure 11-3   *Database Output pane of the Create script executed against the server*

NOTE

Unfortunately, this solution does not prevent another developer from using some other tool to change a database object directly in the database. You can even open Server Explorer in Visual Studio .NET to change them without source code control. Visual SourceSafe only works through consensus. Loose cannons can still wreak havoc on your development ship.

To promote the change to another server, you can choose the Run On option in the context menu of the change script.

TIP

When I first started to use Visual SourceSafe, the directions implied by the terms "Check Out" and "Check In" sounded inverted to me. Just think of Visual SourceSafe as an actual safe from which you are taking your code and into which you subsequently return your code after you are done with it.

8. Now, go back and check out the same stored procedure again.

9. Open it and reverse your previous changes.

10. Save the stored procedure.

11. Run the Change script against the server to test it (right-click the Change script and select Run).

Assume that you are not satisfied with these changes and that you want to abandon them. (Assume that you have tested them and the result is not what you expected.) To do so:

1. Select Undo Check Out from the context menu. The Visual SourceSafe Server locks the file again and uses the previous copy from Visual SourceSafe to reverse the changes in the local file.

2. To reverse changes to the database, you must Run the change script again.

NOTE

Undo Checkout does not actually change any code already deployed, but merely reverses the check out process.

Visual SourceSafe Explorer

The full power of Visual SourceSafe can only be realized through one special tool—Visual SourceSafe Explorer. Take a look at this tool by following these steps:

1. Open Visual SourceSafe Explorer from the Windows Start menu (depending on the version that you have: Start | Programs | Microsoft Visual Studio .NET | Microsoft Visual SourceSafe | Visual SourceSafe) or from Visual Studio .NET (File | Source Control | Microsoft Visual SourceSafe).

2. Expand the Asset project and drill down until you reach Stored Procedures (see Figure 11-4).

The following sections examine some of the most interesting features of the Visual SourceSafe Explorer, particularly history, labels, and versions.

History

Visual SourceSafe keeps an audit trail of changes made to a file. To view this history of changes:

1. Right-click the stored procedure that you edited earlier in this chapter and select Show History from the pop-up menu.

2. Visual SourceSafe prompts you to define the history details you would like to display:

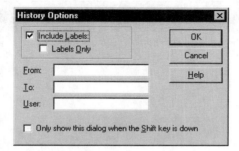

3. In this case, accept the defaults and click OK.

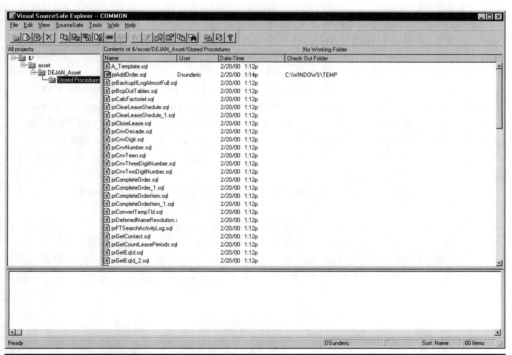

Figure 11-4   *Visual SourceSafe Explorer*

Visual SourceSafe Explorer displays a list of the different versions of the stored procedure, along with the name of the user responsible for each action.

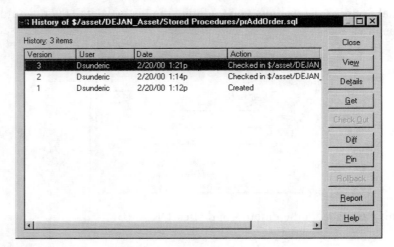

Now you have several options. If you select one version, you can view (click View) the code in an ASCII viewer. You can also see details (click Details) of the selected version such as comments and timestamp. The Get button lets you obtain a version of the stored procedure in a text file.

You can also temporarily or permanently set one of the previous versions to be a current one. The Pin option is usually applied as a temporary measure to test the behavior of an older version of a procedure. If you find that changes you made in your code are introducing more problems than they are solving, you can use the Rollback function to return to an earlier version of the code. Note that all newer versions will be deleted.

My favorite option is Diff. It compares two versions of a file. To use it:

1. Select two versions of a stored procedure (for example, version 2 and version 3) in the History window. You can select multiple versions by pressing the CTRL key and then clicking them.

2. Click the Diff button. The Difference Options dialog box appears.

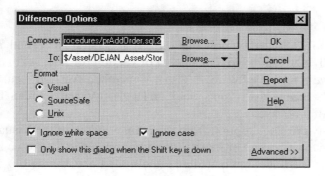

3. This dialog box lets you specify parameters for comparing files. If you wish to ignore case and white space, click OK to accept the defaults; Visual SourceSafe Explorer displays a window in which the differences between the two versions are highlighted (see Figure 11-5).

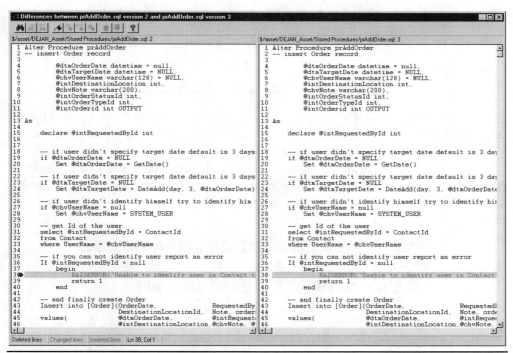

Figure 11-5   *File differences in Visual SourceSafe Explorer*

Labels and Versions

You have probably realized by now that the term "version" in Visual SourceSafe does not actually correspond to the concept of version (or release) that we generally think of when we consider software. A Visual SourceSafe "version" actually corresponds to a change in the source code. You should use labels in Visual SourceSafe to implement the equivalent of a release.

You can apply the Label option from the main window of the Visual SourceSafe Explorer. You can select one or more files and/or one or more projects (folders). When you apply the Label option (File | Label), the Label dialog box appears and prompts you to specify the text of the label (your official release number, for example).

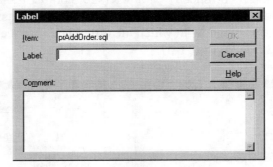

The current versions of all selected files will be labeled. Later, you can use these labels to collect the code that belongs to a particular version. This feature can be very important for supporting or testing the product.

Even more exciting is the opportunity to view the complete history of a project (right-click the project folder and select Show History from the pop-up menu) and determine many historical facts about the project, such as which changes were performed on it after a particular release.

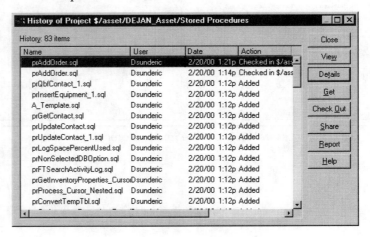

Adding Database Objects to Visual SourceSafe: Traditional Approach

Unfortunately, if you do not have Visual Studio .NET, it is not easy enough to manage the code of individual database objects with only the tools built into SQL Server and Visual SourceSafe. The process involves two steps:

1. Generate scripts from SQL Server.
2. Check in files into Visual SourceSafe.

Therefore, I've created a tool that loops through database objects and scripts them into separate files—TbDbScript. It's written in VBScript and you can download it from www.TrigonBlue.com/sqlxml/sqlxml_download.htm. To run it, you must use Windows Script Host and cscript.exe. Execute from the command prompt:

```
cscript TbDbScript.vbs .\ss2k sa password c:\dbscripter\ Asset
```

The parameters are: server, login, password, destination of database files, and, optionally, the database name. Use the space character as a parameter delimiter. If you omit the last parameter, the program will script all nonsystem databases on the server.

When scripting is finished, you will find database objects in the set of Create scripts in the folder named after the database (see Figure 11-6).

The tool also creates *deployment scripts.* They contain Create scripts grouped by type. You will read more about them in the "Deployment Scripts: Traditional Approach" section, later in the chapter.

It is true that the Generate SQL Scripts Wizard in Enterprise Manager will perform similar actions, but there are several significant differences:

► TbDbScript follows naming conventions used in Visual Studio.

► Generation does not require user intervention and therefore is less prone to errors. The resulting files are always the same.

► The script generates individual database object Create scripts and deployment scripts at the same time.

► You can also schedule usage of TbDbScript, which may be very useful when the development team is not using Visual SourceSafe religiously—as when the team is making changes live to the development database.

► Every deployment script file begins with a Use *database_name* statement and they can even be deployed manually using Query Analyzer.

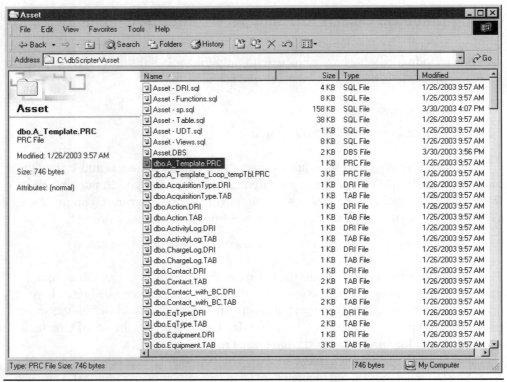

Figure 11-6   *Database object scripts generated by TbDbScript*

Now that Create scripts and deployment scripts are created, all you need to do is check them into the Visual SourceSafe database. You can do this manually with Visual SourceSafe Explorer or automatically with a little VBScript tool—TbDir2Vss.vbs. You can download the tool from www.TrigonBlue.com/sqlxml/sqlxml_download.htm. To run it, you must use Windows Script Host and cscript.exe. You need to specify the location of the srcsafe.ini file, username, password, Visual SourceSafe project/folder, and local folder:

```
cscript TbDir2Vss.vbs "C:\Program Files\Microsoft Visual
Studio\Common\VSS\srcsafe.ini" admin password $/Asset/ c:\dbscripter\Asset
```

The TbDir2Vss.vbs tool can also be scheduled along with TbDbScript.vbs to script databases and put them in Visual SourceSafe.

Database Deployment

Traditionally, RDBMS installation is perceived as complicated, and your customer will understand that you need to send a database administrator (or a couple of them) to set up the environment. When you work with a file-based database system such as Access, database deployment is not a big issue. You usually create a setup program for your client application, and your database (*mdb*) file is just one more file that must be installed on the computer. When you are working in a client/server environment with SQL Server, you first have to install and configure the database server and then install databases.

Fortunately, installation of SQL Server has been simplified significantly. Almost anyone can perform it and there are usually no problems. In fact, SQL Server can be configured to be installed unattended. Microsoft SQL Server Desktop Engine (MSDE) is designed to be deployed on client computers using a special set of setup files that can be included in your setup program.

Some early versions of SQL Server required that all dependent objects be present on the server before a new object could be created. Administrators had to use many tricks to transfer a database from one server to another. The introduction of Deferred Name Resolution has reduced the complexity of database deployment in the SQL Server environment. For example, a stored procedure can be created even if it references a stored procedure that is not yet on the server. Unfortunately, it is not perfect yet. For example, it is not possible to create a foreign key that references a table that is not yet in the database.

The methods for database deployment can be divided into two groups:

- ▶ Deployment of a complete database
- ▶ Deployment of individual objects

Deployment of a Complete Database: Traditional Approach

The idea behind this method is to use some means of moving the complete database so that relationships between individual database objects do not have to be managed once they are established. There are several options:

- ▶ Detach and reattach the database
- ▶ Use the Copy Database Wizard
- ▶ Back up and restore

The idea behind the first two options is to detach the database from the server, copy the database files to the production server, and then attach the database files to the new server (and reattach the database files to the original server, if applicable). To detach the Asset database manually, you can use the following script:

```
EXEC sp_detach_db 'Asset'
```

SQL Server checks the integrity of the database, flushes everything that is in memory to disk, stops further changes to the database, and releases database files.

NOTE

You must have exclusive use of the database to perform this function.

You can then copy the files (in this case, Asset.mdf and Asset_log.ldf) from the \mssql\data folder to a data folder on the target server. To attach the Asset database, you can use

```
EXEC sp_attach_db @dbname = 'Asset',
                  @filename1 = 'c:\Program Files\Microsoft SQL ',
                      + 'Server\mssql\data\Asset.mdf'
                  @filename2 = 'c:\Program Files\Microsoft SQL '
                      + 'Server\mssql\data\Asset_log.ldf'
```

If your database consists of more files, simply add them to the list of parameters. But if your database contains just one data file, you can use an alternative command:

```
EXEC sp_attach_single_file_db
            @dbname = 'Asset',
            @physname = 'c:\Program Files\Microsoft SQL ',
                + 'Server\mssql\data\Asset.mdf'
```

TIP

There is no harm in dropping the transaction log file and attaching just the data file (as long as you do not have some special reason, such as replication, to preserve the log).

You can execute these Transact-SQL statements manually in Query Analyzer or from the setup program. The setup program can use the command-prompt utility osql.exe to run a script file or use ADO to execute the script.

NOTE

I have chosen this method for deployment of the sample database to your computer.

A new feature found in SQL Server 2000 is the *Copy Database Wizard.* You can use it to copy (or move) a database on a known (production, testing, or some other) server. Behind the scenes, the wizard uses stored procedures for detaching and attaching the database. It also contains features for copying logins, error messages, jobs, and system stored procedures, which may be useful for completing server configuration. The disadvantage to this wizard is that it can be used only between servers on the same network. It is useful for deployment of databases used internally in a local department or organization, but not for deployment of databases that are required for shrink-wrapped software.

Another solution is based on creating a backup of the database on a development server and then restoring the database on a production server. Again, this can be performed manually or it can be scripted and included in the setup program.

Unfortunately, these techniques will not restore the links between server logins and database users. Server logins are stored in the *master* database; on different servers, different logins will have different IDs. Database users are stored in each user database. One of the parameters for a database user is the ID of the login to which it is attached. However, that ID is likely to refer to a different login on the production server. The simplest way to handle this problem is either to create all users again using Enterprise Manager or a script that you have prepared in advance, or to use roles instead of users as the foundation of your security solution. See the "Security" section in Chapter 10 for more information. SQL Server offers another solution to this problem—see "Synchronization of Login and Usernames" in Chapter 10.

Another disadvantage to these methods is that you have to maintain a "clean" database—a database that contains just database objects and seed data. Such a database can be delivered to a customer, but it cannot be used for development and testing. In both development and test environments, you need to add test data in order to test all features. You need to develop either scripts for adding test data or, alternatively, scripts for removing test data from a development database.

Deployment of Individual Objects

Some organizations choose to manage the code for individual objects and to deploy the database piecemeal by executing the code on the production server. This provides more flexibility, but requires more effort.

Deployment Scripts: Traditional Approach

Individual object scripts can be grouped in files with all objects of a particular type or even with all objects in a database. Such files can be created using the Generate

SQL Script tool in Enterprise Manager. It can be set so that the group of objects of the same type is saved in a single file. It is also possible to use a custom tool to aggregate individual database object files from the Visual SourceSafe database. Most ERD modeling tools can also produce such scripts (but their scripts often require manual intervention). You can also use TbDbScript, described earlier in this chapter.

To have better control, I like to use the TbDbScript tool, or the Generate SQL Script tool in SQL Server, to create one deployment script for each type of database object. When the system contains more than one database, I find it very useful that TbDbScript names deployment script files using the *Database - DbObjectType*.sql convention (see Figure 11-7).

Scripting Data: Traditional Approach

Some tables contain data (seed, static, or lookup data) that needs to be deployed along with the database schema. To assist in deployment and to facilitate storing the data with the source code, use the setup_DataGenerator stored procedure, described in Chapter 9.

Use the setup_DataGenerator procedure on all tables with data that need to be scripted:

```
set nocount on
exec setup_DataGenerator 'AcquisitionType'
exec setup_DataGenerator 'EqType'
exec setup_DataGenerator 'Location'
exec setup_DataGenerator 'OrderStatus'
exec setup_DataGenerator 'OrderType'
exec setup_DataGenerator 'Status'
exec setup_DataGenerator 'Province'
```

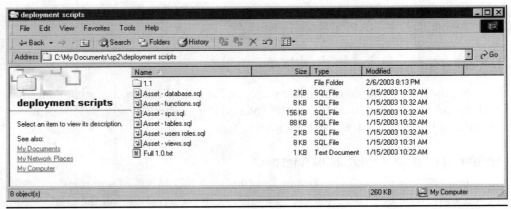

Figure 11-7   *Deployment scripts*

The result will be a script that consists of Insert statements (which had to be cropped to fit the page):

```
------------------------------------------------------------------
Insert into AcquisitionType(AcquisitionTypeId,AcquisitionType) values
Insert into AcquisitionType(AcquisitionTypeId,AcquisitionType) values
Insert into AcquisitionType(AcquisitionTypeId,AcquisitionType) values
Insert into AcquisitionType(AcquisitionTypeId,AcquisitionType) values
Insert into AcquisitionType(AcquisitionTypeId,AcquisitionType) values

------------------------------------------------------------------
Insert into EqType(EqTypeId,EqType) values (1,'Desktop')
Insert into EqType(EqTypeId,EqType) values (2,'Notebook')
Insert into EqType(EqTypeId,EqType) values (3,'Monitor')
Insert into EqType(EqTypeId,EqType) values (4,'Ink Jet Printer')
...
```

Save the resulting scripts in a text file (I often use Database - Data.sql as the name of this file).

Scripting Data in Visual Studio .NET

Alternatively, you can use Visual Studio .NET to script data and add it to Visual SourceSafe:

1. Open Server Explorer, navigate through the nodes, and expand the Tables node in the Asset database.

2. Select the tables with seed data (such as AcquisitionType, EqType, OrderStatus, and OrderType).

3. Right-click the selection and select Export Data from the menu.

4. The program prompts you for Locations For Exported Data File and to confirm that you want to export the selected data. The default location will be the folder that contains the Create scripts you generated earlier.

5. When you confirm the export operation, the program generates a set of DAT files. You typically need to select the files in Solution Explorer and Check (them) In.

These files are not SQL Server scripts but simple binary files (see the content of a file in Figure 11-8).

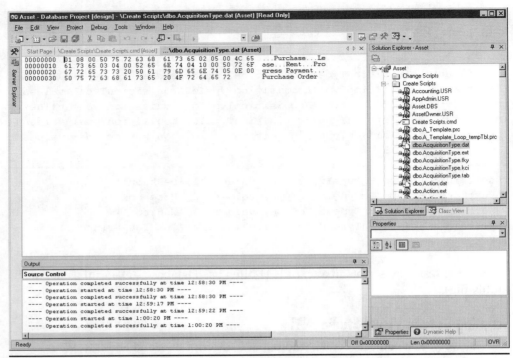

Figure 11-8 *Content of DAT file*

Deploying Scripts: Traditional Approach

The deployment scripts can then be executed manually one by one in Query Analyzer, but I have created a stored procedure that allows me to automate execution of a set of scripts—prBatchExec.

To prepare for deployment, I need to create a list of scripts and save it in a text file. The procedure executes the scripts in the order in which they are listed in the text file:

```
-- list of deployment scripts for Asset database
Asset - database.DBS
Asset - UDT.sql
Asset - Table.sql
Asset - DRI.sql
Asset - Functions.sql
Asset - sp.sql
Asset - Views.sql
```

Although Deferred Name Resolution allows you to ignore the order of creation of stored procedures, there are still some dependencies that must be followed. For example, indexes must be created after tables, tables after user-defined data types, and all of them after the database has been initiated. With this in mind, one of the main advantages of prBatchExec is that it preserves the order of execution of files. No human intervention is required and the opportunity for error is reduced.

The procedure uses SQL Distributed Management Objects (SQL-DMO) to execute individual scripts against the database server. SQL-DMO is a set of COM objects that encapsulate the functionality needed for administering SQL Server. To use SQL-DMO from SQL Server, you have to use the system stored procedures for OLE Automation (COM), described in Chapter 10:

```
create proc prBatchExec
-- Execute all sql files in the specified folder using the alphabetical order.
-- Demonstration of use of OLE Automation.
      @ServerName sysname = '(local)\ss2k2',
      @UserId sysname = 'sa',
      @PWD sysname = 'my,password',
      @DirName varchar(400)='C:\dbScripter\test',
      @File varchar(400) = 'list.txt',
      @UseTransaction int = 0
as

set nocount on

declare @FileSystemObject int,
        @objSQL int,
        @hr int,
        @property varchar(255),
        @return varchar(255),
        @TextStream int,
        @BatchText varchar(8000),
        @FilePath varchar(500),
        @ScriptId varchar(200),
        @Cmd varchar(1000)

--- Get list of files
create table #FileList (ScriptId int identity(1,1),
                        FileName varchar(500))

select  @Cmd = 'cd ' + @DirName + ' & type ' + @File

insert #FileList (FileName)
exec master..xp_cmdshell @Cmd
```

```
-- remove empty rows and comments
delete #FileList where FileName is null
delete #FileList where FileName like '--%'

-- prepare COM to connect to SQL Server
EXEC @hr = sp_OACreate 'SQLDMO.SQLServer', @objSQL OUTPUT
IF @hr < 0
BEGIN
    print 'error create SQLDMO.SQLServer'
    exec sp_displayoaerrorinfo @objSQL, @hr
    RETURN
END

EXEC @hr = sp_OAMethod @objSQL, 'Connect', NULL, @ServerName, @UserId, @PWD
IF @hr < 0
BEGIN
    print 'error Connecting'
    exec sp_displayoaerrorinfo @objSQL, @hr
    RETURN
END

EXEC @hr = sp_OAMethod @objSQL, 'VerifyConnection', @return OUTPUT
IF @hr < 0
BEGIN
    print 'error verifying connection'
    exec sp_displayoaerrorinfo @objSQL, @hr
    RETURN
END

-- prepare file system object
EXEC @hr = sp_OACreate 'Scripting.FileSystemObject', @FileSystemObject OUTPUT
IF @hr < 0
BEGIN
    print 'error create FileSystemObject'
    exec sp_displayoaerrorinfo @FileSystemObject, @hr
    RETURN
END

-- begin transaction
if @UseTransaction <> 0
BEGIN
    EXEC @hr = sp_OAMethod @objSQL, 'BeginTransaction '
    IF @hr < 0
    BEGIN
        print 'error BeginTransaction'
        exec sp_displayoaerrorinfo @objSQL, @hr
        RETURN
    END
```

```
END

-- iterate through the temp table to get actual file names
select @ScriptId = Min (ScriptId) from #FileList

WHILE @ScriptId is not null
BEGIN
    select @FilePath = @DirName + '\' + FileName
    from #FileList where ScriptId = @ScriptId
     if @FilePath <> ''
     BEGIN
       print 'Executing ' + @FilePath

       EXEC @hr = sp_OAMethod @FileSystemObject, 'OpenTextFile',
                              @TextStream output, @FilePath
       IF @hr < 0
       BEGIN
          print 'Error opening TextFile ' + @FilePath
          exec sp_displayoaerrorinfo @FileSystemObject, @hr
          RETURN
       END

       EXEC @hr = sp_OAMethod @TextStream, 'ReadAll', @BatchText output
       IF @hr < 0
       BEGIN
           print 'Error using ReadAll method.'
           exec sp_displayoaerrorinfo @TextStream, @hr
          RETURN
       END

       -- print @BatchText
       -- run it.
       EXEC @hr = sp_OAMethod @objSQL, 'ExecuteImmediate', Null , @BatchText
       IF @hr <> 0
       BEGIN
           if @UseTransaction <> 0
           BEGIN
               EXEC @hr = sp_OAMethod @objSQL, 'RollbackTransaction '
              IF @hr < 0
                BEGIN
                    print 'error RollbackTransaction'
                    exec sp_displayoaerrorinfo @objSQL, @hr
                 RETURN
               END
          END
          print 'Error ExecuteImmediate.' --Transaction will be rolled back.'
          exec sp_displayoaerrorinfo @objSQL, @hr
          RETURN
```

```
        END

        EXECUTE sp_OADestroy @TextStream
    END

    print 'Finished executing ' + @FilePath

    select @ScriptId = Min(ScriptId) from #FileList where ScriptId > @ScriptId
end

print 'Finished executing all files.'
drop table #FileList
EXECUTE sp_OADestroy @FileSystemObject

if @UseTransaction <> 0
BEGIN
    EXEC @hr = sp_OAMethod @objSQL, 'CommitTransaction '
    IF @hr < 0
    BEGIN
        print 'error CommitTransaction'
        exec sp_displayoaerrorinfo @objSQL, @hr
        RETURN
    END
END

RETURN 0
```

Before you can use the prBatchExec stored procedure, you must locate in SQL
Server Books Online sp_displayoaerrorinfo and sp_hexadecimal and store them in
the same database with prBatchExec (in other words, the Asset database).

To execute the prBatchExec procedure, you need to specify values for the parameters
for the SQL Server instance, login, password, folder that contains your deployment
scripts, and the name of the file containing the list of deployment scripts. You also need
to decide whether deployment is to be performed as a transaction. Transactions cannot
be used for initial deployment because database creation cannot be performed by
a transaction. However, using transactions is very useful for incremental builds.

The prBatchExec procedure has one limitation. It can process only short (up to
8000 characters) scripts. I have decided to include it in this the book for two reasons.
First, 8000 characters is probably enough for running an incremental build. Second,
it's educational—it demonstrates use of COM objects from Transact-SQL. For full
builds, you have to use an updated version—prBatchExec3.

You can also download BatchExec.exe program from www.Trigonblue.com/sqlxml/sqlxml_download.htm. This is a console C# application and you can run it on computers that have the .NET Framework installed using

```
BatchExec (local)\ss2k2 sa my,password c:\script\test list.txt
```

Deploying Create Scripts in Visual Studio .NET

Create scripts generated in Visual Studio .NET can also be "glued" together and deployed on other servers:

1. Select the Create Scripts folder in Solution Explorer, and then select Project | Create Command File.

2. Set the Name of Command File and move all or just some of the scripts in the Available Scripts list to the list of Scripts To Be Added To The Command File.

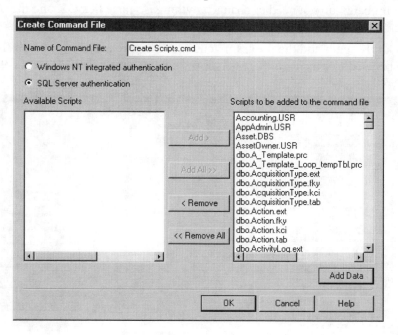

3. If you have moved some of the table files (TAB) that have data files (DAT) associated with them, the Add Data button becomes available. Click the button and the program prompts you to confirm associations between files:

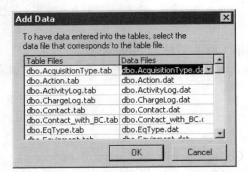

4. You probably do not need to change anything, so just click OK and the program returns you to the previous screen.

5. Click OK again and the program generates a command file (or batch file) that can be used to execute all Create scripts on any server (see Figure 11-9).

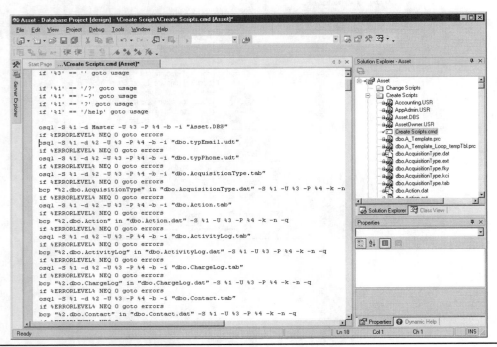

Figure 11-9 *Command file for deploying Create scripts*

Incremental Build: Traditional Approach

Whichever method you choose for performing a full build of the database, you will eventually need to deploy design changes and hotfixes while preserving data in the database. Such changes can even accumulate over time. Typically, code changes for procedures can simply be executed in their latest form against the production database, but changes to the database structure (tables) must be implemented in such a way that they preserve data.

prBatchExec is very useful for deploying incremental changes on the database server. Individual changes to database objects can be grouped by defect number or version number (see Figure 11-10).

It is especially useful to run the process as a transaction in this case. If an unexpected error occurs during the deployment, it is preferable to roll back all the changes, leaving the production system intact.

TIP

Once you assemble deployment scripts, it is critical to perform sufficient unit testing. You can run the scripts against a new server or a new instance on the existing server and test the changes. You should repeat the deployment, fixing issues that you find, until it runs without a glitch. The ultimate test is whether the application can work with the database system without additional intervention.

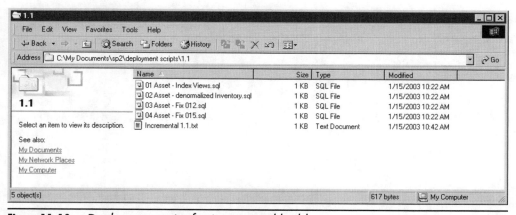

Figure 11-10   *Deployment script for incremental build*

Incremental Build in Visual Studio .NET

Alternatively, you can create incremental scripts in Visual Studio .NET. In this case, you create Change scripts and manage them in the folder of the same name (in Solution Explorer). You should again create a command file, but you should probably name it differently. You will use the same techniques and methods that have already been described regarding the full build in the earlier section "Scripting Data in Visual Studio .NET."

TIP

You should pay special attention to avoid mixing versions of files and to execute database changes in the right order. It is a good idea to add sequential numbers or the date and time at the beginning of filenames. You can store different releases in different folders, or you can have different command files if you keep all change scripts in the same folder. When you are done, test, test, and test again.

Stored Procedures for Web Search Engines

T he search engine is a standard element of every web application. Many tools are available to help web developers create a search engine when information is stored in the form of web pages, but if the information is on a database server, everything has to be customized. This chapter demonstrates some typical problems you may encounter and solutions for them.

Characteristics of the Environment

The following are the characteristics of a typical web-based application environment:

▶ The system has impatient users. Pages must be served quickly or users will leave and go to another web site.

▶ A three-tier architecture is typically used to make the system more scalable.

▶ To be scalable, the system may be deployed on a farm of web and/or middleware servers. If more users need to be processed, you can simply add more servers.

▶ Since it may be deployed on a farm of servers, the application must use stateless connections to the database.

▶ The database server cannot be scaled in the same manner as web and middleware servers. Federated servers allow users to split a database among several servers, but one record will be stored on only one server. It is also not such a trivial matter to add another database server. Tables that are vertically split between servers have to be reorganized so that a new server gets its share of the table. Therefore, the database server is a more precious resource than the web and middleware servers.

▶ Network traffic could be an issue—both internally (between servers) and externally (users could be linked by modem).

A Simple Solution...

Typically, web search engines have two types of web pages—one type for entering criteria and another type for displaying results. The criteria page can sometimes be very simple—a single text box feeding a single table in the database. Sometimes, you may have a web page with a number of objects (such as text boxes, list boxes, and check boxes) that correspond to different fields in different tables. Potentially, all recordset (table) fields could be exposed as criteria fields. A user can use a single field or multiple fields to specify the criteria. I call such pages and corresponding queries *quick* and *full* (or *advanced*), respectively.

The quick criteria page is naturally implemented in SQL Server as a stored procedure with one parameter. In the case of full criteria, the fact that users can specify values for an unknown number of fields, unsurprisingly, leads developers to implement it as a dynamically assembled ad hoc query joining a large number of normalized tables. To illustrate this in the Asset database, I have created a query against Inventory and other associated tables:

```
SELECT Inventoryid,  Make,             Model,
       EqType,       Location,         FirstName,
       LastName,     AcquisitionType,  Address,
       City,         ProvinceId,       Country,
       Phone,        Fax,              Email,
       UserName,     OrgUnit
from Inventory
  inner join Contact
  on Inventory.OwnerId = Contact.ContactId
    inner join Location
    on Inventory.LocationId = Location.LocationId
      inner join AcquisitionType
      on AcquisitionType.AcquisitionTypeId = Inventory.AcquisitionTypeId
        inner join Equipment
        on Equipment.EquipmentId = Inventory.EquipmentId
          inner join EqType
          on Equipment.EqTypeId = EqType.EqTypeId
            inner join OrgUnit
            on Contact.OrgUnitId = OrgUnit.OrgUnitId
where Make = 'Compaq'
  And EqType = 'Storage Array'
order by  Country, ProvinceId, City, Location
```

In the real world, such a query may be designed to run against more tables—I have seen solutions with 20 or more joined tables. Such a design might look elegant during development if it is tested by only a couple of users using only a small number of records per table. Unfortunately, in production, an application will work against tables with thousands (or millions) of records and will have to serve dozens (or hundreds) of concurrent users.

NOTE

One such system that I've encountered in the past had difficulty supporting even ten users. The simplest queries took five to ten seconds. Regular queries often timed out after 60 seconds. Users were so frustrated that they would issue a query without criteria, and then copy the complete result set to Excel or Access to query it on their local machines.

...and Its Disadvantages

The following are the standard problems with a "simple" solution based on a single query:

▶ **The query joins many tables** Specifying a number of tables that is acceptable is difficult, but 15 or 20, and sometimes even 10, is too many. SQL Server has to do a considerable amount of work to join them all. A normalized set of tables is optimal for modifying data, but for querying, designers should explore denormalization of the model.

▶ **(B)locking** If users are accessing the same set of tables for both updating and querying, they will block each other. SQL Server puts a shared lock on records that qualify as a result of a query while the query is in progress. Other queries are not blocked by it and can be executed at the same time. However, those locks will prevent modifications of the records until the query is done. On the other hand, when a transaction is modifying a record, users will have to wait for the transaction to be completed to have the results to their queries returned.

▶ **The complete result set is sent to the client** Too often, users specify criteria that are not selective enough and may return hundreds (or thousands) of records. Such a recordset is seldom required and users will not browse through it. Typically, they will modify the original criteria and make the query more selective to get a subset of the original recordset.

▶ **Sorting** Users expect the result set to be sorted and they also expect to be able to change the sort order on-the-fly. These actions require processing power.

▶ **Table scans** Some queries may contain criteria that are not optimizable (SARG-able). A common example occurs when a user requests all records for which the Name field contains a specified string. The query is implemented using the Like operator with wildcards (%) at the beginning and the end of the string, such as

```
Where name Like '%str%'
```

SQL Server will not be able to use the index on the name field to process such a query.

▶ **Ad hoc queries** Since the user has the freedom to specify an unknown number and combination of criteria, queries are typically assembled dynamically. The disadvantage to this flexibility is that you do not have control over these queries, which opens up code management, optimization, and security issues. On the other hand, a dynamically created query allows an experienced user to restrict the query to only those elements that are really needed. You can drop unnecessary tables and segments of criteria.

▶ **Improper indexes**   You should review indexes that are created on tables. Keep in mind that indexes are optimal for querying but not optimal for modifying data. They become overhead on transactions.

Available Solutions

You can do many things to improve this kind of system:

▶ **Denormalization**   This is probably the most effective way to improve the system. SQL Server will have to query a smaller number of tables. You can create a redundant set of tables (one or more, depending on the subject) and periodically (for example, every hour or every day) transfer data from the normalized tables to it. An additional benefit is that "readers" and "writers" will not block each other.

▶ **Limit the result set**   Most search engines on the Web limit the number of results that the user can return (for example, 200 or 500 records).

▶ **Split results rather than limit result sets**   Users should be able to access records in batches (of, for example, 25 or 50 records). Chances are that the user will browse through only the first couple of pages. There is no need to serve the user with 5000 records that he or she will not review.

▶ **Index**   An additional benefit of splitting tables to provide one table for data modification and another for querying is that the indexes you would need to create on the denormalized tables will not slow down data modification transactions.

▶ **Stored procedures vs. ad hoc queries**   Because of the many performance and management reasons discussed earlier, in "Reuse of Stored Procedure Execution Plans" in Chapter 3, you should use precompiled objects such as stored procedures as much as you can. Often, you can significantly simplify a query by dynamically assembling it. When you reduce the number of tables and parameters, the query optimizer creates a better execution plan.

▶ **Search types**   Good results can sometimes be achieved by using a little psychology. For example, users do not always need to do a "Contains" search on a string (like '%*string*%'). Most of the time, "Begins with" (like '*string*%') and "Match" (='*string*') searches are sufficient. For the latter two, SQL Server does not ignore the index. If you add a list box with "Search types" to the text box and make "Begins With" the default option, users will use it probably 90 percent of the time. SQL Server does a table scan only when users really need to scan the whole field.

I will review in detail some of these options in an Asset database scenario.

Result Splitting

There are three options for achieving result splitting:

▶ On a web server
▶ Using a temporary table on the database server
▶ Using a static denormalized table on the database server

Page Splitting on a Web Server

Some web sites split the result set on a web server. The complete result set is transferred to the web server and components on it create HTML pages with links between them. There are several good reasons to use this technique. A farm of web servers can efficiently balance the load. There are solutions on the market that can be purchased and implemented rapidly. Unfortunately, network traffic between servers is not reduced and SQL Server has to grab and transfer much more than it should. I will not go into the details of how to implement such a solution (you'll need a different book for that).

Page Splitting Using a Temporary Table on the Database Server

The idea of this solution is to collect the complete recordset in a temporary table and then to send to the caller only a subset of records (for example, 25 records) to be displayed on the current page.

In the following example, the query creates a temporary table that has an additional identity field. The second query returns records with identity values between the specified numbers. Initially, these numbers might be 1 and 25. The next time it is called, the client increases the values of the first and the last records to be displayed.

```
Alter PROCEDURE prInventoryByMakeModel_Quick_TempTbl
-- Return a batch (of specified size) of records which satisfy the criteria
-- Demonstration of use of temporary table to perform recordset splitting.
  @Make varchar(50) = '%',
  @Model varchar(50) = '%',
  @FirstRec int = 1,
```

```
    @LastRec int = 25,
    @RowCount int = null output
AS
/* test:
declare @rc int
exec prInventoryByMakeModel_Quick_TempTbl @RowCount = @rc output
select @rc
exec prInventoryByMakeModel_Quick_TempTbl @FirstRec = 26,
                                          @LastRec = 50,
                                          @RowCount = @rc output
*/
SET NOCOUNT ON

Create table #Inv(ID int identity,
                  Inventoryid int,
                  Make varchar(50),
                  Model varchar(50),
                  Location varchar(50),
                  FirstName varchar(30),
                  LastName varchar(30),
                  AcquisitionType varchar(12),
                  Address varchar(50),
                  City varchar(50),
                  ProvinceId char(3),
                  Country varchar(50),
                  EqType varchar(50),
                  Phone varchar(20),
                  Fax varchar(20),
                  Email varchar(128),
                  UserName varchar(50))

insert into #Inv(InventoryId, Make, Model,
                 Location, FirstName, LastName,
                 AcquisitionType, Address, City,
                 ProvinceId, Country, EqType,
                 Phone, Fax, Email,
                 UserName)
SELECT
   Inventory.Inventoryid, Equipment.Make, Equipment.Model,
   Location.Location, Contact.FirstName,
   Contact.LastName, AcquisitionType.AcquisitionType, Location.Address,
   Location.City, Location.ProvinceId, Location.Country,
   EqType.EqType, Contact.Phone, Contact.Fax,
   Contact.Email, Contact.UserName
 FROM  EqType
 RIGHT OUTER JOIN Equipment
 ON EqType.EqTypeId = Equipment.EqTypeId
    RIGHT OUTER JOIN Inventory
    ON Equipment.EquipmentId = Inventory.EquipmentId
      INNER JOIN Status
```

```
            ON Inventory.StatusId = Status.StatusId
              LEFT OUTER JOIN AcquisitionType
              ON Inventory.AcquisitionTypeID = AcquisitionType.AcquisitionTypeId
                LEFT OUTER JOIN Location
                ON Inventory.LocationId = Location.LocationId
                  LEFT OUTER JOIN Contact
                  ON Inventory.OwnerId = Contact.ContactId
where Make Like @Make
and Model Like @Model
order by Location, LastName, FirstName

select @RowCount = @@rowcount

SELECT *
FROM #Inv
WHERE ID >= @FirstRec AND ID <= @LastRec
order by ID
return
```

The stored procedure should be used the first time in the following manner to get the first batch of records and the number of records:

```
declare @rc int
exec prInventoryByMakeModel_Quick_TempTbl @RowCount = @rc output
select @rc
```

The next time, the user must specify the first and last record that he wants to see:

```
declare @rc int
exec prInventoryByMakeModel_Quick_TempTbl @FirstRec = 26,
                                           @LastRec  = 50,
                                           @RowCount = @rc output
```

There are, however, several problems with this solution. You are still executing the query against a large set of normalized tables. You are also creating a large temporary table every time you execute the stored procedure. Because you are working in a stateless environment, you cannot keep the temporary table on the server. Therefore, SQL Server works much harder than it should. The advantage to this technique is that network traffic is significantly reduced.

Page Splitting Using Denormalized Tables on the Database Server

To reduce the number of tables that need to be joined every time, you can create a new table that contains all the fields that you typically need in the query. The InventorySum table has such a role in the Asset database.

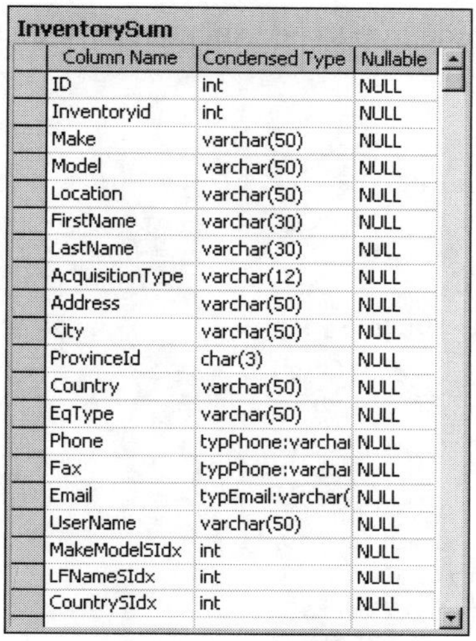

InventorySum

Column Name	Condensed Type	Nullable
ID	int	NULL
Inventoryid	int	NULL
Make	varchar(50)	NULL
Model	varchar(50)	NULL
Location	varchar(50)	NULL
FirstName	varchar(30)	NULL
LastName	varchar(30)	NULL
AcquisitionType	varchar(12)	NULL
Address	varchar(50)	NULL
City	varchar(50)	NULL
ProvinceId	char(3)	NULL
Country	varchar(50)	NULL
EqType	varchar(50)	NULL
Phone	typPhone:varchai	NULL
Fax	typPhone:varchai	NULL
Email	typEmail:varchar(	NULL
UserName	varchar(50)	NULL
MakeModelSIdx	int	NULL
LFNameSIdx	int	NULL
CountrySIdx	int	NULL

Most of the fields are just copied from normalized tables. ID is an identity field, which you will use to request a subset of records and to sort records on. Several records have a SIdx suffix. I call them *surrogate indexes*. They store the position of the record in a set when it is sorted in a particular order. For example, LFNameSIdx is the surrogate index that is used when a recordset is returned sorted by first and last name (see Figure 12-1).

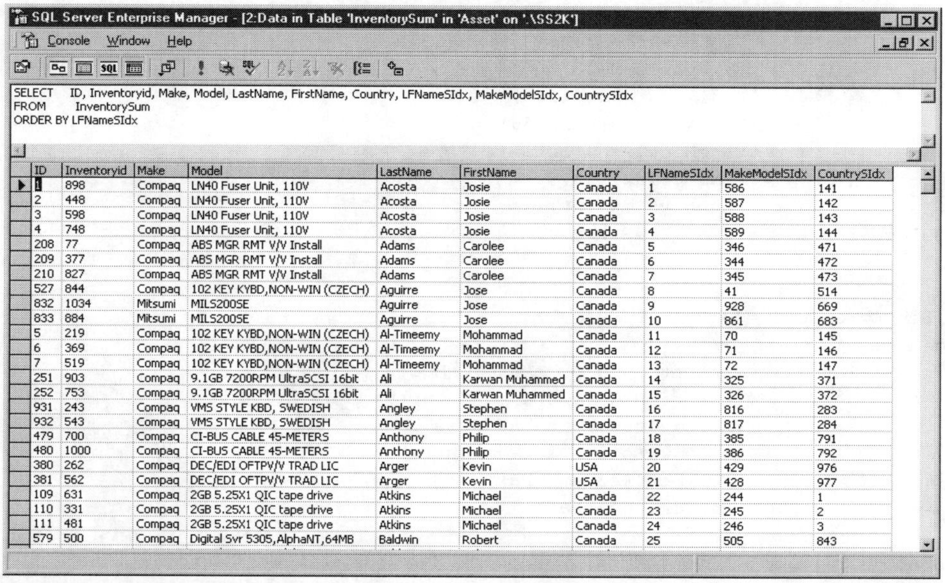


```
SELECT    ID, Inventoryid, Make, Model, LastName, FirstName, Country, LFNameSIdx, MakeModelSIdx, CountrySIdx
FROM      InventorySum
ORDER BY LFNameSIdx
```

ID	Inventoryid	Make	Model	LastName	FirstName	Country	LFNameSIdx	MakeModelSIdx	CountrySIdx
1	898	Compaq	LN40 Fuser Unit, 110V	Acosta	Josie	Canada	1	586	141
2	448	Compaq	LN40 Fuser Unit, 110V	Acosta	Josie	Canada	2	587	142
3	598	Compaq	LN40 Fuser Unit, 110V	Acosta	Josie	Canada	3	588	143
4	748	Compaq	LN40 Fuser Unit, 110V	Acosta	Josie	Canada	4	589	144
208	77	Compaq	ABS MGR RMT V/V Install	Adams	Carolee	Canada	5	346	471
209	377	Compaq	ABS MGR RMT V/V Install	Adams	Carolee	Canada	6	344	472
210	827	Compaq	ABS MGR RMT V/V Install	Adams	Carolee	Canada	7	345	473
527	844	Compaq	102 KEY KYBD,NON-WIN (CZECH)	Aguirre	Jose	Canada	8	41	514
832	1034	Mitsumi	MILS200SE	Aguirre	Jose	Canada	9	928	669
833	884	Mitsumi	MILS200SE	Aguirre	Jose	Canada	10	861	683
5	219	Compaq	102 KEY KYBD,NON-WIN (CZECH)	Al-Timeemy	Mohammad	Canada	11	70	145
6	369	Compaq	102 KEY KYBD,NON-WIN (CZECH)	Al-Timeemy	Mohammad	Canada	12	71	146
7	519	Compaq	102 KEY KYBD,NON-WIN (CZECH)	Al-Timeemy	Mohammad	Canada	13	72	147
251	903	Compaq	9.1GB 7200RPM UltraSCSI 16bit	Ali	Karwan Muhammed	Canada	14	325	371
252	753	Compaq	9.1GB 7200RPM UltraSCSI 16bit	Ali	Karwan Muhammed	Canada	15	326	372
931	243	Compaq	VMS STYLE KBD, SWEDISH	Angley	Stephen	Canada	16	816	283
932	543	Compaq	VMS STYLE KBD, SWEDISH	Angley	Stephen	Canada	17	817	284
479	700	Compaq	CI-BUS CABLE 45-METERS	Anthony	Philip	Canada	18	385	791
480	1000	Compaq	CI-BUS CABLE 45-METERS	Anthony	Philip	Canada	19	386	792
380	262	Compaq	DEC/EDI OFTPV/V TRAD LIC	Arger	Kevin	USA	20	429	976
381	562	Compaq	DEC/EDI OFTPV/V TRAD LIC	Arger	Kevin	USA	21	428	977
109	631	Compaq	2GB 5.25X1 QIC tape drive	Atkins	Michael	Canada	22	244	1
110	331	Compaq	2GB 5.25X1 QIC tape drive	Atkins	Michael	Canada	23	245	2
111	481	Compaq	2GB 5.25X1 QIC tape drive	Atkins	Michael	Canada	24	246	3
579	500	Compaq	Digital Svr 5305,AlphaNT,64MB	Baldwin	Robert	Canada	25	505	843

Figure 12-1 *Surrogate index*

I have created a stored procedure to be executed periodically from a job to populate the denormalized table:

```
ALTER    Procedure prInvSum_Generate
-- Generate denormalized table that will speed-up the querying.
As
set nocount on
Declare @intErrorCode int,
        @intTransactionCountOnEntry int

Select @intErrorCode = @@Error

If @intErrorCode = 0
Begin
  create table #Inv(ID int identity(1,1),
                Inventoryid int,
                Make varchar(50),
                Model varchar(50),
                Location varchar(50),
                Status varchar(15),
                FirstName varchar(30),
                LastName varchar(30),
                AcquisitionType varchar(12),
                Address varchar(50),
                City varchar(50),
                ProvinceId char(3),
                Country varchar(50),
                EqType varchar(50),
                Phone varchar(20),
                Fax varchar(20),
                Email varchar(128),
                UserName varchar(50),
                MakeModelSIdx int,
                LFNameSIdx int,
                CountrySIdx int)
  Select @intErrorCode = @@Error
End

If @intErrorCode = 0
Begin
  insert into #Inv(Inventoryid ,   Make , Model ,
                Location , FirstName , LastName ,
                AcquisitionType, Address ,
                City ,ProvinceId , Country ,
                EqType ,Phone , Fax ,
                Email , UserName
)
  SELECT Inventory.Inventoryid, Equipment.Make, Equipment.Model,
        Location.Location, Contact.FirstName,
```

```
            Contact.LastName, AcquisitionType.AcquisitionType, Location.Address,
            Location.City, Location.ProvinceId, Location.Country,
            EqType.EqType, Contact.Phone, Contact.Fax,
            Contact.Email, Contact.UserName
    FROM   EqType
    RIGHT OUTER JOIN Equipment
    ON EqType.EqTypeId = Equipment.EqTypeId
      RIGHT OUTER JOIN Inventory
      ON Equipment.EquipmentId = Inventory.EquipmentId
          LEFT OUTER JOIN AcquisitionType
          ON Inventory.AcquisitionTypeID = AcquisitionType.AcquisitionTypeId
            LEFT OUTER JOIN Location
            ON Inventory.LocationId = Location.LocationId
              LEFT OUTER JOIN Contact
              ON Inventory.OwnerId = Contact.ContactId
    order by Location, LastName, FirstName

    Select @intErrorCode = @@Error
End


-- now let's do record sorting

---- Make, Model -------------------
If @intErrorCode = 0
Begin
    create table #tmp (SID int identity(1,1),
                       ID int)
    Select @intErrorCode = @@Error
End
If @intErrorCode = 0
Begin
    insert into #tmp(ID)
    select ID
    from #inv
    order by Make, Model
    Select @intErrorCode = @@Error
End


If @intErrorCode = 0
Begin
    update #inv
    set MakeModelSIdx = #tmp.SId
    from #inv inner join #tmp
    on #inv.ID = #tmp.id
    Select @intErrorCode = @@Error
End
If @intErrorCode = 0
Begin
    drop table #tmp
```

```
      Select @intErrorCode = @@Error
End
-----------------------------------------
---- CountrySIdx: Country, Province, City, Location -------------------
If @intErrorCode = 0
Begin
  create table #tmp2 (SID int identity(1,1),
                      ID int)
  Select @intErrorCode = @@Error
End
If @intErrorCode = 0
Begin
  insert into #tmp2(ID)
  select ID
  from #inv
  order by Country, ProvinceId, City, Location
  Select @intErrorCode = @@Error
End

If @intErrorCode = 0
Begin
  update #inv
  set CountrySIdx = #tmp2.SId
  from #inv inner join #tmp2
  on #inv.ID = #tmp2.id

  Select @intErrorCode = @@Error
End
If @intErrorCode = 0
Begin
  drop table #tmp2
  Select @intErrorCode = @@Error
End
-----------------------------------------
---- LFNameSIdx: LName, FName -------------------
If @intErrorCode = 0
Begin
  create table #tmp3 (SID int identity(1,1),
                      ID int)
  Select @intErrorCode = @@Error
End
If @intErrorCode = 0
Begin
  insert into #tmp3(ID)
  select ID
  from #inv
  order by LastName, FirstName
  Select @intErrorCode = @@Error
End
```

```
If @intErrorCode = 0
Begin
  update #inv
  set LFNameSIdx = #tmp3.SId
  from #inv inner join #tmp3
  on #inv.ID = #tmp3.id

  Select @intErrorCode = @@Error
End
If @intErrorCode = 0
Begin
  drop table #tmp3
  Select @intErrorCode = @@Error
End
-----------------------------------------

If @intErrorCode = 0
Begin
    Select @intTransactionCountOnEntry = @@TranCount
    BEGIN TRANSACTION
End

If @intErrorCode = 0
Begin
  if exists (select * from dbo.sysobjects
        where id = object_id(N'[InventorySum]')
        and OBJECTPROPERTY(id, N'IsUserTable') = 1)
  drop table [InventorySum]

  Select @intErrorCode = @@Error
End

If @intErrorCode = 0
Begin
  create table InventorySum(ID int,
            Inventoryid int,
            Make varchar(50),
            Model varchar(50),
            Location varchar(50),
            FirstName varchar(30),
            LastName varchar(30),
            AcquisitionType varchar(12),
            Address varchar(50),
            City varchar(50),
            ProvinceId char(3),
            Country varchar(50),
            EqType varchar(50),
            Phone typPhone,
```

```
            Fax typPhone,
            Email typEmail,
            UserName varchar(50),
            MakeModelSIdx  int,
            LFNameSIdx int,
            CountrySIdx int)
  Select @intErrorCode = @@Error
End
-- copy
If @intErrorCode = 0
Begin
  insert into InventorySum
  select * from #inv

  Select @intErrorCode = @@Error
End


-- create indexes
If @intErrorCode = 0
Begin
  CREATE UNIQUE CLUSTERED INDEX [idx_InvSum_Id]
    ON [dbo].[InventorySum] ([ID])
  Select @intErrorCode = @@Error
End
If @intErrorCode = 0
Begin
  CREATE INDEX [idx_InvSum_LFName]
    ON [dbo].[InventorySum] (LastName, FirstName)
  Select @intErrorCode = @@Error
End


If @intErrorCode = 0
Begin
  CREATE INDEX [idx_InvSum_Location]
    ON [dbo].[InventorySum] (Location)
  Select @intErrorCode = @@Error
End


If @intErrorCode = 0
Begin
  CREATE INDEX [idx_InvSum_ModelMakeEqType]
    ON [dbo].[InventorySum] (Model, Make, EqType)
  Select @intErrorCode = @@Error
End


If @@TranCount > @intTransactionCountOnEntry
Begin
    If @intErrorCode = 0
        COMMIT TRANSACTION
    Else
```

```
       ROLLBACK TRANSACTION
End
return @intErrorCode
```

At first sight, the stored procedure might look a bit unusual to you. I first collect all data in a temporary table and then, within a transaction, drop the denormalized table, re-create it, and copy the collected data from the temporary table into it. I wrote the stored procedure in this way for performance reasons. It is critical for users to be able to query the table without interruption. The whole process typically takes a couple of minutes, and queries will time-out if not completed after 30 seconds (or the limit that is specified on the server, in the ADO connection, or MTS). Therefore, it is critical to shorten the interruption. The process of copying collected data is much shorter than the process of collecting it.

On one project where I applied this solution, the complete process took about three minutes. The transaction that re-creates the table and copies data into it took about 20 seconds.

NOTE

It is certainly possible to perform the loading transaction in other ways. Creating an additional static table and renaming it comes to mind.

Quick Queries

This section walks you through the process of gradually adding the following features to a stored procedure, implementing a quick query:

▶ Result splitting

▶ Sorting

▶ Search type

▶ Counting

I will build a stored procedure that returns a list of equipment with a specified make and model:

```
Alter Procedure prInventoryByMakeModel_Quick_1
@Make varchar(50) = null,  -- criteria
@Model varchar(50) = null  -- criteria
/* test:
exec prInventoryByMakeModel_Quick_1 'Compaq', 'D%'
*/
as
```

```
select Inventoryid ,     Make ,        Model,
       Location ,        FirstName ,   LastName ,
       AcquisitionType,  Address ,     City ,
       ProvinceId ,      Country ,     EqType ,
       Phone ,           Fax ,         Email ,
       UserName
from InventorySum
where Make LIKE @Make
and Model LIKE @Model
```

The preceding is a simple stored procedure that uses the Like operator, and therefore enables the caller to add a wildcard (%) to the string.

Now I'll add sorting to the stored procedure. I can sort only by sort orders for which I have defined surrogate indexes:

```
Alter procedure prInventoryByMakeModel_Quick_2
  @Make varchar(50) = null,  -- criteria
  @Model varchar(50) = null,  -- criteria
  @SortOrderId smallint = 0

/* test:
exec prInventoryByMakeModel_Quick_2 'Compaq', 'D%', 1
*/
as

  select Id = Case @SortOrderId
             when 1 then MakeModelSIdx
             when 2 then CountrySIdx
             when 3 then LFNameSIdx
           End,
       Inventoryid ,    Make ,        Model,
       Location ,       FirstName ,   LastName ,
       AcquisitionType, Address ,     City ,
       ProvinceId ,     Country ,     EqType ,
       Phone ,          Fax ,         Email ,
       UserName
  from InventorySum
  where Make like @Make
  and Model like @Model
  order by case @SortOrderId
        when 1 then MakeModelSIdx
        when 2 then CountrySIdx
        when 3 then LFNameSIdx
      end
return
```

I have also added an ID column to the recordset. I use a Case statement to set it with one of the surrogate indexes. The second instance of the Case statement is a little bit unusual. Note that I am using it inside an Order By clause.

Now I will add code that will return the result set in batches of 25 records:

```
alter procedure prInventoryByMakeModel_Quick_3
  @Make varchar(50) = null,    -- criteria
  @Model varchar(50) = null,   -- criteria
  @PreviousID int = 0,              -- last record from the previous batch
  @SortOrderId smallint = 0

/* test:
exec prInventoryByMakeModel_Quick_3 'Compaq', 'D%', 444, 1
*/
as

  select    top 25 Id = Case @SortOrderId
              when 1 then MakeModelSIdx
              when 2 then CountrySIdx
              when 3 then LFNameSIdx
            End,
        Inventoryid ,    Make ,        Model,
        Location ,       FirstName ,   LastName ,
        AcquisitionType, Address ,     City ,
        ProvinceId ,     Country ,     EqType ,
        Phone ,          Fax ,         Email ,
        UserName
  from InventorySum
  where Case @SortOrderId
      when 1 then MakeModelSIdx
      when 2 then CountrySIdx
      when 3 then LFNameSIdx
    End > @PreviousID
  and Make like @Make
  and Model like @Model
  order by case @SortOrderId
        when 1 then MakeModelSIdx
        when 2 then CountrySIdx
        when 3 then LFNameSIdx
      end
  return
```

I have added Top 25 to the Select statement. I added a parameter that will be used to pass the identifier of the last record seen in the previous batch. I also added a Case function in the Where clause that allows me to return records that were not previously seen by the user.

Next I will add code to support Begins With, Contains, and Match search types. I will simply add different combinations of wildcards to the search parameters:

```
Alter procedure prInventoryByMakeModel_Quick
-- display a batch of 25 assets of specified status
  @Make varchar(50) = null,  -- criteria
  @Model varchar(50) = null,  -- criteria
  @PreviousID int = 0,     -- last record from the previous batch
  @SortOrderId smallint = 0,
  @SearchTypeid tinyint = 0  -- 0: Begins With, 1: Match, 2: Contains
/* test:
exec prInventoryByMakeModel_Quick 'Compaq', 'D', 50, 2, 2
*/
as

if @SearchTypeId = 0
begin
  set @Make = @Make + '%'
  set @Model = @Model + '%'
end

if @SearchTypeid = 2
begin
  set @Make  = '%' + @Make  + '%'
  set @Model = '%' + @Model + '%'
end

select top 25 Id = Case @SortOrderId
          when 1 then MakeModelSIdx
          when 2 then CountrySIdx
          when 3 then LFNameSIdx
       End,
    Inventoryid ,    Make ,       Model,
    Location ,       FirstName , LastName ,
    AcquisitionType, Address ,   City ,
    ProvinceId ,     Country ,   EqType ,
    Phone ,          Fax ,       Email ,
    UserName
from InventorySum
where Case @SortOrderId
    when 1 then MakeModelSIdx
    when 2 then CountrySIdx
    when 3 then LFNameSIdx
```

```
    End > @PreviousID
and Make like @Make
and Model like @Model
order by case @SortOrderId
        when 1 then MakeModelSIdx
        when 2 then CountrySIdx
        when 3 then LFNameSIdx
      end
return
```

Since it is important to display the total number of records that satisfy specified criteria, I will create a stored procedure to return the count to the user. I have two options: I could add the code to the stored procedure that does the search; but the better option is to make code more readable and create a separate procedure:

```
Alter procedure prInventoryByMakeModel_Count
-- display a batch of 25 assets of specified status
  @Make varchar(50) = null,  -- criteria
  @Model varchar(50) = null,  -- criteria
  @SearchTypeid tinyint = 0,  -- 0: Begins With, 1: Match, 2: Contains
  @Count int output
/* test:
declare @count int
exec prInventoryByMakeModel_Count 'Compaq', 'D', 2, @count output
select @count count
*/
as

if @SearchTypeId = 0
begin
  set @Make = @Make + '%'
  set @Model = @Model + '%'
end

if @SearchTypeid = 2
begin
  set @Make  = '%' + @Make  + '%'
  set @Model = '%' + @Model + '%'
end

select @Count = count(*)
from InventorySum
where Make like @Make
and Model like @Model

return
```

Advanced Queries

An advanced query allows users to specify criteria using any combination of input parameters. Therefore, all parameters have default values specified so that they will never become part of the criteria (I can agree with web developers that null means that the user didn't specify a value for the parameter on the web page):

```
Alter procedure prInventorySearchAdvFull_ListPage
-- display a batch of 25 assets that specify the criteria

-- Example of use of dynamically assembled query
-- and denormalized table with surrogate index fields
-- to return result in batches of 25 records.

    @Make varchar(50) = null,
    @Model varchar(50) = null,
    @Location varchar(50) = null,
    @FirstName varchar(30) = null,
    @LastName varchar(30) = null,
    @AcquisitionType varchar(20) = null,
    @ProvinceId char(3) = null,
    @Country varchar(50) = null,
    @EqType varchar(30) = null,
    @City varchar(50) = null,
    @UserName varchar(50) = null,
    @email varchar(50) = null,
    @SortOrderId smallint = 0,    -- 1: Make and model;
                                  -- 2: Country, Prov, City, Loc;
                                  -- 4: LName; FName
    @PreviousID int = 0,       -- last record from the previous batch
    @BatchSize int = 25,
    @debug int = 0
/* test:
exec prInventorySearchAdvFull_ListPage
    @Make = 'Compaq',
    @Model= null,
    @Location = null,
    @FirstName = 'Michael',
    @LastName = null,
    @AcquisitionType = null,
    @ProvinceId  = null,
    @Country = null,
    @EqType = null,
    @City = null,
    @UserName = null,
    @email = null,
    @SortOrderId = 2,   -- 2: Make and model
    @PreviousID = 25,   -- last record from the previous batch
```

```
    @BatchSize = 25,
    @debug = 0
*/
as
set SET CONCAT_NULL_YIELDS_NULL OFF
set nocount on

declare @chvSelect varchar(8000),
      @chvFrom varchar(8000),
      @chvWhere varchar(8000),
      @chvOrderby varchar(8000),
      @chvSQL varchar(8000)

-- order records
set @chvSelect = 'SELECT top ' + Convert(varchar, @BatchSize)
        + '        Inventoryid ,        Make ,           Model,
                  Location ,           FirstName ,
                  LastName ,           AcquisitionType, Address ,
                  City ,               ProvinceId ,     Country ,
                  EqType ,             Phone ,          Fax ,
                  Email ,              UserName,  '
          + Case @SortOrderId
              when 1 then ' MakeModelSIdx '
              when 2 then ' CountrySIdx '
              when 3 then ' LFNameSIdx '
            End
          + ' as ID '

set @chvFrom = ' FROM  InventorySum '

set @chvWhere = ' where '
          + Case @SortOrderId
              when 1 then ' MakeModelSIdx'
              when 2 then ' CountrySIdx '
              when 3 then ' LFNameSIdx '
            End + '> '
          + Convert(varchar, @PreviousID)

if   @Make is not null
    set @chvWhere = @chvWhere + ' AND Make = ''' + @Make + ''' '
if   @Model is not null
    set @chvWhere = @chvWhere + ' AND Model = ''' + @Model + ''' '
if   @Location is not null
    set @chvWhere = @chvWhere + ' AND Location = ''' + @Location + ''' '
if   @FirstName is not null
    set @chvWhere = @chvWhere + ' AND FirstName = ''' + @FirstName + ''' '
if   @LastName is not null
    set @chvWhere = @chvWhere + ' AND lastName = ''' + @lastName + ''' '
if   @AcquisitionType is not null
```

```
       set @chvWhere = @chvWhere + ' AND AcquisitionType = '''
                     + @AcquisitionType + ''' '
if   @ProvinceId  is not null
     set @chvWhere = @chvWhere + ' AND ProvinceId = ''' + @ProvinceId + ''' '
if   @Country is not null
     set @chvWhere = @chvWhere + ' AND Country = ''' + @Country + ''' '
if   @EqType is not null
     set @chvWhere = @chvWhere + ' AND EqType = ''' + @EqType + ''' '
if   @City is not null
     set @chvWhere = @chvWhere + ' AND City = ''' + @City + ''' '
if   @UserName is not null
     set @chvWhere = @chvWhere + ' AND UserName = ''' + @UserName + ''' '
if   @email is not null
     set @chvWhere = @chvWhere + ' AND email = ''' + @email + ''' '

set @chvOrderBy = ' order by '
              + Case @SortOrderId
                  when 1 then ' MakeModelSIdx'
                  when 2 then ' CountrySIdx '
                  when 3 then ' LFNameSIdx '
                End

set @chvSQL = @chvSelect + @chvFrom + @chvWhere + @chvOrderby

if @debug = 0
   exec (@chvSQL)
else
   select @chvSQL
```

The stored procedure dynamically assembles the query using just the Where clause for input parameters that were specified. This technique allows SQL Server to optimize the query and use the appropriate indexes. Similarly, Order By and Select clauses are assembled based on the specified sort order. The Top clause is added dynamically to the Select clause based on the number of records that the user wants to see in the batch.

NOTE

Something that I didn't demonstrate here, but that could also be very useful for joining tables on demand is the following: if some tables are joined just to support some additional search criteria, they might be added to the rest of the From clause only when their values are specified. The query will perform better if the number of joined tables is smaller.

Introduction to XML for Database Developers

IN THIS CHAPTER:

XML (R)evolution
Introduction to XML
XML Document Quality
Linking and Querying in XML
Transforming XML
Why XML?

Microsoft SQL Server has become a giant among the select group of enterprise-ready relational database management systems, but as with those other RDBMSs, its roots are in pre-Internet solutions. The Internet revolution has highlighted a set of old tactical and strategic challenges for the Microsoft SQL Server development team. These challenges include the following:

► Storing the large amounts of textual information that web-based, user-friendly database applications require

► Delivering that textual (and other) stored information to the Web

► Sharing information with other departments and organizations that may not use the same RDBMS system

In earlier editions of SQL Server, Microsoft addressed these issues with features such as Full Text Search, the Web Publishing Wizard, DTS, ADO, and OLE DB. SQL Server 2000 introduces XML compatibility—the new holy grail of the computing industry and the latest attempt to tackle the same old problems.

XML (R)evolution

To communicate with customers in today's rich-content world, you need to provide them with information. Until very recently, such information was inevitably encapsulated in proprietary, document-based formats that are not shared easily. For example, word processor documents are optimized for delivery on paper, and relational databases are often structured and normalized in formats unsuitable to end users.

The first step in the right direction was the *Standard Generalized Markup Language (SGML)*. Although it was designed in the late 1960s (by Charles Goldfarb), it became the international standard for defining markup languages in 1986, after the creation of the ISO standard. In the late 1980s, companies and government agencies started to adopt this tag-based language. It allowed them to create and manage paper documentation in a way that was easy to share with others.

Then, in the 1990s, the Web appeared on the scene and our collective focus shifted from isolated islands of personal computers and local networks to a global network of shared information. SGML's tagged structure would seem to make it a perfect candidate to lead the Internet revolution, but the complexity of SGML makes it difficult to work with and unsuitable for web application design.

Instead of SGML, the developers of the Internet adopted the *Hypertext Markup Language (HTML),* a simple markup language used to create hypertext documents that are portable from one platform to another. HTML is a simplified subset of SGML. It was originally defined in 1991 by Tim Berners-Lee as a way to organize, view, and transfer scientific documents across different platforms. It uses the *Hypertext Transfer Protocol (HTTP)* to transfer information over the Internet. This new markup language was an exciting development and soon found nonscientific applications. Eventually, companies and users started to use it as a platform for *e-commerce*—the processing of business transactions without the exchange of paper-based business documents.

Unfortunately, HTML has some disadvantages. One of the biggest arises as a result of its main purpose. HTML is designed to describe only how information should appear—that is, its format. It was not designed to define the syntax (logical structure) or semantics (meaning) of a document. It could make a document readable to a user, but it required that user to interact with, and interpret, the document. The computer itself could not parse the document because the necessary metadata (literally, data about the data) was not included with the document.

Another problem with HTML is that it is not extensible. It is not possible to create new tags. HTML is also a "standard" that exists in multiple versions—and multiple proprietary implementations. Web developers know that they have to test even their static HTML pages in all of the most popular browsers (and often in several versions of each) because each browser (and each version of each browser) implements this "standard" somewhat differently. Different development tool sets support different versions of this standard (and often different features within a single standard).

In 1996, a group working under the auspices of the World Wide Web Consortium (W3C) created a new standard tagged language called the *eXtensible Markup Language (XML)*. It was designed to address some of the problems of HTML and SGML. XML is a standardized document formatting language (again, a subset of SGML) that enables a publisher to create a single document source that can be viewed, displayed, or printed in a variety of ways. As is the case with HTML, XML is primarily designed for use on the Internet. However, as already mentioned, HTML is designed primarily to address document formatting issues, while XML addresses issues relating to data and object structure. XML is also extensible in that it provides a standard mechanism for any document builder to define new XML tags within any XML document. Its features lower the barriers for creation of integrated, multiplatform, application-to-application protocols.

Introduction to XML

In today's world, words such as "tag," "markup," "element," "attributes," and "schema" are buzzwords that you can hear anywhere (well, at least in the IT industry), but what do these terms mean in the context of markup languages?

Introduction to Markup Languages

In a broader sense, a *markup* is anything that you place within a document that provides additional meaning or additional information. For example, this book uses italic font to emphasize each new phrase or concept that is defined or introduced. I have a habit of using a highlighter when I am reading books. Each time I use my highlighter, I change the format of the text as a means of helping me find important segments later.

Markups usually define

▶   Formatting

▶   Structure

▶   Meaning

A reader has to have an implicit set of rules for placing markups in a document—otherwise those markups are meaningless to that reader. A *markup language* is a set of rules that defines

▶   What constitutes a markup

▶   What a markup means

Building Blocks of Markup Languages

The syntax of markup languages such as SGML, HTML, and XML is based on tags, elements, and attributes.

A *tag* is a markup language building block that consists of delimiters (angled brackets) and the text between them:

```
<TITLE>
```

An *element* is a markup language part that consists of a pair of tags and the text between them:

```
<TITLE>SQL Server 2000 Stored Procedure Programming</TITLE>
```

Each element has an *opening tag* and a *closing tag*. The text between these tags is called the *content* of the element.

An *attribute* is a component in the form of a name/value pair that delimits a tag:

```
<font size="2">
```

Okay, suppose you have created a document and have marked up some parts of it. Now what? You can share it with others. They will use something called a *user agent* to review the document. In a broader context, a user agent could be a travel agent that helps a customer buy tickets for a trip. However, in the IT industry, a user agent is a program that understands the markup language and presents information to an end user. An example of such a program is a web browser designed to present documents created using HTML.

XML Elements and Attributes

The following is a simple example of an XML document:

```
<Inventory>
  <Asset Inventoryid="5">
    <Equipment>Toshiba Portege 7020CT</Equipment>
    <EquipmentType>Notebook</EquipmentType>
    <LocationId>2</LocationId>
    <StatusId>1</StatusId>
    <LeaseId>1234</LeaseId>
    <LeaseScheduleId>1414</LeaseScheduleId>
    <OwnerId>83749271</OwnerId>
    <Cost>6295.00</Cost>
    <AcquisitionType>Lease</AcquisitionType>
  </Asset>
</Inventory>
```

An XML document must contain one or more elements. One of the elements is not part of any other element and therefore is called the document's *root element*. It must be uniquely named. In the preceding example, the root element is named `Inventory`.

Each element can, in turn, contain one or more elements. In the preceding example, the `Inventory` element contains one `Asset` element. The `Asset` element also contains other elements (Equipment, EquipmentType, and so on). The `Equipment` element contains just its content—the text string "Toshiba Portege 7020CT."

Unlike HTML, XML is *case sensitive*. Therefore, `Asset`, `asset`, and `ASSET` would represent different elements.

It is possible to define an *empty element.* Such elements can be displayed using standard opening and closing tags:

```
<Inventory></Inventory>
```

or using special notation:

```
<Inventory/>
```

If an element contains attributes but no content, an empty element is an efficient way to write it:

```
<Asset Inventoryid="5"/>
```

An element can have more than one attribute. The following example shows an empty element that contains nine attributes:

```
<Asset Inventoryid="12" EquipmentId="1" LocationId="2" StatusId="1"
LeaseId="1" LeaseScheduleId="1" OwnerId="1" Lease="100.0000"
AcquisitionTypeID="2"/>
```

You are not allowed to repeat an attribute in the same tag. The following example shows a syntactically incorrect element:

```
<Inventory Inventoryid="12" Inventoryid="13"/>
```

Processing Instructions

An XML document often starts with a tag that is called a *processing instruction.* For example, the following processing instruction notifies the reader that the document it belongs to is written in XML that complies with version 1.0:

```
<?xml version="1.0"?>
```

A processing instruction has the following format:

```
<?name data?>
```

The *name* portion identifies the processing instruction to the application that is processing the XML document. Names must start with xml. The *data* portion that follows is optional and includes information that may be used by the application.

TIP

Although it is not required, it is recommended that you start an XML document with a processing instruction that explicitly identifies that document as an XML document defined using a specified version of the standard.

Document Type Definition

As mentioned earlier, markups are meaningless if defining rules for the following is not possible:

▶   What constitutes a markup

▶   What a markup means

A *Document Type Definition (DTD)* is a type of document that is often used to define such rules for XML documents. The DTD contains descriptions and constraints (naturally, not Transact-SQL constraints) for each element (such as the order of element attributes and membership). User agents can use the DTD file to verify that an XML document complies with its rules.

The DTD can be an external file that is referenced by an XML document:

```
<!DOCTYPE Inventory SYSTEM "Inventory.dtd">
```

or it can be part of the XML document itself:

```
<?xml version="1.0"?>
<!DOCTYPE Inventory [
<!ELEMENT Inventory (Asset+)>
<!ELEMENT Asset (EquipmentId, LocationId, StatusId, LeaseId,
                 LeaseScheduleId, OwnerId, Cost, AcquisitionTypeID)>
<!ATTLIST Asset Inventoryid CDATA #IMPLIED>
<!ELEMENT EquipmentId (#PCDATA)>
<!ELEMENT LocationId (#PCDATA)>
<!ELEMENT StatusId (#PCDATA)>
<!ELEMENT LeaseId (#PCDATA)>
<!ELEMENT LeaseScheduleId (#PCDATA)>
<!ELEMENT OwnerId (#PCDATA)>
<!ELEMENT Cost (#PCDATA)>
<!ELEMENT AcquisitionTypeID (#PCDATA)>
]>
<Inventory>
  <Asset Inventoryid="5">
```

```
      <EquipmentId>1</EquipmentId>
      <LocationId>2</LocationId>
      <StatusId>1</StatusId>
      <LeaseId>1</LeaseId>
      <LeaseScheduleId>1</LeaseScheduleId>
      <OwnerId>1</OwnerId>
      <Cost>1295.00</Cost>
      <AcquisitionTypeID>1</AcquisitionTypeID>
    </Asset>
</Inventory>
```

The DTD document does not have to be stored locally. A reference can include a URL or URI that provides access to the document:

```
<!DOCTYPE Inventory SYSTEM "http://www.trigonblue.com/dtds/Inventory.dtd">
```

A *Uniform Resource Identifier (URI)* identifies a persistent resource on the Internet. It is a number or name that is globally unique. A special type of URI is a *Uniform Resource Locator (URL)* that defines a location of a resource on the Internet. A URI is more general because it should find the closest copy of a resource and because it would eliminate problems in finding a resource that was moved from one server to another.

NOTE

In some cases, it is not important that a URI points to a specific resource, but the string that is supplied must be globally unique, meaning no other XML document (that can be merged with the current XML document) is using the same string for some other resource. However, there are also cases in which a URI points to a specific resource on the Internet and the content of the string is critical for proper processing of an XML document.

XML Comments and CDATA sections

It is possible to write comments within an XML document. The basic syntax of the comment is

```
<!--commented text-->
```

where *commented text* can be any character string that does not contain two consecutive hyphens (--) and that does not end with a hyphen (-).

Comments can stretch over more than one line:

```
<!-- This is a comment. -->
<!--
This is another comment.
-->
```

Comments cannot be part of any other tag:

```
<Order <!-- This is an illegal comment. --> OrderId = "123">
...
</Order>
```

You can use CDATA sections in XML documents to insulate blocks of text from XML parsers. For example, if you are writing an article about XML and you want also to store it in the form of an XML document, you can use CDATA sections to force XML parsers to ignore markups with sample XML code.

The basic syntax of a CDATA section is

```
<![CDATA[string]]>
```

The *string* can be any character string that does not contain the string]]>.

CDATA sections can occur anywhere in an XML document where character data is allowed:

```
<Example>
   <Text>
      <![CDATA[<Inventory Inventoryid="12"/>]]>
   </Text>
</Example>
```

Character and Entity References

Like HTML and SGML, XML also includes a simple way to reference characters that do not belong to the ASCII character set. The syntax of a *character reference* is

```
&#dec-value;
&#xhex-value;
```

The decimal (*dec-value*) or hexadecimal (*hex-value*) code of the character must be preceded by &# or &#x, respectively, and followed by a semicolon (;).

Entity references are used in XML to insert characters that would cause problems for the XML parser if they were inserted directly into the document. This type of reference is basically a mnemonic alternative to a character reference. There are five basic entity references:

Entity	Meaning
&amp;	&
&apos;	'
&lt;	<
&gt;	>
&quot;	"

Entity references are often used to represent characters with special meaning in XML. In the following example, entity references are used to prevent the XML parser from parsing the content of the `Text` element:

```
<Example>
   <Text>
      &lt;Inventory Inventoryid="12"/&gt;
   </Text>
</Example>
```

XML Namespaces

Some entities from different areas of a document can have the same name. For example, you could receive a purchase order document that contains a <name> tag for the customer and a <name> tag for the company. People reading this document would be able to distinguish them by their context. However, an application would need additional information to interpret the data correctly.

A solution to this problem is to create *XML namespaces* to provide the XML document with a vocabulary (that is, a context). After that, customer and company names can be referenced using a context prefix:

```
<contact:name>Tom Jones</contact:name>
<Company:name>Trigon Blue</Company:name>
```

Naturally, before these prefixes can be used, they have to be defined. The root element of the following document contains three attributes, each of which specifies a namespace and a prefix used to reference it:

```
<PurchaseOrders
   xmlns:contact="http://www.trigonblue.com/schemas/Contact.xsd"
   xmlns:Company="http://www.trigonblue.com/schemas/Company.xsd"
```

```
    xmlns:dsig="http://dsig.org">
  <PurchaseOrder>
    <Customer>
      <contact:name>Tom Jones</contact:name>
    </Customer>
<PurchaseDate>2000-09-11</PurchaseDate>
<SalesOrganization>
      <Company:name>Trigon Blue</Company:name>
      <Company:DUNS>817282919</Company:DUNS>
      <Company:ID>1212</Company:ID>
    </SalesOrganization>
    <dsig:digital-signature>78901314</dsig:digital-signature>
  </PurchaseOrder>
</PurchaseOrders>
```

In some cases, it is critical that the namespace points to an actual URL for a resource so that the XML document can be processed correctly, but in some cases (as in the preceding XML document), it is only important that the URI string in the namespace is globally unique (that is, that no other XML document is using the same URI for some other purpose).

Even when you have to use a specific namespace in an XML document, you can still arbitrarily chose a prefix. However, some prefixes are traditionally associated with some namespaces. For example, XML Schema documents traditionally use the xsd prefix and UpdateGrams (see Chapter 15) use the updg prefix.

Structure of XML Documents

XML documents consist of three parts, as you can see in the following illustration:

The first part of the document, called the *prolog* or *document type declaration* (not Document Type Definition), is optional. It can contain processing instructions, a DTD, and comments. The second part of the document is the *body*, which contains the document's elements. The data in these elements is organized into a hierarchy of elements, their attributes, and their content. Sometimes an XML document contains a third part, an *epilog,* which is an optional part that can hold final comments, processing instructions, or just white space.

XML Parsers and DOM

Applications (or user agents) that use XML documents can use proprietary procedures to access the data in them. Usually, such applications use special components called XML parsers. An *XML parser* is a program or component that loads the XML document into an internal hierarchical structure of nodes (see Figure 13-1) and provides access to the information stored in these nodes to other components or programs.

The XML *Document Object Model (DOM)* is a set of standard objects, methods, events, and properties used to access elements of an XML document. DOM is a specification that has received Recommended status from the W3C. Different software vendors have created their own implementations of DOM so that you can use it from (almost) any programming language on (almost) any platform.

Microsoft has initially implemented DOM as a COM component called Microsoft .XMLDOM in msxml.dll. Microsoft used to call it *Microsoft XML Parser*, but at the

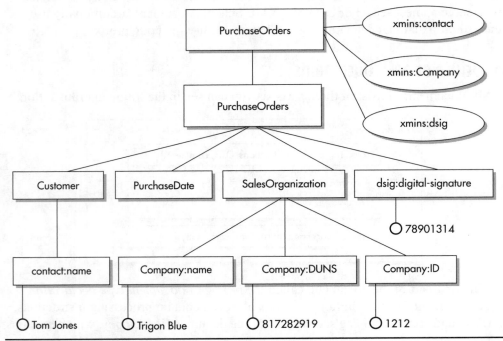

Figure 13-1 *A possible graphical interpretation of a node tree*

time of this writing it is called *Microsoft XML Core Services*. It is delivered, for example, with Internet Explorer, or you can download it separately from Microsoft's web site. Developers can use it from any programming language that can access COM components or ActiveX objects (for example, Visual Basic, Visual Basic .NET, VBScript, Visual C# .NET, Visual J++, JScript, and Visual C++).

Nevertheless, it is unlikely that you will use DOM from Transact-SQL. Microsoft has built special tools for development in Transact-SQL (which are reviewed in the next chapter).

XML Document Quality

There are two levels of document quality in XML: well-formed documents and valid documents.

An XML document is said to be a *well-formed document* when

- ▶ There is one and only one root element.

- ▶ All elements that are not empty are marked with start and end tags.

- ▶ The order of the elements is hierarchical; that is, an element A that starts within an element B also ends within element B.

- ▶ Attributes do not occur twice in one element.

- ▶ All entities used have been declared.

An XML document is said to be a *valid document* when

- ▶ The XML document is well-formed.

- ▶ The XML document complies with a specified DTD document.

The concept of a valid document has been ported to XML from SGML. In SGML, all documents must be valid; in other words, they must comply with the rules defined in the DTD. XML is not so strict. It is possible to use an XML document even without a DTD document. If the user agent knows how to use the XML document without the DTD, then the DTD need not even be sent over the Internet. It just increases traffic and ties up bandwidth.

XML Schema and XML Schemas

The DTD is not the only type of document that can store rules for an XML document. At the current time, several companies (including Microsoft) have submitted a proposal to W3C for an alternative type of metadata document called the *XML Schema*. In fact, there are other proposed standards for the same use, which are all referred to as XML schemas. In May of 2001, W3C published its XML Schema Recommendation, which should gradually replace all other XML schemas. However, some of these schemas (such as the one defined by Microsoft) are already in use.

XML schemas are XML language for defining the business rules with which a class of XML documents (data) must comply in order to be valid.

These are the major differences between a DTD and an XML schema:

▶ XML schemas support data types and range constraints.

▶ XML schemas allow users to define new data types.

▶ The language in which XML schemas are written is XML. Developers do not have to learn an additional language as they do with DTDs.

▶ XML schemas support namespaces (XML entities for defining context).

Why are XML schemas important? A huge portion of application development resources is spent on checking whether data complies with (business) rules about structure and content. If you have a simple language to define the structure and content of data (that is, the business rules by which it is constrained) and you have a *schema validator* (a tool or program that can check compliance), you will be able to reduce development resource requirements significantly, and therefore reduce the cost to implement applications.

XML–Data Reduced (XDR) Schema

When SQL Server 2000 was released, the W3C was still working on its XML Schema specification—it was not even clear which variation would be adopted. Microsoft has implemented a variation of XML schema syntax called *XML–Data Reduced (XDR)* in the MSXML parser (Microsoft XML Core Services) that was delivered initially as a part of Internet Explorer 5, and later in SQL Server 2000.

Microsoft promised complete support for XML Schema when the W3C awarded it Recommended status, but before that could happen, more and more organizations started using XDR. It is also important to note that Microsoft uses XDR in BizTalk, one of the most significant initiatives in the Web Services market. It is an initiative intended to create e-commerce vocabularies for different vertical markets.

At the time of this writing, SQL Server 2000 is using XDR schemas for several features, and support for XML Schema is increasing with each SQL Server 2000 Web Release.

The following is an example of an XDR schema document:

```
<Schema name="Schema"
  xmlns="urn:schemas-microsoft-com:xml-data"
  xmlns:dt="urn:schemas-microsoft-com:datatypes">
<ElementType name="Inventory" content="empty" model="closed">
     <AttributeType name="Inventoryid" dt:type="i4"/>
     <AttributeType name="EquipmentId" dt:type="i4"/>
     <AttributeType name="LocationId" dt:type="i4"/>
     <AttributeType name="StatusId" dt:type="ui1"/>
     <AttributeType name="LeaseId" dt:type="i4"/>
     <AttributeType name="LeaseScheduleId" dt:type="i4"/>
     <AttributeType name="OwnerId" dt:type="i4"/>
     <AttributeType name="Rent" dt:type="fixed.14.4"/>
     <AttributeType name="Lease" dt:type="fixed.14.4"/>
     <AttributeType name="Cost" dt:type="fixed.14.4"/>
     <AttributeType name="AcquisitionTypeID" dt:type="ui1"/>
     <attribute type="Inventoryid"/>
     <attribute type="EquipmentId"/>
     <attribute type="LocationId"/>
     <attribute type="StatusId"/>
     <attribute type="LeaseId"/>
     <attribute type="LeaseScheduleId"/>
     <attribute type="OwnerId"/>
     <attribute type="Rent"/>
     <attribute type="Lease"/>
     <attribute type="Cost"/>
     <attribute type="AcquisitionTypeID"/>
  </ElementType>
</Schema>
```

This XDR schema describes the structure of an XML document that contains
Inventory information. The schema describes just one element—`ElementType`.
The definition also specifies its `name` (`"Inventory"`), `content` (the tag is
`"empty"` because all information will be carried in attributes), and content `model`
(`"closed"`—indicating that it is not possible to add elements that are not specified
in the schema).

The element contains several attributes. Each attribute is first *defined* in an
`AttributeType` element and then *instantiated* in an `attribute` element:

```
     <AttributeType name="Cost" dt:type="fixed.14.4"/>
...
     <attribute type="Cost"/>
```

For each attribute, the schema defines a name and a data type. You can see a list
of acceptable data types in the appendix at the end of this book.

The following listing shows an XML document that complies with the previous XDR schema:

```
<Inventory xmlns="x-schema:Schema.xml"
           Inventoryid="5"
           EquipmentId="1"
           LocationId="2"
           StatusId="1"
           LeaseId="1"
           LeaseScheduleId="1"
           OwnerId="1"
           Cost="1295.0000"
           AcquisitionTypeID="1"/>
```

Schema Constraints

This section reviews XDR schema attributes that can be used to declare elements and attributes. These can be classified as

► Element constraints

► Attribute constraints

► XML data types

► Group constraints

Element Constraints

Elements in an XDR schema can be constrained using attributes of the `<ElementType>` tag:

► `name`

► `content`

► `model`

► `order`

► `group`

► `minOccurs`

► `maxOccurs`

The `name` attribute defines the name of the subelement.

Possible values for the `content` attribute are listed in the Table 13-1.

content	Meaning
"textOnly"	Only text is allowed as content
"eltOnly"	Only other elements are allowed as content
"empty"	No content
"mixed"	Both text and elements are allowed as content

Table 13-1   *content Attribute Values*

An important innovation in XDR schemas (that was not available in DTDs) is the capability to add nondeclared elements and attributes to an XML document. By default, every element of every XML document has its model attribute set to "open". To prevent the addition of nondeclared elements and attributes, the model attribute has to be set to "closed".

It is also possible to define how many times a subelement can appear in its parent element by using the maxOccurs and minOccurs attributes. Positive integer values and "*" (unlimited number) are allowed in the maxOccurs attribute, and "0" and positive integer values are allowed in the minOccurs attribute. The default value for minOccurs is "0". The default value for maxOccurs is "1", except that when the content attribute is "mixed", maxOccurs must be "*".

An order attribute specifies the order and quantity of subelements (see Table 13-2).

The default value for order is "seq" when the content attribute is set to "eltOnly" and is "many" when the content attribute is set to "mixed".

Attribute Constraints

By their nature, attributes are more constrained than elements. For example, attributes do not have subelements (or subattributes), and it is not possible to have more than one instance of an attribute within the element.

The required attribute (constraint) in a schema specifies that the attribute is mandatory in XML documents that follow the schema. The default attribute

order	Meaning
"seq"	Subelements must appear in the order listed in the schema.
"one"	Only one of the subelements listed in the schema can appear in the XML document.
"many"	Any number of subelements can appear in any order.

Table 13-2   *order Attribute Values of <ElementType>*

(constraint) in a schema specifies the default value of the attribute in an XML document (the parser will use that value if an attribute is not present).

The schema can be set so that an attribute value is constrained to a set of predefined values:

```
<AttributeType name="status"
               dt:type="enumeration"
               dt:values="open in-process completed" />
```

XML Data Types

The schema can also enforce the data type of the attribute or element. Table A-2 in the appendix lists data types and their meanings, and Table A-3 in the appendix shows the mapping between XML data types and SQL Server data types.

Group Constraints

The `group` element allows an author to apply certain constraints to a group of subelements. In the following example, only one price (rent, lease, or cost) can be specified for the `Inventory` element:

```
<Schema name="Schema" xmlns="urn:schemas-microsoft-com:xml-data"
 xmlns:dt="urn:schemas-microsoft-com:datatypes">
<ElementType name="Inventory" content="eltOnly"
             model="closed" order="many">
  <element type="Inventoryid"/>
  <element type="EquipmentId"/>
  <element type="LocationId"/>
  <element type="StatusId"/>
  <element type="LeaseId"/>
  <element type="LeaseScheduleId"/>
  <element type="OwnerId"/>
  <group order = "one">
     <element type="Rent"/>
     <element type="Lease"/>
     <element type="Cost"/>
  </group>
  <element type="AcquisitionTypeID"/>
</ElementType>
</Schema>
```

The `group` constraint accepts `order`, `minOccurs`, and `maxOccurs` attributes.

XML Schema (XSD)

In May of 2001, XML Schema was given Recommended status by the W3C. Unfortunately, this stamp of approval happened after Microsoft had already released SQL Server 2000. However, in subsequent web releases of XML for SQL and SQLXML, and in releases of other products such as Visual Studio .NET, Microsoft has added support for XML Schema.

You can find the W3C XML Schema Recommendation specification, tools, and other resources at www.w3.org/XML/schema.html. I will try, however, to introduce the most important concepts.

The purpose of XML Schema is to define a class of XML documents. Each document of a specified class is an *instance* of that XML document class. The Equipment.xsd file contains an XML Schema document that defines instances of XML documents with Equipment information:

```xml
<?xml version="1.0" encoding="utf-8" ?>
<xsd:schema xmlns:xsd="http://www.w3.org/2001/XMLSchema"
            targetNamespace="http://www.trigonblue.com/Equipment.xsd"
            xmlns="http://www.trigonblue.com/Equipment.xsd"
            xmlns:mstns="http://www.trigonblue.com/Equipment.xsd"
            xmlns:msdata="urn:schemas-microsoft-com:xml-msdata"
            elementFormDefault="qualified"
            attributeFormDefault="qualified">
 <xsd:element name="Document">
   <xsd:complexType>
     <xsd:choice maxOccurs="unbounded">
       <xsd:element name="Equipment">
         <xsd:complexType>
           <xsd:sequence>
             <xsd:element name="EquipmentId"
                          msdata:ReadOnly="true"
                          msdata:AutoIncrement="true"
                          type="xsd:int" />
             <xsd:element name="Make" type="xsd:string" />
             <xsd:element name="Model" type="xsd:string" />
             <xsd:element name="EqTypeId" type="xsd:short" />
             <xsd:element name="ModelSDX" type="xsd:string" />
             <xsd:element name="MakeSDX" type="xsd:string" />
           </xsd:sequence>
         </xsd:complexType>
       </xsd:element>
     </xsd:choice>
   </xsd:complexType>
```

```
     <xsd:unique name="DocumentKey1" msdata:PrimaryKey="true">
        <xsd:selector xpath=".//mstns:Equipment" />
        <xsd:field xpath="mstns:EquipmentId" />
     </xsd:unique>
   </xsd:element>
</xsd:schema>
```

You may notice that all elements in all XML Schema documents have an xsd prefix. Therefore, they are often stored in .xsd files and referred to as XSD *schemas*.

An XSD schema defines the structure and the types of data that can be used in a valid XML document instance. The following XML document is a valid instance of the previous schema:

```
<?xml version="1.0" encoding="utf-8" ?>
<Document xmlns="http://www.trigonblue.com/Equipment.xsd"
          xmlns:xsi="http://www.w3.org/2001/XMLSchema-instance"
          xsi:schemaLocation="Equipment.xsd">
   <Equipment>
      <EquipmentId>478</EquipmentId>
      <Make>Compaq</Make>
      <Model>15 Cart. DLT Library Tabletop Conversion Kit </Model>
      <EqTypeId>1</EqTypeId>
   </Equipment>
   <Equipment>
      <EquipmentId>394</EquipmentId>
      <Make>Compaq</Make>
      <Model>2KVA Prestige W/Ext full Bat</Model>
      <EqTypeId>1</EqTypeId>
   </Equipment>
   <Equipment>
      <EquipmentId>347</EquipmentId>
      <Make>Compaq</Make>
      <Model>Deskpro EN CMT PIII 733 10GB 128MB 48xCD nVidia NT</Model>
      <EqTypeId>1</EqTypeId>
   </Equipment>
...
</Document>
```

When an instance of an XML document and an XSD schema are processed together in a schema validator, the program checks whether the instance complies with the business rules defined in the schema and reports the result to the caller.

xsd:schema Element

All XML Schema documents must contain the xsd:schema root element:

```
<xsd:schema xmlns:xsd="http://www.w3.org/2001/XMLSchema"
            targetNamespace="http://www.trigonblue.com/Equipment.xsd"
            xmlns="http://www.trigonblue.com/Equipment.xsd"
            xmlns:mstns="http://www.trigonblue.com/Equipment.xsd"
            xmlns:msdata="urn:schemas-microsoft-com:xml-msdata"
            elementFormDefault="qualified"
            attributeFormDefault="qualified">
...
</xsd:schema>
```

The `xmlns:xsd` attribute notifies a parser (or any other agent) that all elements with an xsd prefix should be processed as XSD schemas. You must be very careful to include a reference to the namespace using the URL indicated in the preceding listing. Otherwise, parsers and validators will not recognize it and will not be able to process the XSD schema properly. All components of an XSD schema (such as elements, types, sequence, schema) are defined in this namespace.

The `targetNamespace` attribute specifies the namespace of a target XML document instance. The XML document instance must have a matching namespace declaration.

The `xmlns` attribute defines the default name of the namespace in the XML document instance. When you set `elementFormDefault` and `attributeFormDefault` to "qualified," all elements and attributes defined in the XSD schema (not just global elements and attributes) will belong to the target namespace in the XML document instance, and they must be namespace qualified (that is, they must contain the appropriate prefix).

Structure Declarations and Definitions

The primary tasks of the developer (or program) writing an XSD schema are to

► *Declare* the components of an XML document instance (elements and attributes)

► *Define* the components that are used inside the XSD schema (such as simple and complex types and attribute and model groups)

Element and Attribute Declaration

xsd:element and xsd:attribute are used to declare elements and attributes in an XML document instance. In their simplest forms, elements and attributes can be defined by name and type (data type). In the following case, the LocationId attribute is defined as int and the Location element is defined as string:

```
<xsd:schema xmlns:xsd="http://www.w3.org/2001/XMLSchema">
  <xsd:element   name="Location"   type="xsd:string"/>
  <xsd:attribute name="LocationId" type="xsd:int"/>
</xsd:schema>
```

Attributes can be declared based only on simple types, while elements can be declared based on both simple and complex types (I will define types in the next two sections).

Attributes and elements can be defined either *globally* (just below xsd:schema), as in the previous example, or inside other elements and complex types.

Simple Type Declarations

Types are XSD schema equivalents of data types. Simple types are XSD components that cannot contain xsd:elements and xsd:attributes. Some simple types like int, datetime, string, ID, IDREF, language, and gYear (Gregorian year) are defined along with the XML Schema in the xsd namespace, while others can be derived from them in the XSD schema (like user-defined data types in TSQL).

A new simple type is derived in an xsd:simpleType element:

```
<xsd:simpleType name="ProdYear">
  <xsd:restriction base="xsd:gYear">
    <xsd:minInclusive value="1990"/>
    <xsd:maxInclusive value="2010"/>
  </xsd:restriction>
</xsd:simpleType>
```

A new simple type is defined by a name (attribute) and a set of *facets* (elements) inside the xsd:restriction element. In this case, the minInclusive and maxInclusive facets define the range of acceptable years.

The enumeration facet can be used to define a lookup list (the list of acceptable values):

```
<xsd:simpleType name="CanProvince">
  <xsd:restriction base="xsd:string">
    <xsd:enumeration value="ON"/>
```

```
    <xsd:enumeration value="BC"/>
    <xsd:enumeration value="MA"/>
    <xsd:enumeration value="NB"/>
    ...
  </xsd:restriction>
</xsd:simpleType>
```

The `pattern` facet uses regular expressions to define the format of values in the element:

```
<xsd:simpleType name="GUID">
  <xsd:restriction base="xsd:string">
    <xsd:pattern value="[0-9a-fA-F]{8}-[0-9a-fA-F]{4}-[0-9a-fA-F]{4}
-[0-9a-fA-F]{4}-[0-9a-fA-F]{12}"/>
  </xsd:restriction>
</xsd:simpleType>
```

In this case, the GUID type is defined as a set of 8, 4, 4, 4, and 12 hexadecimal digits divided by dashes (-).

The W3C Recommendation defines the following facets:

► length
► minLength
► maxLength
► pattern
► enumeration
► whiteSpace
► maxInclusive
► minInclusive
► maxExclusive
► minExclusive
► totalDigits
► fractionDigits

Naturally, you cannot use every facet with every type. Only some combinations make sense.

Complex Types

Complex types are XSD schema elements that can be defined to contain additional attributes and elements. In the following example, the EqType complex type definition consists of two element declarations:

```
<xsd:complexType name="EqType">
  <xsd:sequence>
    <xsd:element name="EqTypeId"   type="xsd:integer"/>
    <xsd:element name="EqTypeName" type="xsd:string"/>
  </xsd:sequence>
 </xsd:complexType>
```

The meaning of the xsd:sequence element is that both elements must be present in the sequence (order) in which they are declared.

Complex types can be built from other simple and complex types:

```
<xsd:complexType name="Equpment">
  <xsd:sequence>
    <xsd:element name="EqId"     type="xsd:integer" minOccurs="1"/>
    <xsd:element name="Make"     type="string" minOccurs="1"/>
    <xsd:element name="Model"    type="string" minOccurs="1"/>
    <xsd:element name="eqType"   type="EqType" minOccurs="1"/>
    <xsd:element ref="comment"   minOccurs="0"/>
  </xsd:sequence>
  <xsd:attribute name="guid"     type="GUID"/>
</xsd:complexType>
```

The first three elements are defined as simple types, but the eqType element is defined as an instance of the EqType complex type defined earlier.

The first four elements are defined *inline*—the definition of each element also contains its type. There is an alternative means of defining elements: you can name an element in one place and reference it in another. For example, the comment element was named somewhere else in the schema and is only referenced here.

NOTE

The advantage of an inline definition is that it is more compact—the definition and the instance of an element are in the same place. The advantage of a named definition is that it can be referenced in many places.

Groups

An xsd:group element allows you to define a set of xsd:elements that will later be referenced together. In the following example, the ExtendedPrice element has been defined as the group of Price, Currency, and Quantity elements:

```
<xsd:element name="OrderItem">
   <xsd:complexType>
...
       <xsd:group ref="ExtendedPrice"/>
...
   </xsd:complexType>
</xsd:element>
...
<xsd:group name="ExtendedPrice">
       <xsd:sequence>
           <xsd:element name="Price"    type="xsd:decimal"/>
           <xsd:element name="Currency" type="xsd:string"/>
           <xsd:element name="Quantity" type="xsd:decimal"/>
       </xsd:sequence>
</xsd:group>
```

An attributeGroup element also allows you to define a group of attributes that can later be referenced together:

```
<xsd:element name="Equipment"  maxOccurs="unbounded">
   <xsd:complexType>
...
       <xsd:attributeGroup ref="EquipmentProp"/>
...
   </xsd:complexType>
</xsd:element>
...
<xsd:attributeGroup name="EquipmentProp">
       <xsd:attribute name="Make"   type="xsd:string"/>
       <xsd:attribute name="Model"  type="xsd:string"/>
       <xsd:attribute name="EqType" use="required">
          <xsd:simpleType>
              <xsd:restriction base="xsd:string">
                  <xsd:enumeration value="Monitor"/>
                  <xsd:enumeration value="Desktop"/>
                  <xsd:enumeration value="Keyboard"/>
              </xsd:restriction>
          </xsd:simpleType>
       </xsd:attribute>
</xsd:attributeGroup>
```

Annotating Schemas

To add a comment to the schema, you can use the xsd:annotation element. It can contain two subelements. The xsd:documentation element is used to mark comments written for people, while the xsd:appinfo element is used to mark information for programs (such as style sheets and SQLXML). The content of the appinfo element should be well formed XML (so that target applications can parse them).

NOTE

It's not that programs need a valid comment from the developer. The appinfo *annotations simply do not have any meaning for the schema validator, while they might be very important instructions for target programs.*

```
<xsd:annotation>
    <xsd:documentation xml:lang="en-US">
  This element should be linked with Location.LocId.
    </xsd:documentation>
    <xsd:appinfo>
        <TbSql proc="Location.LocId">Link</TbSql>
    </xsd:appinfo>
<xsd:/annotation>
```

You should also use the xml:lang attribute inside the xsd:documentation element to indicate the language in which your comment is written.

Annotations can be placed only:

▶ Before and after any global component (such as schema, simpleType, and attribute)

▶ At the beginning of nonglobal components

XSD Schema Tools

The XML development community, including Microsoft, has developed many useful tools for development and management of XSD schemas. You can find a comprehensive list with links at www.w3.org/XML/Schema#Tools. I will now demonstrate use of three tools developed by Microsoft.

XSD Designer   Visual Studio .NET supports the use of XSD schemas primarily to process ADO.NET data sets. It contains the XSD Designer—a graphical tool that allows you to drag and drop relation tables to link them and then build XSD schema out of them. To use it:

1. Open a new Visual Studio .NET project.
2. Select File | Add Item from the menu.
3. Select XSD Schema. The program will open the XSD Schema Designer with the Schema pane active.
4. Open Server Explorer.
5. Expand the server node until you reach the tables in the Asset database.
6. Drag the Equipment table onto the XSD Schema Designer (see Figure 13-2).
7. You can switch to the XML pane to see the code of the schema.

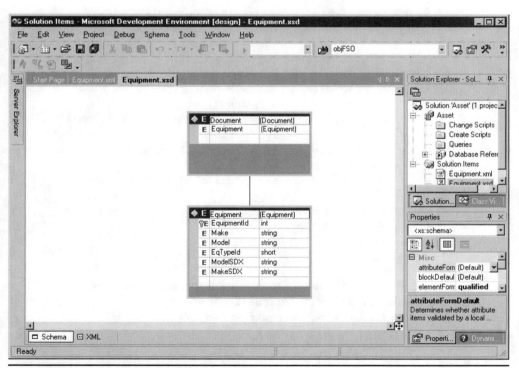

Figure 13-2   *The XSD Schema Designer*

The XSD Schema Designer generates schemas that have some additional elements and attributes that are needed to validate ADO.NET datasets:

```xml
<?xml version="1.0" encoding="utf-8" ?>
<xs:schema targetNamespace="http://tempuri.org/XMLSchema.xsd"
           elementFormDefault="qualified"
           xmlns="http://tempuri.org/XMLSchema.xsd"
           xmlns:mstns="http://tempuri.org/XMLSchema.xsd"
           xmlns:xs="http://www.w3.org/2001/XMLSchema"
           xmlns:msdata="urn:schemas-microsoft-com:xml-msdata">
  <xs:element name="Document">
    <xs:complexType>
      <xs:choice maxOccurs="unbounded">
        <xs:element name="Equipment">
          <xs:complexType>
            <xs:sequence>
              <xs:element name="EquipmentId"
                          msdata:ReadOnly="true"
                          msdata:AutoIncrement="true"
                          type="xs:int" />
              <xs:element name="Make" type="xs:string"
                          minOccurs="0" />
              <xs:element name="Model" type="xs:string"
                          minOccurs="0" />
              <xs:element name="EqTypeId" type="xs:short"
                          minOccurs="0" />
              <xs:element name="ModelSDX" type="xs:string"
                          minOccurs="0" />
              <xs:element name="MakeSDX" type="xs:string"
                          minOccurs="0" />
            </xs:sequence>
          </xs:complexType>
        </xs:element>
      </xs:choice>
    </xs:complexType>
    <xs:unique name="DocumentKey1" msdata:PrimaryKey="true">
      <xs:selector xpath=".//mstns:Equipment" />
      <xs:field xpath="mstns:EquipmentId" />
    </xs:unique>
  </xs:element>
</xs:schema>
```

The XSD is generated with temporary URI (`tempuri.org`) namespace references. You can replace them with your own namespaces:

```
<?xml version="1.0" encoding="utf-8" ?>
<xs:schema targetNamespace="http://www.trigonblue.com/Equipment.xsd"
        elementFormDefault="qualified"
        xmlns="http://www.trigonblue.com/XMLSchema.xsd"
        xmlns:mstns="http://www.trigonblue.com/Equipment.xsd"
        xmlns:xs="http://www.w3.org/2001/XMLSchema"
        xmlns:msdata="urn:schemas-microsoft-com:xml-msdata">
```

XSD by Example: Microsoft XSD Inference   *Microsoft XSD Inference* is a web-based
utility that you can use to create an XSD schema from an XML instance document
(see Figure 13-3). You can think of it as "XSD by example." When you select a well-
formed XML file, the utility generates an XSD schema that can be used to validate
it. You can continue refining the XSD schema by selecting more XML files. At the
end, you might also need to edit it manually to implement additional components
such as *facets* (restrictions) and annotations.

XSD Schema Validator   Another tool that you might find useful when working with
XSD schemas is the *XSD Schema Validator*, a web application (see Figure 13-4) that

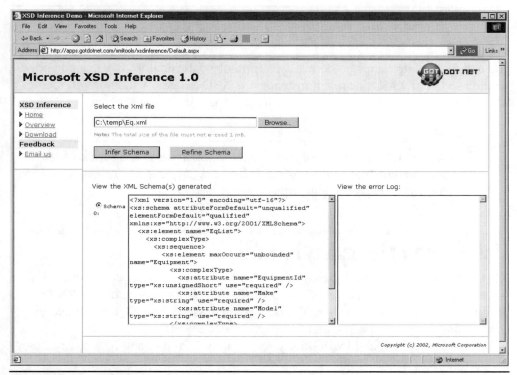

Figure 13-3   *XSD by example*

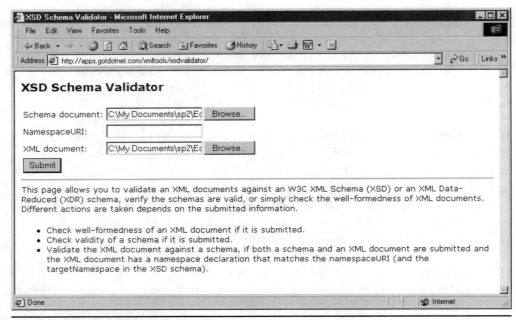

Figure 13-4 *The XSD Schema Validator*

you can find at http://apps.gotdotnet.com/xmltools/xsdvalidator/. If you load your schema and your XML document instance, the XSD Schema Validator will report whether or not the instance complies with rules specified in the schema.

NOTE

You cannot validate an instance if you simply put the instance and schema in a folder on an IIS server and open it using Internet Explorer. Unfortunately, the parser in IE is not set as a validating parser and will simply display the content of the document instance.

Linking and Querying in XML

XML today represents more than a simple language for encoding documents. W3C is working on a whole other set of specifications for using information in XML documents. Specifications such as XLink, XPointer, XPath, and XQL allow querying, linking, and access to specific parts of an XML document.

This is a vast topic, and I will briefly review only XPointer and XPath, since they are used in SQL Server 2000.

XPointer

The XPointer reference works in a fashion very similar to the HTML hyperlink. You can point to a segment of an XML document by appending an *XML fragment identifier* to the URI of the XML document. A fragment identifier is often enclosed in `xpointer()`. For example, the following pointer directs the parser to an element with the `ID` attribute set to `"Toshiba"` in the document at a specified location:

```
http://www.trigonblue.com/xml/Equipment.xml#xpointer(Toshiba)
```

The character # is a *fragment specifier*. It serves as a delimiter between the URI and the fragment identifier, and it specifies the way that the XML parser will render the target. In the preceding case, the parser renders the whole document to access only a specified fragment. To force the parser to parse only the specified fragment, you should use | as a fragment specifier:

```
http://www.trigonblue.com/xml/Equipment.xml|xpointer(Toshiba)
```

Use of the | fragment specifier is recommended because it leads to reduced memory usage.

`xpointer()` is not always required. If a document has a schema that specifies the `ID` attribute of an element, you can omit the `xpointer()` and point to a fragment of the document using only the `ID` attribute value:

```
http://www.trigonblue.com/xml/Equipment.xml#Toshiba
```

Child sequence fragment identifiers use numbers to specify a fragment:

```
http://www.trigonblue.com/xml/Equipment.xml#/2/1/3
```

The preceding example should be interpreted as follows: /—start from the top element of the document; 2—then go to the second child element of the top element; 1—then go to the first subelement of that element; 3—then go to the third subelement of that element.

Child sequence fragment identifiers do not have to start from the top element:

```
http://www.trigonblue.com/xml/Equipment.xml#Toshiba/1/3
```

In this example, fragment identification starts from the element with its `ID` set to `"Toshiba"`. The parser then finds its first subelement and points to its third subelement.

XPath

The full XPointer syntax is built on the W3C XPath recommendation. XPath was originally built to be used by XPointer and XSLT (a language for transforming XML documents into other XML documents), but it has found application in other standards and technologies. You will see in the next chapter how it is used by OpenXML() in SQL Server 2000, but first you need to examine its syntax.

Location steps are constructs used to select nodes in an XML document. They have the following syntax:

```
axis::node_test[predicate]
```

The location step points to the location of other nodes from the position of the *current node*. If a current node is not specified in any way, the location step is based on the root element.

Axes break up the XML document in relation to the current node. You can think of them as a first filter that you apply to an XML document to point to target nodes. Possible axes are listed in Table 13-3.

Axes	Description
parent	The parent of the current node.
ancestor	All ancestors (parent, grandparent, and so on) to the root of the current node.
child	All children of the current node (first generation).
descendant	All descendants (children, grandchildren, and so forth) of the current node.
self	The current node only.
descendant-or-self	All descendant nodes and the current node.
ancestor-or-self	All ancestor nodes and the current node.
attribute	All attributes of the current node.
namespace	All namespace nodes of the current node.
following	All nodes after the current node in the XML document. The set does not include attribute nodes, namespace nodes, or ancestors of the context node.
preceding	All nodes before the current node in the XML document. The set does not include attribute nodes, namespace nodes, or ancestors of the current node.
following-sibling	All siblings (children of the same parent) after the current node in the XML document.
preceding-sibling	All siblings (children of the same parent) before the current node in the XML document.

Table 13-3   *Axes in XPath*

The *node test* is a second filter that you can apply on nodes specified by axes. Table 13-4 lists all node tests that can be applied.

A *predicate* is a filter in the form of a Boolean expression that evaluates each node in the set obtained after applying axes and node test filters. Developers have a rich set of functions (string, node set, Boolean, and number), comparative operators (=, !=, <=, >= <, >), Boolean operators (And, Or), and operators (+, –, *, div, mod). The list is very long (especially the list of functions), and I will not go into detail here. I will just mention the most common function, `position()`. It returns the position of the node.

Let's now review how all segments of the location step function together:

```
child::Equipment[position()<=10]
```

This location set first points to child nodes of the current node (root if none is selected). Of all child nodes, only elements named `Equipment` are left in the set. Finally, each of those nodes is evaluated by position and only the first 10 are specified.

Very often, you will try to navigate from node to node through the XML document. You can attach location sets using the forward slash (/). The same character is often used at the beginning of the expression to establish the current node.

In the following example, the parser is pointed to the Inventory.xml file, then to its root element, and then to the first child called `Equipment`, and finally to the first `Model` node among its children:

```
Inventory.xml#/child::Equipment[position() = 1]/child::
Model[position() = 1]
```

It all works in a very similar fashion to the notation of files and folders, and naturally you can write them all together:

```
http://www.trigonblue.com/xml/Inventory.xml#/child::
Equipment[position() = 1]/child::Model[position() = 1]
```

Node Test	Description
element name	Selects just node(s) with specified name in the set specified by axes.
* or `node()`	All nodes in the set specified by axes.
`comment()`	All comment elements in the set specified by axes.
`text()`	All text elements in the set specified by axes.
`processing-instruction()`	All processing instruction elements in the set specified by axes (if the name is specified in brackets, the parser will match only processing instructions with the specified name).

Table 13-4 *Node Tests in XPath*

XPath constructs are very flexible, but also very complex and laborious to write. To reduce the effort, a number of abbreviations are defined. `position() = X` can be replaced by *X* (it is enough to type just the number). Thus, an earlier example can be written as

```
Inventory.xml#/child::Equipment[1]/child::Model[1]
```

If an axis is not defined, the parser assumes that the `child` axis was specified. Thus, the preceding example could be written as

```
Inventory.xml#/Equipment[1]/Model[1]
```

The `attribute::` axis can be abbreviated as @. Therefore, the following two expressions are equivalent:

```
Inventory.xml#/child::Equipment[1]/attribute::EquipmentId
Inventory.xml#/child::Equipment[1]/@EquipmentId
```

The current node can be specified using either `self::node()` or a dot (.). The following two expressions are equivalent:

```
Order.xml#/self::node()/OrderDate
Order.xml#/./OrderDate
```

A parent node can be specified either by `parent::node()` or two dots (..). The following two expressions are equivalent:

```
parent::node()/Order
../Order
```

`/descendant-or-self::node()` selects the current node and all descendant nodes. It can be abbreviated with //. The following two examples select all `EquipmentId` attributes in the document:

```
Inventory.xml#/descendant-or-self::node()/@EquipmentId
Inventory.xml#//@EquipmentId
```

Transforming XML

In many cases in business, information that is already in the form of an XML document needs to be converted to another XML structure. For example, a client of mine is participating in RossetaNet, an e-commerce consortium of IT supply chain organizations that defines standard messages to be sent between partners. Although messages are standardized, each pair of partners can agree to modify their messages slightly to better serve their needs. Such changes are mostly structural—new nodes (fields) can be defined, standard ones can be dropped, a node can change its type from element to attribute, and so on. Instead of generating completely different messages each time (and developing two separate procedures for performing similar tasks), it is preferable to create a simple procedure that will transform a standard XML message into another form.

Another typical situation occurs when an application uses a browser to display an XML document. Although modern browsers such as the latest versions of Internet Explorer are able to display the content of an XML document in the form of a hierarchical tree, this format is not user-friendly. More often, the XML document is transformed into an HTML document and information is organized visually into tables and frames. Such HTML applications usually allow the end user to modify the displayed information interactively (for example, to sort the content of the tables, to display different information in linked tables, or to present data in different formats). Each of these tasks could be performed by modifying the original XML document.

A typical problem with HTML browsers from different vendors is that they are not compatible. Naturally (well, actually, it seems quite unnatural), even different versions of the same browser behave differently. Each of them uses a different variation of the HTML standard. However, these differences are not major, and instead of generating a separate XML document for each of them, you can create a procedure to transform the XML document so that it fits the requirements of the browser currently in use.

You can think of XML as just one type of rendering language. Some systems use other types of rendering languages and appropriate browsers. For example, more and more PDAs and wireless devices such as cellular phones are offering Internet access. They often use a special protocol (Wireless Application Protocol, or WAP) that has its own markup language (Wireless Markup Language—WML) based on XML. A web server offering information should be able to transform the XML document to fulfill the needs of different viewers.

XSL

The *eXtensible Stylesheet Language (XSL)* addresses the need to transform XML documents from one XML form to another and to transform XML documents to other formats such as HTML and WML. It is based on *Cascading Style Sheets (CSS)*, a language for styling HTML documents. Over time, XSL has been transformed into three other languages:

  ▶   *XSLT* for transforming XML documents

▶ *XSLF* for rendering

▶ *XPath* for accessing a specific part of an XML document

XSLT

XSLT is a (new) language for transforming XML documents. W3C gave it Recommended status in November 1999. XSLT style sheet files are also well-formed XML documents. These files are processed by *XSLT processors*. Such a processor can be a separate tool or part of an XML parser (as in the case of MSXML).

At this point, I will not go into detail about XSL and XSLT syntax. Such topics are really beyond the scope of this book. Refer to www.w3.org/Style/XSL/ and www.w3.org/TR/xslt for more information on this topic. However, I will cover the use of XSLT in SQL Server 2000 later in "Using XSL," in Chapter 14.

Why XML?

I have described XML, which is all well and fine, but of course the questions arise: why do you need XML, and what can you do with it? Two major areas of application are

▶ Exchange of information between organizations

▶ Information publishing

Exchange of Information Between Organizations

XML provides platform-independent data transport for a variety of types of information, from simple messages (commands, information requests) to the most complex business documents. Its extensible nature—the ease with which you can add new nodes or branches, create multiple instances of the same element, and use open schemas to add elements as necessary (provided they comply with schema rules)—makes XML an ideal development language for the rapidly evolving "dotcom" economy. You can use XML to implement solutions that can grow and evolve with an organization and be relatively certain that your solution will not end up on next year's scrap heap and that the organization will not have to replace it at an enormous cost as the needs of the organization grow and change.

It is no wonder that Microsoft has incorporated support for XML in its new releases of applications such as SQL Server, Exchange, Visual Studio, and Internet Explorer. This support allows Microsoft to remain the major player in operating systems and network solutions even as businesses organize themselves into trading communities and industry associations defined by their ability to exchange information seamlessly and securely via the Internet.

EDI: a Cautionary Tale

XML is finding extensive application within the B2B (business-to-business) and B2C (business-to-consumer) arenas, to name but two of this young century's most ubiquitous buzzwords. XML's success in this emerging marketplace is largely due to its platform independence, which translates directly to the bottom line in terms of low implementation costs. Trading partners require only Internet access and a web browser to conduct secure business transactions over the Internet.

One of the buzzwords of the early 1990s was *EDI (Electronic Data Interchange)*. EDI is still around, but it has never fulfilled its promise to make the exchange of paper documents between businesses obsolete. It was the cost of implementation that prevented EDI from fulfilling this promise. The problem that EDI encountered is a variation on the "Tower of Babel" theme: the proliferation of languages and protocols ensured that each implementation would be unique, and therefore costly.

Classic EDI follows a hub-and-spoke model: a large company (the "hub") that must manage business relationships with a large number of suppliers (the "spokes") decrees that the spoke organizations must implement EDI or lose their trading-partner status. The spoke organizations have to bear the considerable cost of implementation or lose a considerable portion of their business income.

A company that is forced to implement EDI by virtue of a trading relationship with a hub company receives an "implementation guide" that describes the EDI standard with which it must comply. One EDI veteran described the difference between classic EDI and XML-based e-commerce succinctly: with EDI, your postal carrier delivers an implementation guide printed on paper; with XML-based e-commerce, the implementation guide is attached to the electronic business document/transaction in the form of a DTD or XML schema.

This comparison is a gross oversimplification of the relationship between these two technologies, but it does highlight one reason that XML-based e-commerce has succeeded with small- to medium-sized businesses where EDI could not, and that is its relatively low cost of implementation.

The other reason for this success is that XML-based e-commerce leverages Internet-based communications. The dial-up *Value Added Networks (VANs)* of the EDI world are more or less glorified (and generally expensive) electronic mailboxes to which you post business documents and from which you download business documents from your trading partners. The XML revolution has spawned Internet-based, third-party *Application Service Providers (ASPs)* and "Infomediaries" to take the place of the VANs and use XML to conduct business transactions between diverse trading partners.

Of course, these ASPs and Infomediaries are in the business of developing data-based applications for the Web, so you can begin to see why it is so important that SQL Server be XML-ready. The new XML features in SQL Server 2000, along with SQL Server's ease of use, make it a leader in this emerging market.

Information Publishing

Just as trading partners can use XML to exchange business documents, organizations and individuals can use XML to develop data-based applications that publish information. The only real difference between business document exchange and information publishing is that the information itself becomes the commodity.

Using XML to publish information located in a SQL Server database combines the easy access of the Internet with the power and data integrity of a mature RDBMS. Browser-based applications allow users to retrieve data dynamically from diverse databases.

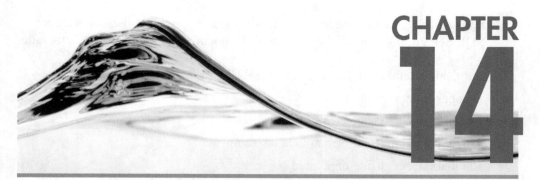

CHAPTER
14

Publishing Information Using SQLXML

IN THIS CHAPTER:

I n this chapter, I will explain the methods you can use to publish and access SQL Server 2000 data in the form of XML documents. These methods include:

► Publishing database information using HTTP

► Database access using URL

► Database access using POST

► Accessing database information using templates

► Database access using annotated schemas

► Client-side XML processing

► Programmatic database access from .NET applications

I will start by exploring the For XML clause of the Select statement.

For XML Clause

SQL Server 2000 can return data as XML. The foundation for all new features related to publishing database information in XML format is the extended syntax of the Select statement.

The Select statement has a new For XML clause:

```
[ For { XML { Auto | Raw | Explicit }
        [ , XMLData ]
        [ , Elements ]
        [ , Binary base64 ]
    }
]
```

This clause allows a caller to request the results of a query as an XML document instead of a recordset. The structure of the resulting XML document depends on the XML mode that the caller has selected:

► Auto
► Raw
► Explicit

Auto Mode

The following example uses Auto mode against the Inventory table in the Asset database:

```
Select *
From Inventory
For XML Auto
```

TIP

*Before you issue such a query against the database yourself, go to Tools | Options in Query Analyzer and open the Results tab. Change the Maximum Characters per Column value to **8192** (the maximum allowed value). The default value is too short. If you do not change it, you will wonder why the resulting XML document is shortened.*

Figure 14-1 shows how Query Analyzer displays the results. To analyze the result, I recommend that you either copy and paste it into some other editor or insert line breaks and tabs to emphasize the structure of the document:

```
<Inventory Inventoryid="5"
           EquipmentId="1"
           LocationId="2"
           StatusId="1"
           LeaseId="1"
           LeaseScheduleId="1"
           OwnerId="1"
           Cost="1295.0000"
           AcquisitionTypeID="1"/>
<Inventory Inventoryid="6"
           EquipmentId="6"
           LocationId="2"
           StatusId="2"
           LeaseId="1"
           . . .
```

Each record in the Inventory table is represented as an element. The `Inventory` element is named after the table, and all columns are represented as attributes of the element. Since there is no other content aside from these attributes, each element is coded as an empty tag: `<Inventory/>`.

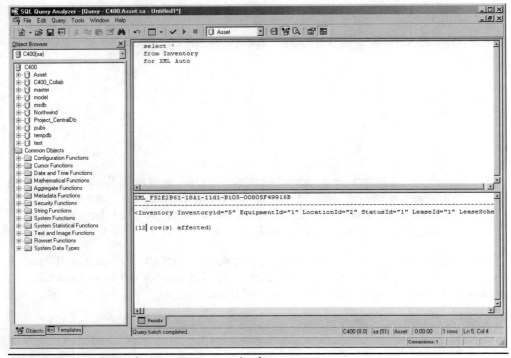

Figure 14-1 An XML document as a result of a query

NOTE

There is one problem with this XML document. Strictly speaking, it is not a valid XML document since there is no root element. The first element, Inventory, does not qualify as the root element because it is not unique within the document (the document has one instance for each record). This type of XML file is often called an XML fragment. Later in the chapter I will show you how to handle this problem.

The following example shows what happens when another table is added to the query:

```
select *
from Inventory inner join Equipment
on Inventory.EquipmentId = Equipment.Equipmentid
for XML Auto
```

I will execute this query and then add some line breaks so that you can more easily see the structure of the resulting XML:

```
XML_F52E2B61-18A1-11d1-B105-00805F49916B
-------------------------------------------------------------
<Inventory Inventoryid="5" EquipmentId="1" LocationId="2"
          StatusId="1" LeaseId="1" LeaseScheduleId="1"
          OwnerId="1" Cost="1295.0000" AcquisitionTypeID="1">
   <Equipment EquipmentId="1" Make="Toshiba"
          Model="Portege 7020CT" EqTypeId="1" ModelSDX="P632"/>
</Inventory>
<Inventory Inventoryid="6" EquipmentId="6" LocationId="2"
          StatusId="2" LeaseId="1" LeaseScheduleId="1"
          OwnerId="1" Rent="200.0000" Lease="0.0000"
          AcquisitionTypeID="3">
   <Equipment EquipmentId="6" Make="NEC" Model="V90"
          EqTypeId="1" ModelSDX="V000"/>
</Inventory>
<Inventory Inventoryid="8" EquipmentId="5" LocationId="2"
          StatusId="1" OwnerId="1" Lease="87.7500"
          AcquisitionTypeID="2">
   <Equipment EquipmentId="5" Make="HP" Model="LaserJet 4"
          EqTypeId="7" ModelSDX="L262"/>
</Inventory>
<Inventory Inventoryid="12" EquipmentId="1" LocationId="2"
          StatusId="1" LeaseId="1" LeaseScheduleId="1"
          OwnerId="1" Lease="100.0000" AcquisitionTypeID="2">
   <Equipment EquipmentId="1" Make="Toshiba"
          Model="Portege 7020CT" EqTypeId="1" ModelSDX="P632"/>
</Inventory>
...
```

This time, the result is a simple nested XML tree. The structure of the XML document is based on the content of the From clause. The leftmost table is mapped to the top element; the second leftmost table is mapped as a subelement of the top element; the third leftmost table (if it exists) is mapped as a subelement of the second-level element, and so on. Again, table columns are mapped to the attributes of the element.

If I now create a query that joins Inventory with all other lookup tables, I get a nested tree with a number of levels (see Figure 14-2).

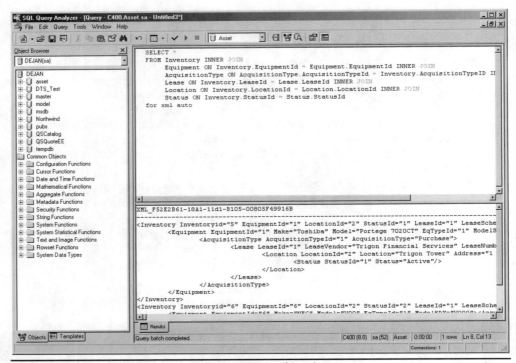

Figure 14-2 *An XML document with a number of levels*

In the preceding case, each `Inventory` element contains one `Equipment` element, which could be very useful for client applications. Each record from the main table is followed by the associated lookup (foreign key) records.

The following example reverses the order of tables in the From clause and uses Left Join:

```
Select *
From Equipment Left Outer Join Inventory
On Inventory.EquipmentId = Equipment.Equipmentid
For XML Auto
```

Now each record in the Equipment table is followed by a variable number of records from the Inventory table. There are records in the Equipment table that are not associated with any Inventory record and Equipment records that are associated with more than one Inventory record:

```
XML_F52E2B61-18A1-11d1-B105-00805F49916B
-----------------------------------------------------------------
<Equipment EquipmentId="1" Make="Toshiba" Model="Portege 7020CT"
           EqTypeId="1" ModelSDX="P632">
   <Inventory Inventoryid="5" EquipmentId="1" LocationId="2"
              StatusId="1" LeaseId="1" LeaseScheduleId="1"
              OwnerId="1" Cost="1295.0000" AcquisitionTypeID="1"/>
   <Inventory Inventoryid="12" EquipmentId="1" LocationId="2"
              StatusId="1" LeaseId="1" LeaseScheduleId="1"
              OwnerId="1" Lease="100.0000"
              AcquisitionTypeID="2"/>
</Equipment>
<Equipment EquipmentId="2" Make="Sony" Model="Trinitron 17XE"
           EqTypeId="3" ModelSDX="T653">
   <Inventory/>
</Equipment>
<Equipment EquipmentId="6" Make="NEC" Model="V90" EqTypeId="1"
 ModelSDX="V000">
   <Inventory Inventoryid="6" EquipmentId="6" LocationId="2"
              StatusId="2" LeaseId="1" LeaseScheduleId="1"
              OwnerId="1" Rent="200.0000" Lease="0.0000"
              AcquisitionTypeID="3"/>
</Equipment>
<Equipment EquipmentId="4" Make="HP" Model="LaserJet 4"
           EqTypeId="6" ModelSDX="L262">
   <Inventory/>
</Equipment>
<Equipment EquipmentId="5" Make="HP" Model="LaserJet 4"
           EqTypeId="7" ModelSDX="L262">
   <Inventory Inventoryid="8" EquipmentId="5" LocationId="2"
              StatusId="1" OwnerId="1" Lease="87.7500"
              AcquisitionTypeID="2"/>
</Equipment>
(6 row(s) affected)
```

TIP

You do not have to use column names as tag names. You can assign aliases to columns and these aliases will be mapped to the attributes.

Aggregate Functions

Aggregate functions and the Group By clause are not supported in Auto mode. However, it is possible to use a simple workaround based on a derived table to pool such values in an XML document:

```
Select Inv.InventoryId, Inv.SumCost
From (Select InventoryId, Sum(Cost) SumCost
      From Inventory
      Group By InventoryId) Inv
For XML Auto
```

In this example, the inner Select statement returns the required data, and the outer Select statement functions as a wrapper with a For XML Auto clause. It is also possible to join the results from the inner Select statement with other tables to provide additional information.

Computed Columns

If the column list of the Select statement includes a column that cannot be directly associated with a table (such as a computed column), SQL Server will map it to the attribute (or subelement) at the nesting level that is current when the column is encountered in the list. For example, if a computed column is included as the first in the column list, it is added as an attribute (or a subelement) of the top element; if it is included after the columns of another table are referenced, the computed column is mapped at the second level.

The Elements Option

Table columns do not have to be encoded as attributes. If you add the Elements option to the For XML clause, all columns will be coded as subelements. You can see the result set of the following query in Figure 14-3. Nested tables are also encoded as subelements.

```
Select *
From Inventory Inner Join Equipment
On Inventory.EquipmentId = Equipment.Equipmentid
For XML Auto, Elements
```

NOTE
The Elements option is supported only in Auto mode.

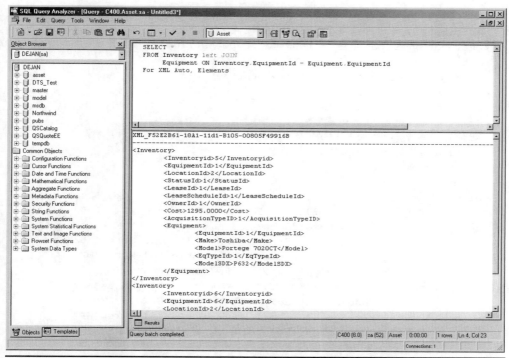

Figure 14-3   Use of the Elements option in the For XML clause

The XMLData Option

If the XMLData option is specified in the For XML clause, the XML document will also contain an XML–Data Reduced (XDR) schema:

```
select *
from Equipment
for XML Auto, XMLData
```

The schema is added at the beginning of the document as an inline schema:

```
<Schema name="Schema"
    xmlns="urn:schemas-microsoft-com:xml-data"
    xmlns:dt="urn:schemas-microsoft-com:datatypes">
<ElementType name="Equipment" content="empty" model="closed">
  <AttributeType name="EquipmentId" dt:type="i4"/>
  <AttributeType name="Make" dt:type="string"/>
```

```
    <AttributeType name="Model" dt:type="string"/>
    <AttributeType name="EqTypeId" dt:type="i2"/>
    <AttributeType name="ModelSDX" dt:type="string"/>
    <AttributeType name="MakeSDX" dt:type="string"/>
    <attribute type="EquipmentId"/>
    <attribute type="Make"/>
    <attribute type="Model"/>
    <attribute type="EqTypeId"/>
    <attribute type="ModelSDX"/>
    <attribute type="MakeSDX"/>
  </ElementType>
</Schema>
<Equipment xmlns="x-schema:#Schema" EquipmentId="1" Make="Toshiba"
          Model="Portege 7020CT" EqTypeId="1" ModelSDX="P632"/>
  <Equipment xmlns="x-schema:#Schema" EquipmentId="2" Make="Sony"
          Model="Trinitron 17XE" EqTypeId="3" ModelSDX="T653"/>
<Equipment xmlns="x-schema:#Schema" EquipmentId="6" Make="NEC"
          Model="V90" EqTypeId="1" ModelSDX="V000"/>
<Equipment xmlns="x-schema:#Schema" EquipmentId="4" Make="HP"
          Model="LaserJet 4" EqTypeId="6" ModelSDX="L262"/>
<Equipment xmlns="x-schema:#Schema" EquipmentId="5" Make="HP"
          Model="LaserJet 4" EqTypeId="7" ModelSDX="L262"/>
```

Data elements also include an attribute with a reference to the schema:

```
xmlns="x-schema:#Schema"
```

TIP

You have to be very careful when generating a schema this way. The schema could be incorrect if, for example, your query specifies a recordset that contains fields (and/or aliases) with the same name (for example, when fields have the same name in both main and lookup tables). SQL Server will not resolve name or data type collisions.

The BINARY Base64 Option

The BINARY Base64 option is designed for encoding binary data such as images, video, and sounds via XML. It is not required in Auto mode, but it must be specified in Explicit and Raw modes of the For XML clause. Figure 14-4 shows an encoded photograph of an employee from the Northwind database.

```
SELECT Photo
FROM Northwind..Employees
WHERE EmployeeID=2
FOR XML RAW, XMLData, BINARY Base64
```

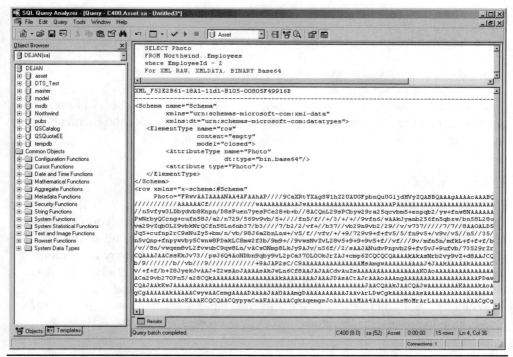

Figure 14-4   *Encoding of binary data in XML*

Raw Mode

Raw mode of the For XML clause returns every row of the result set as an individual XML element named `row`:

```
Select Equipment.Make, Equipment.Model,
       Inventory.InventoryID, Inventory.Cost
From Inventory Inner Join Equipment
On Inventory.EquipmentId = Equipment.Equipmentid
For XML Raw
```

Note that elements in the result set are called `row` and that the mode is called Raw:

```
<row Make="Toshiba" Model="Portege 7020CT"
     InventoryID="5" Cost="1295.0000"/>
<row Make="NEC" Model="V90" InventoryID="6"/>
<row Make="HP" Model="LaserJet 4" InventoryID="8"/>
<row Make="Toshiba" Model="Portege 7020CT" InventoryID="12"/>
```

```
<row Make="Toshiba" Model="Portege 7020CT"
    InventoryID="5"Cost="1295.0000"/>
<row Make="NEC" Model="V90" InventoryID="6"/>
<row Make="HP" Model="LaserJet 4" InventoryID="8"/>
<row Make="Toshiba" Model="Portege 7020CT" InventoryID="12"/>
```

Columns that have a null value are skipped in the list of attributes. Columns are always encoded as attributes because it is not possible to specify the Elements option in this mode. Again, it is important to avoid name collisions.

Explicit Mode

Explicit mode is much more flexible than Auto mode or Raw mode. It allows you to specify all details of an XML document including the shape and data. You are therefore responsible for ensuring that the XML document is well formed and valid.

The process of creating such a document involves writing a query that defines a *universal table*. This table contains all the information (both metadata and data) needed to create the XML document. Table 14-1 shows a universal table.

When the query that generates the universal table is executed with the For XML Explicit option, SQL Server returns an XML document such as the following:

```
<Equipment EquipmentID="1" Make="Toshiba" Model="Portege 7020CT">
   <Inventory InventoryID="5" StatusID="1"/>
   <Inventory InventoryID="12" StatusID="1"/>
</Equipment>
<Equipment EquipmentID="2" Make="Sony" Model="Trinitron 17XE"/>
<Equipment EquipmentID="4" Make="HP" Model="LaserJet 4"/>
<Equipment EquipmentID="5" Make="HP" Model="LaserJet 4">
    <Inventory InventoryID="8" StatusID="1"/>
</Equipment>
<Equipment EquipmentID="6" Make="NEC" Model="V90">
   <Inventory InventoryID="6" StatusID="2"/>
</Equipment>
...
```

The first two columns of the table (Tag and Parent) control the shape (that is, the nesting) of the XML document. The Tag column contains an identifier for the current element. The Parent column contains a tag value for the Parent element. SQL Server uses these columns to create the hierarchy. The top-level element will have a 0 (zero) or null value for the Parent column.

Tag	Parent	Equipment!1! EquipmentID	Equipment!1! Make	Equipment!1! Model	Inventory!2! InventoryID	Inventory!2! StatusID
1	Null	1	Toshiba	Portege 7020CT	Null	Null
2	1	1	Toshiba	Portege 7020CT	5	1
2	1	1	Toshiba	Portege 7020CT	12	1
1	Null	2	Sony	Trinitron 17XE	Null	Null
1	Null	4	HP	LaserJet 4	Null	Null
1	Null	5	HP	LaserJet 4	Null	Null
2	1	5	HP	LaserJet 4	8	1
1	Null	6	NEC	V90	Null	Null
2	1	6	NEC	V90	6	2

Table 14-1   *A Universal Table*

The other columns in the universal table represent the elements, attribute names, and data. Column names have to be specified using the following template:

```
ElementName!TagNumber!AttributeName!Directive
```

Table 14-2 explains the meaning of the components of the template.

The example on the following page illustrates how the Tag and Parent columns are used to form the hierarchy of the XML document and how the AttributeName

Component	Meaning
ElementName	Generic identifier of the element.
TagNumber	The tag number of the element.
AttributeName	The name of the attribute if the Directive is not specified. In the case in which the Directive is specified (as xml, cdata, or element), the AttributeName becomes the name of the contained element. If the Directive is specified, the AttributeName can be empty.
Directive	The optional component. If neither the AttributeName nor the Directive are specified, SQL Server defaults to ELEMENT.

Table 14-2   *Components of Column Names*

component of the column name is used to name attributes (I have already shown the corresponding universal table and resulting XML document):

```
SELECT     1 as Tag,
           NULL as Parent,
           Equipment.EquipmentID as [Equipment!1!EquipmentID],
           Equipment.Make as [Equipment!1!Make],
           Equipment.Model as [Equipment!1!Model],
           NULL as [Inventory!2!InventoryID],
           NULL as [Inventory!2!StatusID]
FROM       Equipment

UNION ALL
SELECT     2,
           1,
           Equipment.EquipmentID,
           Equipment.Make,
           Equipment.Model,
           Inventory.InventoryID,
           Inventory.StatusID
FROM       Equipment, Inventory
WHERE      Equipment.EquipmentID = Inventory.EquipmentID
ORDER BY [Equipment!1!EquipmentID], [Inventory!2!InventoryID]
FOR XML EXPLICIT
```

The Directive has two purposes. When `hide`, `element`, `xml`, `xmltext`, or `cdata` is used, the Directive controls how the data in the column is mapped into the XML document. `id`, `idref`, and `idrefs` are used to allow the XDR schema to enable intradocument links.

The hide Directive

The content of the column with the `hide` directive will not be displayed in the resulting document. This feature is useful when you want to sort information by columns that you do not want to display.

The element Directive

You will likely use the `element` directive most often. It forces SQL Server to generate an element instead of an attribute. If the column contains data that could confuse an XML parser, SQL Server replaces it with entity references (for example, the ampersand character, &, is replaced with & and the < symbol is replaced with <).

The following example illustrates the use of the `hide` and `element` directives:

```
SELECT    1 as Tag,
          NULL as Parent,
          Equipment.EquipmentID as [Equipment!1!EquipmentID!hide],
          Equipment.Make as [Equipment!1!Make!element],
          Equipment.Model as [Equipment!1!Model!element],
          NULL as [Inventory!2!InventoryID],
          NULL as [Inventory!2!StatusID!element]
FROM      Equipment

UNION ALL
SELECT    2,
          1,
          Equipment.EquipmentID,
          Equipment.Make,
          Equipment.Model,
          Inventory.InventoryID,
          Inventory.StatusID
FROM      Equipment, Inventory
WHERE     Equipment.EquipmentID = Inventory.EquipmentID
ORDER BY [Equipment!1!EquipmentID!hide], [Inventory!2!InventoryID]
FOR XML EXPLICIT
```

A partial result of the query is displayed in the following listing. `Make`, `Model`, and `StatusId` information are displayed as elements. Note that the ampersand character has been replaced with & in the `Make` element:

```
<Equipment>
   <Make>Toshiba</Make>
   <Model>Portege 7020CT</Model>
   <Inventory InventoryID="5">
       <StatusID>1</StatusID>
   </Inventory>
   <Inventory InventoryID="12">
       <StatusID>1</StatusID>
   </Inventory>
</Equipment>
<Equipment>
   <Make>Bang &amp; Olafson</Make>
   <Model>V3000</Model>
...
```

The xml and cdata Directives

The xml and cdata directives are similar to the element directive. They just treat special characters differently. If the xml directive is specified, SQL Server does not perform entity encoding but rather leaves the content intact. If the cdata directive is specified, SQL Server encapsulates the content of the column in a CDATA section. In the following example, the Equipment.Make column is displayed three times and is treated each time with a different directive:

```
SELECT    1 as Tag,
          NULL as Parent,
          Equipment.EquipmentID as [Equipment!1!EquipmentID!hide],
          Equipment.Make as [Equipment!1!Make!element],
          Equipment.Make as [Equipment!1!Make!xml],
          Equipment.Make as [Equipment!1!!cdata],
          Equipment.Model as [Equipment!1!Model!element],
          NULL as [Inventory!2!InventoryID],
          NULL as [Inventory!2!StatusID!element]
FROM      Equipment

UNION ALL
SELECT    2,
          1,
          Equipment.EquipmentID,
          Equipment.Make,
          Equipment.Make,
          Equipment.Make,
          Equipment.Model,
          Inventory.InventoryID,
          Inventory.StatusID
FROM      Equipment, Inventory
WHERE     Equipment.EquipmentID = Inventory.EquipmentID
ORDER BY [Equipment!1!EquipmentID!hide], [Inventory!2!InventoryID]
FOR XML EXPLICIT
```

A partial result of the query is displayed in the following listing. Note that the Make data is treated differently each time:

```
...
<Equipment>
   <Make>Bang &amp; Olafson</Make>
   <Make>Bang & Olafson</Make>
   <![CDATA[Bang & Olafson]]>
   <Model>V3000</Model>
...
```

The xmltext Directive

The `xmltext` directive is used to incorporate an XML document (or section of the document) stored in a column of the record into the resulting document.

Imagine a scenario in which you have created a database table, but the nature of the business is such that new information (and new columns) will often be added. In the past, I have used a solution that you can see in the Asset database in the InventoryProperty table:

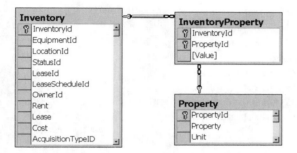

Instead of adding a new field for a property of the equipment entity, I have created a new table in which each property of an asset is stored in a separate record. Instead of storing information in a mostly empty table

InventoryId	Make	Model	CPU	Capacity	HDD	Clock	RAM	Resolution
1	HP	LaserJet 4	Null	Null	Null	Null	4MB	600 dpi
5	Toshiba	Portege 7020 CT	Pentium II	Null	6.4GB	366 MHz	64MB	1024×768

information is stored "vertically":

InventoryId	Property	Value	Unit
1	RAM	4	MB
1	Resolution	600	dpi
5	CPU	Pentium II	Null
5	RAM	64	MB
5	HDD	6.4	GB
5	Resolution	1024×768	Null
5	Weight	2	kg
5	Clock	366	MHz

An XML alternative to this solution is to create a special column to store the "overflow" data. In the following statement, the Inventory table is created with a Properties column to store additional information in XML format:

```
CREATE TABLE [InventoryXML] (
    [Inventoryid] [int] IDENTITY (1, 1) NOT NULL ,
    [EquipmentId] [int] NOT NULL ,
    [LocationId] [int] NOT NULL ,
    [StatusId] [tinyint] NOT NULL ,
    [LeaseId] [int] NULL ,
    [LeaseScheduleId] [int] NULL ,
    [OwnerId] [int] NOT NULL ,
    [Rent] [smallmoney] NULL ,
    [Lease] [smallmoney] NULL ,
    [Cost] [smallmoney] NULL ,
    [AcquisitionTypeID] [tinyint] NULL ,
    [Properties] [text] NULL,
) ON [PRIMARY]
```

You can then insert information in the form of an XML document or its subset into the Properties column:

```
<Inventory CPU = "Pentium II"
           RAM = "64 MB"
           HDD = "6.4 GB"
           Resolution = "1024x768"
           Weight = "2 kg"
           Clock="366 MHz"/>
```

To integrate this information into the resulting XML document, you should use the xmltext directive:

```
SELECT    1 as Tag,
          NULL as Parent,
          InventoryXML.InventoryID as [Inventory!1!InventoryID],
          InventoryXML.StatusID as [Inventory!1!StatusID],
          InventoryXML.Properties as [Inventory!1!Properties!xmltext]
FROM      InventoryXML
ORDER BY [Inventory!1!InventoryID]
FOR XML EXPLICIT
```

The following listing contains a partial result:

```
<Inventory InventoryID="1" StatusID="1">
   <Properties
```

```
         CPU="Pentium II"
         RAM="64 MB"
         HDD="6.4 GB"
         Resolution="1024x768"
         Weight="2 kg"
         Clock="366 MHz"/>
</Inventory>
<Inventory InventoryID="2" StatusID="2"/>
...
```

If AttributeName is specified (as in the preceding example), SQL Server uses this value instead of the tag name specified for the column (in the preceding example they were the same).

If AttributeName is omitted, SQL Server appends the attribute to the list of attributes in the enclosing element:

```
SELECT    1 as Tag,
          NULL as Parent,
          InventoryXML.InventoryID as [Inventory!1!InventoryID],
          InventoryXML.StatusID as [Inventory!1!StatusID],
          InventoryXML.Properties as [Inventory!1!!xmltext]
FROM      InventoryXML
ORDER BY [Inventory!1!InventoryID]
FOR XML EXPLICIT
```

The following listing displays a partial result:

```
<Inventory
   InventoryID="1"
   StatusID="1"
   CPU="Pentium II"
   RAM="64 MB"
   HDD="6.4 GB"
   Resolution="1024x768"
   Weight="2 kg"
   Clock="366 MHz">
</Inventory>
<Inventory
   InventoryID="2"
   StatusID="2"
...
```

The author of a query using the xmltext directive assumes a huge responsibility for the validity of the content of the column. If the column does not contain well-formed XML, the results may be unpredictable.

The `xmltext` directive is permitted (and meaningful) only with columns of character data types (`varchar`, `nvarchar`, `char`, `nchar`, `text`, `ntext`).

The id, idref, and idrefs Directives

The `id`, `idref`, and `idrefs` directives are used to modify schemas when the XMLData option of the For XML clause is specified. When the `id` directive is specified, elements receive an `id` attribute. Attributes specified using the `idref` directive can be used to reference elements with an `id` attribute. This kind of relationship is the XML equivalent of the foreign key relationship that you are used to in relational databases.

The following example links Equipment.EquipmentId to Inventory.EquipmentId. These two columns are also linked by a foreign key relationship in the database.

```
SELECT      1 as Tag,
            NULL as Parent,
            Equipment.EquipmentID as [Equipment!1!EquipmentID!id],
            Equipment.Make as [Equipment!1!Make],
            Equipment.Model as [Equipment!1!Model],
            NULL as [Inventory!2!InventoryID],
            NULL as [Inventory!2!StatusID],
            NULL as [Inventory!2!EquipmentID!idref]
FROM        Equipment

UNION ALL
SELECT      2,
            1,
            Equipment.EquipmentID,
            Equipment.Make,
            Equipment.Model,
            Inventory.InventoryID,
            Inventory.StatusID,
            Inventory.EquipmentId
FROM        Equipment, Inventory
WHERE       Equipment.EquipmentID = Inventory.EquipmentID
ORDER BY [Equipment!1!EquipmentID!id], [Inventory!2!InventoryID]
FOR XML EXPLICIT, XMLDATA
```

A partial result is shown in the following XML document. Note that the data type of the `EquipmentId` attribute of the `Equipment` element is set to `"id"` (it must be unique) and that the `EquipmentId` attribute of the `Inventory` element is set to `"idref"`:

```
<Schema name="Schema" xmlns="urn:schemas-microsoft-com:xml-data"
                      xmlns:dt="urn:schemas-microsoft-com:datatypes">
<ElementType name="Equipment" content="mixed" model="open">
```

```
   <AttributeType name="EquipmentID" dt:type="id"/>
   <AttributeType name="Make" dt:type="string"/>
   <AttributeType name="Model" dt:type="string"/>
   <attribute type="EquipmentID"/>
   <attribute type="Make"/>
   <attribute type="Model"/>
</ElementType>
<ElementType name="Inventory" content="mixed" model="open">
   <AttributeType name="InventoryID" dt:type="i4"/>
   <AttributeType name="StatusID" dt:type="ui1"/>
   <AttributeType name="EquipmentID" dt:type="idref"/>
   <attribute type="InventoryID"/>
   <attribute type="StatusID"/>
   <attribute type="EquipmentID"/>
</ElementType>
</Schema>
<Equipment xmlns="x-schema:#Schema"
   EquipmentID="1" Make="Toshiba" Model="Portege 7020CT">
   <Inventory InventoryID="5" StatusID="1" EquipmentID="1"/>
   <Inventory InventoryID="12" StatusID="1" EquipmentID="1"/>
</Equipment>
<Equipment xmlns="x-schema:#Schema"
    EquipmentID="2" Make="Sony" Model="Trinitron 17XE"/>
...
```

Publishing Database Information Using HTTP

SQL Server 2000 has an external set of components that allow users to access data in the form of XML documents using the HTTP protocol. It is important to understand that these components are external. The most important of these is the ISAPI filter that works within IIS (Internet Information Server—a web server) rather than within SQL Server (see Figure 14-5). It retrieves data through the SQL Server 2000 OLE DB

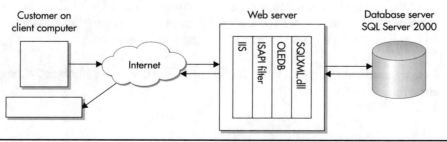

Figure 14-5   *Accessing database information through HTTP and SQLXML*

provider (SQLOLEDB). The SQLOLEDB provider itself has been modified to use a new SQLXML.dll component and to support returning the result in the form of a stream. Figure 14-5 illustrates the transfer of information from a client computer to the server and back.

To continue working through the examples in this book, you first need to install the latest version of SQLXML (XML for Microsoft SQL Server 2000 Web Release). You can find the latest version at msdn.microsoft.com. You can also download files with XML-related examples from www.trigonblue.com/sqlxml/sqlxml_download.htm.

Configuring Database Access Through HTTP

One new component delivered with SQL Server 2000 is an MMC snap-in called *IIS Virtual Directory Management for SQLXML*. This snap-in provides a graphical user interface for configuring database access through HTTP.

This tool can operate on any edition of Windows NT or Windows 2000. Computers with Windows NT must also have IIS 4.0 or higher (or Peer Web Services 4.0 or higher on Windows NT Workstation) and MMC 1.2 or higher.

The configuration of database access requires only one operation—the administrator needs to create a *virtual directory*. Apart from the usual information (such as name and path), this virtual directory must contain information for accessing the database (login, password, database, server name, database name, and the type of access allowed through the URL and virtual names). Before I explain what a virtual name is, first consider the four types of access that end users can accomplish through IIS:

► **dbobject** You can issue a Select statement as a part of an HTTP request and access a database object (such as a table or a view).

► **template** You can specify a template that is a valid XML document and contains one or more T-SQL statements. SQL Server will execute the statement(s).

► **schema** The URL can include an XPath query to be executed against the annotated mapping schema file.

► **SOAP** An application can send SOAP requests. The SQLXML server will execute the associated stored procedure or template and return the SOAP response to the caller. SOAP is used for implementing web services.

A *virtual name* is the part of a URL that specifies and executes a dbobject, a template, a schema, or a SOAP request.

The following steps demonstrate how you can configure IIS to provide access to SQL Server:

1. Launch IIS Virtual Directory Management for SQLXML: Start | Programs | SQLXML 3.0 | Configure IIS Support.

2. When the application appears on the screen, expand the server node and select Default Web Site. From the menu, select Action | New | Virtual Directory. In the dialog box that appears, select the General tab.

3. Set the name and the physical path of the virtual directory.

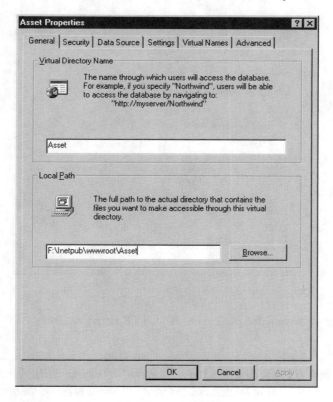

4. Select the Security tab and define the authentication method that the user will use to connect to the database.

5. Select the Data Source tab and define the server and the database for which you want to enable IIS support.

6. Select the Settings tab to specify the type of access to allow through the virtual directory. For purposes of this exercise, allow them all (although on a production server you will probably allow only templates, XPath, and POST).

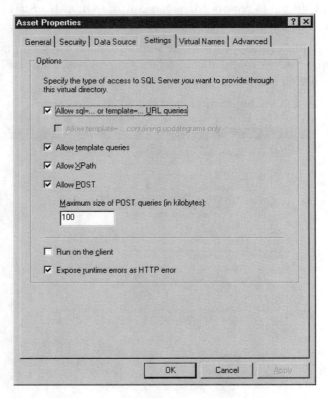

7. Leave the Run On The Client option unchecked.
8. Select the Expose Runtime Errors As HTTP Error option.

NOTE

By default, when a T-SQL error occurs in the query, SQLXML returns HTTP/1.1 200 OK. The error is returned in the body of the response. This setting allows you to change the behavior — instead of indicating a successful query, SQLXML returns HTTP/1.1 512 Runtime error.

9. Select the Virtual Names tab to associate a specific type of access and optional directory to a virtual name.
10. Click the <New virtual name> entry in the list box. Type a new name, specify dbobject as the Type, select an existing Path that will store files, and then save it.

11. Repeat the previous step to create virtual names for schema and template types:

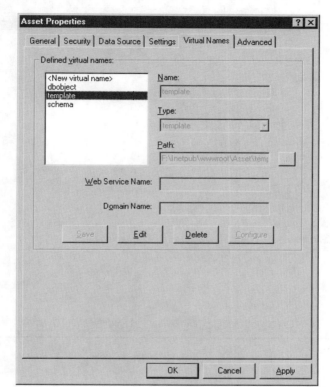

NOTE

The SOAP type requires additional settings and configuration and therefore I will cover it in the "XML Web Services" section of the next chapter.

12. Switch to the Advanced tab. You can disable caching of mapping schemas, templates, and XSLT in your development environment to avoid the need to restart the virtual directory (in other words, the application) every time you make a change. Naturally, in a production environment, caching should be turned on, since it can boost performance of the application up to 40 percent.

13. Click Apply to save the settings and close the dialog box. The application creates a new virtual directory (see Figure 14-6).

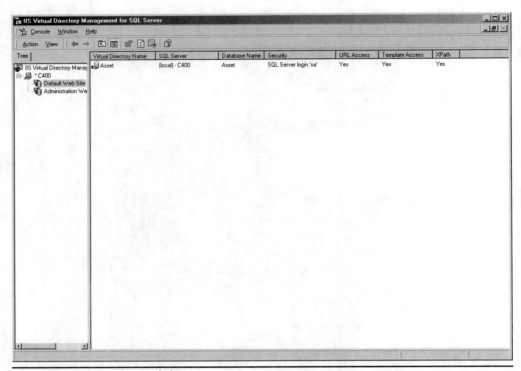

Figure 14-6 *A new virtual directory*

Accessing Database Information Using a URL

After the virtual directory is created, an end user can use a browser such as Internet Explorer (version 5.0 or later) to query the database using HTTP GET and POST methods. The simplest syntax for making HTTP GET queries would be

```
http://server/virtual_directory?sql=tsql_statement
```

Unfortunately, characters such as a blank space, ?, /, %, #, and & have special meaning in URL syntax. Therefore, they must be encoded using their hexadecimal value in the form %xx. For example, the space character can be replaced using %20 or +. Therefore, to query the Inventory table, a user can issue the following statement:

```
http://localhost/Asset?sql=select%20top%201%20*%20
from%20Inventory%20for%20xml%20auto
```

The query returns an XML document that contains just one node (see Figure 14-7).

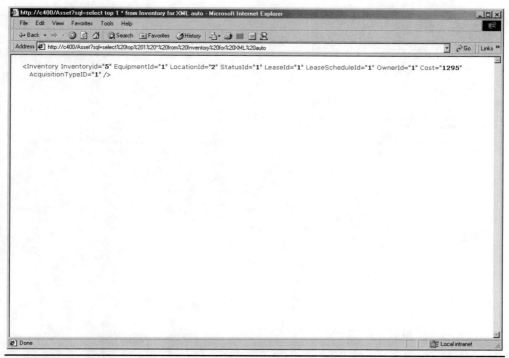

Figure 14-7   *An XML document as a result of a database query in Internet Explorer*

NOTE

You do not have to type %20 instead of a space in the query. If you omit it and use a space instead, Internet Explorer first replaces all spaces with %20 and then executes the URL.

If you leave the clause `top 1` out of the following query, the parser will not be able to process the result:

```
http://localhost/Asset?sql=select%20*%20
from%20Inventory%20for%20xml%20auto
```

The Inventory element in the result string is repeated for each record and there is, therefore, no unique top element (see Figure 14-8).

There are two solutions to this problem. You can add a *root* parameter to the HTTP GET method, and the server will add a root node to the result:

```
&root=root_node
```

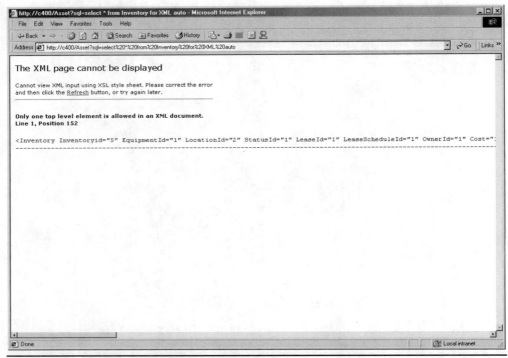

Figure 14-8 *The problem with no unique top element*

In this case, the previous query would be

```
http://localhost/asset?sql=select%20*%20
from%20Inventory%20for%20xml%20auto&root=ROOT
```

The other alternative is to write the T-SQL statement so that it returns the missing root element. In the following example, two additional Select statements were added:

```
http://localhost/Asset?sql=SELECT%20'<Root>';
%20SELECT%20*%20FROM%20Inventory%20FOR%20XML%20AUTO;
%20select%20'</Root>'
```

The results of both methods are identical, as shown in Figure 14-9.

Troubleshooting Virtual Directories

Unfortunately, many things can go wrong when you connect all these components and try to make them work together. Internet Explorer and the XML parser are not

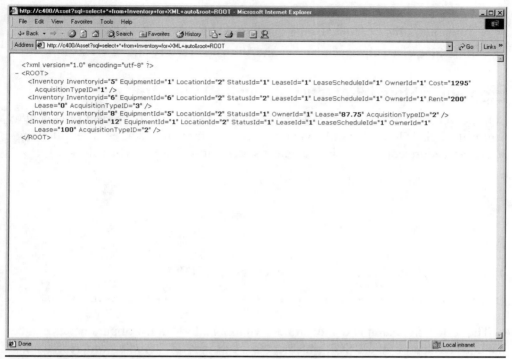

Figure 14-9   *The result as an XML document with root element*

ideal debugging tools, which is understandable considering the number of layers created and the transformations that occurred. The following activities can help you to identify and fix problems:

▶ Try to run a different or less complex type of query (such as `select 1`).

▶ Disable "friendly" messages in Internet Explorer (Tools | Internet Options | Advanced | Browsing and then uncheck Show Friendly HTTP Error Messages).

▶ Make sure that IIS is running (try to open the home page).

▶ Restart the application (right-click the virtual directory name in the IIS Virtual Directory Management snap-in and select Restart Application).

▶ Check the Virtual Directory security settings.

▶ Use SQL Profiler to ensure that the queries are reaching SQL Server.

▶ If you are using templates, make sure that they are well-formed and valid XML documents.

► Try running your URL, template, or schema query from Query Analyzer. Sometimes, the original error is overwritten by subsequent errors.

► If nothing else helps, try to delete the Virtual Directory and re-create it.

Executing a Stored Procedure Through HTTP

SQL Server 2000 and SQLXML do not force you to use only the Select statement to access data via HTTP. Naturally, you can also use stored procedures. The following stored procedure contains a simple Select statement with a For XML clause:

```
CREATE PROCEDURE prListEquipment_xml
AS
select *
from Equipment
for xml auto
```

The stored procedure can then be executed through HTTP:

```
http://localhost/asset?sql=execute%20prListEquipment_xml&root=ROOT
```

The following example demonstrates two things. First, a list of parameters can be included as a part of the T-SQL statement that executes the stored procedure. Second, the root element can be created in the stored procedure as well.

```
CREATE PROCEDURE prGetEquipment_xml
    @EquipmentId int
AS

Select '<Root>'
Select * from Equipment
Where EquipmentID= @EquipmentId
For XML AUTO, elements
Select '</Root>'
```

This stored procedure can be executed using the following URL:

```
http://localhost/asset?sql=execute%20prGetEquipment_xml%20@EquipmentId=5
```

Naturally, you are not required to use named parameters. The following URL is also legal, but a little confusing to read:

```
http://localhost/asset?sql=execute%20prGetEquipment_xml%205
```

Accessing Database Information Using Templates

The preceding section showed how you can incorporate a T-SQL statement as a part of the URL to access data via HTTP. Naturally, you should not use this technique on a production system, because

▶ It is too complicated for end users.

▶ It is prone to errors.

▶ The security of the system could easily be compromised.

▶ Browsers support only a limited URL length (2K).

Fortunately, there is an alternative—templates.

Syntax

A *template* file is an XML document that contains all the technical information such as For XML and XPath queries, parameters, and XSL transformation files required to access, process, and display data. Template files have the following syntax:

```
<ROOT xmlns:sql="urn:schemas-microsoft-com:xml-sql"
     sql:xsl='XSL_FileName' >
 <sql:header>
   <sql:param name=parameter_name>default_value</sql:param>
 <sql:header>
 <sql:query>
   tsql_statements
</sql:query>
 <sql:XPath-query mapping-schema="Schema_FileName">
   XPath_query
 </sql:XPath-query>
</ROOT>
```

The root element of the template file has one mandatory and one optional parameter. All other elements and attributes of the template file are declared in the urn:schemas-microsoft-com:xml-sql namespace. Therefore, all template files must have an xmlns:sql='urn:schemas-microsoft-com:xml-sql' attribute. The xsl attribute is optional. It is used to specify the name of the XSL transformation file.

Using the Query Element

The sql:query element is used to specify one or more T-SQL statements. The following template file queries the Equipment table:

```
<root xmlns:sql='urn:schemas-microsoft-com:xml-sql'>
    <sql:query>
        select * from Equipment for XML auto, elements
    </sql:query>
</root>
```

You can access a template using

```
http://server/virtual_directory/virtual_name/template_name
```

So, if the template file is saved as ListEquipment.xml in the template folder, it can be executed using the following URL. You can see the result in Figure 14-10.

```
http://localhost/asset/template/ListEquipment.xml
```

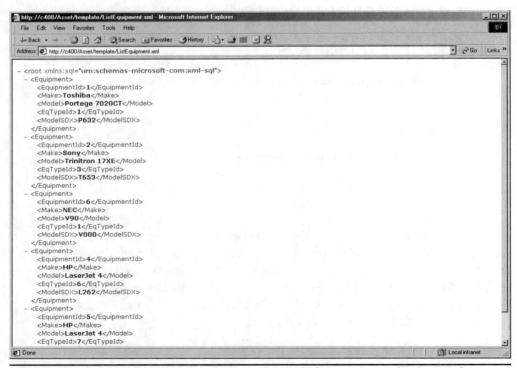

Figure 14-10   *The result of an XML template designed for accessing database information*

NOTE

The template file can contain more than one `sql:query` *element (and more than one* `sql:XPath-query` *element). It is important to note that all queries contained within separate elements are treated as separate transactions. Even if some of these transactions fail, the others will be executed independently.*

Using Parameters

If the T-SQL statements contain parameters, they are defined in the `sql:header` element. Each parameter definition contains the name of the parameter and the default value to be assigned if a value is not supplied:

```
<sql:param name=parameter_name>default_value</sql:param>
```

The following example defines a simple template file with two parameters:

```
<root xmlns:sql='urn:schemas-microsoft-com:xml-sql'>

  <sql:header>
     <sql:param name='Make' >Toshiba</sql:param>
     <sql:param name='Model'>Portege 7020CT</sql:param>
  </sql:header>

   <sql:query>
       exec prGetEquipment2_xml @Make, @Model
   </sql:query>
</root>
```

Assume that the template is saved as GetEquipment.xml in the template folder. As usual, the *parameter list* in the URL starts with a ? character. If multiple parameters are listed, they should be delimited with an & character. Parameters such as *strings* (that are delimited with quotes in T-SQL) must be delimited without quotes, as shown in the following URL:

```
http://localhost/asset/template/GetEquipment2.xml?Make=Toshiba&Model
=Portege%207020CT
```

You can see the result in Figure 14-11.

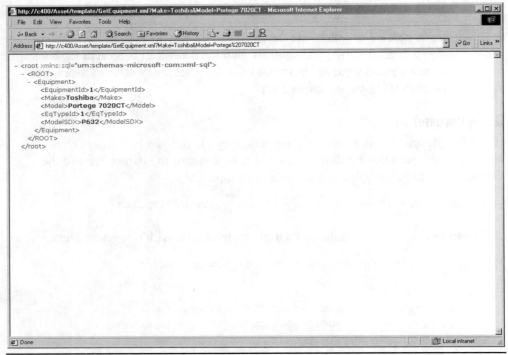

Figure 14-11 *The result of an XML template with parameters*

Using XSL

It is possible to use XSL files to change the way information is presented in a web browser. The following template references a query (stored procedure) that provides an XML result and an XSL file, Equipment.xsl, that converts it to HTML:

```
<?xml version ='1.0' encoding='UTF-8'?>
 <root xmlns:sql='urn:schemas-microsoft-com:xml-sql'
      sql:xsl='/Equipment.xsl'>
   <sql:query>
      exec prListEquipment2_xml
   </sql:query>
 </root>
```

If you execute just the stored procedure (for example, from Query Analyzer), you can see the simple XML document it produces:

```
<Equipment
    EquipmentId="1"
```

```
   Make="Toshiba"
   Model="Portege 7020CT">
   <EqType EqType="Desktop"/>
</Equipment>
<Equipment
    EquipmentId="2"
    Make="Sony"
    Model="Trinitron 17XE">
    <EqType EqType="Monitor"/>
</Equipment>
<Equipment
    EquipmentId="6"
    Make="NEC"
    Model="V90">
    <EqType EqType="Desktop"/>
</Equipment>
...
```

The XSL file shown in the following code listing describes how the XML file
is converted:

```
<?xml version='1.0' encoding='UTF-8'?>
 <xsl:stylesheet xmlns:xsl='http://www.w3.org/TR/WD-xsl' >
    <xsl:template match = '*'>
        <xsl:apply-templates />
    </xsl:template>
    <xsl:template match = 'Equipment'>
       <TR>
         <TD><xsl:value-of select = '@EquipmentId' /></TD>
         <TD><xsl:value-of select = '@Make' /></TD>
         <TD><xsl:value-of select = '@Model' /></TD>
         <TD><xsl:value-of select = './EqType/@EqType' /></TD>
       </TR>
    </xsl:template>

    <xsl:template match = '/'>
<HTML>
<HEAD>
<title>Equipment</title>
</HEAD>
<BODY>
<TABLE border = "1" width="100%">
<TR><TH colspan="4" bgcolor="#000000">
    <p align="left"><font color="#FFFFFF" face="Arial">
                      <b>Equipment</b>
                  </font>
```

```
      </p>
   </TH></TR>
<TR>
    <TH align="left" bgcolor="#C0C0C0">
        <b><font face="Arial" size="2">
            Equipment ID
        </font></b>
    </TH>
    <TH align="left" bgcolor="#C0C0C0">
         <b><font face="Arial" size="2">
            Make
        </font></b>
    </TH>
    <TH align="left" bgcolor="#C0C0C0">
         <b><font face="Arial" size="2">
            Model
        </font></b>
    </TH>
    <TH align="left" bgcolor="#C0C0C0">
         <b><font face="Arial" size="2">
            Equipment Type
        </font></b>
    </TH>
</TR>
<xsl:apply-templates select = 'root' />
        </TABLE>
      </BODY>
    </HTML>
    </xsl:template>
</xsl:stylesheet>
```

You can distinguish two segments within the XSL file. The last xsl:template match = '/' element defines the static part of the HTML page. It consists of the <HEAD> and <BODY> tags of the HTML page and the definition of the table (using the <TABLE> tag). Because of the match = '/' attribute, the described transformation is performed on the root node of the XML document.

The second xsl:template match = 'Equipment' element is applied to each element node called 'Equipment'. Each node is converted to a row within an HTML table (using row <TR> and column <TD> tags):

```
<xsl:template match = 'Equipment'>
   </TR>
      <TD><xsl:value-of select = '@EquipmentId' /></TD>
```

```
        <TD><xsl:value-of select = '@Make' /></TD>
        <TD><xsl:value-of select = '@Model' /></TD>
        <TD><xsl:value-of select = 'EqType/@EqType' /></TD>
    </TR>
  </xsl:template>
```

The `xsl:value-of` elements define the source from which the parser obtains the values for the table cells. Recall that in the "XPath" section in the previous chapter, `'@EquipmentId'` referred to an attribute called `EquipmentId` (not a T-SQL local variable). The last node reference (`'EqType/@EqType'`) is most interesting. It first points to a child node named `EqType` and then to its attribute named `EqType`.

To execute the template file, you can specify the following URL:

```
http://localhost/asset/template/ListEquipmentWithXSL.xml
```

Unfortunately, Internet Explorer displays HTML code, as shown in Figure 14-12.

To see how everything works together, you must prompt Internet Explorer to treat the content received from the web server as an HTML file rather than an XML file.

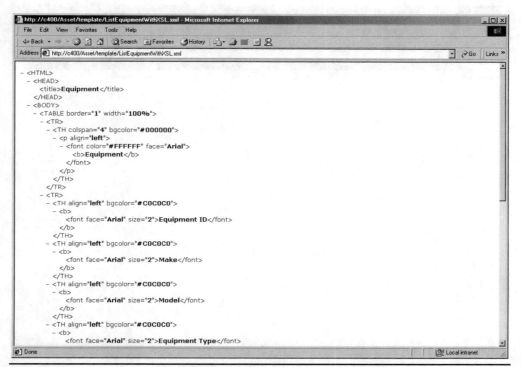

Figure 14-12   *HTML code obtained using an XML template with XSL*

You must specify an additional parameter (`contenttype=text/html`) when you specify the URL:

```
http://localhost/asset/template/ListEquipmentWithXSL.xml?contenttype=text/html
```

You can see the result in Figure 14-13.

Using Schemas and XPath Queries

The `sql:XPath-query` element of the template is used to specify XPath query expressions and mapping schema against which the XPath query expression should be executed. I will not describe mapping schemas until the next section, so I will demonstrate XPath queries in this section on the simplest possible schema.

If you execute a simple Select statement with a For XML clause that contains an XMLData option against the Equipment table,

```
Select EquipmentId, Make, Model from Equipment For XML auto, XMLData
```

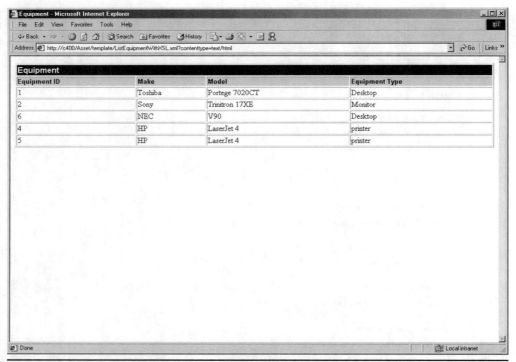

Figure 14-13 *HTML page as a result of XSL transformation*

you get an inline XDR schema at the beginning of the XML document:

```
<Schema name="Schema" xmlns="urn:schemas-microsoft-com:xml-data"
                      xmlns:dt="urn:schemas-microsoft-com:datatypes">
<ElementType name="Equipment" content="empty" model="closed">
<AttributeType name="EquipmentId" dt:type="i4"/>
<AttributeType name="Make" dt:type="string"/>
<AttributeType name="Model" dt:type="string"/>
<attribute type="EquipmentId"/>
<attribute type="Make"/>
<attribute type="Model"/>
</ElementType>
</Schema>
<Equipment xmlns="x-schema:#Schema"
           EquipmentId="1" Make="Toshiba" Model="Portege 7020CT"/>
...
```

To get a proper mapping schema in this case, you need to extract the schema into a separate file and add another namespace to it (`xmlns:sql="urn:schemas-microsoft-com:xml-sql"`):

```
<Schema name="Schema" xmlns="urn:schemas-microsoft-com:xml-data"
                      xmlns:dt="urn:schemas-microsoft-com:datatypes"
                      xmlns:sql="urn:schemas-microsoft-com:xml-sql">
<ElementType name="Equipment" content="empty" model="closed">
<AttributeType name="EquipmentId" dt:type="i4"/>
<AttributeType name="Make" dt:type="string"/>
<AttributeType name="Model" dt:type="string"/>
<attribute type="EquipmentId"/>
<attribute type="Make"/>
<attribute type="Model"/>
</ElementType>
</Schema>
```

NOTE

This is not the only operation usually needed to create a mapping schema. It is successful in this case only because the target XML document is so simple. The following section explores the details of mapping a schema.

Now it is possible to create a template file to use the XPath query to get information using this schema:

```
<ROOT xmlns:sql="urn:schemas-microsoft-com:xml-sql">
   <sql:xpath-query mapping-schema="EqSchema.xml">
```

```
        Equipment
    </sql:xpath-query>
</ROOT>
```

The schema is referenced in a `mapping-schema` attribute, and the XPath query is specified as the content of the `sql:xpath` element. The XPath query in the template references only the `Equipment` node. If the template and the schema are saved as EqTemplate.xml and EqSchema.xml, respectively, in the template virtual directory, they can be executed using

```
http://localhost/asset/template/EqTemplate.xml
```

Figure 14-14 shows the result.

We can use more complicated XPath queries in a template:

```
<ROOT xmlns:sql="urn:schemas-microsoft-com:xml-sql">
    <sql:xpath-query mapping-schema="EqSchema.xml">
        Equipment[@EquipmentId=1]
    </sql:xpath-query>
</ROOT>
```

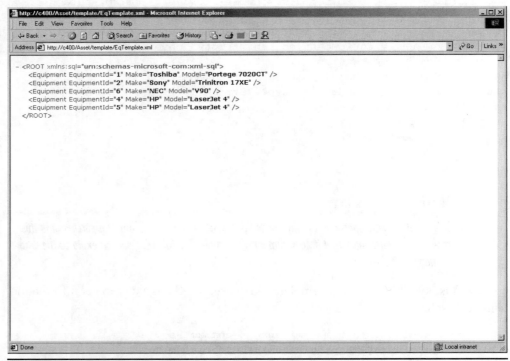

Figure 14-14   *Using an XPath query in a template file*

This query filters `Element` nodes that have an `EquipmentId` attribute with a value set to 1. Figure 14-15 shows the result.

POSTing Queries to the Server

In preceding sections, I demonstrated how you can access database information over HTTP using the GET method. This method is easier to use for testing purposes—you supply parameters in the URL after the ? sign in the form of an ampersand-separated list. Unfortunately, this database access method has two problems:

▶ You cannot expect even the most skilled users to be able to type proper queries in the form of a URL address.

▶ The size of the URL is limited to 2K, thus limiting the number of parameters and complexity of the query.

HTTP's POST method does not set limitations on the size of a query, but it is even more difficult to use. You need a custom application (or component) to pass parameters to the web server.

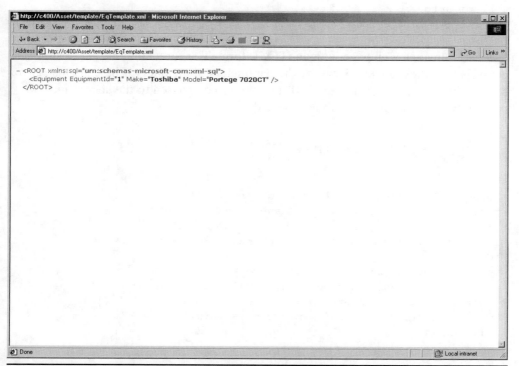

Figure 14-15   *Using an XPath query to filter results*

NOTE

Before you can start using the POST method, you must set the virtual directory to allow POST queries.

The simplest version of such an application is an HTML form that uses the POST method to pass the content of its controls to the server. In this case, instead of passing the query to an ASP page or some other component on the server, you need to pass the query to the virtual directory that processes XML requests. This technique can be demonstrated using the following stored procedure with two parameters:

```
CREATE PROCEDURE prListEquipment3_xml
    @Make varchar(50),
    @Model varchar(50)
AS
select EquipmentId, Make, Model, EqType
from Equipment inner join EqType
on Equipment.EqTypeId = EqType.EqTypeId
where Make like @Make
and Model like @Model
for xml auto
GO
```

Next, I create a web page with an HTML form. The form contains two visible controls that allow a user to specify the parameters of the query. There are also two hidden controls that specify an XML template to be passed to the server and the content type in which the result is expected:

```
<head>
<TITLE>Query Equipment</TITLE>
</head>
<body>
<H3>Query Equipment (use % as wild card).</H3>
<form action="http://localhost/Asset" method="POST">
Make:
<input type=text name=Make value='Tosh%'><BR>
Model:
<input type=text name=Model value='Por%'>
<input type=hidden name=contenttype value=text/xml>
<input type=hidden name=template value='
<ROOT xmlns:sql="urn:schemas-microsoft-com:xml-sql" >
<sql:header>
```

```
      <sql:param name="Make">%</sql:param>
      <sql:param name="Model">%</sql:param>
</sql:header>
<sql:query>
    exec prListEquipment3_xml @Make, @Model
</sql:query>
</ROOT>
'>

<p><input type="submit">
</form>
</body>
```

When a user opens this form, he or she is prompted to supply parameters (see Figure 14-16).

After the form and query are submitted, Internet Explorer displays the result shown in Figure 14-17.

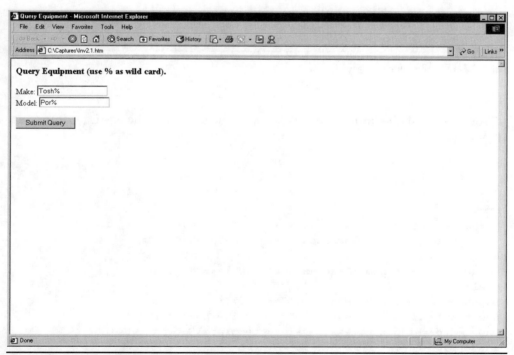

Figure 14-16   *An HTML form for querying the database*

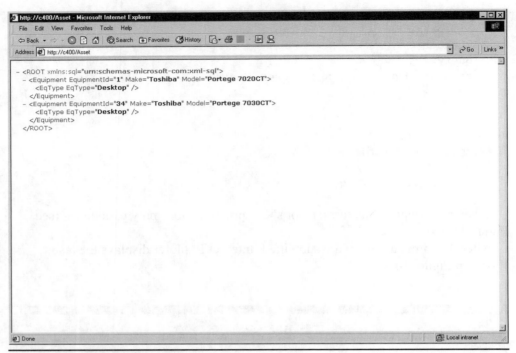

Figure 14-17   *Result of query*

You can polish this form if you add an XSL file to convert the XML result into an HTML form:

```
<head>
<TITLE>Query Equipment</TITLE>
</head>
<body>
<H3>Query Equipment (use % as wild card). </H3>
<form action="http://localhost/Asset" method="POST">
Make:
<input type=text name=Make value='Tosh%'><BR>
Model:
<input type=text name=Model value='Por%'>
<input type=hidden name=contenttype value=text/xml>
<input type=hidden name=xsl value="template\Equipment.xsl">
<input type=hidden name=template value='
<ROOT xmlns:sql="urn:schemas-microsoft-com:xml-sql" >
<sql:header>
```

```
    <sql:param name="Make">%</sql:param>
    <sql:param name="Model">%</sql:param>
</sql:header>
<sql:query>
    exec prListEquipment3_xml @Make, @Model
</sql:query>
</ROOT>
'>

<p><input type="submit">
</form>
</body>
```

Now, you can assemble a more complex application by adding more forms, security, links between pages, and other elements, but this type of solution is really more suitable for simple search pages than for such complex applications.

XML Views Based on Annotated XDR Schemas

The "Using Schemas and XPath Queries" section, earlier in the chapter, demonstrated how XDR schemas and XPath queries can be used to retrieve data from a database. This section now examines in greater detail the use of XDR schemas for mapping.

The main purpose of an XDR schema is to define the structure of the XML document. SQL Server 2000 extends the XDR schema language with *annotations* designed to *map XML nodes* (elements and attributes) and *database objects* (tables, views, and columns). Other annotations enable features such as the definition of *hierarchical relationships* between XML nodes, the change of a target namespace, and the retrieval of XML-encoded data from a database. Such XDR schemas produce XML documents that behave in a fashion similar to database views and, therefore, are sometimes called *XML views*.

The basic idea is that all metadata needed to generate and validate an XML document should be stored in one place—a schema document. The basic features of schemas define the structure, and annotations-based features extend that definition by providing mapping information.

Mapping Tables, Views, and Columns

The XDR schema used in the "Using Schemas and XPath Queries" section was based on default mapping between tables and elements, and between columns and attributes. Because SQL Server was able to find a table that corresponded to the specified element and attributes that corresponded to the table's columns, the result was an XML document containing information from the database table.

In the case in which an element is named differently than a table (or a view), you must add a `sql:relation` annotation (an attribute of the `<ElementType>` tag) to the XDR schema. In the case in which attributes of the element are named differently than the columns of the table (or the view), you must add a `sql:field` annotation (an attribute of the `<attribute>` tag) to the schema. In the following example, the Equipment table is mapped to the element `Part`, and the columns EquipmentId and Make are mapped to the attributes `PartNum` and `Manufacturer`:

```
<Schema name="Schema"
        xmlns="urn:schemas-microsoft-com:xml-data"
        xmlns:dt="urn:schemas-microsoft-com:datatypes"
        xmlns:sql="urn:schemas-microsoft-com:xml-sql">
<ElementType name="Part" sql:relation="Equipment"
             content="empty" model="closed">
<AttributeType name="PartNum" dt:type="i4" />
<AttributeType name="Manufacturer" dt:type="string" />
<AttributeType name="Model" dt:type="string"/>
<attribute type="PartNum" sql:field="EquipmentId"/>
<attribute type="Manufacturer" sql:field="Make"/>
<attribute type="Model"/>
</ElementType>
</Schema>
```

The following template can use the preceding schema:

```
<ROOT xmlns:sql="urn:schemas-microsoft-com:xml-sql">
    <sql:xpath-query mapping-schema="PartSchema.xml">
        Part
    </sql:xpath-query>
</ROOT>
```

The result is shown in Figure 14-18.

`sql:field` annotations can be applied to elements as well. The following schema is not attribute-based, but element-based:

```
<Schema name="Schema"
        xmlns="urn:schemas-microsoft-com:xml-data"
        xmlns:dt="urn:schemas-microsoft-com:datatypes"
        xmlns:sql="urn:schemas-microsoft-com:xml-sql">
  <ElementType name="Part" sql:relation="Equipment"
               content="eltOnly" model="closed" order="many">
    <element type="PartNo" sql:field="EquipmentId"/>
    <element type="Manufacturer" sql:field="Make"/>
```

```
    <element type="Model"/>
</ElementType>
<ElementType name="PartNo" content="textOnly"
            model="closed" dt:type="i4"/>
    <ElementType name="Manufacturer" content="textOnly"
                model="closed" dt:type="string"/>
    <ElementType name="Model" content="textOnly"
                model="closed" dt:type="string"/>
</Schema>
```

You can use this schema through the following template:

```
<ROOT xmlns:sql="urn:schemas-microsoft-com:xml-sql">
    <sql:xpath-query mapping-schema="PartElementSchema.xml">
        Part
    </sql:xpath-query>
</ROOT>
```

The result is shown on the following page in Figure 14-19.

Figure 14-18   *The result of the annotated schema*

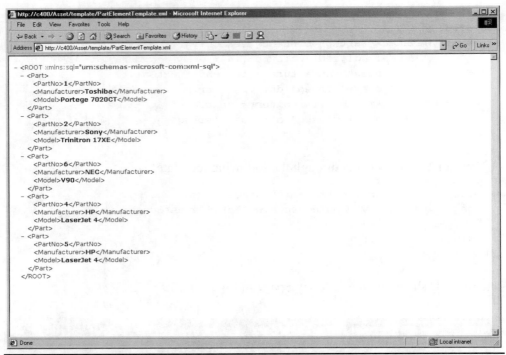

Figure 14-19   *An element-based XML document as a result of an annotated schema*

Required Namespaces

All XDR schemas are defined in the `urn:schemas-microsoft-com:xml-data` namespace. Therefore, each schema must contain a reference to that namespace. The XDR data types are defined in the `urn:schemas-microsoft-com:datatypes` namespace. SQL Server annotations that allow you to map relational objects with XML components are defined in the `urn:schemas-microsoft-com:xml-sql` namespace. The typical XDR schema needs a root element similar to the following:

```
<Schema name="Schema"
        xmlns="urn:schemas-microsoft-com:xml-data"
        xmlns:dt="urn:schemas-microsoft-com:datatypes"
        xmlns:sql="urn:schemas-microsoft-com:xml-sql">
...
</Schema>
```

Mapping Relationships

So far, I have demonstrated only schemas based on a single table (or view). When the XML document has to map to more than one table, that relationship has to be annotated using the `<sql:relationship>` tag. This process is similar to the creation of foreign keys in relational databases. The following attributes of the `<sql:relationship>` tag need to be defined:

Attribute	Description
key-relation	Name of the primary relation
key	Node (field) in a primary relation (table) that serves as the primary key
foreign-relation	Name of the foreign relation (table)
foreign-key	Node (field) in a foreign relation (table) that serves as the foreign key

The following schema contains the definition for a relationship between the `Contact` and `Inventory` elements:

```
<Schema name="Schema"
        xmlns="urn:schemas-microsoft-com:xml-data"
        xmlns:dt="urn:schemas-microsoft-com:datatypes"
        xmlns:sql="urn:schemas-microsoft-com:xml-sql">

<ElementType name="Contact" content="eltOnly"
            model="closed" order="many">
<element type="Inventory" maxOccurs="*">


        <sql:relationship
        key-relation="Contact"
        key="ContactId"
        foreign-key="OwnerId"
        foreign-relation="Inventory" />


</element>
<AttributeType name="ContactId" dt:type="i4"/>
<AttributeType name="FirstName" dt:type="string"/>
<AttributeType name="LastName" dt:type="string"/>
<AttributeType name="Phone" dt:type="string"/>
<AttributeType name="Fax" dt:type="string"/>
<AttributeType name="Email" dt:type="string"/>
<AttributeType name="OrgUnitId" dt:type="i2"/>
<AttributeType name="UserName" dt:type="string"/>
<AttributeType name="ts" dt:type="i8"/>
<attribute type="ContactId"/>
```

```
<attribute type="FirstName"/>
<attribute type="LastName"/>
<attribute type="Phone"/>
<attribute type="Fax"/>
<attribute type="Email"/>
<attribute type="OrgUnitId"/>
<attribute type="UserName"/>
<attribute type="ts"/>
</ElementType>

<ElementType name="Inventory" content="empty" model="closed">
<AttributeType name="Inventoryid" dt:type="i4"/>
<AttributeType name="EquipmentId" dt:type="i4"/>
<AttributeType name="LocationId" dt:type="i4"/>
<AttributeType name="StatusId" dt:type="ui1"/>
<AttributeType name="LeaseId" dt:type="i4"/>
<AttributeType name="LeaseScheduleId" dt:type="i4"/>
<AttributeType name="OwnerId" dt:type="i4"/>
<AttributeType name="Rent" dt:type="fixed.14.4"/>
<AttributeType name="Lease" dt:type="fixed.14.4"/>
<AttributeType name="Cost" dt:type="fixed.14.4"/>
<AttributeType name="AcquisitionTypeID" dt:type="ui1"/>
<attribute type="Inventoryid"/>
<attribute type="EquipmentId"/>
<attribute type="LocationId"/>
<attribute type="StatusId"/>
<attribute type="LeaseId"/>
<attribute type="LeaseScheduleId"/>
<attribute type="OwnerId"/>
<attribute type="Rent"/>
<attribute type="Lease"/>
<attribute type="Cost"/>
<attribute type="AcquisitionTypeID"/>
</ElementType>
</Schema>
```

It can be used through the following template:

```
<ROOT xmlns:sql="urn:schemas-microsoft-com:xml-sql">
   <sql:xpath-query mapping-schema="OwnerSchema.xml">
      Contact
   </sql:xpath-query>
</ROOT>
```

The result is shown in Figure 14-20.

Naturally, you can join more than two tables.

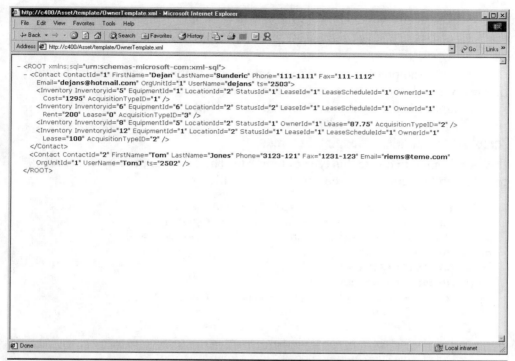

Figure 14-20   *Relationship as an annotation of an XDR schema*

Other Annotations

There are other annotations that you can also use in mapping schemas: `sql:is-constant="1"` annotations are used on static nodes such as the root node; `id`, `idref`, and `idrefs` attributes can be used to create intradocument links in XML documents; `sql:id-prefix` annotations can be used to make ID attributes unique; `sql:use-cdate` annotations can be used to specify a `CDATA` section in the XML document; `sql:overflow-field` attributes are used to retrieve data from fields that contain XML tags; `sql:map-field` attributes are used to prevent nodes from being mapped in the schema; and so on.

Retrieving Data Using XDR Schemas

There are many ways to retrieve database information using XDR annotated schemas, including:

▶ Templates that contain XPath queries

▶ Templates with inline mapping schemas

▶ A URL that refers to the mapping schema and specifies an XPath query

▶ Applications that refer to mapping schemas and use XPath queries

So far, all examples have used the first method—templates that contain XPath queries. We will now explore the next two. The last method is covered in the "Programmatic Database Access" section later in this chapter.

Templates with Inline Mapping Schemas

It is very simple to create this type of template. The following example merges template and schema files used earlier into one file:

```
<ROOT xmlns="urn:schemas-microsoft-com:xml-data"
      xmlns:dt="urn:schemas-microsoft-com:datatypes"
      xmlns:sql="urn:schemas-microsoft-com:xml-sql">
<Schema name="Schema"
    sql:id="InlineSchema"
    sql:is-mapping-schema="1">
    <ElementType name="Part" sql:relation="Equipment"
            content="empty" model="closed">
      <AttributeType name="PartNum" dt:type="i4" />
      <AttributeType name="Manufacturer" dt:type="string" />
      <AttributeType name="Model" dt:type="string"/>
      <attribute type="PartNum" sql:field="EquipmentId"/>
      <attribute type="Manufacturer" sql:field="Make"/>
      <attribute type="Model"/>
    </ElementType>
</Schema>
    <sql:xpath-query mapping-schema="#InlineSchema">
        Part
    </sql:xpath-query>
</ROOT>
```

The schema is identified using the `sql:id` attribute and described using the `sql:is-mapping-schema` attribute of the `Schema` element. The identifier is used later in the `mapping-schema` attribute of the `sql:xpath-query` element. The template can be used with a simple URL reference to the file, as shown in Figure 14-21.

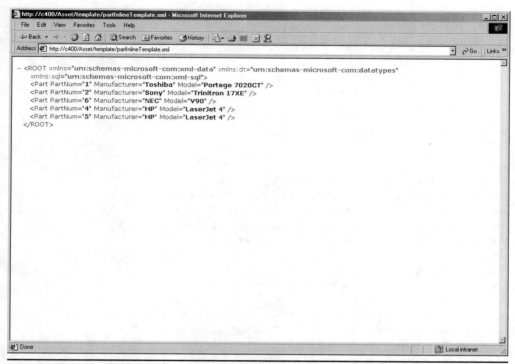

Figure 14-21   *Using a template with an inline mapping schema*

A URL with a Reference to a Mapping Schema and an XPath Query

To refer to an XDR-annotated schema in a URL, you must first create a virtual name for the schema of the type described in "Configuring Database Access Through HTTP," earlier in this chapter. Such a URL has the following structure:

```
http://server/virtual_directory/virtual_name/schema_file/XPath_query
```

The following schema joins three tables (Inventory, Equipment, and EqType). They are related using the <sql:relationship> tag.

```
<Schema name="Schema"
        xmlns="urn:schemas-microsoft-com:xml-data"
        xmlns:dt="urn:schemas-microsoft-com:datatypes"
        xmlns:sql="urn:schemas-microsoft-com:xml-sql">
```

```
<ElementType name="Inventory" content="eltOnly"
            model="closed" order="many">
<element type="Equipment" maxOccurs="*">

      <sql:relationship
        key-relation="Inventory"
        key="EquipmentId"
        foreign-key="EquipmentId"
        foreign-relation="Equipment" />

</element>
<AttributeType name="Inventoryid" dt:type="i4"/>
<AttributeType name="EquipmentId" dt:type="i4"/>
<AttributeType name="LocationId" dt:type="i4"/>
<AttributeType name="StatusId" dt:type="ui1"/>
<AttributeType name="LeaseId" dt:type="i4"/>
<AttributeType name="LeaseScheduleId" dt:type="i4"/>
<AttributeType name="OwnerId" dt:type="i4"/>
<AttributeType name="Rent" dt:type="fixed.14.4"/>
<AttributeType name="Lease" dt:type="fixed.14.4"/>
<AttributeType name="Cost" dt:type="fixed.14.4"/>
<AttributeType name="AcquisitionTypeID" dt:type="ui1"/>
<attribute type="Inventoryid"/>
<attribute type="EquipmentId"/>
<attribute type="LocationId"/>
<attribute type="StatusId"/>
<attribute type="LeaseId"/>
<attribute type="LeaseScheduleId"/>
<attribute type="OwnerId"/>
<attribute type="Rent"/>
<attribute type="Lease"/>
<attribute type="Cost"/>
<attribute type="AcquisitionTypeID"/>
</ElementType>

<ElementType name="Equipment" content="eltOnly"
            model="closed" order="many">
<element type="EqType" maxOccurs="*">

      <sql:relationship
        key-relation="Equipment"
        key="EqTypeId"
        foreign-key="EqTypeId"
        foreign-relation="EqType" />
```

```
</element>
<AttributeType name="EquipmentId" dt:type="i4"/>
<AttributeType name="Make" dt:type="string"/>
<AttributeType name="Model" dt:type="string"/>
<AttributeType name="EqTypeId" dt:type="i2"/>
<AttributeType name="ModelSDX" dt:type="string"/>
<AttributeType name="MakeSDX" dt:type="string"/>
<attribute type="EquipmentId"/>
<attribute type="Make"/>
<attribute type="Model"/>
<attribute type="EqTypeId"/>
<attribute type="ModelSDX"/>
<attribute type="MakeSDX"/>
</ElementType>

<ElementType name="EqType" content="empty" model="closed">
<AttributeType name="EqTypeId" dt:type="i2"/>
<AttributeType name="EqType" dt:type="string"/>
<attribute type="EqTypeId"/>
<attribute type="EqType"/>
</ElementType>

<ElementType name="ROOT" sql:is-constant="1">
    <element type="Inventory"/>
</ElementType>

</Schema>
```

In the preceding examples with template files, it was not necessary to define a unique root element in the schema. The template took care of that requirement. In this case, you have to define the root element explicitly in the XML schema:

```
<ElementType name="ROOT" sql:is-constant="1">
    <element type="Inventory"/>
</ElementType>
```

You can see the complete tree of the XML document by using the following URL:

```
http://localhost/asset/Schema/InvSchema.xml/ROOT
```

The XPath query refers to the <ROOT> node and all nodes that it contains. The result is shown in Figure 14-22.

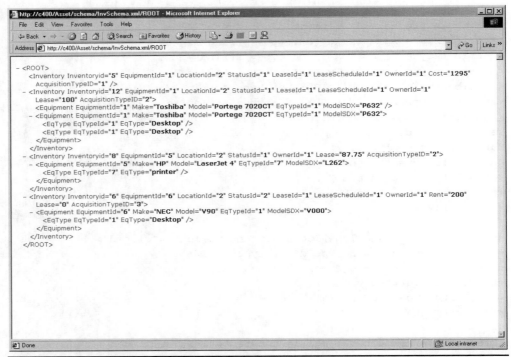

Figure 14-22 *Using a URL with an XDR schema and an XPath query*

You could use XPath to further filter the result. The following URL retrieves only Inventory nodes that have a `StatusId` attribute set to 2:

```
http://localhost/asset/Schema/InvSchema.xml/ROOT/Inventory[@StatusId=2]
```

The result is shown in Figure 14-23.

XML Views Based on Annotated XSD Schemas

Since the W3C gave the XML Schema Recommended status in May of 2001, Microsoft has been adding support for XSD schemas in SQL Server 2000. If you install SQLXML on your server, you will be able to create XML views using XSD annotated schemas.

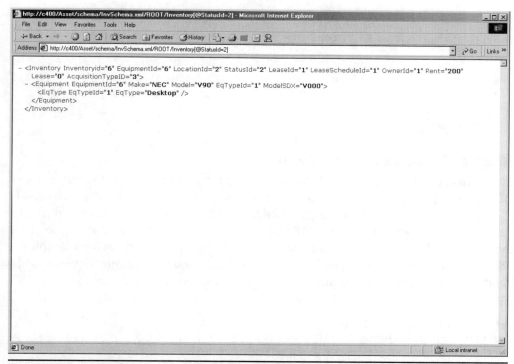

```
- <Inventory Inventoryid="6" EquipmentId="6" LocationId="2" StatusId="2" LeaseId="1" LeaseScheduleId="1" OwnerId="1" Rent="200"
    Lease="0" AcquisitionTypeID="3">
  - <Equipment EquipmentId="6" Make="NEC" Model="V90" EqTypeId="1" ModelSDX="V000">
      <EqType EqTypeId="1" EqType="Desktop" />
    </Equipment>
  </Inventory>
```

Figure 14-23   *Filtering XML documents using an XPath query*

NOTE

If you have already made an investment to develop a number of XDR schemas (for example, on a BizTalk project), you can convert them to XSD schemas. SQLXML 3.0 (and newer versions) includes the CvtSchema.exe tool in the \Program Files\SQLXML 3.0\bin folder, which enables you to convert the XDR schemas to XSD schemas.

I will now delve into the design details of XSD annotated schemas. You will see that they are not much different from XDR annotated schemas.

Required Namespaces

XSD schemas are defined in the `http://www.w3.org/2001/XMLSchema` namespace. SQL Server annotations are defined in the `urn:schemas-microsoft-com:mapping-schema` namespace. If an XSD schema also specifies SQL Server data types, it must contain a reference to the `urn:schemas-microsoft-com:datatypes` namespace. Therefore, a typical XSD schema will have a root element similar to the following:

```
<xsd:schema xmlns:xsd="http://www.w3.org/2001/XMLSchema"
            xmlns:dt="urn:schemas-microsoft-com:datatypes"
            xmlns:sql="urn:schemas-microsoft-com:mapping-schema">
...
</xsd:schema>
```

Mapping Tables, Views, and Columns

In the case in which an element is named differently than a table (or a view), you must add a `sql:relation` annotation (as an attribute of the `xsd:element` element) to the schema. Its value must match the table (or the view) name. In the case in which attributes or elements are named differently than the columns of the table (or the view), you must add a `sql:field` annotation to the schema. In the following example, the Equipment table is mapped to the element `Part` and the columns EquipmentId and Make are mapped to the attributes `PartNum` and `Manufacturer`:

```
<?xml version="1.0" encoding="UTF-8" standalone="no" ?>
<xsd:schema xmlns:xsd="http://www.w3.org/2001/XMLSchema"
xmlns:dt="urn:schemas-microsoft-com:datatypes"
xmlns:sql="urn:schemas-microsoft-com:mapping-schema">
    <xsd:element name="Part" sql:relation="Equipment" type="Part_type" />
    <xsd:complexType name="Part_type">
       <xsd:all>
          <xsd:element name="PartNo" sql:field="EquipmentId" type="xsd:int" />
          <xsd:element name="Manufacturer" sql:field="Make" type="xsd:string" />
          <xsd:element name="Model" type="xsd:string" />
       </xsd:all>
    </xsd:complexType>
    <xsd:element name="PartNo" sql:field="PartNo" type="xsd:int" />
    <xsd:element name="Manufacturer" sql:field="Make" type="xsd:string" />
    <xsd:element name="Model" type="xsd:string" />
</xsd:schema>
```

The name of the `Model` element is the same as the name of the database field, so there is no need to include annotations to link them. SQL Server will use *default mapping* to automatically link XML and SQL Server components.

Mapping Relationships

XSD schemas can map to more than one table. As previously discussed, table relationships are annotated using the `sql:relationship` element. This tag must be contained within the `xsd:appinfo` element inside the `xsd:annotation`

element. In XSD Schemas, the `sql:relationship` element has four attributes
that link elements in a manner similar to the creation of foreign keys between tables
in relational databases:

Attribute	Description
`parent`	Name of the primary relation
`parent-key`	Node (field) in a primary relation (table) that serves as the primary key
`child`	Name of the foreign relation (table)
`child-key`	Node (field) in a foreign relation (table) that serves as the foreign key

The following schema contains the definition for a relationship between the
`Contact` and `Inventory` elements:

```
<?xml version="1.0" encoding="UTF-8" standalone="no" ?>
<xsd:schema xmlns:xsd="http://www.w3.org/2001/XMLSchema"
            xmlns:dt="urn:schemas-microsoft-com:datatypes"
            xmlns:sql="urn:schemas-microsoft-com:mapping-schema">
  <xsd:element name="Contact"
               sql:relation="Contact"
               type="Contact_type" />
<xsd:complexType name="Contact_type">
  <xsd:all>
    <xsd:element name="Inventory"
                 sql:relation="Inventory"
                 type="Inventory_type">
      <xsd:annotation>
        <xsd:appinfo>
          <sql:relationship parent="Contact"
                            parent-key="ContactId"
                            child="Inventory"
                            child-key="OwnerId" />
        </xsd:appinfo>
      </xsd:annotation>
    </xsd:element>
  </xsd:all>
  <xsd:attribute name="ContactId" type="xsd:int" />
  <xsd:attribute name="FirstName" type="xsd:string" />
  <xsd:attribute name="LastName" type="xsd:string" />
  <xsd:attribute name="Phone" type="xsd:string" />
  <xsd:attribute name="Fax" type="xsd:string" />
  <xsd:attribute name="Email" type="xsd:string" />
```

```xml
        <xsd:attribute name="OrgUnitId" type="xsd:short" />
        <xsd:attribute name="UserName" type="xsd:string" />
        <xsd:attribute name="ts" type="xsd:long" />
    </xsd:complexType>
    <xsd:element name="Inventory"
                 sql:relation="Inventory"
                 type="Inventory_type" />
    <xsd:complexType name="Inventory_type">
      <xsd:attribute name="Inventoryid" type="xsd:int" />
      <xsd:attribute name="EquipmentId" type="xsd:int" />
      <xsd:attribute name="LocationId" type="xsd:int" />
      <xsd:attribute name="StatusId" type="xsd:unsignedByte" />
      <xsd:attribute name="LeaseId" type="xsd:int" />
      <xsd:attribute name="LeaseScheduleId" type="xsd:int" />
      <xsd:attribute name="OwnerId" type="xsd:int" />
      <xsd:attribute name="Rent" type="xsd:decimal" />
      <xsd:attribute name="Lease" type="xsd:decimal" />
      <xsd:attribute name="Cost" type="xsd:decimal" />
      <xsd:attribute name="AcquisitionTypeID" type="xsd:unsignedByte" />
    </xsd:complexType>
</xsd:schema>
```

NOTE

XML views have one significant advantage over relational views — they are updateable. You can use UpdateGrams or XML Bulk Load to load XML documents into multiple tables.

Other Annotations

`sql:is-constant="1"` annotations are used on static nodes. This annotation is useful for defining the root node or other nodes that are not linked to table columns.

In the following schema, the root node (`EqList`) is artificially added as a container for all other nodes:

```xml
<?xml version="1.0" encoding="UTF-8" standalone="no" ?>
<xsd:schema xmlns:xsd="http://www.w3.org/2001/XMLSchema"
            xmlns:sql="urn:schemas-microsoft-com:mapping-schema">
  <xsd:element name="EqList"
               sql:is-constant="1">
    <xsd:complexType>
      <xsd:sequence>
        <xsd:element name="Eq"
                     sql:relation="Equipment"
                     maxOccurs="unbounded">
          <xsd:complexType>
```

```
                <xsd:attribute name="EqId"
                               sql:field="EquipmentId"
                               type="xsd:integer" />
            <xsd:attribute name="Make" type="xsd:string" />
            <xsd:attribute name="Model" type="xsd:string" />
          </xsd:complexType>
        </xsd:element>
      </xsd:sequence>
    </xsd:complexType>
  </xsd:element>
</xsd:schema>
```

The `sql:mapped` attribute serves an opposite purpose. It is useful in cases in which you have a schema that contains a component that cannot be mapped to a database object. SQL Server will not return XML view components that are annotated with `sql:mapped = "0"`:

```
<?xml version="1.0" encoding="UTF-8" standalone="no" ?>
<xsd:schema xmlns:xsd="http://www.w3.org/2001/XMLSchema"
            xmlns:sql="urn:schemas-microsoft-com:mapping-schema">
  <xsd:element name="EqList"
               sql:is-constant="1">
    <xsd:complexType>
      <xsd:sequence>
        <xsd:element name="Eq"
                     sql:relation="Equipment"
                     maxOccurs="unbounded">
          <xsd:complexType>
            <xsd:attribute name="EqId"
                           sql:field="EquipmentId"
                           type="xsd:integer" />
            <xsd:attribute name="Make" type="xsd:string" />
            <xsd:attribute name="Model" type="xsd:string" />
            <xsd:attribute name="GTIN" type="xsd:string"
                           sql:mapped = "0"/>
          </xsd:complexType>
        </xsd:element>
      </xsd:sequence>
    </xsd:complexType>
  </xsd:element>
</xsd:schema>
```

The `id`, `idref`, and `idrefs` attributes can be used to create intradocument links in XML documents; `sql:id-prefix` annotations can be used to make ID attributes unique; `sql:use-cdate` annotations can be used to specify a `CDATA` section in the XML document; `sql:overflow-field` attributes are used to retrieve data from fields that contain XML tags; `sql:limit-field` and `sql:limit-value` annotations are used to filter result sets; `sql:identity` and `sql:guid` are used to control whether SQL Server uses values supplied by DiffGram and UpdateGram or generates new ones; and so on.

Programmatic Database Access

SQLXML contains two data providers that can manage SQL Server data using XML:

▶ **SQLXML Managed Classes**   For creating .NET applications using the .NET Framework

▶ **SQLXMLOLEDB Provider**   For creating database application using ADO and ADO.NET

Retrieving XML Data Using SQLXML Managed Classes

The SQLXML Managed Classes assembly contains three main classes:

▶ **SqlXmlCommand**   Used to specify a query and retrieve XML from SQL Server 2000

▶ **SqlXmlParameter**   Used to set parameters to SqlXmlCommand

▶ **SqlXmlAdapter**   Used to retrieve a DataSet object based in a SqlXmlCommand query

To use these classes in your .NET application, you must add to your project a reference to the `Microsoft.Data.SqlXml` namespace (implemented as the Microsoft.Data.SqlXml.dll assembly in the \Program Files\SQLXML 3.0\bin folder).

NOTE

Although these managed classes were initially delivered with SQLXML 2.0, you should install the newest version. Earlier versions were designed to work with the Beta 2 version of the .NET Framework, and you will resolve some compatibility issues when you install the latest version.

Figure 14-24 shows the architecture of a .NET application that uses SQLXML Managed Classes.

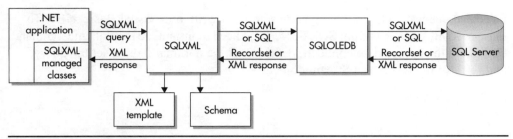

Figure 14-24   *Retrieving data using SQLXML Managed Classes*

Retrieving XML Data Using the SqlXmlCommand Class

You can use the SqlXmlCommand class to specify a SQL query (with the For XML clause), a template, or an XPath query (against the mapping schema) to retrieve an XML document (or fragment) from SQL Server 2000.

The query itself has to be specified using the CommandText property of the SqlXmlCommand class. The type of query is specified using the CommandType property. Possible values are

► SqlXmlCommandType.SQL (default)

► SqlXmlCommandType.Template

► SqlXmlCommandType.TemplateFile

► SqlXmlCommandType.XPath

► SqlXmlCommandType.UpdateGram

► SqlXmlCommandType.DiffGram

The next chapter discusses how you can use the SqlXmlCommand class with UpdateGrams and DiffGrams; this chapter focuses on the rest of the available properties.

There are three methods for returning XML data using the SqlXmlCommand class:

► **ExecuteToStream**   The resulting XML fragment is written to an existing Stream object (typically a file)

► **ExecuteStream**   The result is returned as a new Stream object (typically console)

► **ExecuteXmlReader**   Returns the result as an XmlTextReader instance (to be used in data-bound controls)

Each of these options has its advantages and can be used in different circumstances.

Relational Queries   The following code sample is written in Visual Basic .NET. To retrieve XML fragments from SQL Server, you need to instantiate the SqlXmlCommand class with the appropriate connection string, set the command type, set the query, and retrieve the result as a Stream object:

```
'SqlXml_SqlQuery
Imports System
Imports System.IO
Imports Microsoft.Data.SqlXml 'The SQLXML managed classes

Module Module1
    Sub Main()

    'Instantiate the SqlXmlCommand object and the connection
    Dim objSqlXmlCmd As New SqlXmlCommand("Provider=SQLOLEDB;" _
        & "Server=(local)\SS2K;Database=Asset;" _
        & "Integrated Security=SSPI")
    'Set type of query
    objSqlXmlCmd.CommandType = SqlXmlCommandType.Sql
    'Set the query
    objSqlXmlCmd.CommandText = "SELECT * FROM Inventory FOR XML AUTO"

    'Execute the query and retrieve result as a stream
    Dim objResult As MemoryStream = objSqlXmlCmd.ExecuteStream()

    'Write result to the console
    Dim objStreamReader As New StreamReader(objResult)
    Console.Write(objStreamReader.ReadToEnd)
    End Sub
End Module
```

If you build this project in Visual Studio .NET, it will create an executable file in the bin subfolder of the project. If you execute it from the command prompt, it will return an XML fragment to the console:

```
<Inventory Inventoryid="5" EquipmentId="1" LocationId="2" StatusId="1"
LeaseId="1" LeaseScheduleId="1" OwnerId="1" Cost="1295"
AcquisitionTypeID="1"/>
<Inventory Inventoryid="6" EquipmentId="6" LocationId="2" StatusId="2"
LeaseId="1" LeaseScheduleId="1" OwnerId="1" Rent="200" Lease="0" AcquisitionTypeID="3"/>
<Inventory Inventoryid="8" EquipmentId="5" LocationId="2" StatusId="1"
OwnerId="1" AquisitionTypeID="2"/>
...
```

Output from the console can be redirected to a file:

```
...\sqlxml_sqlquery> sqlxml_sqlquery > Inventory.xml
```

The other option for directing XML results to a file is to create a FileStream object, use the ExecuteStream method, and write the XML directly to a file:

```
'SqlXml_SqlQuery2File
Imports System
Imports System.IO
Imports Microsoft.Data.SqlXml 'The SQLXML managed classes

Module Module1
 Sub Main()
    'Instantiate the SqlXmlCommand object and the connection
    Dim objSqlXmlCmd As New SqlXmlCommand("Provider=SQLOLEDB;"
        & "Server=(local)\SS2K;Database=Asset;"
        & "Integrated Security=SSPI")
    'Set type of query
    objSqlXmlCmd.CommandType = SqlXmlCommandType.Sql
    'Set the query
    objSqlXmlCmd.CommandText = "SELECT * FROM Inventory FOR XML AUTO"

    'execute into a stream reader
    Dim objStrmReader As New StreamReader(objSqlXmlCmd.ExecuteStream())
    'prepare destination file
    Dim objResult As New FileStream("Inventory.xml", FileMode.Create)
    Dim objStrmWriter As New StreamWriter(objResult)

    'write result into destination file
    objStrmWriter.WriteLine(objStrmReader.ReadToEnd)

    objStrmWriter.Close()
    objResult.Close()
    objStrmReader.Close()
 End Sub
End Module
```

The SqlXmlCommand can also return data to a StreamReader instance. It is designed to read forward efficiently through an XML document. To use it, you must define a StreamReader object and instantiate it using the ExecuteStream method of the SqlXmlCommand class. Then you need to instantiate a FileStream object that points to the file that you want to create. You also need an instance of the StreamWriter object that will allow you to write in a file through the FileStream object. You will glue everything together when you read the content of the StreamReader object and write it into the StreamWriter object:

```
objStrmWriter.WriteLine(objStrmReader.ReadToEnd)
```

Naturally, the SQL query used in CommandText is not limited to the Select statement. It could also be a stored procedure that returns a result set using a For XML clause (in a Select statement):

```
ALTER   PROCEDURE prListEquipment2_xml
AS
Select EquipmentId, Make, Model, EqType
From Equipment inner join EqType
On Equipment.EqTypeId = EqType.EqTypeId
For XML Auto
```

To use it, add an Execute statement in the CommandText string:

```
objSqlXmlCmd.CommandType = SqlXmlCommandType.SQL
objSqlXmlCmd.CommandText = "exec prListEquipment2_xml"
```

If you want to add the root element to the result, you can use the RootTag property:

```
objSqlXmlCmd.RootTag = "CompleteInventory"
```

When the root tag is specified, SqlXmlCommand will also add a processing instruction that defines the XML version and the encoding of the document. The default encoding is UTF-8. If you want to change it, you must use the OutputEncoding property (alternatives are Unicode and ASCII):

```
objSqlXmlCmd.OutputEncoding = "Unicode"
```

To add a default namespace, use the Namespaces property:

```
objSqlXmlCmd.Namespaces = "xmlns:inv = ""www.TrigonBlue.com/Xml/Inv"""
```

NOTE

Since double quotes (") have special meaning in Visual Basic .NET, you must double them so that they appear in the final XML string.

Templates   You can also use an inline template as a query. You need to specify CommandType as SqlXmlCommandType.Template and provide a string with the template as a CommandText:

```
objSqlXmlCmd.CommandType = SqlXmlCommandType.Template
objSqlXmlCmd.CommandText = _
& "<root xmlns:sql='urn:schemas-microsoft-com:xml-sql'>" & vbCrLf _
& "    <sql:query>" & vbCrLf _
& "        select * from Equipment for XML auto, elements"  & vbCrLf _
& "    </sql:query>"  & vbCrLf _
& " </root>"
```

The template can also be in an external file, in which case you must use SqlXmlCommandType.TemplateFile constant and set CommandText to the location of the template file:

```
objSqlXmlCmd.CommandType = SqlXmlCommandType.TemplateFile
objSqlXmlCmd.CommandText = "ListEquipment.xml"
```

The template can also be a stream, in which case you need to assign the template to the CommandStream property (instead of CommandText). You also need to set CommandType to SqlXmlCommandType.Template, even if the origin of the stream is a file, as in this case:

```
Dim objStrmTemplate As New FileStream ("ListEquipment.xml", _
                          FileMode.Open, FileAccess.Read)
objSqlXmlCmd.CommandType = SqlXmlCommandType.Template
objSqlXmlCmd.CommandStream = objStrmTemplate
```

XSL Transformation   SqlXmlCommand calls can also transform XML documents using XSL files. In the following example, the prListEquipment2_xml stored procedure returns an XML stream that will be converted using Equipment.xsl into an HTML stream to be saved in the Inventory.htm file:

```
Imports System
Imports System.IO
Imports Microsoft.Data.SqlXml 'The SQLXML managed classes

Module Module1
 Sub Main()
    'Instantiate the SqlXmlCommand object and the connection
     Dim objSqlXmlCmd As New SqlXmlCommand("Provider=SQLOLEDB;" _
```

```
            & "Server=(local)\SS2K;Database=Asset;" _
            & "Integrated Security=SSPI")
      'Set type of query
      objSqlXmlCmd.CommandType = SqlXmlCommandType.Sql
      'Set the query
      objSqlXmlCmd.CommandText = "exec prListEquipment2_xml"
      objSqlXmlCmd.RootTag = "Root"
      objSqlXmlCmd.XslPath = "Equipment.xsl"

      'execute into a stream reader
      Dim objStrmReader As New StreamReader(objSqlXmlCmd.ExecuteStream())
     'prepare destination file
      Dim objResult As New FileStream("Inventory.htm", FileMode.Create)
      Dim objStrmWriter As New StreamWriter(objResult)

      'write result into destination file
      objStrmWriter.WriteLine(objStrmReader.ReadToEnd)

      objStrmWriter.Close()
      objResult.Close()
      objStrmReader.Close()

  End Sub
End Module
```

XML Views and XPath Queries   You can also use XPath queries against XML views (or annotated schemas) to retrieve data from the database. You need to specify CommandType as XPath, point to the schema file, and specify the XPath query, before you execute the SqlXmlCommand object in the usual manner:

```
'Set type of query
objSqlXmlCmd.CommandType = SqlXmlCommandType.XPath
'Point to schema file
objSqlXmlCmd.SchemaPath = "InvSchema.xsd"
'Set the XPath query
objSqlXmlCmd.CommandText = "/ROOT/Inventory[@StatusId=5]"

objSqlXmlCmd.RootTag = "DefectiveInventory"
```

Retrieving XML Data Using the SqlXmlParameter Class

Relational queries (including stored procedures) and templates can have parameters. The SqlXmlParameter class is used to pass values, for which the user has been prompted, to SqlXmlCommand query objects.

In the following example, a T-SQL statement (in this case, a stored procedure) is prepared for execution with ? as a placeholder for the parameter. A SqlXmlParameter object is declared, instantiated (in the context of a SqlXmlCommand object), and named. After the user is prompted, the value is assigned to the parameter, and finally the query is executed:

```
'SqlXml_Param
Imports System
Imports System.IO
Imports Microsoft.Data.SqlXml 'The SQLXML managed classes

Module Module1
    Sub Main()

    'Instantiate the SqlXmlCommand object and the connection
    Dim objSqlXmlCmd As New SqlXmlCommand("Provider=SQLOLEDB;" _
        & "Server=(local)\SS2K;Database=Asset;" _
        & "Integrated Security=SSPI")
    'Set type of query
    objSqlXmlCmd.CommandType = SqlXmlCommandType.Sql
    'Set the parameterized query
    objSqlXmlCmd.CommandText = "exec prGetEquipment_xml ?"
    'define parameter
    Dim objParam As SqlXmlParameter
    'instantiate parameter
    objParam = objSqlXmlCmd.CreateParameter()
    objParam.Name = "EquipmentId"

    'prompt for the value
    Console.WriteLine("Equipment Id:")
    objParam.Value = Console.Read()

    'Execute the query and retrieve result as a stream
    Dim objResult As MemoryStream = objSqlXmlCmd.ExecuteStream()
    'Write result to the console
    Dim objStreamReader As New StreamReader(objResult)
    Console.Write(objStreamReader.ReadToEnd)
    End Sub
End Module
```

Retrieving DataSet Using the SqlXmlAdapter Class

A DataSet object is very convenient for further processing since many other classes and methods (in other words, data-bound controls) are designed to use it. The following example is a simple Windows application that consists of a form (frmGrid) that contains a grid (gridTable) and a button (btnLoad). When the user clicks btnLoad, the application connects to the database using the SqlXmlCommand, retrieves data in the form of SqlXmlAdapter, fills the data set, and finally passes the data set content to the grid (only one line is needed):

```
'SqlXml2Grid.frmGrid
Imports Microsoft.Data.SqlXml 'The SQLXML managed classes

Public Class frmGrid
    Inherits System.Windows.Forms.Form
#Region " Windows Form Designer generated code "
...
#End Region
    Private Sub btnLoad_Click(ByVal sender As System.Object, _
          ByVal e As System.EventArgs) Handles btnLoad.Click

Dim objSqlXmlCmd As New SqlXmlCommand("Provider=SQLOLEDB;" _
        & "Server=(local)\SS2K;Database=Asset;" _
        & "Integrated Security=SSPI")
        objSqlXmlCmd.CommandType = SqlXmlCommandType.Sql
        objSqlXmlCmd.CommandText = "exec prListEquipment2_xml"
        objSqlXmlCmd.RootTag = "Root"

        Dim objAdpt = New SqlXmlAdapter(objSqlXmlCmd)
        Dim objDs = New DataSet()
        objAdpt.Fill(objDs)

        'load it to grid
        gridTable.DataSource = objDs.Tables(0).DefaultView
    End Sub
End Class
```

NOTE

Typically, there is no need to use SQLXML to retrieve a data set. You can use standard methods like ADO.NET to achieve that. SqlXmlAdapter is more important in cases in which a stored procedure or template already has a For XML clause (or when you want to use it to modify data, but that is a topic for the next chapter).

Retrieving XML Data Using ADO.NET

Developers are able to retrieve data in XML format without SQLXML. They can use standard relational access methods based on ADO.NET.

Using SqlCommand

The SqlCommand class is used in ADO.NET to execute SQL commands against a database server. To use it against SQL Server, you must include a reference to System.Data.SqlClient in the application. You need an instantiated SqlConnection object and SQL query to define the SqlCommand object.

The SqlCommand class's ExecuteXmlReader method can be used to pass the result of SQL queries with a For XML clause to an instance of the XmlTextReader object. In the following example, the XmlTextReader object is used to write the XML result through a FileStream object to a file:

```
'SqlCommand_Simple
Imports System
Imports System.IO
Imports System.Data
Imports System.Data.SqlClient
Imports System.Xml

Module Module1

  Sub Main()
    'Instantiate the SqlCommand object and the connection
    Dim objConn As New SqlConnection("Server=(local)\SS2K;" _
        & "Database=Asset;" _
        & "Integrated Security=SSPI")
    objConn.Open()
    Dim objCmd As New SqlCommand( _
    "SELECT * FROM Inventory FOR XML AUTO", objConn)

    'read the result as XML
    Dim objXMLReader As XmlTextReader
    objXMLReader = objCmd.ExecuteXmlReader()

    'prepare the destination file
    Dim objFile As New FileStream("Inventory.xml", FileMode.Create)
    Dim objStrmWriter As New StreamWriter(objFile)
```

```
'skip processing instructions, etc.
objXMLReader.MoveToContent()
'write xml line by line to file
While objXMLReader.IsStartElement
  objStrmWriter.WriteLine(objXMLReader.ReadOuterXml)
End While

objStrmWriter.Close()
objFile.Close()
objXMLReader.Close()
objConn.Close()

 End Sub
End Module
```

Using DataSet Objects

DataSet objects from ADO.NET are typically used in .NET applications to access the result of a relational query. One of their features is also to *serialize the result as XML* using the WriteXML method. The query that the DataSet object is based upon does not need to contain a For XML clause.

In the following example, a DataSet object is created using SqlConnection, SqlCommand, and SqlAdapter object instances. The WriteXML method is then used to write XML data without schema in a file to a FileStream object.

```
'SqlCommand_DataSet2XML
Imports System
Imports System.IO
Imports System.Data
Imports System.Data.SqlClient
Imports System.Xml

Module Module1

    Sub Main()
        'Instantiate the SqlCommand object and the connection
        Dim objConn As New SqlConnection("Server=(local)\SS2K;" _
            & "Database=Asset;" _
            & "Integrated Security=SSPI")
        objConn.Open()
        Dim objCmd As New SqlCommand( _
        "SELECT * FROM Inventory", objConn)
```

```
Dim objAdpt As New SqlDataAdapter(objCmd)
Dim objDs As New DataSet("CompleteInventory")
objAdpt.Fill(objDs, "Inventory")

'prepare the destination file
Dim objFile As New FileStream("Inventory.xml", FileMode.Create)
Dim objStrmWriter As New StreamWriter(objFile)

'write dataset
objDs.WriteXml(objStrmWriter, XmlWriteMode.IgnoreSchema)

objStrmWriter.Close()
objFile.Close()
objConn.Close()

End Sub
End Module
```

Client-Side XML Processing

Since SQLXML 2.0, it has been possible to move XML processing from SQL
Server to the client (meaning in this case an application on the client or an object
in the middleware or on the web server). In this scenario (see Figure 14-25), a
client application executes a SQL query that includes a For XML clause. The
SQLXMLOLEDB provider strips the For XML clause out and sends the rest of
the query down the line. SQLOLEDB then passes the SQL query to SQL Server.
After execution, SQL Server returns a result set. SQLOLEDB passes the recordset
to the SQLXMLOLEDB provider, which performs the conversion to an XML
document based on the For XML clause and returns the XML response to the caller.

Client-side processing is important in the following scenarios:

▶ To move processing from SQL Server to a middleware component or web server

▶ To reduce network traffic (an XML response is large, because it contains metadata)

▶ To use SQLXML against SQL Server 7.0

▶ To access existing stored procedures and queries that do not contain a For
  XML clause

Server-side XML processing

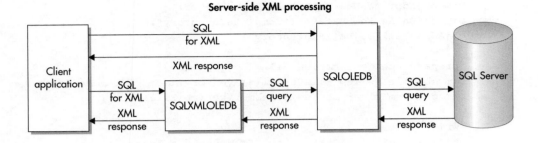

Client-side XML processing

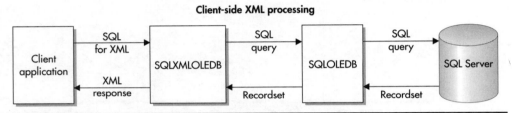

Figure 14-25 *Server-side vs. client-side XML processing*

Using URL Queries

The easiest way to force client-side XML conversion is to set the Run On The Client option for the virtual directory in the IIS Virtual Directory Management for SQLXML tool (see Figure 14-26).

Using Templates

The result of a query referenced in a template will be converted to XML data on the client if you add a `client-side-xml` attribute to the template and set the value to `"1"`:

```
<root xmlns:sql='urn:schemas-microsoft-com:xml-sql'
     client-side-xml = "1">
  <sql:query>
     select * from Equipment for XML auto, elements
  </sql:query>
</root>
```

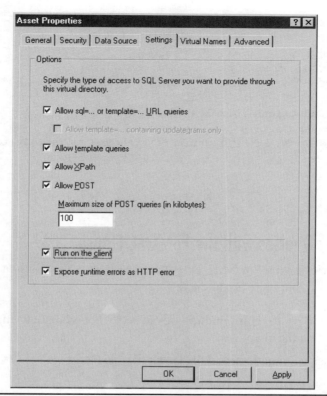

Figure 14-26   *Setting the Run On The Client option for the virtual directory*

Using SQLXML Managed Classes

You can force a .NET application that is using SQLXML managed class to access database information to process record set to XML on the client side if you set the ClientSideXml property of the SqlXmlCommand managed class to True:

```
Imports System
Imports System.IO
Imports Microsoft.Data.SqlXml 'The SQLXML managed classes

Module Module1
    Sub Main()
    'Instantiate the SqlXmlCommand object and the connection
    Dim objSqlXmlCmd As New SqlXmlCommand("Provider=SQLOLEDB;" _
```

```
                & "Server=(local)\SS2K;Database=Asset;"_
                & "Integrated Security=SSPI")
        'Set the query
        objSqlXmlCmd.CommandType = SqlXmlCommandType.Sql
        objSqlXmlCmd.CommandText = "SELECT * FROM Inventory FOR XML ROW"
        'convert to XML on the client
        objSqlXmlCmd.ClientSideXml = True
        'write result to file
        Dim objResult As New FileStream("Inventory.xml", FileMode.Create)
        objSqlXmlCmd = objSqlXmlCmd.ExecuteStream(objResult)
        objResult.Close()
        End Sub
End Module
```

Processing of Queries with the For XML Clause

Processing queries with a For XML clause on the client is very similar to processing them on the server, but there are a few differences:

▶ It is illegal to try to return multiple result sets when you are trying to process the queries on the client.

▶ You can use aggregations and the Group By clause:

```
select EquipmentId, Count(*) [Count]
from dbo.Inventory
Group By EquipmentId
for XML ROW
```

▶ All sql_variant fields are converted to Unicode strings: their base types are ignored.

▶ If you try to process a query that has a For XML Auto clause on the client, SQL Server will process it on the server. When you want to process the query on the client, use the For XML Nested clause instead. It is very similar to For XML Auto.

The For XML Nested clause, although very similar to For XML Auto, has some important differences:

▶ You can add it to a string that executes a stored procedure:

```
exec prListEquipment2
FOR XML Nested
```

▶ The resulting XML fragment will have element names based on base tables, not on their aliases or view names.

▶ Keywords behind For XML Nested do not have to be separated with commas. It is perfectly legal to separate them with spaces only:

```
select * from dbo.Inventory
FOR XML NESTED XMLDATA ELEMENTS
```

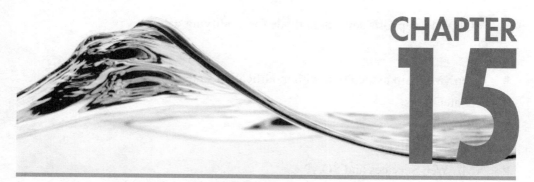

CHAPTER
15

Modifying Databases Using SQLXML

QLXML supports several methods for modifying data:

- ▶ OpenXML(), in association with modification statements
- ▶ UpdateGrams
- ▶ DiffGrams
- ▶ SQLXML BulkLoad
- ▶ XML Web Services and SOAP

OpenXML()

OpenXML() is a new function in Transact-SQL. It provides access to an in-memory rowset similar to a view or a table. Since it is a rowset provider, OpenXML() can be used in Transact-SQL statements in any place where a table, view, or rowset provider such as OpenRowset() can be used. It is a replacement for DOM that Transact-SQL developers can use to parse, access, and return the content of an XML document. By itself, it cannot modify data, but it can be part of a modification statement.

Document Preparation

Before an XML document can be accessed using OpenXML(), the document must be loaded into memory using sp_xml_preparedocument. This stored procedure has the following syntax:

```
exec sp_xml_preparedocument hdoc OUTPUT
                        [, xmltext]
                        [, xpath_namespaces]
```

The stored procedure reads the XML document provided in *xmltext*, parses the document using the MSXML parser, and places the document into an in-memory structure that is ready for use with the OpenXML() statement. This structure is a tree that contains assorted nodes such as elements, attributes, comments, and text. The stored procedure returns a handle for the XML document *hdoc* that OpenXML() can use to access the information, and that sp_xml_removedocument uses to remove the document from memory.

The *xmltext* parameter accepts any type of character data (`char`, `varchar`, `nchar`, `nvarchar`, `text`, or `ntext`).

xpath_namespaces is an optional parameter that is used to provide a namespace declaration for row and column expressions in OpenXML(). The default value is as follows:

```
<root xmlns:mp="urn:schemas-microsoft-com:xml-metaprop">
```

The stored procedure returns a non-zero value when SQL Server cannot prepare the document. You should use this return value to perform error handling in the usual manner.

In the following example an XML document is loaded in memory and its handle is recorded in the @intDoc variable:

```
DECLARE @intDoc int
DECLARE @chvXMLDoc varchar(8000)
-- sample XML document
SET @chvXMLDoc ='
<root>
  <Equipment EquipmentID="1" Make="Toshiba" Model="Portege 7020CT">
    <Inventory InventoryID="5" StatusID="1" EquipmentID="1"/>
    <Inventory InventoryID="12" StatusID="1" EquipmentID="1"/>
  </Equipment>
</root>'
--Load the XML document into memory.
EXEC sp_xml_preparedocument @intDoc OUTPUT, @chvXMLDoc
```

Closing the Document

As soon as it is no longer used, the document should be removed from memory using sp_xml_removedocument. This stored procedure uses very simple syntax:

```
exec sp_xml_removedocument hdoc
```

The *hdoc* parameter is a handle for a loaded XML document:

```
remove the XML document from memory
EXEC sp_xml_removedocument @intDoc
```

NOTE

The memory is not released until sp_xml_removedocument is called, and hence it should be called as soon as possible.

Retrieving the XML Information

OpenXML() is a rowset provider that provides access to the internal tree memory structure that contains the information in an XML document. It has the following syntax:

```
OpenXML(hdoc, rowpattern, flags)
[With (SchemaDeclaration | TableVariable)]
```

hdoc is a handle that points to the tree containing the XML data. *rowpattern* is the XPath string used to identify nodes that need to be processed. *flags* is an optional parameter that controls the way that data from the XML document is mapped to the rowset and how data is to be copied to the overflow property (I will explain this a little later).

SchemaDeclaration is a declaration of the structure in which data will be returned. Alternatively, it is possible to use the name of a table variable (*TableVariable*) instead. The rowset will be formed using the structure of the table variable. The *SchemaDeclaration* can be composed using the following syntax:

```
ColName ColType [ColPattern | MetaProperty]
[, ColName ColType [ColPattern | MetaProperty]...]
```

ColName is the name and *ColType* is the data type of the column. This structure is very similar to the table structure of the Create Table statement. *ColPattern* is an optional parameter that defines how a column is to be mapped to the XML node. A *MetaProperty* is specified to extract metadata such as data types, node types, and namespace information.

Finally, take a look at an example that uses all these constructs:

```
DECLARE @intDoc int
DECLARE @chvXMLDoc varchar(8000)
-- sample XML document
SET @chvXMLDoc =
'<root>
  <Equipment EquipmentID="1" Make="Toshiba" Model="Portege 7020CT">
   <Inventory InventoryID="5" StatusID="1" EquipmentID="1"/>
   <Inventory InventoryID="12" StatusID="1" EquipmentID="1"/>
  </Equipment>
  <Equipment EquipmentID="2" Make="Sony" Model="Trinitron 17XE"/>
  <Equipment EquipmentID="4" Make="HP" Model="LaserJet 4"/>
  <Equipment EquipmentID="5" Make="Bang &amp; Olafson" Model="V4000">
   <Inventory InventoryID="8" StatusID="1" EquipmentID="5"/>
  </Equipment>
```

```
  <Equipment EquipmentID="6" Make="NEC" Model="V90">
    <Inventory InventoryID="6" StatusID="2" EquipmentID="6"/>
  </Equipment>
</root>'
--Load the XML document into memory.
EXEC sp_xml_preparedocument @intDoc OUTPUT, @chvXMLDoc

-- SELECT statement using OPENXML rowset provider
SELECT *
FROM    OPENXML (@intDoc, '/root/Equipment/Inventory', 8)
        WITH    (InventoryID int '@InventoryID',
                 StatusID int '@StatusID',
                 Make varchar(25) '../@Make',
                 Model varchar(25) '../@Model',
                 Comment ntext '@mp:xmltext')
-- remove the XML document from memory
EXEC sp_xml_removedocument @intDoc
```

The result is shown in Figure 15-1.

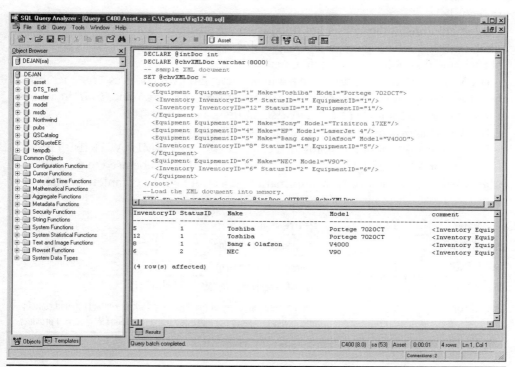

Figure 15-1   *Use of OpenXML() as a rowset provider*

In the preceding example, the OpenXML() rowset provider is used in a Select statement:

```
SELECT    *
From Openxml (@intDoc, '/root/Equipment/Inventory', 8)
    WITH      (InventoryID int '@InventoryID',
              StatusID int '@StatusID',
              Make varchar(25) '../@Make',
              Model varchar(25) '../@Model',
              Comment ntext '@mp:xmltext')
```

The *rowpattern* parameter specifies that information will be extracted (mostly) from Inventory nodes (`'/root/Equipment/Inventory'`).

The third parameter of the OpenXML() clause sets the way in which the overflow property is to be filled. In the preceding example, the last column (Comment) was filled with metadata provided by the XML parser (since the column is associated with the `@mp:xmltext` attribute). Because the third parameter of OpenXML() is set to 8 (the XML_NOCOPY constant), the overflow property does not contain the nodes that are extracted into the rowset. Only nodes that are not included in the rowset are recorded.

Other columns in the rowset are filled from the attribute data. If you remember XPath (see the "XPath" section in Chapter 13), the @ character is used as an abbreviation that points to attribute nodes.

The Make and Model columns are not in the same group of nodes as `InventoryID` and `StatusId`. Since they are attributes of the `Equipment` node, *ColPattern* has to refer to the parent node (`'../@Model'`) first.

Table 15-1 shows a list of possible values of the *flags* parameter.

XML_NOCOPY could be combined (logical OR) with XML_ATTRIBUTES (1 + 8 = 9) or XML_ELEMENTS (2 + 8 = 10). This flag can be used to generate either a string with the overflow information or a string with a complete branch of

Mnemonic	Value	Description
XML_ATTRIBUTES	1	Attribute-centric mapping
XML_ELEMENTS	2	Element-centric mapping
XML_DEFAULT	0	Default—equivalent to XML_ATTRIBUTES (1)
XML_NOCOPY	8	Overflow metaproperty of the document (@mp:xmltext) should contain only nodes that were not extracted using the OpenXML() rowset provider

Table 15-1 *Values of the* flags *Parameter of OpenXML()*

the XML document. The following example extracts the branch of the XML document/tree that describes a node with EquipmentID set to 1:

```
Select *
From Openxml (@intDoc, '/root/Equipment', 2)
      With      (EquipmentID int '@EquipmentID',
                 Branch ntext '@mp:xmltext')
Where EquipmentId = 1
```

SQL Server 2000 returns the following:

```
EquipmentID Branch
----------- ----------------------------------------------------------
1             <Equipment EquipmentID="1" Make="Toshiba"
Model="Portege 7020CT">
   <Inventory InventoryID="5" StatusID="1" EquipmentID="1"/>
   <Inventory InventoryID="12" StatusID="1" EquipmentID="1"/>
</Equipment>
(1 row(s) affected)
```

XML_ATTRIBUTES and XML_ELEMENTS can also be combined. The first level of (selected) nodes are mapped as attributes and others are mapped as elements.

Metaproperties in OpenXML()

After the parser loads the XML document into memory, SQL Server allows the OpenXML() rowset to access a set of properties that describe attributes of the data. These properties are defined in a special namespace (`urn:schemas-microsoft -com:xml-metaprop`). Table 15-2 shows the list of possible values and their meanings.

Metaproperty	Description
@@mp:id	System-generated identifier. It could be used as a unique identifier on the level of the document (until the document is reparsed).
@@mp:localnamed	Name of the current node.
@@mp:namespaceuri	Namespace URI for the current element.
@@mp:Prefix	Prefix of the namespace for the current element.

Table 15-2   *Metaproperties in OpenXML()*

Metaproperty	Description
@@mp:xmltext	String containing the XML branch of the current element, its attributes, and subelements. It could be set not to contain nodes that have already been read by other columns of the OpenXML() provider.
@@mp:prev	ID of the previous sibling of the node.
@@mp:parented	ID of the parent node (equivalent of ../@mp:parentid).
@@mp:parentlocalname	Name of the parent node (equivalent of ../@mp:localname).
@@mp:parentnamespaceuri	Namespace of the parent node (equivalent of ../@mp:namespaceuri).
@@mp:parentprefix	Prefix of the namespace of the parent node (equivalent of ../@mp:prefix).

Table 15-2 *Metaproperties in OpenXML() (continued)*

The following example and Figure 15-2 demonstrate the use of metaproperties.

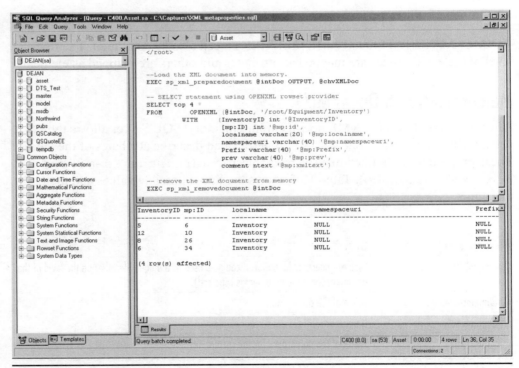

Figure 15-2 *Use of metaproperties in OpenXML()*

```
DECLARE @intDoc int
DECLARE @chvXMLDoc varchar(8000)
-- sample XML document
SET @chvXMLDoc ='
<root>
  <Equipment EquipmentID="1" Make="Toshiba" Model="Portege 7020CT">
   <Inventory InventoryID="5" StatusID="1" EquipmentID="1"/>
   <Inventory InventoryID="12" StatusID="1" EquipmentID="1"/>
  </Equipment>
  <Equipment EquipmentID="2" Make="Sony" Model="Trinitron 17XE"/>
  <Equipment EquipmentID="4" Make="HP" Model="LaserJet 4"/>
  <Equipment EquipmentID="5" Make="Bang &amp; Olafson" Model="V4000">
   <Inventory InventoryID="8" StatusID="1" EquipmentID="5"/>
  </Equipment>
  <Equipment EquipmentID="6" Make="NEC" Model="V90">
   <Inventory InventoryID="6" StatusID="2" EquipmentID="6"/>
  </Equipment>
</root>
'


--Load the XML document into memory.
EXEC sp_xml_preparedocument @intDoc OUTPUT, @chvXMLDoc

-- SELECT statement using OPENXML rowset provider
SELECT top 4 *
FROM      OPENXML (@intDoc, '/root/Equipment/Inventory')
          WITH      (InventoryID int '@InventoryID',
                     ID int '@mp:id',
                     localname varchar(20) '@mp:localname',
                     namespaceuri varchar(40) '@mp:namespaceuri',
                     Prefix varchar(40) '@mp:Prefix',
                     prev varchar(40) '@mp:prev',
                     comment ntext '@mp:xmltext')

-- remove the XML document from memory
EXEC sp_xml_removedocument @intDoc
```

What if an XML Document Is Longer Than 8000 Characters?

You have probably noticed that we used long varchar strings (8000 characters) in
the preceding examples to store XML documents. Naturally, XML documents could

be longer than this arbitrary figure. The trouble is that you cannot define local variables of the `text` data type (and `varchar` is limited to only 8000 characters).

Fortunately, sp_xml_preparedocument and OpenXML() can handle *text* parameters. Instead of using a local variable of the `text` data type, you can use an input parameter of a custom stored procedure as a parameter for sp_xml_preparedocument. The following stored procedure illustrates this method:

```
Alter  Procedure prTestXML
-- Extract Inventory info. from long XML document.
-- Demonstration of usage of text input parameters
-- to parse long XML document.
   @chvXMLDoc text

As
set nocount on

Declare @intErrorCode int,
        @intTransactionCountOnEntry int
        @intDoc int

Select @intErrorCode = @@Error


--Create an internal representation of the XML document.
EXEC sp_xml_preparedocument @intDoc OUTPUT, @chvXMLDoc

-- SELECT statement using OPENXML rowset provider
SELECT     *
FROM       OPENXML (@intDoc, '/root/Equipment/Inventory', 8)
           WITH    (InventoryID int '@InventoryID',
                   StatusID int '@StatusID',
                   Make varchar(25) '../@Make',
                   Model varchar(25) '../@Model',
                   comment ntext '@mp:xmltext')
EXEC sp_xml_removedocument @intDoc
return @intErrorCode
```

Figure 15-3 demonstrates the use of the stored procedure. A large XML document was created by copying and pasting the same set of nodes into the string (XML document) over and over.

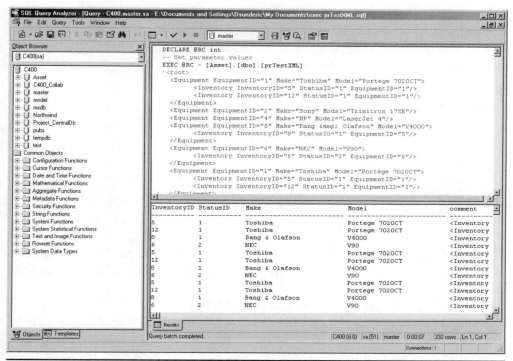

Figure 15-3   *Use of a text input parameter*

UpdateGrams

UpdateGrams are a special type of XML document that allow users to modify tables in SQL Server. They are defined using the urn:schemas-microsoft-com:xml-updategram namespace. The namespace defines three elements: sync, before, and after. These elements allow users to control how data is processed in SQL Server. The sync element initiates a transaction; everything within one sync element is treated as a single transaction. The before element specifies how the data looked before the change. The after element specifies how the data should look after the change. These elements traditionally use the updg: namespace prefix, but you can change this convention in the namespace declaration.

It is probably easier to demonstrate the features of UpdateGrams in an example. UpdateGrams that update existing data must contain both before and after elements. The `before` element must contain the data that will allow SQL Server to identify the record(s) to be changed. The `after` element specifies the new values. The table is identified by the name of the element and columns are identified by attributes of the element:

```
<root xmlns:updg="urn:schemas-microsoft-com:xml-updategram">
  <updg:sync>
    <updg:before>
      <Contact ContactId = "1"/>
    </updg:before>
    <updg:after>
      <Contact ContactId = "1" Phone = "(416) 123-1234"/>
    </updg:after>
  </updg:sync>
</root>
```

This UpdateGram sets a new phone number for any record that has a ContactId value of 1. Naturally, to be properly processed, the UpdateGram needs the namespace that is defined in the `root` element.

To delete a record, an UpdateGram needs only the `before` element. In the following example, the Contact table will delete any record with a ContactId value of 1212:

```
<root xmlns:updg="urn:schemas-microsoft-com:xml-updategram">
  <updg:sync>
    <updg:before>
      <Contact ContactId = "1212"/>
    </updg:before>
  </updg:sync>
</root>
```

To insert a record into a table, only the `after` element is needed:

```
<root xmlns:updg="urn:schemas-microsoft-com:xml-updategram">
  <updg:sync>
    <updg:after>
      <Contact FirstName = "Tom" LastName = "Jones" OrgUnitId = "2"/>
    </updg:after>
  </updg:sync>
</root>
```

The SQLISAPI driver converts the UpdateGram internally to a Transact-SQL batch, which is processed as usual. In the previous example, since the ContactID is the identity field, we do not need to specify its value.

Executing UpdateGrams

The UpdateGrams can be posted to the server using any of the means already described. I will first describe how to do it using HTTP, and then programmatically using SqlXml managed classes.

Executing UpdateGrams Through a URL

The least secure way to execute an UpdateGram is to pass it as a part of a URL. To execute them, XML files with UpdateGrams must be in the folder that is associated with the virtual name of the template type or you must specify the template as a part of the URL:

```
http://localhost/asset?template=<root xmlns:updg="urn:schemas
-microsoft-com:xml-updategram">
  <updg:sync>
    <updg:after>
      <Contact FirstName = "Tom" LastName = "Jones" OrgUnitId = "2"/>
    </updg:after>
  </updg:sync>
</root>
```

If the UpdateGram is successful, SQL Server will return:

```
<root xmlns:updg="urn:schemas-microsoft-com:xml-updategram" />
```

NOTE

As you can imagine, this is very insecure. Anybody can connect to the database and do anything they want.

If the previous UpdateGram is saved as InsertContactUpdategram.xml in the template folder, it can be executed using the following URL:

```
http://localhost/asset/template/InsertContactUpdategram.xml
```

If the UpdateGram is successful, the browser will display an empty screen.

Executing UpdateGrams Using SqlXml Managed Classes

You can execute UpdateGrams through the SqlXmlCommand object. In this case, you need to set the CommandType to SqlXmlCommandType.UpdateGram and pass the text of the UpdateGram to the CommandText property. Since there is no result to be returned, you should use the ExecuteNonQuery() method:

```
'SqlXml_UpdateGram
Imports System
Imports System.IO
Imports Microsoft.Data.SqlXml 'The SQLXML namespace

Module Module1
    Sub Main()

        'Instantiate the SqlXmlCommand object and the connection
        Dim objSqlXmlCmd As New SqlXmlCommand("Provider=SQLOLEDB;" _
            & "Server=(local)\SS2K;Database=Asset;" _
            & "Integrated Security=SSPI")

        'Set type of query
        objSqlXmlCmd.CommandType = SqlXmlCommandType.UpdateGram

        'Query is UpdateGram
        objSqlXmlCmd.CommandText = "<root " _
    + " xmlns:updg=""urn:schemas-microsoft-com:xml-updategram"">" _
      + "<updg:sync>" _
        + "<updg:after>" _
        + "<Contact FirstName = ""Tom"" LastName = ""Jones"" OrgUnitId = ""2""/>" _
        + "</updg:after>" _
      + "</updg:sync>" _
    + "</root>"

        'Execute the UpdateGram
        objSqlXmlCmd.ExecuteNonQuery()

        'since there is no result to return
        Console.Write("Completed.")
    End Sub
End Module
```

Since both Visual Basic .NET and XML use double quotes (") as string delimiters, you have to use double pairs of double quotes ("") or use single quotes as attribute delimiters in your string literal.

If you need to read the result stream and return it to the screen, you can use the ExecuteStream() method instead of ExecuteNonQuery(). As in the case of execution through HTTP, SQL Server returns:

```
<root xmlns:updg="urn:schemas-microsoft-com:xml-updategram" />
```

Element-centric vs. Attribute-centric UpdateGram

So far, we have been using attribute-centric UpdateGrams to demonstrate its features—
in other words, columns have been mapped using XML attributes. If it is more
convenient, you can use element-centric UpdateGrams instead:

```
<root xmlns:updg="urn:schemas-microsoft-com:xml-updategram">
  <updg:sync>
    <updg:before>
      <Contact>
        <ContactId>
         1
        </ContactId>
      </Contact>
    </updg:before>
    <updg:after>
      <Contact>
        <ContactId>
           1
        </ContactId>
        <Phone>
           (416) 123-1234
        </Phone>
      </Contact>
    </updg:after>
  </updg:sync>
</root>
```

UpdateGrams with Parameters

There is not much sense in posting a static UpdateGram to SQL Server. UpdateGrams
really become useful only when you use parameters. The parameters must be declared
using the updg:param element, after which they can be used in before and
after elements:

```
<ROOT xmlns:updg="urn:schemas-microsoft-com:xml-updategram">
<updg:header>
  <updg:param name="ContactId"/>
  <updg:param name="Phone" />
</updg:header>
  <updg:sync>
    <updg:before>
```

```
        <Contact ContactId = "$ContactId"/>
    </updg:before>
    <updg:after>
      <Contact ContactId = "$ContactId" Phone = "$Phone"/>
    </updg:after>
  </updg:sync>
</ROOT>
```

If the preceding UpdateGram is saved as UpdateGramPhone.xml in the template folder, it can be executed using the following URL:

```
http://localhost/asset/template/UpdateGramPhone.xml?ContactId=1&
Phone=416-123-1217
```

Alternatively, you can execute it programmatically:

```
'SqlXml_UpdategramParam
Imports System
Imports System.IO
Imports Microsoft.Data.SqlXml 'The SQLXML namespace

Module Module1
    Sub Main()

    'Instantiate the SqlXmlCommand object and the connection
    Dim objSqlXmlCmd As New SqlXmlCommand("Provider=SQLOLEDB;" _
        & "Server=(local)\SS2K;Database=Asset;" _
        & "Integrated Security=SSPI")
    'Set type of query
    objSqlXmlCmd.CommandType = SqlXmlCommandType.UpdateGram
    'Set the parameterized query
    objSqlXmlCmd.CommandText = "<ROOT " _
    + " xmlns:updg=""urn:schemas-microsoft-com:xml-updategram"" > " _
    + "<updg:header>" _
    + "   <updg:param name=""ContactId""/>" _
    + "   <updg:param name=""Phone"" />" _
    + "</updg:header>" _
    + "  <updg:sync>" _
    + "    <updg:before>" _
    + "      <Contact ContactId = ""$ContactId""/>" _
    + "    </updg:before>" _
    + "    <updg:after>" _
    + "      <Contact ContactId = ""$ContactId"" Phone = ""$Phone""/>"_
    + "    </updg:after>" _
```

```
   + "   </updg:sync>" _
   + "</ROOT>"
   'define parameters
   Dim objParam1 As SqlXmlParameter
   Dim objParam2 As SqlXmlParameter
   'instantiate parameter
   objParam1 = objSqlXmlCmd.CreateParameter()
   objParam1.Name = "ContactId"
   objParam2 = objSqlXmlCmd.CreateParameter()
   objParam2.Name = "Phone"

   'prompt for the value
   Console.Write("Contact1 Id: ")
   objParam1.Value = Console.ReadLine()
   Console.Write("Phone: ")
   objParam2.Value = Console.ReadLine()

   'Execute the query and retrieve result as a stream
   Dim objResult As MemoryStream = objSqlXmlCmd.ExecuteStream()
   'Write result to the console
   Dim objStreamReader As New StreamReader(objResult)
   Console.Write(objStreamReader.ReadToEnd)

   End Sub
End Module
```

In this case, as confirmation that the update has been successful, the program displays

```
<root xmlns:updg="urn:schemas-microsoft-com:xml-updategram" />
```

Setting Parameters to Null

SQL Server designers have developed a special method for setting the values of UpdateGram parameters to null: the UpdateGram template must contain the `nullvalue` attribute of the `updg:header` element, which must be set to the string that will be used in the URL as an alias for null:

```
<ROOT xmlns:updg="urn:schemas-microsoft-com:xml-updategram">
<updg:header nullvalue="isnull">
  <updg:param name="ContactId"/>
  <updg:param name="Phone" />
</updg:header>
```

```
<updg:sync>
  <updg:before>
    <Contact ContactId = "$ContactId"/>
  </updg:before>
  <updg:after>
    <Contact ContactId = "$ContactId" Phone = "$Phone"/>
  </updg:after>
</updg:sync>
</ROOT>
```

If you save the UpdateGram as UpdateGramPhone.xml in the template folder, you will be able to set the value of a parameter to null using a URL like the following:

```
http://localhost/asset/template/UpdateGramPhone.xml?
ContactId=1&Phone=isnull
```

Returning Identifier Values

One of the basic operations that developers need to be able to do is to insert a record with a unique identifier into the database. Earlier chapters reviewed Transact-SQL methods for returning an identity value to the caller and for inserting a global unique identifier. All of those examples were based on the use of stored procedures. Unfortunately, UpdateGrams cannot access stored procedures. However, SQL Server's designers did not forget this requirement.

Identity Values

Two attributes are used to process identity values—updg:at-identity and updg:returnid. The updg:at-identity attribute is used to name and capture the value that will be inserted in the Identity column. The captured value can be used in other places in the UpdateGram or be returned to the caller using the updg:returnid attribute. You just have to be very careful not to use a name that you might later try to insert as a field value.

In the following example, the identity value obtained from the Order record is first named "x" and then passed to the Foreign Key column OrderId in the OrderItem record:

```
<ROOT xmlns:updg="urn:schemas-microsoft-com:xml-updategram">
 <updg:sync>
  <updg:before>
  </updg:before>
  <updg:after updg:returnid="x">
```

```
       <_x005B_Order_x005D_   updg:at-identity="x"
                                RequestedById = "1"
                                TargetDate = "1/1/2004"
                                DestinationLocationId = "10"
                                RequestedById = "1"
                                OrderTypeId = "3"
                                OrderStatusId = "1"
                                OrderDate = "11/3/2004" />
      <OrderItem OrderID="x"
            InventoryId="90"
            EquipmentId="10"
            Quantity="1"
            Note="B123112" />
  </updg:after>
 </updg:sync>
</ROOT>
```

If you need to return the identifier to the calling application to do some additional processing, you should use the updg:returnid attribute. If you add it to the updg:after element, the calling application will receive a response in the form of an XML document with the identity value:

```
<ROOT xmlns:updg="urn:schemas-microsoft-com:xml-updategram">
  <returnid>
    <x>11091</x>
  </returnid>
</ROOT>
```

It is possible to process more than one set of records—in the preceding example, more than one order is processed. Each identity value would need to be named differently. The updg:returnid attribute needs to contain a list of all identity value names (separated by spaces) that will be returned to the caller:

```
  <updg:after updg:returnid="x y" >
   <_x005B_Order_x005D_   updg:at-identity="x"
 ...
      <Order_x0020_Details OrderID="x"
 ...
   <_x005B_Order_x005D_   updg:at-identity="y"
 ...
      <Order_x0020_Details OrderID="y"
 ...
```

The result will again be an XML document:

```
<ROOT xmlns:updg="urn:schemas-microsoft-com:xml-updategram">
  <returnid>
    <x>11091</x>
    <y>11092</y>
  </returnid>
</ROOT>
```

Uniqueidentifiers

UpdateGrams can also process uniqueidentifier values. They first need to be initialized and named using the `updg:guid` attribute of the `updg:after` element. Then you can use this attribute to set one or more fields and even return it to the caller. In the following example, the record will be inserted and the GUID returned to the caller:

```
<SessionGuid updg:guid="x" >
```

The caller will receive the GUID inside an XML document:

```
<ROOT xmlns:updg="urn:schemas-microsoft-com:xml-updategram">
  <returnid>
    <x>7111BD1A-7F0B-4CEE-B411-260DADFEFA2A</x>
  </returnid>
</ROOT>
```

TIP

You will be able to save some time if you generate the GUID (in the middleware or client) before you send it to the database.

Special Characters

You have probably noticed in the preceding examples that I encoded some values using `_x`Hex-value`_`. The `Hex-value` stands for a four-digit hexadecimal USC-2 code. For example, the characters [and] are encoded as `_x005B_` and `_x005D_`. You must use such codes for characters that are legal in Transact-SQL, but illegal in UpdateGrams.

UpdateGrams Behind the Scene

You can run SQL Profiler to evaluate the way that UpdateGrams are converted to Transact-SQL code. Here is an example that I have captured:

```
SET XACT_ABORT ON
BEGIN TRAN
DECLARE @eip INT, @r__ int, @e__ int
SET @eip = 0
DECLARE @V1 nvarchar(40);INSERT [Order] (RequestedById, TargetDate,
DestinationLocationId, OrderTypeId, OrderStatusId, OrderDate)
VALUES (N'1', N'1/1/2004', N'10', N'3', N'1', N'11/3/2004');
SELECT @e__ = @@ERROR, @r__ = @@ROWCOUNT
 IF (@e__ != 0 OR @r__ != 1) SET @eip = 1
SELECT @V1 = SCOPE_IDENTITY( );INSERT OrderItem (OrderID, InventoryId,
EquipmentId, Note) VALUES (@V1, N'90', N'4', N'B123112');
SELECT @e__ = @@ERROR, @r__ = @@ROWCOUNT
 IF (@e__ != 0 OR @r__ != 1) SET @eip = 1

select '<returnid>'+ '<x>' + cast(@V1 as varchar(4000))+ '</x>'
+ '</returnid>'
IF (@eip != 0) ROLLBACK ELSE COMMIT
SET XACT_ABORT OFF
```

Optimistic Locking with UpdateGrams

There are two basic ways to solve concurrency problems using optimistic locking
with UpdateGrams:

► By comparing all fields

► By comparing only timestamp fields

In the first scenario, the updg:before element should contain the original
values of all fields. The updg:after element contains only the changed values.
SQL Server performs the update only if the record contains all of the original values
specified in the updg:before element:

```
<root xmlns:updg="urn:schemas-microsoft-com:xml-updategram">
 <updg:sync>
   <updg:before>
     <Contact ContactId="1013" FirstName="Tom"
              LastName="Jones" OrgUnitId="2" Phone = "(416) 123-1217"/>
   </updg:before>
   <updg:after>
     <Contact Phone = "(416) 123-1234"/>
   </updg:after>
 </updg:sync>
</root>
```

The second scenario is based on the use of the timestamp field in the `updg:before` element (along with the key value). Again, the `updg:after` element contains only the changed values. SQL Server performs the update only if the timestamp value matches the one found in the record:

```
<root xmlns:updg="urn:schemas-microsoft-com:xml-updategram">
<updg:sync mapping-schema="UpdategramContact_TS.xsd" >
<updg:before>
   <Contact ContactId = "1013" ts = "0x0000000000001907"/>
</updg:before>
<updg:after>
   <Contact OrgUnitId = "1"/>
</updg:after>
</updg:sync></root>
```

However, timestamp values require special care because they are essentially binary fields, and UpdateGram needs to treat this attribute value as a binary (not a string) value. You must assign the `sql:timestamp` data type to them using a mapping schema. The UpdateGram must reference the schema in the `mapping-schema` attribute of the `updg:synch` element:

```
<?xml version="1.0" encoding="UTF-8" standalone="no"?>
<xsd:schema xmlns:xsd="http://www.w3.org/2001/XMLSchema"
            xmlns:dt="urn:schemas-microsoft-com:datatypes"
            xmlns:sql="urn:schemas-microsoft-com:mapping-schema">
  <xsd:element name="Contact" sql:relation="Contact" type="Contact_type"/>
  <xsd:complexType name="Contact_type">
    <xsd:attribute name="ContactId" type="xsd:int"/>
    <xsd:attribute name="FirstName" type="xsd:string"/>
    <xsd:attribute name="LastName" type="xsd:string"/>
    <xsd:attribute name="Phone" type="xsd:string"/>
    <xsd:attribute name="Fax" type="xsd:string"/>
    <xsd:attribute name="Email" type="xsd:string"/>
    <xsd:attribute name="OrgUnitId" type="xsd:short"/>
    <xsd:attribute name="UserName" type="xsd:string"/>
    <xsd:attribute name="ts" sql:datatype="timestamp" type="xsd:hexBinary"/>
  </xsd:complexType>
</xsd:schema>
```

In cases where the timestamp in UpdateGram matches the timestamp in the record, SQLXML returns the usual confirmation:

```
<root xmlns:updg="urn:schemas-microsoft-com:xml-updategram" />
```

In the case of nonmatching timestamps, you will receive the following error:

```
<root xmlns:updg="urn:schemas-microsoft-com:xml-updategram">
  <?MSSQLError HResult="0x80040e14"
Source="Microsoft OLE DB Provider for SQL Server"
Description="SQLOLEDB Error Description:
Empty update, no updatable rows found Transaction aborted "?>
</root>
```

Unfortunately, the nature of the problem is not clear from this error message. Someone may have changed the record or it could be something more fundamental such as an attempt to update a nonexistent record. It would have been better had the authors of SQLXML used the TSEqual function (described in the section "Optimistic Locking Using Timestamp Values" in Chapter 9).

Multiple Records and Multiple Tables in a Single UpdateGram

You can change multiple records in a single UpdateGram. If multiple records are contained in a single updg:sync element, they will be executed in a single transaction:

```
<root xmlns:updg="urn:schemas-microsoft-com:xml-updategram">
  <updg:sync>
    <updg:before>
      <Contact ContactId="1013" />
      <Contact ContactId="1014" />
    </updg:before>
  </updg:sync>
</root>
```

Alternatively, you can put statements into multiple updg:sync elements and SQL Server will process them in separate transactions:

```
<root xmlns:updg="urn:schemas-microsoft-com:xml-updategram">
  <updg:sync>
    <updg:before>
      <Orders OrderId="1013" />
      <OrderItem OrderId="1013" />
    </updg:before>
  </updg:sync>
  <updg:sync>
    <updg:before>
```

```
      <Orders OrderId="1014" />
      <OrderItem OrderId="1014" />
    </updg:before>
  </updg:sync>
</root>
```

Multiple Insert or Delete operations on the same table in a single transaction are not problematic since all data is in either `updg:before` or `updg:after` element. But when you want to update multiple records in a single transaction, you must first link elements (records) in `updg:before` or `updg:after` elements. It is easy to link them using key values, but you can do so only when keys are not being changed. If you cannot use keys, you can do it using the `updg:id` element:

```
<root xmlns:updg="urn:schemas-microsoft-com:xml-updategram">
  <updg:sync>
    <updg:before>
      <OrderItem ItemId="1013" updg:id = "c1"/>
      <OrderItem ItemId="1014" updg:id = "c2"/>
    </updg:before>
    <updg:after>
      <OrderItem EquipmentId="12" updg:id = "c2"/>
      <OrderItem EquipmentId="16" updg:id = "c1"/>
    </updg:after>
  </updg:sync>
</root>
```

Alternatively, items in the `updg:before` or `updg:after` element can be linked using the `sql:key-fields` annotation in a mapping schema.

TIP

You will not be able to update multiple base tables if you execute a single UpdateGram against a view because of SQL Server limitations. You also won't be able to create a mapping schema that will map a single UpdateGram to multiple relational tables because of the UpdateGram implementation. There is an alternative. You can create a view with an instead-of trigger on top of it. When you execute UpdateGram, the trigger will kick in and distribute data to base tables.

DiffGrams

DiffGrams are very similar to UpdateGrams in both structure and function. They are designed as an internal format of the DataSet class for persisting and executing data set changes.

A typical DiffGram document has a structure like this:

```
<?xml version="1.0"?>
<Root xmlns:sql = "urn:schemas-microsoft-com:xml-sql
      sql:mapping-schema = "Inventory.xsd">
<diffgr:diffgram
        xmlns:msdata="urn:schemas-microsoft-com:xml-msdata"
        xmlns:diffgr="urn:schemas-microsoft-com:xml-diffgram-v1"
        xmlns:xsd="http://www.w3.org/2001/XMLSchema">
    <DataSetName>
       ...
    </DataSetName>
    [<diffgr:before>
         ...
    </diffgr:before>]

    [<diffgr:errors>
         ...
    </diffgr:errors>]
</diffgr:diffgram>
<Root>
```

The first element (*DataSetName* in the previous example) will get its value from the Name property of the data set from which DiffGram was generated. To a certain level, it is the functional equivalent of the updg:after element. This element is mandatory and it could contain both elements that were changed and elements that were not changed. SQL Server will process only elements that have the diffgr:hasChanges attribute set to an appropriate value. The diffgr:before element is the functional equivalent of the updg:before element. It is used to identify records that need to be changed. The diffgr:errors element is optional and it will not have any effect on data changes.

The DiffGram must contain a reference to a mapping schema to be able to map the data in the DiffGram (if you plan to run it against a database). The annotation for mapping (sql:mapping-schema) must be placed at the root element of the DiffGram.

Using DiffGrams to Insert Data

DiffGrams that insert data do not need the diffgr:before element. All elements (records) inside the *DataSetName* element (CompleteInventory in the following case) must have diffgr:hasChanges="inserted".

```
<?xml version='1.0' ?>
<AddInv xmlns:sql='urn:schemas-microsoft-com:xml-sql'
        sql:mapping-schema='Inventory.xsd'>
<diffgr:DiffGram xmlns:msdata='urn:schemas-microsoft-com:xml-msdata'
                 xmlns:diffgr='urn:schemas-microsoft-com:xml-diffgram-v1'>
  <CompleteInventory>
    <Inventory diffgr:id='Inventory1'
               diffgr:hasChanges='inserted'>
      <EquipmentId>246</EquipmentId>
      <LocationId>14</LocationId>
      <StatusId>4</StatusId>
      <LeaseId>8</LeaseId>
      <LeaseScheduleId>185</LeaseScheduleId>
      <OwnerId>161</OwnerId>
      <Lease>2209</Lease>
      <AcquisitionTypeID>2</AcquisitionTypeID>
    </Inventory>
  </CompleteInventory>
</diffgr:diffgram>
</AddInv>
```

Identity and uniqueidentifier columns must be treated uniquely in DiffGrams.
You cannot simply skip these columns because SQL Server would interpret that as
a null value. You must set sql:identity and sql:guid annotations for those fields. The
annotations use these values:

Annotation	Effect
sql:identity="ignore"	Ignore value supplied by DiffGram — Identity constraint will set the value. You can even omit the value in DiffGram.
sql:identity="useValue"	Use value from DiffGram (similar to Set Identity_Insert On).
sql:guid="generate"	SQL Server will generate value behind the scenes using the NewID() function. The value can be omitted in DiffGram.
sql:guid="useValue"	Use value from DiffGram.

NOTE

*Unfortunately, it is not possible to retrieve and use identity values from SQL Server using
DiffGrams.*

The following schema maps the Inventory element to the InventoryBulkLoad table. The Identity field will be passed as an attribute and SQL Server will ignore the value if it is set in the DiffGram.

```xml
<?xml version="1.0" ?>
<xsd:schema xmlns:xsd="http://www.w3.org/2001/XMLSchema"
            xmlns:sql="urn:schemas-microsoft-com:mapping-schema">
  <xsd:element name="Inventory" sql:relation="InventoryBulkLoad">
    <xsd:complexType>
      <xsd:sequence>
        <xsd:element name="EquipmentId" type="xsd:int" minOccurs="1" />
        <xsd:element name="LocationId" type="xsd:int" minOccurs="1" />
        <xsd:element name="StatusId" type="xsd:unsignedByte" minOccurs="1" />
        <xsd:element name="LeaseId" type="xsd:int" minOccurs="0" />
        <xsd:element name="LeaseScheduleId" type="xsd:int" minOccurs="0" />
        <xsd:element name="OwnerId" type="xsd:int" minOccurs="1" />
        <xsd:element name="Rent" type="xsd:decimal" minOccurs="0" />
        <xsd:element name="Lease" type="xsd:decimal" minOccurs="0" />
        <xsd:element name="Cost" type="xsd:decimal" minOccurs="0" />
        <xsd:element name="AcquisitionTypeID" type="xsd:unsignedByte"
                    minOccurs="1" />
      </xsd:sequence>
      <xsd:attribute name="InventoryId" type="xsd:integer"
                    sql:field="InventoryId" sql:identity="ignore" />
    </xsd:complexType>
  </xsd:element>
</xsd:schema>
```

Using DiffGrams to Update Data

DiffGrams that update data need to have both the *DataSetName* and diffgr: before elements populated. Elements in the *DataSetName* element must have diffgr:hasChanges="modified" or they will be ignored. Elements in the *DataSetName* and corresponding diffgr:before elements must be linked using the diffgr:id attribute.

In the following example, I am trying to change the StatusID of the record. The *DataSetName* element is again called CompleteInventory.

```xml
<Root xmlns:sql="urn:schemas-microsoft-com:xml-sql"
            sql:mapping-schema="InventoryUseId.xsd">
<diffgr:diffgram xmlns:msdata="urn:schemas-microsoft-com:xml-msdata"
                xmlns:diffgr="urn:schemas-microsoft-com:xml-diffgram-v1">
  <CompleteInventory>
    <Inventory diffgr:id="Inventory1"
```

```
                    msdata:rowOrder="0"
                    diffgr:hasChanges="modified">
        <Inventoryid>3</Inventoryid>
        <EquipmentId>246</EquipmentId>
        <LocationId>14</LocationId>
        <StatusId>2</StatusId>
        <LeaseId>8</LeaseId>
        <LeaseScheduleId>185</LeaseScheduleId>
        <OwnerId>161</OwnerId>
        <Lease>2209</Lease>
        <AcquisitionTypeID>2</AcquisitionTypeID>
      </Inventory>
  </CompleteInventory>
  <diffgr:before>
    <Inventory diffgr:id="Inventory1"
                    msdata:rowOrder="0">
        <Inventoryid>3</Inventoryid>
        <EquipmentId>246</EquipmentId>
        <LocationId>14</LocationId>
        <StatusId>4</StatusId>
        <LeaseId>8</LeaseId>
        <LeaseScheduleId>185</LeaseScheduleId>
        <OwnerId>161</OwnerId>
        <Lease>2209</Lease>
        <AcquisitionTypeID>2</AcquisitionTypeID>
      </Inventory>
  </diffgr:before>
</diffgr:diffgram>
</Root>
```

Both copies of the record have all fields defined. This forces SQL Server to check if someone has changed the record in the meanwhile (*optimistic concurrency control*). It is not possible to force SQL Server to do pessimistic locking (because of the disconnected nature of the system). It is also impossible to ignore changes on the record by dropping elements from the `diffgr:before` element. SQL Server will consider those columns as null and no record will match the criteria.

You cannot use an XSD schema with `sql:identity="ignore"` in a DiffGram to update a record. SQL Server would replace the identity value with null and the update would fail. You must create a new schema that contains `sql:identity="useValue"`:

```
<?xml version="1.0" ?>
<xsd:schema xmlns:xsd="http://www.w3.org/2001/XMLSchema"
```

```
                 xmlns:sql="urn:schemas-microsoft-com:mapping-schema">
<xsd:element name="Inventory" sql:relation="InventoryBulkLoad">
  <xsd:complexType>
    <xsd:sequence>
      <xsd:element name="Inventoryid" sql:field="InventoryId"
                   type="xsd:integer" sql:identity="useValue" />
      <xsd:element name="EquipmentId" type="xsd:int" minOccurs="1" />
      <xsd:element name="LocationId" type="xsd:int" minOccurs="1" />
      <xsd:element name="StatusId" type="xsd:unsignedByte" minOccurs="1" />
      <xsd:element name="LeaseId" type="xsd:int" minOccurs="0" />
      <xsd:element name="LeaseScheduleId" type="xsd:int" minOccurs="0" />
      <xsd:element name="OwnerId" type="xsd:int" minOccurs="1" />
      <xsd:element name="Rent" type="xsd:decimal" minOccurs="0" />
      <xsd:element name="Lease" type="xsd:decimal" minOccurs="0" />
      <xsd:element name="Cost" type="xsd:decimal" minOccurs="0" />
      <xsd:element name="AcquisitionTypeID" type="xsd:unsignedByte"
                   minOccurs="1" />
    </xsd:sequence>
  </xsd:complexType>
</xsd:element>
</xsd:schema>
```

Using DiffGrams to Delete Data

To delete a record using DiffGram, reference the record only in the `diffgr:before` block. The other element will be empty:

```
<Root xmlns:sql="urn:schemas-microsoft-com:xml-sql"
          sql:mapping-schema="Inventory.xsd">
<diffgr:diffgram xmlns:msdata="urn:schemas-microsoft-com:xml-msdata"
                 xmlns:diffgr="urn:schemas-microsoft-com:xml-diffgram-v1">
  <CompleteInventory />
  <diffgr:before>
    <Inventory diffgr:id="Inventory1" msdata:rowOrder="0">
      <Inventoryid>83</Inventoryid>
      <EquipmentId>246</EquipmentId>
      <LocationId>14</LocationId>
      <StatusId>4</StatusId>
      <LeaseId>8</LeaseId>
      <LeaseScheduleId>185</LeaseScheduleId>
      <OwnerId>161</OwnerId>
      <Lease>2209</Lease>
      <AcquisitionTypeID>2</AcquisitionTypeID>
    </Inventory>
  </diffgr:before>
```

```
</diffgr:diffgram>
</Root>
```

Again, you must use a schema that contains the `sql:identity="useValue"` annotation for an identity field.

Processing Multiple Records Using DiffGrams

DiffGrams may process multiple records at the same time. In the case of updates, it is essential to link records in both the *DataSetName* and the `diffgr:before` block using the `diffgr:id` attribute.

A data set could contain records from more than one base table. If a DataSet object is used to generate a DiffGram, it will group records by table. In this case, you typically need to use a mapping schema as well. You need to reference the schema using the `sql:mapping-schema` attribute in the root element of the DiffGram.

The order of modification operations is often very important for successful completion. A standard example is the deletion of records in two tables linked by a foreign key. In that case, you must use the `diffgr:parentID` attribute in the child element and the `diffgr:id` attribute in the parent record (the data set). This attribute must be used in the `diffgr:before` block. The DiffGram must also point to the XSD schema with a `sql:relationship` annotation. Such DiffGrams will not follow the order of records in the document, but rather the order dictated by `diffgr:parentID` attribute.

DiffGrams Behind the Scene

All changes in a DiffGram will become part of a single transaction. If any of them fail or if any of them do not modify a single record, the transaction will be rolled back.

You can use SQL Server Profiler to display the Transact-SQL batch generated for a DiffGram. The following batch was created to insert three records into the InventoryBulkLoad table:

```
SET XACT_ABORT ON
BEGIN TRAN
DECLARE @eip INT, @r__ int, @e__ int
SET @eip = 0
INSERT InventoryBulkLoad (EquipmentId, LocationId, StatusId, LeaseId,
 LeaseScheduleId, OwnerId, Rent, Lease, Cost, AcquisitionTypeID)
```

```
VALUES (246, 14, 4, 8, 185, 161,  NULL, 2209,  NULL, 2);
SELECT @e__ = @@ERROR, @r__ = @@ROWCOUNT
 IF (@e__ != 0 OR @r__ != 1) SET @eip = 1
INSERT InventoryBulkLoad (EquipmentId, LocationId, StatusId, LeaseId,
LeaseScheduleId, OwnerId, Rent, Lease, Cost, AcquisitionTypeID)
VALUES (126, 14, 4, 8, 185, 160,  NULL, 1200,  NULL, 2);
SELECT @e__ = @@ERROR, @r__ = @@ROWCOUNT
 IF (@e__ != 0 OR @r__ != 1) SET @eip = 1
INSERT InventoryBulkLoad (EquipmentId, LocationId, StatusId, LeaseId,
LeaseScheduleId, OwnerId, Rent, Lease, Cost, AcquisitionTypeID)
VALUES (286, 14, 4, 8, 185, 151,  NULL, 2500,  NULL, 2);
SELECT @e__ = @@ERROR, @r__ = @@ROWCOUNT
 IF (@e__ != 0 OR @r__ != 1) SET @eip = 1

IF (@eip != 0) ROLLBACK ELSE COMMIT
SET XACT_ABORT OFF
```

Unfortunately, SQL Server will not roll back the transaction and finish processing as soon as an error occurs, but will do so only when all modification statements have been executed.

The following batch was created for an update DiffGram:

```
SET XACT_ABORT ON
BEGIN TRAN
DECLARE @eip INT, @r__ int, @e__ int
SET @eip = 0
UPDATE InventoryBulkLoad SET StatusId=2, Rent=NULL, Cost=NULL
WHERE ( InventoryId=3 )  AND  ( EquipmentId=246 )  AND  ( LocationId=14 )
AND  ( StatusId=4 )  AND  ( LeaseId=8 )  AND  ( LeaseScheduleId=185 )
AND  ( OwnerId=161 )  AND  ( Rent IS NULL )  AND  ( Lease=2209 )
AND  ( Cost IS NULL )  AND  ( AcquisitionTypeID=2 ) ;
SELECT @e__ = @@ERROR, @r__ = @@ROWCOUNT
 IF (@e__ != 0 OR @r__ != 1) SET @eip = 1
 IF (@r__ > 1) RAISERROR ( N'SQLOLEDB Error Description:' +
'Ambiguous update, unique identifier required  Transaction aborted ', 16, 1)
 ELSE IF (@r__ < 1) RAISERROR ( N'SQLOLEDB Error Description: ' +
'Empty update, no updatable rows found  Transaction aborted ', 16, 1)

IF (@eip != 0) ROLLBACK ELSE COMMIT
SET XACT_ABORT OFF
```

Note how the Update statement includes a Where clause to verify that all column values are unchanged. The batch will also verify that exactly one record was updated and raise an error if that is not the case.

Executing DiffGrams Programmatically Using SqlXmlCommand

DiffGrams are executed in the same manner as UpdateGrams. You must set the CommandType property to SqlXmlCommandType.DiffGram and you will typically execute it using the ExecuteNonQuery() method. In the following example, CommandText() will be set by reading the DiffGram from the file:

```
'SqlXml_DiffGram
Imports System
Imports System.IO
Imports System.Xml
Imports Microsoft.Data.SqlXml 'The SQLXML namespace

Module SqlXml_DiffGram
    Sub Main()

        Dim objSqlXmlCmd As New SqlXmlCommand("Provider=SQLOLEDB;" _
            & "Server=(local);Database=Asset;" _
            & "Integrated Security=SSPI")

        'read DiffGram from file
        Dim objFile As StreamReader = New StreamReader( _
                    File.OpenRead("DiffGramInvInsert.xml"))
        objSqlXmlCmd.CommandText = objFile.ReadToEnd()

        'execute DiffGram
        objSqlXmlCmd.CommandType = SqlXmlCommandType.DiffGram
        objSqlXmlCmd.ExecuteNonQuery()
    End Sub
End Module
```

Executing DiffGrams Using URLs

DiffGrams can also be executed through HTTP in the same manner as UpdateGrams. You need to save the DiffGram file and XSD schema file in the template virtual directory. Then you can execute them by referencing the DiffGram file in the URL:

```
http://localhost/asset/template/DiffGramInvInsert.xml
```

IIS will return the page with the root element of the DiffGram:

```
<?xml version="1.0" ?>
<AddInv xmlns:sql="urn:schemas-microsoft-com:xml-sql" />
```

In case of an error, you might get a message similar to this one:

```
<Root xmlns:sql="urn:schemas-microsoft-com:xml-sql">
<?MSSQLError HResult="0x80004005"
Source="Microsoft XML Extensions to SQL Server"
Description="Specified attribute or element ('Inventoryid')
does not have a corresponding mapping in the schema,
and no overflow field defined"?>
</Root>
```

Generating DiffGrams After DataSet Change

I have mentioned before that DiffGrams are designed primarily as an internal format for storing DataSet changes. Therefore, I have created a program that loads a DataSet object, makes a change in it, and then stores the change in a DiffGram file:

```
'SqlCommand_DataSet2XML
Imports System
Imports System.IO
Imports System.Data
Imports System.Data.SqlClient
Imports System.Xml

Module Module1

    Sub Main()
        'Instantiate the SqlCommand object and the connection
        Dim objConn As New SqlConnection("Server=(local);" _
            & "Database=Asset;" _
            & "Integrated Security=SSPI")
        objConn.Open()

        'prepare a data set
        Dim objCmd As New SqlCommand("SELECT * FROM Inventory " _
                                    & "where InventoryId = 83 ", objConn)
        Dim objAdpt As New SqlDataAdapter(objCmd)
        Dim objDs As New DataSet("CompleteInventory")
        objAdpt.Fill(objDs, "Inventory")
```

```
                'prepare the destination file
                Dim objFile As New FileStream("DiffGramInvDelete.xml", _
                                                & FileMode.Create)
                Dim objStrmWriter As New StreamWriter(objFile)

                'delete row
                objDs.Tables(0).Rows(0).Delete()

                'write DiffGram that will delete the record
                objDs.WriteXml(objStrmWriter, XmlWriteMode.DiffGram)

                objStrmWriter.Close()
                objFile.Close()
                objConn.Close()


        End Sub
End Module
```

Debugging DiffGrams

DiffGrams are relatively difficult to debug. There are two groups of DiffGram-related errors:

► **XML parsing errors**   DiffGram and XSD schema files might not be valid
► **SQL Server errors**   SQL Server constraints are preventing the change

When your DiffGram is not giving you the result that you expect, you should use SQL Server Profiler to see if the DiffGram is able to generate a valid query, and then execute the query against the database. If you execute the query in Query Analyzer, you will see the error that SQL Server is returning. If there is no query generated in Profiler, you will have to determine why the system is unable to parse and process the DiffGram. Investigate the following:

► Is the DiffGram a well-formed XML file?
► Is the DiffGram pointing to an XSD schema file?
► Is the XSD schema valid?
► Do the DiffGram and XSD files contain all required namespace references?
► Does the XSD schema map the XML components to database objects?
► Did you map all columns to elements and attributes?

▶ Do the elements and attributes in the XSD schema match the elements and attributes in the DiffGram (remember that the XML parser is case sensitive)?

▶ Are all target table columns referenced in the DiffGram?

▶ Does the DiffGram contain a proper value for the `diffgr:hasChanges` attribute?

▶ Does the DiffGram have a root element and the *DataSetName* element?

SQLXML BulkLoad

BulkLoad is a SQLXML variant of bcp (Bulk Copy Program) and the Bulk Insert statement. It is designed for fast loading of large XML documents (or XML fragments) into SQL Server 2000. It is implemented as a COM object and, therefore, can only be used programmatically. You can use any COM-compatible language, including Visual Basic, Visual C++, VBScript, and all .NET languages such as Visual Basic .NET and Visual C# .NET. Since the component is designed for programmatic access, this section immediately dives into its programmatic use.

Executing SQLXML BulkLoad from a .NET Application

You must include a reference to the Microsoft SQLXML BulkLoad 3.0 Type Library in your program before you can start using it in your code. After the project has been opened (or created), select Project | Add Reference. In the Add Reference dialog box, switch to the COM tab, select Microsoft SQLXML BulkLoad 3.0 Type Library, click Select, and click OK. If the component is not present, you can browse for it. You should be able to find xblkld3.dll in the \Program Files\Common Files\System\Ole DB\ folder.

After you have added the reference to the project, you can declare an object of the SQLXMLBULKLOADLib.SQLXMLBulkLoad3 type.

NOTE

The number 3 at the end of the PROGID string represents the version of the component. If you want, your application can be set to always use the latest version by using the PROGID without the number. However, Microsoft has been changing features and interfaces between versions, and it is probably better to specify the version.

Before executing, you need to specify the `ConnectionString` and `ErrorLog` attributes of the object. In the following case, we also set the object to accept XML fragments, and to drop and generate the target table, by setting the XMLFragment, SGDropTables, and SchemaGen attributes to True:

```
'XmlBulkLoad_Simple
Module Module1

    Sub Main()
        Dim objBulk As New SQLXMLBULKLOADLib.SQLXMLBulkLoad3()

        objBulk.ConnectionString = "provider=SQLOLEDB.1;" + _
            + "data source=(local)\ss2k;database=Asset;" _
            + "integrated security=SSPI"
        objBulk.ErrorLogFile = "error.log"
        objBulk.XMLFragment = True
        objBulk.SchemaGen = True
        objBulk.SGDropTables = True

        'do the load
        objBulk.Execute("Inventory.xsd", "Inventory.xml")
        objBulk = Nothing


    End Sub
End Module
```

Error Log File

During the load, the BulkLoad component will write fatal and nonfatal errors to the file specified by the ErrorLogFile property. The file is naturally an XML document:

```
<?xml version="1.0"?>
<Result State="FAILED">
    <Error>
      <HResult>0x80004005</HResult>
      <Description>
          <![CDATA[No data was provided for column 'Cost' on
                   table 'InventoryBulkLoad', and this column
                   cannot contain NULL values.]]>
      </Description>
      <Source>General operational error</Source>
      <Type>FATAL</Type>
    </Error>
</Result>
```

Executing BulkLoad from DTS (Using VBScript)

DTS is my tool of choice for implementing data transfer applications in SQL Server. The current version of DTS does not have a specialized connection or task object for using XML documents as a data source. Fortunately, you can use an ActiveX Script Task (which allows you to write VBScript or JScript code) with the SQLXML BulkLoad component to achieve this objective.

I created a DTS package with global variables for the XML document, XSD document, error log file, and connection string. Then I created an ActiveX Script Task (see Figure 15-4) to perform the load using the following code:

```
Function Main()

Dim objBulk, objDTS, s

Set objDTS = DTSGlobalVariables.Parent
Set objBulk = CreateObject("SQLXMLBulkLoad.SQLXMLBulkload.3.0")

objBulk.ConnectionString = objDTS.GlobalVariables("ConnectionString")
objBulk.ErrorLogFile = objDTS.GlobalVariables("ErrorLog")
objBulk.XMLFragment = True
objBulk.SchemaGen = True
objBulk.SGDropTables = True

objBulk.Execute objDTS.GlobalVariables("XSD"), _
        CStr(objDTS.GlobalVariables("XML") )

Main = DTSTaskExecResult_Success

End Function
```

The statement for initializing the object is slightly different in VBScript, but you still need to reference the same component. The properties of the bulk load object are set from the global variables of the DTS package. The location of the XML document had to be converted to a string before it could be used in the Execute method.

After the object is prepared, the procedure uses the Execute method to load the document. The Execute method requires the name of the XML data file and the name of the mapping schema that maps the XML file to the relational tables. The mapping file can be either an annotated XSD schema or an annotated XDR schema.

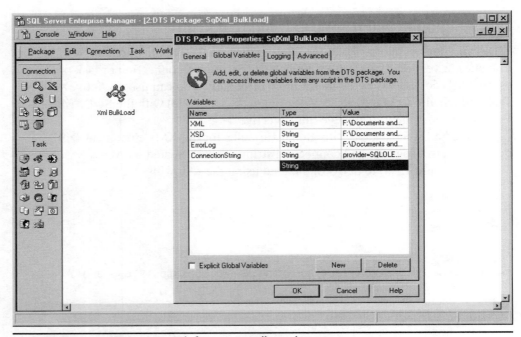

Figure 15-4   *ActiveX Script task for using BulkLoad component*

NOTE

The preceding ActiveX script uses a hard-coded version (3.0) of the SQLXML BulkLoad component. Again, if you want your package always to use the latest version, use the PROGID without the number.

Schema Generation

The preceding examples have demonstrated how you can set the `SGDropTables` and `SchemaGen` attributes to True to force the bulk load process to first drop the target tables and then to generate them using information in the mapping schema file.

SGUseID can only be used when the SchemaGen property is set to True. If SGUseID is set to True, the component will set, as primary key on the new table, the column with `dt:type="id"` in the mapping schema. The default is False.

BulkLoad is used in scenarios in which you want to use the object with SchemaGen and SGDropTables set to True, just to re-create tables. If it is set to False, the component will not load the document. By default, it is set to True.

BulkLoad Transactions

In the case of a nontransactional load, the BulkLoad component creates and executes an Insert statement as soon as it parses an element. In the case of a transactional load, it first writes data to a set of temporary files—it creates a separate file for each table involved. These temporary files will later be loaded into the permanent tables in a single transaction.

You must set the Transaction property to True if you want to force the BulkLoad component to roll back the transaction in case of an error.

The TempFilePath property is used to specify the folder that will be used to store the temporary data files. These files are needed when BulkLoad component is set to load data within a transaction. If a value is not specified, the process will use the folder specified in the TEMP environment variable. Naturally, there should be enough space in that folder, and the user account that is used to run the bulk load process must have appropriate privileges for that folder.

NOTE

You should not attempt to load records with binary and image columns (with XML data types such as bin.hex and bin.base64) in a transaction.

Data Integrity

The CheckConstraints property is used when data needs to be loaded and verified at the same time against constraints such as foreign keys and unique indexes. By default, this property is set to False. Alternatively, you could load the file with CheckConstraints set to False to speed up the load and then use DBCC CHECKCONSTRAINTS to verify the records.

The KeepIdentity property controls how SQL Server handles identity values during the bulk load operation. If it is set to False, SQL Server ignores records supplied in the XML document and assigns the identity values. The default value is True, in which case SQL Server preserves the values specified in the XML document. (It is equivalent to Set Identity_Insert On.)

NOTE

Unfortunately, you will not be able to set BulkLoad to insert a parent record, obtain the identity value generated, and then use it in a child record. If that is required, you will have to convert your XML document to an UpdateGram, but you will pay a severe performance penalty.

KeepNulls controls how values are set for attributes and subelements that are missing in the XML document. If you set this attribute to True, the BulkLoad component will assign null values to them. The default value is False and, in that case, values will be assigned by SQL Server using constraints defined on the column (such as default and null).

IgnoreDuplicateKeys can only be used when the Transaction property is set to False. It forces the BulkLoad component to regard the existence of duplicate keys in the XML document as a nonfatal error.

Table Lock

By default, BulkLoad component acquires and releases an exclusive lock during each record insertion. If you set ForceTableLock to True, you will improve the performance of the load operation by putting an exclusive lock on each database table for the duration of the load. Keep in mind that this also prevents other processes from both reading and modifying data in the tables during the load.

Using SQLXML BulkLoad

BulkLoad component is able to process large XML documents because it does not need to load the complete document into memory. It reads documents element by element and processes each element individually.

Although SQLXML BulkLoad component is significantly faster then UpdateGrams, DiffGrams, and OpenXML(), it is not as fast as the Transact-SQL Bulk Insert statement and the Bulk Insert task in DTS. The reason is the amount of overhead associated with XML parsing.

Mapping Schema

What should you do when someone sends you a large XML document to load to the database? The most important task, and the most difficult, is to create an XSD schema to map the XML components of the document to database tables and columns.

If you can extract a chunk that is smaller than 1MB, you could use Microsoft XSD Inference 1.0 at http://apps.gotdotnet.com/xmltools/xsdinference/ to infer (generate) the XSD schema automatically for you. If you cannot extract a chunk smaller than 1MB, you could download the command-line utility from the same site and try to perform the operation locally on your computer.

If your document is simply too large, you might start from the target table(s). XSD Schema Designer in Visual Studio .NET can create a schema for you if you drag and drop a table into it.

After the initial version of the XSD schema has been created, you will probably need to improve it. If the names of the XML elements and attributes do not match those of the tables and columns, you will have to use `sql:relation` and `sql:field` annotations to map them. If the XML document contains multiple tables, you will need to use the `sql:relationship` annotation to establish the relationships between parent and child elements.

Another source of problems is the nullability of columns. You might need to remove `use="required"` from the schema for columns that do not require data.

You should add a `sql:overflow-field` annotation to point to a large field (typically of the `text` data type) that will collect all the data not mapped to specific columns. You might need it later. More importantly, this is a safety net in case your partner organization decides to change the structure of the XML document they send you.

You will also need to investigate whether data types are compatible. The size of some types, such as numbers and strings, can be an issue. Microsoft also recommends that you explicitly map `xsd:dateTime` and `xsd:time` types to `datetime` or `smalldatetime`, and `xsd:GUID` to `uniqueidentifier` so that the bulk load process performs the necessary conversions.

```xml
<?xml version="1.0" encoding="utf-8" ?>
<xs:schema attributeFormDefault="unqualified"
           elementFormDefault="qualified"
           xmlns:xs="http://www.w3.org/2001/XMLSchema"
           xmlns:sql="urn:schemas-microsoft-com:mapping-schema">
  <xs:element name="Inventory" sql:relation="InventoryBulkLoad"
                               sql:overflow-field ="Note" >
    <xs:complexType>
      <xs:attribute name="Inventoryid" type= "xs:unsignedByte"
                    sql:datatype ="int" use="required" />
      <xs:attribute name="EquipmentId" type="xs:unsignedByte"
                    sql:datatype ="int" use="required" />
      <xs:attribute name="LocationId" type="xs:unsignedByte"
                    sql:datatype ="int" use="required" />
      <xs:attribute name="StatusId" type="xs:unsignedByte"
                    sql:datatype ="tinyint" use="required" />
      <xs:attribute name="LeaseId" type="xs:unsignedByte"
```

```
                          sql:datatype ="int"  />
      <xs:attribute name="LeaseScheduleId" type="xs:unsignedByte"
                          sql:datatype ="int" />
      <xs:attribute name="OwnerId" type="xs:unsignedByte"
                          sql:datatype ="int" use="required" />
      <xs:attribute name="Cost" type="xs:unsignedShort"
                          sql:datatype ="money" />
      <xs:attribute name="AcquisitionTypeID" type="xs:unsignedByte"
                          sql:datatype ="tinyint" use="required" />
    </xs:complexType>
  </xs:element>
</xs:schema>
```

When you are done with the schema, running the load is easy. If there are no errors, you will end up with a table like the one shown in Figure 15-5.

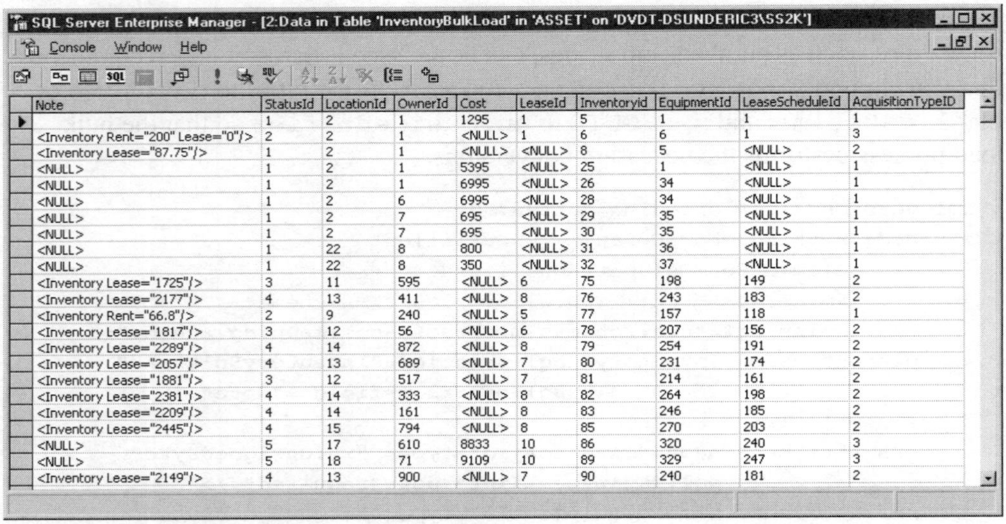

SQL Server Enterprise Manager - [2:Data in Table 'InventoryBulkLoad' in 'ASSET' on 'DVDT-DSUNDERIC3\SS2K']

Note	StatusId	LocationId	OwnerId	Cost	LeaseId	Inventoryid	EquipmentId	LeaseScheduleId	AcquisitionTypeID
	1	2	1	1295	1	5	1	1	1
<Inventory Rent="200" Lease="0"/>	2	2	1	<NULL>	1	6	6	1	3
<Inventory Lease="87.75"/>	1	2	1	<NULL>	<NULL>	8	5	<NULL>	2
<NULL>	1	2	1	5395	<NULL>	25	1	<NULL>	1
<NULL>	1	2	1	6995	<NULL>	26	34	<NULL>	1
<NULL>	1	2	6	6995	<NULL>	28	34	<NULL>	1
<NULL>	1	2	7	695	<NULL>	29	35	<NULL>	1
<NULL>	1	2	7	695	<NULL>	30	35	<NULL>	1
<NULL>	1	22	8	800	<NULL>	31	36	<NULL>	1
<NULL>	1	22	8	350	<NULL>	32	37	<NULL>	1
<Inventory Lease="1725"/>	3	11	595	<NULL>	6	75	198	149	2
<Inventory Lease="2177"/>	4	13	411	<NULL>	8	76	243	183	2
<Inventory Rent="66.8"/>	2	9	240	<NULL>	5	77	157	118	1
<Inventory Lease="1817"/>	3	12	56	<NULL>	6	78	207	156	2
<Inventory Lease="2289"/>	4	14	872	<NULL>	8	79	254	191	2
<Inventory Lease="2057"/>	4	13	689	<NULL>	7	80	231	174	2
<Inventory Lease="1881"/>	3	12	517	<NULL>	7	81	214	161	2
<Inventory Lease="2381"/>	4	14	333	<NULL>	8	82	264	198	2
<Inventory Lease="2209"/>	4	14	161	<NULL>	8	83	246	185	2
<Inventory Lease="2445"/>	4	15	794	<NULL>	8	85	270	203	2
<NULL>	5	17	610	8833	10	86	320	240	3
<NULL>	5	18	71	9109	10	89	329	247	3
<Inventory Lease="2149"/>	4	13	900	<NULL>	7	90	240	181	2

Figure 15-5 *Overflow field*

XML Web Services

Simple Object Access Protocol (SOAP) is a platform-independent, XML-based protocol for cross-system component communication. There are other protocols for carrying out such communication (for example, COM/DCOM, CORBA, .NET Remoting, and Internet Inter-ORB Protocol), but they are typically tied to a single component technology. SOAP, on the other hand, is intended to be truly platform independent. To this end, a working group was formed under the W3C to define a protocol for the exchange of structured, typed information between peers in a distributed, decentralized environment using XML. The result of its work is the SOAP protocol for implementing web services. In SQLXML 3.0, Service Pack 1, and in the .NET Framework, Microsoft implements SOAP version 1.1. W3C's XML Protocol Working Group has already defined SOAP version 1.2, and soon new versions of Microsoft tools will add support for it.

Before I describe the details of SOAP implementation within SQL Server, I'll review the web services architecture.

SOAP Messages and XML Web Services Architecture

XML Web Services are components that expose functionality to callers using standard web protocols. SOAP defines messages to be used when a client (component) sends a request message to an XML Web Service component. The SOAP message is parsed and the request is processed by the XML Web Service. The service returns a response message to the caller, also using a SOAP message.

An XML Web Service component must describe its interfaces to (potential) callers. A standard way to describe these interfaces is to provide an XML document that follows the Web Services Description Language (WSDL) standard. Developers can then build applications using any language on any platform to use the exposed services.

To help potential users find WSDL documents, web services need to be registered using Universal Discovery Description and Integration (UDDI, standard for registering and discovery of descriptions of web services).

Using SQLXML to Create XML Web Services

SQLXML 3.0, and newer, can be used to create a web service. You can expose stored procedures, functions, and XML templates using SQLISAPI. Web services are implemented as a SOAP type of the SQLISAPI virtual directory.

To create a web service, you can configure an existing virtual directory to support SOAP, or add a new virtual directory that supports SOAP:

1. Use the Configure IIS Support application to open the Properties sheet of the existing virtual directory.

2. Switch to the Virtual Names tab.

3. Create a new virtual name of the SOAP type.

4. As soon as you choose SOAP, the program enables the Path, Web Service Name, and Domain Name text boxes.

   The Web Service Name text box allows you to set the name of the web service to be used in the WSDL document. By default, the program sets it to the virtual name, but you can change it to something more meaningful.

   The Domain Name text box entry will be used as a namespace for the web service and as the Location attribute in the Service element of the WSDL document. The default is the name of the IIS server that hosts the virtual directory. If you use the server on your local network, you can leave the default, but if you are going to expose it to the Internet, you should add a domain name to it.

   As soon as you save the virtual name, the program enables the Configure button.

5. Click Configure. The program opens the Soap Virtual Name Configuration dialog box (see Figure 15-6), which is used to configure the methods of the web service. Methods can be based on XML templates or stored procedures (including user-defined functions). A web service will not function properly if you use stored procedures that contain the For XML clause.

6. Select the Type of method (SP or Template) and click the Browse button (indicated by "...") to the right of the SP/Template list box. If you selected the SP radio button, the program prompts you to choose a stored procedure or function.

7. Select the format that will be used for converting a recordset to XML (using the For XML Row or For XML Row Nested clause) and the format for returning

Figure 15-6   *The Soap Virtual Name Configuration dialog box*

the output (XML elements, array of DataSet objects, or single data set). Methods based on XML templates are always returned as XML elements.

If you select the Return Errors As Soap Faults check box, the web service returns all errors as *SOAP Fault* elements of the response. SOAP-aware clients, like those developed using the .NET Framework or SOAP Toolkit from Microsoft, can trap exceptions. If the option is not checked, error messages will simply be returned as XML elements (if they originated in a stored procedure) or processing instructions (if they originated in a template). Stored procedures configured to return output as a single data set must return errors as SOAP faults.

8. Click Apply and close the Configure IIS Support application.

The program creates *web service description* (.wsdl) and *configuration* (.ssc) files in the folder associated with the SOAP type of the virtual name. The WSDL file contains a description of the web service created. The configuration file contains the mapping information entered in the Soap Virtual Name Configuration dialog box. SQLISAPI will use this information to map the web service's methods to stored procedures and templates. These files are updated each time you make a change to the virtual name of the web service.

Creating .NET SOAP Clients

Using the .NET Framework, this section demonstrates the creation of SOAP clients that access methods configured to return data via different methods and using the following formats:

▶ Return values and output parameters
▶ XML elements
▶ Array of data sets
▶ Single data set

If you are planning to run the code examples, you will need to map the following functions to web service methods:

Method	Stored Procedure	Output
OrderAdd	prOrder_Add	XML elements
fn_DepartmentEquipment	fn_DepartmentEquipment	XML elements

Method	Stored Procedure	Output
prOrderItemByOrderId_List	prOrderItemByOrderId_List	Single data set
prOrderRequestedBy_List	prOrderRequestedBy_List	Array of data sets

Adding a Web Service Reference in Visual Studio .NET Project

To create a SOAP client in Visual Studio .NET, you need to create a new project, and then add a reference to the XML Web Service using Project | Add Web Reference. The program opens the Add Web Reference browser window to allow you to connect to the UDDI directory of the web services (see Figure 15-7), or you can simply type the web address of the web service:

```
http://localhost/Asset/soap?wsdl
```

The *wsdl* parameter of the URL compels the program to open the file containing the web service description.

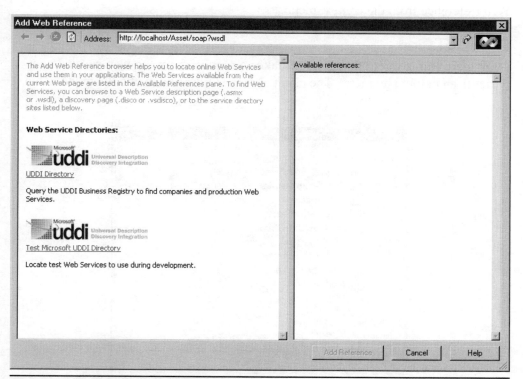

Figure 15-7   *The Add Web Reference browser window*

The program opens the WSDL file and displays it on the screen. You can browse it or simply click Add Reference and the program adds it to your solution as a web reference. The web reference is named after the server that hosts the web service (localhost in this case). Use this opportunity to give it a more meaningful name (see Figure 15-8).

Based on information found in the WSDL file, Visual Studio .NET generates a proxy class in your project, which you can use to access web service methods.

NOTE

The proxy class does not allow non-string output parameters to get null values from XML Web Services. If your service returns nulls, you can either assign it to string values or rewrite the proxy class to accept nulls.

If you ever make a change to the web service, you can refresh the web reference and the class it creates: open Solution Explorer, open Web References, right-click the service name (in the example, localhost, or AssetOrderService), and select Update Web Reference from the context menu.

Simple .NET Client

I will start with a client that simply makes a request from the web service and retrieves an output parameter. The client uses the OrderAdd method mapped to the

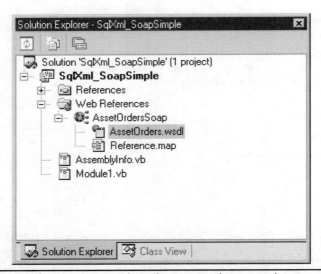

Figure 15-8 *A web reference in Visual Studio .NET Solution Explorer*

prOrder_Add stored procedure. It accepts several parameters and returns the OrderId that was assigned to the order during the insert.

```
alter procedure prOrder_Add
-- insert Order and return Order id
-- used in soap demonstration

  @OrderDate smalldatetime,
  @RequestedById int,
  @TargetDate smalldatetime,
  @DestinationLocationId int,
  @Note varchar(200),
  @OrderTypeId smallint,
  @OrderStatusid tinyint,
  @OrderId int output
as
declare @intErrorCode int

INSERT INTO [Order]([OrderDate], [RequestedById], [TargetDate],
[DestinationLocationId], [Note], [OrderTypeId], [OrderStatusid])
VALUES(@OrderDate, @RequestedById, @TargetDate, @DestinationLocationId, @Note,
@OrderTypeId, @OrderStatusid)

select @OrderId = scope_identity(),
    @intErrorCode = @@Error

return @intErrorCode
```

The following Visual Basic .NET console application instantiates a web service proxy object (objWSProxy) based on the class that was generated using WSDL. The application needs to set the Credentials property of the proxy object when a web service does not accept anonymous users. Finally, the method of the web service is executed through the proxy method of the proxy object. As an application developer, you do not have to worry about the intricacies of the SOAP protocol. The proxy object takes care of it.

```
'SqlXml_SoapSimple
Imports System
Imports System.IO

Module Module1

Sub Main()
  Dim objResponse As Object()
  Dim iOrderId As Integer
```

```
    Dim objWSProxy As New AssetOrdersService.AssetOrders()
    objWSProxy.Credentials = System.Net.CredentialCache.DefaultCredentials
    objResponse = objWSProxy.OrderAdd("3/3", 1, "5/5", 1, _
                                       "URGENT!", 1, 1, _
                                       iOrderId)

    Console.WriteLine("OrderID: " & iOrderId)

End Sub

End Module
```

Function That Returns Data Sets as XML Elements

The next project uses a table-valued, user-defined function mapped to the method that returns output as XML elements:

```
'SqlXml_Soap_XmlElements
Imports System
Imports System.IO

Module Module1

Sub Main()
  Dim objResponse As Object()
  Dim objError As Object
  Dim iElem As Integer
  Dim objResponseElement As System.Xml.XmlElement

  Dim objWSProxy As New AssetOrdersService.AssetOrders()
  objWSProxy.Credentials = System.Net.CredentialCache.DefaultCredentials
  objResponse = objWSProxy.fn_DepartmentEquipment("dejans")

  For iElem = 0 To objResponse.GetUpperBound(0)
   Select Case objResponse(iElem).GetType().ToString()
     Case "System.Xml.XmlElement"
         objResponseElement = objResponse(iElem)
         Console.WriteLine(objResponseElement.OuterXml)
     Case "SqlMessage"
         objError = objResponse(iElem)
         Console.WriteLine(objError.Message)
         Console.WriteLine(objError.Source)
   End Select
```

```
    Next

End Sub

End Module
```

The application loops through the XML elements of the response and writes them to the screen. It differentiates between data set and error and writes them separately.

In the case of a function that returns a scalar value, or a stored procedure that returns a value as a data set, you can add the following code in the Select Case statement:

```
Case "System.Int32"
     iReturn = objResponse(iElem)
     Console.WriteLine("Return Value: " & iReturn)
```

Stored Procedure That Returns a Single Data Set

This is probably the easiest case to code. The proxy method returns a data set that you can use to fill any data-bound control such as a grid:

```
'SqlXml_Soap_SingleDateSet
Public Class Form1
    Inherits System.Windows.Forms.Form

#Region " Windows Form Designer generated code "

Private Sub Button1_Click(ByVal sender As System.Object, _
          ByVal e As System.EventArgs) Handles Button1.Click

  Dim iReturn As Integer
  Dim dsResponse As DataSet

  Dim objWSProxy As New AssetOrdersService.AssetOrders()
  objWSProxy.Credentials = System.Net.CredentialCache.DefaultCredentials
  dsResponse = objWSProxy.prOrderItemByOrderId_List(CInt(TextBox1.Text), _
                                                    iReturn)

  'load it to grid
  gridTable.DataSource = dsResponse.Tables(0).DefaultView

    End Sub
End Class
```

Since the proxy method returns a DataSet object, the return value of the stored procedure has to be returned as a parameter of the proxy method.

Stored Procedure That Returns Array of Data Sets

In this case, you have to combine approaches from the preceding two examples. You will be able to extract data sets and use them to populate grids, but first you have to parse XML elements to find them. Look for "System.Data.DataSet" to identify the XML element with data set information:

```
'SqlXml_Soap_DateSetArray
Public Class frmOrders
    Inherits System.Windows.Forms.Form

#Region " Windows Form Designer generated code "

Private Sub btnLoad_Click(ByVal sender As System.Object, ByVal e As
System.EventArgs) Handles btnLoad.Click
  Dim iReturn As Integer
  Dim dsResponse As DataSet
  Dim objResponse As Object()
  Dim objError As Object
  Dim iElem As Integer
  Dim objResponseElement As System.Xml.XmlElement

  Dim objWSProxy As New AssetOrdersService.AssetOrders()
  objWSProxy.Credentials = System.Net.CredentialCache.DefaultCredentials
  objResponse = objWSProxy.prOrderRequestedBy_List(txtUserName.Text)

  For iElem = 0 To objResponse.GetUpperBound(0)
      Select Case objResponse(iElem).GetType().ToString()
    Case "System.Data.DataSet"
        dsResponse = objResponse(iElem)


        ...
        grdOrders.DataSource = dsResponse.Tables(0).DefaultView()
        ...
        grdOrderItems.DataSource = dsResponse.Tables(0).DefaultView()
        ...

    Case "System.Int32"
        iReturn = objResponse(iElem)
        Console.WriteLine("Return Value: " & iReturn)
    Case "SqlMessage"
        objError = objResponse(iElem)
```

```
        MsgBox(objError.Message)
        Stop
      End Select
  Next


    End Sub
End Class
```

The application gets two data sets from the web service and uses them to populate grids on the form.

NOTE

Visual Studio .NET is not the only tool that you can use to create SOAP clients. You can use Microsoft's SOAP Toolkit to create COM-based SOAP clients using Visual Studio 6. There is also an Office XP SOAP Toolkit that you can use to create VBA applications.

```
'SqlXml_Soap_DateSetArray
Public Class frmOrders
    Inherits System.Windows.Forms.Form
#Region " Windows Form Designer generated code "
Private Sub btnLoad_Click(ByVal sender As System.Object, _
                     ByVal e As System.EventArgs) _
        Handles btnLoad.Click
Dim iReturn As Integer
Dim dsResponse
Dim dtOrderItems As DataTable
Dim objResponse As Object()
Dim objError As Object
Dim iElem As Integer
Dim dsOrderItems As DataSet
Dim objResponseElement As System.Xml.XmlElement

Dim objWSProxy As New AssetOrdersService.AssetOrders()
objWSProxy.Credentials = System.Net.CredentialCache.DefaultCredentials
objResponse = objWSProxy.prOrderRequestedBy_List(txtUserName.Text)

For iElem = 0 To objResponse.GetUpperBound(0)
  Select
    Case objResponse(iElem).GetType().ToString()
    Case "System.Data.DataSet"
      'put both tables in dsResponse
      If dsResponse Is Nothing Then
        'process Orders
        dsResponse = objResponse(iElem)
```

```
            dsResponse.Tables(0).TableName = "Orders"
        Else
          'process OrderItems
          dsOrderItems = objResponse(iElem)
          dtOrderItems = dsOrderItems.Tables(0)
          dsOrderItems.Tables.Remove(dtOrderItems)
          dsResponse.Tables.Add(dtOrderItems)
          'link tables
          Dim custOrderRel As DataRelation =_
              dsResponse.Relations.Add("OrderItems", _
              dsResponse.Tables(0).Columns("OrderID"), _
              dsResponse.Tables(1).Columns("OrderID"))
          'assign new datasets to grids
          grdOrders.DataSource = dsResponse '.Tables(0).DefaultView()
          grdOrders.DataMember = "Orders"
          grdOrderItems.DataSource = dsResponse
          grdOrderItems.DataMember = "Orders.OrderItems"
        End If
      Case "System.Int32"
        iReturn = objResponse(iElem)
        Console.WriteLine("Return Value: " & iReturn)
      Case "SqlXml_Soap_DatasetArray.AssetOrdersService.SqlMessage"
        objError = objResponse(iElem)
        MsgBox(objError.Message)
        End
      End Select
    Next
End Sub
End Class
```

T-SQL and
XML Data Types in
SQL Server 2000

In this appendix, you will find four tables that provide an overview of the data types in use in SQL Server 2000. Table A-1 lists all Transact-SQL data types, their synonyms, their most important attributes (range and size), as well as sample constants. Table A-2 lists XML data types that you can use in XDR schemas. Table A-3 provides a mapping between Transact-SQL and XML (XDR) data types. Table A-4 lists XSD Schema built-in data types.

Data Type and Synonym	Description	Range or Length	Storage Size	Sample Constant
Character Strings				
char (character)	Character string	1 to 8000 chrs	1 to 8000 bytes	'D12-D13A36'
varchar (character varying)	Variable-length character string	1 to 8000 chrs	1 to 8000 bytes	'Toronto'
text	Long variable-length character string	1 to $2^{31} - 1$ chrs	16 bytes + 0 to 2GB	'SQL Server'
Unicode Character Strings				
Nchar (national character or national char)	Unicode character string	1 to 4000 chrs	2 to 8000 bytes	N'Никола'
Nvarchar (national character varying or national char varying)	Variable-length Unicode character string	1 to 4000 chrs	2 to 8000 bytes	N'Никола'
Ntext (national text)	Long variable-length Unicode large character string	1 to $2^{30} - 1$ chrs	16 bytes + 0 to 1GB	N'Никола'
Date and Time				
datetime	Date and time	1-Jan-1753 to 31-Dec-9999; precision: 3 ms	8 bytes	'6/27/1998 10:20:17.31'
smalldatetime	Small date and time	1-Jan-1900 to 6-Jun-2079; precision: 1 min	4 bytes	'Oct 30, 1993 14:30'
Integer Numbers				
tinyint	Tiny integer	0 to 255	1 bytes	17
smallint	Small integer	-32,768 to 32,767 $(-2^{15}$ to $2^{15}-1)$	2 bytes	23017
int	Integer	-2,147,483,648 to 2,147,483,647 $(-2^{31}$ to $2^{31}-1)$	4 bytes	343013

Table A-1   *SQL Server Built-in Data Types*

Data Type and Synonym	Description	Storage Size	Range or Length	Sample Constant
Integer Numbers				
bigint	Big integer	8 bytes	–9,223,372,036,854,775,808 to 9,223,372,036,854,775,807 (-2^{63} to $2^{63}-1$)	3222121343013
bit	Logical	1 bytes (up to 8 bits per byte)	0, 1, or Null	1
Exact Numbers				
numeric (decimal or dec)	Numeric or decimal	5 to 17 bytes	-10^{38} to $10^{38}-1$ (depends on precision and scale)	–352.4512
Approximate Numbers				
real	Real (single-precision) number	4 bytes	$-3.40\ 10^{38}$ to $3.40\ 10^{38}$	–232.212E6
float	Float (double-precision) number	8 bytes	$-1.79\ 10^{308}$ to $1.79\ 10^{308}$	34.2131343E-64
Monetary				
smallmoney	Small monetary data type	4 bytes	–214,768.3648 to 214,748.3647	$120.34
money	Monetary data type	8 bytes	–922,337,203,685,477.5808 to 922,337,203,685,477.5807	$120000000
Binary				
binary	Fixed-length binary string	1 to 8000 bytes	1 to 8000 bytes	0xa5d1
varbinary	Variable-length binary string	1 to 8000 bytes	1 to 8000 bytes	0xA5F2
image	Long variable-length binary string	1 to 8000 bytes	1 to $2^{31}-1$ bytes	n/a
timestamp	Database-wide unique number	8 bytes	n/a	n/a
uniqueidentifier	Globally unique identifier (GUID)	16 bytes	n/a	6F9619FF-8B86-D011-B42D-00C04FC964FF

Table A-1 *SQL Server Built-in Data Types (continued)*

Data Type and Synonym	Description	Range or Length	Storage Size	Sample Constant
Special				
cursor	Cursor reference	n/a	n/a	n/a
sql_variant	Variant	n/a	n/a	n/a
table	Table	n/a	n/a	n/a

Table A-1 *SQL Server Built-in Data Types* (continued)

XML Data Type	Description
bin.base64	Binary BLOB MIME-style Base64-encoded.
bin.hex	Hexadecimal digits.
Boolean	0 (false) or 1 (true).
char	One character–long string.
date	Date in a subset of ISO 8601 format (no time data). For example: 2000-12-25.
dateTime	Date in a subset of ISO 8601 format, with optional time. Time zone is not allowed. Time can be specified to the level of nanoseconds. Data and time segments are delimited with "T". For example: 2001-02-12T13:29:19.
dateTime.tz	Date in a subset of ISO 8601 format, with optional time and time zone (specified as time difference from GTM). Precise as nanoseconds. For example: 2001-02-12T13:29:19-06:00.
fixed.14.4	Decimal number with up to 14 digits left and up to 4 digits right of decimal point. Optional leading sign.
float	Real number; no limit on digits; optional leading sign, fractional digits, and an exponent. Value range: 1.7976931348623157E+308 to 2.2250738585072014E–308.
int	Integer number.
number	Real number, with no limit on digits; optional leading sign, fractional digits, and an exponent. Value range: 1.7976931348623157E+308 to 2.2250738585072014E–308.
time	Time in a subset of ISO 8601 format. No date and no time zone. For example: 04:12:17.
time.tz	Time in a subset ISO 8601 format, with no date but optional time zone. For example: 14:18:1237-03:00.
i1	Signed integer represented in 1 byte.
i2	Signed integer represented in 2 bytes.
i4	Signed integer represented in 4 bytes.
r4	Real number; 7-digit precision; optional leading sign, fractional digits, and an exponent. Value range: 3.40282347E+38F to 1.17549435E–38F.
r8	Real number; 15-digit precision; optional leading sign, fractional digits, and an exponent. Value range: 1.7976931348623157E+308 to 2.2250738585072014E–308.
ui1	Unsigned integer represented in 1 byte.
ui2	Unsigned integer represented in 2 bytes.
ui4	Unsigned integer represented in 4 bytes.
uri	Universal Resource Identifier (URI). For example: urn:schemas-microsoft-com:datatype.
uuid	Hexadecimal digits representing octets, optional embedded hyphens that are ignored. For example: 331B7AB4-630B-11F4-AD03-0720B7052C81.

Table A-2   *XDR Data Types*

SQL Server Data Type	XML Data Type
bigint	i8
binary	bin.base64
bit	Boolean
char	char
datetime	datetime
decimal	r8
float	r8
image	bin.base64
int	int
money	r8
nchar	string
ntext	string
nvarchar	string
numeric	r8
real	r4
smalldatetime	datetime
smallint	i2
smallmoney	fixed.14.4
sysname	string
text	string
timestamp	ui8
tinyint	ui1
varbinary	bin.base64
varchar	string
uniqueidentifier	uuid

Table A-3   *Mapping Between XDR Data Types and SQL Server Data Types*

Data Type and Synonym	Description	Range	Sample Constant
Logical			
`boolean`	n/a	1, 0, true, false	`1`
Numbers			
`decimal`	n/a	Arbitrary precision (minimum 18) decimal positive and negative numbers	`-2.45,3001021.212`
`double`	Double-precision 64-bit floating-point $m \times 2^e$	+0, −, INF (infinity), −INF (negative infinity), NaN (not-a-number), $\pm m \times 2^e$ (floating-point number where $m <= 2^{53}, -1075 < e < 970$)	`-00, -2E200, -2.00000002e200, -200.000002, INF, NaN`
`float`	Single-precision 32-bit floating-point $m \times 2^e$	+0, −0, INF (infinity), −INF (negative infinity), NaN (not-a-number), $\pm m \times 2^e$ (floating-point number where $m <= 2^{24}, -149 < e < 104$)	`-200, -2E2, -2.00000002e2, -200.000002, INF, NaN`
`integer`	Whole number	Infinite set of integer numbers	`0, 1, -1, 2, -2`
`nonNegativeInteger`	n/a	Derived from integer	`0, 1, 2`
`nonPositiveInteger`	n/a	Derived from integer	`0, -1, -2`
`long`	Long (8-byte) integer	−9,223,372,036,854,775,808 to 9,223,372,036,854,775,807 (-2^{63} to $2^{63}-1$)	`3222121343013`
`int`	4-byte integer	−2,147,483,648 to 2,147,483,647 (-2^{31} to $2^{31}-1$)	n/a
`short`	2-byte integer	−32,768 to 32,767 (2^{15} to $2^{15}-1$)	`-19281, 0, 23131`
`byte`	1-byte integer	−128 to 127 (-2^7 to 2^7-1)	`-81, 0, 31`
`unsignedLong`	Long (8-byte) integer	0 to 18,446,744,073,709,551,615 (0 to $2^{64}-1$)	`3222121343013`
`unsignedInt`	4-byte integer	0 to 4,294,967,295 (0 to $2^{32}-1$)	n/a
`unsignedShort`	2-byte integer	0 to 65,535 (0 to $2^{16}-1$)	`-19281, 0, 23131`
`unsignedByte`	1-byte integer	0 to 255 (0 to 2^8-1)	`-81, 0, 31`
Dates and Times			
`date`	Calendar date	CCYY-MM-DD	`2001-01-01`
`time`	ISO 8061 time with time zone offset	hh:mm:ss-hh:mm	`17:35:00-05:00` (17:35 ET -5h)

Table A-4 *XSD Built-in Data Types*

Data Type and Synonym	Description	Range	Sample Constant
dateTime	ISO 8061 data and time with time zone offset	CCYY-MM-DDThh:mm:ss-hh:mm	`2001-01-01T17:35:00 -05:00 (17:35 on Jan 1, 2001 ET -5h)`
duration	Duration	±PyYmMdDThHmMsS	`P3Y (3 years), -PT30M30S (-30 min 30 sec)`
gYear	Gregorian year	0001 to 9999	`2010`
gMonth	Gregorian month	--m-- (--1-- to --12--)	`--02-- (Feb)`
gDay	Gregorian day	--d (--1 to --31)	`--15`
gMonthDay	Gregorian month and day	--m-d	`--02-21 (Feb 21)`
gYearMonth	Gregorian year and month	yyyy-mm	`2010-5 (Feb 2010)`
Binary			
hexBinary	Hex-encoded binary	Finite set of binary octets (octet consists of pair of hex characters [0-9a-fA-F])	`A7F4, 0b7c`
base64Binary	64-base encoded binary	Finite set of binary octets	`A7F4, 0b7c9812aa`
Text			
string	Character string	n/a	`asdasd`
anyURI	Uniform Resource Identifier Reference	Absolute or relative	`http://www. trigonblue.com/ sqlxml`
normalizedString	Normalized string	String that does not contain the carriage return, line feed, nor tab	n/a
token	Token	Normalized string that does not have leading and trailing spaces and no internal sequences with two or more spaces	n/a
language	Language tokens	n/a	`en, fr`
XML Types			
Name	XML names	n/a	n/a
NCName	XML noncolonized names	n/a	n/a
NOTATION	n/a	n/a	n/a
Qname	XML qualified names	n/a	n/a

Table A-4   *XSD Built-in Data Types* (continued)

Data Type and Synonym	Description	Range	Sample Constant
XML Types			
ENTITY	ENTITY attribute type	n/a	n/a
ENTITIES	ENTITIES attribute type	n/a	n/a
ID	ID attribute type	n/a	n/a
IDREF	IDREF attribute type	n/a	n/a
IDREFS	IDREFS attribute type	n/a	n/a
NMTOKEN	NMTOKEN attribute type	n/a	n/a
NMTOKENS	NMTOKENS attribute type	n/a	n/a

Table A-4 *XSD Built-in Data Types* (continued)

Index

Symbols

prefix, 269-270
prefix, 270
< and > operators, 94
@@ prefix, 104
@@cursor_rows, 127
@@error, 62, 105, 234, 237, 242-246
@@fetch_status, 125, 127
@@identity, 104, 151, 378-380
@@nestlevel, 365
@@rowcount, 106, 232
@@trancount, 191-192
@debug, 222-227
@ErrorCode, 113
@intErrorCode, 244
@TransactionCountOnEntry, 246

A

ACID test, 182, 196
AcquisitionType table, 15
Action table, 17
ActiveX Script Task for using BulkLoad, 641-642
ActivityLog table, 18
Ad hoc queries, 470-471
admin password, setting, 440
Administrators, notifying in e-mail, 415
ADO.NET, using to retrieve XML data, 597-599
after element (UpdateGrams), 615-616
after (keyword), 288
After triggers, 52, 283
design of, 284-291
full syntax of, 288-291
triggering, 287
Aggregate() function, 383
Aggregates, 164-165, 309-311, 383, 534
Aging of execution plans, 68, 70
Alerts, 406-407, 415
AllowNull property of ColumnProperty() function, 297
Alter Function statement, 271
Alter Procedure statement, 56-57
Alter Trigger statement, 301
Alter View statement, 313
And operator (&), 290
Annotated schemas, 571-588
ANSI SQL-92, 86
Application roles, 436
Application security, managing, 432-436
Application service Providers), 525
Approximate numbers, 93-94
ASCII viewer, viewing code in, 448
ASCII() function, 161
ASPs (Application Service Providers), 525

Asset management system, 7
Asset sample database, 7
asset deployment tables, 12-14
asset description tables, 11-12
design of, 10-18
downloading, 6
entity relationship diagram, 10
installation, 7-9
leasing tables, 14-15
order tables, 15-18
purpose of, 7, 9-10
running book's examples against, 170
Assignment (=), 62, 94
At sign (@), 58, 86, 100
Atomicity requirement (ACID test), 182
Attribute constraints (XDR), 505-506
Attributes (markup language), explained, 493
Audit trail, triggers to create, 306
Author's web site, 7
Auto mode (of For XML clause), 529-534
Autocommit transactions, 183-184
Autoparameterization, 68-70
Avg() function, 144-145
Axes (in XPath), 520

B

Backups, transaction log, 187
Base name, of stored procedure, 52
Batches, 42, 170-179
creating using the Go command, 171
defined, 170
errors and, 172-176
execution steps, 173
scope of comments in, 177-179
scope of objects in, 176-177
scope of variables in, 177
self-sufficient content in, 176-179
transactions spanning, 203
BatchExec.exe program, 463
bcp (Bulk Copy Program), 128, 639
before element (UpdateGrams), 615-616
Begin Distributed Transaction, 202
Begin...End, 111-112
Begin Transaction statement, 184-185, 252
Berners-Lee, Tim, 491
bigint data type, 93
Binary And operator (&), 290
BINARY Base64 option, in For XML clause, 536-537
Binary constants, 95
Binary data encoding (in XML), 536-537
Binary data types, 95
Binary_CheckSum() function, 142-144
bit data type, 92-93
BizTalk, 502

Blocked resources, 197
Body (of stored procedure), 40, 54
break statement, 117
Breakpoints, in debugging, 218-219, 221-222
Browser-based applications, XML and, 526
B2B (business-to-business), 525
B2C (business-to-consumer), 525
Bugs, explained, 208
Bulk Insert statement, 639
BulkLoad (SQLXML). See SQLXML BulkLoad
Business rules, consistent implementation of, 83
Business-oriented terminology, in naming, 47

C

CAL (Client Access License), Server/Per-Seat, 6
Cascading deletes, 305, 306-309
Cascading referential integrity constraints, 307
Case function/expression, 136-139
in an Order By clause, 483
in a Where clause, 484
Cast() function, 146-149
CDATA sections (XML document), 497, 542, 577, 588
Changes committed to the database, 184
Char() function, 160
Character data types, 89-90
Character references (XML), 497
Character strings, 89-91
character varying data type, 89
ChargeLog table, 17
CharIndex() function, 157-158
Check constraints, 324, 331
functions as, 134
and partition key ranges, 332
on triggers, 306
Check Out dialog box (Visual Studio .NET), 444
CheckConstraints property, 643
Child sequence fragment identifiers, 519
Client Network Utility, 28-29
Client-side cursors, 128
Client-side XML processing, 599-603
ClientSideXml property, 601
Close statement, 127
Closing tag, 493
Coalesce statement, 309-310
Coalesce() function, 145-146, 350
Code (source). See Source code
Column aliases, 533

INTERNATIONAL CONTACT INFORMATION

AUSTRALIA
McGraw-Hill Book Company Australia Pty. Ltd.
TEL +61-2-9900-1800
FAX +61-2-9878-8881
http://www.mcgraw-hill.com.au
books-it_sydney@mcgraw-hill.com

CANADA
McGraw-Hill Ryerson Ltd.
TEL +905-430-5000
FAX +905-430-5020
http://www.mcgraw-hill.ca

GREECE, MIDDLE EAST, & AFRICA
(Excluding South Africa)
McGraw-Hill Hellas
TEL +30-210-6560-990
TEL +30-210-6560-993
TEL +30-210-6560-994
FAX +30-210-6545-525

MEXICO (Also serving Latin America)
McGraw-Hill Interamericana Editores S.A. de C.V.
TEL +525-117-1583
FAX +525-117-1589
http://www.mcgraw-hill.com.mx
fernando_castellanos@mcgraw-hill.com

SINGAPORE (Serving Asia)
McGraw-Hill Book Company
TEL +65-6863-1580
FAX +65-6862-3354
http://www.mcgraw-hill.com.sg
mghasia@mcgraw-hill.com

SOUTH AFRICA
McGraw-Hill South Africa
TEL +27-11-622-7512
FAX +27-11-622-9045
robyn_swanepoel@mcgraw-hill.com

SPAIN
McGraw-Hill/Interamericana de España, S.A.U.
TEL +34-91-180-3000
FAX +34-91-372-8513
http://www.mcgraw-hill.es
professional@mcgraw-hill.es

UNITED KINGDOM, NORTHERN,
EASTERN, & CENTRAL EUROPE
McGraw-Hill Education Europe
TEL +44-1-628-502500
FAX +44-1-628-770224
http://www.mcgraw-hill.co.uk
computing_europe@mcgraw-hill.com

ALL OTHER INQUIRIES Contact:
McGraw-Hill/Osborne
TEL +1-510-420-7700
FAX +1-510-420-7703
http://www.osborne.com
omg_international@mcgraw-hill.com